PROBLEMS IN LABOR RELATIONS

Problems in Labor Relations

BENJAMIN M. SELEKMAN
Kirstein Professor of Labor Relations
Graduate School of Business Administration
Harvard University

SYLVIA KOPALD SELEKMAN
Former Fellow, Social Science
Research Council

STEPHEN H. FULLER
Associate Professor of Business Administration
Graduate School of Business Administration
Harvard University

SECOND EDITION

McGRAW-HILL BOOK COMPANY, INC.
New York   Toronto   London
1958

PREFACE

When the first edition of this book was written in the tense atmosphere of the immediate postwar years, the question may well have been asked whether collective bargaining was an enduring institution. The year 1946, for instance, was marked by repeated, costly strikes in one basic industry after another. Indeed, in a reaction against this thrust of power on the part of new, industry-wide unions, the Taft-Hartley Act was enacted in 1947. It marked a reversal of the trend started with the validation of the Wagner Act by the Supreme Court in 1937. For now trade unions, too, were under surveillance and could be made subject to charges of unfair labor practices as only management had been under the Wagner Act. Other restrictions were placed upon them by the Federal law, and a number of states enacted even more stringent legislation in the form of so-called "right-to-work" laws.

At this writing, ten years later, it can safely be said that, whatever legislation may still be forthcoming, collective bargaining has nevertheless survived as a permanent institution. Hardly any responsible managements would be willing to say now, regardless of their feelings in the past, that they preferred to function without unions or that they *could* do so even if they so desired. Problems still continue, some of them serious in nature. Whereas in the first five or six years after the war it was repeated strikes, some of an emergency nature, that troubled the nation, now it is "creeping" inflation. Indeed, many observers think that the continuous inflationary trend can be traced in large part to the periodic wage settlements, including fringe benefits, entered into by large unions and large corporations which establish patterns for the economy as a whole. The debate goes on as to whether unions are the primary cause of the inflationary trend or whether it is caused by corporations when they translate wage increases into price increases which, it is charged, are greater than just the wage component. To this management replies, "Well, surely, prices must be greater than the amount of the wage increase because our wage increase creates a cycle which makes everything we buy cost more. It costs us many times more to replace plants and machinery we built before the inflationary cycle began, not to say anything about raw and semifinished material."

The truth of the matter is that problems will always be with us: this or that issue will continuously arise in the highly dynamic industrial environment that characterizes this nation. Collective bargaining does not in itself solve major economic and social problems. What it does provide is a procedure by means of which problems can be identified and handled.

v

And so the day-to-day work of labor relations and collective bargaining goes on. New agreements are negotiated, grievances processed, seniority problems handled, new machines and better methods of increasing productivity introduced, men disciplined for infractions of rules, and through all these activities management and men learn to live together from day to day with the rules and practices of their own making.

All these complex phenomena can best be understood if presented through actual living situations as portrayed in the cases here recorded. And since so much has happened since 1949, when the first volume was published, the time has come for a revision. Accordingly, this new edition, while retaining cases which in a sense portray timeless situations, describes new significant events, such as the massive negotiations in steel and automobiles, as well as those in smaller industries like food, soap, chemicals, and oil. Suggestions as to how these cases can most profitably be studied are indicated in Part I.

This book is truly a cooperative effort. It consists primarily of the record of activities carried on by individuals in companies and unions at all levels from president and chairman of the board to foreman and shop steward as well as rank-and-file workers. They, therefore, deserve chief credit for the material. They are the ones who live, day in and day out, that which the rest of us record as collective bargaining or labor relations or industrial relations. But if we are to be free to use these cases, these individuals must in most instances remain anonymous. In addition to these anonymous collaborators, the authors wish to express their thanks to those who helped in gathering and recording these cases—Professors John Cooley, George C. Homans, and E. Robert Livernash, and Research Associates John M. Baitsell, Robert B. McKersie, and Richard E. Walton—and to Catherine C. Ellsworth, Ruth C. Hetherston, and Nadine Rodwin, assistants in courses. Selena Gardner and Nanette Gillis undertook all the chores that go into the secretarial part of the job, from hammering the numerous drafts away on the typewriter to seeing the final ones through the press.

In particular, for substantial assistance on this second edition, very special credit is due our research associates, Messrs. Baitsell, McKersie, and Walton.

These cases have been the foundation of our courses in labor relations at the Harvard Graduate School of Business Administration. In original form many of them were copyrighted by the President and Fellows of Harvard College. We wish to express our appreciation for permission to make them available in this book.

Professor Benjamin M. Selekman
Sylvia Kopald Selekman
Professor Stephen H. Fuller

CONTENTS

PART I.   FRAMEWORKS FOR STUDY OF CASES IN LABOR RELATIONS

One of the virtues of the case method is its flexibility.   Accordingly, an instructor and his students may use this book in such a way as best fits their orientation.

Economics.   If one's approach is that of the economist, the material lends itself to an exploration of the economic factors that go into the negotiations and administration of trade-union agreements.   We have here such cases, for instance, as those portraying the dealings between the United Auto Workers and General Motors and Ford; the United Steel Workers with the steel corporations; the Chemical Workers with Lever Brothers; and companies and unions in metals, oil, textiles, clothing, and food.   Inevitably, one finds criteria advanced by both sides with regard to wage determination, such as cost of living, standard of living, productivity, profitability, capacity to pay, competitive rates, etc.   We read not only the arguments and supporting data presented by corporations and unions, but also their elaborate discussions, their briefs, their appeals to public opinion—and, finally, their compromises in arriving at actual settlements.

On the subject of patternmaking, to take a specific example, a vivid understanding of this process is seen in actual life as we read how at one time Ford, at another time General Motors, and again at another time Bethlehem Steel, negotiate with their respective unions a settlement—be it wage increase, fringe benefits, pensions, union security, or supplementary unemployment benefits, or some combination of these—to be followed in short order by other corporations and unions.   Here, indeed, we see what amounts to a process of economic legislation.

Again, the debate going on for the past twenty years with regard to the inflationary impact of trade unionism can best be read in its full scope in the negotiation cases, particularly those in automobiles and steels.   The unions articulate one set of principles; business, another; fact-finding boards and government agencies, still another.   To be sure, these arguments do not point to definitive answers.   Indeed, is there a final answer to this question?   The best thing the instructor can do is to expose the student to the material in these actual negotiations, together perhaps with assigned readings from various schools of economics.

If instructor and student would like to experiment with bargaining models which are being developed by theoretical economists, where could they find more challenging material?   What could be more sobering to any tendency to "overtheorize" than the record of how the parties actually bargain?   This is

I

not to deprecate theory. On the contrary, the cases actually may serve to help hammer out a working concept of the logic of bargaining.

Similarly, issues of productivity constantly confront companies and unions. Some of the most tense negotiating sessions deal with this thorny problem. In addition, a number of cases deal specifically with shop obstacles to new incentive systems, modernization programs, or other attempts to increase output. How the procedures of collective bargaining are utilized to secure the introduction of such programs can again best be realistically grasped as those rough-and-tumble experiences are explored from shop to shop.

Behavioral Sciences. Similarly, other orientations, whether sociological, anthropological, or psychological, can be profitably applied in these cases. The basic fact is that we are dealing here with human behavior. The problems recorded are authentic slices of life. Accordingly, the materials lend themselves to an exploration in terms of any discipline that deals with human relationships. Every shop is in reality a community made up of various individuals and groups with differing personalities, backgrounds, emotions, and sentiments. Thus, the social psychologist or sociologist will find here cases which teem with small-group formations. Indeed, Bartolo Brothers, to mention only one case, shows how two small groups struggle for status or supremacy over a period of seven or eight years, how both management and union officials are baffled by this internal conflict, and how the collective-bargaining machinery gradually helps resolve this tense situation. Nor does one overlook at the same time the economic aspects of competitive wages and costs as the union is trying to increase wages, in line with those paid by competitors in other markets, and management pleads inability to absorb such costs and stay in business. There are also wildcat strikes and insubordination; thus the system of jurisprudence inherent in the collective-bargaining agreement is challenged. How this community of management and men survives this struggle turns out to be a fascinating chapter in human relations. Indeed, it throws a vivid light on collective bargaining as an adaptive system.

If personality and its influence are of major interest, ample opportunity is afforded to explore the problem presented by the overaggressive or nonconformist personality, against the fact that the day's work must be done and the values of a community conserved. Similarly, the case situations point up the maturity required of management and union personnel so as to avoid becoming punitive, with the risk of upsetting the stability and efficiency of the entire work community.

Political Science. If political science or government is the instructor's primary framework, here indeed is a rich harvest before him. Essentially these cases embody experiments in constitutionalism. For the first time in all their history, major corporations and unions have had to learn how to deal with one another, to negotiate, to develop common rules, to codify these rules in contracts, to decide on divisions of power, to establish a judicial machinery binding on all parties without the sanctions of fines or imprisonment. One has only to recall the "Battle of the Overpass" in the Rouge plant of Ford in 1937 and the negotiation to establish SUB in 1955. What a change from raw power to law and order in a short period of less than two decades!

Administration as a Framework of Action. We who use these cases in our courses at the Harvard Business School are oriented to an administrative point of view. We are training men who will occupy executive posts. We aim, therefore, to help them develop skills in strategy and tactics that will enable them to carry on their jobs as successfully as possible. We take it for granted that in a typical company not only the director of industrial relations but every official will have some responsibility for labor relations. They will have to make decisions and initiate programs dealing with wages, costs, the making and selling of goods and services, the negotiation of contracts, and taking and settling strikes. Above all, they will develop patterns of relationship over the years. Obviously, the understanding of human behavior is a prime requisite for our men. Hence, we use any or all disciplines which throw the greatest illumination on the particular problem and task at hand.

At the same time we attempt to give a logical core to the material and to the various approaches through two dynamic concepts: (1) power relations, and (2) human relations.

POWER RELATIONS: CORPORATIONS AND UNIONS AT THE BARGAINING TABLE

It is by mobilizing their power—economic, political, and moral—that workers and their leaders compel management in the first instance to deal with them and then to grant, in whole or in part, the demands which they make upon the corporation. It is by countering with power—economic, political, and moral—that corporate management determines how much and to what extent it will deal with its employees through organized unions; and, once it deals with these unions, how much of the demands it will grant, consistent with the necessity of maintaining competition, efficiency, and freedom to conduct the enterprise. Indeed, management may find it desirable, if not necessary, to make proposals of its own to the unions.

Not to recognize these power components as the critical element in determining relationships is to be naive and, indeed, to run the risk of jeopardizing effective and positive relationships between corporations and unions. This is not to say that other values do not enter into any given situation, such as the nature and history of a particular industry, the types of personalities that occupy the positions of leadership, the political and moral climate of the times, the long-range economic outlook, and so on. Essentially, however, power remains primary; these other factors only help shape the way in which power will express itself.

Since power is the chief factor, we place a great deal of emphasis upon the strategy and tactics conceived and employed by corporations and unions in planning and executing their negotiations as well as in projecting the administration of the agreements which they have signed. We look upon negotiation and administration as a unitary activity, one phase inseparable from the other. We hasten to add that by giving primary emphasis to power components, we do not look upon strategy and tactics as being directed exclusively to the conduct of conflict. On the contrary, just because a showdown of power is latent in every negotiation, the strategy must be all the more carefully planned and the tactics all the more skillfully employed so as to avert recourse to raw power. Indeed, conflict and cooperation are interrelated. Just as diplomacy and war are but two phases of relations between nations, so conflict and cooperation are two interdependent phases of continuity in institutional relations between corporations and unions.

Moreover, only by recognizing explicitly the reality of power as a primary determinant is it possible not only to develop the pattern of relationships most suitable at a given time but also to enable leadership to make a transition from conflict to some type of accommodation, if not cooperation.

The acceptance of power as a reality also helps prevent oversimplification —that is, polarizing dealings as either "good" or "bad." Herein lies the value of studying the bargaining sessions recorded in these cases. We soon begin to realize that a "model" of cooperation may prove effective in one situation but not necessarily fit the requirements of another. The practices that recommend themselves to one union and company may seem just the wrong ones to others having different needs and goals. The structure of institutional relationships that serves well during the uncertainties of early stages of collective bargaining may, if continued too long, thwart the potentialities of a later stage.

Structures of institutional relationships are to be studied, in a word, as adaptive mechanisms. At least nine types, in our opinion, may be distinguished: (1) the structure of balance of power, (2) the structure of containment, (3) the structure of conflict, (4) the structure of accommodation, (5) the structure of cooperation, (6) the structure of deal-bargaining, (7) collusion, (8) racketeering, (9) ideology.

The Structure of Power-bargaining. Power-bargaining continues an old-style pattern of conflict with roots extending far back in industrial history. But unlike the basic conflict patterns stemming from nonacceptance of the bargaining institution as such, the parties to power-bargaining generally accept not only one another but also the unqualified logic of the market place. Indeed, the outstanding representatives of power-bargaining among the unions are often conservatives, even in their politics, with little interest in idealistic "trimmings" that might "dress up" their hard-boiled willingness to exact by every pressure within their power the last ounce of advantage that economic conditions at any given time make possible.

Indeed, throughout the joint dealings the frank manipulation of relative power dominates relations. Whatever the background development behind any specific structure of power-bargaining, strong and securely established unions face strong, and often associated, employers. The implications of strength and relatively balanced power are faced; each side "accepts" the other as sovereign spokesman for its side. And they accept each other as practical men and economic realists.

The Structure of Containment. In this structure, the union aggressively presses to extend its scope of action; and management strives with equal determination to contain it within bounds. The modes of joint dealing reflect in early years of relationships the responses of leaders on both sides to the sheer newness of the relations into which they suddenly have found themselves plunged by legal compulsions and organizing force.

By the nature of things, every characteristic phase of bargaining practice is held to the strict limits of legal obligation. In negotiating the agreement, management gives way as gradually as possible. The scope of negotiation is not only rigidly defined but consistently held to the traditional subject matter of wages, hours, and conditions of employment. Agreements are strictly construed. Legalistic interpretation and insistence upon disciplined observance of contractual obligations characterize daily administration.

The Structure of Conflict. The conflict structure that arises from the determination of a management to refuse to deal with unions dominated industrial relations before 1933. Today it has become a secondary pattern in collective bargaining. Nevertheless, employers still remain who hold onto the earlier determination to bar unions by all means at their disposal.

Whenever the union receives a majority mandate from the employees to whom it is appealing, the employer must embark upon joint dealings and collective relationships. Under a conflict structure, however, such an employer usually never really accepts the union. In contrast to containment, he does not yield to the union even a narrow, restricted scope until he literally has to; and he looks for the first opportunity to get rid of the intruder. His acceptance of joint dealings is an "imposed acceptance," imposed by law and by union power.

It should be borne in mind, however, that containment or conflict as a tactic is employed even when relationships are cast on the balance-of-power pattern or even accommodation or cooperation. In any given negotiation of a new contract, the union's demands may be excessive in the judgment of management. The union risks a strike; but management may prefer the losses incurred by a showdown of power as against potential losses in its competitive position if it accedes to the men's demands. Likewise, management may decide to contain a union's attempts to interfere in what is deemed essential to its capacity to keep the plant productive and efficient.

The two structures just described—containment and conflict—may be said to be on the left side of the balance of power. As such they are characterized by using power primarily for a sort of coexistence or a holding action to see what are the possible next steps in the evolution of relationships. The parties are always on the verge of a showdown and recourse to naked power.

We come now to those structures which are on the right side of balance of power. These are characterized by an attempt to use power to bring about positive relationship and to avoid any recourse to naked power. These structures are accommodation, cooperation, and deal-bargaining.

The Structure of Accommodation. The structure of accommodation has many likenesses, as would be anticipated, to the structure of cooperation. Accommodation may be differentiated from cooperation in joint dealings by two broad tests: (1) the scope of mutuality; and (2) the intangibles of underlying spirit.

By and large, managements and unions who deal together within relationships of accommodation tend to confine their cooperative approaches to what may be termed the traditional agenda of collective bargaining. They still concentrate practice and procedure upon establishing wages, hours, and conditions of employment and then upon administering the jointly established standards. Although not unduly alarmist about the potential of every demand for encroaching upon managerial prerogatives or of every counter-demand for affecting shop rights, the parties to accommodative bargaining do maintain alert watchfulness upon these ramparts of principle, these orbits of respective equities and privileges.

But within these bounds the leaders, the ranks, and the organizations linked by relationships of accommodation interact within comfortably "customary," familiar patterns of behavior. They have evolved their routines of recognizing functions and settling differences. They have learned how to adjust one to another in daily affairs, to accept the reduction of conflict as an accomplishment without demanding its total elimination. They have proved themselves willing to compromise whenever possible, to conciliate whenever necessary, and to tolerate at all times.

The Structure of Cooperation. This structure is characterized by the fact that the parties extend mutual concerns beyond the familiar matters of wages, hours, and conditions. They also recognize productive efficiency, the solvency of business, elimination of waste, advance of technology, and so on, as components in their common interest. The union accepts managerial problems as being of concern to labor; management recognizes its stake in stable, effective unionism; together they dispose of problems as they arise. Differences are recognized elements of cooperative dealings, whether at the negotiating table or the grievance meeting. Similarly, mutual acceptance carries over to active subscription, on the part of the union, to the right and the need of business profits, and on the part of the company, to the right and the need of union participation.

The Structure of Deal-bargaining. Deal-bargaining undoubtedly requires a high degree of cooperation and mutual understanding between the management and the union leaders who engage in it. By the very nature of the deal, it is a device limited to top leadership. This is at once the source of its strength and its weakness. Belonging to the secret diplomacy of bargaining, it naturally does not reveal itself explicitly in the records. Yet all familiar with concrete experiences can testify to the wide prevalence of the deal—in negotiation, in grievance settlement, in arbitration, in rate setting, in strike settlements, and in other joint activities. Indeed, deal-bargaining represents a rooted American habit: we have always enjoyed making "good deals." In case study, indices of its existence must be sought between the lines of the record or in the recurrent troubles in the ranks: the misunderstandings and wildcat strikes that must be faced by the leaders who have failed to communicate adequately to the ranks the reasons for and the results of their "deal."

So far we have dealt with six structures which represent phases in a continuum of power relations. But the power used by the parties is legitimate power, that is to say, within the legal and moral framework of American industrial democracy. No one relishes the use of the strike weapon or the lockout, but these are legal actions and win moral validation by a considerable segment of the community. Similarly, we all wish that unions and corporations paid more attention to economic consideration in setting wages and costs, but in the final analysis we recognize that they have the right to arrive at those terms which enable them to work together with a maximum of productivity and mutual satisfactions.

We now consider three structures which also are characterized by the exploitation of power but in these instances the power is illegitimate—that is, either illegal or outside the pale of American morality or both. The structures are collusion, racketeering, and ideology.

The Structure of Collusion. While collusion is a form of cooperation and deal-bargaining, the resulting "cooperation" generates problems that extend beyond the specific structure of relationship to affect adversely the legitimate interests of other employers, other workers, and the consuming public. For the collusive parties to collective bargaining connive to control their market, supplies, or prices, or to engage in practices of mutual interest to serve their exclusive advantage. They cooperate, but through a form of jointly established monopoly which is frankly unconcerned with every legitimate interest except their own. The courts have already declared certain types of these collusive deals illegal; and the watchfulness of competitors, rival unions, and public representatives no doubt will continue to curb these questionable deals.[1]

It must be recognized, of course, that American experience with such collusive relationships has been concentrated in small-scale industry. The potentialities of collusion between big unions and giant corporations loom far more formidable; but so far there is little evidence of such developments. If the cases contain no clear-cut instances of collusion, the student may be interested in watching for the conditions that seem favorable to its possible appearance or those that completely discourage its emergence in American labor relations.

The Racketeering Structure. From time to time sensational investigations uncover collusive arrangements—particularly in such industries as shipping, transportation, and construction—between trade-union leaders, underground criminal forces, or corrupt political officials, with or without the tacit consent of business, by means of which relationships are determined and administered.

---

[1] The best-known court decisions, *United States v. Brims*, 272 U.S. 549 (1926), and *Allen Bradley Co. v. Local Union No. 3, I.B.E.W.*, 325 U.S. 797 (1945), show the persistence of the underlying problem in the almost two decades that separate the two cases.

Indeed, a certain type of peace is imposed upon the industry and the community. It is one of the sordid aspects of American life. It represents extreme pathology. But pathology is as characteristic of social as of individual life. Only by recognizing such phenomena can we deal with them effectively.

The Structure of Ideology. This structure is relatively infrequent, especially since 1949 when the CIO came to grips with those unions led by Communist sympathizers. But as long as any given structure of joint dealings remains in the hands of the ideologists, inevitably it remains also a *conflict pattern.* Of course, ideological unions—unions dedicated primarily to an ideology like socialism, or the transcendence of class over national considerations—are no new phenomena in American industrial relations. But the Communist and left-wing unions of the present day loom more formidable, because the party line they seek to serve via union policy ties in with an expanding imperialistic movement dominated by a powerful Communist state. Repeated observations have now made widely familiar the fluctuations of the party line with the changing issues of foreign relations stemming from the Kremlin throughout the defense period, the war, and the postwar years. Beyond any short-term changes in the bargaining program, accordingly, the ideological structure constitutes the most undeviating and ineradicable conflict pattern in industrial relations. For the party-line leaders accept neither the system of free collective bargaining nor the American democracy of which it is part.[1]

Diversities of Structure. These nine structures, overlapping as they are, blurred though the boundaries between them may be, nonetheless suggest the variety of present-day industrial relations in individual plants and industries. Each instructor or student may think of further structures or may modify these tentative classifications. Moreover, "local" relations do not necessarily parallel those that characterize top levels. Instead, one often uncovers dealings at the work level proceeding from day to day within a structure of easy, accommodative relationships, though top-level bargaining is tough and wary; or a highly militant local relationship may be watched anxiously by top leaders who deal together in a structure of accommodation or even cooperation. The combinations and permutations are many and varied; they emphasize the diversities amid uniform trends of development that constitute the realities of present-day bargaining. Once again, the content of bargaining experience is to be probed, not by abstracting this concrete element or that, but by viewing them all in terms of the human behavior that we label "industrial relations."

HUMAN RELATIONS: THE UNION AGREEMENT IN THE SHOP COMMUNITY

Our second orientation, that of human relations, is employed in the exploration of problems at the shop level. The key to understanding here

---

[1] For further description of these structures, see the author's forthcoming book, *Labor Relations, Human Relations, and Power Relations,* to be published by McGraw-Hill.

lies in the day-to-day operation of the trade-union agreement in a particular shop. The shop is regarded as the communal environment within which problems arise and must be handled. The agreement and its clauses must, therefore, be administered in terms of the people who make up the community—workers, foremen, shop stewards, and business agents, as well as higher company and union officials. Issues regarding seniority, wage rates, vacations, holidays, discipline, productivity—all of them are constantly arising in the highly dynamic complex which goes to make up the typical American plant. The trade-union agreement lays down working rules and guides. The people involved may not always act according to these rules. The logic, therefore, becomes compelling. Just how is the shop organized as a unit in collective bargaining? What about the union involved, its affiliation, its internal organization? What similarly about the company: Is it a small company, closely owned, or a large multiplant corporation? In what sector of industry is it functioning—in basic production? In consumers' goods? In distribution? What light does the history of the union-management relationship throw upon behavior in the problem to be currently handled? How did the union gain entry? How long have relationships existed? Does shop behavior contain any hang-over, or residual hostilities and suspicions, from the organizing period or from any previous experience? Are any shop groups, cliques or factions, actual or potential, functioning in the situation? Are they formed around the work organization, ethnic or race ties, age or sex interests, or political factions? How are these groups related to the purposes of the management and the union? What unwritten group codes, if any, shape shop behavior within the formal rules and contract provisions?

Certain extrashop factors add another and often different set of forces influencing the internal situation being diagnosed. They must be integrated into the effective patterns of shop relations, because external forces manifestly help to fashion the motivating drives, the sentiments, and the feelings of the people at work together, and hence help explain their on-the-job behavior. For instance, how about economic factors, such as trends in production demand, labor demand, prices? How about technologic and engineering factors? How about social and political influences?

Exploration of a shop problem through such questions—and others that the instructor or student may add—now permits evaluation of its true dimensions, its dimensions both as a situation to be understood and as one to be actually handled. The initial problem defined and classified as "seniority," or "discipline," or "wage determination," or whatever, may prove predominantly what it had been presented to be from the outset: an objective dispute over concrete rights and obligations in shop relations amenable to settlement by the formal procedures of collective dealings. But it may also prove something quite different, taking on additional, deeper, and more relevant meanings as a result of the student's careful survey of the shop territory from which it springs. Indeed, such a diagnostic examination may now require a redefinition of the problem. New clues now may be discovered as to its nature. On re-examination does the problem take on significance beyond what might be deemed the normal expectancies of its label as a wage dispute or difference over seniority or whatever? Does its content seem unduly affected by emotions and sentiments on the part of the individuals and groups? Does the behavior evoked seem repetitive, that is, impervious to prior "settlements," or current offers; or excessive, that is, transcending the intrinsic importance of the issue involved? Do the problems themselves prove expansible, that is, do they seem to grow and multiply as the parties deal with them? In a word, does truly effective handling of the situation require recognition of latent disorders in individual, group, or shop relationships?

Recommending a Program of Effective Action. Just as each situation in this book gives the student the opportunity of exploring labor relations in operation, so also it places him in a situation which he must not only evaluate but within which he also must act effectively to further continuing objectives. The decision maker seeks the kind of understanding of a problem that facilitates responsible action. In like manner, as each new problem situation is presented, the student faces the responsibility of deciding what he himself, not as a student but rather as an individual in the specific situation, would do. Obviously, from the many facts of any one case, each student will draw his own interpretation of its "true nature" and, hence, his own individual plan for dealing with it. But in planning effective action, all students face common questions that each must answer.

For instance, what are the possible alternatives to resolve the situation which are feasible within the formal provisions of the agreement or the institutional considerations of the contract negotiation? Is the recommended program of action a specific one applicable to the concrete situation described in the case? Are the recommendations acceptable to the top leaders of both union and management? To foremen and shop stewards? To rank-and-file union members? Does the proposed action fulfill the institutional needs of the company and the union? Does the solution engender further problems, and, if so, have all the consequences been adequately weighed and prepared for? Is the handling of the specified problem integrated into the underlying internal *and* institutional relationships currently existing between the management and the union? Is the plan of action keyed to the objectives of either side, or both, in shaping the continuing relationships? Are provisions incorporated into the plan that will assure adequate follow-up after it is instituted? Is the program sufficiently flexible to allow for future changes if the need for them arises? Has adequate consideration been given the proper timing of the initiation of the program? Does it encompass a reasonable sequence among its various steps? Who, in terms of the existing social structure, are the most effective individuals and groups to assume responsibility for carrying out the resolution of the problem?

Not all these questions, of course, will need facing in every case, though action in industrial relations should never be a one-dimensional answer by formula to a problem "reduced" to headlining identifications by labels. Even less should it be an emotionalized response to anger, however justified, or to indignation, however valid. For after each problem has been handled, men must continue to live with collective bargaining; and every past action leaves its impress upon continuously evolving relationships. That is why the student does well to keep always in mind the sheer range of test questions to which recommended action may fairly be subjected. That is also why evaluation of the situation always precedes action; and action is related, not only to the problem to be acted upon, but also to the relationships underlying both.

At any rate, clue questions such as these for action in case situations should, at the least, suggest the far-ranging reach of industrial policy and behavior encompassed in present-day labor relations. In much the same way, the questions appended to each case attempt nothing more than to suggest helpful clues for uncovering the problem and its requirements in action. The fundamental aim remains always to stimulate the thinking that leads a student to make administrative decisions *for himself*—and in situations drawn from the *real* world of industrial relations. Thus, he may *experience* in the classroom the realities of collective bargaining in operation.

PART II.   INTERNAL RELATIONS: PROBLEMS IN THE SHOP

SECTION 1.   TRANSITION IN LABOR RELATIONS: A SOCIAL CHANGE

JOSEPH TODD COMPANY [1]

A NEW AGREEMENT IN A RETAIL CHAIN

The Joseph Todd Company operates a chain of retail stores in Cleveland under a three-year contract negotiated on May 1 of the current year with the Amalgamated Association of Mercantile Employees. Excerpts from an arbitration hearing held in June to deal with a dispute over the discharge of William Lee Fisher, a salesman, follow:

Present for the Company	*Present for the Union*
Philip Bartlett, President	Frank Marvin, District Director of the Amalgamated Association of Mercantile Employees
George Bartlett, Vice President of Labor Relations	
Harry Poole, Manager of the Lincoln Store	Anthony Corelli, Regional Staff Member of Union under Mr. Marvin
Charles Matthews, Attorney	William Lee Fisher, Discharged Salesman

Arbitrator [after some preliminary remarks]: I take it the union will present its case first, since it appealed the grievance to arbitration.

Matthews (m) [2] [breaking in]: The Joseph Todd Company operates a number of stores in this city, including the Lincoln store, the Cartwright store, and the Culver store. Three years ago the company employed William Fisher, placing him in the Lincoln store. But his record there proved so unsatisfactory that in February of the following year he was transferred to the Culver store. During his employment there from February to June, the manager filed constant complaints about him. In June, he was transferred to the Cartwright store; but several months later the company had to transfer him once more—this time back to the Lincoln store.

About two months ago, in April, he informed Mr. Poole, the Lincoln manager, that some difficulty had arisen between the employees and the company at the company's store in Allerton, some 60 miles distant, and he proposed to go there to straighten it out. The company has been dealing in these matters with Sullivan, the union's business agent. Accordingly, Mr. Philip Bartlett, to whom Fisher's request was referred by phone for decision, forbade him to leave the store. Nevertheless, he went to Allerton. The following morning, after quite a rumpus, the company agreed to give Fisher another chance.

On May 10th, about a month ago, a dispute arose in the Lincoln store

---

[1] In most of the cases in this volume names of persons, places, unions, and companies are disguised.

[2] The letter (u) or (m) after a name designates the speaker as a representative of union or management, as the case may be.

14

over the discharge of a salesman. Fisher immediately rushed in and announced to Mr. Poole that he was going to the company's main office, located on Colby Square, to discuss the matter. Though Mr. Poole told him definitely not to leave, he walked out. When he returned, he was informed that he was through. Thus the sole issue, as we see it, revolves around this question: against such a background, did the company have the right to discharge Fisher or not?

The man has been a consistent troublemaker, souring the atmosphere of every store in which he worked. Indeed, since he has been out, we find morale in the Lincoln store measurably improved. Moreover, his work record has been consistently below average. To this you must add deliberate insubordination. This is not the first time Fisher has coolly disobeyed unmistakable orders.

The company was reluctant after the Allerton incident to take him back. But to be fair and cooperative, the company finally agreed when the union pleaded. However, it was a last chance, and now the company says the chapter is closed. There is nothing in our contract that requires us to keep a man indefinitely. On the contrary, we have the clear right to discharge any employee for violating instructions.

The union, in turn, has the right to apply for arbitration, within seven days. In Fisher's case, even though the seven-day limit had expired, the union asked the company if it could defer arbitration, and—again we tried to be more than fair—the request was granted.

And that, in essence, is the issue in dispute. The company has discharged a man who for more than two years has been a chronic troublemaker, affected adversely store morale, failed to achieve even an average sales record, and has twice been guilty of undeniable insubordination. The company feels that it has the right not to give Fisher still another chance. We don't want apologies, promises, or explanations. We simply want to use our clear right of discharge in an unarguable case.

Marvin (u): The union cannot agree that this recital gives the whole story. We feel it highly important not to judge by single incidents, but in terms of the entire situation. For two years prior to the signing of our present contract just last month, we had difficulties with the company. We had two strikes, and Fisher was active on the picket line each time.

We were, of course, highly gratified when both sides arrived at an amicable agreement. It is a union shop agreement and stabilizes relations between us after considerable conflict and disturbance. During the whole period, Fisher has been a very militant union member. This current contract was concluded between the company and the international headquarters of the union. Dealing directly with national officials gives the company a substantial security in joint dealings. But Local 137, to which Fisher and the workers belong, still possesses real rights.

Now, in dealing with Fisher's discharge, the union feels that the strikes which took place before we reached this present stage, and Fisher's part in them, should enter into consideration. The company has long given evidence of bitter feelings against Fisher. But the new contract specifically states that the company and union should make an earnest attempt to settle all disputes. The company did not make an earnest effort to settle this dispute. They allowed their resentment of the past to influence their judgment about Fisher.

We also feel that the incident which gave rise to Fisher's discharge, the discharge on May 10th of a salesman named Kendrick, fell within the duties of a shop steward. What you really had was a difference of opinion between Mr. Poole and Fisher as to the proper duties of the shop steward. Fisher had the right to question Mr. Poole's judgment in dealing with the agreement. It was Fisher's duty to take up Kendrick's case and seek his reinstatement. In fact, he was told the night before by the proper union representative to handle the case. Kendrick has been put back. Unfortunately, when we came together to straighten Fisher's case out, remarks were made to intimidate Fisher and to arouse his emotions.

We want to make it clear that we want to maintain a friendly attitude. We have no desire to antagonize; we want no bitter feelings. But if we can convince the company, much more so than the arbitrator, that this trouble about Fisher has been a matter of antagonism, we feel this hearing will be worthwhile. In fact, it would be better if we could conciliate this difference, much better.

Philip Bartlett (m): I would like to say a few words for I have to leave. To begin with, my brother [George Bartlett] does not work for peanuts. He gets a good salary, and the time he spends on labor cases such as this costs the firm hard cash. We had several conferences in regard to this controversy, and made an earnest endeavor to settle it. Marvin begged, pleaded, promised, did everything in his power to have me out of the goodness of my heart take the fellow back, urging upon me that the fellow had a wife and family, there was sickness in the family, etc. But the fellow had no right to do what he did. We have a large business. We cannot be annoyed by malcontents.

Mr. Marvin says we are prejudiced. Yet we called Marvin in and said we wanted to do business with the union. We proposed giving them the union shop they wanted if we could deal directly with the national union office. Does this seem like prejudice?

As a result of Mr. Fisher's discharge, our setup has improved. I am happy to tell Mr. Marvin that I see a very great favorable change. Our stores had been showing a drop in sales, due mainly to personnel difficulties. We just can't employ this type of chap. We haven't singled out Fisher. In fact, when I first spoke with Fisher when he walked out in April, to be fair I said, "If I were you, I wouldn't go to Allerton." Then I came down to his level and I said, "Don't go to Allerton." The next day, when my brother decided he should be discharged, I said, "Give him another chance."

On the second occasion on May 10th, my brother was out of town. They called me. Fisher had left the store for a cup of coffee. Yet he told the manager he wanted to go to the main office and the manager told him he had no right to leave. He didn't come near the office. Subsequently, the union brought to my attention the fact that it was Fisher's half-day off. But he had taken his half-day off before to take his wife to the doctor.

They tried for weeks and weeks not to come to this arbitration. Marvin begged not to come to arbitration. We don't want to take him back unless we have to. I insist he is a disorganizer and a demoralizer. We have a three-year contract. We have accepted the union. Certainly that's no issue. Now what prejudices do I have against this boy? We still have fellows who did more harm, and we accept them. They have no real case. This arbitration is pure facesaving—to save their faces in the eyes of the local. That's all it is.

Arbitrator [to George Bartlett]: You knew, didn't you, that Mr. Fisher was a shop steward?

George Bartlett (m): Our new contract that we just signed in May is not with the local. There is absolutely no provision—not one word—in the contract for the local or for shop stewards. Prior to this contract, we had another contract—our first—and under it grievances were coming up continuously. The stewards looked for grievances, and they took a great deal of my time.

We deliberately made this contract with union headquarters in New York because it was more substantial. The only representative I am to recognize under the new contract is Mr. Marvin who represents national headquarters and whomever they appoint as business agent. As for shop stewards, they changed almost weekly. I couldn't say whether I knew Fisher was a shop steward. We had so many.

Arbitrator: What sort of record has Fisher as a salesman?

George Bartlett (m): When he first worked at our Lincoln store, no month went by without a complaint from the manager. He had low production, was tough to handle, showed sloppiness in his work. He always had an answer; he just could not accept criticism.

After his transfer, he was low man in the Culver store every single week. In spite of that he was put on the regular staff a year after he was hired. Isn't that evidence of no prejudice?

Matthews (m): I would like to know just what provision of the agreement the union charges us with violating. The union has the conventional setup of a business agent. The business agent before our present union-shop contract was Mr. Sullivan, and he was in the stores every day. Under that first contract disputes were always taken up with the business agent or Mr. Marvin. For practical reasons, the company designates one officer to handle these disputes, Mr. George Bartlett.

A shop steward is nothing but a dues collector. That a steward in one store has a right to go to Allerton to straighten out troubles is simply poppycock. Fisher was a store employee. As for Fisher, or any other store employee, we must use every man for sales or stock purposes. Before we start taking evidence, I want to know from the union what contract provision we violated.

Corelli (u): We are not saying much about violating the contract. After all, this contract hadn't been given a chance to work one week when Fisher was discharged. Mr. Bartlett said his stores are in better condition today. This contract had a lot to do with that improvement. Before, they used to be half union and half nonunion. Therefore, it took a lot of nerve and guts in these stores to uphold the union. These boys like Fisher were the leaders.

The thing hasn't really been given a chance to work yet. Probably the store leaders of the union made some blunders. People new in unionism sometimes let power go to their heads. Perhaps the union officers should not have given Fisher instructions to handle Kendrick's case. Fisher went to meet Mr. Sullivan, the business agent, in a restaurant, not to have a cup of coffee, but to report to him as business agent. I heard no complaint about his salesmanship before this hearing. To me, it seems just a question of misunderstanding.

Philip Bartlett (m): It has cost the company $150,000 in the last few years.

Marvin (u): Fisher is a strong union member—a shop steward. He is also a vice president of the local union. When a fellow first becomes an officer, he feels important.

But he didn't do anything to hurt the concern intentionally. I say he was instructed wrong. We admit he had no business to go to Allerton, but he was instructed to try to put Kendrick back—to reinstate a man discharged in his own store.

Arbitrator: Who is Kendrick?

George Bartlett (m): Kendrick is a clean-cut, fine chap. He has worked for us many years. He was not a union man. Without question, he was coerced and intimidated when the unionization campaign began, and after the second strike he joined the union. He became very insubordinate, although for years he had been an excellent salesman. During one of these altercations he was told to go to the main office. The manager always tells the men to go there before they are discharged. Managers do not themselves have the power of discharge. Mr. Kendrick came to the office and we took him back because we found out that he was ill. He himself suggested that he take a few days off to rest up and become himself again. Fisher was fighting Kendrick's case.

Corelli (u): Isn't there a real point in the fact that if Fisher did wrong, he did it under instructions of superior union officers? My honest conviction is that Fisher was not guilty of conscious insubordination. Seeking to reinstate a fellow worker in his line of duty, Fisher simply stepped out to meet the business agent.

Arbitrator: As I make it out, the union is trying to frame the issue upon the fact that Mr. Fisher is a novice in union dealings and therefore would make mistakes.

Philip Bartlett (m): Why should we train their novices?

Corelli (u): Fisher isn't exactly a novice; he's a rank and file leader in a young union. But the purpose of this arbitration is not to create disharmony. Maybe the matter can be conciliated. Wouldn't that give us a

better chance to create the harmony we all want without stirring up antagonism, without having one side win and the other lose?

Marvin (u): We are anxious to eliminate the feeling on the part of the
people that there is prejudice. Our men believe Fisher is a good fighter in
their cause. He has quite a following. The men are very worked up about
his discharge; they are watching this case. But I am sure we can straighten
this thing out. We don't want to go back to our men and say we beat the big
Joseph Todd Company in an arbitration. We would rather say: "See how
harmoniously everything is going; the company has very graciously shown a
big spirit."

Philip Bartlett (m) [to Fisher]: Fisher, you know my position in the
company. Have you ever borrowed money from me?

Fisher (u): Yes, you once lent me $200 when I had large medical bills.

Philip Bartlett (m): You spoke to me when the Allerton case arose. From
my conversation, what inference did you draw about going to Allerton?

Fisher (u): You said that if I went to Allerton, I didn't go as your representative.

Philip Bartlett (m): On the day Kendrick was discharged you went out.
You weren't taking your half-day off.

Fisher (u): I walked out at 9:15 to meet Sullivan. He said we should go
back to the store, but he hadn't had any breakfast and wanted a cup of
coffee.

Philip Bartlett (m) [to Mr. Poole]: Didn't you warn him not to go?

Poole (m): Yes, I told him you had given orders no one was to leave the
store.

Fisher (u): Sullivan and I came back to the store ten minutes after I
left. Mr. Poole told me I was to go to the main office.

Poole (m): I said you could not report back to work.

Fisher (u): I was talking with Mr. Poole between 9 and 9:15. I told him
I was given instructions by Frank Marvin to take Kendrick up to the office
with Sullivan and talk over his case with anybody in charge of the office.
Mr. George Bartlett was not in town. Then when I was told I could not
come back to work, our business agent at that time, Mr. Sullivan, phoned
Mr. Hillyer, the district manager of Todd, and asked if he could see him.
He told us to come right up. No time was wasted on fooling, such as Mr.
Bartlett seems to bring out. Any time I wanted a cup of coffee I asked the
manager and I was allowed to go out. I'm not dumb enough to jeopardize
my job for a cup of coffee.

Philip Bartlett (m): This is nauseating—I'm leaving. [He leaves in
anger.]

Fisher (u): I spoke to Mr. Hillyer about the matter, but he didn't want
to do anything about it.

Arbitrator: Mr. Marvin, who instructed this man to take up the Kendrick
matter?

Marvin (u): I instructed him the night before. I said, "I can't make the
Kendrick conference tomorrow. Why don't you go with Sullivan and if you
have any difficulty, I'll step in."

Matthews (m): Mr. Marvin says he talked to Fisher about Kendrick's case. They know where their union executives are. Was there any emergency? There were stock requirements—there were customers. Why is it necessary for this man to walk out on union business? This is old stuff. What shop stewards do has nothing to do with us. Salesmen cannot be permitted to do this sort of thing.

George Bartlett (m): Some time ago we discharged a man named Lederer. Mr. Marvin said we were right, but "It will create a lot of bad feeling if you fire him. I'll straighten him out." The union and Lederer wrote me letters waiving all future rights to bring the case to arbitration. We took him back on probation.

Arbitrator: I take it, that the union would like to do the same for Mr. Fisher.

George Bartlett (m): Fisher was fired once, then taken back. We are basing the discharge on the fact that this man twice flagrantly disobeyed instructions. As long as Fisher sets such an example in the store, he ruins employee morale.

Corelli (u): If it is a question of improving morale, we don't want to use this boy as a guinea pig. By discharging Bill Fisher, you will create hard feeling in the store. The employees have great respect for Fisher because he fought so hard for them during the strikes. If he is not taken back, I tell you there will be hell to pay. The officers won't be able to hold the men down. I told you I didn't want it to go to arbitration.

Marvin (u): I tell you the employees think a lot of Fisher, and you will find a real good effect on morale if you show bigness and put him back to work. Everyone will feel better.

Matthews (m): We were told by the president of the national union that Marvin could be relied upon. If they made a mistake and got into this kind of situation, then let them place Fisher with some other company. After going through that strike last fall and seeing what some of your members did and said on the picket line, the company has shown a very considerate attitude.

Arbitrator [to Poole]: Will you tell me what happened?

Poole (m): Fisher has been under my supervision for two years. After he came back from Allerton and was admonished, he was on his guard. He wasn't looking for any trouble. When the Kendrick matter came up, I particularly stressed the fact that he didn't have to leave the store. He could have phoned Mr. Sullivan.

George Bartlett (m) [to Poole]: At the time of the Allerton incident you were standing beside Fisher when he spoke to my brother?

Poole (m): I said to Fisher, "Have you Mr. Bartlett's permission to leave?" He said he had. I didn't call back to verify it.

Arbitrator [to Fisher]: Just why did you take it on yourself to go to Allerton?

Fisher (u): I received a call from the men in Allerton at the time; they said they were going out on strike.

Arbitrator: Why did you receive such a call from Allerton? Why not the union officers?

Fisher (u): I used to live in Allerton. I knew all those boys. When a man told me they were going to strike, I thought he knew what he was talking about. I knew that if they did go out on strike that eight men would not go back to work. I couldn't get in touch with Marvin. I told Mr. Philip Bartlett what had transpired. He said—these are exactly the words he used: "To hell with them. If the eight walk out, they won't be put back to work." He said to me, "Fisher, if you do go to Allerton, you don't go as my representative." I said that I was only going to see that no men walk off the job. I thought I was doing the company a good turn. Was I really so guilty? The company gained. I persuaded those men not to walk out.

Matthews (m): It's apparent Fisher is imbued with the idea that a job is a necessary evil only as long as it doesn't interfere with his desire to do as he wants.

Fisher (u): From the inferences of Mr. Bartlett and Mr. Matthews, I was a chronic troublemaker in their stores. But Mr. Poole will agree that since I came back to his store I never once had words with him. Time and time again, I straightened out a man, Mallinson, who was hard to handle. I was the only man who could talk with him.

Mr. Poole asked me before Columbus Day if I would have the men come in before the store opened to get stock ready and he knew I could refuse him. The fellows weren't "hepped up" about it, but I pleaded and got practically every one to come in before one o'clock. On another holiday the same thing happened. Then there was the time when Mr. Poole asked me to get the men to work after six on stocktaking during inventory and I did. Is that being detrimental?

Poole (m): How about the times I didn't fire men who were hard to handle?

Fisher (u): I was only proving that I wasn't such a detriment. I'll admit my selling wasn't exactly at high standard at first. But after I was put in a different store and learned how to take on more customers, my sales greatly improved. Then I asked to go back to my first store. I was unhappy in the other store. I had lost eighteen pounds running downstairs and upstairs—that was after the strike.

George Bartlett (m): He asked me as a personal favor to transfer him back. I was so "prejudiced" against him that I granted his request.

Arbitrator [to Fisher]: There was some mention of your taking your wife to the doctor on your half-day off, and getting a loan.

Corelli (u) [interrupting]: His wife is ill. One of his boys was also.

Fisher (u): A year ago I thought I would lose my boy. Now my wife is laid up; she needs an operation. But I don't want to bring her into this.

George Bartlett (m): Did you ask for a loan again recently?

Fisher (u): I asked Philip Bartlett for a loan and he said, "I'm not telling you 'no,' Fisher; I'll see." I thought if he meant to tell me no, he would not keep me waiting. I told him I wanted the money for my wife's operation.

George Bartlett (m): You got a loan last year from the loan fund. But didn't these last incidents occur after he refused you another loan?

Matthews (m): We were afraid that Fisher's family difficulties would be dragged in as appeals to sentiment and pity. When I was attorney general trying criminal cases, the defendant would usually claim he had trouble at home. But I always used to argue, "Why didn't this man think of his family before he committed his crime?"

Fisher (u) [to George Bartlett]: The statement was made to me that you yourself said you were lending other salesmen money, but how could you have any real feeling for picketers?

George Bartlett (m): Six men have had loans since that strike.

[The hearing was adjourned but the arbitrator asked Messrs. George Bartlett, Matthews, Marvin, and Corelli to remain for an informal conference.]

INFORMAL CONFERENCE

As the arbitrator canvassed the possibility of arriving at a mediated settlement, the following supplemental evidence was presented:

Corelli (u): The manager has been sore at Fisher. He made statements that he was going to get him. And Sullivan, too, tried to get Fisher out of a job. All the men know that for two years Sullivan said he was going to get Fisher.

George Bartlett (m): Sullivan fought for those men. Sullivan stood up for the stores too, and protected their interests.

Matthews (m): The Joseph Todd Company made its first contract covering stores in this city two years ago as the result of a strike. That contract covered four stores. It was extended to two other stores that were later added. That contract expired a year ago. There was another strike. They wanted a union shop.

George Bartlett (m): We rejected the demand for a union shop because the local officers didn't control their members.

Matthews (m): Then a month ago a new contract was signed granting the union shop in return for restricting all our dealings to national union representatives. So for all practical purposes we have been working with this union for over two years.

George Bartlett (m): In 41 of our stores we have contracts with this union and no disagreements whatever. We have had to go to arbitration only in Cleveland.

Marvin (u): I would like to clarify the question of company morale. It doesn't make any difference what the company thinks about Jim Sullivan, but it makes a difference what the union thinks about a business agent. Jim Sullivan was removed from office as business agent because everybody in the union believed he was out to get Fisher. He was found guilty on no less than six charges.

Now if Fisher is discharged, every single employee of the Joseph Todd Company will feel that Jim Sullivan got Fisher. What does the company think will happen with all the men thinking that? The whole city is watching this case. Our boys think the company always liked to work close with Sullivan. That's what they think, rightly or wrongly, and they just ousted Sullivan because he actually said he was out to get Fisher.

George Bartlett (m): Corelli and Marvin will agree that the union went to the salesmen's heads. What we went through was terrific. No one could have handled them. But now all but two or three have settled down. I am supposed to have 66 stores under my control; instead of that, I handle only six because they take all my time. But I haven't fired anyone without absolutely good cause.

Marvin (u): I'd rather we work these things out quietly between us. But if the company is going to take an absolutely arbitrary stand, the union can make plenty of trouble too.

Corelli (u): This case will wreck the local union in the city. There is deep union feeling in this case. We have to preserve the union.

Marvin (u): The moment Fisher was fired there was a lot of feeling stirring. They were going out on strike, but I sent a bulletin to the stores telling the men to be loyal to the company and to the contract.

DISCUSSION QUESTIONS

1. How would you evaluate the new union agreement as fitting the Joseph Todd Company as a working community?

2. How would you evaluate the handling of this whole situation (*a*) by the company; (*b*) by the union?

3. How would you evaluate the process of communication in this case?

ABBOT–PEABODY COMPANY

WILDCAT STRIKES AND A NEW AGREEMENT

Abbot-Peabody is a producer of quality cabinets with a custom trade and a long-established reputation for expert workmanship. One of its skilled craftsmen, Charles Lane, was discharged after participating in a wildcat strike. The United Craftsmen of America disputed the company's decision regarding Lane and ultimately sought arbitration. Present at the hearing before the arbitrator were the following:

For the Company	For the Union
Barton Kent, Plant Manager	Michael Westerly, Chairman of the District Council
	Christopher Moreland, Business Agent
	George Cooper, International Representative
	Charles Lane, Discharged Employee

Westerly (u): The workers at Abbot-Peabody are skilled craftsmen. Yet they were paid less than the prevailing wage in the city. The company operated without a union until February of this year when the workers decided the only way to improve conditions was to join the union.

Lane came to our office to request that we organize Abbot-Peabody. He has been cabinet-maker in the special-order department for 11 years and never had any trouble. We assigned Christopher Moreland, a business agent, to organize the Company. After a meeting, the workers signed cards designating our union as bargaining agent. Moreland then approached Mr. Kent. After some negotiation, the union was accepted and the workers were granted an increase of $2.40 per week, which brought them up to the market wage level.

Chairman: Which was what?

Westerly (u): $48.50 per week.

However, we did not succeed in obtaining a signed agreement then, and when Mr. Kent objected to Moreland's visiting the shop, we had our first difficulty. That controversy over the right of access resulted in a stoppage. But it was immediately settled, with the understanding that an agreement would be negotiated to get everything down formally in writing.

In the meantime, I was negotiating an agreement covering all member companies of the Employers' Association. All firms here are on a 40-hour week. Hence the standard market contract we negotiated with the Association provided: "The 40 hours per week shall be worked in 6 days of 6 hours and 40 minutes each."

Shortly afterward Business Agent Moreland approached Abbot-Peabody with a copy of this standard contract just negotiated with the Association of which Abbot-Peabody was not a member. In urging acceptance of its terms, he overlooked the fact that Abbot-Peabody employees had for years been working their 40 hours in 5½ days. Moreland never realized the seriousness of this issue, and how the change would affect these workers. They were accustomed, you see, to working 5½ days and taking Saturday afternoons off. For reasons best known to Mr. Kent, he notified his employees that *beginning September 1*, working hours would be divided equally into six days per week, thus ending Saturday afternoon off. There was a great deal of resentment to that change. Brother Moreland will go on from here.

Moreland (u): On the first Saturday in September, the entire group stopped working at 12:30, the same time they had stopped for years. The following Monday at 9:30 A.M., they all came to the union office. I told them to go right back to work—that I could do nothing unless they observed the contract on handling grievances.

That same morning Mr. Kent called me for all new workers. I told him I had already sent the people back to work. He put them all back to work except one cabinet-maker. That was Harriman, not Lane. About 11:00 A.M. I went to Abbot-Peabody and found Harriman outside. He said he was fired; so I contacted Mr. Kent. He was very much upset. He told me Harriman was finished, though he had worked there ten years. I called a meeting that night. I told them that according to our agreement they could not stay away from work as they had that morning.

Chairman: Had they all gone back that morning?

Moreland (u): Yes, and all were put back to work immediately except Harriman. At our evening meeting I explained the contract clause providing for arbitration of differences. Then I told them all to report back to work the next morning. Harriman was then put back to work, but Lane was fired. Mr. Kent phoned for a cabinet-maker saying that if I didn't send him one within 48 hours, he would advertise in the papers. I asked him why. He had Lane, didn't he? He said, "This man is too radical to work for me." We claim Lane was discharged without cause.

Chairman: Mr. Kent, let us hear from you.

Kent (m): Let me give you some history. Although these employees were paid less than the established wage before they joined the union, they had many extra benefits. For instance, if they were out sick for several days, they got their pay. If they were out for more than a week, they got half pay. That was rather indefinite—in some cases, it ran up to a sick leave, or other leave of five or six months. They were also given the Saturday half holiday, while the rest of the market was on a 6-day week. During the summer, when we close on Saturday, they worked 35 and one-half hours a week but received 40 hours' pay. They were permitted to leave early when necessary and were excused on stormy days and hot afternoons. We also carried insurance for these people—and many other considerations were shown them. Our minimum wage for cabinet-makers was $46.10; elsewhere the minimum was $48.50.

They joined the union because they wanted more money. When they joined they spoke to me, and I said I would be glad to pay the established union wage, but they would then have to work under the same conditions which union employees throughout our market worked; that is, instead of being paid a weekly wage, they would go on an hourly wage. That was about all that was said. In my opinion, I thought the slight difference in the union rate would hardly see them with any more money in their pockets. Moreland told me the minimum wage per cabinet-maker was $48.50, but because of the quality of our work, he asked that we pay $50.00. I finally agreed to that.

Now I didn't want Moreland to come into our shop because it was not then a union shop. We had three women who were not union members. They are not young—two are in their 60's—one has turned 70. Moreland has spoken to them of joining—and they were annoyed and disturbed. In addition, once when I was away from the shop, two other union men came with Moreland and tried to sell the union to our salesmen and office help. Now, it is against our policy, right or wrong, to let union officials come into the shop to organize. Therefore, I denied Moreland the privilege of coming to the shop—except to ask particularly for me.

When I denied Moreland this privilege, Moreland called a strike. After they were out a couple of days, Moreland and I got together and I agreed that we would let him come if he let those three older women alone. I think that takes care of that point.

Now, we come to Mr. Lane.

Chairman: Before you get to that—I gather you now operate under a written agreement. Will you tell me about it?

Kent (m): I will be glad to. In July, Moreland told me that the Employers' Association was going to increase pay to $52.50 and that it was up to me to do the same thing, although this time he didn't suggest a quality differential. I got in touch with Mr. Anderson, Marshall Company's manager and chairman of the employers' group in labor negotiations. He said, "Yes, the union has asked for $52.50 and our group has agreed to it." So I told Moreland that we would bring our minimum wage up to $52.50. At the same time, I asked him for a written agreement. Since we were now employing on the same terms as others, I said, we should have the same contract they had. He agreed and presented me with the standard contract. We signed it in August. We have lived up to that contract. It calls for a standard 40-hour week to be worked 6 hours and 40 minutes a day for 6 days. And that's the way we are working.

When our employees came to me and asked to continue Saturday afternoons off, I said that I did not see how I could. It would hardly seem fair to other shops. Our men are all members of the same union; our shop now is a member of the Employers' Association. We are all paying the same money, and we should all be considered in the same light. Incidentally, these contract hours suited us better than our former arrangement. They give an evenly balanced day every day of the week. We know just what we have to do.

We have lived up to the contract. But unfortunately, our employees have not liked it. They have resented it very much. They protested about the hours. Then finally, on this particular Saturday, I went out to the workroom between twelve and one o'clock. They are usually at lunch then, but this day they were still working. "What's this?" I asked. "Aren't you taking any lunch hour today?"

"No," they said, "we are going to leave at twenty minutes of one."

I said, "You can't do that. You will be losing two hours' pay." Well, they seemed perfectly willing to lose two hours' pay. They were leaving at twenty to one! I was very much disturbed. I had counted on that full day's work. I said I was sore, and I probably sounded that way.

In any event, I said, "All right, if you want to lose pay, go ahead." But I said to Lane, "Here are orders that simply have to be finished today; they must be done for Monday morning." But he walked out and didn't touch them.

Monday morning they didn't come in. I called Moreland and told him the men had walked out and that in accordance with our contract I was asking him to supply the workers I needed. I specified one cabinet-maker less than we had when they walked out.

He said, "How about sending back your own workers?"

I said, "That's fine. Can you get them here in 15 minutes?"

He said, "I will have to look them up. I can't do it in 15 minutes."

I understood him to say a moment ago that they were there in his office at 9:30 A.M.; that is not what he told me then. They came back at a quarter of eleven. When I asked them if they were going to work, they said they would start at eleven o'clock.

I went over to John Harriman and said, "I am afraid I will have to let you go."

The next morning Harriman came back. I said, "I told you yesterday I didn't need you. I still don't."

He just said, "All right." When Harriman walked out, Lane and two others also walked out, but the rest of them who had walked out before decided they didn't want to walk out again.

Then I called Moreland again and told him I needed a cabinet-maker and one jointer. In accordance with the contract, I have to give them 48 hours to supply someone; otherwise, I can go into the open market.

Shortly afterwards Mr. Anderson called me, more or less interceding, and we conversed about what had happened. Apparently, Mr. Westerly had talked to him, asking him to try his good offices.

Mr. Anderson said: "Why don't you change your hours back to your old schedule?"

I said, "I don't feel I should."

After a while he asked, "Why don't you take back these men?"

I replied, "I don't need the jointer, and I don't want the cabinet-maker."
He said, "Would you settle for one?"

And I said, "Well, all right, and if it doesn't make any difference, I'll take Harriman and the other two back."

I said then, and I repeat now, that I cannot take Lane back. He is discharged because he has been a troublemaker for a long, long time. We had great difficulty with him, even though we treated him most liberally. He is not a well man. He has been out sick a great deal; he has had other troubles which took him away from business. Before he belonged to the union, he was paid during such absences. Since that time, he has lost such pay.

He is very difficult to get along with; he has a temper; he is not cooperative. I feel Abbot-Peabody would benefit greatly without his services. I think the other employees are tickled to death that he isn't there. They all are working today and have been since he's been out—just as nice as you please, and they are all happy.

You may wonder why I let Harriman go. You see, we in cabinet manufacture must maintain quality, meet high costs, increased wages, and try to keep prices down. Consequently, to survive we must increase volume or get greater efficiency. In our custom trade increasing volume doesn't offer much hope. So we have to watch expenses. When things were on an "easy come, easy go" basis, when we were on a personal basis with our workers, and they got a little below the standard wage, there were many times we didn't need everyone. We kept them all just the same. Now we have to watch our step.

We have more efficient management. I have just put a new man in to supervise one department. Our former supervisor is ill—has been for three weeks. It is doubtful if he will be able to come back, and I had to get another man. I now have a man who has more ability to manage. We talked over the situation and concluded that we could do the same work with one less man since the walkout, so we let Harriman go.

Westerly (u): According to one paragraph of our agreement, "The employer should not employ any regular employees covered by this agreement who are not members in good standing in the union."

Kent (m): That is right.

I have conscientiously kept a union shop. Three women did not join in the beginning. Mr. Moreland spoke to me about them. He said he would waive their initiation fee, but they weren't interested. When we signed the written agreement, I told them, "I'm sorry, but this has got to be a union shop. You've got to join the union if you want to stay."

They said, "All right." I gave them the cards and they signed them. I talked to Moreland about them again, and said, "These people can't give me $3 all at once." He said, "It isn't $3 now; it is $5." I said, "You told me $3, the same as the other people paid." He said, "It's been changed."

I still have their three signed cards and I have $3 from each one. He agreed to $3 and then changed to $5.

Westerly (u): No dues were paid for these members up to now?

Kent (m): You haven't asked me for their cards.

Westerly (u): You stated a while ago you asked exemption for these three in spite . . .

Kent (m): I didn't ask for exemption. I asked that they be taken in without initiation fee, because Moreland had offered to waive that.

Moreland (u): I never told Mr. Kent I would waive it. I told him the others who came in as a group each paid $3, and I didn't see why those women should not pay. Mr. Kent said he had the initiation fee for the women, and handed me $3, installments of $1 each. I said, "I cannot take $1 each, and besides they will have to pay $5 because we changed the fee."

Westerly (u): In the meantime, you permitted those women to work without paying the union fees?

Moreland (u): I did.

Westerly (u): You didn't enforce the contract on this matter?

Moreland (u): No, I overlooked it.

Westerly (u): Now to the matter of the hours. [To Mr. Moreland.] Mr. Kent didn't request during negotiations that the 40 hours should be worked in 6 days instead of 5½ days? That was simply overlooked on your part?

Moreland (u): Correct.

Westerly (u): Right after the stoppage, I received a call about it from Mr. Kent. We discussed the situation and I told him the whole trouble arose from a misunderstanding on hours. If the schedule could be brought back to 5½ days—which the shop was accustomed to—that would be the end of our dispute. Mr. Kent took the attitude that he would concede the hours. I told him that since the hours were settled, all the people would go back to work. Mr. Kent said they were all discharged—"since they walked out of my shop last Saturday, they are no longer considered employed."

As you know, such an attitude on the part of management generally throws a picket line about the shop. I realized that Mr. Kent did not have much experience with the union, nor did our people there have much experience with our union. I phoned Richard Anderson, chairman of the Employers' Association, to ask if he would intervene. Mr. Anderson contacted Mr. Kent who said he would take everyone back but Lane. I sent the workers back and told Mr. Kent that we would arbitrate Lane's case.

That evening, the men came to my office and said when they got back to the shop, Mr. Kent claimed that the hours would remain on the 6-day schedule. I immediately contacted Mr. Kent who insisted we had not reached any understanding about hours. I thought we had. But Mr. Kent said, "If you will drop the arbitration regarding Lane, I may consider the reinstatement of the 5½ day schedule."

Remember that Lane has worked for the firm eleven years. He must have been a faithful employee; he never had any dispute with the firm until he joined the union. Now, as a result of that two-hour stoppage, he is fired. We insist he should be reinstated with wages lost since his discharge.

Chairman: Mr. Kent, do you want to make any further comments?

Kent (m): We have a club called the "Quarter Century Club." It has about 75 members. I am a member myself. Clearly we don't discharge employees unless we have cause. Our company is 103 years old, and we are proud of our record with both employees and customers. I wouldn't have discharged Mr. Lane if I didn't honestly believe I was justified in doing so.

Chairman: On the hours of work, have you anything further to say on that issue?

Kent (m): When Mr. Westerly and I talked that over, I said I would change the hours but that I expected the consideration and treatment I was entitled to under the contract. Their contract calls for 6 hours and 40 minutes per day, and Lane walked out on me in spite of the fact he was told not to go. Mr. Westerly says Lane has never had any trouble before. He has had trouble with his fellow employees—lots of trouble. I ask you to take my word for it.

I don't know anything else I can say. I do not think that these men who have been in the union for six months should have done what they did. They have been in long enough to know what the contract requires. I believe the union has been negligent. I don't think the union has dealt fairly with us. I see no reason why I should make concessions to them, since this is a contract identical for all shops in this area, and we are now paying the union wage.

Cooper (u): I feel that there's no reason why Mr. Kent and the union can't learn to work together. Mr. Kent said he would be satisfied to have the hours the same as they used to be, but the firm did not want to violate the contract. We agreed to change that paragraph.

Kent (m): If it were agreeable to Mr. Anderson and the other companies in the Employers' Association.

Cooper (u): So we said, "Okay, the hours issue is eliminated. Let us get them back to work and we will forget about it."

Mr. Kent said, "I will not have them back."

Kent (m): When I discovered that I could not have the sympathy and co-operation of the union to support me in a justifiable claim regarding the work force, I felt there was no use trying to play ball with you fellows, and I would stand on my contract. I would consider the hours when I felt satisfied the union would play ball with me.

Cooper (u): Lane has worked at Abbot-Peabody's eleven years. So he must have been satisfactory.

Kent (m): We put up with him, that's all.

Cooper (u): The point is this: After he joined the union, he became a troublemaker; he became a sick man. After eleven years, all the bad in him came out. If he did not join a union for another eleven years, I don't believe there would be any action against him.

Chairman: Mr. Kent, when did Mr. Lane become a problem as an inefficient man?

Kent (m): He will loaf on the job when nobody is watching him. It is an old game for men in the special-order department to let work pile up and make overtime.

Chairman: When did he start that?

Kent (m): That has been a matter of four or five years.

Lane (u) [interrupting heatedly]: It is not the truth.

Kent (m): I do take special exception to these things now. For now, you see, he represents a higher investment, a greater expense to Abbot-Peabody. Before, it wasn't too serious.

Chairman: Would you like to say something, Mr. Lane?

Lane (u) [rises and exclaims vehemently]: I have been working here eleven years. I am the father of seven children. I am a strong fellow, and I work like a horse. My work was always finished on time. I never went on a drunk as some of the others, and my work went off like clockwork.

Chairman: If there are no further comments, we will declare the hearing adjourned.

DISCUSSION QUESTIONS

1. How would you diagnose the situation underlying this dispute between the company and union?

2. Evaluate critically the way in which management and union representatives handled themselves.

LAKETOWN POWER COMPANY

AN INTERNATIONAL REPRESENTATIVE'S ASSIGNMENT

I

By vote of the executive board of the Electrical Workers' Union, J. C. MacTavish, international representative, was directed to investigate the discharge of Edward Weston. He was empowered to conclude the most favorable possible settlement compatible with the maintenance of good relationships with the company. The duties of an international representative are not sharply defined. He usually assists local unions in matters demanding a specialist's knowledge and experience. He aids in the negotiation of contracts and in the handling of grievances of major significance.

Laketown Power employed some 1,000 men. The local union had been in existence for two and one-half years, and was operating under its second contract. MacTavish sized up union-management relationships as "average—not especially good and not particularly bad."

Weston, a boiler operator employed by the Laketown Power Company, was also the president of the recently organized local union. From the beginning he had taken an active and aggressive part in union affairs.

II

In preparing to handle the dispute, MacTavish arranged a special meeting with the union for the evening of his arrival, and a conference with company representatives the following morning. At the union meeting John Thomas, vice president, presided. Upon the request of the members, MacTavish agreed to act as chairman of the grievance committee to meet with the company if Thomas and Frank Hunter would serve as its members. Hunter, a member of the local union's executive board, was a boiler-room foreman, while Thomas held the job of a company lineman and thus worked outside the plant. They accepted membership on the committee.

Thereupon the following findings of the executive board with regard to Weston's discharge were read by the secretary:

Near shut-down time on the morning of April 14, Weston asked Bilk [plant operator, and direct supervisor of Weston and Fry] to assign Fry [oiler] to assist him [Weston] in taking boiler meter readings. Bilk told Weston that he had Fry busy on other work and to remember that meter reading was the duty of boiler operators. Weston argued that Fry should be helping him with this kind of work so that he could be trained for promotion. Bilk refused to give in. As he went back to his work, Weston noticed Fry removing soot from a fire box door. Thereupon he returned to Bilk to protest that Fry was doing work belonging properly to maintenance men. Bilk repeated that Fry was busy and that the work he was doing was solely his [Bilk's] responsibility. The two fell to arguing over the duties of the various men on the shift and the need for giving them training that would qualify them for promotion. Finally Weston informed Bilk that he intended to take the matter up with Carver [plant superintendent] the next day. Bilk replied he would meet Weston in Carver's office at 2 o'clock.

When Weston arrived at Carver's office, he found Bilk already there. Carver immediately informed him that Bilk had recommended, on Personnel Form 18,[1] his discharge for insubordination. Carver refused to discuss the matter, telling Weston to take it up with Mr. Johnson [division manager].

Although Johnson was unable to see Weston that afternoon, he gave him an appointment the next morning. When Weston arrived in Johnson's office, he found Carver and Bilk with Johnson. As discussion got under way, Weston interjected, "You fellows just have it in for me for taking time off last week." Johnson replied, "That is not so. We have closed that case. But if that's the way you feel about it, Bilk has recommended your discharge, and I now concur in his recommendation. There is nothing more to be said."

III

After the union meeting had adjourned, the grievance committee stayed to plan procedure. Hunter told MacTavish that Weston had been officious around the plant. He had made himself unpopular in the company by pushing too aggressively his ideas about exclusive job duties. Weston's father had been a railroad union man, while Weston himself had worked previously in construction. In contrast to the railroads and the building trades, where rigid craft lines prevailed, there was considerable latitude in utilities regarding work assignments. Yet Weston persistently attempted to introduce more job rigidity, and thus had made himself unpopular with management. As for that statement of Weston's that had caused Johnson to explode, everyone in the boiler room had heard that Weston had been "on the carpet" some weeks ago, but neither Hunter nor Thomas knew the exact details.

IV

When he met alone with the union members of the grievance committee, Weston took no exception to the report of the executive board regarding his discharge. MacTavish asked Weston to explain his charge that management "had it in for him." Some two weeks ago, Weston explained, he had gone to Bilk's house to arrange for the next night off to attend to union business. Bilk had told him his request was too late to arrange for relief. Moreover, he doubted whether Weston really had to take time off for the purpose alleged— to go to a neighboring town to learn the results of an arbitration over wage rates in another division of the company. Upon Weston's insistence, however, Bilk finally had agreed, provided Weston could make proper arrangements

---

[1] A form on which supervisors rated men every four months for purposes of promotion. Specific offenses were also noted. Employees were permitted to enter remarks on the back. The use of this form was unpopular because the workers felt that "the slate was never wiped clean."

with Carver. Unable to locate Carver, however, Weston phoned the boiler operator whom he was to relieve, and told him he would not be in. Both of the following two nights were Weston's regular times off. When he returned to work on his regular shift, he was called to Carver's office and rebuked in the presence of Bilk. Admitting that he had been wrong, Weston offered to reimburse the company for the overtime paid to the man who had worked in his stead. Carver refused the offer, with the warning not to let it happen again.

Bilk also confirmed the accuracy of the executive board's report to the union committeemen. In his opinion, moreover, Weston would not have been discharged except for his attitude in Johnson's office. Although he would not rescind his recommendation that Weston be discharged, Bilk was willing to do anything to help Weston find another job. He refused any information regarding the attitudes of Carver or Johnson as expressed to him personally.

V

The union grievance committee coming to meet with management the next day found Messrs. Mitchell (sales manager), Burnes (division engineer), and Johnson (division manager) present as members of the company committee. The union members objected to Johnson as an unsuitable member of a joint committee to pass judgment upon appeal from a discharge that he himself had already confirmed. Johnson replied that MacTavish, as international representative, was just as biased as he. Throughout the discussion that followed, Johnson insisted upon his right to participate. The union finally withdrew its protest, and Johnson presided at the hearing.

Carver thereupon opened the hearing by declaring that Weston had been a disturbing element. He cited the refusal of other operators to accept Weston on their shifts, which proved Bilk more patient with Weston than most other supervisors. Weston always seemed to feel employees were doing work that didn't belong to them; yet *he* always wanted the chance at work that would give him training to qualify for promotion. In fact, he had asked transfer out of Bilk's shift because Bilk would not let him run the switchboard, and accordingly was "unduly limiting," as Weston put it, "his chances for promotion."

As soon as Carver concluded, Johnson, without consulting his own management members, declared that the company committee had decided "to stand on the discharge." MacTavish protested that they were meeting in joint conference; but as yet nothing had occurred that could be considered either joint or conferring. Thomas joined MacTavish in requesting opportunity to question both Johnson and Carver. Johnson refused to accede to these protests. Thereupon Hunter, speaking for the first time, accused Johnson of acting in a very unfair manner. If he persisted, Hunter said, the union executive board would carry the case to arbitration. On that note, the meeting adjourned.

VI

Taking the next step in appeal procedure, the union presented a written grievance to the company president. The contract gave him ten days in which to determine management's final decision.

MacTavish hardly expected President Horne to reverse the decision of his subordinates unless the union could uncover further evidence. The apparent inconsistency of Hunter's reactions to the situation led him to suspect, moreover, that he himself had yet to learn the whole story. When the grievance committee first met, Hunter had been quite critical of Weston's attitudes, and almost seemed to justify management's dissatisfaction with him. Yet, at the joint conference, when Johnson declared management would uphold Weston's discharge, Hunter had protested vigorously.

MacTavish decided to investigate further. As matters stood, he did not believe arbitration could be averted. Yet, although the union's position was strong, he wanted, if possible, not only to save the time, money, and effort involved in arbitration, but even more important, to avoid the effects on relationships that such an arbitration might have.

MacTavish began by another talk with Hunter. In its course, Hunter made the following remarks:

Mac, I am somewhat on the spot. Weston has made it tough for the foremen because he insists on trying to run a utility along the lines of a building trades organization. Then he hollers like hell because he doesn't get a chance to work as switchboard operator. Bilk has been a plant operator only a short time and hasn't yet been willing to take the responsibility for recommending anybody's promotion. Bilk told me he had no idea they would fire Weston on his recommendation. He just wanted to throw a little fear into a fellow whose head was getting too big for his hat. A reprimand would have been enough about the fire box door. But Johnson has been anti-union all the time and has been waiting for a chance to crack down. Bilk is a good man and I hate to make any statement before an arbitrator that would hurt him. On the other hand, I know that what Carver said is not so—the other plant operators would not object to accepting Weston if he were transferred. If the case goes to arbitration, I will have to tell the arbitrator what Bilk told me, so I hope you can do something to keep it from getting that far.

VII

MacTavish then interviewed Bilk. The record of this interview follows:

MacTavish: Bilk, this Weston affair is a mess. What's the real trouble here anyway?

Bilk: Mac, I wish I really knew. I haven't been on this job long and I'm anxious to make a go of it. Good jobs like this don't grow on trees, and I'm making more money now than I ever did in my life. With a couple of kids to support, I can't take any chances. Ed needled me for a long time about not giving the men a chance to learn better jobs. Fry wasn't the first by any means. But I'm responsible for over $4,000,000 worth of equipment, and I'm not going to take chances on a green man blowing it up.

MacTavish: You say Ed needled you?

Bilk: Did he! Why, he was after me all the time for a chance to take over the switchboard. And another thing, do you know what Ed told me after the meeting in Carver's office? He said he was going to prefer charges against me in the union for disclosing union business. All I had said was that I did not think he really needed that time off for a trip. As a matter of fact, I think he simply wanted a night off and this one looked as good as any—better perhaps because it came just before his regular time off and gave him a nice stretch. I've read the contract, and if the union suspends me, the company will have to fire me, won't they? [1]

MacTavish: No, you always have the chance to appeal. Anyway, the union would never suspend you for anything like that.[2] Ed must have been kidding you.

Bilk: I never thought of that. [Pause.] You know, I had no idea that they would fire Ed. In fact, I didn't even intend to recommend him for a discharge. When I went home though, later on, I got thinking of how Ed had been needling me constantly and maybe needed a little disciplining. I talked the matter over with Mr. Carver and he suggested that a recommendation for discharge and a talk from Mr. Johnson might do Ed some good. We had no idea that Mr. Johnson would get angry and discharge Ed when he said management had it in for him. Why, Mr. Johnson had told us we were foolish to bring in a recommendation for discharge on such a small matter. He said that maybe Ed should have been suspended and lose a few days' pay, but he thought it was too late for that. I wish I knew what to do. You're not going to say anything to Mr. Carver or Mr. Johnson about this, are you?

MacTavish: No, Bilk. I'm simply charged with presenting the case for Weston in behalf of the union.

Bilk: You know, I've a good notion to tell Mr. Johnson we can't get by with this. He just lost his temper. By golly, it's not fair, and I'm going to see him right now.

That night Bilk called MacTavish to inform him that he had seen Johnson, who had told him to forget the whole thing until Mr. Horne returned to the city. He also said that he got the impression Johnson had "cooled off."

---

[1] The contract with the union provided that "all employees within the terms of this agreement must become and remain members of the union in good standing as a condition precedent to continued employment with the company."

[2] The contract also included this provision: "The parties hereto recognize that because of the requirements of the public service, certain employees, such as working foremen and higher grade workmen, are required from time to time to enforce discipline, to supervise and direct the work, and to instruct and train other employees. Accordingly, it is agreed that nothing herein contained shall serve to hinder or obstruct such employees in the lawful discharge of their duties, nor shall this agreement alter or diminish the right of the company to remove such designated employees when they repeatedly or inexcusably fail in the discharge of their responsibilities to the management."

VIII

The next morning, before leaving town, MacTavish called on Ed Clancy, company vice president, to discuss the matter.   Clancy told him that since he had to live with the union in negotiations, he did not want to be involved in grievance matters.   However, he promised to talk with Johnson, and if he felt it necessary, with Carver and Bilk.

Five days later Clancy called MacTavish to report Horne's decision.   The president had decided management had been "too hasty in discharging Weston."   He wanted to know if the union committee would accept for Weston a 10-day layoff, without pay, and a return to work with all rights unimpaired.   Weston had been out 23 working days, but the union had found a construction job for him three days after he was discharged.

The offer of the company was accepted, and Weston returned to his job as boiler operator.

DISCUSSION QUESTION

1. Trace in detail and evaluate the steps utilized by MacTavish in handling this situation.

EXHIBIT 1

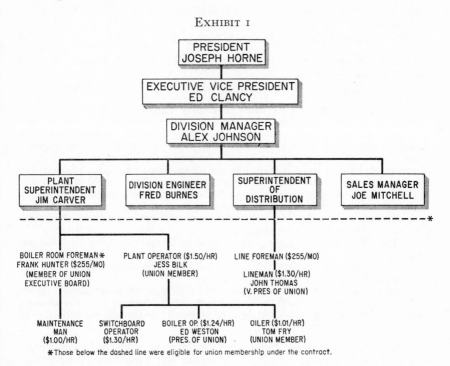

* Those below the dashed line were eligible for union membership under the contract.

ELLISON SHOE COMPANY

A CRAFTSMAN QUITS

Ambrose Vitek approached his foreman Saturday morning for his wages; he wished to quit. Foreman Cooley refused to finalize the resignation without knowing Vitek's reason, which Vitek would not share.

Vitek then went to the employment supervisor, Gerald Smith, who in turn took him to see the superintendent. Learning that Superintendent Lawrence would be away for a few days, Smith talked with Vitek. Vitek alleged that the union grievance committee and many of his fellow operators had made his life miserable. The union, affiliated with the AFL, had recently won a representation election, superseding the independent union with which the company had been dealing for some two years.

Vitek was excited and talked a great deal about his abuse at the hands of his fellow employees. He also complained that he had not been getting his share of "centers," and that he had been getting large sizes while other cutters were given small sizes, which enabled them to earn more than he. Smith urged Vitek to remain an employee and take up the case with Lawrence when he returned on Wednesday.

The following bulletin had recently been posted:

1. The position of this company regarding each and all the unions in the shoe industry is *entirely neutral*.
2. The company will not advise an employee whether or not to join a union or any particular union.
3. The company retains its rights to employ qualified workers regardless of membership or nonmembership in any particular union. There have now been two elections in our plant. The company has abided by the wishes of its employees in dealing impartially with the unions successively certified as their chosen majority spokesmen—even though management still feels that the history of this company demonstrates that no union is needed to protect employee interests. The company asks the same observance from our union employees. They should abide loyally to their contractual pledges not to "intimidate or coerce employees into membership in the union," and not to "recruit new members on company time."
4. All employees have the right to the same treatment, regardless of whether they do or do not belong to any organization.
5. The policy of this company with regard to becoming a union shop *has not changed*.
6. We believe that the most satisfactory solution of problems arising can be had only by frank, open conferences with employees.
7. In conformity with this belief, there will always be the freest possible opportunity to discuss problems with the management either personally with the foreman, employment supervisors, superintendent, or president; or through regularly elected union representatives.

On Wednesday morning, Superintendent Lawrence convened a conference. The foreman, the union grievance committee, and Vitek himself were summoned.

Vitek repeated the complaints he previously had made. He also stated that the grievance committee of the union had told him not to take anything up with the management except through the committee.

The chairman of the grievance committee replied that Vitek was lying, and charged him with breaking union rules. Lawrence suggested that such a charge could not affect Vitek's employment; it was for the union and not for the company to discipline a man who broke union rules.

Lawrence closed the conference after assuring the union representatives that he would take the matter up with them as soon as he was able to get the facts concerning the assignment of work to Vitek.

Two days later Lawrence talked privately with Vitek and told him the results of the investigation regarding the discrimination he had alleged in the allotment of "centers" and "sizes." The superintendent also stated his decision regarding Vitek's status with the company.

These points were restated in a conference held later the same day with the grievance committee, at which the following were present:

For the Company	*For the Union*	
Frederick Lawrence, Superintendent	Anatole Newell,	⎤
Paul Cooley, Foreman	Chairman	⎥
Gerald Smith, Supervisor of Employ-	George Kelley	Grievance
ment	Martin Moore	Committee
	Edward O'Brien	
	James Cody	⎦

Excerpts of this conference follow:

Lawrence (m): I will tell you what we did in the matter of Ambrose. I had them make up a complete list of what every man has cut by weeks, and Ambrose has had just as good a deal as anybody else, and even a little better. As far as that's concerned, he's got no kick.

We have been able to prove that he got his share of "centers." He kicked on "sizes." For four weeks he had had two size 7, one 10, and one 11. That averaged up fairly well. So we told him that on coming back to work he would be on exactly the same basis as he has been, and could expect exactly the same treatment as in the past. That settles the matter as between this man and the company.

Now comes the question between you folks and this man. The company has no grievance against him. We recognize that he is a faultfinder; and the foreman would, frankly, just as lief that he weren't with us. But we can't fire a man simply because of that. He is a good cutter. I think you folks will admit that. But you folks feel that the man should not be retained and we therefore are asking you to give us reasons why we should not retain him.

The other day you said that he was behind in his dues and had broken the union rules. But that is not something that we can deal with. If the man breaks the rules of the union, you can do anything to him that you want, and that's none of our business. But unless he has also broken company rules we can't discharge the man. We haven't got a union shop. Now, then, what is your side of the case?

Newell (u): As a fellow employee, he is unfair from every way you take him. He is a troublemaker, leaving the union part of it entirely out.

Lawrence (m): Let's do that, because, although he may have broken the bylaws of the union, we, of course, know nothing about that. But why should we discharge him from the company's standpoint?

Newell (u): I should think when you have a foreman in the room you want to see him obeyed and respected, and that fellow doesn't do it.

Lawrence (m) [to Cooley]: What have you to say about that?

Cooley (m): The only thing that he has been disrespectful about is when he talks about stock, and finds fault. The other day he didn't exactly refuse to cut stock; he simply quit.

Lawrence (m): Hasn't any man a right to quit? I mean, if he isn't satisfied with the way things are going, he can come and say, "I'm through!"

O'Brien (u): Well, do you think it is a fair and square deal for a man to quit without notice? When this company discharges a man, they don't do it on a minute's notice.

Lawrence (m): No, we expect to give a man a reasonable notice.

O'Brien (u): So he left your employ at a minute's notice. He was not fair to the company, was he?

Lawrence (m): He didn't leave us. He came and said he wanted to get "through." We talked and talked and talked with this man. We wanted to be absolutely fair. But now we have told the man, "We don't feel that you have been discriminated against. As far as we are concerned, if you come back, it will be under exactly the same conditions."

Kelley (u): Does he want to come back?

Lawrence (m): He says he does. Frankly, I didn't expect he would, but he does. I am going to tell you the report has come to us in a round-about way that you want this man discharged because you feel that he has been reporting to the company what has gone on in union meetings. Mr. Cooley states that he has not reported anything. Isn't that true, Mr. Cooley?

Cooley (m): Correct.

Lawrence (m): We aren't hiring spies; we don't want people to come and tell us things.

Kelley (u): I don't think that charge was ever preferred against him.

Lawrence (m): No, it was reported to us through another department.

Kelley (u): He is unfair to the men he is working with; he wants to get ahead of them and doesn't care if he knocks a man down and steps on him. Another thing, he won't obey the rules of the union or the company, that is, when they both have the same rule. For instance, in regard to working from whistle to whistle. Originally this man wanted everyone to wait until the whistle blew and to stop when the whistle blew. Then he was one of the very first to break that rule. Some of the cutters complained and he got sore.

Lawrence (m): Did he continue doing that? We asked the foreman to enforce that ruling 100%.

O'Brien (u): He is the first person who broke that rule; I spoke to him about it at the time.

Lawrence (m): As I was telling you, some men said, "We understand you've got a man who has been playing the spy, and the grievance committee has demanded he be discharged." We want you to know that he hasn't been going to Mr. Cooley with any tales. Also, here in the foreman's book these instructions exist:

It is against the policy of this company to employ or encourage informers, spies, plotters, detectives, or other persons for the purpose of reporting to the management on employment problems or labor administration. You are especially cautioned to discourage tattletales, voluntary informers, and employees who endeavor to ingratiate themselves with you by reporting the actions of other employees in a disloyal manner.

I just wanted to get that out of the way. Now as this matter stands, you are asking us to discharge a man against whom we have no complaint. I agree that the man is a troublemaker. He is not always as truthful as he might be because we have discovered quite a few statements he has made that wouldn't stand investigation. But he isn't the only man working here about whom those things could be said.

Kelley (u): It's true there may be others. But the men haven't been bothered directly by them, and they have been by Ambrose.

Lawrence (m): That's what we want to get. Just what has he done or said? He insists he hasn't said anything.

Kelley (u): We are suspicious of him because from the very first he was strong for the union and he wanted everyone else to be in it. He was always talking against the independent while it was in here. Now he's doing just the opposite. For a man to make such a right-about-face would naturally make men distrust him.

Lawrence (m): I agree with you on that, but that to my mind is from the standpoint of the union.

Kelley (u): No, as a man to work with.

Lawrence (m): Well now, how would those particular points injure you folks working with him? Most of the time this man has had very little to say. [To Mr. Cooley.] Is that the truth?

Cooley (m): I guess so, as a general thing, yes.

O'Brien (u): I think he runs my job more than I run it myself. Let me tell you. When we organized this place, and won in the election over the independent, they made me representative in that room. Instead of me acting in that capacity, he acted in it; he proposed all the rates. I was willing to keep him in good humor if I could. He explained everything to the men. He took the job off my hands and ran it. When I didn't get him "centers," and he couldn't get them himself, he went to work and made a kick.

He wouldn't pay his dues; we didn't press him. The first thing we knew he paid his dues. Everything was all right. Then he wouldn't pay them again.

Then he didn't speak to me for a long time. Then all of a sudden, he changed around again. Every day he would ask me if I wouldn't have him changed over to "centers." I said to him, "Go to Mr. Cooley." He says, "You have more power than Mr. Cooley." I laughed at him, and kept putting him off.

This last Saturday he really demanded that I should get him "centers." Somebody told me that he was on the warpath. I tried to get away from him, but he keeps hold of me. I says to him, "Just wait for a second and I'll get Cody and send him down to Mr. Cooley. We'll get it straightened out now." I went to look for Cody. By the time I was back, he was up here in the office, saying he was quitting. Now, if you had called that fellow's bluff, he would have been back, and we would have forgotten all about it.

Lawrence (m): You agree to that.

O'Brien (u): Yes. I'll tell you; I used to take that fellow into my own home and talk to him—told him that he had to work for a living. He was at my home only last Sunday. As far as the foreman is concerned, he has no respect for Mr. Cooley; I know it.

I have tried to humor him in every way. I said to him: "Your turn is coming; wait." But no, he got it in his head that he would go among these Polanders.

Newell (u): He made the remark: "Give me 'centers'; give them to a friend of mine, then the rest of the line will feel all right."

Lawrence (m): When was this supposed to have occurred?

Cooley (m): I should say a little while before the 4th of July vacation. There was readjustment of prices; that was the time we raised "centers" 5% and "hind shanks" 15%.

O'Brien (u): From the start this man has been selfish all the way through. He was working for himself and nobody else.

Newell (u): There is another case that shows how he can't be trusted. One time this summer, two men had a mistake in their pay; they were short something. They told the grievance committee. The grievance committee took it up, but didn't make much headway, and those two men came up to the office and fixed it up themselves. Vitek said they should be suspended because they had not handled their grievances through the committee. The other day he made the statement that to stay in office we were packing the union with French and Irish. Just look at that for the way he makes things up. Yesterday one of our fellows asked him, "What's the matter?" Ambrose says, "You know, on my case, I'll have to be paid until it's settled."

Lawrence (m): He has never been discharged. We asked him to stay, and we said we would pay him while we kept him waiting. Why didn't you just kick him out of the union and let him go on working down there?

O'Brien (u): That's up to the men, not up to us. He can speak Polish, and he organized practically the whole sole leather amongst the foreigners. He was the first man to congratulate me when I joined. Now he says he was trapped into it. He thought by putting me on this committee that he could get the cream.

Lawrence (m): Well, if he is out of your union, he can't bother you with his grievances. And we haven't offered him any "sops" to come back.

O'Brien (u): If he is allowed to get away with this, you will have every man in the department saying, "Well, if this fellow can do that kind of thing, why can't I?"

Lawrence (m): What do you mean?

O'Brien (u): I mean you are going to have your whole department trying to dictate to the foreman what they shall do and what they shan't do, like Vitek did.

Lawrence (m): We told him, "You come back just exactly as you started out. If the foreman tells you to cut 'hind shanks,' you must do it; and if the foreman gives you any run of sizes, those are the sizes you cut."

Newell (u): That man Vitek knew the score absolutely Saturday when he said, "It's all off." He knew the game was up; he knew he was wrong.

Lawrence (m): Of course I wasn't in on Saturday.

Newell (u): Well, he knew the game was up. But he wasn't allowed to go; the company wouldn't let him go. The men feel that he is an undesirable. That room feels that way 100%.

Lawrence (m): Is that true of the Poles?

Newell (u): No man in the room wants to work with that man.

Lawrence (m): But look, the supervisor of employment induced him to come back.

O'Brien (u): That was poor policy. It makes it disagreeable all around when he won't speak to anybody. I'm sorry for his wife and children, but you have to teach him a lesson.

Mr. Lawrence, if you had let him quit, in a week or so if he didn't come himself, he would send his wife. We would then have straightened it out. But if he is going to be so damned stubborn, somebody's got to show him his mistake.

Kelley (u): Why is there so strong a desire for the company to keep this man?

Lawrence (m): We are not wildly anxious to have this chap working for us. But there is a principle involved. The union is asking us to discharge a man whom we have no cause to discharge. The union feels that they have grievances against him as a union; this brings up the principle of the union shop. I am not arguing for Vitek at all; I am just sticking up for this particular principle.

Newell (u): But we feel strongly that he is an undesirable man to work with.

Lawrence (m): Why don't you kick him out of the union?

Newell (u): He's done this against the firm too. Why don't the firm kick him out?

Lawrence (m): We don't feel that we have sufficient reason.

O'Brien (u): He has done this repeatedly. As I say, perhaps in a couple of weeks from now—I don't know how the rest feel but I naturally feel for his wife and children.

Lawrence (m): We don't care a thing about the individual in this case. He is a kicker and a troublemaker. But from the firm's standpoint there isn't any real grievance against him. We have got to defend this particular case, not only against you people, but against the management. They are going to ask, "Why did you discharge that man?" We would have to say, "The union insisted that they wouldn't work with him." Isn't that really the situation? Look at it from my standpoint. There's a principle involved.

O'Brien (u): Yes, but don't you think you have a good grievance just the same as we have? He's a kicker; he quit without notice; he tries to hog the "centers" and small "sizes"; he gets the men all stirred up.

Newell (u): Mr. Lawrence, every few minutes he kicks up a rumpus, and yet you go out of your way to get him to change his mind when he wants to quit without notice. You say: "We haven't got a thing against you, Ambrose; you're fine and dandy; go back to your job."

Lawrence (m): We don't say that.

Newell (u): It comes down to that. He don't do any of his dirty work himself. He will suggest a committee to do this and a committee to do that, and so forth—all that stuff.

Kelley (u): A man of his disposition, a troublemaker to the company and the men—I would think that was cause enough to let him go when he put up such a bluff as that, and when you called it you found he wasn't right in anything he'd been saying. And also consider the fact that his coming back is going to stir up a lot of trouble among the other men.

Newell (u): You must realize that if he comes back, the others will go out. That's sure.

Lawrence (m): I'll tell you; the principle of the union shop involved is very important. If it is left to me, I can only decide in one way.

Newell (u): We can't require you to discharge him, but if he returns to work our men won't work with him. Just as soon as he goes to the machine, the rest go out.

Cody (u): It isn't the cutting room alone that feels this way; it is all sole leather.

Lawrence (m): Mr. O'Brien said that if he had gone home last Saturday and stayed home and thought it over, and come back, it would have been all right. What has he done since then?

Kelley (u): He got reinstated and he's given the rest of us a chance to think.

O'Brien (u): If you had not urged him to return to work, everything would have been all right. You must take that into consideration.

Kelley (u): Why do you want him to come back?

Lawrence (m): There is a principle involved there.

Kelley (u): Why isn't it a good principle to have agreeable men in the factory?

Lawrence (m): A darned good principle. I'll tell you; I want a chance to go over this with the foreman and some of the others. We will not put him back to work until we have gone over this matter with you again. In the meantime, I would like to have you folks think it over and see if you won't be willing to stretch a point.

Kelley (u): There is considerable tension right now; it won't take much to snap the string.

O'Brien (u): This union will stand back of the foreman 100%. Is that what I told you, Mr. Cooley?

Cooley (m): Yes, Ed.

O'Brien (u): Anything that goes wrong in that room, he can always know we will handle it. We know we haven't got a union shop here, but we will stand back of him 100%.

Lawrence (m): We appreciate the way you people have worked with us. We haven't any complaint.

O'Brien (u): One day we were discussing Vitek's cutting, and he says, "I don't want the boss behind my machine." He said if the boss came behind his machine he would tell him to get out.

Cody (u): I don't really believe it will do to have him come back to work now, until things cool down.

Lawrence (m): Well, I'll tell you; I want to talk the matter over with the foreman and some of the others. Let's meet sometime tomorrow. Is that agreeable to you folks?

Newell (u): I don't like to see this come to a showdown, but it has come to that point. There is no use trying to smooth it over.

Lawrence (m): We are not necessarily trying to smooth it over; we are trying to see if there is some way to settle the thing. You folks feel that if a little later on he came around and asked for a job, you would be able to fix it up. Couldn't we arrive at some definite understanding?

Newell (u): I'm afraid it might be too late for that now. But you, Mr. Lawrence, have already told him he can come back to work. The other employees say they will not work with that man. There it is and he's probably boasted all over the room already that you said this morning he could come back. You really had evidence enough not to reinstate Ambrose. You could have accepted his notice to quit; since you didn't, you've got enough evidence now not to reinstate him.

Lawrence (m): We have evidence enough that the man certainly should be discharged from your union for breaking the union rules. Admitting that he is a troublemaker and that he ought to be punished for some of the things he's done outside, ought *we* to give that punishment? Consider that being kicked out of the union is sufficient punishment. Mr. Newell, see if you can't find some way of straightening the thing out with your crowd.

Newell (u): That puts me in a tough position. It's beginning to look as if the firm is putting us to a test.

Lawrence (m): It isn't a case of the firm putting it to the test. If anybody is doing it, I'm the one, and I'm certainly not trying to start any trouble. There is this principle involved, and it is you folks who are starting the thing. You are asking us to do something, leaving personalities out of account, that you are only justified in asking us to do if we would have a union shop.

Moore (u): We recognize the fact that we haven't a union shop. But we have a certain amount of principle, too, and there is a big principle involved in this for us.

Kelley (u): It looks very much like a test case. You apparently have reason enough to let this man go—and you won't.

Lawrence (m): I don't agree with you in that. I am inclined to feel that you folks are presenting the issue of the union shop in insisting that we discharge him. Can't we get together again tomorrow?

When they met the next day, Superintendent Lawrence refused to discharge Ambrose Vitek and advised the members of the committee, if they still were interested in the case, to appeal to the president of the plant.

Two days later, on Monday morning, the following note was received by the president of the company:

We, the cutters, refuse to work with Ambrose Vitek.

He is unfair, untruthful, a troublemaker, agitator, and altogether an undesirable man to work with. He has shown himself to be a man who would not hesitate to literally step on his fellow workman in order to reach a little higher up on the ladder of success.

The president called a meeting of Lawrence, Cooley, Smith, the grievance committee, and Ambrose Vitek. After hearing a review of the history of the case, the president proceeded with an investigation. The representatives of the employees produced evidence to show, beyond reasonable doubt, that Vitek had been one of the men most prominent in the organization of the union at Ellison's. During the past few months, however, he had taken no part in the union's activities, and had spoken against the organization. The union grievance committee brought into the conference several outsiders who testified that Vitek had told them he had joined the union against his better judgment, and believed the independent union that had preceded it in the plant was far superior.

The union representatives also repeated their charge that Vitek had said: "Give me 'centers'; give them to a friend of mine, then the rest of the line will feel all right." Further questioning developed the fact that prior to the controversy about Vitek, the cutters had complained about their rates and had asked management for an adjustment. They were told that management realized the piece rates on this particular work were out of line, and that as soon as a study could be made they would be adjusted.

Shortly after this, Vitek had approached the foreman and had stated that, if Mr. Cooley would give him centers, he would arrange matters with the men so that the company would hear nothing more about their request for an increased piece rate. The president asked the foreman if he recalled such a proposition. Mr. Cooley replied that Vitek had made this proposition. Several employees of the company, who had no immediate interest in the rate issue, volunteered the evidence that shortly after this incident Vitek had told them he would fix it with the foreman so that he could make more money than the rest of the cutters, and the company would not have to increase its piece rates.

It was further testified that Vitek had advised one of the committee members not to turn out too much work per day as that might have an adverse effect on future piece rates. Vitek had also offered a motion in a union meeting to the effect that one of the committee members should see each operator's pay envelope each week in order to detect the men who were working excessively and to influence them to slow down. This motion had not been carried. Several days later, Vitek had told the foreman that one of the committeemen had introduced this motion at the meeting and that he, Vitek, had had a hard fight to keep it from passing.

The president told the grievance committee that he would give his decision the following afternoon.

DISCUSSION QUESTIONS

1. Evaluate, from the viewpoint of management's objectives, Mr. Lawrence's handling of the situation created by the quitting of Ambrose Vitek. Include in your consideration the conduct of the conference with the union grievance committee.

2. If you were the president, what would be your decision after completing your investigation?

PART II. INTERNAL RELATIONS: PROBLEMS IN THE SHOP

SECTION 2. ADMINISTERING THE AGREEMENT

HILTON CLOTHING CORPORATION

THE DISCHARGE OF A SHOP STEWARD

The Hilton Clothing Corporation, from which Joseph Ascola, shop chairman, was discharged on February 19, had been dealing with the Amalgamated Clothing Workers for some 20 years. When the parties failed to negotiate a settlement of the dispute that followed, it was submitted to Philip Milton, impartial chairman in the market for the past 17 years. The following were in attendance at the arbitration hearing:

For the Union	For the Company
Edward Bellando, Assistant Manager of the Joint Board	Alfred Waterman, President
Vincent Tonati, Business Agent	Harley Stone, Company Counsel
Joseph Ascola, Discharged Employee and Shop Chairman	Nicolas De Marco, Foreman of the Pressing Room

Bellando (u): A week ago my manager called me. "Ascola has been fired," he said, and he wanted me to have him reinstated. I had a talk with Mr. Waterman. He told me Ascola called him a fool during a dispute between Ascola and the foreman. Two people were talking at the same time, and Ascola just said, "Let one fool talk at a time." When those words came out, Waterman told Ascola, "You have been working for a fool long enough." Ascola insists that he didn't call Waterman a fool. Ascola, you tell the story.

Ascola (u) [rising and speaking heatedly]: I said, "Just a moment, one fool at a time." Upon that statement Mr. Waterman shot me dead economically.

For three months since I became shop chairman, I have had many disputes with Mr. Waterman. So far as I know I have never offended him, and he has never offended me. Mr. Waterman and Mr. De Marco were talking last Wednesday at the same time, and I said, "One fool at a time." Sometimes I think in Italian even though I talk English. Among Italians such talk is very common; we get excited easily. I don't think it was grounds for offense on the part of Mr. Waterman, and I certainly don't think that it was justification for discharge. If you should find that he was right in discharging me, then my job—or any shop chairman's job—is hanging by a thread. I should not only be reinstated, but I should be compensated for a loss of $68—a week's pay.

I don't know what Mr. Waterman is going to say, but this is the reason they gave me. If other things happened during the past six months, they should be discussed separately from the discharge issue.

I have been zealous in the discharge of my duties as shop chairman. It is my job to protect the workers. Some seven weeks ago, Mr. Waterman made a statement that if I lost my job, I could not get another in the city. He even said he would give me ten days off to look for another job, and pay me for those ten days, as well as $30 more, if I could find another job. If he is right that I cannot get another job, then this discharge is way out of proportion for the remark I made in anger.

I am not only a worker—I am a shop chairman. I have often thought since I have been in office and protecting the people, "Gee, I would like to bust that guy in the nose," but I kept it to myself. Now Mr. Waterman has interpreted a single remark as an offense and has thrown me out. I have been out a week and $68 is money to me. Working as a presser is not a hobby with me. I work because I have to! That's all I have to say.

Chairman: Thank you. Does the union have any more evidence?

Tonati (u): I say that the man be reinstated with compensation. Mr. Ascola has told the whole story very well. We haven't anything more.

Chairman [to Mr. Stone]: Do you want to go ahead?

Stone (m): Mr. Ascola, you were employed as a presser for seven and one-half months—twenty-nine weeks and two days to be exact. Do you feel that you have done your job properly?

Ascola (u): That is not the issue. I don't think . . .

Chairman: The company must demonstrate justification for your discharge. They have a right to bring evidence directed to the question of "just cause."

Stone (m): Do you consider that you performed your job properly?

Ascola (u) [hesitating]: Am I required to answer this?—Yes, I do!

Stone (m): There were 147 working days during that period. How many days were you absent?

Ascola (u): I don't know. Three or four, I guess.

Stone (m): If I showed you that you were absent sixteen days, what would you say?

Ascola (u): I don't think that is true.

Stone (m): You were absent from work on the 11th of December; the 5th and 6th of January, and the 29th because of illness. The period from October 30 to November 12 you were out.

Ascola (u): The whole pressing department was out, and I was out with them.

Stone (m): We'll come back to that. Now you were at work 131 days. How many days did you come in on time?

Ascola (u): I merely want to say that my attendance and punctuality is equally as good as anybody's in the department.

Stone (m): If I told you that 66 days out of 131 you were late, what would you say?

Ascola (u): I don't know. My record of punctuality is as good as anyone else's.

Stone (m): Then I'll tell you that seventeen times you were late by five minutes or less, fifteen times by more than five minutes, and thirty-four times by ten minutes or more.

Ascola (u): Some people came in after I did. Mr. Waterman complained to me as shop chairman about the general lateness of everybody.

Stone (m): Was there a stoppage in the pressing section between October 30 and November 12?

Ascola (u): I think there was.

Stone (m): Before they went out, did you discuss it with them?

Ascola (u): I was not shop chairman at that time.

Stone (m): When did you become chairman?

Ascola (u): I don't have the exact dates.

Stone (m): Was there any interference with production on December 30?

Tonati (u): I will answer that. You went home sick on that afternoon. If I recall correctly, the rest of the department left the shop at the end of the day.

Ascola (u): I left at a quarter of three.

Stone (m): On January 27, was there a two-hour stoppage in your section, while you were chairman?

Ascola (u): You have my time records. I think that is the morning I didn't come in at all.

Stone (m): Did the pressing section stop work on the 17th of February?

Ascola (u): Yes, and let me tell why. There is a condition we complained about for six weeks. On the floor below, the tenants [another company] use some chemicals and the fumes seep through in the pressing department. I complained about it many times. I went to Mr. Waterman, and he said, "Open the window." On the 17th, the stench was unbearable. I called over the men, and said, "Come here! Smell this gas." Four of the pressers were there, and we all agreed it was impossible to work. I told Mr. Waterman that, and he said, "There's nothing I can do. If you don't like it, go home." And we went.

Stone (m): Did the rest of the shop go home?

Ascola (u): No. The stench concentrates itself around the pressing department.

Stone (m): Did anybody else want to go home?

Ascola (u): I don't know—just the pressers.

Stone (m): How do you explain the spool of thread you threw at your foreman?

Ascola (u): That was after working hours. We had an argument, and Nick called me a stool pigeon. That was a personal affair. It did not involve any shop problems.

Stone (m): Is it within the jurisdiction of a shop chairman to tell people when they can go home?

Ascola (u): I think it is proper for a shop chairman to do that when men have waited around for an hour or more and no work has been prepared for them.

Stone (m): Is it the prerogative of the shop chairman, when management tells a woman to stay on her job, for you to tell her to go?

Ascola (u): That was the case of Martha. I happened to come along, and Mr. Waterman was having a hot argument with this girl. I said, "What's the trouble?" The girl said she had to go home because her father was ill. She hadn't been in that morning, but came in at noon to inquire about work the next day. She said she would come in the next morning. Mr. Waterman said, "You go to work now, or don't come back at all." I told the girl to go home and come in the next morning.

Stone (m): Did you know that prior to your coming to work on that job that it was the practice of management . . .

Tonati (u) [interrupting]: I think this is all irrelevant. This is childish. This is not according to the agreement. Let's stick to the merits of the case.

Chairman: Mr. Stone, why don't you just develop your case systematically from now on.

Stone (m): All right. Do you want to state your case, Mr. Waterman?

Waterman (m): It is my business to keep that shop running at all times, and I try to do as fair a job as I know how. Let us begin with the stoppage on October 30th. It has been our practice to make no daily check on the pressers; they work on contract accounts. If the contract called for 50,000 coats and the pressers had received pay in the period for 50,100, they would reimburse the company for the 100 coats on our side of the ledger. On the other hand, if they had received pay for only 49,900 coats, we would make up the underpayment. On October 30th we found that there had been an overpayment of $143 to seven pressers. After so informing them, I deducted $143. The boys said if they didn't get the money, they would walk out. I said to Ascola, who was clearly the ringleader, "I am willing to put the money in your hands in the form of a certified check. When the union has time to go through our books, we can see whether we are right." Ascola refused; he said, "I don't want any part of it." There was a stoppage from October 30 to November 12. It's true Ascola wasn't shop chairman then, but he was elected shop chairman very shortly after that stoppage.

Stone (m): On December 30th, wasn't there a one-day stoppage?

Waterman (m): It started about three o'clock. We had called the pressers in that morning to explain that if we used up certain materials, there would be a loss of time. Therefore we asked them to stagger their work. We were bluntly told the practice was all or nothing, and we'd have to pay the usual make-up time of $1.58 per hour. I refused, and they went out.

Stone (m): Was there any request for discussion with Mr. Bellando, or for arbitration?

Waterman (m): No. They simply walked out.

Stone (m): Is it the practice in your shop for each man to change the padding on his machine?

Waterman (m): Yes. One morning Ascola refused to do it. He said he didn't care if he had to pull the whole section out, he wouldn't change the padding, as his foreman had told him to.

Stone (m): On January 22 was there another stoppage?

Waterman (m): It really involved a minor question about wages. The point is that Ascola stopped work in the pressing room for two hours until he got his way.

Stone (m): What happened on February 19?

Waterman (m): It is my practice in the morning to inspect the plant. I found an argument going on between the foreman, Nick, and Ascola. I just listened; then I asked what the trouble was. There were 32 coats involved that went from Ascola's section to another section. They had been done improperly, and Nick wanted them repressed. Ascola said, "I don't give a damn about those coats—I won't do them unless I get paid for it." I tried to offer a suggestion, and then Nick interjected something. Ascola said, "One fool at a time." That proved the straw that broke the camel's back. I ordered my foreman away. I said to Ascola, "You have worked for a fool long enough. You are discharged."

Stone (m): Did he have any objections to good relations with your employees? Didn't your employees give a present each Christmas to your father until Ascola stopped it?

Waterman (m): Yes. My father has worked with our people for years—since he started the business. They always liked him a lot. But Ascola said openly that employees should not buy bosses presents, or be on good terms with bosses.

Stone (m): Prior to his coming, did you ever have any stoppages?

Waterman (m): No. Our firm has never had any complaints about our relations with the union. We get along well.

Chairman: Did you ever try to have a real talk with Mr. Ascola?

Waterman (m): Yes, I have bent over backwards to work with him. I asked him, "Why is it we have these stoppages?" Ascola told me that bosses should be done away with. "If bosses were eliminated," he said, "business would run a hell of a lot better." He suffers from "boss-hatred."

Chairman: Did you ever warn him that you would discharge him if he did not improve?

Waterman (m): Yes, I spoke to Mr. Tonati about him many times. I felt it was imperative that he go out of the shop, or I would go out of business. I have been fed up, practically been on the verge of a nervous breakdown. There has been continuous bickering and squawking since Ascola came.

Ascola (u) [rising to speak]: I would like to ask Mr. Waterman a question, Mr. Milton, before I rebut Mr. Stone's arguments.

Chairman: Go ahead.

Ascola (u): Mr. Waterman came to me and said he needed seven girls to work overtime. Didn't I get the girls? Then a girl wanted to leave, and didn't I cooperate in keeping that girl on the job? Then on another occasion, didn't you say, "This may not be within your duties as shop chairman, but will you round up some finishers for us?"

Waterman (m): Yes.

Ascola (u): Wasn't there a time when you had a tough problem and one of the men said, "Why don't you call in Ascola?" Mr. Waterman said, "I don't think I can talk to Ascola." But I came in and we talked for about two hours. You must have thought that time was useful, for you paid me for it! Didn't you find me cooperative in those instances?

Waterman (m): Yes.

Ascola (u): Mr. Waterman and I have had several philosophical talks. I told him that bosses were unnecessary nuisances. I said I believe in the cooperative system instead of the capitalist system.

Waterman (m): I didn't take it as personal—it just reflects your general attitude.

Ascola (u): You said that I preach "boss-hatred." That is ridiculous. On four distinct occasions I went out of my way to help you. I did it not because I was interested in the company but because I was interested in the workers. The suggestion that I have sown seeds of insurrection is not true.

About your father—one woman came up to me. I said I didn't approve of giving presents to bosses, that bosses should give presents to employees.

Mr. Waterman has made it just as difficult for me as he says I have made it for him. Take the question of loss of work time on December 30. I told the workers to come in the next morning, and I collected for loss of time from the boss. It was hard fighting to get it. They said I was overzealous. I was not chairman when that big stoppage occurred from October 30 to November 12, but Mr. Waterman was told that I got them to walk out. If management would pay less attention to rumors, it would be a healthier situation.

When I became shop chairman, we had a talk about how to get along. Mr. Waterman said, "You know how these things are. Sometimes I will give in, and sometimes you will give in." I said, "I don't believe in that. What is yours is yours; what is ours is ours." This business about my sowing hatred is farfetched.

Chairman: I would like to know about the stoppages that occurred after you became shop chairman.

Ascola (u): The only one I know of was about the stench. Mr. Waterman said, "I can do nothing about it. If you don't like it, you can go home."

Waterman (m): If I told you to go home, you will admit it was in impatience. I was about fed up: nobody else complained; the Board of Health found nothing harmful; it was not a condition over which we had control. You simply were always looking for complaints, and keeping the pressers stirred up.

Ascola (u): I don't remember anything about any other stoppage. I do remember that—maybe December 30—I went home at three o'clock, and the boys may have gone home afterwards.

I want to bring out one more point. It is news to me that Mr. Waterman complained to the business agent about me. Only on one occasion did Mr. Waterman intimate to me that he wanted me out of the shop. It's true, when

I complained about the stench, he said, "Ascola, this is the wrong shop for you. You complain about the lights, the pressing machines, and now the stench—always something."

He did also say once that I was overzealous in regard to my duties. I assumed an attitude Mr. Waterman wasn't used to. Let me ask Mr. Waterman if I ever made a complaint that didn't have some sort of grounds?

Chairman: How about your refusal to pad your machine when Mr. De Marco told you to change the padding?

Ascola (u): I am glad you brought that up. It was not a simple case of putting another pad on. It was padding the machine in a new way Nick thought would be better. I went to Mr. Waterman. I said, "If it is a question of experimenting, it shouldn't be done on my time."

I want to conclude by saying that I have not had too many run-ins with the boss. There isn't a shop chairman in the city—or any other market— that doesn't have a run-in with the boss. Waterman is not accustomed to this sort of thing. In the previous six years before I took office he had another kind of chairman.

You may think this is none of my business, but two-thirds of the trouble is because the firm has mismanaged the shop. Sections are overcrowded. Operators are losing time. They all come to me, and I have to believe this girl—believe that girl. When I told Martha to go home because her father was ill, I did it for her as well as for the dignity of the shop chairman. I try to follow the contract too.

Stone (m): I should like to ask some questions of Nick De Marco, our foreman. Nick, tell us about the padding incident.

De Marco (m): I told Ascola that with his padding the coats would not come out right. He said, "I am not going to change this machine." I told him that every presser has to change his own machine. He said, "I don't care; I am not going to." I came back from lunch and Mr. Waterman said, "Nick, you change that machine; we must get on with the work. I don't want any trouble." I padded the machine, and everything came out satisfactorily.

Once I showed him some coats and how badly they'd been done. I sponged them, and did them over. He said, "You must have magic in your fingers." I continued to show him how, but he wouldn't accept my suggestions. "You must have magic in your fingers," he kept on saying. He couldn't or wouldn't do the work right.

On another morning his sponging machine was not right, and I said, "We don't want to lose production, so we will use another machine." But he wouldn't change and of the coats he did, not one was passable.

Stone (m): You heard the discussion about the October 30 stoppage. Did you see Ascola talk to the men that day?

De Marco (m): He came out there among the boys. I remember definitely that Mr. Ascola said, "I want the money for these coats, and if I don't get it, we will walk out."

Stone (m): Was there a stoppage at the end of December over paying makeup time?

De Marco (m): Yes.

Stone (m): Was there an occasion that the coats were improperly pressed, and when you told Mr. Ascola so, he started an argument and then said he was sick?

De Marco (m): Yes, there was a stoppage. That was in early January. I was going the rounds, and I looked at the coats on his rack, and said, "These coats are not pressed; they are not passable." He began arguing; then he said, "I feel sick; I am going home." I went to Mr. Waterman about it, and came back and the whole pressing room was out.

Stone (m): Was there a stoppage on January 27?

De Marco (m): I don't recall that.

Stone (m): Okay. Tell us your version of Mr. Ascola's discharge.

De Marco (m): At five o'clock I looked over the coats that had been done that day, and I thought there were thirty-two coats on which the fronts were not pressed. I showed Ascola the coats and told him the fronts were not done right. He said, "I will not do them over unless you pay me. I don't care!" Mr. Waterman came along, and we tried to explain the trouble. Mr. Waterman then talked to him. Ascola said, "I don't care if I have to pull the whole pressing section out—the whole shop out, I will not do these coats!" And it wasn't so casual either that he said, "One fool at a time."

Chairman: What happened to the coat fronts?

De Marco (m): We brought someone else in to do them, and I stayed around and we got them out.

Stone (m): That is our case.

Bellando (u): I want to bring up a few points about the stoppage on October 30. I am not taking Ascola's part right now; it's just the situation.

Stone (m) [interrupting]: Did Al say to you "I'll put the $143 that's in dispute in your hands"? Isn't that the point—how to handle such disputes?

Bellando (u): Yes, but when you work in a place, there are a lot of things you get to know that go against the firm. As much as I like Waterman personally, he has made a lot of blunders.

Waterman (m): Name one case!

Bellando (u): You waited six months to pay three boys.

Waterman (m): But I paid them. Nobody says we never have our differences.

Bellando (u): The boys were ready to fight, you waited so long.

Waterman (m): It wasn't any six months anyway; you exaggerate.

Bellando (u): Say it was three months—what's the difference; you didn't pay them for a long time! Then there was that 12½-cent increase we got in the last contract. Mr. Waterman wanted to check the contract. [To Waterman.] You told me you were going to write to New York. It took you three months.

Waterman (m): You are wrong there again!

Bellando (u): Another case: A fellow happens to be sick. Colds are going the rounds. You said that the man who doesn't come in on Wednesday cannot get time-and-one-half when he comes in on Saturday. Every other employer pays it. One boy had a vacation coming for several months. He only stayed until he got it; then he left.

Tonati (u) [interrupting]: It's not as bad as all that; don't get so hot under the collar, Eddie. We've done business with the firm for years; and we intend to continue good relations.

Bellando (u): Of course we do. Mr. Waterman and I are really good friends. Tomorrow I may even take him to dinner.

Tonati (u): Let's not get away from the issue. I am still going to be Mr. Waterman's friend. We came in here today to discuss the question of discharge of a certain Ascola. The man was discharged specifically for a comment he made during working hours. But today Mr. Stone takes a lot of dead cats out of the bag—a lot of things which I consider irrelevant. As business agent, I have leaned over backwards many times in dealing with the company because I do not like to see stoppages. If Mr. Waterman had any intention of discharging Mr. Ascola, he should have done it in the past when he had grounds to discharge the man, and not on the pretense of a remark.

Waterman (m): Have you ever asked me not to fire Ascola when I definitely spoke to you about the trouble he made?

Tonati (u): That is beside the point. As I was saying, haven't I also leaned over backwards in many instances? If one of our men, like Ascola, sometimes hasn't observed the contract, the firm has done likewise. We have had arguments. Mr. Waterman has a temper, and I have a temper too. But I know his nature pretty well by now; I can go to him now and talk with him. Believe me, there have been many instances that had it not been for my efforts, there would have been a strike. Both the firm and Ascola are at fault.

Chairman: Did you know about these stoppages?

Tonati (u): Yes, and they would have been more serious if it hadn't been for me because of provocations from the firm.

Waterman (m): Oh, we agree that things would have been worse since Ascola came if it weren't for you.

Tonati (u): Ever since we have gone into civilian production, unfortunately the shop has not worked continuously. Mr. Waterman could not get materials. When there isn't plenty of work, everyone gets upset. They must earn a living. People get nervous and upset and there are bound to be altercations. Some individuals are told to come in. They work a while, and then there is no work. The foreman says to wait around—and naturally being shop chairman, it is Mr. Ascola's duty to see that these conditions are eliminated as quickly as possible.

Chairman: How about his troubles with his foreman?

Tonati (u): Insubordination is something I just don't believe of the man. He is not stupid!

Ascola (u): May I say a few words in my own defense? This talk that I tried to hurt the business with walkouts and insubordination is a falsification. I admit that on the day I was discharged I said, "I am not going to press those coats." I said other unpleasant things. I said, "I didn't care if the shop stopped; I am not going to press those coats." The picture is that I have been a disrupting influence since I have been chairman. But I showed Mr. Waterman four or five instances where I went out of my way to cooperate.

Chairman: I am interested in the stoppages that occurred when you were shop chairman.

Ascola (u): They talk as if there were stoppages only after I became shop chairman. On one occasion even while I was chairman, but was absent —January 27—there was a rampage.

I want to inject something here—it is serious. I think the firm has been playing politics against me. On the day of my election Mr. Waterman told two or three girls not to vote for Ascola. Later I said to Mr. Waterman, "Well, I don't think you spoke to enough girls before the election." On another occasion when Mr. Waterman was talking with the chairman of the pressers about pay he said, "You wouldn't get this if your friend Ascola were here." The firm has been playing politics! Several other times he has tried to win the people away from me.

Chairman: What about refusing to comply with instructions from your supervisor?

Ascola (u): I want you to know that every presser in there has had trouble with the foreman. Also the trouble is because we changed from army uniforms, which are easy to press, to civilian coats which are more difficult.

Stone (m): It's a question how such things should be handled, whether through the grievance machinery or the way you did.

Ascola (u): The stoppage on October 30 was not my responsibility. Are you going to pick on Ascola who was not chairman? As a matter of fact, some of the fellows felt that Waterman was acting too high-handed generally. There are a number of instances showing that the firm should be penalized—one man had $9 coming to him for months.

Waterman (m): He certainly didn't!

Ascola (u): Why did you pay him then?

Waterman (m): To get rid of you. It had gotten to the point where I found it easier to pay money than to have you around all the time.

Ascola (u): Why, there was the time when the war was over. I was told Mr. Waterman came around and said to the pressers, "I don't want you any more. You can all get out. I'm running my own shop now."

Waterman (m): That's a malicious lie!

Tonati (u): Mr. Waterman is right—there is no truth to that statement. Don't say things like that, Ascola.

Ascola (u): Well, that's what I was told. Everyone said that Mr. Waterman was a difficult man. Then there was also the question of prejudice. Mr. Waterman told me one day, "If I had known who you were, I would never have hired you. But I found out too late."[1]

I told you about these times I tried to cooperate. I never ordered any stoppage. When I was discharged, the pressers wanted to go out. I said, "Men, go back to your work. You will only make my case worse."

Stone (m): Have you ever had trouble with any of your other men, Mr. De Marco?

De Marco (m): Without Ascola it would be an ideal shop. I get along fine with the others. We are friends outside the shop, even though I am foreman.

Stone (m): I would like to sum up. This is the first arbitration Mr. Waterman has had in six years, which speaks very well for his shop. I would not recommend to a client that if some worker once gets excited, that would be cause for discharge. We are all working for a living. But when we look at the over-all picture, we find a serious accumulation of grievances. The employer cannot be wrong all of the time. But whoever was wrong, there is a grievance procedure which should have been followed. Then if he had been wrong, Mr. Waterman would have had to learn the hard way. The union has a right to be wrong as well as the management. There either were stoppages, or there weren't stoppages. Our friend, Mr. Ascola, admits there were stoppages, admits there was a threat in connection with his discharge—"I don't care if the whole shop stops!" When you take that with a record of poor attendance and tardiness, in a shop which previously had harmonious relations, you have a serious case of disruption.

I am talking about day-to-day things that make for production or nonproduction. When you add up all these day-to-day things, Ascola is constantly interfering with production. Mr. Ascola wasn't fired because he was shop chairman; he was fired in spite of the fact that he was shop chairman. A good shop chairman patterns his conduct according to the contract. I am only interested in the effect of his conduct upon production. We are all trying to do business under trying circumstances. If the workers are on edge, as Mr. Ascola and Mr. Tonati urge, management has reason for nerves these days too.

Ascola (u): I would like to have the cards of the other pressers checked on this issue of lateness.

Tonati (u): I think the firm has made a mistake in what they say about tardiness. There is one individual who has been absent and late more than Mr. Ascola.

---

[1] There were rumors and suspicions that Mr. Ascola was of left-wing persuasion. Political speculations also revolved about him. He had become president of the pressers' local in the market during the seven months of his employment at the Hilton Company, and his name was prominently mentioned as a probable contender for the post of manager of the joint board at the next election.

Stone (m): A man who is just late, you can put up with it—men are hard to get these days. But a man who is constantly tardy among other more serious things—then I say we have had enough.

DISCUSSION QUESTIONS

1. Analyze the situation underlying the discharge of Joseph Ascola.

2. Compare with the situation underlying the discharge of William Fisher in the Joseph Todd case and that underlying the discharge of Kent in the Abbot-Peabody case.

MERRILL MANUFACTURING COMPANY

AN IMPASSE OVER SENIORITY

The Merrill Manufacturing Company manufactures small products used in a variety of electrical equipment. For one product the company constituted one of few sources of supply. Until the time of the difficulty recorded in this case, this article always went to customers with whom Merrill had established uniform specifications regarding types, sizes, and quality. The Carlton-Wheeler Company, a newcomer to the field, requested the Merrill Company to supply this item, but with quality specifications higher than those generally required by the trade.

The Merrill management determined that the quality item required could be selected with careful inspection from regular production runs. A group of special inspectors, however, would have to be set up, each member to be instructed regarding the standards to be met. This posed the problem of additional expense. The cost problem for the extra inspection was submitted to Carlton-Wheeler executives. They readily agreed to meet the additional expenditures and their order was accepted.

Merrill thereupon prepared to put its program into operation. With the industry expanding, management foresaw that it might have to meet further problems involving "extra quality specifications." If the program of the special inspectors proved successful, it might provide a method of flexible production adjustments. Management accordingly proceeded to plan carefully the organization of the special inspection group. Inspectors normally worked on inspection lines next to the production lines. The supervisor of inspection, John Brooks, demonstrated that the special inspectors could not continue their new work at their established locations without impeding the flow of regular work. Therefore, a "special inspection room" was outfitted, adjacent to the warehouse.

Mr. Brooks chose from among the regular inspectors 36 girls, 12 to a shift, for the special work. Since the isolated location would make regular supervision impracticable, he gave careful consideration to individual ability. Although the union contract provided for seniority, management conceived the proposed shifts as only temporary departmental assignments. Nonetheless, seniority was taken into consideration, and the selectees were girls of relatively long service. Fearful, however, that the older women might find transfers back and forth from regular to special work a more difficult adjustment to make, Mr. Brooks restricted his choices to the younger inspectors. The selections completed, each girl was interviewed by Mr. Brooks and the personnel manager, George Ashley.

It was explained to them that they would receive a few days' special training, would work in a special room until the order was finished, and then would return to their former places on the regular inspection line. They would continue to accumulate seniority in the inspection department and receive all regular benefits but no special privileges. It was also explained that girls from production would be temporarily transferred to do the special girls' regular jobs.

The special order took a little over six months. During that time the average monthly quit rate in the regular inspection department was 4.1; none of the special inspectors quit. Absenteeism at the regular inspection lines averaged 6.8%; in the special inspection room, 2.3%. Although Mr. Brooks was able to make only occasional supervisory visits, on each occasion he was impressed with the high morale among the special inspectors. They worked with gusto; he saw them coming and leaving in chatting, laughing groups. The Carlton-Wheeler Company expressed satisfaction with the product.

During the fifth month of this period, Mr. Ashley made a visit to the special inspection room shortly before the end of the first shift. A mild influenza epidemic had been felt in Centerville, and the employees had been circularized with a bulletin setting forth precautionary measures. Mr. Ashley decided to take the occasion for a meeting with the special inspectors. He suggested that as a precautionary measure, if any of the group felt a cold coming on, they should stay home a day to avoid becoming really ill and substitutes could be trained for the special inspection room. To his surprise the girls protested strongly at the idea of any new girls in their group. To prove that they could make out all right they described how they had, on several occasions, switched shifts to help each other out although this was against the company rules. The group had obviously developed a close relationship. As one girl, Betty Barton, said, "You see, we girls got to know each other pretty well these past months. And we've had lots of fun together outside—dances, and theatre parties, and things like that. We all even spent a weekend together once in New York. We really have awfully good times together."

Some six weeks later the order for Carlton-Wheeler was completed. Mr. Ashley suggested that he and Mr. Brooks meet with the special inspectors. They read to them extracts from letters sent by the Carlton-Wheeler Company affirming Merrill's success in meeting the extra quality specifications. Now, the executives informed the girls, they would be transferred back to their former positions on the regular inspection lines. But they could expect to receive a call to return to the special inspection room as further "special orders" came in.

About three weeks later, Mr. Brooks appeared in Mr. Ashley's office, obviously perturbed. The following conversation developed:

Brooks: Well, here's a surprise for you! You won't believe it, but things seem to be going haywire with the special inspectors! It seems Rose Townley finally went to Bill MacIntyre, the shop steward for the inspectors, with what she called "a grievance" for all the special inspectors. They all claim they should be on one regular inspection line. If we want the right to move them between the regular lines and the special room, we owe them some privileges too. They even feel they should have special seniority rights. I gather Rose is quite active in the union and has a considerable following. But Mac's going to have trouble if we move those regular inspectors too. I warned him he'd better watch Mrs. McKenna and her side-kick, Mary Hammond.

Ashley: You mean McKenna will make trouble if she's "bumped" to make a place for the special inspectors?

Brooks: Well, I wouldn't be a bit surprised. She is always crabbing—but she's a good inspector too, always 100%. She thinks she's very good, too, and I know she's been pretty sour over not having been chosen as a special inspector. I was in a tight spot explaining we chose younger girls—McKenna's over 40. We're in for trouble, George, and I wonder what we should do next.

Ashley: At least we're absolutely solid in our position. We have planned this thing carefully; we explained matters at every step to the girls; we prepared them from the start that they simply couldn't ask for privileges. We're right and they're wrong and we'll just have to stand pat. The whole thing amazes me.

Brooks: Mac told me those 36 girls were long-service employees and good union members. If the company couldn't grant such a simple request in return for their fine work, he said he would have to put the whole matter before their president, Lloyd Parsons.

Ashley: Well, why don't you ask Lloyd Parsons and Mac in for a talk—take the initiative. Parsons is usually a pretty level-headed fellow. Coming from the outside he may see the whole problem with us.

Mr. Brooks arranged a meeting with Messrs. Parsons and MacIntyre for the same week. In the meantime, Mr. Ashley asked Mr. Brooks to get all the data that seemed relevant concerning Mrs. McKenna and Rose Townley. The record revealed the following:

Mrs. Agnes McKenna had been an inspector for 14 years; she was now 44 years old. She was a member of the union since its entry; before then she had three times led protests against rate adjustments when new products had been added. Mrs. Mary Hammond, eight years with the company, had been placed opposite Mrs. McKenna when promoted to inspection and had remained Mrs. McKenna's work partner. She was seconding Mrs. McKenna in the current disturbance, just as she did in most shop matters. Both women, but particularly Mrs. McKenna, were considered "money-hungry" by the other employees. The husbands of both women had steady jobs.

Mrs. McKenna was known to be lazy except when there was an opportunity to make money. She and her husband lived in a one-room furnished apartment because, it was said, she refused to "slave" for anybody unless she got paid for it. Her personnel record showed she had lived for 12 years on a farm, acted as nurse to an invalid relative for 4 years, and had several jobs as a housemaid for well-to-do families during the next 10 years.

Mrs. Hammond was 17 at the time she was hired at Merrill. She had previous experience only as salesgirl in the five and ten, where she began working upon receiving her working papers at the age of 14. She had learned quickly at Merrill, had always carried a high efficiency rating, and had been promoted to inspection from assembly. She was married two years later, when she was 19, but continued to work to get a "start." At times she had intimated an intention of quitting. Her husband, classified 4F shortly after his induction into the armed services, had been discharged.

Rose Townley had come to Merrill upon graduation from high school. Like many of the younger employees, she entered the shop during war-production days; moreover, in the small town of Centerville, Merrill offered a large proportion of the jobs available to girls who had both to work and remain with their families. Rose was known to be devoted to her family, and proud of her gifted younger brother. Although engaged, she was determined to work to finance him through engineering school.

Not only in her own home, but in the shop and in the small-town circles, Rose was a person of many close ties. She was very "popular"; fellow workers of her own age turned to her when problems arose, and she proved resourceful in helping friends. She had considerable skill in planning "sociables" both in the shop and the union; many outings, parties, dances, and during the war, "relief" and similar activities seemed to originate with and be "managed" by her. Mr. Brooks considered her one of the department's best workers; her output records proved her both quick and accurate. She had seven years' service in the department.

When the union officers appeared for their scheduled appointment, Mr. Brooks had ready the seniority records of the department and other relevant data. When they left, he dictated the following summary of the discussion to present to Mr. Ashley:

Parsons (u): I understand you expect to send those girls to the special room any time you get an order requiring extra quality. It might be worth your while to keep them together on a single line in the regular runs. That's all they ask; it's not much in return for what the company gets from this arrangement.

Brooks (m): Well, maybe it doesn't seem so much, but any such scheme would disrupt the whole department. We can't understand why the union backs these girls up on this thing. Management played fair and square with them and each agreed to go back to her regular place when the order was finished.

Parsons (u): Rose Townley says all those girls are long-seniority employees; they have rights in such a transfer.

Brooks (m): But look here, Lloyd. If you bring up seniority, just remember that there was no obligation on us to consider seniority at all. There was nothing like a transfer. We were simply setting up a special arrangement to meet a special production problem.

Parsons (u): You say you didn't have to consider seniority at all, but maybe you should have considered it. You certainly have to consider it now. If you *had* considered it, we wouldn't have this problem on our hands. Seniority always means a lot to the union. We can't permit our members to suffer any infringement on their job rights.

Brooks (m): I don't know what the problem really is. Those girls, I don't mind telling you as we told them, did a fine job in the special room. And they have been doing their usual satisfactory work now on the regular runs. Somehow they feel entitled to special privileges, although they agreed at the start there would be nothing like that. That's what you've got to help us show them they just can't ask. This was not a question of promotion, or rehiring, or even transfer. It was just a production adjustment in one department.

Parsons (u): Well, as soon as you considered seniority, the union had a right to be consulted. Maybe if you had called us in we could have helped avoid this trouble.

Brooks (m): But look here, Lloyd; the very fact that older women aren't as adaptable shows we couldn't make seniority a controlling consideration.

Parsons (u): Well, to the extent you did consider it, couldn't you give it equal weight in meeting the demand of these girls for a single inspection line? That would simply recognize them as a special inspection group. It isn't very much they're asking.

Brooks (m): No, we couldn't—and for two reasons. As I told you, it would simply disrupt the whole department production-wise. Then, secondly, once we admit seniority in such rearrangements the girls would have to give way to many senior inspectors. The longest service employee among the special inspectors had 8 years. In the regular group there are inspectors with 9 years, 10 years, and so on. Agnes McKenna has 14 years, and she's already warned me she won't let anybody bump her.

MacIntyre (u): Say, just between us, she's always griping.

Brooks (m): I know just what you mean, Mac, and generally I too would be inclined to listen more to Rose Townley than to Agnes McKenna. But this time Agnes is right and Rose is wrong. In fact, I can't understand what got into Rose. I'm sure the other girls would follow her lead, and apparently she's been the one pressing this demand for them all. It just isn't like Rose to go back on her word—and that's what it is.

MacIntyre (u): Well, Rose is just expressing what they all feel. They all want to work together in the regular room too. I know; they're after me all the time.

Brooks (m) [smiling]: Oh, you needn't defend Rose to me, Mac. I like her too. But in this thing she's really all wrong. Let us transfer some girls, and soon we'd be swamped with requests for transfers. Other girls would want to work next to their friends, or next to the door, or away from the windows.

If we put management's decision on seniority those special inspectors could be bumped by the older women. Just study those seniority lists I've drawn up, and would you put it beyond Agnes McKenna to demand the right to "bump" one of those girls off the special line, if we set one up for them? You know Agnes. Why, you'd be in for just as much trouble in the union as we would in the department.

Parsons (u): I didn't realize the special inspectors had less seniority than the regular ones. I think Rose thinks she has seniority on her side. Why don't we talk some more to the special inspectors and show them these lists? I can't help saying once more, and don't think I'm just rubbing it in, that if the company had called the union in, we could have warned you seniority would arise sooner or later. You'd have done better to choose on straight seniority; maybe those older women had a right to the special assignments.

Brooks (m): But remember it was purely a production problem, Lloyd. No promotion, no extra pay, no special privileges, no transfer out of the department, nothing like that. Flexibility was the main thing.

Parsons (u): Well, even if we had had those charts we could have put Rose—and the others—straight when they first brought up the demand. If management only wouldn't be afraid to call in the union—at least for consultation.

Brooks (m): Well, Lloyd, we get along pretty well together; and you know management simply must keep its right to manage. We'll be glad if you will help us straighten this out.

Two days later, Mr. Parsons informed Mr. Brooks that he had been unable to persuade the special inspectors that their demand was unwarranted. Shortly thereafter, Bill MacIntyre came to see Mr. Brooks. He said things were getting "more tangled up" every day. Now the regular inspectors wanted "a showdown" to see just where they stood. Everybody was talking "seniority" to him. The two men agreed to arrange a conference at which spokesmen for each side would meet with Messrs. Brooks, Ashley, Parsons, and MacIntyre. When this conference convened three days later in Mr. Ashley's office, Rose Townley and Catherine Grey were present to speak for the "special" group; Agnes McKenna and Mary Hammond for the "regular" group. After Mr. Ashley and Mr. Parsons both said they were sure this chance to talk the situation over would straighten things out, the following discussion took place:

Ashley (m): I'm glad we're all having this chance to talk this situation out. I'm sure we'll work things out together.

Parsons (u): Mr. Ashley, we're sure, too, that all of us here will be able to straighten this trouble out.

Agnes (u): There'd never have been any trouble if some people's heads didn't get too big for their hats. I don't know why some people feel they're so much better than anybody else they have to work off by themselves.

Rose (u): Now, Agnes, let's not get personal. It's just a matter of our rights. I brought the union contract along and if you don't mind, I'd like to read the seniority clause so you can see just how we girls look at it: [She reads from the contract.]

(1) Seniority is defined as the length of an employee's service in a department in respect to length of service with the company.

(2) The purpose of seniority is to help establish, with ability, a jointly recognized policy of preference as to promotion, demotion, layoff, and rehiring.

(3) In the event of such promotion, demotion, layoff, rehiring, the company and the union will take into consideration departmental seniority and ability, and when ability is relatively equal, seniority will prevail.

(4) In the case of an employee-requested transfer, seniority shall be retained in the employee's regular department until six months' service in the new department has elapsed, at which time accumulative service in the new department shall become effective and shall cancel seniority in the old department.

(5) In the case of company-ordered transfers, seniority shall be effective as of hiring date.

(6) An employee temporarily transferred to any department other than his regular department at the request of such other department shall continue to cumulate seniority in his regular department. When such employee is requested to return to his former regular department he may refuse such request without any penalty other than the loss of departmental seniority in his former regular department.

We girls feel we have very plain rights by these terms. We didn't ask to be transferred to the special room; the company transferred us. Now we were in the special room a little over six months. That means by Section (6) we can refuse to return to our regular department without any penalty except loss of seniority in that old department. But by Section (5) on a company transfer, we have seniority as of hiring date. So we have the right to demand that we be kept as a new department, with seniority in it as of our hiring dates. And that's all we ask.

Brooks (m): Well I'm glad to get your ideas, Rose, and I will say you've built a plausible case. But those were not the terms of our bargain, were they? Didn't each of you agree that this was a temporary arrangement, and when the order was finished you'd return to your former places?

Rose (u): Maybe we did, Mr. Brooks, but we feel just as if we are a new department. That's why we want to stay together.

Agnes McKenna (u): Well, just a minute, if there's any new department formed, we have the right to bid for promotions under the seniority clause. I have 14 years' seniority, and Mary here has 8.

Rose (u): But under Section 3, seniority prevails only if ability is equal. Now, we don't say we girls have more ability than any of the rest. But for this special assignment Mr. Brooks, and Mr. Ashley too, said the company needed girls who could be flexible. Flexibility then becomes a factor in ability under Section 3, and counts over seniority.

Ashley (m): But we explained, didn't we, that the program couldn't work unless you girls returned to your regular places? And if we transfer you, how could we refuse to transfer other girls for still other good reasons?

Rose (u): But we ask transfer for a good production reason. We're a special inspection group. Anyway, it did turn out to be a real transfer; you will have to send us into the special inspection room when new orders come in. That's why we think it will work out for everybody's good if we're kept together on a special line.

Parsons (u): Well, now that we have heard just how you girls on both sides feel about it, maybe it would be a good idea for Mac and me to talk it all over with management.

[The girls thereupon left.]

Brooks (m): Rose worked up a good case but she's just all haywire. I didn't want to argue it too much before Agnes and Mary, but I'm afraid to let things go on this way. That department's fast getting demoralized. I think a meeting with the special girls might bring them around. I'd like to try it anyway.

Parsons (u): Mr. Brooks, I really think this is union business now. Seniority is a strong union principle.

Ashley (m): Well, Lloyd, the company has to insist likewise this is a production problem, not a seniority issue. If seniority safeguards job rights, our ability to bring in more orders safeguards jobs. I hope you'll see we're in this together. Well, let's all sleep on it tonight. Suppose you draw up a list of concrete, detailed suggestions on next steps—and we will too. Then we can come to a decision tomorrow.

DISCUSSION QUESTIONS

1. Give in detail your diagnosis of the disturbance that arose over seniority in the inspection department of Merrill Manufacturing Company.

2. Interpret and evaluate the behavior of the people who play focal roles in the situation. Support your answer by reference to the evidence presented in the record, noting particularly the sentiments that seem to weigh most with the union officials, the management executives, and the leaders of the special and regular inspectors. Do you think management executives or union officials involved realized fully the nature of the disturbance confronting them? Explain your judgment of them on this aspect of the situation.

3. If you had been a member of the management at Merrill responsible for follow-through on the Carlton-Wheeler order, at what point would you have been quite sure, on the basis of the behavior of the special inspectors, that there would be difficulties when the order was terminated? Why?

4. Assume that you were called in as a consultant by the Merrill Company. What would have been your advice: (*a*) if you had been called in upon receipt of the order from the Carlton-Wheeler Company, regarding the planning of the program and the objectives to be sought in each of the conferences with the inspectors and the union; (*b*) if you were called into the situation as it is at the end of the record, regarding its handling from then on?

SHERIDAN CHEMICAL COMPANY

SENIORITY IN OVERTIME ASSIGNMENTS

The Sheridan Chemical Company produces a broad line of industrial chemicals. At one of its plants, management was confronted with a series of seniority grievances arising from assignments of workers to different jobs, to different shifts, and to overtime. All but three of these were settled in the three-step grievance machinery, established by the Agreement with the International Chemical Workers' Union, AFL, which provided conferences among (1) the aggrieved employee with his steward and foreman; (2) the employee with steward and superintendent of the department; and (3) the union grievance committee of Local 499 covering the plant and the "Plant Management."

The three grievances still unsettled were appealed to arbitration under Article XII, which provided, however, for a final attempt at resolution by a Settlement Committee composed of one member appointed by the union and one by the company. Charles D. Heinrichs, industrial relations director, represented management and Andrew T. Reilly, chairman of the grievance committee, represented the union. The two had asked Lloyd R. Wilcox, plant manager, and John Carmichael, union secretary and grievanceman, to join them in these discussions. Excerpts follow:

Heinrichs (m): It's just hard for me to believe we can't reach a satisfactory decision on these cases. But you think our foremen have used bad judgment, or haven't consulted you, or haven't followed some past plant rules. Now, it isn't the money; there is less than $200 involved in these grievances. But let us once pay penalties and we've conceded what we refused to write into the agreement in our last negotiations.

Wilcox (m): It boils down to the minimum amount of flexibility management feels it must have. We have now been working for years in a manner fair to the men—and the plant. We feel that the union and the management see pretty well eye-to-eye on seniority. Problems of assignment must arise in the day-to-day operation of a plant which makes 50 or 60 chemicals with thousands of varieties and variations coming up every day. We do not want to bind our hands to say that overtime will always be distributed, regardless of circumstances or the foremen's judgment, to the senior men—and I do not believe that the union wants that either.

Reilly (u): We're not trying to tie the company's hands. The company has paid off on mistakes in overtime in the past and, so, recognized its mistakes. It is not the money for us either. But, all of a sudden, the company takes the attitude that it is not going to continue to pay for mistakes. Let me tell you, you did scare us when you started arguing like that.

Besides, if and when a problem comes up where there is a difference of opinion and there's no immediate emergency, well, in such cases, I say there should be courtesy enough not to let some foreman—who does not understand labor relations any better than a kid in the fifth grade—decide and interfere with the contract.

When we make rules with you for dividing overtime, under Article III, Section 12, of the contract,[1] "as equally and impartially" as possible in each classification, we try to hold our fellows to some decent standards of fairness too. In a plant like ours, with jobs pretty well known as "candy jobs" and "dirty jobs," well, rules help us when overtime on the dirty jobs comes up. Naturally, everybody wants "candy jobs." We can say to the fellows when overtime assignments come up that each man gets his opportunity in his regular turn. If he refuses, whatever his reason, he's charged anyway. That's why we insist men must be asked, so they can't come "beefing" to us and say, "Look, I've been passed." That was why "red overtime"[2] came in. That was to discipline our own men. It wasn't the company that brought that up. It was the union. Guys were picking their overtime and to avoid grievances and a lot of wasted time, we said, "All right, you'll be charged if you don't work, so you can't pick the spots. It's a red mark against you. You take it as it comes. If you don't like it, you still take it—or leave it—but as it comes."

Carmichael (u): I think if we get to the cases we'll be able to show you why these are important issues.

I. First Grievance

Reilly (u): Sicone's grievance is a good one to start off with. For it involves the rule to distribute available overtime as equally as possible among the employees in each classification, the pipe fitters in Sicone's case. First, we have agreed, haven't we, that the low man, as far as total cumulated overtime assignment opportunities are concerned, shall be offered what overtime work is available, if possible?

Now, the company needed two men on the particular Monday; one man was the lead man, and, by our understanding, he stays on for the overtime. So far, so good. But it also so happened that the two lowest men in overtime in that group *were tied* for the amount of hours. Accordingly, we come to another rule and to the *determining factor. Two men are tied.* What is the marker for a decision on who shall work? *Seniority*—departmental seniority! Sicone happened to be the senior man. Even worse, at 4 o'clock Sicone asked his foreman, "Is there going to be any work tonight?" Callahan said, "I don't know yet. I'll let you know." At 4:20, he calls in the other individual, Basuto, and tells him to work. Sicone is grieved right there, because he was not allowed to work. But the company contends that, a few days later, he

---

[1] "All overtime, holiday, Saturday, and Sunday work shall be as equally and impartially distributed among the employees of each classification in a department as possible."

[2] The cumulative overtime record for each man originally included only the number of hours he actually worked overtime. At the union's suggestion, the hours offered but refused were also included and posted in red.

was asked to work overtime and refused. He is an alderman and had to attend an official meeting scheduled for that night. He was charged with red overtime for refusing—which would have been O.K. *if*, and here's the big *if*, there had not been that matter of Foreman Callahan's slip the Monday before. Management now contends they gave Sicone a chance to make up the time. But it cannot be made up! Since Sicone had not been given the opportunity to work on that first night when it was his turn, the man should be paid six hours for the lost overtime. And the fact that the second time round the guy just couldn't work but is charged with overtime is rubbing a little more salt into the wounds.

Heinrichs (m): Well, Andy, we agree with all your facts. But the interpretation—well, that's another matter.

In general, we try to go on the basis of the senior men with low overtime being offered the job. But it is no contractual requirement. To formulate such a rule would be to go beyond the intention of the parties in their negotiations. In fact, the union made a demand during our negotiations last fall, the substance of which asked an amendment that would require the company to pay for all overtime hours lost. We refused. We feel you are now trying to get it through the grievance and arbitration procedure. . . .

Carmichael (u): But management does pay penalties for supervisory "slips." Isn't this case practically the same as for a man to be given a short notice of change of schedule? If a man isn't given a 24-hour notice, the company would pay. This is practically the same position.

Reilly (u): Remember that the practice of *red overtime* helps us in the union to maintain discipline. It's our own traffic rule on overtime. If a man is asked to work and refuses, he is charged with that overtime just as though he worked. But the man who took his place and did the work, he likewise has been charged, so he can't say "I'm *low man*, since I only took what my buddy refused." That's why the union insists that the company cannot make up overtime to an individual.

The union did ask in negotiations that all mistakes be payable. The company came out and said "If we make a mistake, we'll pay for it, but we won't be tied down in black and white." Maybe it is "rocking chair" money; maybe it does look as if we're trying to get paid for work not performed. But we're really trying to set up rules together to get order into these assignments.

Carmichael (u): With hard work, we worked out a method whereby we get along pretty well on the distribution of overtime. You say that yourself. Nothing in the contract requires a list be posted where the workers can see it. But, to keep peace in the family, we post a list in every department of names, dates, and total hours. Now, we have a clause in the contract that overtime is going to be distributed as equally as possible. Every year that list starts over. If a man is low and he gets a tough assignment, he might refuse it. He gets marked in red, and the hours go into his total. He cannot make up what he loses; he simply must wait for his regular turn again.

We know nothing in the contract says anything about the red marks.

That is something we worked up. But here is a man, Sicone, with a good reason for refusing his second overtime—and he gets penalized. But, if his foreman hadn't made a mistake, the night when he had duties as a city official wouldn't have been his chance at overtime. Isn't the penalty going on the wrong side?

Wilcox (m): We just don't see any hard and fast obligation for that first Monday assignment. We are obligated to keep overtime distributed as equally as possible among the men, and we recognize that seniority is as practicable a guide to follow as any. Now, Sicone was overlooked by a human slip, but we gave him a chance the next time. We just can't be tied down too rigidly, especially in a chemical plant.

Our understanding is that overtime will be offered to the man with the lesser amount of overtime. But it does not follow that every day it is going to be equal. We try to balance this up over a period. We have to have some leeway.

The company agrees that you fellows have all worked out a damned fine understanding. I also think it's tough, too damn tough, that Sicone had to be assigned red overtime. But it was done in accordance with your long-standing practice. If a man is a city officer, maybe he shouldn't be penalized because he has to attend a meeting. But penalizing him is in accord with the rules on overtime assignments. You have allowed only two permissible reasons for refusing overtime: shop stewards' meeting and the union executive board meeting.

Reilly (u): Well, let me refresh your memory by reading from the company's minutes on our meeting when we drew up this rule. We agreed that:

Generally an employee is charged with refusal of overtime whenever it is offered while on the company premises, the number of hours being determined by the length of time the job ran. The sole exception is when there is to be a Union Shop Stewards' meeting or to attend the regular Executive Board Meeting. The past practice of not charging while off the company premises will be continued. The above will be reduced to writing and signed by the parties as a special agreement.

Now, those are the company's minutes.

Carmichael (u): If the union is satisfied for members to be charged with red overtime when they refuse, that's no concern to the company. The company does not lose any money by it. We are the ones who are willing to agree by that strict penalty. We do that to keep the records straight.

Wilcox (m): I think the foremen are trying hard to make an equitable distribution. But we don't want a system so rigid that we have to equalize to the closest minute. A foreman has to have some latitude. In case of a breakdown at night, it is unpracticable to call a man 35 or 40 miles away. Yet we have agreed to try to work at least from the bottom half of the list. The union thought that was reasonable. It's live and let live.

Reilly (u): Well, before we go to the next case, can you, Mr. Wilcox and John [Carmichael], agree to the submission we drew up, in case we decide to call in an arbitrator?

Stipulation. The parties have agreed that the question to be put to the Arbitrator is as follows:

Did the company violate Article III, Section 12, of the contract by failing to assign certain overtime to S. Sicone, and, if so, what, if any, additional compensation is due him?

Statement of Facts. On Monday afternoon, Mr. Sicone and Mr. Basuto, two first-class pipers, were working together on a job. Mr. Basuto was asked to work overtime. On the following day, Mr. Sicone protested to his foreman that he should have been awarded the overtime work. No grievance was filed at that time. On the following Friday, overtime was offered to Mr. Sicone. He refused the overtime but was charged for his refusal on the overtime records.

Mr. Sicone then presented the grievance, alleging that, had he been asked to work on the previous Monday, he would not have been asked to work overtime on Friday, and therefore, would not have had to be charged with a refusal. He claims pay for overtime equivalent to that which Basuto had worked. Mr. Basuto and Mr. Sicone had exactly the same hours of overtime prior to the overtime assignment on April 14. Mr. Sicone is the senior man.

Wilcox (m): It sounds O.K.

II. SECOND GRIEVANCE

Reilly (u): O.K. Let's go to our case on the sulfuric acid mixer. You know, Chuck, it might be a good idea to present the stipulation you and I composed together first:

Did the company violate Article X, Section 4,[1] of the contract by the work schedule assignment of P. Mahoney during the week beginning August 27? If so, what, if any, additional compensation is due Mahoney for that work week?

Statement of Facts. It became necessary to schedule 2-shift operations of the batch mixer in the OV Filling Department beginning Thursday, August 31. Because of operating difficulties attendant on starting up a new plant, the mixer had to be operated 16 hours a day. The 2 men assigned to the classification charged with the operation of this batch mixer were P. Mahoney and F. Donahue. Both men had been offered to work on an overtime basis and both have refused to work. In order to keep customers supplied, a 2-shift schedule was set up with Donahue assigned the day shift and Mahoney the 4–12 shift on Thursday and Friday. Mahoney has the greater department seniority. On the second shift of August 31 and September 1 the mixer was manned by a utility man assisted by the foreman, Hoffman. Mahoney assumed his duties on the second shift the following day.

This grievance was brought by Mahoney, alleging that he should not be scheduled on the 4–12 shift, but that he should be given his choice of schedules, since he was the senior man. Both men normally work the day shift, 8–4 P.M.

Wilcox (m): I can't see why you define the main issue between us here as a violation of the management clause. Certainly, you do not think Hoffman, the foreman, assigned Donahue to deprive Mahoney of work?

Reilly (u): This whole thing is another example of why we must insist on rules. We grant there were personalities involved here, a hot-headed Irish-

---

[1] Section 4 was the management clause and included the following: "Supervisory employees on the salaried payroll shall not do work in order to deprive hourly paid employees of jobs regularly performed by the latter. This does not prevent such supervisory employees from performing the necessary functions of instruction, or from operating equipment or processes in emergencies or for experimental purposes."

man and a dictatorial German.   O.K., but Hoffman must be made to observe rules like anybody else.

Wilcox (m): Well, we'll get to that in a minute.   But don't those rules really concern the administration of overtime assignments, with regard to shift preferences and seniority?   What has the management clause to do with it?   We're pretty anxious to see no questions arise from our rights under general management functions.

Carmichael (u): Well, if Hoffman hadn't been so all-fired bent on his own way against Mahoney, he would not have needed to assign the utility man, and to help the utility man do Mahoney's work.   That's why we think Hoffman violated Section 4 of Article X.

Reilly (u): But I think Mr. Wilcox has something.   We're so mad at Hoffman we're forgetting the central issue ourselves.   [To Heinrichs.]   Can't we add the question of seniority?

Heinrichs (m) [after writing hastily for a few moments, as the others do likewise]: How's this: "Did the company deviate from the practice of seniority and violate Article X, Section 4, of the contract, etc., etc."

Reilly (u): Sounds O.K. to me.

Carmichael (u): Me, too; that does it.

Wilcox (m): Well, no!   I'd like to leave room for management to argue before any possible arbitrator that what Hoffman did was quite within our managerial rights.

Carmichael (u): Well, the union thinks foremen like Hoffman need to learn that they can't do work belonging in the bargaining unit just because they mess things up.

Reilly (u): Well, why not leave both possibilities open—say, with an "and/or."

Heinrichs (m) [writing, and then reading]: Like this, eh?   "Did the company deviate from the practice of job assignment on the basis of seniority and/or violate Article X, Section 4, of the contract etc., etc."

Wilcox (m) [after a moment's thought]: I guess we can buy that for the time.

Reilly (u): I certainly can't understand how any question even arose over whether we operate under a system of preferential choice on shift assignments. Hoffman agreed that Mahoney, being senior man, should not have to work the 4–12 shift as overtime on the days when he had the day-shift assignment. But, when Hoffman set the work up on two shifts, he took the attitude "I am boss—there is nothing in the contract that says anything about senior preference, and you'll go on 4–12." Now, time after time, when the company has had to assign day workers to a 4–12 shift, we have always been able to work out the conditions satisfactorily.   But this particular time the senior man did not choose to go on, and yet he was forced to take it.   Past practice seems to have been thrown to the winds.   The thing that has got the union so concerned is the unwritten contract.   Management seems to be demanding the right to disregard it now.

Carmichael (u): Although the company originally raised the issue of relative qualifications, after the first discussions they quickly dropped it. Since that time, it is a little difficult for me to understand just exactly what the company's position is.

Heinrichs (m): But, Johnny, you and Andy are practical men. We had just recently started a big new plant and, in the starting-up operations, we had fallen seriously behind in shipments. We had to get our customers supplied by operating that mixer for 16 hours a day, rather than the usual 8. The two men assigned to the classification in charge of the operation were Mahoney and Donahue. Both men had been offered the work on an overtime basis, but both refused. There was no deviation from the existing practice, because our practice has always been in such cases, for the supervisor involved to exercise his best judgment. Nowhere in the contract is set forth a requirement that assignment to shift must be done in strict accordance with seniority. Our shift schedule throughout the entire plant will reflect the fact that your senior man, for example, might take Saturday and Sunday for his days off for a period of three months and then change to two other days off during the week. The schedules rotate. Besides, the job to which Mahoney was assigned was the lighter of the two jobs. We believe that there is an even more important consideration, however. To concede now that Mahoney was improperly assigned would invite the senior man in every department of the entire plant to bring up arguments like, "Well, I'm the senior man and I want all day shifts." In operating a chemical plant, that could cause a considerable amount of grief.

Reilly (u): True, nothing about seniority preference was written in the contract, but how about past precedent? Now, I understand you to say, Mr. Wilcox, that as far as you are concerned you don't operate on past precedent. Well, we did operate on past precedent for quite a few years. Of course, the reason the union let Mahoney continue working on the undesirable shift like he did was for the simple reason that we couldn't keep on haggling with the supervisor until we settled it. We had no choice; and we decided we would, if we had to, carry the issue to arbitration.

Heinrichs (m): I would infer from your comments that the union hopes that by arbitration, if necessary, that it will have the equivalent of a contractual obligation establishing seniority right to shift preference—which is, in effect, amending the contract that the parties negotiated.

Reilly (u): That is not the conclusion to be drawn at all. We have, of course, our written contract. But we also have many parts of that contract that are unwritten; they arise in daily applications, under the precedents established and recognized on many cases. The unwritten contract is to be respected; a precedent, established and recognized, is to be honored. Now, the company contends that, if this case is decided in favor of the union, the senior men on shift jobs would elect to have all preferable shift assignments. Now that is not the question at all. For there are all kinds of rules and precedents to govern that. The union and the company are both always aware there are three types of workers: shift workers, day workers, and exception-to-the-workweek workers. A day worker's and the shift worker's week is

Monday through Friday; the week of an exception-to-the-workweek employee can be Tuesday to Sunday, or Monday to Saturday, or any schedule required by production. A day worker can be assigned to shift work on the Monday-through-Friday basis only if he volunteers, except when he is the only man in the classification needed. Then he can be forced to go on another shift even though he is a senior man. But he cannot be laid off on any of the scheduled workdays and be required to work on Saturday and Sunday for straight time. We expect supervision to respect the rules.

Generally, we have harmony, too. If a junior day worker had something planned from 4–12, the senior man usually would offer to take it. In this case, it was the antagonistic attitude of the superintendent that got Mahoney's back up. He took the attitude "I'm the boss—you're going on 4–12." Mahoney is a day worker, and by practice seniority governs in their assignments to shifts—if disputes arise. It is the status of the unwritten contract that must be cleared up, or we're going to have to start negotiating every little thing that comes up in this plant.

Heinrichs (m): But you always leave out one thing we regard as very important. We must have sufficient leeway, so that if we require a certain man, who may have special knowledge, to work on a night shift, say, we would expect to assign him without regard to seniority.

Carmichael (u): Are you talking qualifications? Mahoney broke Donahue in on the job. You agree that Mahoney is qualified. What the company is saying is not that they want a qualified man to fill a particular job. The company is saying, "We want the *particular* man that our supervisors say we want."

Reilly (u): Management admitted to us that it was done wrong, and were they to do the thing over, they would apply the rule that the senior man gets the preferable shift. Is there any need of arguing when management agrees that the foremen had done wrong? We are just hashing it over and over again. For us, we only want to know your answer to the question of the unwritten contract and whether it is going to be honored or not.

III. Third Grievance

Heinrichs (m): O.K. Shall we go to Ev Smith's grievance, then? It's another gripe, but, also, more of the same.

Reilly (u): Oh, no. It isn't something you can just dismiss like that! We have to get a real understanding now about just where we both stand on these rules of our unwritten contract. That's what we're really after—not money. Arbitration expense will be more than the damages will amount to, even if we win.

Carmichael (u): Yes, look. About Sicone, you say his foreman *just blanked out*. With Mahoney, it's a foreman who *just* gets into a *personality* clash. Now with Smith, his foreman *just didn't have time* to phone around the plant, or, at least look for a union representative, before he decided to assign the next day's overtime to the wrong man. What kind of a run-around are you giving us, or, rather, our plant rules? What's this business of *fore-man's judgment* got to do with them?

Heinrichs (m): Here is the agreed stipulation:

Stipulation. The parties have agreed to the following stipulation:

Did the company violate Article III, Section 12, of the contract by failing to assign certain overtime work to E. Smith, first-class carpenter, and if so, what if any additional compensation is due him?

Statement of Facts. At approximately 4 P.M. on the Friday day shift, it became apparent to the foreman of the Carpenters that certain overtime work would be necessary on Saturday. Messrs. Hight and Randall were in the Carpenter shop when the call for the work came, and were asked to take the overtime assignment. The aggrieved, Mr. Smith, was out in the plant on another job. The foreman asked Randall and Hight to work because they knew the details of the work to be per-formed.

The aggrieved, Everett Smith, claimed that he and not Hight should have been asked to work, since Hight had 5½ hours of overtime for the year, and he had 4½ hours. In his discussions with the foreman, the aggrieved claimed that he should be paid the same amount of money which Hight received for the Saturday overtime work.

Wilcox (m): Sounds O.K. After all, it was the end of the shift, and there was only one hour's difference in the overtime credited to Hight as against Smith. Certainly they'd balance that out before the end of the year!

Heinrichs (m): Yes. The company's position does remain pretty much the same in these cases. The language in Section 12 of Article III requires that the company distribute overtime "as equally as possible" among the men in the carpenter's classification. But, if the union's position in this matter should be sustained, we feel it would be the equivalent of writing into the contract a mandate that it should be distributed exactly from day to day.

Now, let's not forget that this was still early in the year, the middle of June, I believe. We had still a half year ahead. The foreman could see that it would be quite possible during the year to even out things; and, further-more, he knew good and well that there was only a very small difference in the overtime between the two in question. We didn't agree that this distribu-tion of overtime had to be done to the minute, or hour, or half-hour, but equally over a period of time.

The foreman proceeded on three considerations: First of all, the men who were there in the shop knew the job in question. Secondly, this was late Friday afternoon, and doubtless the foreman had other things to do other than try to trace Mr. Smith somewhere in the plant. Finally, it was his judgment, and he frankly admits it in his own writing here, "There was only an hour difference, and I took the man I could immediately reach in the shop knowing I could even up the overtime later on as it was only June."

Carmichael (u): I don't understand the company's position in interpreting that contractual obligation, "as equally as possible." I don't think we ever negotiated an understanding that you have the rest of the year to try to even up the overtime. How do you know it is going to be possible to make it up at all?

Heinrichs (m): I have the record right here. The carpenters worked 32 hours' overtime in January, 39 in February, none in March, 26 in April, 15½ in June, none in July, and 153 in August. I have the individuals here too. As of the first of August, you have Hight with 30½ hours; Randall has 11½; Lombardi has 29; MacDonald, 25½; Smith, 27½; Hill, 25; Benson, 27; Lawrence, 29; and Mitchell, 33.

Reilly (u): Well, let's go back to the contract too. In this same Article III, Section 13,[1] is where the union comes in on the distribution of overtime. We insisted that the records, made monthly, be kept by department and posted on the departmental bulletin board each month to assist in the impartial distribution of overtime. Such records are subject to examination at any time by the grievance committee or the shop steward.

Now, there was one hour's difference between Hight and Smith. What guarantee was there that there would be any more overtime? Even your records show there was none in July.

Wilcox (m): Now, you know, Andy, we have never gone lower than a total overtime hours of 2,000 per month, and last month we worked 13,000 hours of overtime. The foreman knew damn well he was going to have some overtime work in the next half year.

Carmichael (u): You must bear in mind that carpenters hardly ever get overtime. Most of their work can be carried along on straight time.

Heinrichs (m): I disagree. In August, for example, carpenters worked 153 hours of overtime.

Carmichael (u): Well, since the Korean war, there have been more emergencies requiring overtime.

Reilly (u): The contract is for the whole plant. You can't set aside one department when you apply plant rules!

Carmichael (u): There was no valid reason to pass up the low man in this case. The fact that the man was out of the shop makes no difference. The foreman could be pretty sure, since it was so close to 4 o'clock, that the locker room would find the man he wanted. I don't think it is a hardship for the foreman to contact the man and ask him to work; and, assuming the man did not want to work, foremen usually ask a second man tentatively, "Will you work if Smith won't?" Had he done that easy little thing, the foreman would be covered. Or he could have discussed the assignment with a union representative.

In the vernacular of the plant, you know we have the so-called "candy jobs" and the so-called "stinky jobs." You must be impartial, because some overtime jobs around here are tough. They are "blood-money jobs." I don't think you'll dispute that. But follow the rules and no man can complain of partiality.

Wilcox (m): That is a good argument, and management doesn't defend discrimination. I am not sure that this case bears you out. Do you see this

---

[1] "Monthly and yearly overtime records of each employee will be kept by his department and posted on the departmental bulletin boards each month to assist in the impartial distribution of overtime. Such records are subject to examination at any time by the Grievance Committee or Shop Steward."

case as a failure to make an impartial assignment, or is it an issue of distributing overtime?

Carmichael (u): I raised that point as a rebuttal to the company's argument that, after all, what is an hour's difference? I'm trying to show why, for the union, even an hour's difference is important.

Wilcox (m): But, remember, too, that for 5, 10, 20 or more years, the foreman distributed the overtime on the basis of getting the job done as well as possible. During these same years we've had a gradually evolving system of rules for complying with the contractual provision for its impartial distribution. We didn't agree that we were *required* to have the low man work. We set up a system to try to help foremen to distribute the overtime as impartially as possible.

DISCUSSION QUESTIONS

1. What important factors in the Sheridan situation determined the establishment of a system for distributing overtime?

2. Evaluate management's plea for "flexibility" in making overtime assignments.

3. Why did the union seek a highly systematized arrangement?

4. How would you decide each of the cases? What position do you think an arbitrator would take?

SEDGEWICK–COLE CORPORATION (A)

JOB EVALUATION AND LOCAL UNIONS

I

The Sedgewick-Cole Corporation, a major manufacturer of floor coverings, operated two plants, one at Craftown, and the other, about 60 miles away, at Kingsville. In anticipation of extensive demand for a new product, NuCrest, as well as for its regular products, the company initiated plans for improvements and new equipment to cost $5,250,000. While the proposed improvements were being effected, the Craftown local of the United Rubber Workers (CIO) entered a grievance regarding a job-evaluation plan that its membership had rejected but that the Kingsville membership had accepted.

II

The company was organized in 1930 to continue businesses formerly conducted independently by the Sedgewick Company at Craftown and the Cole Company at Kingsville. During the depression of the 1930's, the company suffered substantial losses, reduced wages, and abandoned an incentive system installed at Craftown in 1928 which had promised substantial benefits for all.

In 1937 some Craftown employees requested the Rubber Workers to organize the plant. A few months later the company recognized the Craftown local and granted an increase of five cents an hour. The Craftown local then organized the Kingsville workers, and the two locals formed a joint committee that negotiated a company-wide agreement, effective February 15, 1938. Less than a month later, management, citing losses, announced a five-cent hourly wage reduction. When negotiations failed, the Craftown employees struck and the Kingsville men walked out to support Craftown. The strike lasted one day, work being resumed after joint agreement to choose a fact-finding board consisting of two union, one company, and two federal representatives. This board did not find the reduction justified, and the company withdrew it. However, the board did report as follows:

The company has inadequate reserves to weather even a short depression, and it has not been able to raise capital necessary to keep equipment abreast of competition. Wage rates have averaged less than in competitors' plants, but Sedgewick-Cole gets less production per man-hour than its competitors.

The contract negotiated in 1939 provided for a union shop and for a substantial number of upward adjustments in rates to go into effect at both plants. No horizontal increase in hourly base rates was granted. The union based demands for rate revisions upon the company's past practice of setting

81

rates in relation to "going community rates," or at the whims of supervisors, particularly with respect to new jobs.

During 1938, financial conditions had improved sufficiently to permit installation of new equipment, which had changed jobs throughout the plants. In anticipation of grievances resulting from production changes, the following clause was written into the 1939 contract:

All special grievances concerning a speed-up, slow-down, or other serious matter shall be deemed of emergency nature and the usual procedure on grievances shall be dispensed with. These matters will be handled immediately through the shop committee and the management.

Grievances regarding wage inequities increased sharply during 1939. The contract negotiated in 1940 ran for three years, providing for reopenings on wages only. Because grievances had involved wage rates so extensively, this contract provided:

ARTICLE 4, SECTION 2, PARAGRAPH "d"

In any case where a speed-up occurs, through increasing speed of present equipment or revamping of same, whereby the company's costs are lowered and maintained for a period of 90 days, the employees affected will receive a fair share in the savings involved, such share to be distributed at the discretion of company and union officials.

This clause, however, proved unsatisfactory because of the difficulty of allocating the "share in the savings" upon greater effort or upon improvement in equipment. As a result only those employees working in departments where such improvements were made enjoyed increased pay, which, in turn, gave rise to a multitude of alleged inequity grievances in other departments.

III

After the 1940 contract had been signed, the company offered the position of personnel director to Albert C. Tedrick, treasurer of the Craftown local, editor of its paper, and member of the international's executive board. As one of the organizers of his local, Tedrick had been active in the formulation of union policy, and had always served as chief union spokesman in negotiations. After serious consideration, Mr. Tedrick accepted the company's offer.

Shortly thereafter, Mr. Tedrick enrolled in evening courses to study job evaluation and incentive systems. Upon completion of his course, he was convinced that solution of the company's wage problems lay first in effecting a sound job-evaluation program, and then in building a well-conceived incentive system. His first objective was to dispel any suspicion that his program would be similar to the previous incentive plan at Craftown. Accordingly, Mr. Tedrick began informally to suggest to union officials at weekly grievance meetings the merits of job evaluation.

During the war, operations differed radically from regular work, and the "haggle" system of rate setting continued. Repeatedly, wage rates were submitted to arbitration. To reduce arbitration, the parties concluded a new agreement providing: "In the event new equipment is installed for any operations, rates for jobs on same will be settled by mutual agreement." Wage rates continued, however, to be arbitrated rather than settled by mutual agreement.

IV

In their postwar contract, the union and the management agreed, with the assistance of a federal conciliator, to include the following clause:

ARTICLE 4, SECTION 2, PARAGRAPH "c"

The company will undertake a job evaluation study with a view of eliminating intraplant inequities. The job evaluation and wage adjustment is to be subject to the mutual agreement of both parties with the provision that any disputes thereunder will be subject to impartial arbitration by an arbitrator to be selected by the parties. In the event new equipment is installed for any operation, rates for jobs on same will be decided by a mutually satisfactory job analysis and evaluation.

A joint job-evaluation committee composed of two union and two company representatives from each plant was formed, and a former federal conciliator was retained by the company as consultant. Within four months this committee had completed a job-evaluation manual and had agreed on evaluation for all jobs.

The locals in Kingsville and in Craftown, however, rejected the plan. At the time, wage-increase demands of 30%, equivalent to about 33 cents per hour, were pending.

Two months later the contract was extended for another year, by a joint stipulation which provided as follows:

JOINT STIPULATION

There is to be inserted in place of Article 4, Section 2, Paragraph "d" [1] a paragraph calling for the development of an incentive plan to be worked out between a union committee and a company committee with the usual arbitration clause. The company agrees immediately to increase by 15 cents hourly wage rates applicable to all members of the union alike.

Under this extended contract, the job-evaluation committee at Craftown applied job-evaluation standards despite the previous vote of rejection, to establish rates for 16 new jobs and to review one old job. Vincent Rosetti, president of the Craftown local, signed acceptance stipulations for the union. Four months after the extension of the contract, Mr. Rosetti refused to sign any other acceptance stipulations or to accept new rates thenceforth set by the evaluation unless they were higher than the prevailing base rate.

Three months later, a consultant engaged to install an incentive system under the terms of the joint stipulation also reviewed the evaluation plan. He recommended that higher credits be allocated to physical effort, which the union had protested as "rated too low." Union leaders thereupon agreed to present the revised evaluation plan to their members. The revised plan was approved by the Kingsville local, but Craftown again voted rejection.

---

[1] See p. 82.

Notified of these votes, Mr. Tedrick informed union officials that notwithstanding rejection at Craftown, evaluation would be used in setting rates on new jobs. Before such rates were applied, however, union representatives on the job-evaluation committee would be invited to check them, and disagreements would be submitted to arbitration.

During the next month, accordingly, union representatives on the Craftown committee reviewed one job and approved evaluations on five new jobs. James O'Hara, vice president, and William Phillips, secretary, did not sign acceptance stipulations on these rates. Mr. Tedrick nevertheless put them into effect.

V

Four weeks later, Mr. Tedrick received the following grievance at Craftown:

After investigating the plastic tile job we feel that since the job formerly had three men and now has two, the job has been revamped and speeded up in more ways than one, so that production has been doubled without any chance for the men to gain a fair share of the profits such as in our Contract (Article 4, Section 2, paragraph "d").[1] We must ask to arbitrate this case since company refuses to compensate these men accordingly.

Mr. Tedrick replied immediately as follows:

We assume the job in question is the pressing of Nu-Crest tile by the double platen process instead of on single platen presses with a crew of two men, each of whom worked about half their time due to the heats.[2] This job is one on which the company cannot make any great profit and therefore there is no share in the profits to be considered.

We will gladly re-evaluate the job according to Article 4, Section 2, paragraph "c"[3] and if additional wages are agreed upon, we will pay same. Our job analyst has prepared his analysis for discussion by the job evaluation committee. We are willing to meet at any time.

Furthermore, our joint stipulation calls for the elimination of Article 4, Section 2, paragraph "d" and in its place we are to substitute a wage incentive clause;[4] therefore, the clause you refer to is no longer a part of our agreement. We will agree to have the job time studied and determine a rate of pay. To do this, this job would first be evaluated.

We suggest that the company-union job evaluation committee set a rate; if no agreement can be reached, submit the question to arbitration. We do not intend to set any rates by guesswork, nor pay increases unless justified by systematic methods. The present process of curing Nu-Crest tile is a temporary expedient to get this product on the market and will be discarded when multiplatened presses are installed.

The outcome of this grievance, Mr. Tedrick believed, would be crucial in establishing job evaluation as the method of determining new rates. Other-

---

[1] See p. 82.
[2] A platen is a flat molding plate which holds the tile during the application of heat and pressure. The time period during which the tile is under pressure is referred to as a "heat."
[3] See p. 83.
[4] See p. 82.

wise, the haggle system would inevitably return and wage inequities would continue a serious problem.

Five months prior to the filing of this grievance, the company had notified the union that press crews would be reduced from three to two men, and that twelve men thus released would be transferred elsewhere. A better product could be turned out if molds were left longer in the presses and the number of heats reduced. If the union opposed this change, the company warned it might be necessary to lay off all 36 men until new presses were installed. The union responded that the men would not comply and requested that action be withheld until the officers explained the situation to them. The company agreed but added that in the event the union did not cooperate the company would request arbitration. Within a few days, crews were reduced. A multi-press had been ordered a week before the union filed the above grievance.

Two weeks after receipt of the grievance, Mr. Tedrick informed the union that the company had evaluated the disputed jobs, that the results indicated that the jobs were overpaid, but that, in spite of that, the rates would not be reduced. The union requested arbitration and the following submission was jointly drawn up:

Are the employees pressing Nu-Crest entitled to a rate adjustment as the union contends, pursuant to Article 4, Section 2, paragraph "d" or pursuant to paragraph "c" of the same article, as the company contends?

The union supported its claim to a "share in the savings" by three major arguments:

1. The company changed the one-platen process to a two-platen process, increasing output. Article 4, Section 2, paragraph "d" applies.

2. This is not a new job, nor is new equipment used.

3. The local has twice rejected job evaluation. Therefore, Article 4, Section 2, paragraph "c" cannot apply.

The company supported its position that the new rates be determined by job evaluation on four main grounds:

1. The job is a new operation, and even if it were not, it is subject, as are all jobs, to the job evaluation provided for in the contract.

2. The union accepted job evaluation as proved by acceptance stipulations signed by Mr. Rosetti on a reviewed old job and 16 new jobs.

3. One old job was reviewed and 5 new jobs were approved by the joint evaluation committee, and made effective.

4. Article 4, Section 2, paragraph "c" does not require complete mutual agreement for it provides for arbitration of disputes.

In his first finding the arbitrator stated, "The contract does not clearly express the method to be followed. The arbitrator urges the parties to expedite the conclusion of job evaluation for more harmonious relationships." Both the union and management thereupon requested the arbitrator to render a decision. Since both parties preferred an award, he ruled that the job was subject to evaluation.

Mr. Tedrick believed that through arbitration he had accomplished at Craftown the long-sought objective which had been impeded by the negative votes of the Craftown local union. Following the arbitration, Mr. Tedrick discussed the case with a friend who was interested in union-management co-operation. He invited him to interview the principal individuals who had been concerned with the job-evaluation program. Several of the interviews follow.

INTERVIEWS AT THE CRAFTOWN PLANT

James O'Hara, President of the Craftown Local
(Mr. O'Hara was a mechanic.)

O'Hara: I can talk my head off but it does no good. The company co-operates, the union agrees, and we tell the men, but they don't pay any attention.

Interviewer: How did the evaluation program start?

O'Hara: We were in negotiations, getting no place. The company wanted to give only certain departments increases. The union couldn't go that. After the federal conciliator came, he told us about evaluation. He had been here many times before and helped us, so we formed a joint job evaluation committee. However, most of the men in the shop didn't want anything to do with it. Some sections were for it because management had sold the gang leader. If they sold him, the gang went along.

When the consultant came to our department he evaluated the jobs, determined the requirements for an "A" mechanic, and decided that four men were to get "A" ratings. After that, we had a meeting to decide who would get these four "A" jobs. I was the representative for the mechanical department. The foreman picked out four men he thought qualified. I asked about men I had in mind. But the foreman didn't agree with me.

Today I do one job and one of these "A" men does another, and tomorrow he does the thing I did yesterday and I do the thing he did. You can't say his job is harder than mine and so [slowly and with emphasis] the foreman was evaluating the men, not the jobs. That's just the foreman picking out his favorites and "mechanical" voted in a block against the job evaluation proposal.

Take that one department [inspection department]. They were all against it, even some who would have gotten 10 cents more per hour.[1] They were afraid of cuts. Let me give you an example. Suppose I'm getting $1.35 an hour and you're working as my helper. Well, *my job* is evaluated down to $1.30, but *I* would still get $1.35 [as a "red-circle" rate]. Now you were making $1.20 and are evaluated up to $1.28. When you are promoted to my job on another machine, when there is an opening, you would only get $1.30! You see, you'd only get a 2-cent raise instead of a 15-cent raise! You'd be

---

[1] Most references to inspection at Craftown in plant interviews indicated its widely held reputation as a "trouble spot."

doing the same work as I am and I'd be getting $1.35 on the next machine, and the union always stands for "equal work, equal pay."

Interviewer: Were there many of these "cuts"?

O'Hara: No. That's the strange thing. Most of the jobs, 60 per cent of them, were to get better rates. The men are beginning to realize now how much money was involved.

Interviewer: You have evaluation on new jobs, don't you?

O'Hara: That's reasonable. They used to give you whatever they wanted to. It's their right to set rates on new jobs, and we'd rather have a fair method so we see why a job is rated so much.

Interviewer: Why did Kingsville accept evaluation when you turned it down?

O'Hara: They don't have that inspection department down there or things would be different. The committee tried to do a job in selling evaluation here, but the men just yelled, "We don't want no part of it." When we are introduced at Kingsville as officers from Craftown, everyone applauds. When we introduce a Kingsville officer here, the fellows boo and someone shouts, "Go on home." The Kingsville company was always good to work for, even before the two plants consolidated. Kingsville as a city has fewer problems. Take the Craftown plant of the Crocker Company. There isn't a company in America which is more antiunion. Our union had an "in" there once but that company beat it down.

Edward Diffin, Former Vice President of the Craftown Local
(Mr. Diffin, an older employee, was a mechanic. At one time
he had been a railroad employee.)

Diffin: When the union was formed, I was very active. Some wanted a one-man union; they thought officers should run everything. I thought each department ought to have its own union committee. When the others did not agree, I got out. Too many unions have been destroyed because of fights between officers.

History proved I was right. We had a one-man union. When that one man went over to management, it hurt the union. Al Tedrick knew everything about the union and everyone in it, so management got along O.K. It's just like a dictatorship: when the leader dies, the country has no leader. In a democracy a great man like Roosevelt can die and the people can continue because they all have had a part in the show. When Al did go over on the other side, the boys did not like it. If you fight alongside someone and then find, all of a sudden, without warning, that he is on the other side, you naturally don't like it.

Al has brains and plenty on the ball politically. He can put an idea across if he wants to. Our fellows can hardly read or write, so what we need is an educated person to negotiate for us. It takes a liar to catch a liar, and a robber to catch a robber.

Interviewer: Could you tell me something about the evaluation plan?

Diffin: It would have split the men and the union apart. When a fellow would be promoted he might not get the same rate if the job had been lowered by evaluation. Then fellows would be getting different pay for the same work and start fighting. The union would be split. It's happened at the Crocker Company. That company got the AFL and the CIO unions fighting each other. Now they don't have either union.

> Stanley Gardner, Organizer of the Craftown Local
> (Stanley Gardner, 60 years old, worked in the black-
> smith shop in the mechanical department.)

Gardner: I organized this union. We were getting the lowest wages around and the efficiency engineers had been in with time watches and had done a job on us. That's when I got the union. Then I went to Kingsville and they signed up.

A lot of foremen used to be union members. If any of them want to, they can come back to the union. Any guy who moves up [pauses]—well, almost any of them—can come back. Mr. Tedrick used to be in the union. He had his chance and ran the whole show once, but he left. He and Rosetti were real thick, but Rosetti isn't nearly as smart as Al is.

Interviewer: Can you tell me anything about evaluation?

Gardner: I was against evaluation. Our foreman had his nose in it all the way while our mechanical department representative just sat and didn't say anything. The foreman picked out his fair-haired boys for favors rendered.

Interviewer: Were any departments for it?

Gardner: Sure, the print room. The gang leader got sold. In the print room all the boys are Italians. Most guys who work here only went to the third grade. We've got a League of Nations here. Over in the presses there are Italians, Hungarians, Poles, Serbs, a little of everything. We have some colored workers, and there are a few women.

> Vincent Rosetti, Former President of the Craftown Local
> (Mr. Rosetti, worker in the pipe shop, was union president
> when votes were taken on the evaluation program.)

Rosetti: What do you want? Who sent you?

Interviewer: I am studying your labor problems. No one sent me.

Rosetti: You aren't a snoop? Someone didn't send you?

Interviewer: No.

Rosetti: I thought someone was getting information through the back door. You are not a snoop?

Interviewer: No. That is not playing the game.

Rosetti: O.K., if you aren't a spy, we get along pretty good. At one time the company used to be lousy on wages. Then we got the organization and they couldn't push us around any more.

Interviewer: You were union president when they voted on evaluation?

Rosetti: Yes, but we didn't go for that. The company was going to get the cream and give the men skimmed milk. We say "equal work, equal pay." How were they going to evaluate guys in the pipe department? We all work on the same pipes. The company said no one would be cut—that the evaluated pay, if lower, would apply only to new men. Who the devil did they think the new men were going to be? Paper boys they dragged in off the street? The new man was going to be the guy who had worked here nine years, and who had earned a promotion. There weren't going to be new men because the union wouldn't stand for it. But they thought we were dumb.

[After the interview.]

O'Hara: Rosetti and Tedrick used to be union leaders. They lived on the same street. Their wives knew each other; the kids played together. They don't go together since Tedrick moved.

William Phillips, Secretary of the Craftown Local
(Mr. William Phillips worked in the pattern department.)

Phillips: We were in on evaluation from the very first. We talked with the men, got their ideas. From my work on the committee I learned more about the plant than any single foreman. If we had proposed the evaluation, we could have sold it. But because the company proposed it, the men didn't want it.

Interviewer: Why did they oppose it?

Phillips: Oh, they never say *why*. They just yell it down. It was a case of a vocal minority. All the people who wanted evaluation and would have gotten increases didn't bother to vote. Of course, all the minority voted. We put in a rule that any member missing three meetings would be fined, but it doesn't help. It was too bad that Pat Kelly died; he would have been the difference. We seldom elect a president for more than one term, but he was always re-elected.

Interviewer: How did evaluation ever start in the first place?

Phillips: It was Tedrick's idea. He studied about it. Then he started talking and it seemed like a good idea to Kelly.

The trouble goes back more than 15 years. Wages were low and many days there wasn't any work. Men thought there was favoritism shown in who got to work. That's all changed now, but the inspectors never changed. They don't trust anybody. They were even against the union at first. Now they are against the company.

They didn't like it when Al Tedrick changed over. At the time, he was representing the union in negotiations. The company wanted a three-year contract. When we had a meeting, it was clear nobody wanted it. Tedrick sold it to the members. It turned out to be a good thing. Wages were frozen so we could not have gotten increases anyway. But it wasn't more than six months later that Tedrick became personnel manager.

Things that happened since haven't helped. Things have tightened up a lot in the last few years. There is more discipline. Also, to get a foreman they used to promote one of the men. Lately they have gone outside. I don't resent it, though it happened in my department. The people they bring in don't know anything. That's half the trouble in inspection, too; the foreman is weak.

INTERVIEWS AT THE KINGSVILLE PLANT

Elder Morgan, Personnel Manager at Kingsville

Morgan: I was the first union president here. For a depression period things weren't too bad here. We had a few men who wanted to remain outside the union. We thought we would have better union members in the long run if we didn't force the issue. I was president for four years when I told the boys, "'You've got a fine contract, a strong union, and a cooperative company." I explained I would rather step aside for someone else. I agreed to continue on the executive board and they saw my point. Soon I was offered the job as personnel manager to work under Albert Tedrick.

I knew the only way was to let the boys decide. I told them I wouldn't accept unless they felt I was acting in good faith. I said if I did take the job, I would represent the company with my full energy. They answered, "Go ahead and take that job, Elder. We don't expect any favors."

At first a few were skeptical. I insisted that workers handle problems through their union representatives and that foremen handle their own problems on the floor. I would not discuss a problem unless it had been first discussed with them. I told the foremen when they did not feel qualified to decide, they should come to me.

Interviewer: What about your relationship here?

Morgan: We have less than a dozen grievances every year, not more than six in writing. Since the union came we have had only one stoppage and one arbitration. We are proud of the record, and I keep reminding the union about their part in it. Now they remind me about *their* record and how it is *my* responsibility to live up to it!

Interviewer: How is the job evaluation working out?

Morgan: We feel it is working well. The saturation department took a beating because a number of men had their jobs evaluated lower there. However, Carl Wilson explained it to them in terms of the best interests of all workers in the plant. Of course, the men turned it down on the first vote. They were probably waiting to see if they could get a better deal. It may be they were waiting on Craftown to accept.

Interviewer: Do you have regular grievance meetings?

Morgan: No, we meet as soon as the grievance comes up. Many times I get an idea of what's troubling the men from Carl Wilson, for I often have a beer with him on the way home. We have no groups in our plant. Of course, we have good union officers here. Occasionally they make a mistake, but so do we. Several months ago they brought a grievance. We fought it hard and they fought it harder. To continue might have thrown us back in building good feelings, so we gave in.

Josiah Blakely, President of the Kingsville Local
(Mr. Blakely, 65 years of age, was a class A machinist.)

Blakely: We have an excellent relationship. The union is very proud of it. We try to remind the management what a good record we have so we can make them proud of it, too. We have never had a strike here, not one of our own. Craftown got into trouble once and spoiled our record.

Since I have been president we have had only two grievances where the vice president in charge of operations was called in. Do you know what he did once? Management was on one side of the table and we were on the other, and after we presented our case, even before management answered, the vice president got up and said, "Boys, I like to be on the right side so I am going to move my chair over and argue with you." You see our company believes in unions and in paying good wages.

Interviewer: How long have you been president?

Blakely: I have been re-elected seven times. Of course, I was thrown out of office once. A new fellow—a loud mouth—told the boys what he would do if he was president. He won, but when he learned the men didn't want to shake the buildings down, he quit. The real function of a trade union is to work so that both the company and the workers prosper. When we negotiate it might be possible to get a 50-cent increase, but there wouldn't be any jobs next year after we put the company out of business. People used to look down on union members, but they don't any more. They are looking to us to do a good job.

Interviewer: Didn't you reject job evaluation the first time?

Blakely: Well, we may have waited for Craftown to make up their minds.

Carl Wilson, Secretary of the Kingsville Local
(In the opinion of both company and union officials
at the Craftown and Kingsville plants, Mr. Wilson
was "the real leader of the Kingsville union.")

Wilson: We needed a systematic method to develop a wage structure. Management, failing to educate foremen, permitted them to be sole judges of wage increases. Their favoritism and lack of knowledge gave the union an effective means of increasing wage rates by claiming B's wage was too low in relation to A, A's wage having been improperly set by management itself. As soon as management conceded, C, D, E, and F immediately had complaints with regard to their pay. By playing the wage inequity game we sowed seeds of multiple grievances throughout the union. That is why the union accepted job evaluation.

Interviewer: What was the program of installing evaluation?

Wilson: We kept the membership informed why evaluation was necessary. We indicated the substantial advances it would mean in total payroll. We called in the man who had complaints, explained the system, and had him evaluate his own job. As a rule he evaluated himself too low, in which case the committee's evaluation prevailed.

The engineer hired by the company to assist us was not a production man. We had to do a great deal toward assisting him. Yet his problem was common to any man who might have come in from the outside.

Interviewer: Why did Kingsville accept job evaluation when Craftown turned it down?

Wilson: People will tell you Craftown is different from Kingsville. I cannot agree. People everywhere are pretty much the same. First, the Craftown union does not do a good educational job, and second, Craftown officers have abdicated their position of leadership. They listen too much to various opinions and express their own ideas too little, and the result is chaotic thinking.

It was unfortunate that Pat Kelly, the Craftown union president, died. Jim O'Hara, who succeeded him, was new and uncertain about the program. Craftown did not explain the system as well to their membership. If we had their inspection department here, we would be much firmer. We would have been glad to have their criticisms, but we would not permit them to shout us down. The union hasn't done an education job at Craftown. That is in part due to management.

Discussion Questions

1. List in order of their occurrence factors which you think contributed to the difficulty encountered in gaining acceptance of job evaluation at Craftown.

2. Whom would you designate as (*a*) the focal individuals and (*b*) the focal groups at Craftown?

3. Evaluate critically the various contract clauses cited in this case. What is your interpretation of Article 4, Section 2, Paragraph "c"?

4. Why did the Kingsville union accept job evaluation while the Craftown union rejected it?

5. If you were Mr. Tedrick, what problems would you consider as unresolved at the time of the receipt of the arbitrator's decision? What would be your program to resolve each of these remaining problems?

SEDGEWICK-COLE CORPORATION (B)

INCENTIVE WAGES AND LOCAL UNIONS

I

The Sedgewick-Cole Corporation considered it necessary to offset wage increases through increased productivity to maintain its competitive position. Some 17 months after authorization to develop an incentive system had been incorporated into the union agreement, Mr. Tedrick, company personnel director, met with the union officers of the Craftown local, United Rubber Workers (CIO), and filed the following grievance:

> A definite effort is being made by certain groups of employees to control to a predetermined number of units the production in the inspection department. One has only to look at the level of production on the "C" inspection to feel certain these crews are not making a reasonable effort to attain and maintain the production as agreed upon.
>
> In view of the union's repeated assurance that they will not approve *any* control of production we request some reason for the actions of these inspection crews. We can see no reason for them to refuse to make some incentive on the present standard. The whole group is determined to sabotage the agreement between the company and the union. Will you kindly reply to this grievance in writing at your earliest convenience?

II

The contractual provision empowering the development of an incentive system read:

> There is to be inserted in place of paragraph "d" [1] a paragraph calling for the development of an incentive plan to be worked out between a union committee and a company committee with the usual arbitration clause.

Thereupon the company had hired D. K. Coates as consultant to develop the plan. Within 9 months he had a group of incentive rates and standards ready to install. The union requested a delay until the completion of contract negotiations, which were to open the next month. Without citing any specific objections, they said they wished to review the situation.

During the new negotiations, in addition to the pattern agreed to by basic industry, the company offered an *additional* increase of 6 cents per hour if the union would accept the proposed production norms. Although management

---

[1] The superseded paragraph "d" had provided: "In any case where a speed-up occurs, through increasing speed of present equipment or revamping of same, whereby the company's costs are lowered and maintained for a period of 90 days, the employees affected will receive a fair share in the savings involved, such share to be distributed at the discretion of company and union officials."

estimated that only 40% of the work force could increase their output, Mr. Tedrick did not consider it feasible to limit the additional 6 cents to them. The union negotiators rejected this offer, reporting that an informal membership survey indicated the offer inadequate, inasmuch as proposed norms would necessitate a 15% increase in output before the bonus would begin.

After two months of discussion, the union finally agreed to consider the proposal if the additional increase were to be 10 rather than 6 cents. The company offered 7 cents. The union amended its counterproposal to 9 cents. Both parties agreed on 8 cents, and the incentive joint stipulation shown in Exhibit 1 was incorporated into the new contract.

III

With this agreement, the company put into immediate effect production standards for all direct-production workers. For those operations which he had time-studied, Mr. Coates first determined the rate of output reasonably to be expected of the normal operator working under the inducement of the incentive wage. He then established as the production "standard" a level of output 30% less than the output expected of the normal operator. Thus management anticipated that most operators would produce 30% over standard, and earn 30% over the base rate, which included all increases granted at the most recent negotiations. For operations not yet time-studied, management established a temporary estimated standard equal to the average of the past performance of the department increased by 15%. Starting from this estimated standard, the company would give pay increases directly proportional to increases in production. For a few departments in which the nature of the process allowed no decrease in production time, the management established a temporary standard which, when increased by 30%, would equal the prior production rate. Thus such workers would receive a 30% bonus for the same amount of work which they had previously performed. Where operations were not process controlled, management expected a 15% increase in output over past performance to justify the extra 8-cent increase it had granted in base rate.

Reviewing subsequent developments, Mr. Tedrick recalled that many workers, especially inspectors, did not like the new system. "One inspector who had griped for years clammed up. Another announced, 'I know when I'm licked. I quit.' He had been with us 20 years. Another inspector asked, 'Why should we speed up just to give the mechanics a raise? Give it all to us, and we'll do the job.' The inspection department was in a state of internal warfare over acceptance of incentives."

IV

Several days after incentives were installed, Craftown averaged but 68% of the new standard, while the company's other plant at Kingsville was averaging 90%. The Craftown plant manager told Mr. Tedrick that the situation would improve with time. Nevertheless, Mr. Tedrick decided to talk with the men.

Mr. Tedrick selected the pulling-out department as the first for such a conference. This small department, always cooperative, and working under a foreman considered firm but fair, was producing 70% of standard. Accompanied by the union vice president, a "quiet, stable" production worker, Mr. Tedrick spoke to the workers. Mr. Tedrick told them they were "laying down on the job" and if they didn't attain standard within one day, every one of them would lose his 8-cent increase. He said, "This is an ultimatum."

One man answered, "This isn't what the union told us." The union vice president interjected with: "You didn't understand. Mr. Tedrick is right."

Output in the pulling-out department reached standard within 4 hours after Mr. Tedrick's talk. The talk was repeated the next day in the inspection department with similar results on all inspection tables except those assigned to "C" inspection. Output there continued at exactly the same level registered before the installation of incentives. It remained exactly the same each day. Often the inspectors did nothing for the last 30 minutes of each shift if they had already reached their daily level. After three months, Mr. Tedrick entered the grievance set forth above and stated, "If no action is taken, the company will be compelled to eliminate employees willfully holding up any jobs."

V

After receiving the company's grievance, the union announced that a union time-study engineer would make independent studies. After six weeks, the union engineer submitted his report objecting to methods the company had employed in establishing standards for the inspectors. The company restudied the operation and reaffirmed its standard fair. The union requested arbitration.

Two months later the standard developed by the company was upheld in arbitration. Pending this arbitration, problems had continued to arise. A typical situation is presented in Exhibit 2. Interviews held during this same period appear below.

Four days following the arbitration, the Craftown inspectors held a departmental meeting at the union office. Following this meeting, the department committeeman advised the foreman that the men felt they had no obligation to produce any more than the standard. Mr. Tedrick immediately informed the union officers that control of production was continuing, and unless they corrected the situation within two days, the company would take drastic action.

VI

Two days later Mr. Tedrick filed another grievance against the Craftown union:

After six months' discussion, negotiation, and finally arbitration, a standard of production is established for "C" inspection. Employees are refusing to make more than standard. This refusal is a violation of our agreement. Unless these crews decidedly improve by tomorrow, it will be necessary to dismiss those controlling production. The reluctance of the union to control the actions of its members will be taken up as a separate grievance.

The following morning Mr. Tedrick read this latest grievance to all inspectors in the presence of local union officers and the international representative. The following discussion took place:

International Representative (u): We want the names of those employees who supposedly are controlling production.

Tedrick (m): Henry Perry and Thomas Dowler are among those present whom we accuse. However, we will discipline any other employees whom supervision names.

International Representative (u): How are the union officers to know what employees are controlling production?

Tedrick (m): The union was given ample time to make their own investigation.

Committeeman (u): If the company is making a charge, it should point out the offenders. The company is all wrong in making its charge against Perry and Dowler. They should not be held responsible for the poor production of an entire crew. They have never been given a fair standard to shoot at.

Tedrick (m): This morning Perry's table did not work for 22 minutes with no apparent reason. If Perry, as inspector, had ordered another roll to be placed on the table for inspection and the men refused, then it would be up to supervision to take action.

Committeeman (u): Does a man have to make over standard?

Tedrick (m): Yes.

Committeeman (u): If production does not increase tomorrow, will Perry and Dowler be accused of controlled production?

Tedrick (m): Yes, and any others inspection supervision accuses. Dismissals will be made. I suggest this department meet with your international representative to discuss this matter before it becomes necessary for the company to take final action.

The next day production was 10% above standard on the "C" inspection tables. Eleven days later, output was 34% above standard, having increased a little each day. Thus increased productivity had been achieved in the inspection department 11 months after the incentive stipulation was incorporated in the contract, and 14 months after the first incentive standards had been formulated.

INTERVIEWS

James O'Hara, President of the Craftown Local

O'Hara: Some of the boys are pushing for more production under the incentive. They argue, each blaming the other if they don't make the bonus. We are in for trouble.

Interviewer: How did the incentive come in?

O'Hara: The inspectors didn't want it. They fought hard, but everyone got an eight-cent increase. The inspectors said, "It stinks." It was discussed, and finally voted in. The inspectors were very mad. Yet I know inspectors right now who are doing all right. They make the bonus. They wouldn't talk against it any more, but they couldn't say anything for it.

Interviewer: What about the inspection department?

O'Hara: When I first came, they were the biggest department. They always demanded things and got it. Almost everyone was in inspection then. Of course it's smaller now, but they still have over 100 men. They always got their own way before—special privileges. They always voted in a bloc. They never elected any officers, but what they were against didn't go through. They are breaking up now though. This incentive is splitting them. There are only three tables which aren't doing anything, and I know they could.

The consulting engineer has taken months to put in this incentive system. He is a "blow-hard." He is doing his best to drag his job out to last as long as it can. I'll bet the company is paying him plenty. No wonder the company can't afford to give us a wage increase.

The fellows are anxious to get the incentive set up. The maintenance men can't get anything until the whole system is in operation. Half the trouble we have—all these grievances—could be eliminated if incentives had been put in faster. Grievance meetings are costly. The arbitration on the incentive will cost us at least $100. We are a small union. I'm going to have to do something to get this thing hurried up.

William Phillips, Secretary of the Craftown Local

Phillips: The inspection department has never been for the incentive. The only word for them is "aginners." They are "agin" everything. The incentive arbitration will be their last chance to save face.

If the standard is put down where the inspectors think it ought to be, they might make it. They never have tried to make it. They could if they wanted to. Some inspectors were doing all right and the others got mad at them.

Interviewer: How did the incentive get started?

Phillips: No one wanted it at first. It was forced down our throats. The men needed more money with prices going up. The company offered eight cents more if the incentive plan was accepted, and the men wanted money. They accepted it to get money but lots of them think it's glorified piecework. The inspectors didn't want the indirect men to share. The company shifted men around in inspection and the men against the incentive didn't like that.

Two "C" Inspectors, Perry and Dowler

Dowler [to interviewer]: I don't know anything to tell you. [Perry leaves his work place and joins discussion.] Perry, I was saying I don't know about things that go on here. You tell him what he wants to know.

Perry: I don't know that we are going to have much time to talk. They complain we don't make the standard so we had probably better get on the job.

Interviewer: I don't want to interfere with your work, Mr. Perry; in fact, I would be very interested in seeing what you do. Would you mind if I just watched?

Perry: It is not interesting and there is nothing to it. I don't think you'd learn much. Besides we are about through for the day.

[The time was 2:30. The shift was scheduled to go off duty at 3:00. At the time there was no indication of any work.]

Interviewer: You think the incentive standard is too high?

Perry: We can work as hard as a man can and still not make it. There is no use to try.

Interviewer: How are they doing on the other inspection tables?

Perry: Not very good.

Dowler [to Perry]: I thought they were making around 20% bonus.

Perry: No, nothing like that. I don't know what *they* do. Did you want to know anything else?

Interviewer: You were here when they proposed evaluation?

Perry: Yes.

Dowler [interrupting]: I don't know anything about that.

Interviewer: Could you tell me how you felt about that?

Perry: I don't remember anything about it. Is there anything else you want to know?

Interviewer: No, but if you don't mind, I would like to come down again.

Perry: You can come but you won't find out anything. The arbitrator came down, but he didn't find out much.

Herbert Furst, Inspector

Interviewer [to William Phillips, Craftown secretary]: There must be some inspector who likes to talk.

Phillips: Herb Furst loves to talk; in fact, if he gets started you can't stop him. He is on a crew that isn't trying to make standard. Here he is. Herb, tell this man about the incentive.

Furst: We always turned out 106 pieces a day. The company brought in engineers who timed us and set a standard of 123. I don't know how they ever got that number. We complained and they admitted they were wrong because they changed the standard to 121. But that was no change and there is absolutely no use in trying to make 121. It is just a way to get old quick.

Phillips: I am going to walk down here where I can't hear in case you want to talk confidentially.

Furst: That is about all I know anyway. Stay, Phillips. Don't go walking away or the fellows will think something is funny.

Interviewer: You were speaking about the incentive plan.

Furst: I was saying there is no use to even try it. Some of the boys are making bonus. We feel sure that their standards have been set differently, so just because they make them is no reason why we should make them.   Say, I can't talk to you any longer.   The boys are wondering what I am saying to you.   They won't like it at all, so I'd better get over there and explain it to them.   You know how it is, don't you?   We work in teams.

Peter De Lucca, a "D" Inspector

Interviewer: How is the incentive working out on your table?

De Lucca: We are making 30% bonus.   Of course, I have a young crew. The men who have worked here 15 years and always work the same way don't like incentives.   They find it difficult to change.   The foremen say they have to make the incentive, so a lot would rather shut up and try it instead of finding another job.

Interviewer: Do the men have to change the way they do their jobs?

De Lucca: No, but now they work faster and steadier.   They can't talk as they used to.   The younger ones can change, but it's not easy on the others. There are some who don't want to try to make the incentive, but most of them could if they tried.

Vincent Rosetti, Former President of the Craftown Local

Interviewer: What do the men think about the incentive system, Mr. Rosetti?

Rosetti: Some are doing all right; some are too lazy.   We had these time-study men once before, and the boys went along.   After a few months under the old incentive we got production up and were making some money.   Then the company said, "Fine, boys.   We see what you can do.   Just keep on and we'll pay you less than we ever did."   Out went the bonus, and if you didn't keep up the pace, they got rid of you.

Interviewer: How is it going now?

Rosetti: They can't get away with that now.   But they're playing games all right.   They told the indirect men like us in the pipe department, "You'll get in on this bonus, so vote with us."   We sold the thing to the membership, and now we would be better off without it.   They were to build a common fund to be divided among all the indirect men.   The production men on incentive were to get 30% bonus.   We were to get one-half of what the production men got.   So if the whole plant made 30%, we would get 15%.   We didn't expect to get anything the first week because it wouldn't be much, but the company was to build up this fund and distribute it in 90 days.

Interviewer: The stipulation provided that indirect men would participate 90 days after the incentive was installed?

Rosetti: That was it, and it's not been 90 days either.   Hell no.   It's been 7 months, and what have we gotten?   Nothing.   The company is getting fat by keeping all our money for themselves.

Interviewer: How do the production men feel about the indirect men sharing in the bonus?

Rosetti: That makes me so damn mad.   [Rosetti becomes excited.] That's what the production men say.   They are dumb—just plain ignorant.

They don't understand a thing. They would like to hog it all themselves. Where in hell do they think my pay has been coming from all along? Out of production, hasn't it? We are all on the same production wheel, and as the wheel turns, we all move together. Just let them have a breakdown. We'll take our good old time to fix it up and see how much incentive they make then. They're going to have to learn the hard way. They can't make more than 30% incentive anyway, and what's left over they would rather give to the company. At least, with the indirect men sharing, we get some of it instead of the company keeping it all.

Edward Diffin, Mechanic and Former Vice President of the Craftown Local

Diffin: An incentive is a speed-up system. That's all it is. The boys wanted money and the only way to get it was to agree to incentives. The membership didn't want anything to do with it. We turned it down several times.

Interviewer: You voted on it?

Diffin: The only way it passed was the print department all voted for it. The company got the votes where the standards were set so low it was easy to make the standard. The standards were set loose in some departments to get votes.

Interviewer: Why were the inspectors against it?

Diffin: They were afraid of working themselves out of a job. You can only print so much linoleum on the machines. What will happen if the inspectors speed up and finish ahead of the machines? Print machines can't turn out more just because the inspectors hurry. Someone will have to be laid off.

The company says they need incentives for more production. What they need is foremanship. If you have good foremen, you don't need incentives. But they won't have good foremen if they keep bringing them in from outside.

D. K. Coates, Consultant

Coates: The time watch will soon be a thing of the past. It won't be long until we have only synthetic standards. After we develop curves for all factors we will have a scientific basis for establishing incentives.

Interviewer: I am interested in problems you encounter which affect the attitudes of workers or relations with the union.

Coates: We emphasize that. The first thing I did here was to give a training course for supervisors. It is important we educate management first, so we always give a course. The thing wrong with incentive installations that have soured is there are no human relations. We do a constant selling job, especially to top management.

Let's look at the course outline. [Coates reads the course outline.]

1. Rules for straight thinking.
2. Progress and people.
3. Does the existing distribution of income tend to promote or retard progress?
4. Are we merely machine tenders?

5. Does the machine throw men out of work?
6. The industrial accountant and the need for incentives.
7. Types of averages.
8. Time-study techniques, including
    a. The Bedaux system
    b. History of time and motion
    c. Types of charts
9. Motion study.
    a. Twenty rules or principles of human motion
    b. Standard therbligs

The course was made especially for this plant. You will notice each page has the name Sedgewick-Cole in the corner. At the beginning, we state the basis for the course. [Coates reads from his lecture notes.]

This course will reaffirm the high purpose and the important responsibilities which beset the industrial engineer. Time and motion study is the one common denominator for the measurement of endeavor on a factual basis.

One of the first things we must consider are the human motors—people—and the things that affect them. What is wrong with people? There are two outstanding things that are wrong. They are that it is human nature (1) to resist the new, and (2) to resent criticism. Like the parachute, the mind functions only when open.

We teach 23 workable rules of human relations. [Mr. Coates reads the following 11.]

1. Indirectly introduce the new idea so that the person accepts it as his own. (Sell 'em; don't tell 'em.)
2. Show respect for the other person's opinions. Never tell him he is wrong.
3. To get the best of an argument, avoid it. Nobody ever wins.
4. Try to see things from the other person's point of view.
5. Praise every suggestion or improvement, no matter how small.
6. Give the person a fine reputation to live up to.
7. Never accept a challenge.
8. Call attention to people's mistakes indirectly.
9. Make sure you pronounce and write his name correctly.
10. Remember we are all egotists, more or less.
11. Smile. Less effort required than to frown.

Interviewer: I have a good idea of the training you give.

Coates: This course gets us rolling. Then we start taking times. We didn't analyze plant layout or methods prior to making our time study here because there wasn't enough time. The company was anxious to have the system installed.

Interviewer: What do you do in a department before you use the stop watch?

Coates: We send a notice to the vice president in charge of operations, the plant manager, the director of personnel, and the foreman. When we go into the department, we tell the men to go on just as usual.

Interviewer: Have you had any problems?

Coates: In one department they were not making standard. I had the foreman come up to my office and asked him what was wrong. I told him his poor performance was a reflection on his ability. One of the problems is the failure of foremen to back up the standard. Of course a foreman won't have his department make 200% because it means something is wrong with the standard, and if he used his head he will peg his production at 130%.

Exhibit 1

Sedgewick-Cole Corporation (B)

Excerpts from Joint Incentive Stipulation

I. (1) The company agrees to increase the hourly rates of all employees by 8 cents per hour to compensate employees for the additional effort needed to increase present production to the standard production "norms" as established by the time study engineers.

(2) Having accepted the principles of establishing wage rates by evaluation and time study, it is agreed that employees will be expected to make every effort to maintain quality and production norms. Where employees fail to make reasonable effort, they shall be warned, and failure to comply with reasonable requirements shall be subject to disciplinary action, jointly agreed upon by the company and the union.

II. New or revised standards shall be presented to the union for two working days after which they shall become effective. A reasonable trial period of two weeks shall follow during which no grievance shall be filed. If during the first twenty-one days following the trial period the employees desire to protest the standard, they shall do so in writing, after which the union and the company time study men may review the standard together. If retiming shows a loosening of production standards would be justified, the new rate shall be retroactive.

III. Questions regarding incentive standards shall be settled on the basis of factual information developed by standard time study method. Union employed time study men may take time studies at any time.

IV. *Cooperation by the Union.* The union recognizes that high wages can be maintained only by maintaining productivity. The union will cooperate in maintaining as high productivity as is consistent with the health of employees and will also assist in effectuating economies.

V. The amount of pay received shall be commensurate with the amount of production; that is, for each 1% of output above the standard as established by time studies, 1% additional pay shall be received by the employee.

VI. Time study information will be made available by the company to the union.

VII. Standard time values shall not be changed unless there has been an accumulated change in any portion of an operation which affects the over-all standard time by ten (10%) per cent.

VIII. Disputes which arise that cannot be settled as outlined in paragraph No. II shall be subject to the regular grievance procedure.

IX. The company may at any time make the following changes in rates and job procedures or introduction of rates on new jobs:

(a) Make changes in the motions or methods of job procedures.

(b) Effect changes in incentive rates when the over-all standard time is changed 10%.

(c) Set new rates for new jobs.

X. The company has the right to study any worker performing the task under normal conditions. The studies will be normalized to the performance of an average worker (normal 100%) as established by time study.

XI. The rates shall be set so that this normal operator with an increased maintainable effort with proper allowance for personal fatigue shall have the expectation of earning 30% above the base rate.

XII. Indirect workers shall be covered by this incentive plan as soon as possible and their incentives shall be based wherever possible on the particular operation or group of operations which they service.

It is recognized that the level of activity of a worker who is not on incentive is usually at/or below standard effectiveness; therefore in all fairness to employees on direct incentive, indirect employees shall receive one-half for each one per cent of the incentive earned by the group or groups which they service.

The general increase of 8 cents is conditioned upon the attainment of the production increases specified in the standards and may be withdrawn if employees refuse to cooperate in maintaining the minimum production requirements as established by the standards.

EXHIBIT 2

SEDGEWICK-COLE CORPORATION (B)

Dispute between Two Workers at Craftown

Mr. John Thomas, assistant to Mr. Tedrick, called a conference between two employees of the pulling-out department. Both Benton Allen, union vice president, and the foreman were present.

Thomas (m): Ed Mazzoco claims Mike Stanos threw a wedge at him from the top of the heater.[1]

Allen (u): What's up, Stanos?

Stanos (u): I'm not saying anything until I hear what people have been saying about me. [Mazzoco enters with Pinkie, another crew member.]

Thomas (m): Mazzoco, tell them what you told me this morning.

Mazzoco (u): Well, Stanos has been throwing wedges at me. This isn't the first time. He knew I was down on the plant floor. I looked up and saw him throw the wedge. I yelled at Pinkie and ran.

Stanos (u) [yelling and moving forward with fists clenched]: You be careful what you say! [Mazzoco backs into a corner. Stanos laughs.] You're crazy.

Thomas (m): You say you saw him? It seems unlikely that someone would throw a wedge at you.

Mazzoco (u): It was a wedge. Ask Pinkie.

Thomas (m) [to Mazzoco]: You say you saw him?

Stanos (u) [interrupting]: He doesn't know what he's saying, but he'd better be careful. He can't prove it. He couldn't have seen me throw it.

Mazzoco (u): I looked up, saw him throw it, yelled, and ran.

Stanos (u): Now listen to him! He must be a magician! He couldn't see me because I was on the other side of the roller.

Mazzoco (u): I saw him.

Stanos (u): You think you're pretty good, don't you? You must be a genius! You see me when no one else can.

Allen (u): You were on the other side of the roller, Stanos?

Stanos (u): Sure I was!

Mazzoco (u): We've been having arguments. He keeps yelling at me all the time.

Stanos (u): If I didn't, I'd be working for nothing. I can't make any money waiting on you.

---

[1] The disputants, Ed Mazzoco and Mike Stanos, were members of a crew of six. After linoleum is processed through print machines, it is hung in 90-feet-high heaters to be dried. Once dried, the linoleum is pulled to the *top* of the heater by four crew members, moved over a roller, and lowered to the plant floor where the other two crew members roll it for inspection. Wedges are used on top of the heater to assist crew members in "pulling-out" the linoleum.

Mazzoco (u): Well, I just can't do it, then. I'm doing my very best. Look at my fingers from pulling that linoleum down. I do the best I know how

Thomas (m): You know what you are saying? If someone hit you, it might kill you. It would be murder. You are accusing Stanos of trying to murder you.

Pinkie (u): It fell close to me. Mazzoco yelled and ran. I didn't have time to move.

Stanos (u) [speaking to Mazzoco]: You think I'm crazy? If I threw a wedge at you I ought to be in a nuthouse.

Mazzoco (u): Well, I saw it coming.

Thomas (m): Then you didn't see Stanos throw it?

Mazzoco (u): I saw it coming and Stanos was up there. He doesn't think I work fast enough.

Stanos (u): I am not going to the poorhouse for you. If someone doesn't keep after you, we wouldn't make a cent.

Thomas (m): You boys ought to take care of this stuff on the outside. What you do on the outside is your business, but you ought not to bring it into the factory.

Foreman (m): Then, Mazzoco, you didn't actually see Stanos throw it, did you?

Pinkie (u): Those things are always falling. It fell close to me.

Thomas (m): That is all, boys. You can go back. [Stanos, grinning, slaps Mazzoco on the back.]

Foreman (m): What is wrong with Mazzoco? We had him in another department, and he didn't like it so we put him on the presses. He "blacked out" there so we put him in the pulling-out department.

Thomas (m): He wants to be changed again. He doesn't want to work. If you keep moving him, it will set a bad example.

Allen (u): Someone has been razzing him and he can't take it. Keep him where he is.

Thomas (m): Mazzoco is lucky that Stanos was feeling good. Stanos was in the marines, and he gets rambunctious at times. Something is bothering Mazzoco. I will find out sometime, but I won't bother him now.

DISCUSSION QUESTIONS

1. Evaluate Mr. Tedrick's handling of the installation of the wage-incentive plan at Craftown. What, if anything, would you have done differently?

2. How do you explain the actions of the inspectors?

3. Should companies have and utilize the right to initiate grievances?

4. What effect is the introduction of incentive wages having on the social organization of the Craftown plant?

5. If you had been the management consultant hired to install the incentive program, what would you have done? What would you do were you to be hired at the conclusion of this case?

SENECA PAPER COMPANY

A REBUILDING PROGRAM AT BOONE

I. Introduction

The chief operating executives of the Boone plant of the Seneca Paper Company met in emergency session with Graham Scott, assistant plant manager in charge of administration and industrial and public relations, during the entire afternoon of Thursday, March 8, 1956, to consider an impasse which had developed with the Boone local of the United Paperworkers of America, AFL–CIO. Eight of the nine men present felt that on Monday unauthorized work stoppages would occur in several departments, paralyzing the entire plant by Tuesday. Management did not want an "interruption of work." It did have two objectives: (1) further modernization of the plant and (2) development of a constructive, affirmative relationship with the union. If these required management to "take a strike," it was willing to do so. However, Scott was anxious to do everything possible within the framework of good labor relations to avoid a shutdown.

The company, starting in 1827 as a manufacturer of writing paper in the Catskills, became over the years a large producer of high-grade magazine stock, fine wrapping paper, specialized cardboard, and by-product chemicals. The main offices were moved to Philadelphia and by 1956 the company operated seven plants located in the Appalachian, Allegheny and Catskill areas. The local managements were virtually autonomous and competed with each other in producing the company's complete line. The work forces varied from about 700 to 2,000, represented a substantial part of the labor supply in each town, and carried seniority averaging 15 to 20 years.

Organized labor representation began in the mid-thirties when management quickly recognized incipient independent plant unions. These were later replaced by successions of international unions as the International Brotherhood of Papermakers, AFL, and the United Paperworkers of America, CIO, battled each other and District 50 of the United Mine Workers to represent all employees at various plants, and as several AFL craft unions sought to carve out segments of their own. By 1956, the situation had been stabilized for over three years. The UPWA, currently AFL–CIO, represented all employees at Boone, Kentucky; Hillsdale, Virginia; and River Bend, Ohio. The IBP, currently AFL–CIO, and three AFL–CIO craft unions represented workers at two plants. One plant was nonunion and one was organized by District 50, UMW.

Boone, Kentucky, with a population of about 12,000, was the county seat and trading center for the surrounding hilly farm and woodland country. Most of the leading families had lived there for generations and were extremely proud of the social stability and conservative traditions of their community. But they viewed with concern what they considered a weakening of the moral fiber of the community, which they attributed largely to the further industrialization of the area.

Except for the Seneca Paper Company, Foss Textiles with a branch plant built in 1936 was the town's only other large employer. Women in the Boone area had not customarily done factory work and Foss recruited many of its 1,000 employees by advertising in newspapers throughout Kentucky. In 1956, about 100 Foss workers were wives of Seneca Paper employees. Foss' top management had become discouraged by constant disputes over time standards and piece rates, stoppages and strike threats at each contract negotiation. The problem had become aggravated in very recent years when glutted textile markets necessitated short work weeks. In March, 1956, a slowdown had been in effect for over a year, and town leaders feared that if conditions did not improve the entire plant would be closed.

II. The Boone Plant

The Seneca Paper Company had been the core of the town's economy for almost 50 years, employing the greatest number of workers, many of them highly skilled. The Boone plant had seven paper-making machines, each having a crew leader, a second hand, and a third hand. Machines #5, #6, and #7 with higher speeds and greater output had a fourth and fifth hand. On five-men crews the third, fourth and fifth hands were responsible for winding rolls of the sizes required by customers' orders. Such rolls were later rewound in the finishing department to guarantee the proper tension on the rolls for their use by customers on printing presses. The machine crew had to work "as a team," and any changes in crew personnel created serious problems of adjustment. Nor were crews shifted from one machine to another as it was important that they know "their" machine intimately.

Prior to 1940 the Boone plant was one of the largest and lowest cost producers of its kinds of products in the world. However, major competitors, who built large modern plants farther South, began to compete vigorously. By continued experimentation in methods and equipment, these companies achieved far higher operating speeds with greater productivity per manhour than prevailed at Boone. This competition was not immediately effective since Seneca had a reputation for quality and enjoyed excellent customer relations. However, customers were becoming increasingly conscious of cost considerations. Plant managements, therefore, were placing increased emphasis on methods of reducing production costs. For example, at Boone between 1953 and 1955 improvements in methods and minor equipment changes had eliminated 250 jobs.

Edward Hancock, Sr., resident manager, had come to Boone in 1909 immediately after putting himself through M.I.T. From the rank of assistant foreman he had worked his way up, reaching his present position in

1935. Shortly afterwards he had been made a director of the company. Hancock was a recognized leader in the community, devoting generous support to church and civic organizations. He also was president of a local bank.

Graham Scott was Hancock's principal assistant. Reared near Boone and a graduate of Alabama Polytechnical Institute, he had come to the plant as office manager and had been advanced to his present position in 1950. Staff departments reporting to him were real estate, general purchasing, order receiving, main office, accounting, payroll, plant protection, and personnel. In 1954, he had become spokesman for the company in contract negotiations for the three plants organized by the CIO.

Edward Hancock, Jr., became plant personnel officer in 1956. He replaced Cutter, who had been personnel manager for many years but who, after a heart attack, had been advised to take up less strenuous duties. Under Hancock, Jr., were Cutter (training director), and Holmes (records officer).

III. Contract Negotiations, 1954 and 1955, with the Three UPWA Plants

Foremost among the union's 1954 demands were a 35-cent wage increase plus 15 cents for mechanics and the application of plant seniority in promotions, demotions, transfers, layoffs and recalls. The wage increase was refused and the union's debate was prolonged and acrid. When workers at Boone, by following the union's instructions to refuse normal call-ins and overtime, disrupted operations of the mutually interdependent departments, negotiations were suspended. Violence occurred as workers began to heed the company's public appeals to ignore the union's contractually illegal instructions.

A month later, after the company offered the industry's newly established wage pattern of 5 cents plus 3 cents for mechanics, negotiations foundered on plant seniority. Scott argued that the historical seniority by job and department was eminently suitable in a plant utilizing the diverse skills required by wood handling, pulp production, paper making, chemical distillation and reclamation, and the various maintenance operations.

Individual work teams and departmental efficiency would be destroyed if individuals could claim jobs all over the plant. Management had conceded plant seniority *solely in the case of discontinuance of a department* to take care of older workers who would otherwise be terminated. But this was as far as the company could go.

In spite of federal conciliation and compromises by both parties, negotiations were again suspended and both sides resorted to publicity. The company clearly stated its willingness to take a strike on the issue and the union charged the company with union busting and callousness toward its older workers. When the UPWA international president entered negotiations at the contract deadline, agreement was quickly reached, though there was considerable dissent by Boone representatives.[1]

By 1955, it had become apparent, as the quality of competitive products improved and as price competition increased, that the minor changes in equipment and assignment of personnel which had been made since 1953 were inadequate. The problem was complicated by the fact that the volume of production at Boone could not be expanded because disposal of waste, in spite of close attention by disposal engineers, already taxed the capacity of the river. The local management, therefore, determined to regain its competitive position by investing $10 million in new or modernized machinery.

When negotiations opened in April, the union presented a list of 30 demands. The economic demands included a general wage increase of 25 cents, 10-cent and 15-cent shift differentials, overtime at $2\frac{1}{2}$ times for work in excess of 16 hours in any 24-hour period, some specific changes in local job rates, a guaranteed annual wage, and $50 a week sickness and accident benefits. Other demands provided for: joint administration of equal division of overtime,[2] a local practice clause, joint quarterly meetings on contract problems, freezing of work schedules, job sequences and job classifications, no job transfers without employee consent, liberalization of disciplinary provisions with offenses not to accumulate beyond one year, elimination of the principal management rights clause, and a joint committee to work out job descriptions. Plant seniority was to be extended by a revision of Par. F., sec. 2C3.[3] This would have set up a procedure, grouping departments *inside* the plant into three to six divisions within which an employee might exercise plant seniority to move to the lowest level of any job sequence in his division; the bumped employee could bump to the lowest level in any other division; the last man could bump *outside* the plant—as in the woodyard.

Management countered with 13 proposed changes including: tightening of equal division of overtime procedures with elimination of pay for "mistakenly" lost opportunities for overtime, exclusion of hourly paid supervisors from the bargaining unit, tightening of disciplinary provisions, elimination of the union's rights to challenge management's determination of the number of job classifications and the number of workers within a classification and institution of a three-year contract.

Little agreement was reached in eight days of discussion; negotiations were recessed pending the development of a national wage pattern. When the parties met again in September their respective demands were virtually the same. Management stood firm on the seven-cent pattern increase. It also maintained the union's demands would freeze operations whereas new equipment was to be installed and management would need its freedom of action in order to offer jobs and maintain the best wages possible. Scott stated

---

[1] For contract language on seniority, see Exhibit 1, Pertinent Contract Clauses, Paragraph F, pp. 122–123. Material enclosed in brackets represents 1955 additions to the 1954 contract.

[2] At Boone, overtime grievances had totaled 198 in the past year.

[3] See Exhibit 1, Pertinent Contract Clauses, p. 122.

costs at River Bend and Twin Falls (nonunion) were $10 and $20 a ton out of line with competitors and these plants would have to improve or shut down. He also enumerated some of the changes which management had planned. At Hillsdale high-speed machines would replace the present ones in the next year or two. At Boone where the #6 paper-making machine was being rebuilt, #5 and #7 machines were to have a major overhauling, and a new machine would be installed leaving #1, #2, #3 and #4 machines as stand-by equipment. Other Boone plans called for consolidations of work currently being done on opposite sides of the river.

The new two-year agreement provided: a seven-cent general wage increase, increase in shift differentials from four cents and seven cents to five cents and ten cents, and extension of sickness and accident insurance from $20 to $25 a week. Wages would be increased 5% in September, 1956.

IV. Work Stoppages, Arbitrations and Grievances at Boone

Of the 11 work stoppages between 1953 and 1955 there were three in 1955 which management considered significant in the light of the major changes required to further increase production. In one 1955 stoppage 28 man-hours were lost when 11 employees sat down in one department after the supervisor posted, as was his usual custom, the number of batches to be processed. A second stoppage occurred when the superintendent told a shop steward in the finishing department that production of one of the supercalenders was behind 15% to 20%. The supercalender crew were joined by 92 employees involving a loss of 182 man-hours. The third 1955 stoppage was initiated by 55 electricians when four of their number were transferred from work in buildings on "this side of the river" to work in similar classifications on "the other side of the river." The 55 electricians were joined in their sit-down by 266 mechanical and construction workers in eight other departments. The protest of the electricians ultimately went to arbitration where the union based its case on a contract appendix listing in perpendicular form two identical electrical job sequences separated by a vertical line. This line was, according to the union, an embodiment of an oral promise not to transfer workers from one side of the river to the other. Management denied the alleged promise, and noted that electrical assignments had previously been made back and forth between the two sides of the river and that the work loads on the two sides were disproportionate to the number of workers on each side. Management also pointed out that there was nothing in the contract to abridge its right to direct workers.

Of the 26 arbitrations in 1953–1955, management considered another 1955 arbitration as pertinent. The loaders and the rewinders for #1 to #5 machines had protested changes entailed in converting the loading operation from a daywork, five-day operation to around-the-clock work. For many years paper orders were filled from inventory and the loading department's work consisted of: (1) moving finished rolls from the rewinder department into storage, and (2) moving finished rolls out of storage into freight cars.

But the former part of the work during night tours and weekends was done by rewinder operators and rewinder helpers. In recent years, however, orders had changed from small lots of miscellaneous products to quantity orders processed on a job lot basis, enabling most shipments to move directly from the rewinders to freight cars. As a result the loading crew was idle a good part of the time and studies revealed that the amount loaded per man-hour persistently declined. The company therefore decided to have *all* handling of finished rolls done by loaders only on a shift basis. The loading sequence was to consist of three rather than four jobs. As a result, 12 fewer people would be required in loading and 8 fewer in rewinding; rate increases would be given to those remaining in the loading department. Management's announcement of its proposals was followed by nine months of discussion. Finally, after top international officers had refused to accept the proposed work assignments, management notified the union that it was putting the changes into effect. The union immediately filed a formal grievance; nevertheless the company instituted the change. At the arbitration hearing the company cited Paragraph D, sections 4 and 6; and Paragraph S, section 1.[1] The union challenged management's right to make the changes unilaterally during the life of the contract. Furthermore, it took the position that, since the dispute arose out of differences in contract interpretation, management did not have the right to institute the changes pending a determination as to which contract interpretation was valid. The union cited Paragraph P, section 1; Paragraph C, section 6a; and Paragraph D, sections 1 and 3.[2]

In finding for the company the umpire wrote in part:

> The provisions in the contract . . . cannot be construed to imply that the existing job confines, classifications and sequences in effect at the time the contract was signed, were to continue without any change during the entire life of the contract, unless the union acquiesced, or unless an arbitration decision was handed down, if the union filed a grievance. . . . The arbitrator is unable to find any language in the contract indicating that the union is authorized to process a grievance concerning matters before they occur.

During the 1954–1955 contract, production changes resulted in 84 grievances, or about one-quarter of all the grievances at the Boone plant. Most production change grievances were settled in favor of the company; a few (job rates) involved compromises, and fewer still favored the union. Of the 84 cases, 32 were pressed to arbitration.

V. A MEETING WITH MR. ROBERTS

In early February, 1956, Scott reviewed the problems which the Boone management was to face in its program of new equipment, changed work methods and consolidations. All of these changes would result in a substantial reduction of the working force. In view of previous experiences with the union, Scott knew that such a reduction in personnel would be very

---

[1] See Exhibit 1, Pertinent Contract Clauses, pp. 122 and 123.
[2] *Ibid.*, pp. 121 and 122.

troublesome unless a realistic approach were taken in formulating manage-ment's plans. He concluded the assistance of an outsider with a fresh view-point would be beneficial. Hancock concurred and plans were made for management representatives from Philadelphia and from Boone to meet with Douglas Roberts, a well-known consultant.

Present at the February 16 meeting with Roberts were the company's president and the vice-president in charge of personnel, and Hancock and Scott. In addition to the facts thus far provided Roberts was given the fol-lowing data:

(1) The primary effect of modernization would be the scheduled termina-tion of employment for 459 workers in groups of 6, 12, 20, etc., of varying skills, throughout 1956, and in larger groups, also of varying skills, through-out 1957 and 1958.

(2) Seniority provisions of the union contract would require many "bumps" across departmental lines, multiplying the number of "moves" re-quired, and could spread into several departments the resulting effects of a single initial change.

(3) Fluctuations in market conditions, and consequently in employ-ment, would cause both "bumps" and "recalls," which would crisscross with the effect of layoffs due to the modernization program itself.

(4) Similar modernization was planned at the company's other plants. Boone management hoped that its plans for effecting changes would set the pattern for other mills.

(5) Management was uncertain of how to deal with the union. Should it attempt to negotiate the contemplated changes "piecemeal" as they arose, or to try to reach an advance settlement, at least in principle?

(6) In certain situations it would be necessary to insist on "qualifica-tions" ahead of "seniority" in making layoffs. In the past, however, man-agement had not been severe in insisting on qualifications and the union could be expected to oppose any such effort. Scott did not know how he could develop a firmer stand on qualifications or how to settle questions of disputed qualifications.

(7) During the shrinkage of the work force, it might be preferable to increase overtime rather than issue temporary recalls. If this were done, division of time problems might be aggravated, not only in number but also by exciting resistance to overtime as such, despite the extra pay.

(8) Consolidations would involve transfer of several hundred employees from each side of the river to the opposite side.

(9) Operating less equipment would enable a substantial reduction among maintenance and construction employees after modernization was completed. About one-third of such employees terminated should be first-class workers, one-third second-class, and one-third trainees and laborers. If layoffs of maintenance and construction employees were made on a de-partmental basis,[1] considerable downgrading of long-service employees

---

[1] A mechanic, electrician, etc., held seniority in a skilled trade, rather than in a produc-tion department.

would be necessary if contractually established ratios among skill classifications were maintained.

(10) With fewer hourly paid employees, a substantial reduction in supervisors would be necessary.

(11) The new equipment would have much higher operating speed capacities.

(12) All construction work entailed in the modernization program would go to outside contractors as the company did not possess either the personnel or the know-how.

(13) The company had hired no new employees at Boone since October, 1954.

(14) Accidents, though rare, were often serious.

(15) While Boone workers knew vaguely that changes were contemplated, no specific discussions detailing future plans had been held with anyone except that Mr. Hancock had spoken with his divisional superintendents.

(16) The company was prepared to consider *any* suggestions for lessening the impact of the reduction of its work force. This did not mean, however, that the program could be compromised or long delayed. The first change was scheduled for March 5, 1956.

After discussing various aspects of management's problems with those present, Roberts made two tentative recommendations: (1) That Boone management discuss with the union the first step involved in its rebuilding program. Roberts felt that the facts presented to him made very questionable any discussion of the entire three-year program with the union at this time. (2) That an investigating team of three consultants from his office visit the plant to gain other information and make additional suggestions. Both recommendations were accepted.

VI. First Meeting with the Boone Union, February 20

Present for the Company	*Present for the Union*
Scott, Assistant Plant Manager in charge of Administration and Public and Labor Relations	Mattson, Plant Committeeman and acting Union President
Norris, Assistant Plant Manager in Charge of Production	Ladd, Plant Committeeman
Reid, Superintendent, Paper Making	Kane, Vice-President
Parker, Foreman, Rewinding Department for Machines 1 to 5	Howe, Shop Steward, Rewinding Department for Machines 1 to 5
Hancock, Jr., Personnel Manager	Lothrop, Shop Steward, Rewinding Department for Machines 1 to 5

Scott (m): We have asked you to meet with us to tell you about changes in the rewinding department for #1 to #5 machines. As you know, it has always been necessary to rewind the finished rolls of paper in the rewinding department after they have been wound the first time by the machine crew on the paper-making machines. For a long time engineers have been trying to develop a winder which could be placed on the end of the paper-making machine to wind the paper in such a way that rewinding would be unnecessary. One company has recently developed just such an automatic winder. This means that paper as wound on the paper-making machines will be ready for shipment. I am sure you have seen the new winder for the #5 machine. It has been out in the department for about three weeks. We were not surprised when two weeks ago several men in the rewinding department for #1 to #5 machines requested transfers to other departments. Obviously the new machine is going to eliminate some jobs; otherwise we could never justify its tremendous cost. We realize in any deal like this someone will always get hurt. We are sure the union committee as well as your national officers understand we have to make technological changes.

At one time the Boone plant headed the list of the company's moneymakers, but over the past few years Boone, along with the other UPWA plants, has been producing less and less of our total production and profits. We have a program ahead which will, we hope, re-establish Boone's former position. I want to make it clear that our other plants already have these new winders attached to the machines, and they are operated by the third, fourth, and fifth hands on the machine crew. We feel this is a change in equipment and therefore comes under Paragraph D, Section 4,[1] of our contract. If we cannot agree on new rates, the union will have the right to question any rate which management sets.

The rewinding department for machines #1 to #5 will need 16 less people after the change is made. We will be able to eliminate two rewinders and two rewinder helpers on each of our four tours. We wanted to give you as much notice as possible so we will make the effective date of the change March 5.

Norris (m): As Mr. Scott has said, the third, fourth, and fifth machine hands will operate the new winder just as they now operate the winder. The only difference will be the new winder will wind a roll ready for shipment and eliminate rewinding. Recently I visited some of our competitors' plants and saw their setups. They have machines of far greater width than ours and with vastly greater operating speeds. We will have to get competitive or else. As you know, it is impossible to expand our production because the river will not accommodate more pollution. Our only hope lies in reducing costs and improving quality without substantially increasing production.

Reid (m): This new winder will mean far less work for the machine crew.

(The union recessed for approximately 20 minutes)

Mattson (u): We were certainly surprised when you said the third, fourth, and fifth hands would operate the new winder. As you know, it

---

[1] See Exhibit 1, Pertinent Contract Clauses, p. 122.

takes all five on the crew to handle any emergency when the paper breaks. We knew you had to make some changes, but we had no idea you planned to use the machine crew for work that belongs to the rewinding department and cut off people to whom that work belongs. Now the union wants to cooperate, but we just can't see this thing at all.

Scott (m): But the machine crew is already winding and with the new machine it will be even easier. Other people are doing this in our competitors' plants.

Reid (m): At present when you have a break, you have to either leave the winder going or shut it off and wait until it stops. With this new winder you merely throw a switch and it automatically slows itself to a stop.

Norris (m): Other UPWA mills in our own company have already accepted the setup. At Brentwood (District 50) their #1 machine is producing 500 tons a day compared to 80 on our #5 machine.

Mattson (u): What sort of wages do you pay at Brentwood?

Scott (m): As you know, the rate is higher, but it is a far cry between our 80 tons and their 500 tons.

Howe (u): Doesn't a man have a right to work in his own department? Rewinding work is going to be done on a new rewinder even though you call the machine a winder.

Norris (m): We still plan to rewind rolls in the rewinding department for the #1, #2, #3 and #4 machines. The new equipment is only being added to #5 machine. The new winder, because of its size, won't fit in the machine department. We plan to locate it about halfway between the two departments.

Scott (m): Our stiffest competition uses this same setup. Boone is falling behind and the pressure is on us to improve.

Mattson (u): For years the machine crews have been trying to get rid of winding. What will they say if we give them both winding and rewinding?

Norris (m): The new machine will definitely be smoother. While they will have some added duties, they will have much less trouble with wrinkles and things of that nature.

Kane (u): What will happen when you convert #1 to #4 machines? If you can do this on #5 machine, you can do it on all of them.

Ladd (u): Will rewinders be laid off or downgraded who are older than people left on the machine crew to do work that doesn't belong to them?

Lothrop (u): It will certainly be hell for a man with 15 years' job seniority in rewinding to step back in his job and see some young fellow across the aisle on a machine crew who has only been here several years doing his work.

Scott (m): There are different kinds of job security; one is job seniority; another is to make sure a job will remain. If we fold up the plant, there won't be jobs for anybody.

Mattson (u): Our contract establishes job sequences and department confines. What you plan is not allowed by our contract. We can't go by other mills.

Scott (m): The company cannot give up its right to make these changes. The union has protested these things before, and the arbitrator has upheld the company. We do hope the union will see that what the company is doing is best for all and that you will try to convince the people.

Mattson (u): Nobody can prevent hard feelings if you try to do this. You can't tell a man somebody else is going to do his work and everything will be all right. We just can't go along with it.

Scott (m): We feel some of our past trouble is due to somebody saying to the employees, "We're not going to let the company do this." Let's don't do that this time. Give Hancock, Jr., a ring after you have had an opportunity to get together and talk this thing over.

VII. Second Meeting with the Boone Union, February 21

Present for the Company	*Present for the Union*
Scott, Assistant Plant Manager in Charge of Administration and Public and Labor Relations	Luis Machetti, State Director for Kentucky and Virginia
Norris, Assistant Plant Manager in Charge of Production	Mattson, Plant Committeeman and Acting Union President
Reid, Superintendent, Plywood and Paper-Making Operations	Paine, Vice-President
Miller, Foreman, Rewinding Department for Machines 1 to 5	Kane, Vice-President
Hancock, Jr., Personnel Manager	

Machetti (u): Yesterday I couldn't come. I would like to have you explain the rewinder situation again to me.

[Management thoroughly explained the new setup, the fact it was in use by plants within and outside the company, and the need for the change.]

Machetti (u): I want it understood the union is not fighting progress. However, we can't see this move at all. Now if the company wants to replace its old rewinder with a new one, that is perfectly O.K. with the union, but when people in a department are laid off and are told that somebody in another department will do their work, the union can't go along. I personally feel the rewinding job belongs to the rewinding department, and the company has a contractual obligation to give the available work first to the people in the rewinding department according to seniority. Since the one new winder is going to take the place of *two* old rewinding machines, it would seem that only eight rewinders and helpers would have to be laid off. We can work that out. We can also work out new rates for these new jobs.

Scott (m): Do you mean you would be willing to transfer people from rewinding over onto the machine crew to replace those third, fourth, and fifth hands who might have less seniority?

Machetti (u): Of course not, that would be taking work away from the machine department and giving it to people in the rewinding department. However, if you want to leave the present five men on the machine crew and then have eight men from rewinding operate the new winder, we could work out plans to lay off the eight other rewinders. There is no need for the company to be a whole hog in this situation. Why don't you just be a half a hog? If you didn't want to do that, you could add a sixth and seventh hand on the machine crew.

Scott (m): We realize it is tough for the people who are to be laid off and for those who get lower rated jobs because of the contraction. We also appreciate this is tough for the union. If we find our new setup is not economical, we will be willing to change, but it is necessary to try it. We are perfectly willing to discuss rate increases and we know that additional training will be required.

As far as the departmental confines are concerned, we can look at this change as coming under Paragraph F, Section 2c3 [1]—that is, a consolidation. We agree we are taking a duty from the rewinding department and putting it in the machine department, but this is no violation of the contract. Let me read the umpire's decision on the loading arbitration:

> The provisions in the contract pertaining to job seniority involving promotion and demotion, etc., cannot be construed to imply that the existing job confines, classifications and sequences in effect at the time the contract was signed, were to continue without any change during the entire life of the contract, unless the Union acquiesced, or unless an arbitration decision was handed down, if the Union filed a grievance.
>
> The arbitrator accordingly holds that the Company, by changing the job classifications and sequences in the departments named, merely exercised its authority customarily exercised by Management, and not specifically abridged by any expressed provision of the existing agreement.

We believe that the union took a similar position to the one it is now taking once before, in the loading case; and I have just read the arbitrator's decision on that.

Machetti (u): There is not the remotest connection between the two cases.

Scott (m): Let me re-read that decision. [Scott re-read the two paragraphs.]

Machetti (u): That has no bearing at all. That case involved changing jobs within a given department. Your present proposal involves changing jobs between two different departments.

Scott (m): In the loading arbitration departmental confines were involved. Work was being transferred from the rewinding department to the loading department.

Machetti (u): There is no use to prolong this conversation; I have checked with international headquarters and we can't go along. We will fight this thing to the end.

Scott (m): You mean through the grievances procedure?

Machetti (u): I don't have anything else to say.

Scott (m): How do the other international officials justify the position you are taking. Do they know the full details?

---

[1] See Exhibit 1, Pertinent Contract Clauses, p. 122.

Machetti (u): I have explained everything to them.

[The union took a recess.]

Mattson (u): We suggest the new winder be placed in operation and operated by the present force in the rewinding department. No one would be laid off. The paper machine would be operated by the five men on the machine crew. Then we would discuss this thing in detail at our next negotiations.

Scott (m): We appreciate your idea, but we couldn't delay that long.

Mattson (u): Let me give you another alternative—get the umpire's opinion as to what is right before any change is made.

Scott (m): If this were the only change, that might not be so bad. But, as you know, we are making several changes, and we would always be short-cutting the grievance procedure.

We have already checked with several arbitrators who feel we are within our rights. Have you told the machine people to follow orders when we put this new winder in operation?

Mattson (u): We always tell our people to follow orders, but so far no one has told the machine crews to run the new winder. And we don't know what they might do as individuals when they are told to operate it.

Reid (m): I plan to tell them as of 7:00 A.M., March 5.

Mattson (u): If the union loses on this one by arbitration or otherwise, then nobody's job in the plant is safe. We realize that you must make progress, but we wish you would agree to some middle ground as we proposed. If you go ahead with this change people will stay bitter a long time and you will not get the production you want. It looks like we are going to have trouble.

Scott (m): Luis, I hope you and the committee will discuss this thing and that you will also discuss it with your higher union officials. However, we feel that we are right in making this change and that the loading decision by the umpire is a strong precedent in our favor.

VIII. Three Consultants Visit the Boone Plant

Following this meeting, management decided to take no further action until the three consultants from Roberts' office arrived on March 1.

On February 27, Machetti phoned Scott requesting that installation of the new winder be delayed until the union could explore the company's position and explain the change to the union membership. In agreeing to postpone the change until March 12, Scott said the delay was granted to give the union every opportunity to analyze the situation in the hope it would decide to support management in the change.

At the conclusion of their visit the consultants recommended that the plant management schedule another meeting with the union to explain to the union leadership all the changes planned for Boone over the next three years.[1]

---

[1] Information underlying the recommendation is given in Exhibit 2, p. 123.

IX. THIRD MEETING WITH THE BOONE UNION, MARCH 5

Scott arranged a meeting with union officials for March 5. Prior to it, Scott explained to the divisional superintendents the developments to date. Scott also arranged to discuss the situation with the foremen in the presence of their superintendents on March 7. Hancock, Sr., was not present at these meetings inasmuch as he was on vacation from March 3 to March 30.

At the March meeting, management purposefully kept its committee small. Union representatives at any one time numbered about 20, but 35 in all were present during at least a part of the discussions.

Present for the Company	*Present for the Union*
Scott, Assistant Manager for Administration	Machetti, State Director, PWA
Norris, Assistant Manager for Production	Mattson, Acting Pres., Boone local
	Ladd, Plant Grievance Committee
Childes, Director of Research & Supt. of By-Products Operations	Paine, Vice-Pres., Boone local
	Kane, Vice-Pres., Boone local & Shop Steward, Rewinding Department
Keene, Supt., Raw Material Preparations	for #1 to #5 Machines
Cook, Supt. of Engineering and Maintenance	Also five Shop Stewards, Rewinding Department for #1 to #5 Machines
Howard, Supt. of Chemical Operations	

Scott (m): We have a problem in which you men have an interest so we feel it is only fair to tell you just what we plan to do. Our whole idea is to solicit your help in our undertaking and we sincerely hope you will make suggestions. Mr. Norris will tell you our plans.

[Norris factually explained in detail the shift in Boone's competitive position, the advantages Boone still possessed, and expressed the hope that the $10 million modernization program would ensure continuance of well-paid work.]

Norris (m) (continuing): We've gone into the background carefully so that you'll understand why we must modernize. We would also like to explain the whole program itself slowly and in detail. Don't hesitate to interrupt at any point where you have a question.

Before we get into it, let's recognize that it will take two or three years to complete and since it's impossible to schedule accurately that far ahead, any dates or numbers of jobs to be eliminated are only approximate.

[For nearly an hour, he painstakingly described, one after another, some 15 major equipment changes, in the sequence contemplated, and detailed the number and types of jobs eliminated by each change. No department would be unaffected; many consolidated; some eliminated. Skills affected ranged from top to bottom. The number of jobs to be eliminated by groups varied from 4 to 175.]

Norris (m) (continuing): From the above outlines it appears it will be necessary to eliminate approximately 490 jobs over the next two or three years. This does *not* mean that 490 employees will be laid off, for, during the two to three-year period, the normal attrition of the work force—voluntary quits, deaths, retirements—will absorb an appreciable number. This reduction in the number of jobs, however, is absolutely essential if we are to successfully meet the competition of the highly efficient mills located in the South.

Please bear in mind that all of these plans are subject to modification and change should conditions warrant, and minor deviations from the pattern indicated above are almost certain to occur.

All of us—the union, the employees, the company, the community—face a common problem—that of restoring the competitive strength of our mill. If we are to succeed, we must succeed together, working out our problems in a spirit of mutual confidence and trust. We of management invite the fullest possible degree of participation on the part of the union and you men in effecting our plans. We, more than ever before, shall want to consult with you of union leadership, the shop stewards, and the men, and to give careful and thorough consideration to any proposals that you make. We know that we must have the cooperation of the union. We know that we've made mistakes in our relationships with the union. We are honestly sorry about them. However, we've been seeking lots of advice and as we try to do a better job, we hope we'll make it easier for you to do a constructive job. Only in such a way can we both make the jobs of our employees secure and worthwhile.

[Not a word was spoken by any union member during this entire exposition. Machetti took copious notes. The union took a recess.]

Machetti (u): Have you anything further to tell us?

Scott (m): No, but you must have some comments you would like to make. Do any of you have any questions to put to the production men? They planned the changes and are here to answer questions.

[No questions were asked.]

Scott (m): You may want to think things over a while and then make some suggestions which we would be most anxious to entertain. While management is firmly committed to the production changes and the job elimination which Bryant has outlined, the union can offer valuable suggestions as to the way these things could be done. We will welcome your ideas for lessening the impact of these changes on you men and on the community. We would like to arrange a meeting as soon as possible after your weekly union meeting. Could we get together Wednesday, day after tomorrow?

Machetti (u): Not very well. I am leaving town tomorrow for two weeks. The grievance committee and the shop stewards have plans for the week and will be too busy. We will get in touch with you later. In the meantime we shall consider that our problems are still under negotiation.

X. The Crisis Is Reached

Management was disappointed that the conference was not more fruitful. The union's apparent lack of willingness to set a date for another meeting was not interpreted optimistically. By Wednesday, March 7, rumors of a strike scheduled to take place at 7:00 A.M. on Monday, March 12, were widespread. Townspeople were phoning to ask whether the strike rumor was true. Foremen reported several instances of arguments between groups of workers and their shop stewards. Some members of machine crews had torn up their union cards and thrown the pieces at the shop stewards. The supervisor in charge of the electricians reported that he had been told by some of them that they were not going to support the workers in the rewinding department for machines #1 to #5 because the rewinder operators had refused to support the electricians when the latter group called a work stoppage in 1955.

On March 8, Mattson requested that management schedule fourth step grievance meetings for the entire days of March 8, 9, and 12 to resolve grievances which had been pending for some time. Since Scott had previous commitments for the mornings of March 8 and 9, he suggested meeting on those afternoons and all day the 12th. This was not convenient for the union committee, according to Mattson, since it was meeting with employees from selected departments every afternoon at 3:30. Mattson requested that the fourth step hearings be scheduled for the mornings of the 8th and 9th. Scott re-scheduled his other appointments to make himself available those mornings.

At 9:00 A.M. on March 8, Kane, a union vice-president, called the personnel office to say that unless management could meet all day on the fourth step grievances, the union committee would not meet. The meetings were postponed.

New developments kept Scott busy the morning of March 8. Three letters, each sent by registered mail with return receipt requested, were received from the union. The first was a copy of a letter to the standing umpire requesting hearings on 13 arbitration cases then pending. The second was a copy of a letter to the executive board of the Boone local wherein Paine tendered his immediate resignation as a union vice-president. The third letter informed the company that all of the shop stewards in the paper machine departments were resigning, effective March 11. The company was concerned for until the office of shop steward was filled in these departments, effective communication with the union at the departmental level was impossible.

The editor of the Boone Journal called requesting a statement regarding the situation at the plant. He pointed out the community had a vital interest in the plant's operation and the newspaper had had many requests for information.

Superintendent Reid submitted two additional problems for Scott's decision. (1) Reid pointed out the need for training the machine crews on the

#5 machine in the proper methods of operating the new winder. Reid felt that this should be done prior to putting the winder in actual operation on March 12. While Scott recognized that a question of safety was involved, he also was uncertain as to the outcome of any attempt to give the machine crews such training prior to the 12th. (2) What action should the foreman of the #5 machine department take if the third, fourth, and fifth hands did not operate the new winder on Monday morning? Reid reported that in the past when the workers did not wish to go along with a change they never explicitly refused to work, but merely stood in silence with their hands in their pockets. What should the foremen do if the workers repeated this pattern on the 13th?

Scott recognized that within 24 hours he would have to resolve several other questions. For example, if the crew on the #5 machine refused to operate the new winder and the #5 machine were shut down, other departments would eventually have to be shut down. What would be the proper time for management to shut down these departments? And should the personnel office try to avoid call-in pay penalties as stipulated in the contract, by early notice to workers on the 3:00 P.M. tour not to report?

Scott also felt that he should decide whether or not the company could win if it were necessary to go to arbitration on the issue of the new winder. And would the union be in a position to claim that the company had, in bad faith, unilaterally made the change at a time when negotiations were still pending? Scott also felt that the company should define its own proposals for lessening the impact of the modernization program on the employees and the community.

On the afternoon of March 8, Scott called together the chief operating executives of the plant to decide what program of action should be adopted.

Exhibit 1

Seneca Paper Company

Pertinent Contract Clauses, September 13, 1955–September 13, 1957 [1]

Paragraph C—Hours of Work

Section 6: The Company agrees to discuss suggestions on work schedules from the Union.

   a. As a general policy, changes in work schedules which affect an entire department or substantial portion thereof will be discussed with the Union prior to the change, but such discussion shall not be used to delay the effective date of the change.

Paragraph D—Rates of Pay and Wage Scale

Section 1: The established wage rates are attached hereto as Appendix "B" and shall become a part of this Agreement and, except as they may be revised under any provision of the contract, shall remain in effect for the life of the Agreement.

---

[1] Material enclosed in brackets represents 1955 additions to the 1954 contract, which was otherwise unchanged.

Section 3: During the life of this Agreement, the Company and the Union will consider proposals for job rate adjustments, when said proposals are supported by relevant facts and data. Such proposals may be processed as a grievance through, but not beyond, the fourth step of the grievance procedure.

Section 4: When a bona fide new job is created, or when changes are made in equipment and method of processing or production which result in a substantial change in job duties, the Management shall evaluate the job and inform the Union of the proposed new rate. Differences shall be settled by collective bargaining and subject to the Grievance Procedure.

Section 6: The number of employees in each classification and the number of classifications shall be determined by Management. However, the Union shall have the right to question such determination through the established Grievance Procedure.

Paragraph F—Seniority

Section 2: If an employee is to be laid off, recalled, promoted or demoted to other hourly paid jobs, seniority will prevail, but the affected employee must have the ability and job qualifications. Changes shall be made along the following lines:

a. Job Seniority:
1. The job sequence for promotion and demotion of hourly paid employees is set forth in Appendix "F" annexed hereto. Job sequence changes may be negotiated by mutual agreement or upon request signed by 75% or more of the employees in the sequence.
5. Job seniority shall govern in cases of promotion and demotion. In the event that job seniority is equal, departmental seniority shall prevail.
7. Grievances in regard to promotions or demotions shall be made in writing within sixty consecutive days after the employee is classified and receives the job rate on a permanent basis, after which no grievance will be considered.

b. Departmental Seniority:
1. Seniority in a department starts with the day an employee begins work in the department on a permanent basis and gives precedence through the department. At the time a job in a department becomes permanent, the employee will be given credit for unbroken service from the last date he started work in the department. In the event that departmental seniority is equal, plant seniority shall prevail.
2. The confines of and the job classifications in each department are as set forth in Appendix G annexed hereto.

c. Plant Seniority:
1. Seniority in the plant starts with the day an employee begins to work at the plant and applies only where specifically stated in the Agreement.
2. In case of layoffs caused by the discontinuance of an operating job or department, employees with more than fifteen years' plant seniority, if they can qualify, will be placed on jobs which are occupied by employees with up to five years' plant seniority, and they shall have five years' job and departmental seniority in the new department; then employees with more than ten years' plant seniority, if they can qualify, will be placed on jobs which are occupied by employees with up to three years' plant seniority, and they shall have three years' job and departmental seniority in the new department; then employees with from five to ten years' plant seniority, if they can qualify, will be offered transfer, within ten days after layoff, to jobs at the lowest level of any job sequence occupied by employees junior to them in plant seniority, displacing those with the least plant seniority. [In any such case, however, an employee with ten or more years' plant seniority may elect either the procedure provided by this section or that provided by Section 2. c. 3 below, whichever he prefers.]
3. In case of layoffs, other than those caused by the discontinuance of an

operating job or department, employees with more than five years' plant seniority, if they can qualify, will be offered transfer within ten days after layoff, to jobs at the lowest level of any job sequence occupied by employees junior to them in plant seniority, displacing those with the least plant seniority.

Paragraph P—Grievances and Arbitration

Section 1: Issues subject to the grievance procedure are differences arising out of the interpretation, application or alleged violation of any provision of this Agreement. Differences relative to working conditions not specifically covered by this Agreement, which are of such a detailed or minor character as not to involve fundamental principles or relationships or any substantial economic advantages or disadvantages to the parties, are also subject to the Grievance Procedure.

Section 2: An effort will be made to present issues subject to Grievance Procedure in writing within five days after they occur, and they shall be adjusted promptly within the periods specified below through negotiations taken in the following order, it being understood that the sole reason for the time limit herein set forth is the desire of both parties to assure prompt settlement of grievances.

f. Grievances growing out of discharge, layoff, promotion, demotion, hiring, re-hiring and transfer, shall be subject to the Grievance Procedure, but no arbitrator shall have the power to substitute his judgment for that of Management, unless he finds that the Management has acted arbitrarily or for an ulterior motive or through a mistake in fact or in violation of this Agreement.

Paragraph Q—No Strikes or Lockouts

In view of the foregoing Paragraph P for the settlement of grievances, there shall be no strikes or lockouts while this Agreement is in effect. The Union agrees that if any strike or concerted stoppage of work which is unauthorized or unratified by the Union occurs, the Union will immediately and publicly disavow such strike or stoppage and direct the employees engaged therein to return to work forthwith. In the event of any such unauthorized or unratified strike or stoppage, the Company may discipline any employee participating therein, and any such discipline shall not constitute a grievance within the meaning of Paragraph P unless the union claims that the Company has exercised such discipline in a discriminatory manner.

In consideration of the foregoing undertaking by the Union, the Union and its officials will not be liable in damages and the Company will not bring suit against the Union or its officials in connection with any such unauthorized or unratified strike or concerted stoppage of work.

Paragraph S—Management

Section 1: The direction of the working force is vested in the Company through its supervisory personnel. The Company reserves all the rights, powers and authority customarily exercised by Management except insofar as they are specifically surrendered or abridged by express provisions of this Agreement.

Exhibit 2

Seneca Paper Company

Information Requested by Roberts' Consultants

1. Is the company locally regarded as a good place to work?

An important segment of the community would so consider the company. Most workers have long service. Brothers, cousins, sons, etc., work in the plant. It would be difficult to assess the opinion of the union leadership.

2. Has stock been sold on any basis to employees?
   No.
3. How do your wage rates compare with other local industries?
   Ours are generally higher by a comfortable margin.
4. How do your rates compare with other companies in the same industry, nation-wide?
   Ours are equal or better for comparable jobs.
5. Does the company follow or set the industry wage pattern?
   We generally follow the pattern, depending somewhat on when contracts expire in the various companies. The industry has, in recent years, followed the national wage pattern in cents per hour. This has meant that our industry has absorbed proportionally larger increases than most basic industries because average wage rates in our industry have been typically lower.
6. Does the company have a job evaluation plan?
   No. The union requested at the last negotiations that job descriptions be developed jointly by the union and the company. But, because most of the jobs are about to be changed substantially, the company believed descriptions of present jobs might introduce rigidities.
7. Does the company have a wage incentive plan, time and motion studies, or a formal employee merit rating plan?
   No.
8. Does the company have a recreational program for employees?
   Yes, the company maintains an employee club house and a golf course. Two baseball teams, one for white and one for colored workers, are supported by profits from Coca-Cola machines in the plant.
9. Does the company submit annual reports to employees?
   Yes. In addition, we discuss the annual report with supervisors.
10. What has been the principal point at issue between the union and the company during the last four years?
    The application of mill seniority. The variety and range of skills required in different operations render wholesale transferring and bumping throughout the plant impossible. In addition, women hired during the war can qualify for only a limited number of jobs. Another problem would be senior employees in the wood-yard trying to bump into skilled jobs inside the plant. Of course, the contract already provides for a rather liberal application of mill seniority.
11. What is the company's attitude toward publicity in regard to labor relations problems?
    It has attempted to keep its plant communities fully informed of any developments whatsoever which might affect the towns. Mr. Hancock outlined the Boone modernization program to the local Chamber of Commerce in January and his talk was later broadcast on the Boone radio station.
12. What has been the plant's experience with quits, discharges, etc., over the past five years?
    See Exhibit 3.
13. How many employees are 60 years old or over?
    See Exhibit 3.
14. Has the company arrived at new job rates on the new winder for the third, fourth, and fifth hands?
    The company is prepared to offer increases as follows: third hand to be increased from $1.76 per hour to $1.85 per hour; fourth and fifth hands from $1.67 to $1.72 per hour. These compare with the present rewinder operators' rate of $1.79 and the rewinder helpers' rate of $1.68. These rates have not been proposed to the union for it was hoped that the union would choose to "bargain" over new rates.
15. Is the company prepared to take a strike on its right to effect the changes?
    Yes. A strike at Boone costs about $100,000 per week.

16. What is the attitude of the workers toward having a union?

At Boone they want a union as shown by every representation election to date. On the other hand, the employees take little interest in union affairs or in attending the weekly union meeting.

17. What is the present status of the international union?

It is somewhat smaller than IBP, its chief rival, and a significant segment of its membership derives from the plants it has organized in our company. It recently lost representation rights at the Beaufort Company. The LaGrange Company, also in Kentucky, has been on strike for the last three months. In Michigan an equally long strike over seniority may end in the liquidation of the Winn Company.

EXHIBIT 3

SENECA PAPER COMPANY

Boone Employees: Number by Plant Seniority and by Age 60 and Over; Permanent Separations, by Cause

Employees by Plant Seniority, March 1, 1950				Age 60 and Over (Total 128)			
Years	Male	Female	Total	Age	Number	Age	Number
1 to 2	71	0	71	60	18	68	8
2 to 3	136	0	136	61	17	69	5
3 to 4	206	0	206	62	11	70	1
4 to 5	146	6	152	63	9	71	3
5 to 10	602	72	674	64	9	72	4
10 to 15	130	0	130	65	10	73	1
15 and Over	601	7	608	66	10	74	3
				67	13	75–81	6
Totals	1,892	85	1,977				

Permanent Separations, November 1, 1944—January 1, 1950

Fiscal Year Ending	Average No. of Employees	Quits		Deaths		Pensioned		Discharged		Total of Separations	
		No.	%	No.	%	No.	%	No.	%	No.	%
October, 1945	1,675	570	34.0	6	.4	1	.06	66	3.9	643	38.4
October, 1946	2,124	522	24.6	4	.2	1	.05	45	2.1	572	26.9
October, 1947	2,234	277	12.4	7	.3	1	.04	32	1.4	317	14.2
October, 1948	2,285	173	7.6	7	.3	2	.1	20	.9	202	8.8
October, 1949	1,979	60	3.0	13	.7	16	.8	7	.4	96	4.8
Five-Year Averages	—	320	16.3	7	.4	4	.2	34	1.7	365	18.6
Quarter, January, 1950	1,975	6	0.3	4	0.2	4	0.2	2	0.1	16	0.8

DISCUSSION QUESTIONS

1. What has been the company's previous experience with introducing technological change? Why are the workers resisting the introduction of the new rewinding equipment?

2. What significance do you place on the resignation of the stewards?

3. What is the company's ability to take a strike?

4. What action would you recommend that management take at the Thursday meeting? Specifically, what action would you recommend with respect to the following areas: response to the request for a statement for the local paper, training of crews, wage rates, layoffs, and instructions to foremen?

5. Given the decision to modernize, describe the manner in which you would introduce the change.

6. What are some of the specific problems that will arise as the company attempts to carry out the modernization program?

7. How well prepared is the company to handle these problems?

INTERSTATE STEEL CORPORATION

THE ROLLING CREWS AND THE EXPANSION PROGRAM

I. INTRODUCTION

E. B. Benson, umpire under the Agreement between Interstate Steel and United Steelworkers, received a phone call in August from Douglas J. Marshall, company counsel. The latter apologized for "breaking into his vacation at his summer home," but Thomas J. Guthrie, union district director, joined him to ask how soon arbitration hearings could be scheduled at the Halsey Plant. They were facing a serious situation in the cold strip mill—not for the first time, as he well knew. Benson regretted he could not hold any hearings before September; the last Thursday and Friday in September were thereupon scheduled.

Excerpts from the testimony of the following persons, who, among others, testified at the hearings.

For the Company

Douglas J. Marshall	Company Counsel
Stanley H. Powell	Superintendent, Strip Mill Division
Clifford Rogers	Time Study Analyst
Harold C. Lee	Time Study Analyst
Philip I. Cullom	Superintendent, Cold Strip Mill

For the Union

Thomas J. Guthrie	District Director
Walter A. Adams	Chairman, Grievance Committee Inspector
Daniel C. Deacon } Donald N. Ellis }	Rollers, Skin Mills
Lawrence F. Stewart	Roller No. 1, Sheet Mill; Relief Roller, Coil Mills; and Grievance Committeeman
Franklin Ritchie	Roller, 75-inch Tandem Mill; and Grievance Committeeman

II. THE SKIN MILLS

On Thursday morning the dispute over revised incentive rates in the skin mills was presented. The dispute had arisen when the company introduced new standards in three re-equipped skin mills.

At the time the program was launched in February, two of the skin mills, Nos. 2 and 5, were rolling coils; one skin mill, No. 3, was rolling sheets. The conversion process entailed shifting mill No. 3 to coil work and re-equipping all three mills for higher rolling speeds.

During the change-over all three mills were identically re-equipped. Improvements were also instituted in auxiliary equipment for feeding coils into the mills and taking away finished product. Maximum rolling speed was doubled: each mill was able to roll at a rate up to 2,500 feet per minute, as compared to the former maximum of 1,250 feet.

No. 2 mill was taken out of service on February 21, re-equipped, and placed back in operation on March 18. Similarly, No. 3 mill was converted during July and No. 5 mill during July and August. By August 21, all three mills had been identically re-equipped.

Under the new rates the bonus part of the roller's pay was changed from $.0457 to $.00586 per pay ton; the bonus factor for other members of the crew was changed comparably. The hourly base rate remained unchanged.[1]

Since the mills handled a wide range of steel at various gauges and widths, pay tonnage was calculated by application of a number of factors. These factors of multiplication compensated for the fact that the weight of material rolled might not have any relationship to the time required to complete the operation. Under the old rates, the highest total factor (for narrowest widths and thinnest gauges) was 4.3; under the revised rates it was 25.25.

FROM THE THURSDAY MORNING SESSION

The Union's Presentation. [Fifty pages of the transcript were taken up by this testimony, from which the following represent typical passages.]

Adams (u): Before March, we were called to the superintendent's office and told they intended to time study these improved skin mills so as to put new rates into effect. Superintendent Powell suggested having the men paid a straight hourly rate during the study period. We protested; we feared a loss of money.

The superintendent said he didn't want to see "take-home" drop. So he suggested the men work for 75% of the old rates applied to the increased volume of production. Again, we protested. We felt we should work at the old rates until the company established new rates. Management wouldn't agree. We finally agreed that management would pay a flat hourly rate, during the study, based on average earnings for the 13 weeks prior to the study period, which came to $3.91 an hour for the rollers.

The company put the new incentive rate structure into effect on August 7. It was first presented to the union stewards. The stewards heartily disagreed with these rates. But under the agreement, the company had the right to put them into effect. Shortly thereafter, the union filed grievances; there were a number of incidents which led to highly excited grievance proceedings.

After the study, when the new rates went into effect on August 7, the earnings of the men dropped considerably. The men have continued to lose money. It is no secret that there have been a few walkouts over it. In fact,

---

[1] See Exhibit 2.

after the men got their first pay under the new rates, there was a walkout. The trouble brewing was the reason for hastening this arbitration.

A vital point is the way various gauges and widths are handled in computing tonnage upon which our pay is based. In the old incentive system, relatively few mathematical factors were used to adjust actual tonnage for anything less than the heaviest width and gauge. We aren't able to compare the old pay rates with the new ones, for the company has complicated the tables of factors.

I cannot, for the life of me, see how the company ever arrived at their rates. The company complained in the fourth step that the skin mill rates have been out of line with other jobs in the industry for years. We claim the opposite. They claim this is management's chance to bring them back in line.[1]

The following excerpts from testimony of the rollers indicate the nature of the objections raised about the new rolling mills:

Ellis (u): We have been keeping tab, and I took a $25 to $40 a week cut under the new rate. I process the steel in the same way I did before—for a less amount of money. That is all I can say.

We get a lot of loosely wound coil. During the study period, our mill got the cream of the crop, tightly wound coils. After the study, loose coil came again. You can't have great speed on that. You have to wait for the crane to push the coil in. The coil vibrates. You have to slow down or you might harm the machinery and damage the rolls.

Marshall (m): Hasn't production on your mill improved since Mr. Cullom spoke to you about not operating efficiently?

Ellis (u): We increased quantity last night; but, as for quality, inspection will decide today.

Stewart (u): In the first place, the company's replacement of the machinery was a must, because the old machinery was worn out. But the processing now is identically the same as it was, except that the coils are bigger now.

The speed alone has changed. But speed cannot be maintained at all times. "Stickers," for instance, which means one lap is sticking into another, cause delay. The coil then cannot be run at full speed, for the coil could tear off and cause an awful accident. It is hazardous to the men and damaging to the steel. The management's only interest in the time study seemed to be to bat it out for speed. Quality was strictly secondary. In the past, responsibility for quality was shared with the inspector. But now, on all types of steel except O.K. ship, inspection is eliminated from the job, and the responsibility lies wholly with the roller and catcher. Naturally that's slower.

Marshall (m): Would you be surprised if I said that the occurrence of stickers has decreased about two-thirds?

Stewart (u): That wouldn't surprise me none; it's due to the loosely wound coils—they don't stick.

---

[1] See Exhibit 1 (excerpts from the agreement) to evaluate fully the contractual obligations with respect to introduction of new standards.

Deacon (u): Our incentive rate per pay ton has been decreased, and our take-home has diminished approximately $40 a week. This new setup requires more alertness; and we are responsible for the steel; and it is kind of hazardous. The new hydraulic system at times is very inadequate. The coils are coming in unusual shape: the sides are damaged, water and oil are on the coils, sometimes splices from the tandem mill are marked and sometimes not. We have difficulty with the new saddle that enters the coil into the feed reel. It is a metal, hitting metal, and causes a big gouge in the steel, which requires attention. But the main thing which is giving difficulty is loose coil. The equipment plus loose coils require more work, more operation, more controls—the rate is inadequate.

Marshall (m): Is everything under your control being done on that mill to get maximum production?

Deacon (u): Well, we are doing our best.

Marshall (m): Is it your position that these new rates just don't give any incentive?

Deacon (u): Oh, we make over the day rate, if that is what you mean; but, with these rates, a man cannot come anywhere near what he made before. Remember that half of our pay is the hourly portion of our rate. The other half is incentive, so that, when a man produces twice as much, he couldn't possibly receive twice as much pay.

Marshall (m): If the rates were increased, would we get more production?

Deacon (u): Possibly somewhat. Under the present conditions—not too much.

The Company's Presentation

Marshall (m): Dr. Benson, I once attended a meeting on a problem relating to rollers. Philip Murray himself characterized it as, "not a labor dispute, but an argument between capitalists." The average earnings, $3.91 per hour, paid these men during the study period were high, but it was not our intent to reduce earnings. The purpose of the new rates is to increase earnings.

These grievances have been processed almost as speedily as the maximum speed of the converted mills! The grievances, dated August 17 and answered in Step 2 on August 19, were also discussed in Step 3 on August 19 and in Step 4 on August 21. The reason was that we had a series of work stoppages. We have had a slowdown since these rates went into effect. We are not getting production.

We have not had the usual discussion of these grievances or any definition of issues—something that I think should have been done.

I would like to ask the union whether it questions the company's right to replace the old rates, to adjust to the technical improvements?

Guthrie (u): Dr. Benson, I thought the union made it clear enough that we are not challenging management's right to change the rates. The Agreement clearly gives the company that right. But it also gives the union the right to challenge the new rates as inequitable.

Marshall (m): Good! Now, on the next issue, I want unmistakable clarification. I have explained that there is a difference in basic *structure* between the old rates and the new ones, which might be interpreted as a "new" incentive *plan*.

Guthrie (u): Dr. Benson, we are not in disagreement on the establishment of a new plan. We *are* in disagreement with its results—the earning potentials under these rates. Management seems to believe that now is the opportune time to reduce the earnings of these men. They are attempting to achieve double production for about the same amount of earnings as the men made prior to the change-over.

Our contention is that these earnings should increase, not in direct proportion to the increase in the tonnages, but in whatever proportion the umpire may see fit to grant the union as fair and equitable. We recognize that a direct proportion would be unrealistic. But we maintain that these new rates do not comply with the contract, which provides that whenever incentive rates are changed they shall be in equitable relationship to the rates displaced.

Marshall (m): I am sorry if the union has got the idea that the company wished to cut earnings. The company has said many times that the earnings of skin mill rollers are definitely on the high side. I think the union also recognizes that. That condition is fairly common throughout the industry. But, rather than cut that level of earnings, the company's intent, which I hope to be able to demonstrate, was that the earnings of all crew members would be substantially increased.

To clarify the issue, my understanding is that we are apart solely on whether the new rate schedule is in equitable relationship to the old schedule, and whether it affords equitable compensation within the meaning of that term as contained in the Agreement. In plain English, are the new rates so designed that, in comparison with the old ones, they give the men enough money?

Guthrie (u): Yes.

Marshall (m): Very well. First, I would like to give a bird's-eye view of what we were trying to accomplish. We were trying to get up a uniform schedule of rates, applicable to the three skin mills. As a result of time studies, we developed actual expected production, for the average width and gauge of steel processed during the preceding year. At that average width (46″) and gauge (.036″), we found that the potential production of the re-equipped mill, as established by time study, was 75 tons per hour.

Now, we also found difficulties, which the union has alluded to, in the installation of new equipment. You always run into obstacles to the attainment of potential maximum production. We recognized that these men were not going to achieve 75 tons per hour immediately. But we wanted them to have some increase in earnings, in recognition of their turning out greater production. As a practical matter, even though rates are based upon studies, it is frequently realistically necessary, where you have an increase in production as a result of technical improvements, to grant an increase in total earnings for that increased production in order to maintain a proper incentive.

We found that other plants, both in and out of this company, with similar equipment were rolling around 55 tons per hour, at average widths and gauges. We developed a rate structure based upon those points, 55 tons and 75 tons— frankly, on a more or less empirical basis. We aim at a reasonable increase, without making earnings astronomical. By trial and error, keeping under a $5 an hour earnings level for the roller, we finally came out with an ultimate objective of $4.83 per hour for the roller at 75 tons per hour and a present objective of $4.142 per hour at 55 tons, which the management is confident should be realized now.[1]

I will say flatly that there has been, until the last couple of days, a concerted slowdown, which has been responsible for failing to achieve production, and which explains the difference between the present and the old pay checks.

Guthrie (u): I think you will recognize, Doctor, that, when management calls in the crews and threatens them with discharge unless they speed up the mill, that those men would then simply throw caution to the winds and open up those mills, taking a chance on whatever injury and damage may happen. These men do not want to lose their jobs.

[The session adjourned for lunch.]

FROM THE THURSDAY AFTERNOON SESSION

Marshall (m): Mr. Cullom, what is the effect of all these changes upon the potential production of the mill?

Cullom (m): The potential certainly is doubled. You have doubled the speed. You have the addition of a man to the crew, the utility man. There is much less manual labor. The job now is mostly automatic.

Marshall (m): The rollers testified that they have not had good material since the mill was re-equipped.

Cullom (m): By and large, they have had better material than ever before. They mentioned coils that have laps in them, occasioned by broken welds at the tandem mill. By actual figures, broken welds have been reduced from 4½% to 1½%. Further, where before we slit from 40% to 50% of our material in the pickler to maintain uniform width, we are now slitting 80%. That reduces damaged edges and so also delays, by maintaining uniformity of widths.

Marshall (m): How about stickers?

Cullom (m): A sticker is steel that has been wound too tight on the tandem mill; and, in heat-treating these coils, the laps become fused. When you get them to the skin mills, they become difficult to open. If the stickers are bad, I would insist that the mill be run slowly to prevent damage to the equipment, the rolls, or the material itself—or hazard to the men. But, in most cases, you can run them just as fast as ever. In fact, the material has less tendency to break at high speed than at low speed.

Marshall (m): During the time study, was the steel specially selected? Was surface sacrificed in order to get speed of operation?

---

[1] Further evidence compared these averages with prior hourly earnings averages for the final 13 weeks under the old rates of $3.91 at No. 2 mill, $2.89 at No. 3, and $4.28 at No. 5 mill.

Cullom (m): There was no special treatment at all. We did not select material.

Umpire: Were coils more tightly rolled? Some evidence presented was that the coils are looser now than during the time study.

Cullom (m): Some of the coils are loose, due to our experimentation in loose winding. It does hold them up, but to a very small extent.

Marshall (m): There is a proper median between tight winding causing stickers and loose winding; and experimentation is going on to find that tension at which you will have the least stickers. Since the change, have you been getting production out of the mills?

Cullom (m): It doesn't even remotely approach potentialities. I can state frankly that we have had a slowdown—a deliberate, unnecessary slowdown.

Marshall (m): Did you interview all of the crews?

Cullom (m): Yes, the day before yesterday and yesterday.

Marshall (m): What was the effect of your talks?

Cullom (m): I made it a point to do exactly what I told them I would do. I looked over the gauge, the width, and the class of material, and told them how fast it was to be rolled. The tons per hour for the last two days have doubled.

Stewart (u): What about those welds?

Cullom (m): The potential hazard from weld breakage is considerably less.

Stewart (u): Well, it is only common sense to know that a loose coil has a tendency to flap.

Cullom (m): That is your opinion against mine.

Stewart (u): With that flapping the only way is to slow down your mill.

Cullom (m): If you think that, Larry, you are not qualified to roll in the mill.

Stewart (u): I have never been reprimanded or had time off for not doing my job properly.

Guthrie (u): I don't think Mr. Cullom should indulge in such statements. He is intimidating a witness. I don't like it—and, by gad, if that is going to continue, we will know how to proceed from here on!

Marshall (m): Mr. Cullom was not threatening the witness.

Guthrie (u): By golly, I so took it.

Marshall (m): I think you are exceptionally thin-skinned.

Stewart (u): I have been rolling since 1939, and this is the first time I have heard a statement like that.

Umpire: Nerves get kind of frazzled at the end of the day. It would be just as well not to indulge in personalities. From my point of view, there are experts on both sides, equal before the law, testifying here.

Marshall (m): This has been a long day.

Umpire: It seems to me there are many facts here upon which you haven't yet agreed among yourselves.

Marshall (m): As I said at the beginning, we haven't had *any* discussion. The real problem in presenting this case is that some changes are still being made. This whole situation is in a flux. On top of that, while we have made studies, we have been handicapped from the very beginning by the slowdown. The men won't let us check the rates or make observations on the new equipment. We can't tell whether we are losing production because of the men or from a combination of things.

Guthrie (u): Mr. Umpire, every effort has been made by the union to thrash this matter out. These skin mills were put into operation months ago. They had ample opportunity to observe these new mechanisms during the time study period. The *men* have studied the new incentive rates, and they say frankly that they are just no good. Now, whether there is a slowdown or not, nobody can prove. Obviously, when a man has no incentive, there is no power on earth that can compel him to put in that extra effort brought forth by a fair and equitable rate. Isn't that what "incentive" means?

There isn't too much we can give you in the way of proof, Mr. Umpire. We don't have access to time studies, but the machines have been speeded up. The company says to the men, in effect, you people can turn out about double your prior tonnage, and you will be able to make so much more according to our new rates. Now, the men say that they cannot. So we are stalemated. It's a case of the theoretical angle against the practical.

The only way that the men will put in extra effort is by not only giving them the service they had during the test period, but dangling the good old red apple in front of them. So, there you are.

I know you have taken the position that neither side has introduced much evidence. We will concede that. But we are not engineers; we are not mathematicians. We ask you, as the impartial party, to help us resolve this problem.

Umpire: I am perfectly willing to undertake that responsibility. My remarks resulted from this disagreement as to details, operational details, between the men and supervision. However, if you think you have done all you possibly can to resolve this yourself, that is that.

[The hearing recessed at 5 P.M. to reconvene at 9:30 A.M. the following day.]

FROM THE FRIDAY MORNING SESSION

Mr. Marshall presented evidence by Messrs. Rogers and Lee of the time study department. Usual time study procedures were described: (1) Four types of rolls were differentiated. (2) On each type, mill speeds for varying gauges and width were ascertained. (3) Operations, broken down into constituent elements, were measured, as were delays—both inherent and nonrecurrent—and allowances for personal time. (4) Each normal daily shift of 480 minutes was divided into percentages of productive time and nonproductive time. (5) On these measurements, production standards were set. (6) The composition of the rates, to comprise an hourly portion *and* an incentive portion per crew position, was continued. (7) But the conversion of actual tonnage into pay tonnages by factor allowances was extended and refined. *Under the prior rate structure,* the factor tables listed 10 widths of coils, ranging from 65 inches and wider down to 20 to 25 inches. And, for the 5-width classifications on the wider half of this range, 17 gauges were factored; for the 5 on the narrower half, 20 gauges were factored. *Under the new rates,* tables of factors were established for each of the four kinds of roll finish (i.e., process, O.K. ship, rolled to temper, and cut-out welds and rewind). For each of these types, a range of 14-width classifications was tabulated; each, in turn, was correlated with 27 gauges. (8) Against the prior allowance of 25 pay tons for each complete roll change, there were now straight tonnage allowances for each instance of four types of inherent delays: roll change 230 tons, coil entered 22 tons, part coil cut 12 tons, and 16 tons for each splice in an entered coil. (9) Data sheets detailing these underlying components of the prior incentive rates covered two pages, as compared with nine for the new rates.

The standards emerging from these time studies of the new equipment, finally, were converted into money rates, in terms of "target earnings" deemed achievable by the crews when *full operating potential* of the improved mills would be reached. This was set at $4.83 for the roller for an average production of 75 tons of average gauge and width of steel. Management deemed $4.14 for the roller for 55 tons a fair immediate goal. These latter earnings, in management's judgment, should be achievable currently while the "bugs" still remain to be eliminated.

Excerpts from the cross-examination of these staff witnesses follow:

Stewart (u) [speaking to Rogers—a member of the time study staff]: Would you say that your findings were not doctored up by anyone after you handed them over?

Umpire: Your language is strong. I sense in these questions a basic suspicion of time study men. Time study is a professional field, a function of the larger profession of industrial engineering. "Doctoring" is strong language. A "crook" would get short shrift among these professionals and would be exposed by his own colleagues.

Guthrie (u) [with a smile in which all the union men joined]: Well, Doctor, I'm afraid you're a bit naive.

Stewart (u): I didn't really mean to suggest they were doing any crooked work. I meant: were their findings the final findings, or did somebody else work on them?

Rogers (m): These findings are just as we put them in.

Marshall (m): Maybe I can explain. Part of the job of the time study man is to attempt to detect whether the men are trying to put something over on *him;* and, when he finds that the case, that study is apt to be rejected *in toto,* completely. I believe a number of studies were rejected because it was obvious that the crews were doing that, "dogging it." The reason for the foreman's being there was that we couldn't make a study without his being there to assure some degree of cooperation with us.

Powell (m): That is right.

Adams (u) [to Marshall]: I would like to ask a question, and in such a way that it won't get under your skin. Is it true that, after the men have time studied a certain job, then, the powers that be go over the new rate and decide that it is too high and that it may be reduced downward, in spite of time studies?

Marshall (m): I would put it this way. These men are not the final arbiters. They prepare the data. It is reviewed by their superiors in the local plant. After that, I am sure it is no secret that a rate like this would be reviewed by the industrial engineering department at Conway [home office], and they will either approve or disapprove.

Adams (u): In other words, a rate could be reduced downward, if Conway thought it too high?

Marshall (m): It could, of course; just as it is frequently revised upward. You fellows wouldn't even know.

Adams (u): I didn't ask that question.

Marshall (m): I know you didn't ask it, but I am volunteering the information. The study is checked for accuracy, and the rate calculation is checked for accuracy.

FROM THE FRIDAY AFTERNOON SESSION

The company presented exhibits detailing, for the three mills, crew earnings and individual roller's earnings by quarters during the two years preceding the improvement program, during the time study period, and under the new rates. These exhibits showed that the men were not realizing the expected earnings under the new rates.

Excerpts from the record of the session follow:

Marshall (m): Now, as you will see, none of these rollers is averaging $4.14 per hour. Instead, they cluster strikingly around $3.50. Yet management set this current target of $4.142 by reviewing production during the year before conversion. At the average width and gauge of material then rolled, the mills produced 55 tons per hour. At that production and under the revised rates, the roller would now earn $4.142 per hour.

Further investigation showed management that, with the same type of equipment, our own Larkspur Plant and the Centerville Steel Company plant have regularly produced 55 tons per hour. Therefore, while our time study shows a higher ultimate potential, we should be now getting that production. And, at that production, the average earnings under the new rates are adequate and comply with the Agreement. Admittedly we are dealing with new equipment. The bugs have to be taken out. But, until we get the cooperation of these crews, we cannot determine how much the bugs contribute to the reduced production we are getting.

Stewart (u): Well, at the Borderton Plant of the Comerford Company, the skin mill rollers average between $900 and $1,000 per month at an average output of 35 tons per hour.

[Late in the afternoon, Mr. Marshall asked about the next hearing date.]

Guthrie (u): What do you mean, next date! We'll reconvene tomorrow. We're handling an emergency—or did you forget?

Marshall (m) [heatedly]: Tomorrow is Saturday, and the day after is Sunday. We've heard only the skin mill cases in two days—we have nine more to go. I'm fed up with emergencies at Halsey. You've been breathing down our necks on this all summer. I haven't had a vacation yet this year, thanks to you fellows. I'm not going to start Saturday and Sunday sessions!

Guthrie (u): Maybe I, too, am tired of being called back from vacation—to say nothing about nights and Saturdays and Sundays and holidays—to help end walkouts! We're trying to meet dissatisfaction here that has already produced walkouts. We don't want any more.

Marshall (m): The union is contractually pledged to eliminate illegal walkouts.

Guthrie (u): That's why we're using the grievance procedure as speedily as we can. Don't you want to meet the men's dissatisfaction with your new rates and crew changes?

Marshall (m): I don't want to remind you of the record of the strip mill at Halsey! Dissatisfied, indeed—well, it's certainly not the first time. I don't think yielding to the kind of pressure these crews have been applying is good labor relations.

Adams (u): As chairman of the grievance committee, I can tell you we had all better reduce all possible delays and go on with the hearings!

Marshall (m): Well, we might remember our manners and ask the umpire his convenience on Saturday—and [groaning] Sunday sessions!

Umpire: Well, it seems to me that nerves are already frazzled around here. And, if your other cases contain as large an area of disagreement on sheer matters of fact as these skin mill disputes, we won't finish, I'm afraid, by Sunday. But, at any rate, since I am here I shall be at your disposal—though I, too, can think of better week-end activities. The decision rests with you—mutually.

Guthrie (u): It's really for the good of all of us, Doug.

Marshall (m) [resignedly]: O.K.

III. The Tandem Mills

On Saturday morning, the dispute over revised incentive rates in the 75-inch tandem mill was presented. Formerly a three-stand mill, a fourth stand was added in July to raise rolling speed from a maximum of 600 to 2,000 feet per minute. According to company testimony, auxiliary equipment to reduce delays and increase efficiency included a new loading ramp, a coil positioner, a belt wrapper, tension meters between rolling stands, a discharge hoist, and a lengthened exit conveyer for finished coils.

After these changes were completed, time studies were launched. For the study period, the crews were paid the average of their earnings for the three prior months—$3.716 per hour for the roller, with corresponding averages for the rest of the crew. Production standards based upon the new equipment were prepared. Inherent delays were ascertained; allowances for personal time were set. The remaining productive time, per normal shift of 480 minutes, was determined; and the pounds per day, factored for characteristic widths and gauges at new mill rolling speeds, were worked out to yield new tables of pay tonnage factors. Indirect but recurrent production tasks were covered by measured pay-ton allowances. Production standards were then translated into new incentive rates. The underlying data sheets covered four pages as against one for the old rates. As in the skin mills, the hourly rate portion of total pay remained unchanged.

The new rates were submitted to the union on August 29. As the discussions proceeded, an error in the original computations was discovered, and the rates were corrected. The crews walked out over the revised rates [1] and were joined by the three skin mill crews, just as the tandem mill crews had earlier supported the skin mill stoppages. The grievance they filed was also expedited with those from the skin mills.

Excerpts from the record of the Saturday morning session follow:

Guthrie (u): Once again, Mr. Umpire, upon studying the revised rates, these crews came to the conclusion that they could not expect any increase over their previous earnings. The expected tonnages are obviously so high that it is almost impossible to attain them. In your tour yesterday, you probably noticed a number of placards giving the name of the crew and the "record" tonnage attained, that is when company expectations were met. There were only some five or six placards, so evidently such tonnages are quite an event. In other words, the goal that has been set by the company is much too high and the rates much too low. I'll call Mr. Ritchie, who has been a roller on the tandem mill for 15 years.

Ritchie (u): Our average used to be 56 tons an hour. Management says our average now should be 100 tons for $4.13 per hour for the roller and, when all the bugs are out, 120 tons to give the roller $4.67 per hour. I can't see more than 80 to 85 tons, as an average. And I hold the three top records listed on those placards.

These records were made by pushing everything we could. Everybody was really working his head off. The record is 1,039 tons per eight-hour turn on this new mill. Before it was re-equipped, the record was a little over 1,000 tons. To produce 1,039 tons, you have to take a lot of chances; and, when you take chances, you're still responsible for the steel, the equipment—and your crew!

Guthrie (u): Can you exceed 80 or 85 tons per hour in the near future?

Ritchie (u): Not unless they don't want good steel.

Guthrie (u): Are there still so-called bugs?

Ritchie (u): No, not many of a serious nature.

Marshall (m): It is always nice to be able to agree with the union. The company makes no charges of failure of the tandem mill crews to cooperate in trying to attain production. I have observed the plaques on the wall, and three out of six had Mr. Ritchie's name on them. [To Superintendent Cullom.] You have added another man to the crew, have you not?

Cullom (m): That is right, a sticker, because you have one more stand to watch. Then you have another man added at the delivery end of the mill to

---

[1] See Exhibit 3.

band coils and identify them. One feeder was removed, so the net addition is one man—seven instead of six.

Marshall (m): The effect of these changes is to increase tonnage in two ways: by speeding up the mill; and by adding auxiliary equipment to reduce effort.

Ritchie (u): What is it possible to roll on good steel—72" width, .035" gauge?

Cullom (m): A maximum of 1,500 feet per hour.

Ritchie (u): Even if water gets on it?

Cullom (m): No.

Ritchie (u): It is not possible to roll at 1,500 feet without getting water on it.

Cullom (m): At the present time, you are right.

Ritchie (u): Why is the rate so small on heavy gauge?

Cullom (m): You have to talk to the piece rate department on that. They made the study, Frank.

Ritchie (u): We have the rate. We can't talk to the piece rate department now.

Marshall (m): I now have the time studies. The mathematics are slightly different from the skin mills. Is there any reason for that, Mr. Rogers?

Rogers (m): Yes. When the rate was determined for the tandem mill, we were instructed by our Conway office to determine the allowances in a slightly different manner, which is a little more fair and proper than the previous system.

Marshall (m): By "fair and proper," do you mean liberal?

Rogers (m): Slightly more liberal.

Adams (u): There he goes again! You don't like what the man says, and you have to change his words!

Marshall (m): Now, we can go through the mathematics, unless it can be conceded that we do our arithmetic correctly.

Umpire: Let's wait before going through the mathematics, unless the union raises a question.

Marshall (m): For some time there has been a differential, unfavorable to the tandem mill, between their earnings and those on the skin mill. Part of our objective in setting these new rates was to partially eliminate that differential.

Ritchie (u): Mr. Marshall, you are not by any chance bringing the skin mill scale down to meet us in the tandem mill, are you?

Marshall (m): No. If the skin mill crews produce what they should, they will make more money. We also expect you to.

Ritchie (u): We are producing, you admit—yet our pay check shows no more money.

Marshall (m): At average width and gauge, our studies show that you should be ultimately able to roll approximately 120 tons. And I might say, before the union expresses incredulity, that our Larkspur Plant, with a similar tandem mill, is at present averaging 111 tons.

We regard this figure of 100 tons an hour as comparable to 55 tons an hour on the skin mill—both current achievable averages. We set a rate so that, at 100 tons an hour, the roller would earn $4.13—the same as at the skin mills for 55 tons. The rate was recomputed on discovering an error in the width and the gauge used. That happened after this grievance was appealed to arbitration. Mr. Powell explained this to the stewards, and this correction has been put into effect. [The corrected rates are those in Exhibit 3.] The members of the crews are to be paid retroactively, reflecting that correction.

Setting rates, believe me, is a complicated business. It is as complicated as the devil.

Ritchie (u): We admit that, but we know that Interstate never goes overboard. It always squeezes on rates.

Marshall (m): Our people might question that statement, for we try to do a good job.

Ritchie (u): For Interstate!

Marshall (m): We try to be fair with the men, too.

Ritchie (u): When you want twice as much steel for the same money!

Marshall (m): What does twice as much steel cost the company? And we are not asking it for the same money. . . . I am getting into the philosophy of capital investment, which may be far afield. I would like to talk about this over a glass of beer.

The general philosophy of this thing is outside the scope of this meeting. No man ever gets what he thinks he is worth, and an argument as to how much a particular job should be paid is perfectly fruitless.

But these rates are set so that your earnings are going to be increased a minimum of 30 cents an hour. And we know by time study that that can go to 80 cents an hour, and we hope you will make a hell of a lot more.

[The remaining eight cases were heard during the Sunday sessions, which continued to 7 P.M. One protested "management's elimination of the jobs of inspectors, testers, and tester helpers on the skin mills and the assignment of their duties to the roller, the foreman, and the utility man."]

IV. The Interim Decision

The week following these proceedings, the umpire submitted an "interim decision," excerpts from which follow:

. . . Ordinarily, I would wait, as is customary, for the record to be typed and the briefs to be submitted before addressing myself to the issues involved in all these cases. I am departing, however, from the usual procedure . . . partly because of the emotional atmosphere surrounding these grievances, but, even more, because adequate consideration requires a groundwork of agreed fact, which the hearing made clear to me simply does not now exist. . . .

. . . There is no dispute regarding the right of management under the Agreement, as set forth in Section 1 of Article V, to adjust "existing incentive wage rates because of" technological change. But the union contends that the new rates thus inaugurated on the skin mills violate Section 4 of this same Article V, which reads, in its relevant clauses, as follows:

(*a*) The Management shall develop such new incentive wage rate in accordance with the usual practice at the time in effect with it for establishing incentive wage rates at such Plant or Works and on the principle that the new incentive wage rate shall, giving due effect to the change or other events by reason of which the new incentive wage rate shall have been established, be in equitable relationship to the incentive wage rate which it replaced and provide equitable compensation. . . .

The union's case pivots on the two arguments that the new rates are not in equitable relationship to the incentive rates they replaced and that they do not provide equitable compensation.

. . . . .

Mere distillations of the positions which the parties have taken hardly convey the distance between them. Because they are so far apart, I would have to study in precise detail all the voluminous evidence before I could arrive at a decision. It is precisely to avoid otherwise inevitable delays that I am directing the company to undertake a fresh study for determining the new incentive rates to be paid to the crews on the skin mills. This study shall be considered and discussed with the union, as stipulated in Article V, Section 4, of the Agreement. Obviously, time will be saved if the parties could agree on any phases of the studies already made. I therefore urge a re-examination and a prior joint determination, if possible, on which aspects are to be restudied and which need not be reviewed. The study should be so set up as to preclude the challenges already made: what work must be observed to yield typical assignments; what delays are to be accounted for, and so forth. Last but not least, the final figures and methods for determining individual earnings should be as simple and intelligible as possible.

I need not point out that the men have a responsibility for securing accurate results. I am not now deciding whether or not they have resorted to a slowdown in the past. But I must request—indeed, direct—that there be no diminution in normal effort and attention to the job during the period of effectuating the interim award for the purposes of a mutually desired fair decision.

I should like to report within four weeks upon the result of these studies and conferences.

The grievance arising out of new rates on the tandem mill is similar to the grievances filed on the skin mills, with two important exceptions. For one thing, management does not charge a slowdown. For another, management has already instituted an upward revision of the original "new rates."

The men complain that their present rates are inequitable within the meanings of the contract, since they do not realize the earnings which prevailed before. Here, again, there are differences as to facts—as to the potential output of the reconstructed mill, etc.

Although I am directing that new studies be made here, too, I am not certain that they need be as comprehensive as those on the skin mills. . . . But earnings experience under those new rates should obviously be reviewed. Apparently the anticipated results of the rate increases have not yet shown themselves in payroll data.

If I hesitate to suggest a complete new study on the tandem mill, I shall, nevertheless, direct the parties to review jointly its various new elements and phases and to make fresh studies on points of disagreements. The parties are to report to me within four weeks. . . .

V. SUBSEQUENT DEVELOPMENTS

A second arbitration hearing was held on December 7. Excerpts of the record of the proceedings follow:

Marshall (m): Dr. Benson, we are glad to report progress. Of the 11 grievances brought before you in September, only 5 are left. Five were adjusted by agreement; one was withdrawn by the union. There remain for decision, therefore, the rate disputes and the protests of the inspectors and testers.

Following your interim decision, management and the union held two meetings with the skin mill crews. We reviewed the studies. The union challenged the accuracy of the inherent delays and the coil entry allowance. All other data were conceded to be accurate and reasonable.

After the first meeting, the company re-examined the protested standards by further time studies. Those studies showed justification for liberalizing the allowances for coils entered from 22 to 25 tons and for spliced coils from 16 to 17 tons. At a later meeting with the union, we proposed to make rate adjustments to reflect the new standards, but the union rejected the proposed rate schedule.[1]

With respect to the tandem mill, although we have met twice, the union still insists that these new rates do not stand in equitable relationship to the rates they replaced and do not provide reasonable compensation. Yet, here too, the facts are undisputed. Prior to the addition of the fourth stand to the mill, the average straight-time hourly earnings of the roller approximated $3.71 per hour. The roller should eventually earn under the new rates $4.467 per hour. The company attempted to increase levels of earnings for the tandem mill employees, in order to reduce the differential which existed between their earnings and the earnings of the skin mill crews.

And so, Dr. Benson, we are asking you to carry us forward to a fair settlement.

[The discussions at the hearing revealed the same differences as at the September hearings.]

The company submitted its brief on February 19. Counsel also submitted hourly earnings' data for the rollers. The brief pointed out that, if the skin mill crews had accepted the upward revisions proposed by the company after the interim decisions, their average earnings per hour would be 7 cents higher at the time of the submission of the brief.

The union did not submit a brief.

. . . .

On March 19, the umpire sent the following letter to Mr. Marshall:

I should like both additional data and clarifications, as follows:
(1) Further data on "earnings experience" of the rollers in the four mills involved for February and as far into March as is feasible.
(2) Am I right in assuming that the parties agreed that the earnings experience of the rollers indicates the trend of earnings for all crew members?
(3) One of the aims of management in setting rates for the tandem mill is to narrow the gap between the earnings of the tandem mill rollers and the skin mill rollers. The respective average hourly earnings prior to the change-over were $3.71

---

[1] The upward revisions proposed by the company would have raised the bonus portion of the roller's incentive rate from $0.00586 to $0.00606 per pay ton and of the other crewmen from $0.00336 to $0.00348 per pay ton.

for tandem mill rollers and $3.91 for skin mill rollers. The target is now set at average hourly earnings of $4.13 and $4.14 currently, and ultimately, at $4.46 and $4.83. On the basis of the latter target, the differential works out to approximately 8%, as compared to approximately 5% before the change-over. Will the parties clarify this situation for me, so that I can understand it better in terms both of (a) management's aim to narrow the earnings gap and (b) the contractual requirements regarding equitable compensation and rates?

(4) Have the "bugs," alluded to at the hearings as militating against full capacity utilization of the skin mills and the tandem mills, respectively, been eliminated? If not, what bugs still remain?

On May 2, Mr. Marshall sent his reply:

I regret the long delay. I have been ill and out of the office.

(1) Enclosed are separate sheets which contain further data, complete through April 22, on the earnings experience of the rollers on the skin mills and the tandem mill.[1]

(2) The earnings experience of the rollers indicates the trend of earnings for the other crew members. . . .

(3) While the ultimate targets for the skin mill crews and for the tandem mill crew are farther apart than the former differential in earnings, it is not expected that the differences between the rates will be reflected exactly in differences between earnings. It is extremely difficult to reduce differentials in the earnings of two groups of employees working on different operations and producing different products. Such differentials are not always traceable to the rates themselves. Variations in efforts and in skills of employees are also reflected in earnings.

As we explained, in establishing the new rates, management tempered its judgment by experience which operators of other similar equipment had reported to it. Other steel plants with similar skin mills reported that their average performance was considerably below the performance which the Halsey time studies indicated was possible. Mills which operated tandem mills comparable to the 75-inch tandem mill had experienced average production much closer to the time study findings. Therefore, the management was guided by that reported experience and established the incentive pay rates for the skin mills at a somewhat higher level than the rates established for the tandem mill. We believe that the management's judgment in that respect has been shown to be sound.

Large differentials appear between earnings on different mills, and the reasons for such differentials are difficult to explain. The mechanical characteristics and equipment of all three of the skin mills are substantially similar and they all roll the same types of materials and produce the same sort of products.

However, it will be found that the earnings of the rollers on the tandem mill normally fall within the same range as the earnings of the skin mill rollers. At times the earnings of the rollers on the tandem mill have been higher than the earnings of rollers on the skin mills. That indicates that the practical results of the rates have approximately eliminated any material difference which previously existed between earnings on the skin mills and on the tandem mills.

It is the company's position that it is unnecessary for the umpire to make a finding as to whether the company has succeeded in eliminating the earnings differential between the tandem mill rollers and the skin mill rollers. The test by which the umpire must measure the new rates is set forth in Section 4 of Article V of the Agreement, which requires that "the new incentive wage rate shall, giving due effect to the change or other events by reason of which the incentive wage rate shall have been established, be in equitable relationship to the incentive wage rate which

---

[1] See Exhibits 4, 5, 6, and 7, pp. 146–149. These tables were drawn up by the umpire to summarize 66 pages of figures submitted by Mr. Marshall.

it replaced and provide equitable compensation." Each rate schedule must be tested individually and separately against the old rate which it replaced.

If the management has erred in any respect, we believe it has been on the side of excessive generosity. The testimony in the hearing showed little, if any, increase in workload on the employees. However, giving practical recognition to the fact that the mill crews were expected to turn out substantially higher production, the management incorporated into the new incentive rate structures provision for large increases in incentive earnings.

(4) The "bugs" have now been removed, in the opinion of the management. There still remains the possibility that the upward trend in production may continue and that the mills have not yet found their ultimate normal level. While that is not strictly a "bug," it is a factor in assessing the effect of the passage of more time upon the earnings of the employees under the rates in question.

EXHIBIT I

EXTRACTS FROM THE AGREEMENT

Any new incentive shall be established in accordance with the following procedure:

1. The management shall develop the incentive and furnish to the steward . . . such information . . . as shall reasonably be required to enable him to understand the new incentive. After notifying such steward of the date on which the incentive shall be made effective, the management may put the incentive into effect.

2. Any incentive may be installed on a trial or experimental basis, provided the management and steward so agree. . . .

3. The union may, at any time after 30 days but not later than 60 days following the effective date of the new incentive, initiate a grievance regarding such incentive. . . .

4. If the management . . . shall cancel an existing incentive applicable to any work prior to the establishment of the new incentive which is to replace it . . . during the period preceding the establishment of the new incentive on such work each employee who shall perform such work shall be paid, for all such work performed by him, at an interim hourly rate that shall be equal to the average hourly earnings . . . of all who were assigned to the job on which the work was performed during the three (3) month period next preceding the cancellation or nonpayment of such existing incentive or it shall be such other interim hourly rate as shall be agreed to by the management and the union steward for the applicable department. . . .

EXHIBIT 2

PRIOR AND NEW RATES

Skin Mills Nos. 2, 3, and 5

Position	Hourly Rate Portion (Unchanged)	Incentive (Bonus) Portion	
		Prior Rates Per Pay Ton *	New Rates Per Pay Ton †
Roller	$1.940	$.0457	$.00586
Sticker	1.400	.0252	.00336
Catcher	1.405	.0252	.00336
Inspector	1.425	.0252	.00336
Tester	1.405	.0252	.00336
Tester's Helper	1.400	.0252	.00336
	[Job added after con- version		
Utility Man	1.400]	. . . . .	.00336

* Pay tonnage before mill improvement equaled total net tons of finished product rolled, as shown by the daily production report, multiplied by tabulated factors for coil widths and gauges, plus an allowance of 25 pay tons for each roll change.

† In computing pay tonnage after mill improvement the total net tons of each of four types of finished product was multiplied by its particular new series of factors for width and gauge. Allowance for roll changes was increased, and new allowances were added for coils entered, part coils cut, and spliced stock coils.

EXHIBIT 3

PRIOR AND NEW EFFECTIVE RATES

75-inch Tandem Mill

Position	Hourly Rate Portion (Unchanged)	Incentive (Bonus) Portion	
		Prior Rates Per Pay Ton *	New Rates Per Pay Ton †
Roller	$1.980	$.0286	$.00422
Asst. Roller	1.690	.0215	.00317
1st Feeder	1.455	.0186	.00255
Catcher	1.535	.0186	.00274
Feeder (2)	1.280	.0129	.00190
Sticker	(New Job at 1.535)	—	.00274
Bander	(New Job at 1.280)	—	.00190

* Pay tonnage before mill improvement equaled actual weight of coils rolled factored for width; plus allowances totaling 20.16%.
Four widths were factored as follows:
All coils 47″ and wider to be base.
All coils 40″ and up to 47″ to be base plus 10%.
All coils 30″ and up to 40″ to be base plus 30%.
All coils under 30″ wide to be base plus 50%.

† Pay tonnage after mill improvement also equaled total net tons rolled but factored for gauge and width as determined by Table of Factors (27 gauges and 14 widths). Allowances were increased to 29.1%.

EXHIBIT 4

SKIN MILL ROLLERS' HOURLY AVERAGE EARNINGS UNDER THE NEW RATES

By Mill and Period

Weeks Ending	No. 2 Skin Mill (Prior Av. $3.91)	No. 3 Skin Mill (Pr. Av. $2.89–$2.99) *	No. 5 Skin Mill (Pr. Av. $4.28)	All Skin Mills (Study Av. $3.91)
Oct. 8 (Before Interim Decision)	$3.595	$3.442	$3.560	$3.532
Oct. 15–Dec. 3 (Between Interim Decision and 2d Arbitration Hearing)	3.782	3.640	3.816	3.746
(After 2d Arbitr. Hearing)				
Dec. 10–Dec. 31	3.862	3.841	4.082	3.928
Jan. 7–Jan. 28	4.114	4.002	4.092	4.069
Feb. 4–Feb. 25	4.185	3.941	4.151	4.097
Mar. 4–Mar. 25	4.454	4.179	4.201	4.281
Apr. 1–Apr. 22	4.347	4.162	4.484	4.374

* Job rated, $2.89; personal rated, $2.99.

EXHIBIT 5

SKIN MILL ROLLERS—HOURLY EARNINGS EXPERIENCE

Roller-Turns Yielding Hourly Earnings below or above
Prior and Target Averages

Period and Total Man-Turns (Weeks Ending)	Roller-Turns Yielding Hourly Earnings At No. 2 Mill (Prior Mill Average $3.91)								Peak Hourly Earnings
	$3.91 (Interim Study Guarantee) or Less		Over $3.91 but Under $4.14		$4.14 (Target at 55 TPH) to Under $4.83		$4.83 (Final Target at 75 TPH) and Over		
	No.	%	No.	%	No.	%	No.	%	
Oct. 8 (18 Man-Turns)	16	88.9	1	5.5	1	5.5	0	0	$4.038
Oct. 15–Dec. 4 (119 Man-Turns)	73	64.6	28	24.7	12	10.6	0	0	4.470
Dec. 11–Dec. 31 (48 Man-Turns)	27	56.2	12	25.0	9	18.8	0	0	4.606
Jan. 7–Jan. 28 (56 Man-Turns)	16	28.6	13	23.2	25	44.6	2	3.6	5.298
Feb. 4–Feb. 25 (55 Man-Turns)	13	23.6	9	16.3	31	56.4	2	3.6	5.104
Mar. 4–Mar. 25 (57 Man-Turns)	4	7.0	8	14.0	35	61.4	10	17.6	5.892
Apr. 1–Apr. 22 (58 Man-Turns)	13	22.4	7	12.1	31	53.4	7	12.1	5.486
At No. 3 Mill (Prior Mill Average $2.89–$2.99)									
Oct. 8 (17 Man-Turns)	17	100	0	0	0	0	0	0	3.741
Oct. 15–Dec. 4 (119 Man-Turns)	97 (1 under $2.99)	81.5	16	13.4	6	5.0	0	0	4.472
Dec. 11–Dec. 31 (54 Man-Turns)	29 (1 under $2.99)	53.6	13	24.1	11	20.4	1	1.8	5.260
Jan. 7–Jan. 28 (52 Man-Turns)	31	59.6	14	26.9	7	13.5	0	0	4.464
Feb. 4–Feb. 25 (53 Man-Turns)	25	47.2	13	24.5	15	28.3	0	0	4.633
Mar. 4–Mar. 25 (54 Man-Turns)	14	25.9	12	22.2	23	42.6	5	9.2	5.266
Apr. 1–Apr. 22 (32 Man-Turns)	10	31.2	3	9.4	16	50.0	3	9.4	5.666
At No. 5 Mill (Prior Mill Average $4.28)									
Oct. 8 (18 Man-Turns)	15	83.3	1	5.6	2	11.1	0	0	4.584
Oct. 9–Dec. 4 (125 Man-Turns)	75	60.0	21	16.8	26	20.8	3	2.4	5.114
Dec. 11–Dec. 31 (54 Man-Turns)	24	44.4	8	14.8	16	29.6	6	11.1	5.172
Jan. 7–Jan. 28 (56 Man-Turns)	23	41.1	10	17.8	19	34.0	4	7.1	5.400
Feb. 4–Feb. 25 (53 Man-Turns)	14	26.4	9	17.0	22	41.5	4	7.5	5.072
Mar. 4–Mar. 25 (59 Man-Turns)	15	25.4	13	22.0	26	44.1	5	8.5	5.405
Apr. 1–Apr. 22 (63 Man-Turns)	7	11.1	9	14.3	35	55.6	12	19.0	6.143

EXHIBIT 6

SKIN MILLS COMPARED WITH 75-INCH TANDEM MILL

Rollers' Average Hourly Earnings under the New Rates

Period (Weeks Ending)	All Converted Skin Mills Prior Average $3.91 Interim Target $4.14 Eventual Target $4.83	75-Inch Tandem Mill Prior Average $3.71 Interim Target $4.13 Eventual Target $4.467
Oct. 8 (Before Interim Decision)	$3.532	$3.827
Oct. 15–Dec. 3 (Between Interim Decision and 2d Arbitration Hearing)	3.746	3.870
(After 2d Arbitration Hearing) Dec. 10–Dec. 31	3.928	3.795
Jan. 7–Jan. 28	4.069	4.117
Feb. 4–Feb. 25	4.097	3.955
Mar. 4–Mar. 25	4.281	4.222
Apr. 1–Apr. 22	4.374	4.205

EXHIBIT 7

TANDEM MILL ROLLERS—HOURLY EARNINGS EXPERIENCE

Roller-turns Yielding Hourly Earnings below or above
Prior and Target Averages

| Period and Total Man-Turns (Weeks Ending) | Roller-Turns Yielding Hourly Earnings | | | | | | | | Peak Hourly Earnings |
| | $3.71 (Prior Average) or less | | Above $3.71 but Below $4.13 | | $4.13 (Target at 100 TPH) but Below $4.467 | | $4.467 (Final Target at 120 TPH) or over | | |
	No.	%	No.	%	No.	%	No.	%	
(Before Interim Decision) Oct. 8 (21 Man-Turns)	11	52.4	3	14.3	4	19.0	3	14.3	$4.827
(Bt. Int. Decision & 2d Hearing) Oct. 8–Dec. 4 (141 Man-Turns)	45	31.9	66	46.8	22	17.0	8	5.8	5.120
After 2d Hearing) Dec. 4–Dec. 31 (65 Man-Turns)	25	38.5	32	49.2	8	12.3	1	1.5	4.752
Jan. 7–Jan. 28 (70 Man-Turns)	9	12.8	29	41.4	21	30.0	11	15.7	5.109
Feb. 4–Feb. 25 (64 Man-Turns)	16	25.0	26	40.6	16	25.0	6	9.3	5.136
Mar. 4–Mar. 25 (58 Man-Turns)	6	10.3	19	32.8	18	31.0	15	25.8	5.368
Apr. 1–Apr. 22 (46 Man-Turns)	4	8.7	11	23.9	20	43.4	11	23.9	4.990

DISCUSSION QUESTIONS

1. Make a step-by-step analysis of management's strategy and tactics in overcoming the resistance to the new equipment in these mills.

2. Interpret the umpire's actions in handling this case.

3. What decision would you consider to be equitable for the skin mill? For the tandem mill?

THE FLETCHER COMPANY

A LONG-SERVICE EMPLOYEE IN A CHANGING JOB STRUCTURE

Andrei M. Basaryck, combination welder in the electrical department of the Fletcher Company, entered a grievance claiming he had suffered a reduction in pay despite the contractual provisions "freezing" the established wage structure for the currency of the union agreement. Arbitration proceedings ultimately were held at which the following representatives were in attendance:

For the Company	For the Union
Martin T. Mallory and John C. Worth, Counsel from Legal Staff	Daniel Kronan, District Representative
Edward G. Bennett, Director of Labor Relations, Bridgton Plant	Howell Lynn, Staff Representative, Bridgton Local
Paul Ashford, Foreman, Welding Department	Joseph Sladek, Staff Representative, Bridgton Local
Henry Fairbanks, Superintendent, Rate Setting Department	Peter MacGregor, Shop Steward, Electrical Department

Mallory (m): This is a grievance of A. M. Basaryck, combination welder, concerning his pay rate. Our employees are paid on an incentive system. Piece rates are based on standards set by time study engineers. Certain tasks, however, cannot be piece-rated because varying conditions make it impossible to estimate accurately *in advance* the volume of work and the amount of time they will require of the employees. Such tasks include plant repairs that must be expedited, jobs in which wide variations of materials occur, and work in which exceptional conditions are encountered.

Employees assigned to such tasks are paid guaranteed minimum earnings for time spent in their performance. If, however, supervision deems the work of outstanding emergency character, or done under exacting conditions requiring unusual skill and ability, or completed in remarkably short time, it may recommend compensation *in excess* of the guaranteed minimum. In shop slang, the excesses above this minimum guarantee are called "bogies."

This set-up will become clear as we discuss Basaryck's grievance, a copy of which is presented in Exhibit 1. Exhibit 2 is the minutes of the step 4 meeting. The union did not sign those minutes.

Kronan (u): That will be explained.

Exhibit 1

The Fletcher Company

REQUEST FOR ADJUSTMENT OF GRIEVANCE

Name of Employee *A. M. Basaryck*	Name of Foreman *Paul Ashford*
Department Symbol and Number *GC–2182*	Date Grievance Presented to Foreman *May 17, —*
Occupation *Combination Welder*	Name of Department Steward *Peter MacGregor*

Employee's Statement for Grievance: *I am a combination welder, and for my added skill the company for some time paid me the highest bogey #31, but recently for no reason at all the company put me on lower rated bogey #28. As a result, I have suffered a wage cut of 3.75 cents per hour. There has been no change in my duties. Adjustment of this grievance should be retroactive.*

A. M. Basaryck   5–17–
Signature of Employee   Date

Disposition of Grievance by Foreman: *The method of computing this man's earnings has not been changed.*

Paul Ashford   5–22–
Signature of Foreman   Date

Disposition of Grievance by Superintendent of Department: *Investigation shows no change in method of pay for the work performed by the welder. The present bogey #28 has been that to which he has charged his time since June of last year. Bogey #31 provides for welding of a different class.*

G. D. Mueller   5–31–
Signature of Superintendent   Date

Date of Appeal by Grievance Committee to Management's Representative: *6–7–*

Exhibit 2

The Fletcher Company

Excerpt from Minutes of Step 4 Meeting, September 28
(Signed for management, October 9. Not Signed for union.)

Grievance No. 885–1454

A. M. Basaryck, a combination welder, stated he was taken off the highest-rated bogey, no. 31, and placed on a lower-rated bogey, no. 28, with no subsequent change in his duties and that as a result he suffered a reduction in earnings of about 3.75 cents per hour. He requests that he be placed back on the highest paying bogey retroactively.

The union appreciates that a change in the number assigned the bogey which Basaryck is paid has no significance; that the issue is the request that Basaryck be paid the highest paying bogey, and that he has heretofore been paid the highest paying bogey but is not now, although he was promised by Superintendent Mueller that he would be paid the highest bogey, in recognition of his skill, if he stayed in the shop rather than going out on piece-rated jobs.

The company pointed out that Basaryck is not doing piece-rated work; that he has a minimum guarantee and is often given, on the recommendation of supervision, a bogey in excess of that guarantee because of the nature of the work he performs. The company contended that Basaryck continues to be paid the third highest bogey in the department. The company stated it had not investigated the union allegation that Basaryck was promised the highest bogey by supervision because it did not know who was alleged to have made the promise, but that it would investigate now because Mr. Mueller is alleged to have made the promise. Such investigation found that Mr. Mueller did not recall promising Basaryck the highest bogey.

Mr. Bennett told Mr. Lynn on the phone on October 9, that the company, in the interest of good collective bargaining, was willing to pay Basaryck retroactively the money difference between bogey 31 and bogey 28 with the understanding that in the future he would not necessarily be kept on his usual work in the shop and he would be instructed to charge his time against piecework or against the bogey applicable to the work he was assigned. This disposition of the grievance was satisfactory to the union.

Lynn (u): Mr. Umpire, we are bringing this grievance under that article of the agreement which provides that rates remain in effect during the life of the agreement. This employee has always been paid the highest welding bogey. Management gave him a lower bogey, but used his skill the same as in the past.

Kronan (u): I might add that management in order to compensate Basaryck for his extraordinary skill had promised to pay him the highest bogey in the plant. I do not recall when management decided to change that policy. But the change resulted in loss of earnings for Basaryck. When he filed a grievance, management decided to make up his loss, with the proviso that from then on the man would be sent out of the department like any other welder. We found out, however, that he is still doing the same work; his status did not change as far as performance was concerned.

The adjustment made by the company covered losses sustained by Basaryck over a 17 months' period and amounted to a total of $44.58. However, we still feel that under the agreement the method of computing his pay should not change because his job did not change. He should still get the highest bogey. That, in brief, sums up our case.

Umpire: All right. Mr. Mallory.

Mallory (m): That this grievance was appealed to arbitration is a complete surprise. The step 4 minutes set forth the terms of settlement reached by the company and the union. The union has cited the amount of the payments already made to this employee—$44.58 for 17 months. We were informed that that settlement was satisfactory.

In the step no. 4 meeting, the primary argument of the union was that this employee was required to remain in the shop and was unable to work on piece-rate or bogies outside the shop on which he could have earned more. When the settlement was made, Basaryck was told that hereafter he could be assigned to higher-rated work—piece rates or higher bogies, both outside and in the shop—in order to increase the level of his earnings. But the employee prefers not to perform any piece-rate work or any outside work. He prefers the type of work that he has done the past few years and he is being paid in accordance with that type of work.

Kronan (u): Management assumed that the union was satisfied with the company's adjustment, but we did not notify the company officially or otherwise that the grievance was settled.

Now we have here the Shop Steward, Pete MacGregor, who knows Basaryck and his job. Where do you work, Pete?

MacGregor (u): In the electrical repair shop—for nineteen years. I knew Andy Basaryck many years, ever since I have been in the shop. He has been there many years before me, about 30 years. Is that right?

Ashford (m): About 28 years.

MacGregor (u): Andy is considered a special man. He has been kept in the shop because whenever any job that no other welder can handle comes in, Andy is called upon regardless of what part of the plant it is in. Andy is a combination welder—an electrical welder, an acetylene welder, and I don't know what he doesn't do. He possesses outstanding skill and for that reason, to my understanding, Andy has been promised the highest bogey. He has been kept in the shop not as a worker but practically as a leader, even giving out different kinds of wires to the other welders. He tests plates of any welders that are learning to be welders. Andy is the one who gives them the test to go to the shipyards. Andy was always a very valuable man and, to my understanding, he was promised the highest bogey for his services to the company. And then, every week his wages became a little less and he made his complaint time after time to his foreman, to the superintendent, and then back to the foreman, and nobody did anything about it. Finally, he came to the union, and the union took the grievance up.

Andy himself was the first welder foreman in the plant. But he doesn't speak English very well, so they put another man in charge. I dare say (and Mr. Bennett and the company officials know this) that when any tough job came up, the foreman had to go to Andy. Now after all these years, he is told he can go out and work piecework with the rest of the straight electrical welders. That is an insult. They tell him, "You go out and climb on the shifter house jobs." The man is getting old now; he can't climb like the young fellows, but he can still use his special skill for special jobs.

I feel keenly that Andy deserves consideration for his skill. The company has been using that skill and the man was kept in the department under a definite promise made to him. We have a low base rate in welding, only 54 cents. That is why they promised Andy, "We are going to keep you on the highest bogey." Why now, all of a sudden, does the company make a change in the method of computing his pay?

Mallory (m): First, I would like to call on Mr. Bennett to testify with respect to the agreement reached at the step 4 meeting.

Bennett (m): At step 4, one of the company's main contentions was that this man should be treated as other welders. If he feels that he has been required to stay in the shop and other opportunities have been withheld from him, the company would see he got the same opportunities as other welders. But we claimed he wasn't due payment other than the bogey given for the type of work he had been doing. The union took the position, "Up to now he has been working under an agreement that he would be paid the highest bogey." I stated that if anybody has made promises, we would pay exactly what was promised.

I couldn't find anybody who had made promises to Andy. I reported that, but the feeling still seemed to prevail, particularly in Andy's mind, that he had been given some promise. Andy seemed so sincerely convinced that I finally decided there was certainly some honest mistaken belief in a promise. Andy seemed to feel that we had broken faith; so I said that the company would grant there was some misunderstanding. We would accordingly pay him the difference between what he had earned and what he would have earned under the highest bogey from the time that welders working in the shifter house were given higher bogeys than any other welders. That was about 17 months to date, and came to a total of $44.58. But from now on there must be no further misunderstanding. He must understand he earns whatever piece rate or bogey is paid for the work he is assigned. If he is so competent, he will make the maximum earnings.

I contacted Mr. Lynn, and certainly I had every reason to believe that this proposed settlement was satisfactory. We notified Andy that we would pay what he felt had been promised, but from now on he wasn't working under any promise. My understanding with Mr. Lynn was so definite that I ordered Andy paid. I was very much surprised when the union finally objected to the minutes. I talked to Mr. Lynn again. He said, "Well, Basaryck still isn't satisfied." But unless the whole grievance was being settled, there was no point in the company's making payment.

Mallory (m): Now, Mr. Ashford, will you tell us something about the job duties of this employee?

Ashford (m): I don't think in a department of our size, we are limited to any one man for particular jobs. Basaryck's ability in welding years ago, when there weren't many with experience, made him a valuable man. But now I don't know of any specific job on which we have to call on Andy for information or ability. We have numerous other men who can do the same as Andy. Also Andy recently spoiled several jobs; we gave those jobs to other men. He took care of glass, but that job too has been taken away. We buy glass now instead of Andy cutting it. He fixes welding clamps, which is not skilled. He bundles wire, which also isn't skilled. That job has been cut to the minimum now and almost eliminated by sending our wire to different departments.

Andy has been asked on numerous occasions, when he felt treated unjustly, to just walk over a few feet and take a piece-rate job to make more money. He said he didn't want that. I gathered from Andy that he didn't know why they brought this grievance up again. He was content. He didn't want to go outside; he wanted to remain in the shop. I would like to say that Andy's welding work doesn't amount to very much at all. He is more or less of a handy man now.

Mallory (m): How much time would you say Andy spends welding?

Ashford (m): If Andy does one hour a day actual welding, he is doing a lot. He now does general utility work, he takes care of minor jobs. We have gotten out of the stage where we have to rely on Andy or any one man. Our outfit now is capable of handling even the most skilled jobs.

Mallory (m): I want to submit extracts of a letter dated October 18 from Mr. Kronan, which deals with the union's refusal to sign the minutes:

> The union refuses to sign the minutes of the 4th step meeting held on September 28. The union is contending against management for discriminating against A. M. Basaryck.
> In a telephone conversation on October 9, Mr. Lynn was informed by Mr. Bennett that this grievance would be taken care of properly. But since this conversation, the union finds that Mr. Mueller and Mr. Ashford have taken a bad attitude toward the employee. The union accordingly contends that this grievance is not properly settled.

Kronan (u): Did you say, Mr. Ashford, that Andy was valuable in the past, but now you have skilled people that can perform the job that Andy previously performed?

Ashford (m): He is an old hand. Andy was a one-man welding department years back.

Kronan (u): Didn't Andy break in many of the welders, including foremen, like yourself?

Ashford (m): Not foremen. He did help new welders get ready for the tests I gave them, but they performed their own work. I would inspect it and see whether the results were satisfactory. Andy does not qualify to pass such men. That is my job.

Kronan (u): How long have you been a foreman?

Ashford (m): Six years.

Kronan (u): During that time Andy was paid the highest welding bogey in the plant?

Ashford (m): I knew he was near the top.

Kronan (u): Andy was in the shop before you became a foreman?

Ashford (m): Oh, yes.

Kronan (u): Sladek, do you know anything about this case?

Sladek (u): Yes. Mr. Ashford stated that Andy fixes welding clamps and bundles wires. He didn't tell you that armatures have to be built up on the shafts, welded both electrically and with acetylene. Mr. Ashford likewise states that today he has any number of men with the same ability as Andy. Maybe so, but they certainly are never around to do the tough work. He claims that Andy spoils jobs. Is there any man who doesn't spoil a job occasionally?

It was stated that Andy does very little welding at times. In the electrical department where Andy works and Mr. Ashford is supervisor, they do all the repair work for the plant. Any shaft that wears down is sent there. That work is set up on a platform above the shop and the only one I ever saw up there working was Andy. That has always been Andy's job.

Kronan (u): With reference to the letter presented by Mr. Mallory, it was sent because Andy was threatened. The superintendent and Andy's foreman, Mr. Ashford, both told Andy, "You will be sorry for what you have done, filing the grievance."

Mallory (m): Mr. Ashford, was this fellow threatened?

Ashford (m): I can't recall saying anything like that.

Mallory (m): Was Andy told that he should no longer feel restricted to work in the electrical shop? He could work outside and could be assigned to piece-rate work in order to increase his earnings?

Ashford (m): Yes, emphatically.

Mallory (m): Mr. Ashford, Mr. Sladek has been describing work that Andy does at various times.

Ashford (m): He referred to the small armature shafts that we do up on the welding balcony. I don't know where it would require any special skill that Andy has. As a matter of fact, there are numerous men who do that, maybe not numerous, but we have two or three.

Bennett (m): Emphasis has been put on the fact that Andy is still in the shop doing the work he has done in the past. My understanding is that he is there by choice. We haven't required him to go outside when he had a preference to stay in the shop. Certainly he should have understood that he would get the same rate for the jobs he was doing as everybody else gets for the same kind of work. There is no reason for perpetuating a preferential rate for this man, especially when all the past reasons for doing that have been eliminated.

Mallory (m): Mr. Fairbanks is our expert on rate structure.

Fairbanks (m): You have heard a lot about this man's change of pay, supposedly. About two years ago the company and the union held a general discussion on welding "bogies." A proposal was made that the company set a list of minimums for each bogey on work done by men who did not move around the shop from job to job—where the man always did about the same kind of work. The rates were posted on the bulletin board and the union accepted those minimums. This employee, known as "Big" Andy, received the highest minimum in effect at the time this list was posted and agreed upon.

Since then, however, certain bogies have increased in value. For instance, the shifter house, where they do the locomotive repair, came to be a particularly vital spot and yielded, therefore, the highest bogey; blast furnace repairs yielded the second highest welding bogey. As the importance of some welders' positions increased, they were also increased in money— in bogies. "Big" Andy stayed the same, but groups (there are more than just individual men) went ahead of "Big" Andy. That didn't mean that "Big" Andy went down. Certainly "Big" Andy is not supposed to go up as other people, for other reasons, go up. But he has taken the attitude that, regardless of what happens elsewhere in the welding department (if others enhance their skill, or their responsibility goes up), he must go up and keep ahead of all of them. I don't think that was the intention of anybody.

Kronan (u): The only answer to Mr. Fairbanks' statement is this: The meeting at which we set minimums has no bearing on this case. The fact remains that Andy was promised the highest welding bogey regardless of where that bogey assignment was worked. That is the understanding and that is the grievance. He was paid the highest bogey not occasionally, but day in and day out for a period of years. That has nothing to do with the minimums all over the shop. We are talking about one individual and his pay.

Umpire: At the time when he was paid the highest bogey, did he work only in the electrical shop or take assignments outside, in the shifter house, for instance, or the blast furnace yards?

MacGregor (u): Nothing has changed. Andy is still doing the same job. The idea of condemning Andy's ability after he has been a one-man welding department is an insult. If he was a teacher and a leader, how can he suddenly be only a handy man? Why, even the previous foreman, Mr. Dickinson, who just died recently, had Andy as his right-hand man.

Mr. Ashford is not telling the truth when he says numerous guys can do that job. Why, no matter where Andy is, they say, "Andy, you have to come in Sunday; we have to do that job in a certain department." Why don't they get the other guys? Because they can't depend on them; they can depend on Andy. I take exception to trying to run a man's skill down after all these years. I take exception to trying to make him just another one of the boys.

Mallory (m): Mr. Fairbanks, was the understanding that Andy should have the highest minimum guarantee, or the highest bogey?

Fairbanks (m): The highest minimum guarantee in the electrical shop was then the highest existing welding bogey. It was after we set those minimums that the welding bogies in the shifter house and the blast furnace repair yards topped the electrical department. There were no personalities involved. I don't see how there could be any impression that "Big" Andy's then top bogey would retain the same relation to the others if other jobs went up.

Sladek (u): We never agreed that any man's contract would be brought down to stay at the minimum set. The company agreed that they wouldn't go below the minimum, yes. But there are ways to get above the minimum.

Fairbanks (m): Andy's bogey hasn't gone down. There has been no change in his method of pay. When we posted the agreed list two years ago, the electrical shop bogey topped all other welding bogies in the plant. Since then the shifter house and the blast furnace bogies went above the electrical shop. If Andy had worked on the shifter house bogey he would have averaged 1 and one-third cents more per hour—the difference between that bogey, now the highest, and his electrical shop bogey, the highest welding bogey two years ago. Now the shifter house and blast furnace welders deserve every cent they get.

Mallory (m): Under no recognized incentive system or job evaluation would such a claim as Basaryck makes be permissible. Remember he is claiming the highest bogey paid anywhere regardless of the kind of welding job he does. And how would employee morale stand up under such an arrangement? How could we maintain a sound wage structure?

Sladek (u): Our case is in the record. I think you can judge from the way Pete MacGregor testified here how the welders feel about the deal "Big" Andy is getting. Even Mr. Bennett admits there's a widespread and sincere conviction that there was such a promise, no matter what supervision says now.

DISCUSSION QUESTIONS

1. Evaluate the problem this case presented to management, and in terms of your evaluation (*a*) appraise the action management took in the case up to and including the proposed settlement of October; (*b*) appraise similarly the positions by which they defended this action at the arbitration hearing; and (*c*) indicate what changes, if any, you would recommend in their action, with your reasons for such changes.

2. Evaluate similarly the problem presented to the union administrators, and appraise their action (*a*) in reaching agreement on the October settlement; (*b*) in retreating from that settlement; (*c*) in defending their whole policy at the arbitration; and (*d*) indicate where you think they should have acted differently from the viewpoint of their relations with their members involved and with management under the contract.

3. On the basis of this case, what would you say are the components of a wage structure (*a*) in terms of the normal concerns of management; (*b*) in terms of typical union interests; and (*c*) in terms of the total responses of bench workers like "Big" Andy and Pete MacGregor?

4. On the basis of this record, how would you characterize relationships at the Fletcher Steel Company at such varying levels as (*a*) top plant officials and local union staff officials, *e.g.*, Bennett and Lynn, Fairbanks and Sladek; (*b*) company officials and district union officials, *e.g.*, Mallory and Kronan; (*c*) bench electricians, *e.g.*, "Big" Andy and Pete MacGregor, with their foreman, Paul Ashford?

CHELSEA STEEL COMPANY

A DEMOTION AFTER A MILL BREAKDOWN

On December 10, an arbitration hearing under the agreement between the Chelsea Steel Company and the United Steelworkers of America (CIO) opened at the Mill Harbor Works of the company. The grievance to be settled arose from the demotion of a roller in the rod- and wire-mill department on April 12.

The following persons were at the hearing:

For the Company	*For the Union*
Peter L. Shaw, of Company Counsel	John C. Howell, Staff Representative
Albert H. Hendrick, Superintendent, Rod and Wire Mill	Francis Milton, Staff Representative
B. Eric Duffield, Assistant Superintendent, Rod and Wire Mill	Daniel Seabury, Chairman, Grievance Committee
Charles A. Reynolds, General Foreman, Rod and Wire Mill	Fred Romano, Zone Committeeman
	Jeremy Campbell, Complainant

For the Union (continued):

Leo Nicora, Rougher
George W. Gilmore, Finisher
Bruce MacElroy, Heater
Nicholas Grozak, Charger
Paul Bremer, Heater and Shop Steward
⎱ Number 1 Rod Mill

Impartial Umpire under the Agreement

Walter A. Robinson

Howell (u) [after some preliminary exchanges]: This grievance concerns a demotion on the No. 1 rod mill, which took place after a mishap on April 8. We feel that the man was unjustly demoted and should be placed back as a roller, together with compensation for his loss of earnings.

In the early part of March, the company installed a new three-strand mill with a flying shear. There was considerable trouble on all turns with its operation.

On April 8, Mr. Campbell was rolling during the 3–11 turn, and about 9:30 something happened to the shear, a mechanical defect, which the mechanics couldn't repair. Management claims that Mr. Campbell was demoted because he failed to report this trouble to the production superintendent. Later they made other charges, too.

We found no just cause for the demotion of Mr. Campbell, and certainly not three positions below his regular job of roller down to rougher. On the No. 1 rod mill the top position is that of roller; the second is that of finisher; the third is assistant finisher; and the fourth is rougher. Below that, to complete the schedule, we have, fifth, roll setter; sixth, spell hand; seventh, shearman; eighth, reelman; ninth, switchman; tenth, scrap puller.

Campbell has *rolled* for over 9 years in this particular mill, and a man with nine years of service surely has proved his ability. We feel only discrimination can explain management's action against a man with Campbell's experience. Supervision in the finishing mill or rolling mill can either make a man or break him if they don't hold all employees to the same requirements. Take the rod mill. If the roller on the turn ahead of a man doesn't take care of the mill and rolls the guts out of it, that leaves the other man in a bad position when he comes on. He has to build his mill up, or change rolls. This has been happening a number of times between General Foremen Reynolds and the Websters, working out a policy of discrimination against Campbell.

I asked management in the Step 4 meeting why they took Campbell off. They argued that instead of being a roller, he was a one-man crew; that, if a man had trouble, Campbell would jump in and do that work. That is the first time in the history of dealing with management that they have said they took a man off because he did too much work.

I would like the chairman for the union of the job evaluation committee to read what duties the roller has.

Seabury (u): As I read the description, I want it specifically noted that nothing says that the roller is responsible for the shears. [Mr. Seabury read the joint job description of the roller's position, detailing his tools and equipment, source of supervision, and working procedures in regard to responsibilities for mill equipment, materials, and crews. The roller's relations *with the crews* were indicated as follows:]

He directs the mill crew for operating procedure and the mill, furnace and billet yard crews for working procedure in absence of foreman; . . .

Works with and directs the crew in necessary changes in setup of rolls, guides, and so forth, to produce desired material;

Signals rougher to operate push-button controls to start and stop the mill;

Works with and directs crew on roll and pass changes, performing such tasks as selecting and positioning rolls, etc., using miscellaneous hand tools, such as mauls, wrenches, and any other auxiliaries necessary.

Works with and directs crew on removal of cobbles, using chains, cables, and so forth.

I think it would be helpful if Mr. Romano of the rod and wire mill mechanical department would explain the mechanical difficulty from which this grievance arose.

Romano (u): At the time this disturbance occurred, I found that this mill was put in operation with only one shear. The company usually provides "extras" to be available in cases of breakdown. This time they bought only one shear, and a spare was being built by us in the plant. Anyone familiar with mechanics knows that no matter how good a piece of machinery may be, especially a new piece, there is always a chance for defects to show up. However, even at that time, April 8, there were still about 8 hours of work remaining to be done on that spare shear before it would be ready for operation.

When this shear broke down about 9:30, the roller naturally contacted the millwright, and the millwright went to see what he could do. [Mr. Romano detailed the efforts by millwrights and maintenance foremen to repair the shears until Mr. Reynolds was summoned on the next turn, around 2 A.M.] Mr. Reynolds called the master mechanic who went over the prints, and questioned the men who had worked on the repairs until he figured out what was left that he might look into. It turned out that a nut on the shaft in the cylinder had worked loose and, since it had been hidden and covered by the housing, the mechanics working on it never thought to take that apart to see what was inside.

Howell (u): Mr. Umpire, I would like to have Mr. Campbell tell you just what happened on April 8.

Campbell (u) [talking quickly, breathlessly, and as if out of his element at the arbitration hearing]: It is pretty hard to say. I don't know. The shears were working just like they explained to you. I worked there for a long time, for about 33 or 34 years. I worked first at Riverside Mills and then was transferred here. I did all I could on the mill. I was getting along all right with the men. The only thing I can say is that I know how to work.

Umpire: Would you mind telling me what happened when this break-down occurred?

Campbell (u): The shears broke down, and I didn't know what to do. I called the boss the week before when I had had some trouble. I thought if Mr. Reynolds came and found we had got the shears working again, he would bawl me out. It is pretty hard for me to think back and tell you now, but I can tell you most anything about the mill.

Umpire: When the shears weren't working, to whom did you report that fact?

Campbell (u): I can't understand how they put the shears on me. The mill was rolling full blast, but the shears broke down. If they had had the old type of shears in the mill, I would be able to go to town, just like that [snapping his fingers]. I know the old shears as a book. When the new shears were set up, there was only one crew working on it. My opinion was that, if the whole crew was out there and you had a master mechanic explain those shears to all the men so they can get little ideas, we might make some headway.

Umpire: How long had you worked on the new mill?

Campbell (u): Ever since it started—about a month or so before. The new shears are complicated. They are nasty things. Every other day we have to put in a new shear blade. They cut off and shoot over the pipe. I like to make good rod and I don't like to have scrap. When you get your mill settled and you have your water pipes nicely set and they are opened up right and your checks are nice, so that the rolls don't eat it up, we don't like that to happen with the shear and mess everything up.

I don't know what else to tell you. The only thing is that I like to work in the rod mill. My whole heart is in that mill, ever since I came down here. That old two-bar mill was really good. This is a good mill, too, but those shears sometimes go down. I am not a mechanic. Do you think that ought to be in my line of work? Tell me the truth.

Umpire: I can't tell you now. I am like a judge hearing all the evidence, before I make up my mind.

Howell (u) [smiling]: We are dealing with an old mill man. This is the first time anything like this has happened to him. He doesn't quite understand the nature of these arbitration proceedings. I think we shall rest our case.

Seabury (u): There is one more statement I would like to make. Mr. Campbell testified that, if he would have called the foreman and the foreman would have come in and found the mill operating, he would have been bawled out. On a Sunday evening prior to this particular instance, Campbell was reprimanded by Reynolds for calling him up on Reynolds' day off. Reynolds said he had one day off and he didn't want to be called on that day off. That was one of the reasons the man was reluctant to report to the foreman.

Umpire: All right, Mr. Shaw.

Shaw (m): The decision which is being challenged by this grievance has been a difficult decision for management to reach. Considerable deliberation preceded the final decision. The particular incident occurred on April 8. But no final decision was reached in Mr. Campbell's case until April 11, and Mr. Campbell was notified the following day of supervision's decision. That indicates that his case was weighed pretty carefully by the members of supervision.

I want to review the facts which were considered in reaching this decision. Primarily, the roller is responsible for the continuous and the efficient operation of his mill. He is a leader, a crew leader, and he is responsible for the production of that mill and for seeing that the mill is kept in continuous operation.

In this particular mill, the No. 1 rod mill, the roller is the highest rated man on the mill at night. There is no mill foreman at night. Therefore, on the particular 3–11 turn, when this difficulty occurred, Mr. Campbell was on his own. The mill was his. The position of roller is the highest rated job in the bargaining unit and has to be filled with highly competent men. They must be skilled in the art of rolling, in keeping their mills operating. They must be men who have good judgment and who are able to maintain crew harmony and to obtain the cooperation of their men.

Mr. Campbell is one of the oldest employees in No. 1 rod mill, and that is why the decision wasn't an easy one. He became a member of the mill crew less than one year after No. 1 mill started operations. He moved up the ladder of promotion until he reached the top some 9 years ago, when he became a regular roller.

The company and the management are quite willing to admit that Mr. Campbell has always been a hard and willing worker, a loyal employee. But, unfortunately, in other respects he has been failing. One of his most serious failings is a lack of supervisory capacity.   He lacks the capacity to direct his mill crew efficiently and to maintain harmonious relations.

I want to emphasize that the decision of management was not based solely on this event of April 8.   It was based on that event, but also on Mr. Campbell's whole past performance in the capacity of roller in the mill.   The action that was finally taken on April 12 was action which had long been deferred.

The failure to obtain crew harmony, crew cooperation, became evident as far back as 4 or 5 years ago.   The members of his crew filed numerous complaints at that time and have continued to file complaints about Mr. Campbell's actions in his capacity as a leader of men.   The earlier complaints finally crystallized into open rebellion.   The situation became so serious that the management was required to call a meeting of the men.

At that meeting the members of Mr. Campbell's crew were afforded the opportunity to air their complaints.   They accused Mr. Campbell of being intolerant, of issuing unreasonable orders, and of countermanding orders without reason.   The thing that irritated them in particular was Mr. Campbell's habit of brushing men aside from their positions on the mill, intimating to them that they did not know how to do their work, and then performing the work himself.

It is a sizable crew.   I think that Mr. Howell mentioned nine crew members beside the roller; and I wish only to add one more, the crane operator.   The roller thus has a crew of 10 men directly under his supervision.

After hearing the complaints of the men, supervision was of the opinion that they might have to remove Mr. Campbell.   However, they also admired his qualities of being a hard worker, of being a fellow who wanted to get things done, and they felt that with further experience and with some assistance by the higher ranking members of supervision, he would develop the executive ability to instruct men how to perform their tasks properly and to handle them in a manner that will assure crew cooperation.

Fortunately, at a second meeting, the men relented.   They said they would be willing to cooperate with Mr. Campbell if he mended his ways with them.   Supervision was perfectly satisfied then to allow Mr. Campbell to continue as a roller.   They felt that with assistance and advice and with his natural drive and ability to work hard he would become a good roller.

For a time there weren't too many complaints.   There seemed to be a higher degree of team spirit.   But later the same trouble developed, although not to the same intense degree.   There was, however, the constant irritation of men coming to supervision and asking to be assigned to other crews and complaining about unreasonable assignments, about the fact that Mr. Campbell had been abusive to them.   Some of them threatened to quit because of Mr. Campbell's tactics.

Mr. Campbell was given warnings later, when he failed to show improvement, that he would have to be replaced as a roller if he didn't mend his ways with his crew.

Aside from not being able to handle men, supervision believes that Mr.

Campbell has not shown the proper regard for the safety of his crew. For example: the mill is equipped with signal lights which are to be used when no more bars are to be fed into the mill, when repairs are to be made on the mill. Members of supervision had seen that Mr. Campbell failed to make use of the signal-light system. He was content to depend on oral instructions. On the other hand, if the signals were on (they consist of red lights) when the repairs were completed, he failed to have them removed, but would instruct the feeding end of the mill to shove the bars through. That is definitely an unsafe practice. Mr. Campbell has been warned about that practice, reprimanded for it, but he continues to make the same mistake.

Supervision also believes that in his haste to secure greater production, he causes his crew to take risks which are in violation of the company's safety rules. An example of that is ordering a man to go behind the mill to make a change in the mill while the mill is operating—change a bearing, for example. In one particular incident, the man who was ordered to do that objected and refused to do it. He saw the members of supervision about it, and the members of supervision warned Mr. Campbell against engaging in such a practice and reprimanded him quite severely.

Another practice is that if cobbles [1] had to be removed and burned out, he would himself (or permit members of his crew to) burn out these cobbles with burn torches without the use of goggles, which is definitely unsafe.

All of this lay in back of the incident of April 8. On that particular night, Mr. Campbell was having trouble with a new shear which had been installed in March. We know from the mill-delay sheets that the mill was down from 8:15 until 8:45, when shear blades were changed on the shear, indicating that the shear was in some sort of difficulty. Operations were resumed on the mill but ceased again at 9:15, and the mill remained completely down until 5:40 the next morning.

The company's case is not that Mr. Campbell ruined the shears or was negligent with respect to their operation. The company's case is that, since this was a new piece of equipment (and the union stresses that point), and since Mr. Campbell admits that he had no knowledge with respect to its workings, it was his responsibility as the top man in the mill, as the roller, to get in touch with his general foreman, Mr. Reynolds. That action should have been taken almost immediately; and Mr. Reynolds, in turn, would have gotten the master mechanic, as he did when he was finally notified.

We think that this was just another one of Mr. Campbell's failings as a roller. Because of all these considerations, the members of supervision reached the decision that Mr. Campbell must be demoted.

The management, in Step No. 3, stated its belief that the original penalty was too drastic. I might add here that the original move to remove Mr.

---

[1] A "cobble" occurs when the hot steel piece in the rolls twists, turns down, buckles, or becomes snarled by some mill accident that thus prevents it from coming through the rolls. The steel then begins to pile up literally in all directions, and the mill has to be stopped as quickly as possible. A crane may then pull out the cobbled steel, or, where too serious for that, it has to be burned out. A cobble creates a grave and hazardous mill condition.

Campbell from the roller's position three steps down to the rougher's position was taken by the members of supervision, because they wanted to make certain that Mr. Campbell would not serve as a roller in case of absenteeism. But, after deliberating on this case for a period of three weeks, in the Step No. 3 meeting, supervision decided and offered to the union to move Mr. Campbell up to the finisher's position on the mill with the understanding that he would not—ever—serve as a roller. The union refused that offer but management is willing to renew that offer.

Mr. Hendrick, suppose you recite briefly your responsibilities as superintendent of the rod and wire department.

Hendrick (m): The superintendent is responsible for getting the necessary materials into the plant, seeing that they are properly processed and shipped to our customers. Of course, one of our biggest responsibilities is the men working for us, and probably one of the hardest jobs we have is getting the proper men in the proper positions. There is one job a whole lot tougher and that is in a case where we have made a mistake and have to correct the situation. A decision such as faced us with Jerry [Campbell] is a tough job. But I do have the responsibility, not only of the product and the quality, but also the responsibility of the safety of the men, the harmony, the good working conditions—anything that goes towards better relationships within the department.

Last November I stopped by Charlie's [Reynolds'] desk. He said, "We had an incident last night." Then he told me of Campbell's asking a man to go behind the mill between the spindles and change a bearing on No. 3 stand. That bearing weighs approximately 50 pounds. It would have to be raised up with the mill in motion.

I told Charlie we were going to have to do something with Jerry [Campbell] before he killed a man. I regret now that something wasn't done at that time.

Shaw (m): Let's go into the roller's responsibilities.

Hendrick (m): The roller's responsibilities are divided into three parts. We have the mechanics of the mill; we have the material of the mill; we have the human end of the mill. The roller has responsibility to see to it that his mill is in good operating condition, that the rolls and guides are properly set, that other auxiliary equipment is in such shape that it will serve his mill properly. He is responsible for seeing that the steel is heated properly, that the section that he rolls is of such quality as is acceptable, that scrap is held down to a minimum. He is responsible for the actions, the harmony in his crew, which, of course, reflect on the whole job that he is doing.

Shaw (m): In what respects was Mr. Campbell failing as a roller?

Hendrick (m): A good bit of this I would get secondhand, because I naturally work through the general foreman. However, we have had numerous complaints that Jerry couldn't handle his crew, that he cursed the men, the safety examples cited. In general, he had a continual turmoil amongst his crew members.

Howell (u): I have a couple of questions. Mr. Hendrick, you said something about the safety angle, as did Mr. Shaw. If you would see a man on day turn, when you were in the plant, run up to get a cobble out and put the mill back in operation, would you stop that man?

Hendrick (m): No.

Howell (u): Isn't that running against the safety rules here?

Hendrick (m): That may be a technical question, where a cobble is involved.

Howell (u): Management has brought up technical issues here.

Hendrick (m): Running to get one cobble out of the way may save another cobble and improve safety.

Howell (u): From our mill experience we know that in any situation whatever can be done the quickest way to get production out, that is what you do. Isn't that the way you want it? More production?

Hendrick (m): More production safely.

Shaw (m): I would like to call on Mr. Duffield to testify.

Duffield (m): Jerry [addressing Campbell], you and I have been friends for 20 years, and I have a job to do and it is a disagreeable job to do. I would rather not talk against you. I would rather boost you than talk against you. I am sorry I have to do it, but I have to do it in fairness to the mill. But I am still your friend.

Campbell (u): I don't see where you have anything on me.

Shaw (m): Mr. Duffield, when were Mr. Campbell's deficiencies first brought to your attention?

Duffield (m): Well, continuously for the past several years.

Shaw (m): What were the nature of those complaints?

Duffield (m): Well, one of the duties of a roller is to direct and control his men. Jerry's failings are in that direction. [Mr. Duffield related concrete instances illustrating Mr. Campbell's inability to win cooperation from his men, even in emergencies.]

The men unfortunately got out of control, got out of hand to such a point that they followed orders if they chose to and ignored them if they chose to, regardless of Jerry being in charge of the mill.

To go a little further, Jerry is very enthusiastic about his work. He is very serious. He thinks an awful lot of the mill. When he gets into difficulties, he hasn't hesitated to talk to me about it. He has come to me on occasions—I know him very well and we have been very friendly—and made statements to the effect that Mr. Reynolds complained to him about the way he was doing his work; and the men had complained to Reynolds about him. I told Jerry that I thought one of his difficulties was that he tried to do too much work. I told him flatfootedly that it wasn't a one-man mill. What he had to do was to get in there and instruct his men and, after he had instructed them, have enough confidence in them to let them alone to do their work and only step into the picture when it was necessary. His men resent the fact that he won't let them handle their own jobs, and they just don't like the way he directs them.

Umpire: Mr. Duffield, it has been testified that, following the second meeting you had to discuss the dissatisfaction with Campbell's handling of the men, he mended his ways for a while and then there was a recurrence. Did you consider again taking action?

Duffield (m): We thought about it several times.

Umpire: Did you have further meetings with the crew?

Duffield (m): No.

Shaw (m): I would like to call on Mr. Reynolds, who is general foreman. Mr. Reynolds, how long have you known Mr. Campbell?

Reynolds (m): I would say 35 years. I have been his supervisor since he came to the rod mill.

Shaw (m): Mr. Reynolds, will you tell us, in your own words, the kind of trouble that Mr. Campbell ran into as a roller?

Reynolds (m): Mr. Campbell would go along for a number of weeks, maybe months, getting along all right, and then something would happen and everything was all wrong. He doesn't seem to be able to get along with any of his men at all—very few of them. He wants to do all the work himself. He wants to push them out of the way, pull cobbles out and throw the tongs without looking, and swear at them. I saw him with my own eyes throw the tongs back and almost hit a man a couple of times. I told him about it. Of course, that was just "hurry-up." Safety was not what it should be.

Shaw (m): Mr. Reynolds, you say you warned Mr. Campbell and reprimanded him on numerous occasions?

Reynolds (m): I have. I have had him in the office several times about his profane language, if you want to call it that. I have asked other men to overlook some of that. That was Jerry's way and he couldn't change that. I said, "Forget it. Names don't hurt you." They said that they could take so much and that was all.

Umpire: All this is rather news to me—that steel men are sensitive to profanity.

Reynolds (m): The biggest part use it, but not so much now as in the olden times.

Howell (u): They use it all the time. That is just mill talk.

Shaw (m): Mr. Reynolds, in what respect do you think that Mr. Campbell was failing on the night of April 8?

Reynolds (m): It certainly was his responsibility to give me a call and get hold of me. I was home.

Shaw (m): Mr. Reynolds, do you object to being called out at night?

Reynolds (m): I have always told my men to call me at any time. I have never said a word to any of the men about calling me at any time of the night. I have been foreman for 30 years. That is one thing I never objected to. I don't say I like it, but I have not objected to their calling me. And I have had thousands of calls in that time.

Shaw (m): Did you reprimand Mr. Campbell the week prior for calling you out?

Reynolds (m): I never reprimanded any man for calling me.

Romano (u): Could I ask Mr. Reynolds a question?

Umpire: Go ahead.

Romano (u): Mr. Reynolds, you say you knew Mr. Campbell for 35 years. You knew him about 26 years before he was up for promotion to roller. You say he always—as finisher, rougher—jumped in to do the job of other workers. Don't you think after 26 years you should have known enough about his ability to handle men to determine whether he should have the job? The time for that decision was 9 years ago, wasn't it?

Reynolds (m): We like to give every man the benefit of every doubt.

Umpire: Did Mr. Campbell in the past have any considerable number of such mechanical breakdowns as that of April 8th? I want to get more evidence on Mr. Campbell's behavior in such situations.

Reynolds (m): As a rule, he has always called me when he got into any great difficulties.

Umpire: On this matter of difficulty with personnel and carelessness regarding safety, did any specific issues arise just about this time when Mr. Campbell was demoted? Was it primarily his handling of the shears, or that plus other concrete incidents?

Hendrick (m): I would say that the demotion was not as a result of this specific act when the shears failed. It was an accumulation of several things as regards his capacity as a leader of men.

Shaw (m): Let's add to that. When did Campbell order the bearing changed while the mill was in operation?

Reynolds (m): The latter part of last year.

Shaw (m): How about this practice of having the men burn cobbles without using goggles?

Reynolds (m): That was periodic, once in a while.

Umpire: Are any members of the crew here?

Howell (u): There are five men as witnesses.

Umpire: Mr. Campbell's leadership and relations with his crew are primary causes motivating the company's action. It might be well to hear them.

Howell (u): I call first Leo Nicora, a rougher. How long have you worked on the rougher position in the rod mill?

Nicora (u): Since 1935.

Umpire: How long have you worked with Mr. Campbell?

Nicora (u): I would say approximately 3 years.

Howell (u): Did you have any kicks about Mr. Campbell jumping in and helping you out?

Nicora (u): Off and on, yes, sir.

Howell (u): Isn't it his job to help you out?

Nicora (u): It is his job to help me. When I am stuck I want him to help me. He is the only man who can do it.

Umpire: Did you complain about Mr. Campbell to supervision?

Nicora (u): A couple of times, yes. I was doing the job right one day and he wanted to make it better. I complained to the boss.

Umpire: When was that?

Nicora (u): About 5 years ago, in that first meeting we had in the office.

Umpire: Have you complained since then?

Nicora (u): I have been away from Campbell's turn 4 years now.

Howell (u): Mr. Gilmore, what is your position?

Gilmore (u): Finisher.

Howell (u): Have you worked for Mr. Campbell?

Gilmore (u): I worked for him about 3 years.

Howell (u): How long is it since you worked with him?

Gilmore (u): Approximately 8 months.

Howell (u): Did you ever have any difficulties with Mr. Campbell?

Gilmore (u): I had a conflict with him when I first went to work on that turn. Mr. Reynolds got us together and we worked that out. We have occasional run-ins. That is about all.

Howell (u): How do you feel about Mr. Campbell's production record as a roller?

Gilmore (u): I think Campbell is a little overanxious. That is his only fault. He is more for the company's side than he is for the men. He is more anxious for production than he is for the men themselves.

Howell (u): Why do you feel that way?

Gilmore (u): Jerry wants to produce as much as the other man, and he wants to produce better quality rod than the other man; and when delays occur he is anxious to get started again. I think that is why the men misunderstand. You have to learn to know Jerry.

Shaw (m): You said you have had run-ins with Campbell? What caused the arguments?

Gilmore (u): Different troubles that we might have. Those things are between the two men to iron out and forget about. They happen in a mill.

Howell (u): Now Mr. MacElroy, state your name and position.

MacElroy (u): Bruce MacElroy, heater; I don't work on the mill. I am with the furnace crew.

Howell (u): Do you work on the same turn with Jerry Campbell?

MacElroy (u): Yes, until he was taken off the job. I think he was all right.

Shaw (m): What heater do you work with there?

MacElroy (u): Lawrence Judd.

Shaw (m): Did Lawrence Judd have trouble with Jerry Campbell?

MacElroy (u): Occasional squabbles about the heat. Jerry was particular about his heat.

Shaw (m): Would he come down and try to regulate the heat—change the instruments, gas valves, and so forth?

MacElroy (u): Sometimes he would.

Shaw (m): And did Lawrence Judd complain about that?

MacElroy (u): I don't know whether he went to the foreman about it. He complained to me about it.

[Mr. Shaw later questioned Mr. Reynolds, who testified that Judd had complained to him.]

Shaw (m): Did Judd have any run-ins with Jerry Campbell in your presence?

MacElroy (u): Yes.

Howell (u): Mr. Reynolds, don't you think it would have been good supervision to separate Judd and Campbell and try to work someone else in there who would have more harmony?

Reynolds (m): It has been done in some cases, but you can't continue to do that all the time. You would have everybody working one turn and nobody wanting to work Campbell's turn.

Howell (u): I will now call Mr. Paul Bremer, a heater. Mr. Bremer, how long have you worked on the No. 1 mill?

Bremer (u): Since 1937.

Howell (u): Did you ever work with Mr. Campbell?

Bremer (u): I did in the position of heater, off and on. I would say I worked with Mr. Campbell approximately 3 years.

Howell (u): You are a shop steward. Was it brought to your attention that Campbell was a "hoggy" roller for the company and always wanted to produce more steel than the other fellow?

Bremer (u): There is a certain competitive spirit on the mill. After a crew gets knit together they all want to produce more than other crews.

Howell (u): Did you have any differences with Mr. Campbell?

Bremer (u): You can't work in a mill without having differences with somebody.

Umpire: A little more than normal with Mr. Campbell?

Bremer (u): When I had differences with anybody, I tried to settle them right there and then. I never have gone to my foreman with respect to a man with whom I had to work. I will admit that we had our differences at times.

Shaw (m): You say you were a heater here? When was that?

Bremer (u): It was about six or seven years ago.

Shaw (m): Were you a shop steward at the time of those meetings when the men were complaining about Mr. Campbell?

Bremer (u): No, sir, but I was at the meetings. I made no complaints. I never went to supervision in regard to difficulties with a roller because a roller is my direct boss. If he is putting me in a spot, I settle it with him. We are out there to work 8 hours, and you have to hit some rough spots now and then. After you are working as a crew, you are all working for tonnage. You have to make your meal ticket out of the tonnage.

Shaw (m): In conclusion, I want to emphasize once more that the position of roller is a highly responsible position. He is responsible for his mill and for the crew that works under him. And he is responsible for seeing that the crew cooperates with him. He is responsible for seeing that the mill operates with a minimum of delay time.

We think that Mr. Campbell has been failing in some of these respects. We think that he has had a long period of trial on the job of roller. We think we have established our claim that he has shown deficiencies as crew leader and in mill operation.

Howell (u): It still seems to us that Mr. Campbell has been portrayed by management's evidence as "a one-man crew" so devoted to his job and to production that he does more work than he should. Since when have these things become deficiencies and failings? I think this is the first time in the history of labor relations that a man has been disciplined so severely for such performance on his job as the company has been charging against Mr. Campbell! Mr. Campbell should be reinstated to his position as roller with retroactive adjustment for the losses in earnings he has suffered.

EXHIBIT 1

CHELSEA STEEL COMPANY

Pertinent Contract Clauses

ARTICLE X—SENIORITY

Section 1. In the promotion of Employees to nonsupervisory positions and for the purpose of layoffs in connection with the decreasing of the working force and of the recalling to work of men so laid off, the following factors shall be considered; and, if factors (*b*) and (*c*) are relatively equal, length of continuous service shall govern:

(*a*) Length of continuous service in the applicable unit determined as provided in Section 2 of this Article;

(*b*) Ability to perform the work; and

(*c*) Physical fitness.

ARTICLE XIII—MANAGEMENT FUNCTIONS

The management of the Plants and the direction of the working forces and the operations at the Plants, including the hiring, promoting and retiring of Employees, the suspending, discharging or otherwise disciplining of Employees, the laying off and calling to work of Employees in connection with any reduction or increase in the working forces, the scheduling of work and the control and regulation of the use of all equipment and other property of the company, are the exclusive functions of the management; provided, however, that in the exercise of such functions the management shall not alter any of the provisions of this agreement and shall not discriminate against any employee or applicant for employment because of his membership in or lawful activity on behalf of the union.

ARTICLE XIV—SAFETY AND HEALTH

The company will continue to make every reasonable effort to provide safe and healthful conditions of work for employees at the plants and to provide employees with any necessary protective equipment in accordance with the practices prevailing at the respective plants at the date of this agreement.

The union will cooperate with the company in encouraging employees to observe the safety regulations which shall be prescribed by the company and to work in a safe manner.

DISCUSSION QUESTIONS

1. As a management representative having read the record of this case, what various areas of management responsibility merit your attention? Have you any specific recommendations for appropriate action which management should follow?

2. As a union representative having read the record of this case, what various areas of union responsibility merit your attention? Have you any specific recommendations for appropriate action which the union should follow?

3. Assume that Jerry Campbell is reinstated (*a*) as a roller, (*b*) as a finisher. In each case what would you do, if anything, to make Jerry more effective in his work situation?

4. If you were the arbitrator, what would be your decision regarding the demotion of Jerry Campbell? Support your conclusion by using evidence from the case.

TRI-STATE GAS AND ELECTRIC COMPANY

THE DIFFICULT CASE OF JEFFREY PORTER

I

During the spring of 1942 the city of Borderton, La., was swept by a wave of bitter feeling against the Society of Jehovah's Witnesses. The Society had maintained a church for some years, but with the war, local sentiment against the Witnesses swiftly intensified. On the one hand, they stepped up their propaganda; on the other, the vast majority of citizens began to identify the proselytizing of the sect with antiwar activity. Local newspapers carried almost daily reports upon the beliefs and "sabotage" of this "unpatriotic organization"; in union meetings, in other gatherings of the local citizenry— both in homes and in more formal sessions—the Witnesses of military age were angrily denounced as "draft dodgers"; and the refusal of the group "properly to respect and salute the American flag" became a symbol of general "un-Americanism."

II

On April 22, Mr. G. W. Bellamy, lineman in the employ of the Tri-State Gas and Electric Company, and president of the local union of the International Brotherhood of Electrical Workers, was informed that Mr. Howland, the president of the company, would like to see him. Mr. Howland came quickly to the point. After some general comments on the war, he said, "And that brings me, G. W., to the matter of Jeffrey Porter, who has become something of a problem. We have received complaints from customers that Jeff is calling on them in their homes, and preaching this Jehovah Witness stuff. He carries a portable phonograph to play recorded speeches —something called, 'Is Hell Hot?' These people became particularly angry and asked him to leave their premises. Instead Jeff got into heated arguments, until they threatened to call the police. Fortunately, Jeff left before any violence occurred although they came pretty close to blows.

"Now I'll grant what you probably are going to say. These visits are made outside Jeff's working hours. I know, too, that Jeff has been with us for over 30 years. He's 63 now, and is due for his pension in 1944. Believe me, I hate to contemplate steps that might deprive him of that pension. You'll agree we've always tried to play fair, and the company doesn't enjoy this kind of situation. In fact Jeff's been worrying us for some time; we don't know how to handle the problem. But you will agree, I'm sure, that we have a special kind of responsibility to customers. We can't just tell them that he's acting as a Jehovah's Witness outside working hours. They feel that he has gained entry to their homes in the first place as our employee, and they are telling us straight-from-the-shoulder that it's up to us to stop his unwelcome visits. You know how the whole city feels about this outfit.

"And now, G. W., matters have taken a serious turn. The sheriff called me yesterday. He has been receiving complaints about these Jehovah Witnesses. His department, accordingly, had been keeping them under surveillance, among them Jeffrey Porter. He himself is convinced they are subversive. He warned me that if his office turned up anything, it would be a matter of public knowledge and might affect adversely the company's public relations.

"Now I want to suggest, G. W., that you take the whole matter up with Jeff. I don't know if anyone can accomplish anything with him, but it does seem up to the union to try. Tell him—I don't want to suggest what you should say—but use words strong enough to let him feel this is very serious. Tell him his activities are hurting the company. Tell him they will hurt the local. Tell him that our agreement is based on a 'continuation of harmonious relations' and that if he causes the finger of public opinion or the strong arm of the law to be pointed accusingly at this company, we will point it right back at the local union. Tell him to 'cease and desist' from these unpopular activities if he wants to retain his position. Don't mince matters. Talk the whole situation over with him from the standpoint of the public, the company, and the union. You may get him to understand, although I doubt it."

Bellamy, who had remained silent, now said, "Mr. Howland, I will take this matter up with the executive board in a special meeting that I will call tonight. I will give them all the information. If the Board authorizes me to see Jeff, I will."

III

At the board meeting the members showed considerable concern over the situation, revealing intense feeling against the Jehovah Witnesses. They closed their discussion with the resolution that "Brother Porter is conducting himself in a manner which may bring the local union much unfavorable publicity" and instructed Business Manager Bellamy to confer with him "in an effort to prevent a breach in union-company relations."

The next morning, Bellamy proceeded to the meter department. Porter, a meter tester, was seated at the test board. After a short greeting, Bellamy plunged immediately into the "problem" he had been "instructed" to take up. Repeating almost exactly what President Howland had suggested, Bellamy concluded, "If you don't stop this foolishness, you will lose your job and the local union won't be able to help you."

Porter continued to work while Bellamy "lectured" him. When the latter had finished, Porter said, measuring each word, "What I do when the company does not pay me is none of the company's business; what I do at any place or at any time, so long as I do not violate union rules, is none of the local's business. I am not violating any law, and I am not afraid of the sheriff. If the company and the local feel they can tell me how to run my private life, they can both go to hell—and that goes for you too."

On leaving, Bellamy replied, "Jeff, I'm sorry you can't see things the right way and won't comply with the executive board's request. As for your advice, you can feel certain that I won't follow your suggestion!"

IV

That afternoon Bellamy called upon Mr. Howland to report his conversation with Porter. Mr. Howland thereupon reviewed the entire matter once more. The two men concluded in regretful agreement. Mr. Howland said, "I wish Jeff had changed his attitude because I am not anxious to discharge him after such long service. But I must conduct the business above reproach in the eyes of its customers, the law, and all good citizens. Entirely in pursuit of that policy I'm afraid we will have to remove him from the payroll. It's a bad, sad business, and I am glad that the local union understands our position."

Jeffrey Porter was discharged the next day. In addition to all payments due him, he was given additional pay in lieu of his vacation. He did not inquire why he was being discharged; nor was he given any explanation.

At the next regular meeting of the local, held five days later, the recording secretary read a letter from Porter in which he requested "the union to use its grievance procedure to obtain my reinstatement for I was discharged without cause." The meeting was thereupon given over completely to discussing the "Porter affair." Bellamy presided but made no comment throughout the proceedings. The executive board presented a full report, including the deliberations and conclusions of its special meeting. During discussions the members again revealed their intense anger with "the activities of the Jehovah Witnesses in time of war." Finally a motion that "the communication from Brother Porter be filed, and that the recording secretary be instructed to notify him that the union does not intend to appeal the case" was carried unanimously. The recording secretary informed Porter via registered mail, with "return receipt requested."

V

Some ten days later, Porter wrote International President Edward J. Brown at union headquarters in Washington. Porter asked that President Brown assign an international representative to investigate "so that I can be reinstated." Porter cited his long record of union membership and his length of service with the company. He pointed out that had his service record remained unbroken, he would have been eligible within two years for a monthly pension of $85 for the remainder of his life. These pensions were paid through an insurance company from a retirement fund financed by the company and the individual employees. In conclusion, Porter noted that upon retirement he would also file application for the pension paid by the union, which amounted to $42 per month.

International President Brown at once routed Porter's letter to the vice president in charge of union affairs in the Southwest, and through him to the international representative, David Owen, who had jurisdiction over the area of which Borderton was a part.

Owen came to Borderton to initiate his investigation some 30 days after Porter's discharge. Owen viewed the Porter case with considerable perplexity. As an experienced union official, he knew that it was most unusual for union members to accept without protest the discharge of a fellow member on the eve of his matured rights to retirement. All the union's dealings with the company made him certain that it did not make such a discharge without discomfort. He was also aware of the strong community sentiment against the Jehovah Witnesses. Nonetheless it did seem as if some way might have been found to persuade Porter to "lay off" his proselytizing, or at least to adjust it to his duties as employee and union member. Owen determined to review every fact that might yield more insight into "how matters could have come to such a pass." With this objective he conferred at length with Porter, Bellamy, and President Howland; he met also with the executive board, with Bellamy present. With these discussions concluded, Owen attempted to reassemble what he knew and had learned into a clearer picture of the situation.

VI

At no point did he hear the slightest criticism of G. W. Bellamy or his conduct of union affairs. On the contrary, President Howland had told Owen how much all company supervisors admired Bellamy; they trusted his fairness in all joint dealings. Union members similarly displayed the utmost confidence in him; he enjoyed among them an unusual popularity as a person and respect as an official.

Bellamy, 40 years old, had been married for 12 years; he had no children. He had been a lineman for 22 years, 14 of which had been in the employ of the Borderton company. His membership in the union began in 1924; from the beginning of his employment by Tri-State he had been an active member of Local Union 293. Until very recently, indeed until 1941, the popularity he seemed always to enjoy was the liking accorded a hearty, vital sort of fellow. He drank, yet could hold his liquor. Although a gambler, he always played fair and took losses even better than gains. Trigger-tempered, he was ready with his fists and usually gave better than he got. Yet he knew also that everything had its place; nothing was permitted to interfere with his duties to his job and his union. He was an expert lineman, and was extremely effective in conducting and promoting union affairs.

In 1941 Bellamy suffered a severe illness, during which his life hung in balance. After his recovery, friends began to note striking changes in his behavior and personality. He became a member of the Nazarene Church, and within a year was a deacon, as well as Sunday school superintendent and church treasurer. He gave up all drinking, gambling, and tobacco; the colorful profanity disappeared from his vocabulary as did his ready belligerency from his behavior. But he was still the most popular man among his associates; indeed his new way of life had added an intense admiration—from fellow employees and superiors alike—to the respect and regard in which he had been held.

From the early days of his affiliation with Local Union 293, Bellamy had played an active role in extending organization among company employees and in participating in internal union affairs. As the local increased its membership, it was torn for some years by a bitter fight regarding the kind of union it should become. Although Bellamy was a lineman, he led the faction which held that all employees engaged in the distribution, appliance, power, and meter departments should be eligible for union membership. The opposition fought strenuously for their conviction—that only skilled journeymen linemen [1] should be members. The leader of this opposition was Jeffrey Porter.

VII

Porter, a lineman or line foreman since 1907, was an exceptionally skilled craftsman with an old-school pride in his craft. He had been a member of the union since 1908 and of the Borderton local since 1915. The father of grown children, he had encouraged his sons to train for the lineman's craft, and one of them, Richard Porter, was a lineman in the employ of the Tri-State Company. Porter also had enjoyed long popularity with his union fellows, although he had few close friends. He was an "easy-going, quiet-spoken fellow," and the older linemen looked upon him as leader and spokesman for the pride of craft they shared with him. From 1925 to 1933 he had served as president of Local Union 293. It was during his presidency that the struggle to transform Local 293 from its craft basis to a wider type of membership gained momentum. During the early 1930's, the international representative had backed the Bellamy faction, until in the election for the local presidency in 1933 the basis of membership was made the sole issue of the contest. Porter was defeated by Bellamy.

With this defeat, Porter retired from all active participation in union affairs, even failing to attend meetings with regularity. He did, however, maintain his membership. As Porter declined in union prominence, Bellamy advanced. He served as president from 1933 to 1937; as full-time, salaried business manager from 1937 to 1940, when he resigned; and as president and business manager, on pay only for time lost from company duties because of union business, since 1941.

During this period, in 1939, Porter reached the age of 60 years. Thereupon the management summoned him "for a conference." The executives told him how they valued his long years of service, and respected his skill as a lineman. But they feared that the lineman's craft entailed inevitable hazards for a man of 60 years. The company did not want to see Porter subjected to such hazards. Accordingly they were proposing now to transfer him—a pro-

---

[1] A lineman becomes a journeyman after four years' apprenticeship, and the ratio of apprentices to linemen by Rule 7 of Article IV of the Agreement is restricted to "not . . . more than one apprentice to each 5 journeymen . . ."

posal, they explained, that most linemen got many years prior to the sixtieth birthday. They offered him the job of meter tester. Congratulating him on his son, Dick, who was "a lineman every inch worthy of his father," they reminded him jokingly that there would continue to be a Porter on the "lineman payroll" to maintain the family tradition of skill and craft.

After this episode, Jeff Porter seemed to withdraw even more from his old associations. His wife had died in 1936, and during 1940 Porter remarried, taking as his second wife a woman some 25 years his junior. She had been a Jehovah's Witness for some time, and apparently soon persuaded her husband to enter the church. Porter and his wife led a very secluded life, cutting themselves off from every association—union, work, former friends—outside the circle of their church interests. But from that circle they projected an assiduous proselytizing that by 1942 had transformed them for many of their fellow citizens into suspect, treasonable enemies. Porter's son, Dick, became particularly aroused, for he was active in all the fields of his father's former loyalties; he was an active union member, an expert lineman, a loyal company employee, and a citizen who shared his community's intense devotion to the nation's war effort. Dick determined to attempt "to bring back" his father from this "Jehovah Witness trash." He called upon his father and in the presence of his stepmother began to argue the policies and practices of the Witnesses. His father responded with increasing anger and passion; one tense word led to another, and the pathetic family conference ended in a fist fight between father and son.

From that time on, Jeffrey Porter literally imposed a self-ostracism upon himself. He attended no union meetings whatsoever. While at work he spoke to no one unless he was addressed, and then made the exchange as monosyllabic as possible. He cut himself off from his children, never noticing Dick, and went his new religious way with his wife.

VIII

International Representative Owen decided that some way should be discoverable by which Porter could regain his pension rights, yet safeguard the company's justified concern over its public relations. He addressed himself to this goal. Two further conferences with President Howland convinced him that although the company feared the impact of Porter's proselytizing on its community relations, its executives would, as Howland phrased it, "like to see Jeff get that pension."

Sensing this disquiet in the company, Owen had a long talk with Porter. He found him not at all uneasy over the protracted negotiations, nor eager to press the company for reinstatement. Indeed, he told Owen, all that really concerned him was his pension. He'd actually prefer not to go back if some way could be found to assure him his retirement rights in 1944, when he would be 65 years old. When Owen explained, however, that reinstatement with restoration of "unbroken service" was essential to receiving his pension, Porter accepted this quietly.

Shortly thereafter, Owen obtained an interview with Sheriff Bailey. The sheriff was uncompromising, almost blusteringly adamant. He would continue to keep a sharp eye on that whole "Jehovah Witness outfit." No, Owen could not have access to the "file" against Porter. And now he was warning the union, as he had warned the company, about that fellow.

When Owen again sought conference with President Howland, therefore, he had to restrict himself to a direct, human appeal for reinstatement of a long-service employee. Howland, still uneasy and reluctant, called in the company's executive vice president, Webster Wright. When Mr. Wright proved similarly unwilling to make any positive recommendation, Owen informed the two executives that he must ask for arbitration. He intended to demand reinstatement with all seniority and pension rights restored, compensation for the 117 days Porter had thus far lost from the job, plus any further time lost until the case was settled. He believed Porter a victim of wartime hysteria, and felt sure the company and union could find a fair adjustment, were the will to adjust actually present. Both Howland and Wright declared themselves averse to arbitration. They doubted, indeed, the technical validity of such a course. But Owen persisted, arguing that the initiation of this case through the office of the company president represented merely management's own choice about skipping the preliminary steps in its negotiation. President Howland then suggested a final conference the next day.

When Howland, Wright, and Owen met in this final conference, the company submitted a proposal of settlement formulated in executive conference the night before. The company would ask that Owen procure "a promise" from Porter that "he would cause no further trouble for the company as long as he remained an employee." In return, management would reinstate him with all seniority and pension rights restored. Since the discharge action was taken in full consultation and agreement with the local union, management would not pay Porter for his time lost. Owen promptly informed the executives he considered their offer a fair one.

Owen thereupon went immediately to Porter's home to convey the terms of settlement. Porter heard Owen through silently, and then accepted the settlement with an expression of gratitude to Owen. As he seemed very much moved, Owen took a friendly leave as soon as he could.

He then sought out Bellamy, who also expressed gratification at this "turn of affairs." When Bellamy reported the settlement to the local union, the members transformed it into "a victory for Local Union 293." They seemed genuinely pleased, and somehow relieved.

Porter returned to his job as meter tester, which he filled satisfactorily until he was "honorably retired from active service" in 1944. During his employment after reinstatement, he attended no union meetings, nor displayed any friendliness toward any union member. After his retirement, Porter remained withdrawn from all his former activities beyond his own home, where he seemed content to keep himself occupied in his garden and house.

DISCUSSION QUESTIONS

1. What clues would you say help explain Jeffrey Porter's behavior?

2. Evaluate the handling of the situation by Mr. Howland up to the time that the international union representative, Mr. Owen, came to Borderton.

3. How would you explain the apparently contrasting reactions of Owen, Howland, and Bellamy to the case? Evaluate the policy pursued by each of these three principals.

4. How would you characterize Mr. Owen's handling of the case?

E. B. LAWTON & CO., INC.

WAGE GRIEVANCES AT THE MASON MILLS

In the course of its expansion during the war period, E. B. Lawton & Co., Inc., a steel fabricating corporation with headquarters in Philadelphia, purchased a number of plants west of Ohio, among them the Mason Mills. Bargaining rights for the Mason employees were secured by the Steelworkers Union in 1943.

As further expansions followed the Korean war, headquarters executives became concerned over the necessity of attaining uniform policies throughout the various plants. George Underwood, vice president of industrial relations, thought that two grievances recently appealed to arbitration from the Mason Mills might serve as a vehicle for advancing the changes that top management was determined to achieve. He noted that these grievances represented only Nos. 46 and 47 in almost ten years of union dealings and that only one case had previously been carried to arbitration. . . . Probably even these grievances would not have come to headquarters if local plant managements had not recently been warned by top management that henceforth the contract had to be rigorously applied. "Exceptions" might be recommended, but simply for consideration by top management at headquarters. In cases of doubt, local supervision was directed to seek headquarters' counsel.

Underwood thought that perhaps a visit to the plant might be desirable before determining what position to take on the two grievances. He decided accordingly to review the situation with Philip Norman, his assistant, who had charge of Step 4 meetings, and Ed Boyle, counsel for the department. They had been in on the Mason cases and might have some impressions to share from the Step 4 meeting. Boyle could brief him on the challenge of timeliness, which management since had raised to bar the union's appeal to arbitration. Then they could project the next step.

Such a meeting was arranged. Excerpts of the discussion follow:

George Underwood [pointing to the thick folders before Norman and Boyle]: Well, I see you are ready.

Philip Norman: On the surface, these two wage disputes from Mason seem to be run-of-the-mill stuff. But, if we are going to tighten up contract administration down there, we'll have to be well fortified.

Underwood: Suppose you give us a quick review, Ed.

Ed Boyle: Well, Phil just gave me the letter Shelton sent him to protest our reminder that the union's request for arbitration was untimely under our agreement and that on that ground we refuse to discuss the merits of their grievances until the arbitrator decides on that procedural issue. Shall I read it to you?

Underwood: I'd like us to take a look first on how those merits might shape up, to all the parties at Mason as well as to the arbitrator, if we decide to go to arbitration. Just where do "the merits" stand, Phil, by precedent, and by our own practice?

Norman: Take Grievance No. 46 first. We have situations like this frequently enough. A worker wants his vacation scheduled across two Monday to Sunday workweeks, instead of within a single workweek as management tries to allocate vacations. O.K., supervision grants it, as they did in this case.[1] The fellow involved is a camera enthusiast, as I recall, and he wanted his vacation at a time he could attend a flower show. No less! Then, he's back on the job on Friday; he works on Saturday, and expects overtime premium rates. That's what the union is claiming for Mr. Joseph Cartek, a "Machinist A," in his Grievance No. 46. Listen [reading]:

> The company violated Article VIII and Article X. Joseph Cartek was on paid vacation from August 11 through August 17. Paid vacation should be counted as days worked. But the company finally paid only straight time for hours worked on Saturday, August 19.

Now, the Step 4 meeting put us on notice, I think, that the union is going to town on that word "finally." Frank Saunders [staff member, assigned to represent the company at this Step 4 meeting] tells me that Harry Shelton, union district director for the Mason Mills, kept reminding us that Cartek's foreman had signed a "bonus slip" for his Saturday hours, that Cartek got the $8.80 overtime premium as a result, and that our "higher-ups" later took the money away. Certainly we haven't got them to admit yet that the best of men can make mistakes and that uniform practice exists throughout the company on overtime.

At any rate, David Scott, who is Cartek's foreman at Mason, filed this answer in Step 1 [reading from the grievance form]:

> I talked with Donald Montgomery in the Payroll Department and he said that they had gone according to their instructions from the Audit Department. There is no other course of action open to me.

At Step 2, Superintendent Sawyer ruled [reading]:

> I see no violation of Articles VIII and X of the Agreement.

Then, our plant manager there, Charles Whiteside, you know, in Step 3 affirmed Sawyer's decision:

> I see no reason to differ from the Step 2 answer.

Here, at headquarters, Saunders says that he had a tough battle from Shelton and his colleagues! They came back again and again to the fact that the "bonus slip" gave Cartek his $8.80 and "the audit department had it taken away again." They wanted to know why "audit" suddenly came into this. They gave examples going back years to show that it had been cus-

---

[1] Article X allowed department heads to grant personal requests for irregularly scheduled vacations.

tomary at Mason to settle such questions without the "auditing department's ever coming into the picture"—why, for the "first time now," they kept asking. Another point Shelton stressed was: "Why shouldn't paid vacation days count as days worked? Anyway, the bonus slip said so in hard cash, $8.80 actually paid."

Underwood: I guess there's the rub, all right. How about those Articles VIII and X, Ed? How do you lawyers figure we stand in applying the relevant sections to Cartek's case?

Boyle: Well, VIII, you know, "Hours of Work," governs our overtime issue, while X relates to "Vacation Schedules." The language of the contract is very clear.

[The three men at this point evaluated the relevant contract clauses.]

Underwood: Well, we certainly seem supported by that contract language. Now let's look at Grievance No. 47.

Norman: That's a more complicated business, I think, even though only one worker again is involved. This fellow, Richard Miller, is a fitter and, like Cartek, has been with us a long time. He's O.K., too, a steady, reliable man. [Leafing his file notes.] He does a sort of special job at Mason. For about half of his worktime, he builds expansion joints for bridges and similar construction. It's recognized as something within the general work load for fitters; and he has been the only one doing that for years, for about fifteen out of the twenty years he's been at Mason. Until this grievance arose, the company was giving him a time-and-a-quarter rate while he was working on such expansion joints. He's a general fitter, which is in Job Class 13 in the mill's job classification, with a standard hourly rate of $1.91. The time-study department at Mason claims that it has tried repeatedly to put an incentive rate on expansion joints, but without success. They claim it's too much a type of custom task; each joint has some special requirements. All our other, smaller, joint work, of course, is on incentive. At any rate, management at Mason gave Miller a special, individual rate—time and a quarter over his standard hourly rate—when he was assigned to expansion joints.

But, ever since our 1947 contract, as I need hardly tell you, such special rates are expressly prohibited. Nevertheless, it also is true that local management at Mason continued to pay Miller as always—until this October. At that time, we called to their attention Article V, which provides for the elimination of all special job rates. Nothing can be paid, for any job, but its incentive rate or its standard hourly rate. I'm afraid it has meant some loss of earnings to Miller to receive only his standard hourly rate for expansion joints—but there it is!

The union counters that, since Miller continued to receive his customary special rate not only before but also ever since the new prohibitions in the 1947 contract, that rate remains his rate by "local plant practice"—as guaranteed in Article III. Step 4 showed we have a toughie here.

Underwood: Yes, I gather that. I told you over the phone yesterday what I have in mind. I'd like you, Phil, to send someone from your staff to Mason to talk again with Shelton and other union people there, and with our local management. I want some clearer inkling, if we can get it, as to just how the union and the local folks really stand on these two cases.

I want us to move carefully, both to play it fair and to safeguard the good local relationships we certainly seem to have there, and, yet, also, to make it absolutely clear that we are a national company dealing with a responsible national union under a national agreement which means what it says—everywhere in the company. How can we act most effectively on these two cases to promote those ends? We have turned the union down thus far. We are trying to bar consideration of the merits of the cases by an arbitrator on the grounds of untimeliness. Are there any other alternatives for getting what we're after? By the way, Ed, how would that "timeliness" challenge sound before an arbitrator?

Boyle: Well, as always, I guess it would depend some on the arbitrator. But legally all the contractual requirements and all the precedents seem to put us in an almost impregnable position, I think, if we decide that the procedural challenge is our best course.

Underwood: Well, let's just review the facts on that, too, so I'll have your slant on everything involved to weigh with the final check-up interviews at Mason.

Boyle: Well, I'll review the timeliness challenge beginning with Step 4 on January 17. The dates tell the story. The minutes of that meeting, where the company finally denied both grievances in Step 4, were signed by Frank Saunders (staff member, industrial relations) on January 25 and were sent to the union by registered mail, return receipt requested. This return receipt shows that the union received the minutes on January 27. Shelton made certain deletions for the union, then signed and returned the minutes on February 1, together with a letter expressing the hope that the changes would prove acceptable. Almost four weeks later, February 27, Shelton wrote this letter:

Dear Mr. Norman:
  On February 1, I sent you four copies of minutes of meeting held January 17, with suggested changes. To date we have not heard from you. I would appreciate a communication immediately as it is the intention of the local union to appeal Grievances Nos. 46 and 47 to arbitration.

Phil replied on March 6, enclosing the minutes with the corrections initialed by Saunders. He pointed out that the time for appeal of the grievances, as stipulated by Article XII of the agreement—20 days from the Step 4 meeting on January 17 or 10 days from receipt of their minutes on January 27—had expired. Consequently, the cases must be deemed settled with the decision of Step 4. *Denied*, in a word. But, on March 9, Shelton wrote:

Dear Mr. Norman:
  Your facts as to dates are all true. But you must remember that changes had to be made in the minutes. Some of them were pretty bad—they changed the whole story. So I made the corrections in agreement with the union committee. We mailed the changed minutes back in the belief that before the cases would be closed

we would have to have a complete draft of the minutes. When you didn't return them, I reminded you; and, as soon as we got them with the changes initialed, we appealed the cases to arbitration!

The union lives up to the contract just the way we expect the company to, and we usually get along here at the Mason Mills pretty well. But we are not going to settle these disputes by saying that the time limits have expired. This isn't a big plant here, and these grievances contain issues that the Mason management has to straighten out. The company headquarters in the East says "This is it," and the union here in the West says "No, this is it." So we want to get an arbitrator's opinion on these cases. The same things may happen again, and there is no sense waiting through Steps 1, 2, 3, and 4 all over again. There are a lot of things in the plant that have to be straightened out. So what is the use of trying to "bar" arbitration. If these cases are settled here and now, it will be easier for the local management to operate the plant; and we will know which way we are going.

Underwood: How would you challenge that before, say, a "liberal-interpretation" arbitrator?

Boyle: We'd begin with the contract, of course. The arbitration time limits set forth in Article XII, which we invoke now, were negotiated in 1947. They were designed to obviate the delays encountered in appeals to arbitration. Such delays stemmed sometimes, as the union alleged at those 1947 negotiations, from failure of company representatives to prepare promptly the minutes of the Step 4 meeting. We cited other occasions when delays originated in arguments over the contents of the minutes. At any rate, we both agreed to the 20- and the 10-day limits, on which we stand in these cases.

Now, we have just recently had an arbitration decision which supports our position. This case, which arose at our Lorimer plant, in fact, involved an identical question of corrected minutes and was barred as untimely by the arbitrator just last week. I copied off some pertinent excerpts, which indicate how strong our position seems to be on this issue at Mason [reading]:

As much as the umpire is disposed wherever possible to avoid a summary dismissal of a grievance, he cannot see how, short of changing or ignoring the time limitation requirements of Article XII, Section 3, he can hold that the appeal of the instant grievances was timely. At the outset, if anything is clear about this Section 3, it is that only two factors may be considered in applying its 20- and 10-day appeal time requirement. The first is the date of the Step No. 4 meeting (or if there be more than one such meeting, then the last one); the other, the date of the union's receipt of a draft of the minutes of such Step No. 4 meeting. All other considerations, including the date of the sending and signing of the minutes, are irrelevant and completely uncontrolling. The very wording of the Section leaves no possible doubt thereon. But, if further corroboration is necessary, it may be had by comparing the comparable time limitation clause of the predecessor agreement with the amendments carried forward into our present Section 3. Whereas, in the former, the 10-day period started as of the date of the signing of the minutes, it now commences from the union's receipt of a draft of the minutes. In short, under Section 3, if the appeal is to be timely, it must be made within 20 days from the last Step No. 4 meeting or within 10 days from the union's receipt of the draft of the minutes of such meeting, whichever of the two periods is the longer. Regardless of the issues concerning the correction of the minutes, it accordingly follows that, in the absence of an agreement to the contrary, the appeal here was late and a dismissal of it mandatory.

[Looking up from this file excerpt.] Of course, we must face the fact that we probably won't have this same arbitrator hearing these cases at Mason. As you know, arbitrators differ considerably on these issues of timeliness. Then, too, we have had a rough time at Lorimer with the district international representative of the union there. You may recall him, Bob Fawcett, who has been playing fast and loose with the contract. He has appealed numerous cases to arbitration, regardless of merit. And this arbitrator, who just barred his latest as untimely, had been in on proceedings there a number of times. Maybe he thought it was time to teach that fellow a lesson.

Underwood: Even so, we seem to be in a sound position on the timeliness issue. These big unions, too, need to learn that they must meet their responsibilities everywhere when they sign contracts. But let's get one more check on these particular cases. I can see that wage administration, as well as contract administration, has been loose somewhere along the line to let such situations develop. But I'm still bothered, Phil, even though I'm convinced we're right on our main objectives. We've got to tighten up. But how can we act best on these two particular cases to do that, and yet be fair and careful of all the other things that may be involved? That's why one more plant visit to help us finally decide seems a good idea.

Norman: Yes, Ed and I agree you've got a good idea there. I shall ask Frank Saunders and young Arthur Peterson [a staff member, Industrial Relations] to make those interviews for us. Peterson, you know, is one of our newest recruits on the staff, pretty fresh out of school but with a good head on him. He's been assigned to Saunders; he tours the plants on grievance meetings, and writes up Step 4 minutes. But he hasn't been in on these grievances. Let's get a fresh point of view. I'll ask Saunders to let Peterson prepare the records of the plant interviews and present his recommendations on the cases for us to review. I know that Saunders is bothered by those developments there; and he'll be glad to get a fresh perspective from Peterson.

EXCERPTS FROM THE MEETINGS AT MASON MILLS

Frank Saunders and Arthur Peterson arrived by plane at the Mason Mills for meetings which Charles P. Whiteside, Plant Manager, had arranged with the union officials for them. Present with them were Shelton and Leo Marino, president of the local union. The following excerpts are taken from Peterson's notes on the meetings.

Shelton (u): Look, Frank. For years the workweek at this plant has been from Monday through Friday. Saturday has always been an overtime day. A man who worked eight hours on Saturday was paid for twelve hours. Dave Scott, the foreman, needed Joe Cartek for Saturday work. Evidently Joe was positive he was going to receive time and a half for coming in that Saturday, or he wouldn't have come in.

Saunders (m): But how can Joe Cartek expect overtime rates for Saturday, August 19, after he had been on vacation through Thursday of that week?

Sure, Joe Cartek received a slip giving him overtime pay for that Saturday's work. But the best of men can make mistakes—even Dave Scott.

The contract is controlling. As I said, it's the union's contract as well as ours. Here's Section 4 of Article VIII.

Manifestly, Subsection (a) of Section 4, concerning daily overtime, does not apply to this case at all. Right? O.K.

Now here's Subsection (b) concerning weekly overtime. Is the union going to argue that Joe Cartek worked more than forty hours that week ending August 19? Joe was off on vacation from Friday of the week before, and from Monday through Thursday of the week in question—and off on those days by his own special request. He reported to work on Friday, the 18th, and he worked on Saturday also, or only two days in the workweek—and only one before the claimed overtime day.

Subsection (c)—work on a holiday—doesn't apply here.

But it is Subsection (d), I believe, that you say chiefly supports this grievance. So let's look at its four major stipulations more closely:

(1) "Overtime compensation shall be paid for all time worked by an employee on any day within any week after he shall have worked on five previous days in that week." Joe worked only one previous day that week.

(2) "For purposes of determining valid overtime days, an employee shall be deemed thus to have worked on any day on which he shall have been scheduled to work but did not work because his schedule was changed after Friday of the preceding week." Not Joe's case, really, was it?

(3) "Changes of schedule due to operating interferences beyond managerial control shall exempt the company from this overtime obligation." It was perhaps an operating interference, but within our control—that change in Joe's schedule—and hardly the kind the union here would blame us for!

Now, finally, (4) "Schedule interferences stemming from voluntary individual or group 'quits,' or 'an Act of God,' shall likewise suspend sixth and seventh day overtime after five days' work." Joe's change of schedule certainly was voluntary, however else we define it.

So, there we are! For I need not tell you that we wrote that language to meet our operating needs for round-the-clock, round-the-calendar continuous operations. We can't rate Saturday or Sunday, as such, as "overtime." But, under union pressure, we have sought as much as possible to assure men two days of consecutive rest after five workdays and, for as many as possible, to make the workweek Monday through Friday. We assign vacation weeks to coincide with the payroll week. The payroll week begins on Monday and ends on Sunday, Monday through Sunday, at Mason.

Yet, Joe Cartek requested that he be granted an exceptional privilege. It was he, your camera enthusiast, who wanted to utilize his vacation for visits to a flower show that was opening that Friday. Management granted his request. He—

Shelton (u) [interrupting]: O.K. Don't throw the contract at us, and don't remind us that management is pretty decent here at Mason. Mr. Whiteside will tell you we always admit that, and we try to play it fair and square with them too. It's a wonder you haven't hit me over the head yet with that "timeliness bar." I'm waiting for it.

Meanwhile, Cartek had his $8.80 from local management, but only just long enough to look at it, I guess. Just a little mistake between friends, eh? Was it really a mistake? Or was it really the carrying out of an arrangement understood between an employee and his foreman that, if he would come in on Saturday, he would get time and a half? You know, we don't ask our foremen to put everything down in writing. Most of the time we understand each other without even saying so in so many words.

Besides, if you are going to force us to be technical, we think we can persuade a fair-minded arbitrator that you did change Joe's schedule after Friday of the preceding week, and, thus by Article VIII, Clause (2) of Subsection (d), Joe is entitled to have his days off counted as days worked. We hate to be technical, but if you force us we shall have to be. Management had the final say as to whether Joe should get off for his vacation in the middle of the scheduled workweek! Of course, you were decent, and let Joe go to the flower show. Still, you could have refused; it was finally up to you. But, then, in this case, you give with one hand and take away with the other.

Saunders (m): Now, Harry, that's a lot of challenge mixed into one blast. Again I say, isn't it the union's contract too? What do you mean not to throw it at you? Why even this Subsection (d) in Section 4 of Article VIII, on interpreting rights to overtime, which is primarily involved in this case, was a result of your union's demand at the bargaining table. I remember how it was written then into the 1947 agreement. There had been some dissatisfaction concerning the work schedules of the employees, particularly in the mechanical and the maintenance forces—of men like Cartek. These men might be scheduled for Monday through Friday. If general repair work needed doing, especially on large operating units, management might reschedule the men after the workweek had begun, giving a day off, say, on Wednesday, or Thursday, and assigning work on Saturday. The union urged, and management agreed, that the men should be able, on the basis of the schedule posted on Friday of the preceding workweek, to plan their days off with some degree of certainty. Manifestly, Cartek has no rescheduling like that to protest. He was rescheduled as a special vacation favor!

Whiteside (m): Well, I do want to say that, when Joe asked for that special vacation, we knew very well what his color photography meant to him. We're not a big outfit here, and Joe's camera shots rate high with all of us. I showed you those flower show pictures. [To Saunders and Peterson.] They *were* good, weren't they?

Saunders (m): They sure were.

Shelton (u): He hung one in the union office and it's really something, that rock garden color shot.

Marino (u): Joe's always doing things like that. He's popular for candid shots at weddings, confirmations, and all kinds of shindigs! Of course, he loves to do that sort of thing.

Whiteside (m): We always have Joe's color shots in the cafeteria, it seems to me. Joe's the camera enthusiast, but it seems to me we all get a kick out of that hobby of his.

Saunders (m): Well, headquarters would certainly agree that this kind of thing is fine. But I see by your records too that thirteen other men at Mason requested this summer, for personal reasons, as did Joe Cartek, a vacation week that ran over into two workweeks. And that's why we've got to get agreement on the right practice when overtime issues arise from such scheduling. Remember, after all, the same situation arises in our other plants also. We've got to have uniform practices.

Shelton (u): Isn't the payroll department the one concerned with the hours of work and the money a person makes? Here is a case where the payroll department did agree to the man's getting time and a half. He's paid twelve hours for Saturday's shift. Then the auditing department comes along three days later and takes it away from him. I can't understand why. That is the first time the auditing department ever came into the picture. How could the payroll department overlook that?

Saunders (m): Men make mistakes.

Shelton (u): No doubt that those other thirteen men were told that they wouldn't get time and a half for working that Saturday, because they didn't come in, did they? I know that Cartek certainly wouldn't have come in for straight time on that Saturday. And the foreman knew it.

Whiteside (m): The foreman knew what?

Shelton (u): That Cartek was coming in because he was going to get time-and-a-half pay, by prior understanding. The foreman turned in that credit slip. That is the only reason he filed a grievance, because the man was positive of receiving time and a half for coming in the next day. He is not on incentive. He is a time worker.

Marino (u): Cartek stated the case in this letter, about taking away his overtime (reading):

I was not told nor did my foreman know that this was to be the case. I, therefore, feel that as long as neither the foreman nor the union nor myself was notified in advance of the rule that I am fully justified in filing this grievance with the union in order to collect $8.80, which the auditing department ordered deducted from my salary.

On Grievance No. 47—Richard Miller

Marino (u): The union feels, not only that the company failed in 1947 to eliminate Miller's special rate when that amendment was written into the contract eliminating any job rates but incentive and standard hourly rates, but also that it confirmed this decision by paying him in the same way ever since. During the war, there were many times when the company had to throw in extra money on certain jobs in order to encourage production. The union knew that. That's why, in 1947, when a general increase was granted, a lot of these jobs with special bonuses were eliminated; and the union didn't argue the point. But Miller's special rate stayed on. The union was of the opinion that, as long as this man was really a special worker, as long as the company needed expansion joints, and as long as the company couldn't calculate a fair incentive rating for it, they'd continue to protect Miller's take-home by agreeing to pay him his customary bonus. We never even had to argue about it. For all these years after management had the contractual right to eliminate the job, or eliminate its "fix-up," they continued the long-established, customary rate on it.

Saunders (m): I think you fellows have given the basic facts and defined the single issue: could the company, this past October, validly eliminate a rate which you concede the company could have eliminated in 1947? You agree that this rate represented a kind of extra allowance of the type that the parties expressly intended to eliminate. Their expression of intention can be found in Article V of the agreement. The introductory sentence of its Section 3 reads:

> . . . the standard hourly wage rate for each job class, as set forth in said Appendix I, shall be
> (a) the hourly wage rate for each job in such class which is not paid on an incentive basis (and any other hourly wage rate, whether higher or lower, for such job is eliminated) . . .

Subsection (c) of that same section further defines the standard hourly rate as:

> (c) the hourly wage rate for any work which shall not be incentive rated and which is not included as a part of the work which is covered by an incentive rate (and any and all other payments for such work are eliminated).

Shelton (u): Now, wait a minute, *wait a minute!* You fellows certainly are going legal on us! But don't put words in our mouth. We do *not* say the union would have agreed that you could just have eliminated Miller's special rate in 1947. We do not think at all that his rate is really the kind that Article V aimed its new prohibitions at! He'd still need some incentive to be willing to accept expansion joint work. You can't ask a guy to do your "special" work—and take a pay cut! But we do say that the management, by not availing itself of the new prohibitions on special rates in 1947, sort of conceded Miller's rate wasn't quite that kind we both agreed was "out." It *was* a kind of incentive. Then, you continued paying him as always for all these years since 1947. By now, we say, his rate has at least the protection of the customary practices clause of the contract—if we've got to be contractual!

Saunders (m): Now, Harry, you know these individual rates were a plague throughout the company. One purpose of the job classification program, even before 1947, was precisely to reduce the thousands of rates and put them into an orderly company-wide structure of work and pay. The company, as well as the union, had learned that they could be plagued by irregular rates such as this one, which were commonly called "fix-up" payments. With the amendment to the 1947 agreement we made their elimination final.

Now, it is true that Miller was paid a special rate for work on the larger, custom-made expansion joints. It is also true that this work cannot be piece rated, because it is complex, and nonrepetitive, differing both in parts to be fitted and in work to be done from order to order. And we find the records support your statement that Miller received a fix-up rate on this work for about fifteen years.

Now, management concedes all that. But we deem it an unfortunate circumstance—that Miller's fix-up was not eliminated when the 1947 agreement became effective. It should have been; and, in other branch plants, fix-ups were then ended. But, for some reason or other, we have encountered rate-setting difficulties in this plant. At any rate, contrary to instructions that were issued from company headquarters with the execution of the 1947 agreement, Miller's fix-up was not eliminated. But, when, this past October, a new acting head of the rate-setting department discovered that fix-up payments were being made and had been continued to be made to Miller, he immediately eliminated the fix-up. So much management concedes.

But we concede nothing further. Instead, it seems to us that, from this point on, it's the union that should do the conceding. Certainly you must concede that Miller has been receiving an irregular type of payment, and has, since 1947, been earning more than his contractual due. Management is willing to leave undisturbed the bit of profit accruing to him from this oversight or error on the part of the rate supervisor of the local plant. It is also our position, however, that, when a mistake of that nature is discovered, the company has the right to correct it. To management it appears, beyond question, that in this case nothing more than such a mistake has been involved, belatedly but validly uncovered, and finally but validly corrected.

Shelton (u): You guys are certainly admitting a lot of mistakes around here. I never knew that Lawton's tolerated mistakes, or, shall we say, failed to discover one for years—and, then, bingo! And you are the guys who want to bar the union from arbitrating the merits of these "mistakes," because of *untimely* appeal! You should dare talk of *untimeliness!* Some bears for timeliness—after *fifteen* years!

Saunders (m): Now, be fair, Harry. We're talking "contract." The contract says there *are* time limits within which grievances must be handled or passed on to the next step. The contract says that fix-ups must be eliminated from our job rate structure. It doesn't say that, if one is not eliminated within one year, or three years, or even fifteen, the company forfeits its rights forever after under the contract.

Shelton (u): O.K., and the contract also says, in Article III, Section 4, that management cannot on its own just "change or eliminate any effective local custom or practice at any plant." A special rate, in effect fifteen years, is *customary!*

Saunders (m): Oh, no, Harry! Section 4 of Article III, as you should know, has been under examination all throughout our industry. Every company, not only Lawton's, finds the unions using local customs to ask many benefits beyond the contracts, at least as management reads the language.

We simply say that Section 4 of Article III cannot be invoked to protect any so-called plant custom where express provisions of the agreement control or govern. [Opening the agreement again.] Here's that Section 4 of Article III, on which you base Miller's claim. It opens by defining the protected customs as "any local practice . . . *not covered* by this Agreement." It repeats those words several times besides incorporating Article XII's timeliness requirements for arbitration! Now, surely none of you at the union could deny that rates of pay, above all things, are subjects of express provisions of the agreement! You certainly battle for the pay rate provisions hard enough. The particular provision that governs in this case is Subsection (c) of Section 3 of Article V of the agreement.

It's really all aboveboard and fair. You yourself say the job classification of Miller's work as a general fitter is Class 13. Since October, Miller has been paid that standard hourly wage rate on his nonincentive work, as specified by the agreement. The prior payment of the fix-up allowance for work on expansion devices had given Miller, for several years, more than he was entitled to under the contract.

Shelton (u): Well, didn't management really continue that fix-up because Miller works only about half his time on expansion joints? The rest of his time is on incentive jobs, where, like most good fitters, he averages 17 or 18 cents an hour above the guaranteed standard hourly rate—isn't that true? But, when he is pulled off his incentive job and is put over on expansion joints, he loses his opportunity for earning at incentive. The company saw that, naturally! And wasn't this plant management doing what seemed to be the practical, sensible thing to do? It was only fair to recognize that it wasn't Miller's fault that management couldn't piece rate these expansion joints. But, anyway, the fix-up just gave him the little extra that assured him his usual incentive earnings. Doesn't Miller usually make about 18 cents above the standard hourly rate on his incentive job? And wasn't that about the amount he was given above the hourly rate when assigned on expansion joints?

Saunders (m): I don't have comparative average hourly earnings showing Miller's pay when he works on incentive work and on this nonpriceable work. But Peterson has been getting the average levels of earnings of fitters who are regularly on incentive, that is, of the other men in the group. How about that, Arthur? How much have you got so far?

Peterson (m): It's been hard to get the satisfactorily comparable figures we, naturally, are after. I've been trying to compile earnings for the pay periods before and after October 15, when Miller's special rate on expansion devices was eliminated. For the three quarters before October 15, the fitters averaged earnings of 21 cents, 22 cents, and 18 cents above the standard hourly rate. Miller, in these quarters, as a whole, averaged 23.6 cents above the standard hourly rate. After October 16, in the last quarter of last year, the fitters as a group had a good run of jobs and averaged 37 cents above the standard hourly rate. Miller averaged 16.9 cents above. I've just been looking into this year's earnings. It shows the fitters earned about 18 cents above the standard hourly rate, and Miller running anywhere from the standard hourly rate to about 13 cents above. It all depends on the job mix assigned to him.

Shelton (u): Exactly, and it seems to me that these earnings' figures certainly prove our point. Miller has taken quite a pay cut—and that's exactly our point. But why should he? He's doing, as he always has, a job mix the company needs. Are you sure you can't set a piece rate somehow for the work on expansion joints? Isn't the union justified in feeling at least this much: Since the company has continued that fix-up for years, longer than they were obligated to, the man must have been earning his extra money on his expansion joint work? Lawton doesn't throw around unearned money. We don't expect the company to pay our members for work they don't do satisfactorily, but neither do we expect the company to cut their pay for the same work they've long been doing. If the company is unable to incentive rate expansion joints, but still needs them in the job mix, let the company find some way, under the contract, of meeting their obligation to Miller. You are the experts on holding to each letter and "bar" of the contract!

For such sticklers on the contract as you guys have become, how can you justify a pay cut to an admittedly good worker doing as well as ever the same work he's been doing for some fifteen years? It's up to you not to cut any man's earnings under the contract!

Whiteside (m): But, Harry, this isn't arbitrary. It really is hard to piece rate that large, specialized, custom-made work. And, as headquarters reminded us, standard hourly rates aren't necessarily low rates or minimum rates. They are standard rates for work we don't piece rate, whether done by machinists or by pattern makers—or fitters!

Shelton (u): O.K. We grant that you pay skilled craftsmen standard hourly rates. But you always have. It's not so on production jobs. And you have some very skilled time-study experts both here and in your headquarters organization. I've never seen them really stumped so long. Might not this reflect another kind of "drifting"? Didn't management say "Well"— in 1942—"there's a war on; we'll just keep that fair special rate on the job." Then, when 1947 gave you the contractual right to eliminate this fix-up allowance with the others, why didn't you? You must have felt, at least in the plant—where management ought to know—that there was still some fairness in this special allowance. We're a small plant and know each other pretty well. If local management paid Miller a fix-up, they knew he was giving them full value. And Miller trusted them. But, now, word comes from headquarters, and they just say "Well, no more fix-ups—that's it! Look at Article V—after all these years." I just don't feel as though that's the proper way to handle such a problem. I'll bet, if local management speaks its mind, it will tell headquarters "You've cut a good worker at least 14 cents an hour for doing essential, hard, disagreeable, complicated work for some 50% of his worktime." Is headquarters going to insist that theirs is the last word? Are you going to say "Denied for untimeliness"?

Saunders (m): No. We say your appeal is untimely under the contract. See—

Shelton (u) [again interrupting]: To hell with timeliness! We'll take a chance on a fair-minded arbitrator! We've also got justice to give to two good fellows in these grievances. Isn't that the real problem for both of us? When can we get together to decide on an arbitrator? We are ready to submit the names of three experienced men. Do you have your three candidates ready?

Saunders (m): We would like to go into a huddle once more at our office in Philadelphia. We'll let you know in about ten days.

DISCUSSION QUESTIONS

1. Compare the positions taken by central and local management on the Cartek grievance. How do you account for the position taken by central management?

2. Following this hearing, what position would you recommend the company take on the Cartek case? On the Miller case?

3. What is your position on the issue of timeliness if the case goes to arbitration?

4. In what way will the outcome of these grievances affect (*a*) interpersonal relations at Mason; (*b*) labor relations at other plants; and (*c*) the contract and its application?

PART III. INSTITUTIONAL RELATIONS: PROBLEMS AT THE BARGAINING TABLE

NATIONAL STEEL CASTINGS COMPANY

THE MANAGEMENT CLAUSE IN RENEGOTIATING THE AGREEMENT

I

In the negotiation of which this case is part, 12 sessions, spread over 10 weeks, were held. At the earlier sessions, proposals and counterproposals were discussed until all projected changes had been canvassed. An adjournment followed to permit preparation of final positions. Negotiations were then resumed to hammer out a final draft.

Excerpts are here presented, only (1) from the first session opening the proceedings; (2) from the first session following the resumption after adjournment.

Of twelve management and twenty-seven union representatives present, the following men participated:

For the Company	*For the Union*
Stanley C. Richards, Manager, Industrial Relations	L. T. Dorinsky, International Representative and leader of the union delegation
Charles Everett, Jr., Vice President	
Martin D. Turner, Comptroller	N. T. Robinson, Director (a Midwest region)
William C. Hysinger, Foundryburg	A. G. Cox, Field Representative (Indiana District)
	Albert Henley, Foundryburg
	Louis Nash, Foundryburg
	Frank Bowman, Foundryburg
	Philip Ogden, Harborville
	George Muller, Allentown
	Donald H. Campbell, Pittsburgh

Richards (m): Mr. Dorinsky, would you start and give us your viewpoints why you want the changes indicated?

Dorinsky (u): Very well. Before I begin, however, may I make this explanation: for two days the union committees sent here have been meeting—going over our old agreement to determine what changes should be made. The boys have all had ample time to discuss the changes they desire.

To expedite proceedings, we had a chairman and a secretary appointed for these discussions, and I will want the chairman, Mr. Henley, to assist me in having the delegations from the respective local unions express their viewpoints.

We request that the words "demote," "suspend," "discharge," and "exclusively," be stricken from the management clause which reads as follows:

Article II. Except as otherwise specifically provided in this agreement, the management of the plant and the direction of the working forces, including the right to plan, direct, and control plant operation; to hire, promote and *demote;* to *suspend* or *discharge* for cause; to relieve employees from duty because of lack of work and for other legitimate reasons; to introduce new or improved production methods or facilities, is vested *exclusively* in the company. The rights herein set forth will not be exercised for the purposes of discrimination against employees because of membership in or activity on behalf of the union.

Whom do you want to call on to discuss that, Mr. Henley? You know who participated in the discussions, and those people should discuss the article as we go along.

Henley (u): I do not remember exactly. Some proposals came from one local union, others came from delegations.

Dorinsky (u): Well then, this clause is open for general discussion now.

Richards (m): Everybody ought to get in on it.

Dorinsky (u): Yes, everybody ought to get in on it. That is why we are here.

Richards (m): We are honestly and sincerely trying to find answers here.

Ogden (u): On these words "demote," "suspend," and "discharge," the management has that right "exclusively." Management goes ahead and suspends, promotes, and demotes without consultation with the union. If we are to be a bargaining unit, we should have a vote as to whether the action should be sustained.

Richards (m): Is not that amply covered under your grievance machinery?

Muller (u): It is all right to say you have a grievance machinery, but you also say that the purpose of the agreement is to promote harmony. We cannot have harmony if we have men demoted and suspended, while everything about it rests exclusively with the company. If we want to establish harmony we should specify that the union will have a chance to bargain before a man is fired, demoted or suspended.

Richards (m): Are not you invading the responsibilities of management? How about demoting a man who clearly lacks the qualifications for a job?

Muller (u): I think your representatives at the plant can say that we have been more than ready to go along. There have been some men discharged for whom we have had to go through the grievance procedure to get them back wages. Under the revision we propose, we will never have to come in and ask for back wages because if we decide the man was wrong there will be no case for us to take up.

Richards (m): Personally I have a feeling you are going to create more grievances by taking that word "demote" out. For in the functioning of management you have to give some liberty on these things to administration. In other words, if we are going to be forced to consult each time there is a promotion or demotion, the management is going to be stifled.

Muller (u): The company has recognized us as a bargaining unit. When we give you this exclusive right, you have immediately taken away our bargaining rights. I don't think either party should have the exclusive right or the final right to say anything.

Turner (m): Have you overlooked the words "except as otherwise provided in this agreement"? They are part of the clause as well as "exclusively"; in fact they start it.

Muller (u): We are just looking at the words that are causing us trouble.

Richards (m): Have you any specific cases that would show instances when they have been abused?

Ogden (u): A new employee comes into the plant and the foreman is a friend of his; regardless of whether he is efficient or not, the foreman will go ahead and promote him. I think the man with seniority rights should be given a chance to show his ability and qualifications.

Richards (m): Don't you have a remedy?

Nash (u): We have not been able to find a remedy yet under this contract. I have such a case right now at the new Foundryburg plant. It is resting until we see what is going to be the outcome of this negotiation. Two employees were hired and given jobs better than the job of a man with seniority in the same occupation. You take up the question with the head of the department, and he refers you to this management clause. But if we could sit down as a bargaining unit and take up Bill Jones and John Doe, we could say that they are entitled to work in the vacancies where you are putting the new men. We don't have that chance because management falls back on this Article II.

Richards (m): It seems to me you are going far afield; you are taking a function away from the management. You do have review machinery provided by the contract. If you object to the acts of management, you can start that machinery through a grievance and pursue to the bitter end the question why any man was promoted or demoted outside of his turn.

Bowman (u): Mr. Richards, our position is this: if there is anything in the contract that disrupts harmony, it not only hurts the worker but it hurts the management. These words "exclusively," "promotion," "demotion," "suspension," in reality all go back to the immediate foreman. Management takes the position his act has to be supported.

Now, you ask for instances. In the Foundryburg plant you no doubt remember a letter dated January 5. A group of white workers threatened to strike if negroes were not removed from a certain job that only paid 97½ cents. Since that time, if you please, better than 20 per cent of those same men who threatened to strike have been made foremen; and then they were put over those very negroes. The negro workers have never risen any further than a 97½ cent job. It goes further than that. Two cases of violence arose because these men were made foremen. In the recent case one of our men was arrested by the plant police, and given four months and costs.

If the change we ask were made, management would not feel it should protect men who should not be foremen to start with. I do not contend that management should not have that specific right of naming foremen. But when you put a man in such a position—with an attitude against the policy of the firm, the law, the times, and everything else—exercising your exclusive right has disrupted harmony.

Richards (m): Would you say that management has not the right to "suspend," or "discharge," but has to throw these questions back into a bargaining group to make the determination? Have you gone that far?

Bowman (u): No, we would not say you did not have the right to discharge or suspend with cause. But we do say the union should have the opportunity of knowing whether the "cause" was just or not. You know, under this clause there are suspensions up to and including five days by a minor foreman. The union is not notified. If the foreman says, "I don't like your looks; you get five days off," you get the five days off. Management has the exclusive right to do that. The only time you have a say is when a man is subject to discharge, and then he has to file written notice for a hearing. We say that is unjust.

Richards (m): You mean to say a man can be penalized for one hour, one day or a week, without the right under this contract to start a grievance?

Bowman (u): Yes, sir, I mean that is being done.

Richards (m): Then that is our collective fault in permitting such a thing to be done. It is your fault and our fault. These are merely the rules of the game and it would not make any difference what you put in this agreement; such a situation still would not be met unless we are willing to use the grievance machinery.

Bowman (u): Mr. Richards, no doubt that is true. You say we have the grievance machinery. But here is a man who has been hurt on the job and goes to the dispensary. He is there about twenty minutes. The foreman penalizes him two hours. The immediate foreman has the privilege of suspension, with no say from anybody. In this case he just called the time clerk and said, "Take off two hours." Out of this penalization an altercation starts up between the man and the foreman. As a result the worker is sent to prison.

Richards (m): I still do not see how the changes you propose would give you any more protection than you have now. You have got to learn to use our agreement. Management, I grant you, perhaps has not fulfilled its full intent on the grievance machinery. But we can be driven to fulfilling it by your intelligent use of the grievance machinery. And we urge that.

You must realize that at your plant, as at any new plant, there are hundreds of brand new men and new foremen. These foremen are being pressed for production. Those things have to be taken into consideration. Therefore we have to come back to the agreement, to use that vehicle to ride upon, to accomplish our end; and the grievance machinery is a means to the end.

Bowman (u): That is right, Mr. Richards. But we are looking at something that we have found disrupts the contract. Let me ask you whether you personally would pick this kind of men to be foremen. Here are some thirty of them, who have signed a statement like this. You make them foremen two weeks after they sign it. Listen to this; this is management itself at our plant speaking:

We received a communication addressed to whom it may concern and reading as follows:

"We the undersigned crane millwrights, electricians, crane operators, employees of National Steel Castings at Foundryburg, do not want negroes operating cranes within the above-mentioned plant, and we shall refuse to work, if necessary, effective ten days from date."

Recently an election was held in the new plant at Foundryburg by the NLRB to determine who is the authorized representative of our workmen and your request covers a subject which should be taken up through the regular channels of those authorized by the Government to deal with the workmen.

The management is very desirous of having your full cooperation to the end of getting the plant in total production and toward creating harmonious relations in the plant for the benefit of all our workmen.

Richards (m): Is there anything that would have denied those men the right to serve that petition upon the management?

Bowman (u): No, but something should be written somewhere that would have denied the management the right to make such men foremen over the very people against whom they petitioned.

Richards (m): You don't think these men were promoted for that reason, do you?

Bowman (u): I don't know. Cameron's name is second on this petition. Cameron was given a foremanship three weeks later to supervise these very people he petitioned against.

Richards (m): What has been his conduct since then?

Bowman (u): Very deplorable. He is the foreman who gave the worker two hours for going to the dispensary after he was hurt on the job. The worker winds up with four months in a penal institution because of the actions of this foreman. The workers threatened to walk out sometime this week if this foreman wasn't removed. That is the situation under which they work.

Richards (m): Who is this boy that got four months?

Bowman (u): Jefferson.

Richards (m): What happened there, Bill?

Hysinger (m): He struck the foreman three times, so Cameron went out and preferred charges against him.

Richards (m) [to Bowman]: Are you trying to defend that man for those acts?

Bowman (u): No, but it is my contention that Cameron should never have been made a foreman. Each one of the foremen who signed this petition is known to the workers; their feeling about negro workers is known, and 80 per cent of that department are negroes. There is a disruption of harmony when you make such men foremen.

I am not defending the worker's acts. Assault and battery is against the law wherever it is performed. But if you create provocation, you have some responsibility for the assault that may result. When you put a supervisor over men whom he didn't want even on 97½ cent jobs, with the threat that the whites will strike, of course you will have violence sooner or later. But then the personnel department defends him. Why not defend the worker who is provoked?

Richards (m): Then you want to put yourself in the position of telling the management who are going to be foremen?

Bowman (u): No, sir; not at all.

Richards (m): Isn't that substantially what you said here?

Bowman (u): If I saw a man in that plant bring in a bomb, and put it under one of the blast furnaces, would management appreciate the fact if I told them about it?

Richards (m): I think you are getting off the reservation.

Bowman (u): Suppose you caught the man with the bomb before it went off. I suppose then you would tell him that if he doesn't plant any more bombs you will make him a foreman.

Richards (m): It still begs the question.

Bowman (u): It does not beg the question at all. The feeling those white men who became foremen publicly expressed against the negroes working under them is just like a bomb. You're bound to get explosions sooner or later.

Richards (m): It resolves itself to this: are you going to put yourself in the position of telling management what it can or cannot do with its normally accepted prerogatives?

Bowman (u): No, sir.

Richards (m): It seems to me you said that. How would management perform then?

Bowman (u): I might ask management then, if every time management gets a group of people who have declared themselves against another group of people, do those people become by their very act supervisors over the people they've publicly declared against?

Richards (m): Sometimes people sign petitions as a matter of pressure. You probably have done it yourself. You sign a petition in order to keep company with those you are going along with. That has always been a rather dangerous thing. We have never recognized any group petition as expressing the intent and purpose of every individual who signed it.

Turner (m): Mr. Richards, the proposal that was given to us mentions the words "demote, suspend or discharge," and "exclusively." There is nothing in the proposal about promotions; yet that is what we are now talking about, is it not?

Richards (m): That is right.

Turner (m) [to the union representatives]: Are you changing the proposal here?

Muller (u): No. What we are after and the only thing we are after is bargaining rights. It's the word "exclusively" that we are after. We have an instance in our plant where a foreman walks up to a man and says, "You are suspended for three days." Management naturally goes along with the foreman. When that man comes back, the foreman says, "Now, you admit you told a lie or I am going to give you three more days." He throws the fear of God into the man. That does not make for harmony—or fairness.

Let us have an equal right in seeing what we are getting in the plant. I don't go along with any foreman using the word "exclusively"; he is going to use it as a whip over our men. I go to the foreman and I say, "Here, that worker is innocent," and he replies, "Well now, Muller, we have the exclusive right to do as we please with that man." Where do we have any bargaining rights there?

Richards (m): I will tell you where.

Muller (u): Just wait a minute. It is all right to say use the grievance machinery. But while I am going through four, five, and six stages, the worker doesn't know whether he is going to hold his job or get back pay or not. Why not go to the steward and say, "We have a man here who is out of order," and lay your case before that steward. If you persuade the steward, he is going to go along with you. Other than that, we have no bargaining power.

Everett (m): You are not bargaining then, Mr. Muller. You are running the shop.

Muller (u): No, I say we are matching every ounce of manpower we have against your dollars in that shop. You cannot operate without our manpower.

Turner (m): The only thing the management clause really does is to retain with the company everything they do not give you explicitly in the contract. The right to institute grievances when men have been treated unjustly is certainly not limited by the management clause.

Muller (u): Yes, I realize that. But don't we want to prevent grievances as well as settle them? Why not take out of the contract those words that promote grievances? You fellows possibly do not deal directly with men but we have to hear all of this stuff. All we want is a bargaining chance to get a man out of this long grievance chain before his case becomes a grievance.

Richards (m): What would you say to this; that we add, as a second paragraph of the management clause, the following:

No changes affecting the rights of members of the union shall be put into effect by the company without the company first informing the union. If the company and the union cannot agree on the proposed changes, the company shall have a right to institute the desired changes and the union shall have the right to make them the subject of grievance, as provided in this agreement. Under this procedure a reasonable time is to be allowed the union representative to consult with the union membership and appropriate officers regarding the proposed changes.

Muller (u): We are going to be called in prior to the time you lay off a man or suspend him, and then if there's a difference between us, you still would like to have us take it up through the grievance machinery?

Richards (m): That is right.

Muller (u): I see nothing wrong with that.

Dorinsky (u): Is that agreeable?

Nash (u): Yes, it is agreeable.

Richards (m): We must confess that neither side has grown up completely, and therefore this will clarify things for us. We had presupposed under the present version we would operate as these added words indicate. Let us go to the next change you propose.

II

In this way the union presented all its proposals for revisions in specific contract clauses, and the company suggested counterproposals. After the adjournment to study the proposals as a whole, the negotiating sessions were resumed, and opened with the following discussion:

Dorinsky (u): The committee at the previous sessions expressed itself on changes that it wants. We adjourned to give the company time to consider. We are in a receptive frame of mind to hear what you have got to say about them.

Richards (m): Does everyone have a copy of the contract now? Now, as to Article I, on the purpose of the agreement. We propose that that article remain as is.

Dorinsky (u): Very well.

Richards (m): On page 2, the management clause; the first paragraph remains as is; then we have added a second paragraph. That added second paragraph reads:

No substantial changes adversely affecting the conditions of employment of members of the Union shall be put into effect by the Company without the Company first informing the Union representatives.

Dorinsky (u): Was that the memorandum that you gave us?

Richards (m): Yes, that is the substance.

Dorinsky (u): Has the company any particular reason for wanting this addition outside of the fact that the union asked for some changes in the management clause?

Richards (m): We had been charged with not taking up with employees things that the men felt they had a right to know before they were done. The purpose of this addition is to inform the union before such things are done.

Dorinsky (u): Now I am wondering whether the addition of this second paragraph may not give the company a right to go actually beyond the things specifically set forth in the first paragraph and whether we won't run into some problems on that basis.

In the first paragraph we say, "except as otherwise specifically provided"; and then we write a broad paragraph; then finally we say that, by the mere fact of informing representatives of the union of changes adversely affecting us prior to making them, they can be made.

Richards (m): What do you suggest we do? Strike the second paragraph?

Cox (u): I would say that second paragraph could be improved if you say that, in the exercise of rights that have not otherwise been specifically provided for, no substantial change adversely affecting the conditions of employment of the members of the union shall be put into effect by the company without first informing the union representatives.

Richards (m): I think we can accept that. The only intent and purpose here is to make this contract work.

Dorinsky (u): It is a decent move to inform our people prior to doing something, if that will prevent problems arising. There is nothing wrong with that, if it is understood that the new provision must be used for that purpose specifically. Our problem has always been with language.

Richards (m): That has been going on, I understand, for about four thousand years.

Dorinsky (u): The more language you get the more problems you have. That is why I would like it specifically stated that the new paragraph carries out the thought the first paragraph originates, as Cox suggested.

Richards (m): We would be willing to accept that.

Dorinsky (u): It seems to me this point must still be raised: here in the new second paragraph, the union is giving the company the right to make substantial changes adversely affecting conditions of employment by the mere fact of informing the union. That is a broad statement.

Richards (m): What do you suggest we do? Cut it out entirely?

Dorinsky (u): Let me say this to our committee. Our present clause is a standard management clause used in all agreements with all companies. We made some suggestions on scratching some words such as "promote" and "demote" and "exclusively." But there is nothing in here that does not appear in practically 99 per cent of the labor agreements in existence. We did raise the question of the right to be informed on some of the changes that management does make under its exclusive privilege. But shall we now set forth that the company has the right to make substantial changes adversely affecting the conditions of employment of members of the union and put them into effect by merely informing the union representatives?

Richards (m): Would you suggest we strike this whole paragraph and try to accomplish what we're after along an educational line?

Dorinsky (u): Just what are you proposing?

Richards (m): Strike the second paragraph entirely and let the first paragraph stand as it is and then develop an educational program to keep our works management in line to the place where we must inform the union on such changes.

Robinson (u): If the company desires to make any substantial change, then let the plant management take it up with the local union committee and let a mutually satisfactory agreement be reached before any change is made.

Everett (m): The scheduling of our working forces, how we are going to place work, whether we are going to take work out of one shop and put it in another—we are not going to discuss such things at all.

Cox (u): The particular operations of the working plant, changes in work schedules, those are matters for collective bargaining.

Everett (m): No, I think you are off there.

Henley (u): What we complain about is the "promote," "demote," "suspend" and "discharge." If we can get this paragraph to say that we get notice on these things, we'll have real bargaining rights.

Richards (m): Mr. Dorinsky has very adequately covered it when he said this is a standard management clause. In order to answer the criticism that was brought up, we endeavored to insert that second paragraph.

Dorinsky (u): The paragraph itself is a strictly negative paragraph. It talks only of things that adversely affect us.

Richards (m): That is right.

Cox (u): It is true this is a standard management clause. But it is being used in some instances in ways that are not standard: to penalize for absenteeism, laying off without notice, and also for insubordination or fussing with the boss, and so forth, especially at Foundryburg.

Everett (m): You always have the grievance machinery to redress such conditions.

Richards (m): Let me suggest that we strike that second paragraph, Mr. Dorinsky, and depend, as I said, on an educational program.

Dorinsky (u): All right.

DISCUSSION QUESTIONS

1. What factors seem to have generated the demand for these changes in the management clause?

2. Compare the men who carry the major discussion at the opening session and after the adjournment. How would you explain the difference? Evaluate the content of the discussion from the same viewpoint of the apparent objectives of the leaders in both sessions.

3. Explain Dorinsky's attitude on the wording of the management clause as finally proposed by management.

4. What clues would you offer to explain the differences in the wording of the modifications of the management clause offered by Richards at the two sessions?

5. How would you characterize the strategy and tactics used by Dorinsky as a discussion leader in the first session? In the second session? How would you characterize those of Richards in both sessions?

UNIVERSAL CASTINGS

THE UNION SHOP AND PRODUCTIVITY COMMITTEES

Relationships between Universal Castings and the Steelworkers had begun in 1937. In 1951, five months prior to the termination of their contract, the parties met to negotiate a new agreement. The union demands were presented and clarified in two sessions.

Present at the third meeting were:

For the Company	*For the Union*
Chicago Headquarters	*District Directors*
B. R. Bishop, Director of Industrial Relations	J. Wolensky, Illinois
	A. Baird, Ohio
W. H. Palmer, Vice President in charge of Production	I. Merrill, Pennsylvania
	H. Kohler, Indiana
E. J. King, Comptroller	R. Russell, New Jersey
Plant Representatives	*Plant Representatives*
Personnel Directors of all nine plants	A. Underhill, Rockford
	B. Peters, Alton
	D. Heimer, Toledo
	F. Gotham, South Bend
	G. Docar, Reading
	I. Parenti, Trenton
	Others from all nine plants

Bishop (m): If you are ready to proceed, on union security we propose:

The company and the Union agree to maintenance of membership as the form of union security until the termination of the national emergency or the expiration of this agreement, whichever date first occurs.

Wolensky (u): No. No, period!

Bishop (m): What then do you suggest, Mr. Wolensky?

Wolensky (u): If there is any intent to do a constructive job, this is one time you can discuss a union shop. You give the specific impression that the minute you can you are going to run and run like hell.

Are we to understand that the only way for any progress on union recognition is by order of a governmental agency, or by force or economic pressure? I don't think it does anything for the relationship we are trying to build. I am wondering whether after all these years of discussion it has been anything other than lip service.

Bishop (m): Mr. Wolensky, these things are evolutionary. You cannot push them into a state of maturity. They have to go through an embryonic stage.

Wolensky (u): If that shows any iota of confidence, I would like you to explain it. It leaves us with only one thing, that we must continue to fight, either through federal agencies or through our own economic strength, to retain our organization. These are cold, hard words. The man who reads them knows what they mean. If we tell the men this is an embryonic proposition, they don't know what the hell we are talking about.

Bishop (m): I know of no union contracts that have granted the union shop absolutely without providing first only for union maintenance.

Wolensky (u): Then let me advise you. It has not been uncommon for a union shop to be secured the very first thing, along with the check-off. But you wouldn't give us even maintenance of membership until the order of the War Labor Board, and that is the very same clause we have today. I recognize that there is a crawling stage, but what about all the other years we have been doing business? What about 1937, 1938, 1939, 1940 and so on through 1950?

Palmer (m): It is action, performance, in the final analysis that counts. We too can use the words "lip service." I think your officers are probably very sincere in wanting these contracts fulfilled. But we are yet to see that demonstrated in our plants. You want a fair day's pay. How about a fair day's work? We aren't getting it anywhere.

Wolensky (u): These things don't just happen. Let's not be so damned naive about it. I am called every time somebody has a problem. I find occasions where we are wrong, yes, but I can show you where you provoked trouble about 70 per cent of the time.

Take the case at Alton. That went down for a week. It was something your own people through their own negligence permitted. Maybe it was necessary, I don't know; but it was predicated on the old theory, "We run the plant and we will do as we damned please," with no thought given to the problem itself.

I don't mean to be critical, but after all these years when somebody hits me between the eyes with a clause like this, I am beginning to wonder whether there are any real honest relationships.

Palmer (m): I am beginning to wonder, too, especially after I go to the shops and see there is no damn work being done at all.

Wolensky (u): I haven't seen it, but if you are right, it is wrong for our people to take advantage.

Russell (u): Wait a minute. I have discussed production methods with Mr. Palmer himself, and he took the position that production should be pegged from the company's standpoint. We have urged our workers to increase production, but they were told to make only so many units. Management insisted it was their right to peg production so they don't have the right to say our people are not doing any work.

Palmer (m): Let's not get confused. You are talking about limitations we have only at Rockford and Alton to balance production. But elsewhere, the union's performance leads us to believe it is all lip service. In your own meetings the men are told how to work and what to do. I will take you to Toledo or South Bend and by God, if you don't hang your head in shame, I will be surprised.

Gotham (u): I want to challenge your statements. At South Bend increased production is always urged. But management indicates that production committees are just a joke.

Wolensky (u): Last year I pleaded with management to establish labor-management committees. If they did nothing but discuss problems on production, it would be worth while. But the company refused. It was a lot of hogwash to them. It is a practical approach to a vital problem. It is management's opportunity to tell their problems to the workers. This is not the place to do it; the place to do it is in the shop.

Russell (u): In the face of what happened at Reading, it may be the people who are not union members who are not giving an honest day's work. Our local is on record as wanting to increase production. The only barriers are management's refusal to approve production committees, and management's refusal to get other people into the union.

Underhill (u): Rockford has production committees and when anything goes wrong, we get together and iron it out.

Palmer (m): Rockford and Fort Wayne do give us good performance. What I am quarreling about are South Bend and Toledo. At Toledo your union has put us out of the coupler business. Other people can make the stuff so much cheaper we can't afford to handle it any more. Poor production and constant walkouts.

Heimer (u): Yes, we have trouble in Toledo. One of the most beautiful buck-passing systems in the world. They throw castings together and don't give a damn how. Why, your foundrymen are supposed to use cores that are not right. Castings come to us and we grinders have to practically make them for you. We saw this all coming. During World War II we asked for a labor-management production committee and were turned down cold. You holler our men are not working. But the company tells us "You make so much money, and then you go home." That is Toledo. Next, the boys can't even go to the toilet without being checked off. Damn it all, our men are human! Straighten out those things and you will get more harmony.

Docar (u): At Reading we elected four production committees. Every time management said, "There is nothing in the contract recognizing such a committee." Now, when management says they won't discuss production with us, I say there is no cooperation. We can discuss safety but nothing else.

Palmer (m): You have a duly elected committee provided for in the contract for promoting harmony and efficiency.

Gotham (u): What are the duties of plant committeemen?

Palmer (m): They have multiple duties. They have other duties besides just handling grievances and trying to stir up grievances.

Wolensky (u): What are they?

Palmer (m): Why can't they function under Article I?[1] They do at Fort Wayne and Rockford, but not at other shops. When committeemen offer suggestions on how to get better efficiency, I want to see it. There hasn't been any so far.

Wolensky (u): Give us the instrument. Write a clause.

Palmer (m): We have written a clause, that for eight hours' work you get eight hours' pay.

Wolensky (u): I want a mutual cooperation clause. Let's elaborate this first article. I want to pin you down. It can only function if it is properly instituted.

Gotham (u): At South Bend, a committeeman offered a recommendation for saving welding rods. When he got back to the shop, his foreman told him it was none of his God damned business how many welding rods they wasted.

Palmer (m): If true, it is very shortsighted.

Kohler (u): This contract provides only for the company and the committeemen to adjust grievances. There is no provision for the performance you talk about. Cooperation comes only with mutual confidence, but we are never going to get that confidence by writing a paragraph that says the instant the emergency is over we are going to cut the heart out of you and throw you to hell out of the place. You are going to cut maintenance of membership out of the contract; there will be no period of negotiation; there will be nothing; just termination of maintenance of membership. You establish distrust and with it, shirking on the day's work; because, if each man knows he is going to get his heart cut out anyway, he has nothing to build for.

Palmer (m): By the time the emergency is over, the union will have had ample opportunity to demonstrate they merit confidence by the company. We won't have so many wildcats.

Parenti (u): In our plant we are trying to get out this fair day's work for a fair day's pay. To find out why all the men could not hit the production goal, we had a meeting last Wednesday, with management. That was the first time although we have asked for labor-management committees. The plant superintendent was there. They found out that machines are breaking here, the sand hopper is stuck there, and things like that. Complaints had been made to the company, but nothing had been done. However, it came out that the more work a man did the bigger bonus there was for the foremen. So what is the encouragement for the men? The foremen get all the dough.

Peters (u): As long as distrust comes out here at headquarters, it passes all the way down to the foremen. The foreman knows so far as headquarters is concerned he has a perfect alibi. The men won't work; they are laying down on the job. Now, it is not the men falling down that is the trouble, it is the lack of proper equipment and proper supervision.

---

[1] "It is the intent and purpose of this agreement to promote harmony and efficiency in the plants of the company so that the employees and the company may mutually benefit, and to facilitate the peaceful adjustment of differences which may arise."

Palmer (m): Peters, aren't you in the core room?

Peters (u): Yes. It is a bad situation.

Palmer (m): At Alton weren't you put on day-rate and given the top rate, and in return you were to give us an honest day's work?

Peters (u): Yes, sir.

Palmer (m): That same thing was done at Toledo. After putting in $800,000 worth of equipment, we get exactly 87 per cent of what we used to get. Is that all management?

Baird (u): At Toledo, why does management put a ceiling on a day's pay? On some units you can get 50 per cent more production, but the management won't utilize it. It is your own policies that are stopping production in Toledo.

Palmer (m): We recently brought a bolster outfit up from Alton where we got 135 bolsters in a day. At Toledo what do we get? One hundred. I would be glad to have you watch the No. 2 slinger gang on axle housings. They just won't give us a day's work. They now have a grievance in because the foreman is driving them to give us a day's work. As to the limitation of earnings, why do we have to resort to such a thing at Toledo? Because you have got the thing around there so that the rates are cockeyed and whipperjawed. Why should we pay 76 cents for chipping when they will chip at another place for 58 cents?

King (m): We are talking about relatively few people in relation to the whole crew. There is not 20 per cent of the whole crew under piecework anyway.

Heimer (u): When you criticize Toledo on chipping, God Almighty, you guys set up your own costs. You put in a gang of rough chippers and paid them 88 cents to work ahead of the other chippers, who get 65 cents to chip the rest off. You used to have only one gang of men who you paid 5 cents more. Suppose you start looking at your own picture.

Palmer (m): I grant we make mistakes, Mr. Heimer.

Bishop (m): Labor costs are normally 50 per cent of production costs, but now they are constantly increasing. Somewhere there is a lack of efficiency, a lack of organization, either on the part of management or the combined efforts of management and men. Today we lose $5 on every side frame we sell, but one of our competitors makes $2.50 on each.

Wolensky (u): I don't know whether rates are out of line or what. Or this drop in production may be because of the turnover in labor. At Alton and Rockford five hundred people turn over in the two mills each month. You pose a production problem; you place the blame for lack of production on the men. I want to ask you point blank whether you will write a clause that will give us the right to be of assistance.

Palmer (m): It is already there, under Article I.

Wolensky (u): Will you, in your Article I, extend the functions of this committee? Let us set up two union committees: one for grievances, and one for production.

Palmer (m): I can't agree with you.

Underhill (u): I want to show you where production committees will be valuable. At Rockford the men were not making their required amount of castings for a day's work on side frames. They were green men. I myself saw the department head. We put on a few old men and made a few corrections. We talked to the men. Now they are getting that work out.

King (m): You did that under this contract, too. There is nothing to be gained by writing additional words when some committeemen at some plants want to break things down.

Palmer (m): We are not saying we are "holier than thou's." We have some weak supervision. We grant that.

Wolensky (u): There are not any corporation policies that might keep this from operating, are there?

Palmer (m): No.

Wolensky (u): Now, about the coming NLRB elections on the union shop. Will the corporation policies allow these to be held inside the various plants?

Palmer (m): Not with all these wildcat strikes and poor production. Your union hasn't yet proved itself responsible.

Bishop (m): I would like a five-minute recess.

Wolensky (u): This negotiation is for the purpose of settling problems for the coming year. The union shop and joint production committees would be long steps forward. We would like to get our people, if they are wrong, thinking in positive rather than negative terms. Now, I cannot impress it enough that we have operated in many companies under these committees. If nothing else came out of it, certainly there would be a better understanding of each other's problems.

We cannot be responsible for people who are not members of the union. I am not kidding about it. It is not just conversation. If we are ever charged with poor production after these negotiations, we are not going to listen to it.

DISCUSSION QUESTIONS

1. Analyze the union's tactics during the bargaining session.
2. What form of union security should the company grant?
3. What do you think are the advantages and disadvantages of union-management productivity committees?
4. Should Universal Castings contractually agree to such committees?
5. Following the recess at the end of the case, what position should the company take?

BARRINGTON OIL COMPANY (A)

NEGOTIATING WITH THE LOCAL COMMITTEE

INTRODUCTION

Collective bargaining relations between the Barrington Oil Company and the Oil Workers International Union at the Wellsbridge refinery of the company began in 1934 with a "Memorandum of Terms," to cover those employees who were members of the union. In 1936, an attempt to negotiate the first formal contract between the parties foundered on a disagreement over coverage.

In 1941, the effort to negotiate a first contract was resumed. Management and union achieved agreement on some "seventy points," but they remained at odds on "four to six" issues.

Excerpts from the seven final sessions, held on February 19 and continued on March 6, 11, 20, 21, 24, and 25, are given in this case.

The major negotiators on each side were the following:

For the Company	*For the Union*
Geoffrey S. Malcolm, General Manager, Wellsbridge Refinery	John B. Cobb, President, Local Union
Charles D. Harris, Superintendent of Production	Arthur S. Stratton, Secretary-Treasurer, Local Union
James J. Boyden, Director of Labor Relations	Oley M. Jenkins, Chairman, Negotiating Committee
Richard L. Carlisle, Superintendent of Maintenance	Nicholas Hawley, Member, Negotiating Committee
	O. A. Knight, National President, Oil Workers International Union (appears in session March 20–21–24–25)

For the U.S. Conciliation Service

Hugh W. Everett (appears in sessions March 21–24–25)

FROM THE MEETING OF FEBRUARY 19

Cobb (u): Well, Mr. Malcolm, do you have it all wrapped up for us?

Malcolm (m): All ready to go! Well, who is your spokesman?

Cobb (u): There has been no spokesman selected from our group. Of course, you have our letter which speaks for itself.

Malcolm (m): Well, I would like to invite somebody to tell me on what basis you are making your request for a 15% increase.

Cobb (u): First, the refinery has been underpaid for a long time. Second, we need an increase to compensate for the cost of living. We believe, also, that the working conditions we have been attempting to negotiate for some time should come into consideration with the settlement of wages. Then there is another reason. Barrington has made fifteen million dollars, and we believe we are entitled to a portion of it.

Malcolm (m): That is one good reason; I would like to have a rake-off myself.

Stratton (u) [rather hotly]: We don't feel like it is a rake-off at all. Until about five years ago this refinery had always been above Amtex. The men feel they have been underpaid, and also that they are entitled to an adjustment of wages to meet their expenses from the standpoint of the cost of living. We know that as of August, 1940, this particular area was the highest in the United States in retail over-all food cost.

With respect to area rates we can go into any detail you want. For example: at the Amtex plant the man that has less responsibility than our helper on the stills is getting $1.10 an hour. Ours are getting $1.07. The junior stillman has less responsibility than he has here. He is getting $1.15. We feel we have never reached the point where we could deal with classifications. The only thing we have had from management is the statement that the over-all average in the plant is in line.

The men don't want a rake-off. There is enough good sound reasoning as to why the men should have some relief in wages without having to discuss company earnings.

Malcolm (m): We would like you to give us more detailed reasons. Again I refer to Mr. Cobb's memorandum, which is written to your members, not to us. [Reading.]

When you insist upon an increase in wages, *DO* take into consideration the increase in the cost of living and *DO* take the company's statement that the refinery is in danger of sabotage and consequently the physical risk of your daily work is increased.

That is the position, undoubtedly, on which you are basing your request, although the statement may be for propaganda purposes. But in order that I may approach the company more intelligently would you be kind enough to tell us on which figures you are claiming a cost of living increase?

Stratton (u): The *Pathfinder* magazine.

Malcolm (m): Are its figures authentic—backed by an authority?

Stratton (u): They are.

Malcolm (m): Any other source?

Stratton (u): The United States Department of Labor.

Cobb (u): There is one source that may be difficult to cite figures from, but it is very convincing. That is your grocer man.

Malcolm (m): I am talking seriously about figures you have at your disposal, that we don't have. You cite the *Pathfinder*. I don't know what magazine that is.

Cobb (u): It is similar to *Newsweek*.

Malcolm (m): What does the Department of Labor show?

Stratton (u): In 32 cities the over-all retail cost of food dropped, 17 increased, and 2 held their position. We are one of the 17 that increased. The August Bulletin of the Department of Labor shows our area has the highest average retail cost of food of any place in the nation.

Boyden (m): That is for food? Not for the over-all cost of living?

Stratton (u): No, food only.

Malcolm (m): Have you any figures available now that the cost of living increased, not only food, but everything? Have you the period of time? Is it right now?

Stratton (u): I quoted you sources that you evidently don't feel authentic. The Department of Labor figures run about two months behind.

Malcolm (m): This increased cost is not realized now, but is expected. Is that right?

Stratton (u): Well, we are already feeling the almost 6% increase the figures show, on the over-all picture.

Malcolm (m): Well, is that all your reasons?

Stratton (u): You asked about the cost of living. If you want facts on the other matters, we will be glad to give them to you.

Malcolm (m): The cost of living has been used by your own organization as the main reason, and I would like to be absolutely impartial on the subject.

Jenkins (u): Say a family has $40 they can spend for food. If the cost of better foods increases, that means they have to reduce the amount of buying, or buy poorer food. Another factor involved is housing. Everybody knows rents are going sky high. You can't find a house that is fit to live in today; and that has happened in the last three months. That means over the next period of six months rent will go up 10% to 25%. In so far as clothing is concerned, I don't have any statistics other than our own experience. For instance, work gloves: a pair selling three months ago for 49 cents is now selling for 64 cents. Our demands are not based altogether on just the present data, already much higher than the official figures quoted to you. We wouldn't want to come up every 30 days for a 3% raise to take care of the cost of living. We would like to try to figure some reasonable figure and base our demands on that.

Malcolm (m): Well, do you care to make any additional explanation or give any other details that would help to substantiate your request?

Hawley (u): It has always been our contention, and is still now, that some of the higher jobs especially have been underpaid as compared to other refineries in the area. Mr. Stratton stated the case of Amtex raising some of their skilled jobs. From information I have been able to get Puritan has made some adjustments and I believe Delico is now contemplating making some adjustments, and Jannifer also.

Malcolm (m): Do you mean to say that Amtex or Delico increased their wages, or made adjustments recently?   Could you mention any?

Hawley (u): I know that the Puritan Treating Plant rates have been adjusted. I don't know exactly how much, but I do know the rate I heard about was one cent above ours.

Malcolm (m): Recently?

Hawley (u): Within the last 30 days.

Cobb (u): Puritan even gave a flat $10 per month raise.

Malcolm (m): I know that. You are referring to Amtex, Delico, and Puritan. I am not aware of any adjustments. I would like to know about it. You say that Amtex has made some adjustments?

Stratton (u): That has been quite a while ago, probably in the early part of the year 1940.

Malcolm (m): And you mention Delico; do you know what positions or what crafts?

Hawley (u): I couldn't give you the exact figures, or exact jobs. But I do know they have increased the rates in some classifications, particularly the crafts.

Jenkins (u): There is one thing I believe ought to have a lot of weight. Heretofore this company has been almost the last to make wage adjustments, and it is just common talk that whenever everyone else gets a raise, Barrington will then take steps. It would change the attitude of the men if Barrington would take the lead.

Malcolm (m): Well, you fully realize I am not in a position to say today "Yes" or "No." It is a question of general policy, and I'll be very glad to submit it to our New York management with the reasons given by you. We will get, I hope, a speedy reply. I would say let's not expect anything within two weeks. It will be necessary to work it up and send it to New York.

There is one thing you just brought up: the question whether Barrington should take the lead. Theoretically, maybe you are right; your intentions are right. But the unfortunate part is—and I have to be personal though I don't give a God damn—some of your people in their over-zealousness for propaganda are distributing statements in public whereby they insinuate Barrington is making a handsome profit and is unfair. There is a personal campaign called the Malcolm Plan for Union Busting. So far as I am personally concerned, I have the same reaction if I see a little old mangy dog barking in the moonlight. But listen to your propaganda: It says: "The committee foolishly believed that even Barrington in New York would observe the fundamental principles of American justice in considering this handsome profit it makes out of Wellsbridge resources." If such information is reaching our president and chairman that haven't the close relationship we have locally, the reaction is distinctly unfavorable. If you fellows would like to discuss wages, then why don't you postpone sticking that kind of thing down our craw until the negotiations are over? It is probably one of the tricks of your trade. I don't mind what you call me, but when you attack the entire company you are handicapping your own people.

Stratton (u): I am glad you mentioned that. This question of undermining works two ways: and since we are all adults we are going to have to face it on that basis. If you put out propaganda and instruct your foremen to do certain things, then we are going to retaliate. When the local management dabbles in the affairs of the local union, then you are going to get reaction from us.

Malcolm (m): You raise the question of retaliation and I fully follow your reasoning, but I am afraid there is one missing link. If you will look at the dates, Mr. Stratton, you will find out that your memorandum came out attacking the company February 10, five days after your letter asking wage increases. You are attacking the whole company in public. Jenkins says the company should lead the parade. Suppose they have it in mind, and get something small like this thrown at them. How would our head people feel?

Cobb (u): I think they should hang their heads in shame.

Stratton (u): We don't have any personal animosity, but the company is pretty shrewd and we have to face it. Union bulletins aren't as bad as you think they are.

Malcolm (m): One day Mr. Cobb and Mr. Jenkins said "Well, let's forget everything. Let's start anew." I said fine. At first, I was suspicious, but the fellows talked until I honestly believed them. That was on December 11, and we said now we can shake hands with each other. On December 13, two days later, we had a command to appear before the Labor Board, and all our belief in humanity was destroyed. Now, there is a propaganda against the company even as you expect the company to step out and meet you more than half-way. If you've got something against me, call me up, tell me what you think about me and I'll tell you what I think about you.

Stratton (u): I talked to you on the phone about the Labor Board. Every time something comes up, you try to confuse us with side issues.

Malcolm (m): I am telling you fellows you are barking up the wrong tree as far as the interest of the men is concerned.

Stratton (u): Well, we agreed to go ahead with negotiations so I think we should get back on concrete issues.

Jenkins (u): There is a place where reasonable men can get together. For three or four years there has been growing dissatisfaction in the plant, yet the majority of the men want to have a good relationship. We have a twofold duty; one is the interest of the men, and second the interest of the management. Management should have, of course, the interest of the management at heart—as I am sure they do primarily—and closely secondary the interest of the men. We have lost many a dollar in the refinery because a fellow just got fed up. The men are prone to make mountains out of mole hills. I know that; I have served on Workmen's Committees. I don't think we can continue on the basis we are going along without both of us getting hurt. It alarms me. I have had hopes at times of getting together; then something happens, and we get further apart.

Harris (m): Do you think 15% will clear it up?

Jenkins (u): I will be frank with you. Fifteen per cent will not clear it up. If you will lay a good agreement on one side of the table and 15% on the other, I would take the agreement in a minute.

Malcolm (m): Well?

Stratton (u): Well, Mr. Malcolm, it is getting near that deadline of four o'clock. Going further into what Jenkins said, I think a real equitable adjustment would help immeasurably. I think sitting down, working out some of these things, and taking for granted we might be a little bit wrong here and you might be a little bit wrong there, we could go a long ways. We respect your ability and intelligence, and whatever the difference in opinion, what you call our propaganda is merely our way of saying things. Maybe we are wrong sometimes, the same as the management is wrong sometimes. But we think a lot of this disturbance can be overcome. Right now I don't know what we can do, other than just notify the membership of your position today and then come back to you with whatever instructions we get from them.

Malcolm (m): I will say that if our answer takes only a week I will be only too happy to call you before. I don't want to be kept to two weeks to the day. I will ask for the speediest possible handling, and I should think two weeks would be enough time.

[The meeting adjourned at 4:02 P.M.]

From the Meeting of March 6

Malcolm (m): Though we tried to speed things up, we are just a few hours late in getting together. I told you it would be about two weeks.

Cobb (u): We will consider it two weeks.

Malcolm (m): Your request for a general increase has been very thoroughly studied, not only by us, but by New York. We made a comparison of all the prevailing rates in the industry. I gave them all the figures, and submitted very thoroughly all your reasons you gave to support your request. The company finds that there is no increase in living costs. It so happens that yesterday, we received official figures by the U.S. Department of Labor giving the cost of living figures up to January 15. We realize that we are now past March 1st. However, on January 15 we find that the cost of living in this district decreased over the cost for November and December. In 1937 we gave an increase to compensate for the increased cost of living at that time. Since 1937 the cost of living went down until September, 1940. From then it continued upward until December, 1940. Now it is slightly going down. So, there is no justification on that basis for a general increase.

Hawley (u): All right. We'll show that to our wives on Saturday—and maybe they'll show the butcher and the baker who don't seem to read the same books Mr. Malcolm does.

Malcolm (m): Even so, there is no justification for a general increase based on cost of living. Now, the second important point is that apparently this is not only our feeling, but that of the whole oil industry. To our knowledge, there is no general increase in wages in the oil industry, neither generally, nor locally, and of course we have to compete with local people.

The third factor is that the weighted average of wage rates at Barrington Refinery is already higher than the weighted average among competitors.

Hawley (u): How do you decide the weighted average?

Malcolm (m): We approached seven other local refineries, and from their employment department we got all wages, got the weighted average, and compared it with our weighted average.

Hawley (u): In other words, the company assumes the responsibility of partitioning the total wage.

Malcolm (m): I am sure you are not trying to imply that we are chiseling—juggling the figures for our advantage. We are fully prepared if questioned by any authority or conciliator to put the figures on the table.

Hawley (u): Go right ahead.

Malcolm (m): We are fully aware that while we have been and still are paying many rates on a higher basis than our competitors, certain of our rates are lower and create discontent among our employees. So, we are prepared to correct certain inequities in our wages effective day after tomorrow.

[Mr. Malcolm then read a list of new job rates, raising those below competitive rates for comparable jobs, and constituting an increase of $1\frac{1}{2}\%$ in the payroll. The proposal would raise the weighted average of rates at Barrington 4.9 cents above competitors.]

Cobb (u): Is this the company's absolute limit on the answer for 15% increase?

Malcolm (m): That is correct. But if there are general increases in the industry based on the cost of living, and I wouldn't be surprised if costs will go up, you know Barrington will meet competition. I suggest that you try to transmit that thought to the employees.

Cobb (u): Are you going to circulate your employees about the revised rate structure?

Malcolm (m): No; you are the first agency to be notified. We are going to notify our supervisors because they should know what the men are going to make, but we are not going to write a letter to every employee.

Cobb (u): I would like to ask if the company has changed its position on the matter of signing an agreement.

Malcolm (m): It is very difficult to enter into now. But I have told you repeatedly the door is not closed if we could get minor modifications on the four clauses on which we still disagree. The next step is up to you.

Cobb (u): Is there any other member of the committee who has any questions he would like to ask?

Hawley (u): No, not until we take these proposals to the membership for their approval or rejection. If the rate structure can be ironed out, we are one step nearer to negotiating an agreement.

Malcolm (m): I might mention two further subjects: one is the extensions to our plant. We are building an additional pentane plant and the toluene plant is going to be increased. In other words, there will be promotional possibilities. The key men will likely be brought in. But I would say the operators will be supplied through promotion.

Cobb (u): Do you have any approximate idea of the number of men that will be employed there?

Malcolm (m): Maybe 100, but that is only the beginning. Also for your information, the company decided to put our gatemen and patrolmen on the monthly payroll. I am just telling you.

Cobb (u): Are we to assume that the company will take the position that they will not be covered by a working agreement?

Malcolm (m): I think the monthly employees will not be covered by a working agreement.

Cobb (u): Regardless of their duties and classification? We were certified as a bargaining agency for those people.

Malcolm (m): To my knowledge, just offhand, under the Act, a group of employees can present their own request or grievance to the management.

Cobb (u): If there are no other matters, I assume we might as well adjourn. We appreciate the meeting and the information, plus the offer of job rate adjustments. When am I to understand this is to go into effect?

Malcolm (m): Day after tomorrow.

Cobb (u): The local union will be prepared to give you an answer, probably in the next week.

[The meeting adjourned at 10:45 A.M.]

From the Meeting of March 11

Cobb (u): Well, Mr. Malcolm, in consideration of the adjustments in rates, which brought them almost in line with the area, the members reduced their demand to 10%, plus a signed agreement.

Malcolm (m): Well, I would like to know why you think an increase of 10% is justified.

Cobb (u): For the same reasons we gave before. Our opinion is the same.

Malcolm (m): If I remember it, you gave the increased cost of living as a main reason, and we produced government figures which indicated that this area had a slight decrease in living costs since 1937, the time of your last wage increase. Therefore, in order to comprehend your request intelligently, I will be happy if you submit authoritative figures.

Cobb (u): Well, I believe that the statements that we gave at the last meeting and the figures we gave you . . .

Malcolm (m) [interrupting]: You didn't give me any.

Cobb (u): There are numerous other things that might be brought in, various other advantages that are enjoyed by other companies' employees that don't apply here.

Malcolm (m): Well, before we go into the other reasons, I would be very pleased if you would give me your figures. I am listening; kindly proceed.

Cobb (u): Well one of the boys in the electric shop gave the best answer. He made the remark that he wasn't able to pay his grocery bill with statistics. Then the majority of our men report to us that the price of clothing . . .

Malcolm (m) [interrupting]: Clothing is going down according to the figures of the United States Department of Labor.

Cobb (u): Maybe our clothing stores haven't gotten those government figures yet.

Stratton (u): Do you take the position that the amount of money we received in 1937 sufficed for the cost of living at that time? The union would say that the cost of living dropped off since 1937, but the wages then did not give a comfortable salary to live on.

Cobb (u): I think it would be worth 15¢ per hour more to work under the working conditions we are working under here.

Malcolm (m): Well, that is very interesting. We had an opportunity recently to talk to some workers from Amtex. We talked about bus transportation. They said, "We have to travel in a regular cattle bus." Apparently the other fellow's pasture always looks the greenest.

Stratton (u): Well, we find them liking it at Amtex pretty well. They have changed that open-air bus condition.

Jenkins (u): There are many factors to be included in the wage question. Each company has its own policy on certain benefits that they grant employees. Some of them have a stock purchasing plan whereby the company gives them a 50% reduction on price of their stock.

Malcolm (m): Does Amtex have it?

Jenkins (u): No, not Amtex. Others have hospitalization benefits. Some places give as much as 20% or more discount on any material purchased. Delico allows 20%. All of those things are certainly important to the employee. If the oil industry takes the attitude that we are all pretty well in line on wages and nobody will raise until the other does, it will be like a law passed up north that when two trains approach an intersection neither one would proceed until the other does.

✗ *Malcolm* (m): Well, if you have nothing else to produce, and I am saying this not to be smart or sarcastic, but sincerely—if you can't produce better evidence or figures furnished by the government, we feel we are in line with our competitors and regret very much we are not prepared at present to grant your request for an increase. And I hope you will take it in the spirit I am saying it. There is nothing personal whatever. It has been discussed very carefully with our people.

Jenkins (u) [jokingly]: I was just thinking about serving an antitrust injunction. You can't do anything until the others do. Why doesn't Barrington take the lead once?

Malcolm (m): Don't forget Delico made four times as much as Barrington. Remember, too, that I am not the fellow who gives increases. I could help if you could produce any reasons. I have asked for the figures but you can't give them. Everybody thinks they have to have more money, and ultimately I believe an increase is bound to come, but now you are too impatient. However, if you say now or never or else, I would say go ahead; we are prepared to take the consequences.

[The committee at this point asked for a short recess.]

Cobb (u): Mr. Malcolm, in connection with the request for a signed agreement, has the company's position changed on any of the points in controversy?

Malcolm (m): I would say that is a very broad question. We said it is not our idea to close the door. But if your position has not changed on four points still at issue . . . For a contract, we have to agree on wage rates. But take the matter of pay periods and rate changes: our position has not changed. (We are not prepared to write any agreement with anybody under any circumstances providing for arbitration of wages.) Then on time worked outside of scheduled hours, we still don't feel we should change our position because our conditions are now better than the competitors.

Cobb (u): Well, our position is when a man is called out on off-schedule day *but given forty-hour notice,* he would not receive rate and a half.

Malcolm (m): Well, on this point I am not prepared to give you an answer today. I would like to calculate and see what it means in dollars and cents. On the fourth point, no cessation of work, I was just about prepared to give in on it, and say we would have the no cessation of work clause. But now you are making me feel again there might be a danger in doing that.

Jenkins (u): Just because you break your word to us, we are not breaking ours.

Malcolm (m): That is the second time you have said I am breaking my word.

[Mr. Jenkins referred to Article XIII of the tentative agreement, stating that no classification paid by the hour would be changed to a monthly pay classification during the period of the agreement. He contended that when the company put the gatemen and patrolmen on the monthly payroll, they had violated this agreement.]

Malcolm (m): That was a tentative agreement. If we had agreed on it, we would never have gone back on it.

Jenkins (u): It was a mutual understanding. We said that it would be possible for you to put everybody on the monthly payroll, and you said, "Just to show you that we wouldn't, we will write it into an agreement."

Malcolm (m): And if we had signed the agreement we would not have gone back on it. Do you think that if we enter a tentative agreement on a certain point and we can't reach a final agreement on it, we are bound forever?

Cobb (u): Is the company's position on the strike and lock-out clause still the same?

Malcolm (m): For the time being, yes.

Cobb (u): Well, the craft seniority is the thing we were not going to discuss, and the reclassification.

Stratton (u): He has said he could not change on that.

Cobb (u): And of course you say the arbitration of wages is out. Does the company have any proposal or anything they would like to submit to the

Oil Workers in the way of a wage increase? Is there any counterproposal?

Malcolm (m): Do you mean a counterproposal with regard to a 10% increase?

Cobb (u): Yes.

Malcolm (m): No.

Cobb (u): Well, Mr. Malcolm, we will convey your answer to the membership tonight in our regular meeting, and we will get in touch with you sometime after the meeting. Thank you for the time, Mr. Malcolm.

Malcolm (m): You are welcome.

[The meeting adjourned at 3:53 P.M.]

DISCUSSION QUESTIONS

FROM THE MEETING OF FEBRUARY 19

1. How would you characterize the evolving relationships and this particular negotiation as a phase of those relationships?

2. Evaluate Malcolm's bargaining procedures with regard to (*a*) the demand for wage increases; (*b*) references to problems of joint relationships; (*c*) union "propaganda"; and (*d*) the discussions regarding "completion of an agreement."

3. How would you describe Malcolm's strategy and tactics?

FROM THE MEETING OF MARCH 6

4. Evaluate Malcolm's presentation of the company's reply.

5. Evaluate the responses of the union representatives to this offer for clues to the union's major objectives in the negotiations.

6. What further clues do you see as to strategy and tactics?

FROM THE MEETING OF MARCH 11

7. Evaluate Malcolm's declaration of willingness "to take the consequences." Relate your reply to the underlying strategy of the company.

8. Evaluate the union's windup of the session, in reply to this implicit "last word." What do you make of Malcolm's response?

9. On the basis of the three sessions with the local representatives, how would you evaluate Malcolm's conferences with company headquarters in New York?

BARRINGTON OIL COMPANY (B)

THE INTERNATIONAL UNION TAKES OVER

FROM THE MEETING OF MARCH 20

Malcolm (m) [to Jenkins]: Well, I understand you are chairman of the negotiating committee.

Jenkins (u): That is right, Mr. Malcolm.

Malcolm (m): Well, I am delighted.

Jenkins (u): Well, locally I think we have said everything we can think of. The International is here, and we hope they can find some avenue of settlement. Locally it is out of our hands, but we are going to assist them and you in any way we can. So we are going to ask them to discuss it and see if they can decide who is wrong.

Malcolm (m) [laughing]: That is unfair, but not to organized labor. I am very glad to have Mr. Knight here. We are old fellow workers.

Knight (u): It has always been the policy of the International Union to attempt to settle disputes by conference in a fair and open-minded manner. We don't care to resort to any other means except conference. At the request of the local group and the Defense Commission we have come into this picture. We want to see if we can't arrive at a solution that will not cause any interruption of work.

As I understand it, there are some four points in a proposed agreement on which you have a difference of opinion. I understand the other sections have been decided on. I propose to see how far we are apart on these points and see if we can't work out some solution that will be fair to all. So I would like to discuss these unsettled points one at a time. Is that agreeable?

Malcolm (m): I appreciate your frankness, and we feel that in the interest of National Defense we should find some common ground. I am agreeable to discuss the points with an absolutely open mind.

Knight (u): The National Defense has called me personally by telephone and we are just as concerned as they are in arriving at a solution that the men can live under and which will let the company run its plant.

I would like to open discussion on this "Forty Hour Notice of Change Dates." It is my understanding that 40 hour notice is a method whereby the normal days off of an individual may be changed without a penalty of time and a half. We have been quite successful in that notice in many companies. We feel we cannot agree to a reduction in notice time because it would take away from the men things they enjoy in other Barrington plants.

Malcolm (m): May I ask you a question? You said this policy is adopted wherever your organization is functioning with Barrington. For my information, have you the same provisions of 40 hours' notice in the California refineries?

Knight (u): I think you misunderstood my statement. I didn't say it was universal in Barrington. I said it was in some agreements.

Malcolm (m): You also realize undoubtedly that this practice of 40 hours is considerably more liberal than the practice in the industry.

Knight (u): I can't agree with you on that, Mr. Malcolm.

Malcolm (m): Has the Amtex Refinery a 40 hour notice?

Knight (u): Amtex has a much more liberal policy on the payment of overtime than at Barrington.

Malcolm (m): But haven't they 16 hours notice instead of 40?

Knight (u): I couldn't say offhand; but there are other factors that more than overbalance any discrepancy in that regard.

Malcolm (m): Recently you told us that we have intolerable conditions at the plant and I asked, how about Amtex? Some of you told me Amtex has pretty good conditions; the men there are pretty well satisfied. Now I understand last week you told Amtex how intolerable conditions were there. But, of course, that is a trick of the trade.

Knight (u): We might just as well say this: our relations with Amtex have been more friendly than with Barrington. As to an agreement, we are not at loggerheads with Amtex. There has never been any thought in my mind, and I don't think in the minds of any other officials, of singling out Barrington and turning on the heat. I worked for Barrington a long time myself. My relation with the company was always fine as an employee. On the other hand, as an official of the organization, I found the Barrington organization a little harder to deal with because I couldn't find out what their policy was, and it was hard to justify the differences in policies in the various areas.

Malcolm (m): Talking about this clause on call-out, in your Rio agreement have you 40 hours notice, or have you 16 hours notice?

Knight (u): Mr. Malcolm, that agreement is contingent on final settlement of wages and negotiations at the various other places where we represent Rio Company employees.

Malcolm (m): I am just wondering.

Knight (u): The 40 hour provision that we are discussing is really an infinitesimal proposition when you consider the tremendous profit of the company for last year.

Malcolm (m): Suppose we should consider a concession on that basis. Would you be willing to say "if you don't make any money, you are entitled to withdraw the concession"?

Knight (u): The experience of labor has been that in periods of small profits their earnings are the first depleted. We try to investigate the profits of the various organizations with which we negotiate. Barrington had a very profitable year, and I think the request of the men is timely for that reason. We have wandered far afield from the forty hour notice clause. We would like to have the management concede that the forty hour notice is fair and will be part of the agreement.

Malcolm (m): The latest request made was that you want overtime paid for two shifts on changing shifts; is that right?

Jenkins (u): We had receded from three.

Malcolm (m) [jokingly]: You should have started at six. Well, for your consideration we would offer you a premium for one shift. That I can tell you—we have been calculating—will cost many thousands of dollars per year. But we are making you an offer of one shift, provided you could reduce somewhat the forty hour notice.

Knight (u): What do you mean when you say reduce the forty hour notice? How much notice would you want to give?

Malcolm (m): That is subject to collective bargaining.

Knight (u): Supposing we say thirty-nine hours.

Malcolm (m): Then we have to start on 12 hours.

Knight (u): Well, let's toss it out and have a look at it.

Malcolm (m): Frankly speaking, I am not clear in my mind how many hours it would be. If you are interested, we could step out for a few minutes; then we can give you the answer.

Knight (u): Well, before you go, I would like to leave this thought. The 16 hour notice isn't any notice. Supposing a man comes to work and works part of his shift. Then you notify him that you want him to work tomorrow which was his scheduled off-day. He will have no opportunity to change his plans.

[The company representatives left the room for a few minutes.]

Malcolm (m): Well, our counterproposal is to limit notice to 24 hours.

Knight (u): Well, Mr. Malcolm, I am sure the committee will wish to see all of the answers we get on the various clauses and make their decision on the aggregate.

Malcolm (m): I didn't expect any answer today.

Knight (u): I think the next thing is the proposal for arbitration of complaints which arise over wages. There has been an increasing tendency to agree that the proper method of settling any and all disputes is through arbitration. We have accepted and endorsed the theory of arbitration and we certainly want to see all of the terms subject to final determination in a manner that will remove completely the necessity of industrial warfare. I am at a loss to understand why Barrington would wish to remove that method of settlement.

Malcolm (m): Well, this question is brought up very frequently and I regret that Barrington—and I am not only referring to our refinery—cannot agree to the arbitration of wages. We believe we can bargain collectively and set the wage standard by mutual agreement. But if there is any necessity to reopen the question of wages, we are not prepared to have an outside agency arbitrate the subject. Even the best umpire is not qualified to arbitrate wages. That is our belief right or wrong; I am explaining how the company feels about it—and feels very strongly.

Knight (u): I am extremely sorry that you have had to tell us that. If you have disputes over the question of wages, how are you going to eliminate conflict as long as you have provided no means for final determination? Since you are against arbitration, I am quite sure that our willingness to become a party to an agreement running for a definite time will be contingent on the wages that become part of the agreement.

We can't enter into a bargain settling wages unless those wages are sufficiently high to meet a portion of the increased cost of living we can safely anticipate during the term of the agreement. So the final determination of the whole thing actually hinges on, "What are going to be the wages for these men?"

Malcolm (m): The committee based its request for an increase in wages mainly on the alleged increased cost of living. We repeatedly invited this committee to produce evidence. We also approached Washington. [Malcolm handed Knight a chart showing that the present cost of living index was below that for 1937 when the last adjustment of wages was made. The company had also made an investigation of the competitive wage structure and found that not only was Barrington's over-all weighted average rate roundly 5 cents an hour higher than the over-all average of competitors, but that the rate for each of its job classifications was in line with or above that of the competitive rate. For these reasons the company was not in a position to make an upward adjustment.]

Knight (u): Statistics, Mr. Malcolm, don't keep up with actualities. I don't think I have much more to say on the increased cost of living. The increase is here, and I think it will go up more in the near future.

Malcolm (m): Exactly. Recently the cost of things *has* been going up, but it still hasn't reached the 1937 level.

Knight (u): The point for a fixed term agreement is the trend. However, it is not our intention to limit all our discussion to the question of the cost of living. Also, it is extremely unfortunate that we ever let ourselves be forced into the position of basing wage rate requests on area rates. A major competitor in this area made a profit of $3,500,000. Compare that with the $15,000,000 that Barrington made. They might not be able to grant wage increases quite as readily as you.

We propose to approach the question of wage increases on the improved ability of the Barrington company to pay over and above their ability to pay in 1937. We think a part of the increase in money made should be given to labor who helped to produce it.

Frankly, my advice to your employees will be not to become a party to any agreement which binds them to their present wages. I don't know whether it is a fair question, but do you have the same instructions on wages that you have on arbitration of wages?

Malcolm (m): Yes.

Knight (u): Well, that is indeed an unfortunate circumstance.

Historically, whenever we have had these periods of rapid increase in cost of living, wages have trailed behind. If you are informed that the price of crude oil is going up, you raise your prices. If the price of a cracking chamber goes up, you pay the price. The only price that is subject to long negotiations happens to be the commodity known as labor. That is the only thing these people have to sell. They are asking that the company increase the price in proportion to other things that they are buying.

We will not enter into an agreement for a year's time on the basis of wage rates that we feel are inadequate today and are going to be increasingly inadequate. However long we argue about it, the position is going to be the same.

If this is a determined policy established elsewhere by the corporation, then it is going to take more than a conference to change that policy, and it devolves upon us to find the manner and means of convincing the management in New York that that change is necessary. I hope that out of our meeting we can arrive at a definite understanding.

So again I ask, is it absolutely impossible for this office to discuss the question or to grant an upward adjustment in the wage bill?

Malcolm (m): There is another question I didn't bring up. If you are interested in a contract, what idea have you as far as the expiration date is concerned?

Knight (u): Of course, you have me at a disadvantage there, Mr. Malcolm. I haven't had an opportunity to discuss that with the members of the committee. I would much prefer if the spokesman for the committee would give us the benefit of their ideas on that.

Jenkins (u): It is historical for us to ask for a year's contract. I don't think there will be a lot of quibbling on that.

Malcolm (m): Our suggestion is to have it run for a year, up to January 1 or if necessary I would say February 1.

[From 12:00 to 1:15 the meeting adjourned for lunch.]

Knight (u): You wanted our idea on the period of agreement before making a final answer on wages. If we arrive at a satisfactory understanding concerning the terms of the agreement, February 1 will be agreeable to the men.

Malcolm (m): Well, what is the next question?

Knight (u): We have arrived at a point where a final settlement rests on our ability to get together on the subject of wages. I don't know that there is anything further we can add. We are at a loss to know how to proceed until we know what the position of the management will be.

Malcolm (m): You are attacking the problem from a different basis than the committee had before. You are giving major emphasis now to different criteria for wage adjustments. But still I have to say at the present time we cannot see eye to eye with you. To develop one thought, say the company made $15,000,000 and on the basis of ability to pay they would make an adjustment. Delico made $60,000,000. Their wages should be four times as great as ours. Then there is the company that made $3,500,000. On that basis their wages should be only a fraction of ours.

Knight (u): Of course, you are picking out one particular phase of our presentation and trying to justify the whole procedure on that one thing. It wasn't our intention that our sole basis was because the company made $15,000,000. That wasn't our thought.

Malcolm (m): But the paramount thought?

Knight (u): The paramount thought, yes. We mentioned the very evident increase—both the increase that is already here and the anticipated increase—in living cost, as one reason. We mentioned the ability of the company to meet the wage increase as another reason. Taking the two together, it makes a pretty logical approach to the question. Taking each one separately is not a very logical approach to the question. I think you can see our position. We would be very foolish to sign an agreement binding us to the present wage rate for a period of a year in the face of those two facts. The company has the money and the men are going to need the money even at their present standard of living.

Malcolm (m): Well, I see certain logic in your procedure, but still as a company we can't see that a wage increase is justified.

Knight (u): We can argue all day long on the question of wages. However, I think we understand each other's position. The men take the position that they are not willing to enter into an agreement binding them to these wages you offer now for any length of time. I don't know what it is going to take to change the management's position. I would like to listen, but if the management's position that there isn't another nickel to kick into the bucket is adamant, then that's that. For the men's position is adamant that they are not willing to enter into an agreement unless the wages are adjusted upward. I am sure Barrington can't afford to have a group of dissatisfied men. We want to have a group of men who are going about their jobs in the right way—doing the best they can to help to make a profit.

Malcolm (m): Well, to summarize the whole thing, as I said before and I wish you would realize, it is not a personal issue. Unfortunately the whispering campaign blames me personally. On certain things, administrative matters, I am given certain freedom. On certain cardinal principles I have to take instructions given me. For the present we cannot see on the basis of your arguments how we could make an upward adjustment.

Knight (u): Well, that forces us to point out one further reason which we had certainly hoped would not be necessary. The injection of such ideas is always regrettable and it is extremely regrettable under these circumstances that it must be mentioned. The policy on the question of wages emanates from sources other than this room. There is only one other argument that we can use to change the decision of the management in a case like this. We must tell you that your employees are not only unwilling to bind themselves to an agreement of this sort for a period of one year. We must also tell you that the dissatisfaction is so great they are unwilling to continue working for your company under the present wage scales. That, I think, should be very carefully considered by the Barrington management. The men have expressed that decision through the democratic processes, through a vote.

This situation is disagreeable to us; it is bound to be to you. It is disagreeable to the entire nation at this particular time. However, it is the one recourse we have in a situation of this sort. The men feel, and I feel as they feel, that to agree to what you offer in view of the circumstances would be unfair not only to themselves but to the rest of the people with prices going way up and wages slowly dangling behind. If there is any misunderstanding as to the thought I am trying to convey I will be very glad to restate it.

Malcolm (m): I think we have no misunderstanding on the position you are taking, and I hope you have no misunderstanding on the position we are taking. I think it seems only logical since we are approaching the subject on a different basis than the one given before by the negotiating committee that I have an opportunity to present your idea to the management.

Knight (u): I think a reasonable time should be given to receive management's answer, and we don't want you to get the opinion that we are saying if we don't get an increase today, that tomorrow the men are all going to quit. Certainly we are going to proceed with these negotiations; we are going to permit ample time for our squabble to get to the top management. I don't think ample time means two hours, but on the other hand I don't think it means a week or two weeks.

Malcolm (m): I think it is fair enough. We understand one another perfectly. What time do you think is a reasonable time as long as we don't meet on Saturday or Sunday?

Cobb (u): After all, I believe this is a rather special occasion. I don't like to interrupt anybody's Saturday or Sunday schedule, but it is a great concern to all of us.

Malcolm (m): I fully realize it. For the last seven or ten years I have been full of special occasions, but I have decided never again. I have to have my rest. I am not a machine.

Knight (u): We still have a day before Saturday and Sunday.

Malcolm (m): Well, suppose we will give you our answer by tomorrow at 1:00 o'clock.

Knight (u): That is fine. In order that there might be no disturbance, I hope we can agree that if any reporters contact any of us, the only statement we make is this conference has adjourned until tomorrow at 1:00 o'clock, and progress has been made. I have been asked to keep the Defense Commission informed. I feel I am obligated to contact it.

Malcolm (m): That is very fair because I had the same request from the Defense Commission.

Knight (u): The determination of any further step will depend on the answer of the management tomorrow.

[The meeting adjourned at 2:07 P.M.]

Discussion Questions

1. What is Knight's opening gambit after the initial pleasantries as he takes over union leadership in the negotiations?

2. Evaluate Knight's bargaining procedure in the manner in which he sets up the "order of discussion" on the issues before the negotiators.

3. How does Malcolm adapt himself to Knight's moves?

4. How does Malcolm assimilate the "unsettled issue" regarding arbitration of wage rates into (*a*) the whole negotiation; (*b*) the underlying problems of relationship?

5. Compare the bargaining on wage increases in this session with that in

the earlier "local" ones in terms of (*a*) the criteria urged; (*b*) Malcolm's response to the union in each situation; (*c*) Knight's handling of the rejection by New York of "increases now"; and (*d*) Malcolm's willingness "to take the consequences" in each situation.

6. Evaluate Malcolm's bargaining strategy in this session, again with reference among other things to its contrast with that in the earlier ones, regarding (*a*) the completion of an agreement; (*b*) timing in reporting back instructions from New York regarding the wage increase; and (*c*) problems of underlying relations.

7. What new factors would you say Knight has brought into the union's strategy? Which would you say promised to exert most potent influence?

BARRINGTON OIL COMPANY (C)

THE FEDERAL GOVERNMENT INTERVENES

FROM THE MEETING OF MARCH 21

Malcolm (m): In answer to your question with which we closed our meeting yesterday, we discussed it with our headquarters, and they feel we should take advantage of the mediation service of the United States Department of Labor.

Knight (u): Well, Mr. Malcolm, insofar as our group is concerned, I hesitate to answer without first consulting them. Any mediation will have to be immediate mediation, because of pressing business which requires the presence of many of us in other places. I am going to suggest that we recess for about five minutes.

Malcolm (m): Although this is beside the point, after walking out of the office about three o'clock yesterday afternoon, we were surprised to find a statement in the newspapers, which according to some misquoting reporter was made by Mr. Jenkins, that you were publicly announcing that Mr. Everett of the United States Conciliation Service was called in.

Jenkins (u): I heard of it first when you did. Mr. Everett, as I understand it, gave a statement that he had been requested to come in.

Knight (u): That was very evidently a misquote of Mr. Everett. I talked to him. He said he had been asked by the Defense Commission to be prepared and stand by.

[After a brief recess, the union representatives informed the management representatives that it would be agreeable to call Everett, and suggested an adjournment until he arrived. Everett arrived at 3:10 P.M., and, as the meeting reopened, he asked which side wanted to speak first. At Malcolm's suggestion Knight reviewed the union case emphasizing that the demand for a 10% wage increase constituted the major remaining barrier in the way of a satisfactory agreement He recapitulated the union's arguments basing the wage demand on actual and anticipated increases in living costs, the company's financial position, and the determination of the men to "refuse to work" on the present wage scale. Malcolm replied with a similar review of the company's position. He emphasized the joint agreement upon some 70 items of the contract, with 4 still in dispute until yesterday when final settlement of all was revealed contingent upon settlement of the wage issue. Regarding wages, he again emphasized that Bureau of Labor indices showed no increased living costs, that the adjustments given were equivalent to a 1½% wage increase and brought the weighted wage average at Barrington's some 5 cents above competitive rates, and that profit rates could not enter into wages arguments since one competitor had made four times the profit of Barrington and another only one-third as much.]

Everett: May I suggest that we have separate meetings. I am way behind on knowing what the facts in the case are. If that is agreeable, I would like for us to separate for a moment or two.

[The two groups separated and Everett remained first with the union group. He then conferred with the company representatives, who showed him their figures on competitive rates and cost of living. He spent very little time, however, reviewing these data.

[He then made two suggestions to the parties: first, that they agree on a neutral fact-finding committee which would investigate the case and make their report; and, second, that the size of the group be reduced to one or two on each side. The union representatives rejected both of these proposals. Everett then suggested to each group separately that they adjourn overnight and meet again Saturday, March 22, or Monday, March 24. Under the impression that this suggestion was agreeable to both groups, he left them. Later the union representatives called the company representatives and insisted on having "an answer" before the union meeting which was called for that (Friday) night. The company representatives informed them that it would be impossible to comply with this request, and that Everett had indicated it was agreeable to adjourn until Saturday or Monday.]

From the Meeting of March 24

Everett: I hope everybody listened to the president the other night. Certainly if a strike can be avoided here, it should be! Remember, if this country ever becomes Hitlerized, there will not be any management or any labor. It will be just like labor and industry over there under the heels of dictators. I think you are good reasonable men. You know what these controversies mean, how costly strikes always are. And above and beyond that, these are not normal conditions. As the president said in his speech, we are confronted with a situation more serious than any we have ever faced.

Knight (u): I appreciate your statements and on behalf of the employees of this refinery and those of all the operations throughout the United States, I tell you they are fully cognizant of their duties in the way of defense. I am sure that you will find, if our fears turn into actualities, that these are the men who will have the guns on their shoulders; and most certainly we want our nation to be prepared to meet any eventuality that might come. Defense to us is a serious proposition. We are trying our best to keep the American workman in a position where he can take a part in defense and will want to take part in defense. In my opinion, if a man is going to have to fight for something, it should be something worth fighting for. The workers are asking that an addition be made to their pay check so they can meet their normal requirements. I think they are right in so doing. I understand we are not too far apart at the present moment. If I have it correct, the company is now in a position to make a counterproposal on wages. My hope is that it will be sufficient to warrant real consideration. I personally am quite grateful for your remarks, Mr. Everett.

Malcolm (m): Well, are you through, Mr. Knight?

Knight (u): Yes.

Malcolm (m): We might just as well get down to business. We have been considering your request very carefully, and we are glad to make an offer on the basis of national defense. You know what contracts we have with the Government and mainly because of national defense, we are prepared to make an offer. Our offer is to increase our hourly paid workers in the amount of 3½% on the hourly payroll. Considering that two weeks ago we made an increase effective March 8, 1941, of roughly 1½%, our total increase would amount to 5%.

Knight (u): Three and one-half per cent, in my opinion, is a long ways from the original request of the employees for 15%. My opinion is that the employees are not going to be satisfied with the 3½%.

Malcolm (m): May I correct you for a moment? That's 5%. Two weeks ago we gave you 1½%.

Knight (u): All right, Mr. Malcolm, we will say 5%. That is one-third of the original request. They tell me that their second proposal, when they dropped from 15% to 10%, is about as far as they could afford to yield. I can't blame them much for not being very elated over 3½%. Incidentally, over the week end, I learned that tank wagon prices are up 1 cent. It was unusual to me that this story came out now, inasmuch as the increase took place three weeks ago. Usually it is in the papers immediately. I am sure the companies are taking full advantage of that 1 cent increase. I wish, Mr. Malcolm, that you would reconsider your offer.

Malcolm (m): We are considering it from all sides and I had a hell of a time getting what we got.

Knight (u): Compare that to $15,600,000. We are still leaving you the $15,000,000 and 90% of the $600,000.

Malcolm (m): That is very kind, but let's not forget one thing. If we were grossly underpaying our employees . . .

Knight (u): But you will soon be.

Malcolm (m): But we are not. We are the leaders now. We are prepared to submit our figures and definitely prove we are leading in wages.

Knight (u): In some classifications and some figures, you are. But Barrington has notoriously been a follower rather than a leader. So seldom does Barrington take the lead that here I think is an opportunity.

Malcolm (m): But our claim is that we have been leading already; and on top of it, we are offering an additional increase and leading again. You know how the rest of the companies feel about it. Undoubtedly, we will be seriously criticized.

[The union requested a brief recess.]

Knight (u): Mr. Malcolm, I have been discussing your proposal with the committee. They don't believe that they can recommend acceptance of the proposal you have offered. I would like, however, to make a counterproposal based, of course, on the final completion of the contract. We are prepared to cut our original demand in half by the following method: First, that this increase you offer be granted and made retroactive to January 1st. Then an additional 2½% be forthcoming in 60 days. Finally we include in our agreement a provision making it possible to reopen the contract if and when an index of the cost of living shows a 5% increase. That is exactly 50% less than the increase the employees originally proposed. We feel on that basis we can arrive at a bargain if it is agreeable to the management.

Malcolm (m): First, with regard to reopening the contract if the index goes up 5%. Do you mean the contract will be reopened, or the question of wages?

Knight (u): If we opened any phase of the contract and failed to reach agreement, it would terminate the agreement. But that doesn't mean that all the other provisions would be subject to negotiation.

Malcolm (m): To a certain degree, I see the logic of it. If prices go up unexpectedly, it seems to me logical to look for protection. So if I know what you have in mind, we will be glad to consider it. I am sorry to state we cannot see our way clear to give any more. You are stating your reasoning on the basis that because the organization asked for 15% they should have at least 7½%. Suppose you start with 30%, does it mean we have to give 15%?

Knight (u): We have made a proposal on the original request of 15% which was not unreasonable. The compromise the men have offered is fair. But I think from their attitude, they consider that a rock bottom proposal. I don't think they are going to reduce their request any lower. I know I shall not ask them to. As an additional argument, it is obvious that in the other industries where wage increases are given, none of them are less than 5%. Most of them are more.

Malcolm (m): I would suggest that you stick to the oil industry. We are not aware that in this district anybody is giving even 5%.

Knight (u): But the oil industry is lagging behind all others.

Malcolm (m): Well, we made a counterproposal, regardless of the fact that we have been accused of stalling for time. If we were stalling for time, we feel that we wouldn't have offered you anything.

Knight (u): Mr. Malcolm, I left early Saturday morning and arrived back at 12:15 today. Obviously, I couldn't have made the statement I was credited with making. I haven't talked to a single reporter in the city for a period of about three months.

Malcolm (m): Likely you made a written statement in this case.

Knight (u): I made no written statement.

Malcolm (m): I was called by the reporters, and they read to me your statement.

Knight (u): I will bet you there isn't a reporter in town who could even identify me.

Malcolm (m): I wouldn't like to have an extended discussion about it. But after we have a gentlemen's agreement that we wouldn't make any statement to the press, I was a little disappointed.

Knight (u): Mr. Malcolm, I am not in the habit of making an agreement and then breaking it. This is the only negotiation I have been in for some time where there have been so many statements and counterstatements in the papers. I don't like it, and certainly hope we can soon arrive at an understanding that will eliminate it.

Malcolm (m): As far as publicity is concerned, I think you can do what you wish at present. Now again, as to your counterproposal, we don't see how we can give it any serious consideration.

Knight (u): Just what features are objectionable?

Malcolm (m): In the first place, the retroactive feature. About this reopening clause, I am in favor of it, but I would like to clear it with our management in New York. I am reasonably certain they can agree to it. I realize you can't bind yourself for a year to something that may not be sufficient.

Knight (u): Mr. Malcolm, if that is your only objection, make it retroactive to the 15th of this month.

Malcolm (m): Of course, the retroactive feature is objectionable, but much more objectionable is the demand for a $7\frac{1}{2}\%$ increase, especially if you can reopen on wages if the cost of living goes up.

Knight (u): Of course, there lies the principal disagreement. We can't give you much on that increase of $1\frac{1}{2}\%$ that was granted a short time ago. It adjusted inequities, but the majority of the men received no wage increase whatever.

Malcolm (m): I disagree with you. I claim at least one-half of our hourly paid employees benefited.

Knight (u): Well, that still leaves a half of them who are not going to gain anything. They are going to view the obvious situation. Wages are being increased throughout the country, most of them at least 5%; some more. They see no reason why the workers at Barrington should be satisfied with $3\frac{1}{2}\%$. I don't like to see disagreement over a matter of wages, especially at this time. It will be useless to say $3\frac{1}{2}\%$ is agreeable, so I think the company should give further concessions.

Malcolm (m): Well, we will give this protective clause favorable consideration and if the cost of living is increased we can still get together. In other words, the door isn't shut altogether.

Knight (u): Well, Mr. Malcolm, to be quite frank, the amount of money is so small, that I believe your officials in charge of policy will agree to meet this request of the men.

Malcolm (m): You can rest assured that I am not making this offer on my own hook. In other words, if you think our officials will agree to $7\frac{1}{2}\%$, you are insinuating I am trying to offer $3\frac{1}{2}\%$, and that if I took it to the people in New York they would say $7\frac{1}{2}\%$ is O.K. You are wrong. I am getting my instructions on the wage question.

Knight (u): Well, by the same token, the 5% and $2\frac{1}{2}\%$ were arrived at, you might say, by instructions given to me.

Malcolm (m): Sure, I realize that.

Knight (u): We try to help the boys formulate a request. When it is made, we help them to stick by it. I have no thought and no desire to recede from that request. I say we are quite willing to remove what seems to be your principal objection.

Malcolm (m): Of course, the retroactive feature is objectionable, but the paramount objection is to the amount of money.

Knight (u): That is the feature that is not acceptable now?

Malcolm (m): And the retroactive clause is not acceptable, the date clause is not acceptable, and the amount of percent isn't acceptable.

Knight (u): That is the 7½%.

Malcolm (m): Yes.

Knight (u): How about the 5%?

Malcolm (m): No.

Knight (u): By making that suggestion, I am not suggesting that the men would forego the 2½%.

Malcolm (m): 3½% is final, and as I have said before, we would be glad to protect the men in a contract.

Knight (u): Mr. Malcolm, I don't think there is much use of us wasting each other's time. I feel the company should let us know what is the best possible offer the company can make. If we have already arrived at that, that is it. If you haven't, we wish you would do so. The proposal you made this afternoon, perhaps 60 days ago would have been accepted. Today, no.

Everett: Wouldn't it be a good idea for both sides to sleep on this tonight and meet again tomorrow afternoon, if that is agreeable.

Malcolm (m): Well, Mr. Everett, it might be agreeable, but I wouldn't like to imply by doing so that there is any promise on our part that we will go higher.

Everett: I didn't mean it in that sense. The idea was for both sides to study it over. It is getting late and you gentlemen have done a nice job of negotiating on a high plane and it never hurts to try it again, say 24 hours later.

Knight (u): If there is a thought in the mind of the company representatives that there is no possibility of a change, I think that would obviate the possibility of sleeping on it. I think, if an agreement to recess 24 hours is made, we have every right to expect that the management in the New York office will be apprised of the situation, and plenty of consideration will be given to the request of the men. We haven't accused the company of stalling and we don't intend to, but I am sure that if Mr. Malcolm feels this is the final answer of the company, he will be frank enough to say so.

Malcolm (m): You have me exactly right, Mr. Knight. I have to advise our management in regard to your proposal. But I would like to say definitely in the same breath, it doesn't mean we are going to grant it. It doesn't mean, if we answer you no tomorrow, that I have been stalling. Get the idea?

Knight (u): I do. I had a telephone call from the National Defense Committee today in which we were requested to lay before the management the rock bottom proposal of the employees. That has been done. I think that our meeting tomorrow should bring about a definite end to our conference either through consummation of the agreement, or otherwise. I feel sure, if the top management of the company who makes the policy could listen to our arguments, it might make their final answer a little different. We are placed in the position of laying our argument before you, and you are placed in the position of being our advocate in the matter. I want to impress it upon you very clearly, if I can, that these men have given every consideration to all of the existing circumstances and they don't feel that they can yield further.

[The meeting adjourned at 4:05 P.M.]

From the Meeting of March 25

Malcolm (m): We will have a very short session. After discussion with our headquarters concerning yesterday's meeting, our management reached a decision which is final as far as the company is concerned. In the interest of national defense, the company is agreeable to granting hourly paid employees an increase in the amount of 5%. We will make it effective next Monday, which is the 31st, because we have to put the payroll machinery into operation. We are also prepared to adopt a clause with regard to the cost of living. That is the whole thing in a nutshell. If you wish to remain alone, we will be glad to retire.

Knight (u): There are several other items. [Mr. Knight thereupon referred back to the 40-hour notice on change of schedule, the "normal work week for day workers," and contracting out maintenance and construction work. A recess was then called, after which discussions were resumed, as follows:]

Malcolm (m): On the definition of "work week," I would invite Mr. Carlisle, Mr. Harris, and Mr. Boyden to discuss that.

Harris (m): We have men starting their work weeks all seven days, so there could be seven separate work weeks.

Knight (u): Our proposal is that we define "work week." For the general group, their "work week" will start on Monday and end on Friday, while the required number of odd schedules will provide for the normal trouble shooting.

Harris (m): We can't, with our present setup, start on Monday and end on Friday.

[There was considerable discussion at this point. The company representatives explained their refinery schedule in detail. The point was passed.]

Malcolm (m): Well, the next point is change of shift schedule. [To Boyden.] Will you give our proposal?

Boyden (m): If a man is scheduled to be off on Wednesday and is told 24 hours in advance that he is to work Wednesday and take Friday instead, he will work at straight rate. If a day worker is scheduled to work the 8–4 shift and is told the same day to work 4–12 or 12–8, he will receive rate and a half for the first day so worked, regardless of notice.

Harris (m): And it is understood that if we change a man's schedule, with agreed notice, it can be done at straight time.

Knight (u): We are not very far apart. But, on the 24-hour notice, couldn't we, from the standpoint of what is fair and right, extend it to 26 hours?

Malcolm (m): What are the pitfalls, Carlisle?

Carlisle (m): As far as we are concerned, 26 hours is the same in practical effect as 40 hours.

Knight (u): Well, I am going to say this. I have known Mr. Carlisle for some time, and if he will make every reasonable effort to notify these men *before* they come to work, I am going to suggest to the committee that they accept 24 hours. I have a lot of faith in Mr. Carlisle's statements.

Jenkins (u): It is agreeable to me.

Stratton (u): That is our recommendation.

[The parties at this point explored varying questions introduced by the union as important to their members: the request to receive first consideration for construction and maintenance work, which now might be "contracted-out"; the job rates of asbestos workers; the appeal of a night-shift operator discharged when caught sleeping at his post. The company would not recede from its positions on any of these questions; nor on the more crucial differences over contract coverage of watchmen, which the union thereupon declared it would carry to the NLRB. The discussions then proceeded as follows:]

Malcolm (m): With regard to the clause permitting reopening of wages under certain circumstances, we have prepared a wording that follows the suggestion of the conciliator.

ARTICLE 12, SECTION 11

Either party to this agreement shall have the right to reopen the question of wages only once during the period of this contract. This right shall be exercisable on or before August 1, 1941 on ten (10) days' notice provided that on or before July 1, 1941 the cost of living index of the United States Department of Labor registers a change for this area equal to or exceeding 5% in comparison with the figures published for March 15, 1941. Should no agreement be reached on the question of wages under such circumstances, this agreement shall become null and void thirty (30) days after the date on which the question of wages has been reopened.

Knight (u): Why limit reopening once? If right between now and July 1, it is equally right after July 1. The index might remain static between now and July 1, and immediately thereafter jump 20% or 10%. Our thought was that if the living cost would justify an increase, management would be agreeable to meet with us.

Malcolm (m): Inasmuch as Mr. Everett made this suggestion, we adopted it. But if we agree to the principle, you immediately want something more.

Knight (u): No, Mr. Malcolm, that is not our thought at all. We agreed to the principle that if the cost of living went up the men could reopen the question of wages. We have every reason to believe there will be an upward movement in the cost of living before July 1, 1941, but we are not sure of it, and we feel that we would be doing the employees an injustice to agree to a 5% increase only at that time.

Malcolm (m): I can't commit myself without consulting my people, but let me get it right.

Knight (u): Well, we object to the date July 1st and the limitation of one time.

Malcolm (m): Would it be acceptable to you, if it would read that either party to this agreement shall have the right to reopen the question of wages during the period of this contract on 10 days' notice, providing the cost of living index registers a change for the area equal to or exceeding 5%?

Knight (u): I think that would be quite acceptable.

Malcolm (m): Well, I would like to contact our management.

Everett: Suppose Malcolm gets the green light from New York on this last proposal. Are we settled?

Knight (u): We are very close to a very good understanding on the whole thing. I am going to suggest that the final decision be made by the men to-night.

[Everett suggested that any statements to the press be limited to the information that results were satisfactory to both sides. Malcolm suggested that reporters be referred to Everett.

[The meeting adjourned at 9:17 P.M.

[At their local meeting, the union members accepted the agreement as negotiated; Malcolm received approval from top management.]

Discussion Questions

1. On the basis of Everett's activity both in the session of March 21 and in later sessions, what would you say with regard to the objective of conciliation and Everett's effectiveness in terms of that objective?

2. If you were a management representative, would you prefer a cost-of-living escalator clause incorporated into a long-term contract as in the 1948 General Motors contract, or a reopening clause parallel to the one negotiated at Barrington? As a union representative, what would be your preference?

3. Appraise the "windup" of this negotiation in terms of the background of relations since the union entered. Give your estimate of the prospects for developing relationships. If you were a member of management, what preparation, if any, would you make for administering the new contract?

4. Appraise the skill shown by Malcolm and Knight in these negotiations as they deployed their tactical maneuvers to attain their strategic goals.

NATIONAL FOOD SPECIALTIES (A)

The New Manager of Industrial Relations

On November 1, 1946, Robert R. Mitchell entered upon his duties as manager of industrial relations at the Laurelton plant of National Food Specialties, Inc. Local 8 of the Amalgamated Meat Cutters and Butcher Workmen had just served notice of its desire to negotiate a new agreement. Even as he organized his office, therefore, Mr. Mitchell prepared for the pending negotiations by exploring background factors. From interviews, community contacts, and a study of available records, he compiled the following account:

1. The Business Is Born

In May, 1929, a well-known chef expanded his business from his restaurant to a small one-room operation.

The business had been started to meet requests of restaurant patrons for its Italian foods. Separate packages of spaghetti, mushroom sauce with meatballs, and Parmesan cheese were provided with simple instructions on how to prepare them at home in 10 to 12 minutes. The food thus packaged was prepared almost entirely by relatives and friends of the owner of the restaurant.

Demand increased rapidly, and the preparation of these packages was soon removed from the restaurant kitchen and made a separate operation. By 1937 it became apparent that much larger production facilities were required. Since tomatoes constituted a base product of the sauce, the management cast about for a location near (1) a tomato-growing area, and (2) relatively low-cost labor.

2. The Business Expands

Laurelton, a community of some 8,000 people, situated in the mid-eastern section of Pennsylvania, promised many advantages. Within a 25-mile radius was one of the finest tomato-growing sections in the United States. The surrounding country was settled about 200 years ago, primarily by Pennsylvania Dutch. With the growth of population, the land could not occupy all members of the farm families, so that in time a pool of surplus labor was created that could be tapped for relatively low wages. Anthracite coal fields also are located within the area, and the women of the mining communities competed with those of the farms for jobs.

In 1918, the Allegheny Silk Mills had built a large, modern plant in Laurelton. The mill was hard-hit by the depression and eventually had to close its doors. It passed into the hands of the creditors, and remained empty with a New York bank holding the mortgage. In May, 1938, the Chicago owner of the "spaghetti dinners" purchased it on his own terms. He easily obtained contracts with farmers for the season's tomato planting, and hired some 250 people to process his materials. The minimum hourly wage rate for men was set at 35 cents, and for women at 30 cents; the maxima were 60 cents and 40 cents respectively. In 1941 the minimum hourly wage rates were 40 cents for men and 30 cents for women; the respective maxima were 65 cents and 40 cents.[1]

[1] By the terms of the Fair Labor Standards Act of 1938, minimum wages had been established at the following levels: [*Continued on next page.*

3. THE WAR YEARS

Beginning in 1942 the business expanded rapidly to meet the demands of the Federal Government. The Italian food products that had been added to the company's "line" since 1938, such as canned spaghetti and meatballs, ravioli, minestrone soup, etc., were nearly all abandoned to meet the demand for K Rations.

The company now for the first time had to compete for labor as the work force increased more than tenfold. The company chartered buses to bring in employees from a distance.

When the operations had been transferred to Laurelton, the owner brought along his "organization," chiefly relatives and friends, trained in the making of Italian foods. These people occupied the key positions. A former chief of police of Laurelton occupied the dual position of chief of plant police and employment manager. There were no systematic records and no job or rate structure. Relatives, friends, and acquaintances usually enjoyed premium pay.

4. THE UNION ENTERS

The Amalgamated Meat Cutters and Butcher Workmen made three attempts to organize the plant before they finally succeeded in August, 1945. Management, supported by the merchants in the community, strongly opposed the union. By the time the union was certified, the local union leaders had become belligerent and militant organizers.

5. NEGOTIATING THE FIRST AGREEMENT

The National Labor Relations Board, in September, 1945, certified Local 8 of the Amalgamated as bargaining agent. On October 12, the parties convened to negotiate their first agreement. Management brought in a lawyer who had had no prior experience in labor relations. From October 12, 1945, to January 28, 1946, the parties bargained, "horse traded," and fought every inch of the way from Laurelton to Chicago and return. The union's spokesmen, apparently, seemed ready to trade anything for a union shop. Management wrung repeated large concessions from the union negotiators on almost every other issue as inducement for granting their central demand.

While this "tough" bargaining was in progress, National Food Specialties made overtures for purchase of the plant.

6. A NEW MANAGEMENT TAKES OVER

National Food Specialties, Inc., informed the owners that no transfer of the property would be considered until the agreement with the union had been signed, and thus were instrumental in getting the local management to settle with the union. However, the concessions already offered by the union remained. The final agreement accordingly represented from the union's viewpoint a "hard bargain." By its terms the conferees had settled—and this in January, 1946—for a horizontal wage increase of three cents an hour, retroactive to October 12, 1945.

In February, 1946, about one month after this first agreement was signed, National Food Specialties, Inc., took over the Laurelton plant. Transition from a loosely operated family concern to the expanded but tightly-knit organization that the new management wanted was a jolting change. The suspicious militancy of the union found fresh targets in the familiar bugbear of "remote ownership." Many in the community also viewed gloomily the "prospects" of absentee owners draining off profits at the expense of local people.

(a) First year (i.e., one year from 120 days after June 25, 1938): 25 cents an hour.
(b) Next six years (i.e., October, 1938–October, 1945): 30 cents an hour.
(c) After seven years: 40 cents an hour.

7. Administering the First Agreement

Administration of the 1946 Agreement became a sequence of sharp disputes over its terms. Grievances multiplied; grievance procedures produced few satisfactory settlements; wage dissatisfactions seethed; conflicts over coverage and intent of the Agreement took new forms with new policies; work stoppages grew into an established mode of protest. Neither party felt the Agreement was "working"; each, bristling at the other, felt sure it knew exactly why.

No attempt was made to settle grievances in the shop at the time they arose. Instead all grievances were held until the weekly meeting on Friday afternoon. These meetings then apparently developed into "knock-down-and-drag-out" bouts. Nothing would be done about the particular grievance; it was carried over to the next Friday meeting, when a few more were added, and so on and on, until each "old" grievance was lost in a web of "new" grievances—real and fancied.

Work stoppages made their appearance in departments where any long-fought grievance had originated. Soon the union was resorting to them to dramatize issues it *intended* to bring into the Friday conference. The union shop stewards, led by a militant chief shop steward, began to tell the supervisory force just what they could do and could not do "under the Agreement." As such small stoppages multiplied, they stalled production by tying up now this strategic sector, now that. Management went "in swinging." The union responded with a stronger and more effective swing. Emotionalism suffused the atmosphere of joint dealings.

During the first half of 1946, sales were unusually good. The press carried stories of other industries granting wage increases of from 12 to 18½ cents per hour. The union chafed and fretted against the three-cent per hour increase they had received under the 1946 agreement. Finally its leaders told management they would be unable to hold their people in line unless the wage clause was opened for further negotiation. In July, 1946, the company increased rates six cents per hour. It was announced to the employees by management; the union was given no credit.

As the tomato harvesting season approached management determined that an additional 400 people would be required to process the tomatoes into puree, and then to can and store the puree. The 1946 agreement had excluded seasonal workers from coverage. As it hired these employees, the company offered wages six cents per hour below the minimum rate of the agreement. To the protest of the union, the company replied that seasonal workers were not included in the bargaining unit.

The resulting tension was heightened when the union saw management giving most of the overtime work of the harvest months to these seasonal workers. The regular workforce, members of the union, maintained that they could and should receive all available overtime they could handle before the seasonal employees were assigned any of it. Pressing this protest, the union contended that this development demonstrated why—even if they did not under the Agreement represent seasonal workers—they *did* have a stake in determining their minimum wage. As it was, management was using the seasonal workers' rate to undermine the contractual wage structure and cut the take-home pay of its members.

As the wage dispute dragged on, the union invoked the union shop clause of the Agreement. Under its terms a new employee had to become a union member 45 days from the date he was hired. The union contended that when a seasonal worker was transferred to a permanent job in the plant his employment must be deemed to have begun when the company first hired him as a seasonal worker, not (as management maintained) when he was placed on the regular payroll. The conflict over this issue generated ill feeling that was further exacerbated when the union sought to extend to probationary employees and seasonal workers transferred to permanent jobs the rate increase of July, 1946. Management denied the union's right to bargain for probationers or such seasonal workers during the first 45 days of "regular employment." Not until November, 1946, was this particular controversy settled, when a conciliator of the United States Conciliation Service affirmed the union's contention and granted the employees involved retroactive compensation at the higher rate.

Acrimonious discussion also focused upon the status of supervisors. The union held that, since the supervisor had been a working foreman before the union was certified and had been excluded from the bargaining unit, he must now under the Agreement stop "working at the bench." The supervisors apparently found it hard to change their wonted ways. They were paid five cents above the highest rate of those they supervised. Early in October, 1946, the company put all supervisors upon weekly salary, at last drawing a line between hourly rated employees and supervision. But it did not change the foremen—many of them continued to work at the bench when they deemed proper, as before.

Against this background, Mitchell took up his duties in November, 1946. The immediate circumstances surrounding his entry into the situation reflected, he soon realized, all that had gone before. Production had reached a new peak. Yet work stoppages were frequent and stubborn. The international representative of the union was in town almost continuously. He had organized the union officials and shop stewards into a well-knit team. On each concrete issue, he took action directed, not toward promoting cooperative relations, but toward gaining a better-than-fair chance to win its possible arbitration.

After attending his first Friday grievance meeting, Mitchell met frequently with supervisors. He talked to them about grievances, what grievances could tell management, and why grievances were best settled immediately in the department in which they occurred. He frowned upon big agenda at the tempestuous Friday meetings; repeatedly he threw back to departmental supervisors the petty gripes and complaints, as well as "real grievances," that he insisted they must try to resolve themselves. It was not easy for these foremen to tackle individual grievances as they got them; but, as they made the effort, the union leaders began to meet them half-way.

Mitchell proposed to the union a series of meetings at which the divisional managers of production, maintenance, and warehousing would appear before the shop stewards. They led to an airing of gripes and "over-all" grievances that accomplished much in clearing the atmosphere.

When the union on November 25 transmitted in writing, 37 days before the expiration of the Agreement on December 31, notice of intention to terminate, Mr. Mitchell felt that the work of the past few weeks had bettered the chances for smoother negotiating.

PREPARING FOR THE NEGOTIATING CONFERENCES

It was agreed by the parties that the first negotiating conference should be held on December 11, 1946. The union had submitted its draft of proposed contract revisions. Mitchell addressed himself to those preliminary activities that he deemed important at this stage.

In making appointments to the negotiating committee for management, he recommended men who would meet three requirements: (1) a representative from each division, so that questions raised by the union negotiators could be adequately handled; (2) positions high enough in the managerial hierarchy to lend dignity and status to the negotiating procedures; (3) representatives able to communicate to their respective departments a sense of wide participation in framing the revised agreement, so that administration of its eventual terms would be in the hands of men who would feel they had played an "effective part in writing them."

The management negotiating committee contained the following eight executives: the vice president in charge of production; the plant manager; the chief of the engineering and maintenance division; the chief of the warehousing division; the personnel manager; the administrative assistant to the personnel manager; the assistant to the manager of industrial relations; and Mitchell himself, who would act as chairman of management's negotiating committee.

Mitchell held preliminary meetings with the members of his committee to discuss "the technique of negotiation." He warned them that, no matter how difficult the circumstances in which the evolving discussions might place them, they should not reply even to the most unreasonable demand in a tense or emotional way. The first meeting, and indeed several thereafter, he pointed out, might well prove heated. The union's international representative, who was to act as chairman of the union negotiators, was a hard-bitten, old-line, acute AFL craft unionist, and his very experiences in the 1946 negotiations at Laurelton probably would lead him to present exaggerated initial demands.

He also discussed the union's negotiators with his committee, to exchange ideas on the kind of person each of them was, his background, and attitudes in joint dealings. Thumbnail sketches, as they emerged from these explorations, follow:

International Representative Thomas Wagner. About 45 years old, Wagner had grown up in the packing-house industry and has been an active unionist for a quarter of a century. Slightly hard of hearing, he uses this handicap to very good advantage when the occasion suggests. He can punch and parry with expert effectiveness; and he possesses a rather rich and broad experience with the National Labor Relations Act, which he tends constantly to invoke. He has without question negotiated many agreements, and so knows thoroughly the language of the shop and all the stock answers to management's typical thinking on shop issues.

President of the Local Frank Shultz. Age 36. At one time Shultz had been a supervisor, but he had been reduced to the ranks by what he called "a kick in the face." He is the son of a union official at a locomotive works in the vicinity. This is his first venture, however, in unionism. He was elected President of the Local because he was one of the chief local organizers and the "toughest guy" in the outfit. He has a leave of absence from the company and spends full time as President and Business Agent of Local Union 8.

Chief Shop Steward Edward Parsons. Age 37. The son of a railroad conductor, Parsons is belligerent and militant. He is smart and fearless, and has an unusual working knowledge of the entire plant and its production process. He also knows all the union and management people with whom he has to deal better than anyone else on either management's or the union's side. He has a nose for information that leads him into many so-called secret channels. Much of his thinking and philosophy seems directly traceable to his father's experience in the railroad brotherhoods.

Shop Steward 1. Age 60. A Pennsylvania Dutchman, he always wants to be "right" on issues, but is contrary. He had not been associated with any union activities. Considered quite a rounder in his younger days, he hit the sawdust trail some 20 years ago and has tried to live up to his convictions ever since. When he has confidence in an individual, he gives him almost unquestioning "faith." An unusually good fighter, somewhat impetuous and emotional.

Shop Steward 2. Age 45. A French Canadian by birth, he came to Laurelton via a job with a plumbing contractor. He married a local girl and settled in the community. Assigned as a plumber to the Engineering and Maintenance Division, he is the highest-rated wage earner in the bargaining unit. The man is well-balanced, has the courage of his convictions, is fair, and should be a stabilizing influence in the union committee. He is known to possess an excellent sense of humor, which management should be able to tap when necessary to lighten any charged atmosphere.

Shop Steward 3. Age 29. A process worker who enjoys the confidence of his fellow employees but never says much either in or out of meetings. While he may not add much to concrete negotiations, he can contribute in his quiet way as a stabilizer.

Shop Steward 4. Age 36. A meat-plant worker. (Nothing positive was brought up about him; and the union in fact dropped him from its committee after the first meeting.)

Shop Steward 5. Age 47. Representing the Warehousing Division, it did not appear that this man, either, would contribute much weight to the committee. (It turned out that about the time of the fourth negotiation conference, he found himself in a rather embarrassing position because the union discovered a "leak" which the other members apparently traced to him. They accused him of talking indiscreetly.)

Shop Stewardess and Secretary of Local 8. Age 28. Representing the women, she is generally considered a fine person. She does her own thinking, never speaks out of turn, is fair, and has the respect of all who had dealings with her under the first agreement. She had done welding for a steel concern in this locality during the war, and thus has had prior exposure to unionism. She is not militant but gains her objectives by a mild form of insistence. She is a hard worker both for the company and the union.

The 1946 agreement had been negotiated at the offices of the local Chamber of Commerce, adjacent to the office of the company lawyer. Mitchell looked them over; he found the rooms dark and dingy, bare of all furnishings but the essential table and chairs, and even then imparting a sense of "crowdedness."

Consulting with the union leaders, Mitchell drew from them the suggestion that negotiations take place on company property if a meeting place could be made available.

Knowing that the office of the chairman of the board of the company was not in continuous use, Mr. Mitchell obtained it for the negotiations. The room was well-lighted, more or less isolated, and had good ventilation. It was planned to assign one end of the table to the three chief union negotiators and the other end to the three chief negotiators of management, with the "overflow" of both groups arranging themselves on either side.

Ten negotiating conferences were held between December 11, 1946, and January 30, 1947. After each meeting, Mr. Mitchell recorded his impressions of its "spirit" and the progress made toward the goal.

The negotiating committees were composed of the following representatives:

For the Company	*For the Union*
Robert R. Mitchell, Manager of Industrial Relations and Chairman	Thomas Wagner, International Representative and Chairman
Adolph Hartmann, Assistant to Mr. Mitchell	Frank Shultz, President, Local 8
H. M. Ulrich, Vice President in Charge of Production	Edward Parsons, Chief Shop Steward
	Carl Yost, Assistant Chief Shop Steward
Charles S. Brooks, Plant Manager	Anatole Docette, Shop Steward
James Greenwood, Chief Engineer	George Page, Shop Steward
Richard Adams, Personnel Manager	Bernard Martin, Shop Steward
William Blenheim, Assistant Personnel Manager	Max Snyder, Shop Steward
Herbert Rogers, Jr., Manager, Warehousing Division	Catherine Lloyd, Shop Steward

An office stenographer took notes of the proceedings. The record did not furnish a verbatim transcript but focused on discussion and disposition of the issues.

DISCUSSION QUESTIONS

1. What would you say Mr. Mitchell was trying to accomplish toward his long-term objectives in addition to obtaining background information by his preliminary survey of plant relationships?

2. In what *structure of relationships* do management and union seem to be dealing together when Mr. Mitchell enters the situation?

3. List the continuing issues or differences which you would anticipate as possible "bones of contention" in the pending negotiations.

4. Review the measures Mitchell took in his effort to prepare for the pending negotiations.

5. What clues are you given in these preparations with regard to the strategy Mitchell is planning in the pending negotiations?

NATIONAL FOOD SPECIALTIES (B)

THE FIRST SESSION: STEERING PAST A ROUGH LAUNCHING

[Meeting opened on Wednesday, December 11, 1946, at 2:15 P.M.]

Mitchell (m): What procedure do you want to follow?

Wagner (u): We should set up the procedure as to what time we will start these meetings and end them.

Mitchell (m): We could have tentative arrangements say every other day from 2:00 P.M. to 5:00 P.M. For this afternoon's meeting I would suggest that you go over your proposal, and we will hear you all the way through. You want to change the 1946 agreement; so we are entitled to know why you want those changes.

Wagner (u): The now existing agreement had so many misinterpretations is the reason we want the changes.

Mitchell (m): But if you won't agree to read your proposals clause by clause and give us your reasons for the changes, then our answer is "No." Where will we be?

Wagner (u): If you have not had time to study the proposal, we can adjourn and let you do that.

Mitchell (m): We've read it all right.

Wagner (u): Then the next move is for you to submit your counterproposal to us.

Mitchell (m): We will have it prepared and submitted to you this week, on Friday. We will meet again next Tuesday at 2:00 P.M. Are you willing to talk about certain sections in your proposal so we can get your thinking?

Wagner (u): Yes.

Mitchell (m): For instance, your proposal for joint job evaluation is agreeable to us.

Wagner (u): New employees are put on jobs. The rates submitted to us are not the true rates. Certainly there is something wrong.

Ulrich (m): The point you raise is right. What we want to know is the "How?" of the questions you raise.

Mitchell (m): Let's look at that proposal of yours. It's Article VII on page 3 of your draft [reading]:

All present Rate Schedules and Job Classifications shall be revised and a clear description shall be made by a joint committee which shall consist of not more than eight (8) people, four (4) from the union, and four (4) from the company. Any job evaluation sheets and consequent job grades and job grade rates which are agreed upon by this committee shall thereby be established for the life of the contract.

We are willing to proceed on that basis now—I mean, to set up that committee. The company is willing to go into it sincerely, honestly, and wholeheartedly. Now, if your four people and our four people disagree as to a job rating, how will we find the answer?

Wagner (u): By a third party, Department of Labor and Industry.

Ulrich (m): What we will arrive at is point values showing the relation between each and every job.

Wagner (u): That is right.

Ulrich (m): When we agree on all of the factors involved in setting up this point system, then the only differences that we can expect are such questions as does the job require one or two years, etc. About 99% of our differences will be dissolved between the union committee and management committee. Then for those differences that remain a third party should come in and help iron out the differences.

Wagner (u): According to these classifications all female employees are classified as common laborers. But there are certain semiskilled jobs that women are performing. Setting up accurate job classifications is the only way to keep these grievances from coming up.

Ulrich (m): There are many factors that enter into it. We are not in disagreement on that.

Mitchell (m): That job rating scheme then is one of the ideas in your proposal on which we can get into action right now.

Wagner (u): Would you like to have the names of our committee today?

Mitchell (m): We would like to have them today, or if not today, then tomorrow.

Wagner (u): I will have those names before the close of this meeting. In all sincerity I would like to say that one of the management men present at last year's meetings, Mr. Torrensi, said that there would be no cut in take-home pay. He very much emphasized that; but throughout the year of 1946 I followed many of the employees, and on the average they had 261 hours less than last year. Even with the 9 cent increase that the company gave, the employees this year are going to wind up with wages just as bad as the year 1945, while there is the increased cost of living and a 69-cent purchasing power in the dollar. When we ask for a general increase of 30 cents for 1947, I don't think we ask for enough. We accepted the 2-cent or 3-cent increase in the 1946 negotiations. This year it will absolutely have to be in dollars and cents, not promises.

Mitchell (m): The food industry is competitive. This management wants to pay a fair and reasonable wage and have stable employment. It is not a question of 30 cents or 10 cents an hour. It is a question of how much the company can stand.

Wagner (u): Here is the reason for the wage demand. You take the yearly earnings for 1945. They averaged $1,961.79.

Mitchell (m): Was the company then working for the U.S. Government on war contracts?

Wagner (u): I realize it was operated for the government. But Mr. Torrensi assured this committee there would be no cut in take-home pay. Then, when I get to the close of this year, I find the 261 hours' less work, with only a 9-cent increase; there is something wrong.

Mitchell (m): It is not the intention of this company to exploit labor in any way. We will examine where we are now and where we are going, trying to find what is a fair and reasonable wage rate in terms of competition. That is the fairest for the long pull.

Ulrich (m): One of the statements that came out very strongly in last year's meeting was that we did not know what kind of a bear we had by the tail. We have not spent one penny on advertising, because of the uncertainties. Mr. Torrensi made a study of our products and was sincere in his promise. What was once definitely a big seller is not now. I don't know if competition is cutting it out or if it is just not drawing preference. I don't think we should say he was insincere on that.

Wagner (u): Back in February, when the hours started dropping, Mr. Torrensi should have called a meeting with the union. He should have told us about the cut in hours and arrived at a solution and not let it drag on.

Mitchell (m): Would the old company at any time on commercial products produce the same volume as the new management now?

Ulrich (m): The answer is no by approximately three times. During the war the volume went up tremendously on Army goods. Immediately after the war we began to increase our civilian products just as fast as we could. We are not going to do the volume we did in 1944, but in civilian products we will do more than in prewar.

Wagner (u): Last September 12 [1945] we submitted our proposal. Then after about three weeks, the proposed agreement was read. Certain parts were tentatively agreed to. Then the company's proposal, or counterproposal, was read; and from there on out we tore the agreements apart and built up from there. If the company has a proposal we would be in a better position to negotiate.

Mitchell (m): You will have ours by Friday. Do you suggest that we adjourn and come together next Tuesday at 2:00 P.M.?

Wagner (u): Yes, then I will make arrangements to be here from Tuesday on, to meet whenever suitable to the company.

[Meeting adjourned at 3:15 P.M.]

The joint job evaluation committee was agreed upon between the company and the union.

Mr. Mitchell's comments on this first session may be briefly summarized from his notes:

As anticipated we were launched by a very rugged meeting. These summary minutes do not convey the atmosphere—the stilted exchanges and the attitudes of the parties, particularly the union negotiators. Of course Wagner and I were the only experienced negotiators present, and I felt from the way Wagner started he was set for some very tough window dressing. He's an adroit fellow; and I met his opening by opening with some pretty fancy, tough window dressing of my own for our side. It almost looked as if we'd crack wide open at the very first meeting as we sparred for yes or no answers.

But we made a detour, and got an open edge by concentrating on one thing we had decided we could agree to among the union's demands. It didn't stop Wagner from giving us some bristling warnings and raking up a lot of accumulated "mads." But I feel we took away even from this Session 1 a valuable symbol of good intention—our "first wagon" to which both union and management can hitch their horses, and head in the same direction at the same time. We'll see.

DISCUSSION QUESTION

1. How would you describe Mitchell's major strategy in this first session? And his tactical steps for implementing that strategy?

NATIONAL FOOD SPECIALTIES (C)

THE SECOND SESSION: COVERAGE, RECOGNITION, AND HOURS OF WORK

[The meeting opened on December 17, 1946, at 2:10 P.M.]

Mitchell (m): Do you want a report on job evaluation? We agreed to set up that committee of union and management. Do you want to hear a report on what they have done?

Wagner (u): The committee is in full charge, and whatever it does is all right with me.

Mitchell (m): How do you want to proceed?

Wagner (u): Well, I got your proposal for a new agreement last evening and I read it over last night and today. I don't know what procedure you follow. Do you want to take your proposal?

Mitchell (m): We would rather discuss yours and ours together, based upon the present agreement. It is easier to follow that way. We could keep account of what we do a little better that way.

Wagner (u): I am willing to take either yours or ours and, by article and paragraph, say whether it is acceptable or not. It makes no difference to me if we take the union's or the company's proposal.

Mitchell (m): As I stated, we must have some place to start. If we start with yours, we have the one extreme and if we take ours, we have the other extreme. If we start with the 1946 agreement we can make better and more understanding headway. It seems to me that in yours you did not follow the 1946 agreement at all.

Wagner (u): There are so many things in this present agreement contrary to our policy. I would sooner set aside the 1946 agreement and start on either yours or ours.

Mitchell (m): Well, then, if you have no objections, we will start with ours and tie yours in.

Wagner (u): That's fine. Do you want me to do the reading? [Wagner reads the clauses on "Parties to the Agreement" and "Purpose of the Agreement," giving the union's approval to the company's versions.]

Wagner (u): [looking up from text]: Now: *Article 2—Union Recognition.* When this article was drafted last year, I don't know why the language wasn't used as given by the NLRB Certification. Do you have an objection to the way we've incorporated it in our draft? [Mr. Wagner read the union draft of *Article II, Union Recognition and Coverage.*]

A. In accordance with the results of the election held by the National Labor Relations Board on August 24, 1945, the Company shall recognize the Union as the exclusive representatives of its employees for the purpose of collective bargaining with respect to rates of pay, wages, hours of employment and other conditions of employment.

B. The term "employee" as used in this contract, shall include all production and maintenance employees, including foremen and foreladies, watchmen, and local truck drivers and excluding office clerical employees, timekeepers, nurses, guards, over-the-road truck drivers, chief engineer, and all other supervisory employees with authority to hire, discharge, promote, discipline or otherwise effect changes in the status of employees or effectively recommend such action.

C. The term "Regular Employee" refers only to the employees in the bargaining unit as defined above, and shall be understood to mean a full-time employee who has been retained after serving his or her fifteen (15) days' probationary period.

D. Any employee who has not worked for fifteen (15) days shall not be considered a "Regular Employee."

Mitchell (m): The only difference is we have made a few changes in it.

Wagner (u): You have sneaked in a few extra phrases. Listen to this [reading from the company's draft of agreement]:

ARTICLE 2—UNION RECOGNITION

A. The company recognizes the union as the sole collective bargaining agency with respect to rates of pay, wages, hours of work, and other conditions of employment for all of its production and maintenance employees, including local truck drivers, and excluding seasonal employees, clerical employees, field contact men, timekeepers, nurses, guards, over-the-road truck drivers, Quality Control and other technical employees, foremen, foreladies, and all other supervisory employees with authority to hire, discharge, promote, discipline, or otherwise effect changes in the status of employees or effectively recommend such action. The term "employee" as used in this agreement refers only to the employees in the bargaining unit as defined above.

B. The company agrees not to interfere with the right of its employees to become members of the union, and that it will not discriminate against any employees because of such membership. The union agrees that it will not engage in any act of intimidation or coercion of the company's employees in order to secure membership in the union, and agrees that no solicitation for membership or other union activities, except as permitted by law and otherwise provided herein, will be conducted on company time or property.

You sneaked in some more groups in the exclusions.

Mitchell (m): No, we did not sneak anything into it. Why are you proposing that repetition of recorded fact in your Section A?

Wagner (u): Refer back to the date of our certification.

Mitchell (m): The union was certified by the NLRB August 24, 1945. That is always a matter of record. It does not have to be in our agreement.

Wagner (u): It gives a recognition and coverage. There were certain people who were excluded in your 1946 agreement that should have been in this coverage.

Mitchell (m): I assume that both parties agreed to the exclusions and the inclusions. Do you have a copy of the certification?

Wagner (u): Yes, I have a copy.

Case No. 0–X–0000, Agreement for Consent Election, payroll period ending July 28, 1945. All production and maintenance employees, including working foremen and working foreladies, watchmen, and local truck drivers and excluding office clerical employees, timekeepers, nurses, guards, over-the-road truck drivers, chief engineer, and all other supervisory employees with authority to hire, discharge, promote, discipline or otherwise effectively recommend such action.

Mitchell (m): So far that follows what we had in the 1946 agreement.

Wagner (u): No, it does not. Excluded in your 1946 agreement were working foremen and foreladies and I notice in your proposal you put in Quality Control and the technical employees to be excluded. That I won't agree to.

Mitchell (m): You have done that already. We are merely confirming what we already have done.

Wagner (u): We did agree to Quality Control but what about technical employees? I don't know what you mean by "technical employees."

Ulrich (m): Quality Control have inspectors to report to management so we can see what condition our goods are in. Now, Quality Control could take a man and put him through elementary courses in bacteriology, spoilage of foods, and drug relations on handling food. I would think that a man who is employed as a technical inspector would not come under the bargaining unit.

Wagner (u): Can we agree to accept the certification by the board with the exception of this Quality Control? I still will not agree to exclude "technical employees" as a category.

Ulrich (m): Can we define a technical employee to be one who has received special training at the expense of the company to perform a function of management?

Wagner (u): I am willing to insert the board's certification plus Quality Control; but I am not willing to insert the wording about technical employees.

Ulrich (m): Would you agree to technical salaried employees?

Wagner (u): Let's leave it out altogether. Now as to foremen: you changed the status of the foremen and foreladies about four months ago and put them on salary. That is when the union started kicking and said salaried foremen were not going to work at the bench.

Mitchell (m): That is one of the things we want to get in the open. That is one of the things on which we are definite; that is that all foremen and foreladies be excluded from the bargaining unit.

Wagner (u): That is something the individual has something to say about. Maybe your foremen and foreladies asked to join the union.

Mitchell (m): Then we would take it to the NLRB for a consent election. The individual has nothing to do with it. The NLRB certified the groups to be excluded, and these people were specifically excluded. We would be willing to take out technical employees.

Wagner (u): Would you be willing to include foremen and foreladies?

Mitchell (m): No, so where do we go from here?

Wagner (u): No place. We only want what was stated by the NLRB.

Mitchell (m): On your interpretation? Your version omits the word "working" before "foremen" that's in the certification. Our foremen now are salaried supervisors. We cannot agree to an organization in which the supervisors are a part of the bargaining unit. Supervisors cannot work for two masters. They certainly cannot pay tribute to you and give loyalty to management at the same time.

Wagner (u): May I ask what you are willing to go along on in Union Recognition and Coverage?

Mitchell (m): Under Article 2 in our version we think we are fair. If we also strike out technical employees, it gives you everything you have right now.

Wagner (u): Are you willing to exclude technical employees?

Mitchell (m): Yes. It may look like a "sleeper" but it was not intended as such in any sense of the word. [The company representatives left the room at 3:00 P.M. for five minutes to permit the union to discuss the company's proposal.]

Wagner (u): Throughout this 1946 agreement we had many disputes on seasonal employees. Would the company be willing to include seasonal employees and exclude the so-called foremen and foreladies?

Mitchell (m): No, we would not.

Wagner (u): You want to exclude seasonal employees from the bargaining unit. When are you going to use such seasonal employees?

Ulrich (m): Let me make a good guess. I know our need, fundamentally, for seasonal employees is during the tomato season. It would be advisable probably to start collecting a crew for clean-up work 10 days before the season.

Wagner (u): Let's say seasonal employees from July 1 to October 31. Charge them 50¢ per week the same as your regular employees pay $2.00 per month.

[The company representatives left the room at 3:20 P.M. to discuss the union's proposal.]

Ulrich (m): We still feel this question should be settled with seasonal employees excluded. We feel we can go along in limiting the period of seasonal workers; that we have all seasonal employees working on tomatoes only and not in any plant operations.

Shultz (u): We are right back where we started from.

Mitchell (m): No, we are not. We have defined the seasonal worker as one employed only from July 1 to October 31.

Wagner (u): Why should these people come in here and have full benefits we won without paying one cent to the union?

Mitchell (m): The point is you have not bargained for those people.

Wagner (u): The union is taking the position that we are going to abide by the NLRB Recognition and Coverage.

Mitchell (m): O.K. Let's pass it for the present.

Wagner (u): O.K. The next is *Article 3—Union Membership*. I guess Articles III and IV in our proposal cover the subjects in your Article. There are some important differences; maybe I'd better read them both.

[Both union and the company versions of these provisions covering "Union Membership" agreed in accepting a union shop under which continued employment required union membership upon a certain interval after hiring. The proposals differed in the following particulars:

(1) The union set the probationary period for new employees, after which they must join the union, at 15 days; the company, at 45 days.

(2) The union made loss of "good standing" under its bylaws a cause for discharge; the company accepted this basic relationship but with two qualifications: (a) any refusal to accept new employees to union membership could be questioned by the company, with reference to the grievance procedures if necessary; and (b) after admission, such employees would not be subject to any fines, penalties, or financial contributions not general for the whole membership.

(3) Finally, the union's draft contained two provisions not in the company's version: (a) a checkoff of initiation fees, dues, fines, and assessments; and (b) the requirement that no seasonal employees be hired between July 1 and October 31—the tomato harvest season—without work permits from the union.]

Wagner (u) [looking up from text]: Now, in the union's proposal we ask for 15 days' probationary period; you keep it 45. I don't know why that 3B [*i.e.,* guaranteeing employees equal union membership] is in your Article. It should not have been put in. Nor should that second paragraph under A be in [company's right to question the union's refusal to accept employees to union membership].

Mitchell (m): We had many grievances during the probationary period. Many hard feelings were created when the probationary employees were approached in the wrong way and asked to join the union. We have set up a program whereby we do the policing for you, so that solicitation on the part of the union is not necessary. We think that will work out very well.

Wagner (u): It should not be in there.

Mitchell (m): Well, that is not a difference we cannot bridge.

Wagner (u): The same on probationary period—it should be 15 days instead of 45 days.

Mitchell (m): This company must have (1) good selection and placement of employees, (2) good administration, and (3) the union and the company living together. We must have time enough to find out what the employee can do and what kind of an employee he will make. We must have 45 days to find that out. Why do you want 45 days changed to 15 days?

Yost (u): We think 45 days is too long.

Mitchell (m): That is not an answer. We gave you our reasons for the 45-day period. You should give a reason for 15. We want to be fair to the employees coming in here. We should have 45 days in order to give the employees a fair chance to see whether or not we have done a good job in selection and placement.

Wagner (u): Can we agree or can't we agree on 15 days?

Mitchell (m): No.

Wagner (u): Take that 3B of your Article. We go by a set of bylaws.

Such provisions about equal financial contributions and penalties, and so forth, do not belong in there.

Mitchell (m): All right; let's strike out that paragraph. How about the second paragraph of Section B of Article 3 [maintenance of membership in good standing as a condition of employment]?

Wagner (u): Yes, that I agree to. Next we have Article 4, *Hours of Work and Working Conditions.* They are long articles, especially in your draft; but I guess we'll have a lot of discussion on them before we're done, so I'd better read them together.

[Both versions agreed in (1) making the normal workday and work week 8 hours and 40 hours, respectively; (2) paying premium rates of time and one-half for work in excess of either; (3) granting 15-minute rest periods after every three hours of work; and (4) guaranteeing a lunch period at least after 5 hours' work. As for the differences between them:

(1) The union made the regular work week Monday through Friday, and provided overtime rates for work on Saturday and Sunday, while the company made the work week a continuous one from Monday through Sunday with overtime on the sixth and seventh days but undertook to restrict continuous or out-of-schedule work to emergency or special needs.

(2) The union included guarantees of 40 hours' work or pay a week, 8 hours' work or pay on every day he reported for work, and no deductions for time losses due to holidays, lack of work, waiting time, etc.

(3) In contrast, the company's proposals were directed to pervasive, flexible adjustments of work schedule, as, for instance, (a) the FLSA right to work 55 hours a week for 14 weeks a year without overtime pay; (b) the right to change regular schedules upon proper notification to the union; (c) 4 hours' call-in time; (d) the spelling out of excusable absences which would not impair an employee's title to premium rates for work on the sixth and seventh day of his scheduled work week.]

Wagner (u): Now you tell us: What is the matter with our article on hours of work?

Mitchell (m): You have just wiped out the 1946 agreement on hours of work. In other words, you propose paying Saturday as such, paying holidays as such; and, regardless of conditions or emergencies, you would nail us down to clauses under which we can't in any way, shape, or form set up working schedules except as Monday through Friday—and this, in the food industry!

Wagner (u): In some departments employees are told to come out at 5:00 A.M. They should be compensated for it.

Mitchell (m): If anyone comes out before the scheduled working time, they get time and one-half. That is provided for in our proposed agreement to you.

Wagner (u): I will agree each department has its own starting time. How about work on Saturdays being paid time and one-half?

Mitchell (m): We have gone farther than some industries in having holidays counted as the sixth day. Your proposals would encourage absenteeism.

Wagner (u): As for absenteeism, I am willing to insert that those being absent without just cause cannot come in for that extra pay.

Mitchell (m): We have covered that in Sections K and L of our proposal [the enumerated causes for "justifiable absences"].

Wagner (u): We don't accept your proposal at all.

Mitchell (m): That puts us even to the board. We say no to yours. Looking ahead at your next Article, you also want double time for holidays worked and straight time for holidays not worked, don't you? [1]

Wagner (u): That is right. Well, you reject ours and we reject yours. Let's go to Wages, and come back to this again later.

Mitchell (m): We are not in a position to discuss wages at this time. We would rather go on over the rest of the agreement first. You want a guaranteed 40-hour week, paid holidays, a 30-cent raise, night bonus of 10 cents, double time for Sundays and time and one-half paid on Saturdays as such. All this makes your demand about a 75-cent raise, doesn't it?

Wagner (u): No, it does not. But if I come in here to work eight hours I should be paid for it.

Mitchell (m): You are asking for guaranteed 52 weeks per year at 40 hours per week. This is a young company. Do you have it with Heinz— do they have a guaranteed annual wage?

Wagner (u): No, they don't.

Mitchell (m): There is not another company in the country that has gone as far with the union in its first year as this company has.

Wagner (u): The "Big Four" guarantee a 36-hour week. You did not give us even a counterproposal.

Mitchell (m): We are not going to give you a counterproposal on this. You are doing some blue-sky bargaining and you know it. What you want us to do is a lot of horse trading. Do you think we should adjourn until tomorrow?

Wagner (u): It doesn't make any difference to me if we continue right on. I want to say in all sincerity that, on all these things we are asking, I would like to have a concrete counterproposal from the company.

Mitchell (m): You have our proposal—our draft of an agreement—all except wages. That is a concrete proposal; it cannot be made any more concrete than that. We are bargaining from the 1946 labor agreement and not from the ceiling, from which you are trying to suspend us. . . .

[Meeting adjourned at 5:00 P.M.]

Mr. Mitchell's notes on this second negotiating conference contained the following comments:

The Joint Job Evaluation Committee has been meeting and launched their deliberations very amicably. We also got several promising indices of changing atti-

---

[1] Both versions enumerated specific holidays: the company's, six; the union's, adding Armistice Day to New Year's, Memorial Day, Fourth of July, Labor Day, Thanksgiving, and Christmas, seven. The company's proposal stipulated payment of time and one-half for work done on the contractual holidays.

tudes on the part of the union in this second contract session. I noted them from the very start of the meeting, and felt a mellowing spirit right through the proceedings. Nonetheless, Wagner is still trying some blue-sky bargaining—on coverage, hours of work, wages, holidays, etc. I pointed out to the management group how skillfully Wagner was trying to set up "trading horses"—claiming things the union never had had, to trade off later to management as price for better consideration on items on which the parties may be expected to do some eventual compromising. I detailed to them the specific trading horses Wagner had introduced into this session, so that they might watch for this familiar trick in our subsequent meetings.

DISCUSSION QUESTIONS

1. Why, in your opinion, does Mitchell open this session with a proposal to review the work of the Joint Job Evaluation Committee thus far? How would you interpret Wagner's response to the suggestion?

2. Compare Mitchell's strategy and tactics in this session with those employed in the first session.

NATIONAL FOOD SPECIALTIES (D)

THE THIRD SESSION: PROGRESS—AND CRISIS

[The meeting opened on December 18, 1946, at 2 P.M.]

Mitchell (m): Let's go back to Article 2. We are willing to take "technical employees" from the excluded categories. As to Article 3, Union Membership, you feel that we are interfering with your constitution in our provision for open membership to all employees; so we are omitting it. Now let's go to Article 8 on Seniority.

Wagner (u): We don't accept your proposal at all. Just compare it with ours and you'll see what I mean.

[Both established straight seniority, save that the company included the proviso that the "senior employee" must be "able to perform the work satisfactorily." Moreover, the company included a special section giving it the right to hire, retain, transfer, and recall men of special training or exceptional ability, regardless of their place on the seniority roster, up to 2% of the total work force and not less than one in any job classification.

[Seniority (defined as length of an employee's continuous service) was applied on two bases in the company's version—company seniority and job-classification seniority—and on only one—departmental seniority—in the union's version; the union, however, also sought separate seniority lists for men and women employees.

[The company's proposals recognized seniority chiefly in making layoffs and spelled out in considerable detail the order of layoff and recall via the seniority rosters from probationary employees up and down, within and across, job classifications to company seniority. Its proposals also differentiated between layoffs of less than one month, designated as temporary, and over one month.

[Promotions were affirmed a prerogative of management, which pledged itself, however, to accord seniority "important consideration"; management also sought the right to use any employee at its discretion in any classification or occupation paid at his regular rate.

[In contrast, the union sought application of departmental seniority, not only to layoffs, but also to promotions, replacements in vacancies enjoying a "higher rate of pay," and advancement to position of leadman, subforeman, foreman.

[The recurrent difference regarding the length of probationary employment was repeated in the seniority article—the company seeking 45 days; the union, 15.

[Both versions accorded a maximum of 50 union representatives top seniority on occasions of layoffs.]

Adams (m): Did we have very much trouble in May when we had to lay off about 200 employees?

Shultz (u): No, not that I know of.

Wagner (u): In Section F—that fourth sentence: "A probationary or seasonal worker laid off for more than one month shall, if rehired, be regarded as a new worker." How did that get in there?

Mitchell (m): As answer to problems which arose when probationary employees were laid off and, on recall, raised the question whether the time they spent with the company counted as probationary days worked. If they were laid off for more than one month, they would be regarded as new employees; but if they were laid off for less than a month, then they would have that previous probationary period to their credit and counted toward their 45 days. It is a question of drawing the line somewhere.

Wagner (u): Why should the probationary people come back and start all over again? You don't want a 45-day probationary period; you want a 12-month period. The way that article is worded the probationary employees could work a whole year without having seniority and this could lead to evasion of the vacation period. I am not saying that you are going to do them; but if not, why put it in the agreement?

Adams (m): By what length of layoff would you go along on drawing the line?

Wagner (u): Anytime within the contract year.

Mitchell (m): A man was hired December 2, 1946, and worked 10 days and was laid off. Let's say 60 days from now we will be able to call him back. Will he have served his probationary period?

Wagner (u): His status with the company should be 10 days. You asked for a 45-day probationary period and we are ready to agree to that, though it's three times longer than what we asked. The disposition of the employee is in your hands until the 46th day. All we ask is that if the employee is retained after the 45th day he shall become a member of the union.

Mitchell (m): I think we can accept that. How about the rest? They are largely the present seniority rules and we seem to be living with them in good shape.

Wagner (u): I don't think so. I have had many complaints on them. Male and female classifications should be set up separately. Then you give seniority one way, and in the next paragraph you take it away. For instance, the union does not have a thing to say about promotions. I certainly think those older employees, if capable, should have the promotions and it should be decided jointly between the union and management.

Ulrich (m): How would you have seniority company-wide? Would that mean that every lead job would have to be filled by the older people?

Wagner (u): No, it would have to be departmental seniority. I would advise we set aside this Article 8—seniority, for further study, agreeing that seniority shall be determined by length of service with the company. Right?

Mitchell (m): We would like a recess of about 10 minutes.

[The company representatives recessed from 3:15 P.M. to 3:30 P.M.]

Mitchell (m): We talked about the points raised on this seniority. We would like to follow your suggestion and review it. Why don't you draw up a fuller draft of the kind of provision you could live with and let us see it? Then we could incorporate some of your draft and some of ours and submit a new article.

Wagner (u): I don't think we will be in disagreement if we go at it that way. Now we can go on to the next article—on vacations.

[Wagner read only the company's proposals. They granted one week's (40 hours') vacation after one year's continuous service of not less than 1,600 hours' work; one and one-half weeks' (60 hours') after three years, and, similarly, two weeks' (80 hours') vacation after five such years of continuous service. The service year began on March 1 of the year preceding the current vacation period, which was set between April 1 and July 15, or October 15 and December 31. In case of emergency, management could request needed employees to accept vacation pay but remain at work.]

Wagner (u): You make no provision for layoff, sickness, leaves, etc. You should allow as time worked up to 50 days of each calendar year for acceptable absences. We put that in our proposal, as you probably saw. You should have a time limit on it.

Mitchell (m): How about cases of pregnancy with the allowance of 180 days' leave of absence in your proposal?

Wagner (u): If you grant a leave of absence don't you recognize that as length of service with the company?

Adams (m): They don't lose their seniority.

Parsons (u): If they don't lose their seniority, why should they lose their vacation?

Mitchell (m): Are we doing as well as any competitor on the matter of vacations?

Wagner (u): Not on the basis of the 40 hours for one year and 60 hours for three and four years. There is only 20 hours difference in vacation time after you put four years in the company. You want to cut absenteeism down. Have your vacations based on average yearly earnings.

Mitchell (m): I am not in agreement with what you say there. This company is still very young to know just what kind of a market it is going to find. We are not stabilized. We don't know where our market is. But we will rewrite this vacation article and the seniority article to meet some of your suggestions. We can begin on these at our next meeting.

[The meeting adjourned at 4:30 P.M.]

Mr. Mitchell's comments on this third session follow:

It seemed to me that discussions are taking on a more settled tone with signs of increasing mutual acceptance. I used the seniority revisions of our draft and that of the union as a means of reinforcing this newly developing change in attitude. We said to the union in substance, "O.K., you write the seniority clause as you want it and think you can live with it. If you can live with it, we can."

I thought I could notice a good effect even in the vacation discussion we opened after that. The discussions were factual; it looks as if the union is getting ready to seek honestly and sincerely joint answers to joint problems both of us can live with. We may still get some fancy window dressing from time to time but I suspect that from now on we can take it in stride as giving just a little local color.

It seems doubly unfortunate that just as we are getting on to this more promising kind of negotiating, the bottom should be falling out of production. Since mid-November the plant has maintained a full production schedule only by putting finished goods into inventory. We're hoping this simply signifies the preholiday seasonal drop familiar in the packaged food trades. But everything produced in the 30 days before this meeting *has* gone into storage inventory.

I talked with our group about the possibilities ahead for negotiations if this trend continues. Most of the group were averse to discussing potential layoffs even though they seemed almost inevitable; they feared the union might suspect management of deliberately cutting back employment in order to drive a harder bargain. I wonder if relations are sufficiently improved to chance frank exploration of this looming production threat; after all we probably will have to lay off hundreds before the agreement is signed.

[These forebodings were realized. Throughout the remainder of the negotiations, until the agreement was signed, production slumped as the whole canning industry struggled against a severe setback. Scores of employees were laid off. Mitchell gave continuous and detailed thought to handling this development with the union negotiators. The reductions in the work force were made in accordance with the provisions of the seniority article agreed upon by the parties after this session; it was thus given effect before the final agreement was completed to meet the production emergency.]

DISCUSSION QUESTIONS

1. Evaluate Mitchell's opening of this session.

2. Evaluate Mitchell's suggestion for further action in seeking resolution of the differences over contract provisions to govern seniority from the viewpoint of (*a*) immediate negotiating tactics, (*b*) restructuring the union-management relationships, and (*c*) productivity and efficiency.

3. Define the crisis looming for negotiations at this point, and evaluate the method chosen by management to avert its potentially adverse effects.

4. Evaluate strategy and tactics as they develop in this session. Are they adaptive?

NATIONAL FOOD SPECIALTIES (E)

THE FOURTH SESSION: INITIAL ECONOMIC OFFERS

[The meeting opened on December 20, 1946, at 2 P.M.]

Mitchell (m): In your draft you presented some of the benefits you wanted—paid holidays, uniforms and laundering of uniforms, etc. We would like to discuss that before we get further into our seniority and vacation articles, which we held over until today.

Let me pause, also, to make very clear a procedural matter. Any agreement we reach on each of the articles does not become binding until the whole agreement has been signed.

Wagner (u): That's right.

Mitchell (m): Benefits are a form of hidden wages, so that if we give two paid holidays that is taken into consideration by the company as a part of the wage demand. It is just a case of where you are going to put the money we can give you.

Wagner (u): There is no denying that they are a part of the increase.

Mitchell (m): With that in mind I am going to ask Ulrich to tell you our thinking on paid holidays and things that go along with it.

Ulrich (m): Well, here's the basic information for both of us: This company is an Illinois corporation. The stock of the corporation is owned by National Food Specialties, Inc. That is a New York corporation. The union has asked just how this company ties in with National Food Specialties, Inc. We report to National Food Specialties, Inc., only in the sense that any corporation reports to its stockholders. The stock of National Food Specialties, Inc., is on the market and the people of the United States own it. In any company the stockholders have their money invested for the same reason that you buy savings bonds, to get income from them. You know as well as anyone this company gets its money from the sale of products. We take last month's sales and they pay our expenses for the present month.

Take December; well, you all already know about the pretty gloomy December picture. We have very carefully considered what we may expect in 1947, and from all of the information that we have, we will arrive at just as generous an offer as possible. It must then be added to our expenses. Part of the dollar must go for raw materials, labor, equipment, etc. We cannot increase the total beyond what we can reasonably expect to take in. I am bringing this up so we have a realistic basis to work on. I do want to make the point that we don't have a drawer full of money; and, if we expend more than we can justify, I am not doing my job for one thing—I will not have a job for another thing. We hope that background will explain our attitude that we cannot have increases in twelve different ways, and each of them big.

We are thinking of having two paid holidays—which ones you choose does not really concern us. But we think it is a fair and just proposition to have two of the six holidays we had in our contract last year paid holidays.

Now on laundering—laundering is not a good term, let's say uniforms and maintenance of them—we think we should have some of our employees wearing uniforms. In our thinking, the production floor where the food is being prepared and handled, in other words the heart of the plant, should be uniformed and present a good appearance, not just for appearance's sake but also for those things required by the health authorities. We should have our people who are engaged in that kind of work wearing uniforms. Our intention is to purchase and launder uniforms where the company requires them. We say that because we think the man loading the box car does not need to wear a uniform.

That is our thinking on the two suggestions you brought up the other day.

Mitchell (m): Do you want to talk about it or let it lie?

Wagner (u): I think the company should submit a specific counterproposal on them.

Mitchell (m): O.K., fair enough. We will submit a written proposal and have it ready for our next meeting.

On seniority, you submitted as a suggestion to us quite a lengthy revision of our proposal to see what we thought about it. We have taken that revision and constructed a final article adopting almost the exact language you used but also keeping some of our clauses. Dick, will you give it to them?

Wagner (u): I would suggest that we continue on, going through the contract. When we arrive at a tentative agreement, we can proofread it and then see just where we are.

Mitchell (m): All right. We are getting down to a working basis; we are in agreement on that.

Wagner (u): Now on *Leaves of Absence:* your proposal is all right.

[This article provided leaves of absence (1) for elected union officials up to one year, with extensions up to three years; (2) for other employees at the company's discretion, upon consideration of reasons for the request, up to 90 days, with extensions up to 60 days more; and (3) for female employees, compulsory in cases of pregnancies, at least 90 days before and 90 days after confinement.]

Wagner (u): Now on your draft of Article II, *Adjustment of Grievances,* there are a few things we'd like to change.

[The company's version provided the following:

No stoppage, but an earnest effort to settle differences promptly by a four-step grievance procedure:

(1) A conference between the departmental foreman and the aggrieved employee, accompanied by his steward; but, if not settled within 24 hours, to be appealed to Step 2.

(2) A conference within 48 hours after appeal between the union representative and the departmental superintendent; but, if not adjusted within 48 hours, to be taken up in Step 3.

(3) The grievance to be "reduced to writing" and presented by the union grievance committee, consisting of not more than four members, to the division manager at the first "regularly scheduled meeting." If not settled under the foregoing steps within 10 working days, the grievance to be submitted to the final step.

(4) An arbitrator, to be designated from a list of names furnished by the United States Conciliation Service; the arbitrator to render his decision within ten days after the hearing. No award of the arbitrator shall be made retroactive beyond the date when the grievance was first presented.

(5) A representative was not to leave his job until necessary relief had been provided by his foreman, and the representative was to receive pay for time lost only in meetings called by the company.

(6) Management stipulated its right to submit grievances against the union to these adjustment procedures.]

Wagner (u) [continuing]: The union would like to leave out "24" and "48" hours as time limits for appealing a grievance to the second and third steps. Under Paragraph 4, "No award of the arbitrator shall be made retroactive beyond the date when the grievance was first presented." Scratch that out. Then, about management's right to submit grievances, I don't know what you mean by that.

Mitchell (m): I have always taken the position that we can do it whether it is in the agreement or not; and, if the occasion requires, take it all the way to arbitration. You have the right of grievance against us but we have none against you. If we do act, we are charged with a lockout. That is the only instrument in our hands. In other words, how are we going to follow through with a grievance against one of the union representatives?

Wagner (u): You have the right to call the local representatives into session.

Mitchell (m): Yes, but we have no machinery on which to ride except to say, "All right, you are fired." Suppose a representative exceeds his power. We don't want to fire that man. What are we going to do? Don't we need some orderly way of bringing a formal charge and seeking an answer even up to going to an arbitrator for a decision?

Wagner (u): I understand the principle of it but to be frank, I don't like the wording. How about this? "Union members, foremen, foreladies, and other recognized representatives of the company are bound to observe the respective covenants in this contract of the company and the union."

Mitchell (m): We'll think about that. Now go back to your first objections. Why do you want to leave out the "24" and "48" hour time limits?

Wagner (u): The general procedure is very good with the exception of the remarks I made. Why the long waiting period? In Paragraph 1 leave out the stipulated hours, then in Paragraph 2 change it from 48 to 24 hours. Then we agree the arbitrator's answer is final and binding but you seem to qualify that by limiting him on retroactive pay. Now let's go to your next Article. [Reads.]

ARTICLE 12—STRIKES AND LOCKOUTS

A. The Company agrees that there will be no lockouts, and the union agrees that there will be no slow-downs, strikes, or other forms of work stoppage during the life of this agreement.

B. In the event the foregoing provision is violated by any employee, the company and the union agree that the employee, or employees, involved may be discharged by the company without any such discharge, or discharges, being subject to the provisions on grievances and arbitration.

You have that tied up pretty tight, don't you? I have never pulled a strike without notifying the company. I have had two in 10 years.

Mitchell (m): Suppose we change in Paragraph B the word "without" to "with" and omit the next word "any." Could you live with that?

Wagner (u): Leave it for a while. Let's finish up the rest of these Articles. Now *Article 13—Company Rules and Regulations.* O.K.

Mitchell (m): *Article 14* on uniforms and work clothing we will reconstruct according to what Ulrich said before.

Wagner (u): *Article 15—Bulletin Boards.* O.K.

Mitchell (m): I think our new bulletin boards should be out some time next week.

Wagner (u): *Article 16—Access to Plant.* O.K. . . .

Article 17—Termination of the Agreement. Now we are back to that issue of retroactive date on termination of the contract again.[1] All your draft provides is the calendar year for everything. [Reads.]

A. This agreement shall be in force and effect for a period of one (1) year beginning the first day of January, 1947, and ending the last day of December, 1947, and thereafter from year to year unless either party hereto shall notify the other in writing not less than thirty (30) days nor more than forty-five (45) days prior to the expiration of the term, or any extended term of this agreement, of an intention to cancel or to change any provisions of the agreement upon the expiration of the term or the current extension of the term.

B. If such written notice is to the company, it shall be addressed to Foods Italienne, Inc., Laurelton, Pennsylvania. If such a notice is to the union, it shall be addressed to Local No. 8, Amalgamated Meat Cutters and Butcher Workmen of North America, A. F. of L.

---

[1] This much disputed clause in the first agreement read:

ARTICLE 17—TERMINATION OF THE AGREEMENT

"*A.* This agreement shall be in force and effect for a period of one (1) year beginning the first day of January, 1946, and ending the last day of December, 1946, and thereafter from year to year unless either party hereto shall notify the other in writing at least thirty (30) days prior to the expiration of the term, or any extended term of this agreement, of an intention to cancel or to change any provisions of the agreement upon the expiration of the term or the current extension of the term.

"*B.* However, for purposes of computing wages only, the effective day of the contract shall be considered as October 12, 1945. The above date in no way invalidates or changes the effective date of the contract as a whole, being from January 1, 1946, to December 31, 1946, but is agreed to solely for the purpose of computing retroactive pay. Notwithstanding the above, the effective date of the contract shall be from January 1, 1946, to December 31, 1946."

Mitchell (m): I don't know what the answer is. We have a strong feeling that we are right. You have a strong feeling that you are right. I would like to suggest we call upon the U.S. Arbitration Service.

Wagner (u): Last year we negotiated an agreement and the entire committee was under the impression the retroactive date on wage increases we negotiated always would be October 12. In other words, they worked under a 15-month agreement this time. So, if you and we cannot get together, instead of signing it from January 1 to December 31, we will go back to the original date of the NLRB's decision of September 12. We actually bent backwards agreeing to October 12 due to the fact that it was V–J Day; and there were problems of processing tomatoes, of reconstruction, etc. We should have asked to go back to September 12, which was the date we were certified by the board.

Mitchell (m): There has never been any doubt about the sincerity of the union and its membership, and their firm conviction. But management's conviction runs just as deep. Such increases as were to be granted under the 1946 agreement were for that year alone. The agreements following after were to run on a year-to-year basis. That's the way management understood it.

Wagner (u): The board would have granted us retroactive pay as of September 12, when we were certified.

Mitchell (m): You could bring that conviction before a U.S. Arbitrator.

Wagner (u) [giving Mr. Mitchell a copy of a membership ballot]: The members took a vote on that. Their answer is no arbitration.

Mitchell (m): This is a unilateral decision. Why take a vote about going to arbitration when in the agreement you agree to go to arbitration? This is a question of interpreting a clause of the Agreement—The Termination Clause.

Yost (u): The agreement says any differences over interpretation *may* be taken to arbitration.

Mitchell (m): We would like to have a recess.

[Management recessed from 3:10 P.M. to 3:45 P.M.]

Mitchell (m): Management recognizes the importance of this honest disagreement between us. To be as fair as possible, therefore, we would now propose to have the contract run from January 1 to December 31 of each year. The whole of the contract, inlcuding all wages, benefits, etc., will run concurrently from the beginning of the year to the end of the year. But, for this year, as a sort of transition we are willing to go to December 1 in applying any wage increase.

We want to get out of this retroactive dispute. We could enter into a separate stipulation setting forth all of this so that it would be absolutely understood and so that there would be no misunderstanding from here on out as to where we are going.

Wagner (u): That is the company's counterproposal in reply to the union's demand for October 12? December 1 for this year only?

Mitchell (m): No, it is not a counterproposal; it is a proposal. A counterproposal would be a confession on the part of the management that October 12 was the established date and that is not admitted.

Wagner (u): If the company has no counterproposal as to who was right and who was wrong, we will go back to our original—to September 12.

Ulrich (m): We cannot agree. We cannot undertake to negotiate a contract during the harvest season.

[After some further discussion it was decided to have the next meeting Monday, January 6, 1947, 2:00 P.M.; and that the 1946 agreement would stand until a new one was reached. Meeting adjourned 4:15 P.M.]

Mr. Mitchell's comments on the fourth session emphasized the growing "feeling" on both sides to get on to those subjects upon which mutual agreement could be recorded:

The "retroactive-date" issue furnished the one still stubborn point of controversy. The union introduced the vote taken on the issue before negotiations began. The vote had been supervised only by the union officers; it produced an 8 to 1 rejection of arbitration with authorization to the officials to call a strike if they deemed it necessary. I sensed that at this point in our negotiations, I would be safe in regarding this as a bargaining club rather than an actual threat. I think we rather boomeranged it back upon the union by taking no cognizance whatsoever of the strike possibility or their attitude on it.

DISCUSSION QUESTIONS

1. Can you note any parallels in Mitchell's opening of this session and the third one that would enable you to formulate a preliminary hypothesis as to his utilization of the session opening as a tactic in his strategy?

2. Why do you think the vice president in charge of production was chosen to present the company's first concrete economic offers to the union?

3. Evaluate the type and dimensions of the "gains" chosen by the company to initiate its "economic" proposals as an element in bargaining strategy and tactics.

4. How would you interpret Wagner's reception of Mitchell's statement regarding the current status of the seniority provisions in the negotiation?

5. Analyze the proposals and discussion on the provisions governing "Adjustment of Grievances."

6. Evaluate the issue on "retroactivity" as management and union see it at this stage of the negotiations.

NATIONAL FOOD SPECIALTIES (F)

THE FIFTH SESSION: STOCKTAKING

[The meeting opened on January 6, 1947, at 2:30 P.M.]

Wagner (u): We went from the Preamble to Article 7 pretty thoroughly; and now you drafted a revised proposal based on these discussions. I have read it over this morning and there is a lot in it. I think we will start with that draft you mailed to the union.

[The parties thereupon reviewed and accepted the versions of the articles on seniority (Article 7), leaves of absence (Article 9), adjustment of grievances (Article 10), company rules and regulations (Article 12), bulletin boards (Article 14), and access to plant (Article 15).

In other articles, some of the original differences persisted; thus the union still insisted on: (1) including in their bargaining unit foremen who did any work at the bench, regardless of their formal status as salaried employees; (2) a probationary period of 15 days as against 45 days; (3) allowances for excused absences and leaves in computing service toward earned vacation rights; and (4) retroactivity to at least October 12.

In still other articles, the parties moved toward tentative settlements: thus (1) the company, while protesting the clerical costs of a check-off, promised the demand further friendly consideration; (2) the company promised to launder, as well as supply and maintain, uniforms it required; while the union withdrew its demand for a specific number of uniforms to be supplied employees; (3) the company offered two paid holidays, to be chosen from among the six enumerated in the Agreement, while the union postponed acceptance of this offer only until it received the company's full wage offer; (4) the major differences on "hours of work" approached compromise settlement as the union agreed to the principle of a Monday-through-Sunday work week, while the company agreed to pay overtime rates for work done on Saturdays or Sundays (with stated occupational exceptions) by employees who had worked on the five prior days, even if on short time for reasons beyond their control; and (5) the parties undertook further to explore a mutually acceptable wording for the "No Strike, No Lockout" provision, on the essential intention of which they were in agreement.]

Mitchell's comments on this session reflected pronounced satisfaction. He wrote:

Wagner brought back the "foreman" issue, but he was manifestly puffing up a lost cause. This window dressing was not for us, I suspect, but for the members. The whole meeting gave every indication negotiations were going along; I'd say there's no danger now of a breakdown. We've reached a good understanding;

there's an attitude of facing mutual problems that's very different from the old tension and emotionalism. I think we've left the old belligerence permanently behind us.

Discussion Questions

1. What do you think were Mitchell's objectives in drafting a "revised . . . tentative proposal" for the union embodying all the agreements reached in the negotiations thus far? Do you approve of such a review?

2. What especially made this session an appropriate one for "stocktaking"?

NATIONAL FOOD SPECIALTIES (G)

THE SIXTH SESSION: FURTHER PROGRESS AND A LOOMING JURISDICTIONAL DIFFICULTY

[The meeting opened on January 13, 1947, at 2:10 P.M.]

Mitchell submitted copies of the check-off provision proposed as the second paragraph of Section B:

> The company shall deduct from the wages of all such employees an amount equal to the monthly union dues, initiation fees and assessments certified in writing by the union to the company. However, the company shall not be required to deduct fines from the wages of any employee. The union agrees to hold the company free and harmless from all claims and damages from any party whatsoever and agrees to indemnify the company against any and all such claims and damages.

Wagner (u): That is all right.

Mitchell (m): Now, on the suggestion which you submitted to us at our last meeting concerning hours of work, there is still a question in our minds. We would like to have you write up and identify the exceptions you would make in the application of the hours of work to permit a continuous work week in emergencies or special occupations.

Ulrich (m): We agree that overtime is a penalty on the company for not having the work planned properly to give its employees a couple days' rest in a row. We are now in a position where some of our business can be planned. We should accept a penalty if we don't plan such jobs right. But we are also in a position where on some certain things we cannot control operations. You already agree with us on such jobs as powerhouse, plant maintenance, etc. However, we are now starting a large operation on mushrooms. We feel pretty sure that when we have nine growing rooms going at once we won't be able to control the picking of mushrooms over week ends. In the same way it is impossible for this company at present to tell its suppliers that under no circumstances will we accept a truck for unloading on Saturday; we are glad to get it. We would be forced to pay a penalty for a situation we cannot control—at least in 1947. I am pretty sure a buyer's market will return wherein we will be able to control those things. At any rate our aim is to guarantee two days off each week, same as yours is to receive them.

Wagner (u): The only thing we are in disagreement on, then, is who are to be included as regularly scheduled employees. Do you want to stipulate firemen and maintenance?

Ulrich (m): We have to allow for all such things which the company cannot control. In addition to those long-established jobs, we shall have to pick mushrooms say on Sundays same as we have to have a watchman's schedule then; and for the present we cannot control the incoming merchandise.

Wagner (u): I will discuss these further exceptions you ask with the committee: mushrooms, incoming goods, powerhouse, watchmen, etc. They will all definitely have a day of rest during the week?

Ulrich (m): Yes, they will have two days together.

Wagner (u): Where do we go from here?

Mitchell (m): Article 11, "Strikes and Lockouts."

Wagner (u): Before we go to that, go back to Union Recognition, "The company recognizes the union as the sole, etc." We want to exclude, "including local truck drivers."

Mitchell (m): Why do you want to exclude them?

Wagner (u): In order to avoid any conflict with the Teamsters' Union. These were definite instructions from the International.

Mitchell (m) [after some discussion]: Well, let's hold that open.

Article 11—Strikes or Lockouts. How does this strike you:

The union agrees to accept and abide by all of the terms and conditions of this agreement and during its term will not permit its members to engage in any walkout, sit-down, slowdown, or other interference with or interruption of work, and that it will not call, countenance or otherwise encourage any walkout or strike. The company agrees to accept and abide by all the terms and conditions of this agreement and during its term will not lock out the employees.

Wagner (u): That sounds all right. Let us study it a bit.

Mitchell (m): All right. Now we come down to the question of wages.

Ulrich (m): Our position has been stated several times. It is a lead pipe cinch this company is not going to be able to continue if it must meet greater expenses than its competitors. If we were to evaluate what we could do on the basis of our 1946 performance, we just would not have anything. So we look ahead to 1947, and with the best thinking we have on it, we think we can take a total of 11 cents per hour and distribute them any way we both agree. And more than that we can't see. That is what we hope and think we can do; we will say we can do it and stick with it. How we distribute this 11 cents is within our joint decision, actually.

Mitchell (m): For instance, we figure that two paid holidays comes to somewhere about three-fourths of a cent, based upon 1946.

Wagner (u): Your offer is 11 cents. Is that in addition to the two paid holidays?

Ulrich (m): No, 11 cents including all benefits, the complete package.

Wagner (u): I would like to talk with the committee about it.

[Management Committee adjourned from the room for the Union Committee to discuss the matter—3:25 P.M. to 4:00 P.M.]

[The application of the 11-cent-an-hour increase was discussed by management and union.]

Wagner (u): The 11 cents clears that part of the program with the exception of the night shift differential and your modified vacation. But we cannot accept two paid holidays. If we can get together on vacations, night shifts, and paid holidays, I am willing to meet with you, with the exception of tomorrow.

Mitchell (m): Let's hold a tentative date, this Friday, for our meeting.

Wagner (u): Will you break the increase down into figures? I don't want to confuse the employees. Do you want me to make an appointment with Yost, myself, and the Teamsters?

Mitchell (m): Yes.

In his comments upon the sixth session, Mitchell noted, again with satisfaction, that the negotiators were "exploring issues" rather than "engaging in sheer controversy." But one new demand introduced by Wagner struck him as highly "unusual":

> To find a union requesting exclusion from contract coverage of a work group assigned to the bargaining unit by the NLRB was so striking to my mind that I feel management has to determine carefully its position.
> In certifying the Butcher Workmen, the NLRB had included "local truck drivers" and excluded "over-the-road truck drivers." These latter, who were handling some customer-finished goods the company was then delivering by trailer truck, were members of the Teamsters' Union, which had made an informal arrangement with the company regarding their wage rates. In August, 1946, the company informed the Teamsters' Union that it would no longer deliver finished goods by trailer truck; shipments, however, would be made from the plant by trailer-truck equipment to the two local railroad stations. The Teamsters demanded all the company's drivers; and a "nice, easy jurisdictional dispute" thus began.
> The Teamsters, however, had not participated in the NLRB election, nor had they placed themselves then on record as a party in interest. But the Butcher Workers had lost two elections before that in which the Teamsters had been recorded as a party in interest. The unions determined upon settlement between them, apparently without consulting management. Indeed from the discussion on the issue at the joint meeting following this negotiating session, I infer that the decision had been made by the "top leadership" of the two unions. Thus it was that the negotiators were obeying orders "to deliver the local truck drivers" to the Teamsters.

Management resisted the whole proposal from there on to final settlement. Indeed, signing of the 1947 agreement was held up from February 7 to February 24, 1947, on precisely this issue, as the company took the position that the recognition clause must stand on the terms of NLRB certification. Five representatives of the Butchers and Mitchell went to Philadelphia to confer with the top union leaders. After varied negotiations, the company's contention was conceded *in toto*. Rumor, as it came to Mitchell, had it that final decision was made in Chicago by the international presidents of the two unions.

DISCUSSION QUESTIONS

1. Why do you think that the company might be willing to check off union dues, initiation fees, and assessments but not fines from employees' wages? Would you support such a differentiation, and why?

2. Analyze the company's proposals on hours of work as a formula for both satisfying union demands and safeguarding management's right to schedule the work.

3. What provisions has the company now eliminated from its original draft

on "Strikes or Lockouts"?   What additions have been made?   How would you evaluate these changes?

4. Evaluate management's presentation of its wage offer and discuss the tactic of the "total package" in bargaining.

5. Discuss the issue of teamsters' affiliation in relation to (*a*) the concrete managerial change that precipitated the jurisdictional issue; (*b*) the manner in which the original interunion adjustment apparently was made and communicated; (*c*) the tie-up of the background NLRB elections; (*d*) management's policy in the situation; and (*e*) the character and manner of arriving at the final decision.   Why do you think management fought to deal only with the Butcher Workmen in this situation?

NATIONAL FOOD SPECIALTIES (H)

THE SEVENTH SESSION: WAGE BARGAINING

[The seventh meeting opened on January 23, 1947, at 2 P.M.]

The following letter, dated January 23, 1947, was given to Thomas Wagner this morning:

Dear Mr. Wagner:

The make-up or composition of the 11 cents wage increase that the company tendered to you on Monday, January 13, 1947, at our joint Union-Company Negotiation Meeting would seem to be as follows:

Total hourly wage increase to cover all benefits such as general or vertical wage increase, paid holidays, job evaluation, et cetera. . . . . 11¢

At the present time the estimated breakdown of the 11 cents per hour would be:

4 paid holidays	1.25 cents per hour
(Converts Christmas gratuity)	
Laundry	.25 cents per hour
Job Evaluation	2.00 cents per hour
Retroactive pay to December 1, 1946	.50 cents per hour

4.00

Leaving a general hourly wage increase of . . . . 7.00¢

You will notice that the cost to the company of checking-off dues has not been included.

The general wage increase of 7 cents only would be retroactive to December 1, 1946, with the understanding that in the 1947 agreement or by a supplement thereto, properly accomplished by both parties, all future money considerations shall run concurrently with the then existing agreement, unless otherwise agreed upon. In other words the controversial retroactive date of October 12, 1945, will be foregone.

That portion of the above-tendered wage increase as applied to the general hourly wage increase, herein estimated at 7 cents per hour, would be withheld from employees known as the "Colton Bus Group." If and when the bus was discontinued, these employees would, of course, come into the estimated 7-cents-per-hour general-wage increase as of the date the bus or buses were discontinued.

Wagner asked for a recess to discuss the letter with the Union Committee.

[The meeting commenced at 2:25 P.M.]

Wagner (u): In our last meeting there was some discussion as to the general wage increase and I believe that when we left the meeting neither side had the exact interpretation as to how it would be applied. This morning when I read your letter on the breakdown of the increase, I saw it did not meet our thinking. We were under the opinion it would be 11 cents plus fringes. We are willing to give you a counterproposal. We are willing to accept 12 cents including everybody and let the Colton people find their own transportation.

276

Mitchell (m): What would be your breakdown?

Wagner (u): You offer a general wage increase of 11 cents and fringes which amount to 4 cents. We are willing to accept 12 cents across the board plus these fringes, which in your language is 4 cents; and in it include the Colton group. Remember that there is no guaranteed work week, no night bonus and no change in your vacation policy.

On the question of the retroactive date, if it is the company's proposal to go back to December 1, we insist on September 12.

Mitchell (m): You want in substance 16 cents an hour. I am quite sure we made ourselves plain that any wage increase would include all fringe issues, so that when we offered 11 cents it was to include the fringe issues. Now you come back and say you want 12 cents across the board but in substance and essence you want 16 cents, which includes the fringe issues.

Wagner (u): In our proposal, the night bonus, seven paid holidays and sick leave in reality would mean a 19-cent increase. But we were of the opinion your offer of 11 cents meant a general increase plus fringes, of which neither you nor we knew exactly what they would be. Now on this letter it is 7 cents plus 4 cents on fringes.

[There followed some further discussion of the respective demands against the business outlook in the whole canning industry.]

Mitchell (m): Well, we will take your whole position under consideration. Let us give it a mulling over and see what comes out of the hat.

Wagner (u): I would like also, inasmuch as we are still in disagreement on the retroactive date, that we sign a 9-month contract or come to an agreement on the 7 weeks retroactivity which are concerned. I don't think we are very far apart on that.

Mitchell (m): You might be surprised on how far apart we are. We certainly must come to an understanding, and for once and for all this October 12 date must go out of the picture.

Wagner (u): What is the next move on the company's part?

Mitchell (m): We would like to talk about Article 2, in the light of the Teamsters' demand. The Teamsters' Union is getting quite adamant and making some rather outlandish demands. [Mitchell reported in detail on his conversations with the teamsters' representative, after which he stated his determination not to be "crowded" into any untenable position. Wagner declared he would meet again with the teamsters' local representatives.]

Mitchell considered this meeting further demonstrated that

on wages, as on other matters, step by step the issues before us have been resolved or are on their way to being resolved.

NATIONAL FOOD SPECIALTIES (I)

THE EIGHTH SESSION: WAGE BARGAINING (*Continued*)

[The eighth meeting opened on January 28, 1947, at 2:03 P.M.]

Mitchell (m): Where do you want to start?

Wagner (u): Your wage proposal was rejected. I think it best we start from there.

Mitchell (m): There is not much to be said except, objectively speaking, that if these negotiations had started today rather than six weeks ago the best offer that this company would be able to make you would have probably been somewhere in the neighborhood of an over-all increase of 5 cents per hour.

Ulrich (m): Our 11 cents' offer was not based on what the company thought it could do as of now but what we could do as of the improvement and volume we foresaw in 1947. I think our lens had a little dust on it. For we believed we were allowing for the worst possible—that business would pick up. Here we are at the end of January and orders are running right now less than our production. We still think maybe it will come through soon; I cannot see it honestly now.

Wagner (u): On the retroactive question, have you discussed that? What thought have you on the matter of October 12?

Mitchell (m): Tom, again based upon the current events, if we could even withdraw December 1, we would do that.

Wagner (u): You mean management is taking the position it is still December 1?

Mitchell (m): That is right.

Wagner (u): If we cannot come together on these two issues, wages and retroactivity, and you say that is your final and best offer, I will ask for a conciliator to come in. Even if the membership was to accept that offer (11-cent over-all increase), we are still in doubt as to the retroactive date. If management is going to take the position it is December 1, we will not sign a year agreement this time, even if the wages are acceptable to the membership. Your agreement which we sign now will expire on the 12th day of September; we will go back to the original certification date unless we can agree in the conference room that the retroactive date will be October 12.

Mitchell (m): Outside the question of wages and the retroactive date, we have things pending which are not insurmountable. On vacations, we will go back to the 1946 arrangement with the difference of advancing the vacation calculations to the period of March 1 rather than of May 1; you gain something by that. We have overtime for Saturdays and Sundays. We assume holidays tie up with wages as a fringe issue and job evaluation so that brings us down primarily to wages and retroactive date. I suggest you grant us a reasonable recess and we will go into a huddle and see whether management has had a change of heart on the retroactive date and we will report back in 15 or 20 minutes.

I might inquire as to the job evaluation committee. I want to say that you people have gone along in pretty fine style there. It is new to you and the reason you are doing well is because you have an open mind. It is a long range objective. It does not matter what position we are in now; we are not as far away as when we started.

Adams (m): I think that within a week we should know just about what our point evaluations of our jobs are. Even after that, it is going to take considerable time to print the material.

Mitchell (m): If we seek a U.S. Conciliator, we should have that (Job Evaluation) also in the picture as part of the clean-up job.

[Management recessed—2:25 to 2:55 P.M.]

Mitchell (m): Tom, what we would like is to be given a little more time to think about this until tomorrow afternoon at two.

Wagner (u): One thing, I don't believe that vacation policy is fair even if we go back to the old one. Employees might be off, through no fault of their own, for 10 weeks; they won't make 1,600 hours. There should be some agreement on that. There should be some modification made on the present vacation clause.

Mitchell (m): From the standpoint of hours?

Wagner (u): This present lay-off, for instance, might have reached some employees with three years' service.

[Mr. Adams called the Employment Manager, Mr. Kales, and was told that on the female seniority list they were back to June 20, 1944, and on the male list, to January 2, 1945.]

Mitchell (m): We will do some thinking on that, Tom.

Wagner (u): Within reason, I know you will see the point. These people laid off do not lose their seniority, so they should not lose their vacation. If employees are off, through no fault of their own, for three months, because your vacation year starts and ends at a certain date, they could not possibly make up those lost hours.

Mitchell (m): We will do some thinking on that. Maybe we can work out a special stipulation to protect the employees from the effects of the slump on 1947 vacation rights.

[Meeting adjourned 3:05 P.M. Next meeting to be held the following day, January 29, at 2:00 P.M.]

Mitchell commented briefly on this session:

We got more evidence today that the parties are trying to find answers each can live with.

DISCUSSION QUESTIONS

1. Evaluate the tactic of (*a*) the total "wage package"; and (*b*) timing wage offers in negotiating strategy.

2. By Wagner's restatement of the union's position on the wage offer in

the eighth session, what would you take as the focus of reconsideration if you were on the management committee and anxious to promote final agreement? Why?

3. Evaluate Mitchell's response to the union's restatement of position on the wage offer in terms of (a) the things he recalls to their attention; (b) the things on which he agrees to "do some further thinking."

THE NINTH SESSION: THE STUBBORN ISSUE OF RETROACTIVITY

[The meeting opened on January 29, 1947, at 2:02 P.M.]

Ulrich (m): Tom, you left yesterday with the request that we take care of things beyond the employees' control in their vacation like this slump in the food industry. We have thought it over somewhat. We do agree in principle that you have a point. We are not going to overlook it but we would like to give it more consideration and have a little longer to frame that thing up.

Wagner (u): All right.

Mitchell (m): Now that we have disposed of that, Tom, on the question of wages and the retroactive date, which is the focal point in the position of both parties at this particular time, management deliberated long and hard and for the life of them they could not see any change in their position as to the retroactive date beyond that which has been offered—the vertical increase going back to December 1.

Wagner (u): When we do arrive at an agreement, then, we will still take the position that it will be signed with the expiration date of September 12. We are entitled to the retroactive due to the fact that we sacrificed a month in our first contract negotiations and we see no reason why we should have worked under a 15-month agreement.

Mitchell (m): To further discuss that particular phase of the question is merely a hashing and rehashing, in which we find ourselves going around in the same kind of circles and not finding an answer.

Wagner (u): I think management should realize the position in which we were placed by the first contract. We did sacrifice four weeks retroactive pay last year—and took very low wage increases. There is no reason why we should throw away two additional months; it is a matter, I believe, of seven weeks.

Mitchell (m): It is pretty hard for you fellows to wash your hands of the thing. You were a party to it. The retroactive pay should have been set up in a separate and distinct stipulation so that it would not appear in the 1946 agreement as such. I cannot understand seasoned labor men, Tom, on your side not seeing that.

Wagner (u): I will blame management as well as the local union. Mr. Torrensi sent me a letter, dated September 14, 1945, saying that due to a Mr. George's not being able to get into the picture, negotiations would be postponed until October 12. Then, due to the peak season, management wanted the contract to expire December 31, because they felt they would not be able to negotiate during a peak season. On the other hand, the retroactive date, each succeeding year would be October 12. We really asked for September 12 but the compromise was October 12.

Mitchell (m): I read the Termination clause without anyone's ideas or interpretations on it, as I wanted to see what my own interpretation on it would be. My thought on it was that it would be for that one year only.[1]

Wagner (u): Then we would not have put it in the agreement.

Mitchell (m): It did not have any business in this labor agreement.

Wagner (u): We said in our contract negotiations that for the year 1946 we would go back to October 12 but there was no necessity of specifying it in the agreement unless there was an intention of its being for each succeeding year.

Mitchell (m): Tom, what do you want to do now?

Wagner (u): I would like a final answer as to the company's position on it. You say you won't give a compromise on retroactive, so we will sign a 9-month agreement.

Mitchell (m): And we say we won't do that.

Wagner (u): It would amount to 19 dollars.

Mitchell (m): Nineteen dollars per what?

Wagner (u): Back pay for each employee. Last year on the 3-cent general increase the union compromised. I would like management to sit down and see what they saved last year on a 3-cent general increase, when the union accepted retroactive pay to October 12, instead of September 12.

Mitchell (m): I don't want to repeat what I said yesterday; but if we were to approach the wage standpoint as of today, there would not be an 11-cent over-all wage increase offered.

Wagner (u): Your answer is no; we still say no, so we are back to the termination of the agreement on September 12.

Mitchell (m): And there we say "no."

Wagner (u): Do you gentlemen feel you want to discuss it? I would like to talk to the committee but you are leaving me no alternative but to file a strike notice. I certainly hate to do it on this retroactive issue. The employees voted on it but I have held the strike notice in abeyance.

Mitchell (m): Do you want us to retire then?

Wagner (u): I would like you to give it careful study, because if we adjourn this meeting without an answer, the strike is the only alternative I have.

[The groups recessed—2:47 to 3:55 P.M.]

Wagner (u): I talked with the committee while you were out; no doubt you discussed the same thing. We are still of the opinion that if we cannot get retroactive wages as of October 12, we will accept your proposal but we will not sign a year's agreement.

Mitchell (m): Complete the thought.

Wagner (u): We will take to the membership the offer given us here; and we definitely know the position they will take on that retroactive date, because they each and every one voted by secret ballot on it. I have no other alternative, much as I hate to see it; we will file a strike notice.

---

[1] Cf. footnote on p. 267.

Mitchell (m): In other words, your position has not changed since we left. If we don't go along on the September 12 termination of the agreement, or on the October 12 retroactive date, then you will file a strike notice.

Wagner (u): I don't think the Conciliators would be of much advantage to us if we ourselves cannot get together on those seven weeks.

Mitchell (m): We will meet again tomorrow at 3:00.

Wagner (u): Do you want me to hold that strike notice in abeyance?

Mitchell (m): I think you must follow your own conscience on that if you think 24 hours is vital to you.

Wagner (u): If you want to meet with us tomorrow, you must have something in mind.

Mitchell (m): All right, but as far as filing a strike notice, that is up to you.

Wagner (u): Take these two months in question, we gave last year the month of September; you give this year December. Between October 12 and November 30 there are seven weeks. Let's go home and sleep on it and see what we can do tomorrow.

[Meeting adjourned at 4:00 P.M. Next meeting to be held January 30, 1947, at 3:00 P.M.]

Again Mitchell commented briefly on this session:

Although this meeting was devoted almost entirely to the thorny, old controversy regarding retroactive date for wage increases, I could trace even in this how both sides are gradually coming together in sincere thinking on what can actually be done.

DISCUSSION QUESTIONS

1. Evaluate the opening of this session again as an element in Mitchell's underlying bargaining strategy.

2. Analyze the differentiation Mitchell makes for the technicalities of negotiation between a contract clause and a "special stipulation."

3. How would you appraise Wagner's introduction of the recourse to a strike, and Mitchell's response to it from the viewpoint of negotiating strategy?

NATIONAL FOOD SPECIALTIES (K)

THE TENTH SESSION: THE NEGOTIATIONS END

[The meeting convened on January 30, 1947. Meeting opened at 3:12 P.M.]

Mitchell (m): Now, Harv, talk about the vacation question.

Ulrich (m): All right. Yesterday I asked you to let us think a little longer on the vacation deal, and we think it is unfair for employees who cannot work because of business conditions to lose the 1,600 hours required for a vacation. We would like for 1947 to allow 30 working days if the employee has been off through no fault of his own. In number of hours, that 30 days would amount to 240 hours.

Mitchell (m): In other words, if an employee, through the fault of the company or business conditions, was not able to work 1,600 hours but would have normally worked those hours, you would take the 1,600 hours, deduct 240 and the result would be the number of hours the employee would have then worked. We want to enter into a separate stipulation outside the agreement and then next year treat it a little differently.

Now the question of retroactive date. After long and deliberate consideration management has come around to a place where in a very simple way we will go back to October 12, 1946. I would like to clarify the whole issue very briefly again. So far as job evaluation and all other fringes, they do not go back to October 12; only the 7-cent increase goes back to October 12. It is definitely a part of the transition; from now on the contract year will be the calendar year for all provisions. This management bent to a heavy degree to accomplish that. I am saying that in all sincerity.

Now to have everything clearly understood from now on I'll just read a "Stipulation on Retroactivity" for this year only.

Wagner (u): I want especially now to say that if I could have worked last year with you men, there would not have been a misunderstanding as to the retroactive date. I very much appreciate what you have done and so does the committee. Now on the question of the Colton people. Let's get that thorn out of our side and discontinue those buses.

Mitchell (m): This would be a good time, as the buses are not running now.

Wagner (u): I am in a position then to tell these people that the 7-cent increase is for everyone and that they are to get their own bus service. Another question, on these four paid holidays, are you going to leave that up to the union to decide what those four holidays will be?

Mitchell (m): Yes, but we think it would be fair for you to take it up with us.

Wagner (u): In other words, the company has no disagreement as to what holidays we pick?

Mitchell (m): No, we don't think so but we would like to have your decision before May 1. There are some few rules, like the working on the day before the holiday to be considered when we get down to writing the agreement.

Wagner (u): Let me say this. You draft up the agreement and we will proofread it. We will compare it with your notes and our notes.

Mitchell (m): Fair enough. I think on the matter of Union Recognition that in the light of the Teamsters' group, we have some ideas that may have some value. We would like to take out the words "truck drivers" and substitute "warehousing and service." As I have previously told you, the Teamsters are gunning for the warehousemen and we don't want any part of it. We must come out of this labor agreement with sound understanding on the part of the union and management.

[Meeting adjourned at 3:35 P.M.]

Mitchell's comments on this session were jubilant:

We've reached understanding locally on all issues. What's more important we've developed a relationship in which the union simply told us to draft the final agreement—and they'd proofread it! If anyone would have prophesied that a second agreement would be negotiated by this union and this company in 10 meetings between December 11, 1946, and January 30, 1947, with a complete job evaluation program, I'd daresay most experienced labor relations men would say it could not be done.

. . . . .

The company prepared a draft as requested by the union, and the latter accepted it in its entirety, save for the issue of jurisdictional dispute with the Teamsters' Union. That, too, as already noted, was soon settled, and on February 24 the parties signed their second agreement without changing one word in management's draft. The weekly "Friday grievance meetings" had been discontinued completely.

Pictures of the negotiators were taken in the conference room; the president of the company sat with the conferees for these pictures. The parties discussed the question of whether to hold a "celebration dinner," but because of the continuing slump decided to forego this. A joint release was issued to the press reporting the successful proceedings, including the job-evaluation program. It noted how negotiations had been carried forward through a period of layoffs and shutdowns in Laurelton, resulting from the slump in the canned-food industry generally.

The press releases quoted spokesmen of the parties:

A company spokesman declared that the negotiation of the 1947 agreement was satisfactory in every respect, that the union was fair and reasonable in their approaches to the many problems that face the industry at this particular time. A union representative said "the company and union are in harmony upon all issues. I don't see how our relationship could be any better. Both sides were tolerant in negotiating the 1947 agreement."

Discussion Questions

1. Evaluate Mitchell's opening again to note a recurrent feature of what seems his general negotiating strategy.

2. Indicate how the company's decision on the retroactivity issue emerges as a way of improving relationships. Would you consider it also effective bargaining strategy, and why?

3. List the dates of the bargaining sessions and the duration of their several openings and adjournments. Spot "trends" as they move forward. Give your interpretations of differences between the earlier and later stages after making due allowances for valid interruptions, such as the Christmas holidays.

4. Evaluate the considerations weighed by the parties in their discussions over ceremonializing the success of their negotiations.

NATIONAL FOOD SPECIALTIES (L)

A YEAR LATER: PREPARING FOR 1948 CONTRACT NEGOTIATIONS

Mitchell received formal notice on October 30, 1947, from the Amalgamated Meat Cutters and Butcher Workmen of North America of their desire "to make certain changes and amendments" in the 1947 agreement. He had told his associates when the current agreement had been signed on February 27: "If management administers this contract effectively, the negotiations of our 1948 agreement will reflect how much we have really accomplished." Yet he recognized, too, the inevitable and natural uncertainties of the situation. There had been changes in management personnel. For long months in 1947, business had been in the doldrums; several hundred union members had had to be laid off before the pickup began about midyear. The Taft-Hartley Act had been passed, too, during the currency of the agreement.

Concrete, positive measures had been taken to promote adjustment and cooperation. Thus a series of 13 two-hour meetings on labor history and labor agreements had been organized, which the entire supervisory force and many of the office division heads attended. Discussions focused on the factors behind the development of labor agreements, on the tactics and strategy of their negotiation, and on the requirements of living successfully with these agreements from day to day.

The men participating in these meetings began to "try out" what they were discussing. Management representatives on all levels began to inform the appropriate union representatives of pending developments about which the union might have a right or even an interest in knowing in advance what was going to be done, why and when.

At the time the Taft-Hartley Act was passed, joint meetings were held from time to time, "to take the mystery out of what the Act might do to us," and so also eased the way for the 1948 negotiations. For instance, when the union informed management it would desire renewal of the union shop, the company discussed with union representatives what would be required to attain this end. After giving notice of their desire to make amendments, the union representatives started to get signatures on a petition for a union shop. Management agreed to permit voting in the cafeteria of the plant.

Under the first agreement, it was recalled, the union had developed the "quickie" walkout as a way of underscoring protests or demands. During 1947, not one single stoppage took place.

Shortly after receiving the union's notice, the company selected its negotiating committee. Once more, as in the 1947 negotiations, management designated representatives of every primary function in the operation of the plant. A meeting was held with this group to portray to them what might be expected in the 1948 negotiation meetings. For only one of them, in addition to Mitchell himself, had engaged in the 1947 negotiations. A new plant manager had come into the picture in mid-1947, but he had so "sold himself" to the union group that he promised to be a real asset in negotiating the 1948 agreement.

Under date of November 5, the union mailed to the company three copies of their "Proposed Changes and Modifications." Mitchell thereupon prepared an analysis of the union's proposals, which he presented to management's negotiating committee.

It was arranged that the negotiation conferences would be held in the offices of the industrial relations division of the company. The following people were named to represent the parties (an asterisk before a name indicates that the representative had participated also in the 1947 negotiations):

For the Company

*Robert R. Mitchell, Director of Industrial Relations

James Hurst, Vice President, Production

Joel C. Bergman, Assistant Manager of Manufacturing

Paul L. Voss, Assistant Manager of Manufacturing

Alfred T. Stanley, Manager, Employment, Health, Safety, and Training

Gerald C. Dewey, Manager of Group Insurance and Assistant Employment Manager

*Herbert Rogers, Manager of Warehousing

Adam Mueller, Manager of Raw Materials

Angus MacDowell, Acting Chief Engineer

Herman Van Buren, Manager of Maintenance

For the Union

*Thomas Wagner, International Representative

*Frank Schultz, President, Local 8

Arthur Holden, Vice President, Local 8

*Edward Parsons, Chief Shop Steward and Trustee

*Carl Yost, Shop Steward and Trustee

*George Page, Trustee

Ann Bremer, Recording Secretary and Stewardess

Nancy Lewis, Press Correspondent and Stewardess

Once again, an office stenographer made notes of the discussions at the negotiating conferences. Excerpts from these records, with Mr. Mitchell's comments, follow in the next case.

DISCUSSION QUESTIONS

1. Discuss Mitchell's statement on the influence of contract administration upon negotiation.

2. List the changes in external and internal conditions impinging on bargaining at Laurelton which Mitchell felt might exert influence on the negotiations; then evaluate the measures taken to facilitate adaptation.

NATIONAL FOOD SPECIALTIES (M)

THE FIRST SESSION: REVIEWING THE UNION'S PROPOSALS

[The meeting opened on November 12, 1947, at 2 P.M.]

Mitchell (m): I think first we should get some understanding on the wages to be paid the representatives of the bargaining unit represented here. If we go overtime in our meetings you don't get paid, but you don't lose anything during the meetings.

It is understood that either side can take a recess. No agreement on any one clause is final until total agreement has been reached. Now let's proceed.

[Wagner asked Yost to read the agreement.]

Yost (u): *Parties to the Agreement:* . . .

Mitchell and Wagner: O.K.; and Article 1, too.

Yost (u): *Article 2—Union Recognition:* . . .

Mitchell (m): Now we are getting down into pay dirt. You have added second and third paragraphs which redefine the seasonal employee. In substance this would give you control over everybody that comes into the plant at any and all times.

Wagner (u): The only thing we tried to do is to clarify the provision so we don't get any arguments raised again like we had 6 weeks ago. We felt that if a regular employee is laid off and put on seasonal work he should not be classified as a seasonal employee. We still include in there that the season is "from July 1 to October 31."

Mitchell (m): We are the only company in the canning field having regular production during the tomato season. Every other concern in our competitive field closes down airtight during the vegetable growing season. They switch the people around and those not needed are sent home. We don't do that. We try to take those people from the lines which must be closed during the season for one reason or another and give them the work available on the seasonal operations.

Wagner (u): We felt that those permanent employees transferred to seasonal work when some production lines were shut down should not be classified as seasonal employees, because they had passed their 45-day probationary period. Why were they classified as seasonal?

Mitchell (m): We had to treat them the same way as all others working on the tomato line. Where have you been hurt as a bargaining unit during the 1947 tomato season?

Parsons (u): What will prevent the company from making chili sauce next year and the next year tomato soup?

Mitchell (m): You can let your imagination grow on that. But it must be a matter of faith. Just how did your people actually get hurt?

Wagner (u): They were hurt to this extent that they didn't belong to the union, although they were permanent employees transferred to this seasonal operation.

Yost (u): The company would not check off dues from their pay.

Mitchell (m): That's right, Carl. That became a matter of control within the union. To check off dues while they were on tomatoes would be a confession on our part that that *operation* was a part of the bargaining unit. As loyal union members they could make any special arrangements personally with their organization.

Holden (u): Wasn't catsup a finished goods?

Mitchell (m): That is one of the points of contention. This company says that the making of catsup is a by-product of the tomato season, but that we give your people the benefit of labeling and anything that comes within the plant operation.

Parsons (u): At Marston's do they close down to make catsup?

Mitchell (m): Yes. I made a visit to their plants among others in the industry to see what our competitors did.

Wagner (u): This is our first agreement where seasonal employees are excluded from the bargaining unit. It has been a headache. In 1946 this company was hiring in December and January and saying those employees were seasonal.

Mitchell (m): We are standing on the record of the 1947 tomato season. Where did the union or members of the union get hurt? Be specific.

Wagner (u): We are talking (1) about regular employees transferred by the company and (2) seasonal employees excluded from the bargaining unit when they have passed their 45-day probationary period.

Mitchell (m): Our agreement differs materially from Marston's, Littell's, etc. They take full advantage of the 14-week exemption.[1]

[There followed a discussion of competitive practices on seasonal work.]

Mitchell (m): My feeling is that we owe it to all regular employees to give them all the work and money we can. We do not have the same interest in these people outside your bargaining unit. We owe the bargaining unit members everything we can give in the way of continuous work. In these last 8 months Jim has done a grand job in stabilizing employment.

Wagner (u): Well, give this article a lot of consideration. We are only trying to protect our regular employees transferred over into seasonal work. It is not a question of jurisdiction over seasonal work. But we should carry jurisdiction over those who have served their probationary period and are transferred to seasonal work.

Yost (u): [Reads] *Article 3—Union Membership:* . . .

Mitchell (m): You changed the time within which new employees must

---

[1] This reference is to Section 7, Subsection (*b*) (3) of the Fair Labor Standards Act, which exempts employees from the requirements of Subsection (*a*) (3) stipulating the 40-hour week "for a period or periods of not more than 14 work weeks in the aggregate in any calendar year in an industry found by the Administrator to be of a seasonal nature." During this exempt period such an employer must pay time and one-half for all hours worked over 12 per day or 56 per week.

become members of the union from 45 to 30 days. We will now make the commitment to go along with the union shop and to help maintain a union shop, even to providing a place where you can hold the election required by the Taft-Hartley Act. We will make available the cafeteria right around the clock. That is going to afford you the opportunity to get everyone on the job to vote, so that you will have a better chance to get the necessary 51%.

Wagner (u): Thirty days for new employees is stipulated in the Taft-Hartley Act.

Mitchell (m): That is the minimum. In other words, those agreements that say 10 to 15 days are out; the unions cannot demand that even if they get the vote for a union shop. Thirty days must be the minimum. Anything above 30 days is acceptable under the act. While you are on the question of this election, Carl, do you suppose you could get some voting booths down here, since you are a good Republican?

Yost (u): Holden can do that because he is a good Democrat. [Laughter.]

Mitchell (m): I think you should get ready because the NLRB, after they accept your petition, acts pretty fast.

Paragraph A, in substance, is what we had before. But the word "good" standing in Paragraph B is going to have to come out, and we'll have to put in "dues" standing instead of "good" standing. We cannot accept "good" standing under the Taft-Hartley Act as a cause for discharge under the union shop.

You should also draft an irrevocable assignment because each of your people is going to have to sign such an assignment of wages for union dues for one year before we can check them off. It is not too difficult to phrase one.

[Wagner showed Mitchell a card with a draft of the irrevocable assignment.]

Mitchell (m): That is O.K. Want to go on, Brother Yost?

Yost (u): Yes, sir. [Reads *Article 4—Hours of Work and Working Conditions.*]

Mitchell (m): I would like to raise this question. What's wrong with our 1947 Article 4?

Wagner (u): We are asking mainly for two improvements: (1) for three additional paid holidays and (2) overtime for Saturday and Sunday.

Mitchell (m): What you are doing is removing all exceptions again from the 5-day week and going back to demanding premium pay for Saturday and Sunday as such.

Wagner (u): Aren't you paying time and one-half for Saturday work now as such?

Mitchell (m): No, only after 40 hours of work, with stipulated allowances. There may come a time when we will be able to do it. But now we can't, because this company is not stabilized enough.

Wagner (u): Don't you feel, Bob, that if a man comes out to work, he should be given 8 hours' pay? If he doesn't get that through the week, then he must work 4 hours or so on Saturday straight time in order to get 40 hours in. That isn't fair either.

Mitchell (m): Tom, who else does it in the food industry?

Yost (u): Maybe if this company did it we would start something.

Mitchell (m): We are very young in the field. I don't see where you have been hurt under Article 4 in 1947—it has worked out very satisfactorily.

Wagner (u): It gives us only 4 paid holidays, and the employees who worked on a holiday were hurt by receiving straight time for that day worked.

Mitchell (m): That is the kind of business we have. We are in a competitive industry. I think if this company had had fair earnings for this year they would go for more holidays. I say "I think," because we want to be a leader in the industry. But we don't want to be so far ahead of the hounds that the competitive industry can't see us. If we price ourselves out of the field, we'll both go down. We want to give the best wages and benefits possible. But we are already ahead in our field by the test of our whole agreement.

Wagner (u): Well, what is the verdict on it?

Mitchell (m): Let's pass it for a while.

On the question of wages, the article in substance is as it was before. But you have asked for 14 cents general increase. We will submit to you our counterproposal. Yes, there will be some kind of wage increase but what it is we don't know. Only remember you can't pump water out of a dry well or get blood out of a turnip.

You have asked for 7½ cents for the second and third shifts as such. No others in the field do that.

Wagner (u): Bob, down in South Carolina they are celebrating Christmas today. You should be down there, maybe you would be in a giving mood then. So far you haven't given us anything. [Laughter.]

Yost (u): Where now? Oh, yes. [He read *Article 6—Seniority.*]

Mitchell (m): What do you think is wrong with our present operation?

Parsons (u): What we have here in our proposal is practically the same thing that we are operating under now.

Mitchell (m): Oh, no! You have gone far out.

Parsons (u): Where?

Mitchell (m): On page 8, "Employees may be used, at the discretion of the company, in any classification or any occupation by mutual agreement between the employee and the company, where no reduction in pay is involved." You mean if an emergency comes up over here, and we must change the line, that we must ask the union and the employee? What if the employee refuses?

Parsons (u): Suppose there is a dirty job to be done, why should a man with greater seniority do it?

Mitchell (m): That is the kind of a place this is. If we must go around and solicit each person we might as well close up.

Wagner (u): Wouldn't you agree we both want to eliminate the so-called abuses? Providing for mutual agreement between the employees and the foreman in such cases would do away with the abuses.

Mitchell (m): When the management doesn't have the right to make assignments on a temporary work basis, the union is going to be in management's shoes telling management what it can do and what it cannot do. Management must keep the right to move a man on temporary assignment so long as his rate isn't disturbed. A permanent job is different.

Wagner (u): As the 1947 agreement is written now this could be abused. There is nothing in it about a temporary basis or a permanent basis.

Mitchell (m): You can't read just the one section in and of itself. A. "The oldest employees in the company shall have the preferred job based upon performance only, providing there is a job open or where the employee's job is out." I say that is essentially the only seniority clause operating in any company. The oldest person gets the job. That is what we are operating under now, except where an emergency job or a temporary job is concerned.

Parsons (u): What is an emergency job?

Mitchell (m): Any job within any 8-hour period where someone fails to show up, someone is sick, someone is not capable of performing, things of that sort.

Tom, on this seniority article we tried to write up seniority provisions in the light of our 1947 experience. Here's the result: We cut out all departmental seniority and put everything on straight seniority plant-wide.

Parsons (u): That is what we thought we had done in our proposal.

Mitchell (m): Well, you eliminated Section G [promotions as a function of management, with union rights of discussion] entirely.

Parsons (u): Paragraph G doesn't mean anything anyway, that is why we eliminated it.

Mitchell (m): It is quite important, we think.

Wagner (u): Will you retype this article on seniority as you propose it?

Mitchell (m): Before you go today we will give it to you. Regarding vacations, I don't think you need read your draft on that. You have qualified every employee, whether working or not, as soon as he has 1,600 hours in.

Wagner (u): If there is a layoff, those people should be given their vacation checks. Moreover, you don't allow for sickness, injury, et cetera.

Mitchell (m): Tom, there wasn't a single employee of ours who was sick or injured but what he or she was given a vacation check.

Parsons (u): You mean a person having 1,600 hours in when laid off isn't entitled to a vacation?

Mitchell (m): Again, in the competitive industry we are way ahead of the field. There isn't anyone in the field who gives as generously as we do.

[The parties at this point reviewed vacation practices in competitive firms and specific experiences of their own under the 1947 agreement.]

Mitchell (m): I suggest that we go on now, Tom. In your proposal on the *Adjustment of Grievances* [Article 9], there is a nice question raised there under the Taft-Hartley Act. You still specify the first step in adjustment as: "By a conference between the aggrieved employee and the foreman of the department involved; accompanied by the steward of his department. . . ." The words "accompanied by the steward of his department" will have to come out as a printed matter because the Taft-Hartley Act says that an employee may seek the remedy of his grievance by himself at the outset. No one knows who is going to police this Taft-Hartley Act and we want to keep clear.

The rest of the articles in your proposal are O.K. I suggest that what we do now, Tom, is give you our counterproposal, which does not yet include wages; and by the next time we meet, Wednesday, November 19, we should have our counterproposal on wages, too.

So, I suggest we meet next Wednesday.

[Meeting adjourned at 4 P.M.]

Mr. Mitchell's comments on this first negotiating meeting follow:

The attitudes and approaches of both groups were so different at this opening meeting from our initiation of 1947 negotiations that it would be difficult to identify the meeting as one in which the same union and the same company were participating. Throughout the meeting not a single personality was engaged in— and not a single recrimination. The union, in preparing its proposal, offered an explanation for every change sought. There was little window dressing and few dramatics.

Nonetheless after our first joint conference was adjourned, the management group had a review meeting. No one of our group felt that a 1948 Agreement could be reached before perhaps sometime in late December, 1947, or early in January, 1948. However good the union's attitude, its representatives, I was reminded, had presented us with some, in fact many, deep-reaching demands.

DISCUSSION QUESTIONS

1. Evaluate the three "understandings" with which Mitchell opens the negotiations as rules to govern these proceedings.

2. Compare the issues regarding seasonal employees embodied in the union's demands in this negotiation with those of the 1947 negotiation. What seem the concerns of management, what of the union?

3. Describe the concrete issues brought out in this first review of the union's draft which involve adjustments to the Taft-Hartley Act, and evaluate the discussion between the parties.

4. Compare the strategy and tactics in this session with those in the opening session of the previous year's negotiation.

NATIONAL FOOD SPECIALTIES (N)

THE SECOND SESSION: REVIEWING MANAGEMENT'S COUNTERPROPOSALS—AND STOCKTAKING

[The meeting opened on November 19, 1947, at 2:05 P.M.]

Mitchell (m): How do you want to start, Tom?

Wagner (u): Inasmuch as you submitted a counterproposal, why don't we see how far apart we are on it and go on from there?

Mitchell (m): Since last Wednesday we have revised some of our thinking. There are at least four such revisions of our proposals. They all involve money and we would like to talk about all of them as one package—and then talk about them one at a time: the question of vacation, the wage increase, holidays and the seasonal workers.

First, vacation—we believe that we are going to give you even more than you ever dreamed of getting. Jim, do you want to talk on our vacation proposal?

Hurst (m): All persons who qualify for a vacation will be allowed to take it beginning with the first of January, 1948, and through to December 31, 1948, excluding the seasonal period. An employee qualified for a vacation but laid off for a period of 30 days or more, continuous days, may claim payment for such vacation. But if laid off for less than 30 days he cannot claim vacation payment during that short temporary layoff. For 1947, in consideration of the long slump we will make special provision to substitute 900 hours for the normal 1,600.

Mitchell (m): Explain, Jim, why you specify 30 days' layoff as the normal allowance.

Hurst (m): Certain times on overhaul of lines or on temporary layoffs we might lay off employees for 2 or 3 weeks, maybe only one week. By specifying 30 days of continuous layoff we will prevent employees laid off for short periods of time from coming in and asking for vacation payment.

[At this point the union sought the precise meaning of this offer by asking the company to apply it to varying situations involving potential claims for 1, 1½, and 2 weeks' vacation.]

Mitchell (m): There is no catch in it. Take any type of situation you can imagine to see if it will work, remembering only that the clause now establishes the calendar year as the period in which 1,600 hours must be worked. We want to establish 1,600 hours as the fair and reasonable minimum of hours that the employees should have in order to qualify under general and normal conditions. This year we will use 900 hours to allow for the 1947 slump; we'll have a special stipulation to that effect. Next year we may *want* to go back to 1,600 hours as fair and reasonable if we have a good year in 1948; and we are hoping that everyone will be able to get at least 1,600 hours.

Wagner (u): If we could keep the qualifying date of March 1, the people who came in August would then have a chance to get the 900 hours in by March 1.

Mitchell (m): But we would not extend our proposal on that basis. One of the reasons why we are knocking off 700 hours is that we want to parallel the vacation with the calendar year.

Wagner (u) [after further specific potentialities had been explored]: I would like to have a recess of about 15 minutes.

[Recess for union from 2:30 P.M. to 2:40 P.M.]

Wagner (u): We will accept your vacation proposal with the stipulation on the 900 qualifying hours attached.

Mitchell (m): O.K. Now I would like to go to paid holidays, Jim.

Hurst (m): We looked at the industry to see what it was doing and it seems to us fair and reasonable that we add 1 more paid holiday to our 1947 agreement. Under last year's contract you had 4 paid and 3 unpaid holidays. We will now offer 5 and 2. That should be a fair settlement, because a paid holiday is definitely a part of the wage structure and we think we can go along on 5 paid holidays for 1948.

Mitchell (m): Of course as in 1947 the union would have the right to select the holiday.

Wagner (u): There is another thing: You have added a paragraph about employees scheduled to work on holidays.

Mitchell (m): Yes. An employee called for work on a holiday, but who fails to come in, shall lose his holiday pay. Some of the boys say that next year they just won't come out when they are scheduled to work. That clause was put in there to settle the question. If an employee defies the management we should be able to do something about it. We don't want to discharge our good employees for not coming out to work on the holiday, but we think they should not get holiday pay if they refuse to work.

Wagner (u): Pay double time if called out to work on holidays. Then we will agree you can discharge those who refuse without good cause.

Mitchell (m): There cannot be any double time. The men will get their 8 hours for the holiday and pay for the hours they work.

Wagner (u): You can hardly blame an employee called out to work on a holiday for straight time pay not liking it when an employee who doesn't work gets paid 8 hours.

Parsons (u): Say a mechanic plans to go away and the day before the holiday he is told he is to work. Then, if he doesn't come out to work, he loses his holiday pay, too.

Mitchell (m): You've got to draw the line some place.

[There followed a lengthy discussion in which the union argued that the company was demanding the right to penalize employees who refused to accept a call to work on a paid holiday by forfeiting his holiday pay, while refusing to penalize management via premium rates for work that should properly not be scheduled on such holidays. The management replied by pointing out that such holiday work actually was scheduled only to meet emergencies and that the company's holiday pay standards were well in advance of competitors.   Both sides reverted to Labor Day of 1947 when maintenance men had been called to work, the union claiming that the repairs they did could have been scheduled on a regular workday or on Saturday, their sixth day, and the management claiming that, unless the repairs were done on Labor Day when the need was discovered, the whole force might have lost the next day's work.]

Mitchell (m): Well, what do you want to do, Tom?

Wagner (u): Pass it for the moment.

Mitchell (m): All right.   Now we are down to the question of wage increase.   Our wage structure here is predicated on three things: (1) what are we paying in relation to the average comparable work in the community; (2) what are we paying in comparison with competitors in the industry; and (3) —about which we are not going to cry—what is the ability of this company to pay.   We feel that we should pay in keeping with the community and in keeping with the competitive wage.   If we are not good enough to pay that then we should fold up and seek work elsewhere.   Jim, will you carry on?

Hurst (m): It looks to me as if we are in pretty fair line now with the local industry scale and the prices of our product.   However, any wage increase must be absorbed somewhere.   I think by the cooperation between the union and management and the development in efficiency we did a pretty good job in absorbing the raise given in 1947.   Any raise that comes in 1948 must similarly be absorbed through efficiency of employees and management, management just as strongly as employees.   In consideration of that it seems that we can give a wage increase of 7 cents across the board.   Taking all the wage structure, including your paid holidays, I hope that we can absorb it by increased efficiency in production.   If we don't or can't, then the old economic picture will return and none of us may be very healthy.

Mitchell (m): That would raise our minimum on women employees to 78 cents, on men to 88 cents.

Wagner (u): That would also increase in proportion all the rates in the appendix attached to the agreement.   In other words, it would be a general 7 cents an hour across the board.

Mitchell (m): That's right.   However, beef boners would stay on $1.54 per carcass incentive basis.

Wagner (u): How many beef boners are there?

Mitchell (m): Three.

Parsons (u): Is there 8½ cents differential between our plant and the car company?

Mitchell (m): All right; but let's look at that from the standpoint of the kind of skills our people have and those required by the car company.   My guess is that 50% of our people couldn't perform at the car company.

Parsons (u): What does Freighting Car Line pay?

Mitchell (m): I don't know that.   Laurelton Machine starts at 86 cents; Chester Steel, at 87½ cents; Farmers' League, 65 cents.

Parsons (u): What about Lawrence?

Mitchell (m): I didn't get them; that is a deep dark secret. Littells' starts at 77½ cents.

Parsons (u): Their employees' rent is $12 per month.

Mitchell (m): Meadowfield, 75 cents.

Parsons (u): I would be willing to take that together with the $12 month rent, heat and everything.

Mitchell (m): On the profit side, it is pretty hard to pump water out of a dry well.

Parsons (u): Dig deeper. [Laughter.]

Mitchell (m): You cannot give that which you do not have, Ed; it is impossible.

Parsons (u): It seems to me that if the company could afford 7 cents last year they certainly can afford more than that this year.

Mitchell (m): We told you last year that, if we had not made the commitment to you, you would not have gotten what you did. The management would not go back on its word. Tom, do you want to go on?

Wagner (u): Yes, we will pass, Bob.

Mitchell (m): Now for the provisions on the seasonal work.

In excluding seasonal employees in 1947, the agreement defined such an employee as one employed during the tomato season running from July 1 to October 31. To clarify this still further we propose to substitute the following definitions: "A seasonal employee is herein defined as being one employed for limited and temporary work directly related to the receiving, processing, packaging and shipping of perishable farm crops during their growing season. The season shall be from July 1 to October 31."

Wagner (u): The first six lines of that provision is O.K. up to the word "processing." Then we'd like to include these words, "of fresh tomatoes and up to and including the canning of tomato puree."

Mitchell (m): In substance then you haven't changed it any from your original proposal. It is the same thing. The same horse, only painted and renamed.

Wagner (u): Not quite. We are willing to take your substitution up to "processing." The words "packaging and shipping of farm crops" is out. We are asking the company to take the last part of our paragraph of "fresh tomatoes up to and including the canning of tomato puree." Then this will take care of those regular people who were transferred during this season. How about that?

Mitchell (m): No soap. The company requests a recess.

[The company recessed from 3:33 P.M. to 3:40 P.M.]

Mitchell (m): On page 3, we would revise that proposal by striking out "perishable farm crops" and substituting "of tomatoes during their growing season." In other words, that takes out all the peas and other things that you say we might want to can.

Parsons (u): All but catsup, tomato soup, and chili sauce.

Wagner (u): You want regular employees transferred to seasonal work to be paid the rate of seasonal people.

Mitchell (m): Right.

Wagner (u): That's no good. Where do we go from here?

Mitchell (m): Tom, are you trying to expand the bargaining unit to include seasonal work?

Wagner (u): In any of the Marston plants, if a regular employee works on seasonal work he gets his regular rate. But you want to take these regular employees, who are entitled to that work anyway before additional new employees are hired, and you want the union to say nothing about the wage rate that they are to have.

Mitchell (m): Tom, my understanding is that in the competitive industry they do not pay one penny of overtime on seasonal work. They get no overtime regardless of how long they work.

Anything else you want to talk about?

Wagner (u): There are three or four main issues: holiday pay, wages, and overtime. I checked on union membership under Section 83 of the Taft-Hartley Act. You requested 45 days. The act calls for a 30-day period.

Mitchell (m): That is the minimum. In other words, those agreements which specify 10 or 15 days are in violation of the act.

Parsons (u): Would it take more than 30 days to find out if an employee is any good or not?

Mitchell (m): It doesn't make that much difference now. I guess now we can go along with 30 days. Do you agree with that, Jim?

Hurst (m): Yes.

Wagner (u): Do you want to go from the beginning of this to see how we stand?

Mitchell (m): Yes.

Wagner (u): I'll just review the major accepted changes and the remaining differences.

Article 2—Union Recognition: Now, we are apart on the question of clarifying the definition of seasonal employees. *Article 3—Union Membership:* 45 days changes to 30 days and "dues" is put in instead of "good" standing, and take out "certified in writing." For checkoff, each member will certify on forms provided him. That's O.K. Now *Article 4—Hours of Work and Working Conditions:* we are apart on our demand for time and one-half for Saturday work and double time for Sundays and holidays. Nor are we together on the paid holidays as yet. *Article 5—Wages:* we are not together. *Article 6:* we have a question on this seniority. Bob, what's wrong with our request that assignment to equally rated jobs be "by mutual agreement between the employee and the company"?

Mitchell (m): No, we can settle that right now. There will not be any mutual agreement on decisions that inherently belong to this management.

Wagner (u): Then we will not agree to J of your proposal—that employees may be used on jobs involving no reduction in pay at your discretion.

Mitchell (m): Let us go on.

Wagner (u): There is also that question of foremen and foreladies doing production work.

Mitchell (m): Tom, we stand on the record, so why start an argument? Do you agree to the rest of our proposal on seniority?

Wagner (u): Yes, with the exception of your J. There was also quite a discussion about the requirement in your Section A, that seniority govern "provided the employee is presently competent to perform and does perform that work satisfactorily." Will you explain to the committee what that "provided" means to you?

Mitchell (m): That is the only way you can have plant-wide seniority. There must be a test by performance.

Wagner (u): That is true. If a man is going to bump someone he must be able to perform satisfactorily. You do not specify in there the time required to demonstrate competence to perform satisfactorily.

Mitchell (m): In a reasonable period of time. Most jobs can be performed within 8 hours and the other jobs would not take more than 10 days. It is in substance what we are doing right now.

Yost (u): We are thinking about the old employees.

Mitchell (m): Carl, we again stand on the record in our treatment of old employees.

Yost (u): In 2 or 3 days they could not perform on new jobs during the layoffs; but in 2 or 3 weeks they did a good job.

Mitchell (m): All right then, isn't that the answer? The rule of reason must prevail.

Yost (u): The soft jobs are running out for these old girls.

Mitchell (m): Carl, it is nice of you to remember that; after all we are not running an eleemosynary institution. Believe me there is a relationship between the money paid an employee and the work performed by that employee.

Yost (u): Yes, but we would like to protect them for a little while on the job. Are you satisfied the way it has been going along?

Mitchell (m): Yes.

Yost (u): Then I won't kick on that.

Wagner (u): All the rest of the agreement is O.K. We should ask for a couple more uniforms, but that's O.K. Now, if you give me seasonal employees and the clarifications on it, two additional paid holidays, time and one-half and double time for Saturdays, Sundays, and holidays, and 14 cents wage increase, we will be all right.

Mitchell (m): Tom, I really don't think we are too far apart; that is, we stay in the same 40 acres. When do you want to meet again?

Yost (u): Let's get it over with this week.

Mitchell (m): Tom, how about meeting tomorrow at 2:00 P.M.

[Meeting adjourned at 4:20 P.M.]

Mitchell's comments on this second negotiation meeting follow:

At the very outset of this meeting, management took the position of giving what it was ready to give. Yet when the meeting ended, it would seem that the parties were a long way off from an agreement. The discussions had gone along very smoothly, however; and for my part, I could see definite signs that we were going to reach an agreement soon. My colleagues, however, disagreed with me.

Nonetheless, I thought well enough of our timing to be willing to hold a negotiation meeting the very next day.

Again, after the joint meeting, the management group held a bull session. Since most of the company negotiators were in their first negotiations, there was some high speculation going on as to where we were in relation to a final agreement.

DISCUSSION QUESTIONS

1. Evaluate Mitchell's opening of this session as a tactic in his bargaining strategy.

2. Why do you think Mitchell asks Hurst to present management's "money proposals"?

3. Discuss the division of management's presentation of its proposals on wages, indicating your judgment upon the subject matter Mitchell chose to present himself, and that which he asked Hurst to present. Evaluate management's wage criteria. Give your judgment upon the effectiveness and validity of Hurst's presentation.

4. Interpret the contract revisions made upon the basis of Taft-Hartley requirements as a factor in building relationships.

NATIONAL FOOD SPECIALTIES (O)

THE THIRD SESSION: WINDUP AND AFTERMATH

[The meeting opened on November 20, 1947, at 2:35 P.M.]

Wagner (u): I think the best thing to do is go over your proposal once more and as we come to those articles on which we disagree we can argue them out.

Mitchell (m): Before we do that, Tom, we have some revised thinking to give you. Jim had a change of heart, and I do not disagree with him, on the paid holiday question. Turn to page 6, paragraph E, second paragraph in the last sentence, "if work is performed on these holidays employees will receive in addition straight time." Jim is willing to go along on this; "shall in addition receive time and one-half the straight time rate *for hours actually worked.*"

Parsons (u): In other words, if I come out and work 8 hours on Monday and Tuesday is a paid holiday but on call I work 8 hours, I get paid time and one-half plus 8 hours' straight pay. That sounds close to what we asked for.

Mitchell (m): All right. Will you give us that paragraph on it?

Wagner (u): Yes, we had a proposal to submit revising our demand for double time, but you have taken it right out of our mouths. Let's go back to the seasonal question and get that out of the road, too. In order to get a clarification of what a seasonal employee is, we suggest the following definition be made: "A seasonal employee is herein defined as hired for limited and temporary work directly related to the receiving, processing, packaging and shipping of fresh tomatoes during the growing season. The season shall be from July 1 to October 31." Am I right on that? That's basically your proposal as we finally got it yesterday.

Mitchell (m): We haven't anything but ripe tomatoes so why specify "fresh."

Wagner (u): O.K., we will leave it out. In addition to that you offered a stipulation. There is quite a debate on that. Could you give us the assurance like last year that the regular and permanent employees won't receive any wage cuts on seasonal work? If you can—and in addition all seasonal employees pay 50 cents a week as dues—I think we will finally get an understanding.

Mitchell (m): Tom, with 50 cents' dues you will be in violation of the Taft-Hartley Act.

Wagner (u): In what way?

Mitchell (m): In that they will be entitled to vote. You will have to include them in the voting that you are going to take now on the union shop; you cannot bargain for people outside the bargaining unit without their consent.

Parsons (u): What about the working card?

Mitchell (m): The working card is out under the Taft-Hartley Act.

Wagner (u): The only thing clearly allowed under the act is the dues; there is some question about initiation fees.

Mitchell (m): Yes, and in order to get dues through a checkoff, it becomes necessary that each employee must sign an irrevocable assignment of wages for one year. That would apply to seasonal workers.

Wagner (u): Bob, let's you and I take a look into this. We feel that the seasonal employees should pay 50 cents per week, same as the regular employees. If there is a possibility that we can collect 50 cents after the seasonal worker is here 30 days, will you go along on it?

Mitchell (m): I am just saying that if you are not careful you will get your neck out and destroy yourselves.

Wagner (u): Another thing, on the permanent or regular employees, in the event you shut down production lines so that production employees work on tomatoes, what assurance will you give us on their wage rate? Under your stipulation you say, "the Union agrees that the rate of wage to be paid such temporary workers, although they be union members, shall be the responsibility of the company."

Mitchell (m): That's right. We, again, stand on the record of last year. We submitted those seasonal rates to the union for their information.

Parsons (u): What we want is your agreement to do the same next year as this year. If you needed them on the tomato line while their regular job was working, you paid them their regular rate. But if there was no work in their regular job, they had a choice of either working on tomatoes at the seasonal rate or going home.

Mitchell (m): We should do a better job in 1948 than in 1947 of giving our regular employees the work. The tomato season is an emergency season. You can take this past season as a symbol; after you have done things once, they are hard to get away from. I don't think we took advantage of you this year, but we must always have a certain amount of freedom in order to operate.

Wagner (u): Here is what the majority of the employees are afraid of. Say next July 1 or between July 1 and July 15 you get 500 truckloads of tomatoes. We know you must process them. On the other hand there is nothing to prevent you from shutting down six or seven departments if you cannot get enough seasonal workers. So you take these permanent employees and put them down on seasonal work at any rate you wish to pay them. There is nothing to stop you from doing that. We are not saying you have done it; we are not saying you are going to do it. But, you *could* shut down the entire production line and put regular employees on seasonal work.

Mitchell (m): We differ from most of the people in this field. We are primarily a production plant and not a processing plant. If a time comes where we can shut down this plant on production for 6 months, or even 3 months, then we will all be looking for jobs, because this company cannot survive on that. We are not primarily a seasonal canning plant. I have been talking about our typical canners, but they, too, know that they must get into production, and as quickly as they can, all around the year, because otherwise they cannot hold their people. Where do they get their people for seasonal work? Wharton's took over a prisoner camp; they also bring in anywhere from 750 to 1,500 colored people and they have a little village next to the plant and within the confines of the plant where they have girls, that too is primarily a colored village. They are brought up from the South. They bring up about 10 plane loads of girls. This last year they brought up a colored girls' college from Georgia and put them in this camp. That is the seasonal workers that they have. Why? For two reasons: (1) they cannot go out and compete for this labor in the community, and (2) they don't want people in their community on a half-time basis. They run their season from April 1 when they start harvesting asparagus until December 1 when they harvest peppers. They are trying to get away from it. We are the only ones that produce, or try to produce, year around every month of the year.

Parsons (u): What do the seasonal workers do at Wharton's?

Mitchell (m): They make anything and everything.

Wagner (u): Marston has the same thing. The employees pay 35 cents a night to stay in cabins.

Parsons (u): Do they make catsup and everything?

Wagner (u): Sure.

Mitchell (m): They close down on regular production tighter than a drum.

Parsons (u): Do they make enough catsup during the tomato season to last the entire year?

Mitchell (m): I saw enough catsup at Wharton's and Marston's to last for the next 10 years, it seemed to me. They even took part of the cafeteria for storage and piled up catsup with canvas over it.

Wagner (u): On this stipulation, is there some assurance that we can get on these seasonal people?

Mitchell (m): I think you should stand on this last year's record.

Wagner (u): Then why put the stipulation in at all?

Mitchell (m): From a bargaining standpoint we must protect ourselves under the Taft-Hartley Act on the bargaining area.

Wagner (u): You are right; if I can't take your word for it, your signature doesn't mean anything. In other words, it is in here for a precautionary measure more than anything else. Will it be O.K. if we take a short recess?

[Union recessed from 3:25 P.M. to 3:42 P.M.]

Wagner (u): We have considered this question of seasonal workers. We think we can charge 50 cents per week after the workers are here 30 days. Will you see what you can find out on that under the Taft-Hartley Act? The other part of the clarification on seasonal workers we accept now.

Now on *Article 4—Hours of Work and Working Conditions*, we will accept what Jim Hurst said on time and one-half on holidays.

Mitchell (m): In other words you accept Article 4 as is, with the 5 paid holidays and the time and one-half the straight-time rate for the holidays worked. Can you tell us what the 5 holidays will be?

Wagner (u): We're adding Thanksgiving.[1] *Article 5—Wages.* The company proposed 7 cents an hour increase with the exception of the beef boners. Why are we excluding the beef boners?

Mitchell (m): Because they are on an incentive rate.

Wagner (u): Inasmuch as we offered, or rather asked, for 14 cents general increase, we will split the other 7 cents difference and make it 10½.

Mitchell (m): Tom, I don't know whether or not you know yet how we bargain. We don't split any differences on wages. We give the maximum that we can afford to give at the outset. You can depend on that.

Wagner (u): Maybe we also mean 14 cents when we say 14 cents.

Mitchell (m): O.K., if you mean it, you mean it. That is as far as we can go.

Parsons (u): A fellow can't get rich very fast on that.

Mitchell (m): No, you are right, Ed, you can't. One of the jobs in negotiating a labor agreement is to go out and try to sell management on what they should give when they cite their losses, and then try to sell the union on what they should take when they cite their needs. Tom, the real fact about the business is that this puts us at the top of our class in the competitive industry.

Wagner (u): You said the toughest job is to sell management. Do you wish to adjourn and see what you and Jim and your committee can do?

Mitchell (m): That is the best we can do. No use kidding you by taking a recess. But we will give the 7 cents to the beef boners, on their incentive.

Parsons (u): Seven cents per carcass?

Mitchell (m): That is right. We will go to $1.61, because we can see where you might have difficulty if those few fellows felt excluded.

Wagner (u): That is your final proposal?

Mitchell (m): That's right. We could talk to management until our eyes popped out.

Wagner (u): Well, then, we will hold that open. We cannot give you an answer until after our membership meeting.

Under *Article 6—Seniority,* a question was raised on the number of stewards. It was never discussed in the negotiations.

Yost (u): We don't have near 50 stewards now.

Wagner (u): The company raised the question; now is the time to iron it out.

Parsons (u): I don't think 50 is too many.

Yost (u): We had 38 at one time and needed more.

Mitchell (m): On that, we are not disturbed too much. You have not abused it. We think you should have enough to service your union and we just raised the question in connection with top seniority to get some idea of the limit.

Wagner (u): You have no objection to the 50?

---

[1] The five paid holidays thus became, by the union's selection, New Year's Day, Independence Day, Labor Day, Thanksgiving Day, and Christmas Day. The unpaid holidays became Memorial Day and Armistice Day.

Mitchell (m): No.

Wagner (u): Well, then, that's fine. *Article 7—Vacations:* as Jim Hurst said 900 hours would be the qualifying time, vacation period starts with January 1 to December 31, except that specified period of seasonal work, and on a layoff of more than 30 continuous days the employee can draw his vacation check.

Mitchell (m): Right.

Wagner (u): That's O.K. then. And all the rest is O.K., except that on one article we are deadlocked, that is on Wages.

Mitchell (m): Can we go back to seasonal work on the stipulation? Jim has raised a question that the word "unemployed" be inserted, to read "that unemployed employees of the union," etc. In other words, the unemployed members of the union shall have first consideration.

Wagner (u): We have a membership meeting tomorrow, Bob, and at the termination of that meeting we will give you our answer.

Mitchell (m): As soon as you find out, we will write the agreement in its final form. How many copies of the agreement do you want?

Schultz (u): Three.

Mitchell (m): One thing more: In 1948 we want to start something new in administering the agreement, and it is a big job for the Industrial Relations Division: When the union asks for management's interpretation of what the agreement means in some situation or grievance we will endeavor to give you a written answer on our interpretation and application. That doesn't mean, however, that our answer is final. If you want, you can quarrel with it. What we want to do is get away from this "you said so and so."

Wagner (u): All right. Do you mind giving us a copy of these negotiation minutes?

Mitchell (m): The only thing, Tom, you must remember that they are only high lights and not a verbatim report. On that basis we'll see that you get a copy.

[Meeting adjourned at 4:14 P.M.]

Mr. Mitchell's comments on this third negotiating meeting follow:

The management group reviewed the two previous negotiation meetings. We had something to give, and at the outset of the third meeting we again gave what we had to give.

I could sense a feeling of acceptance on the part of the union that perhaps this might be the last meeting of the joint committees. And it so developed. The union had a membership meeting scheduled for Friday, November 21. This gave us a clue to a possible acceptance.

On Friday night, November 21, we were informed that the union, in a membership meeting, had accepted the agreement.

The negotiation meeting reflected the fine relationship of the union and management in the past year.

. . . . . .

On the following Monday, November 24, President Frank Schultz, speaking for the members of the local, communicated formally at a final joint meeting of the negotiating committees the union's acceptance of the proposal the company "submitted to us on November 20."

The agreement itself was submitted to the union committee "for proof-reading" on Tuesday morning. The following day, the parties affixed their signatures to the document and its special "stipulations" for 1948. As in 1947, President Ford P. Kennedy joined the committees at these "signing formalities." A photograph was taken of the assembled representatives as Mr. Wagner, for the union, was writing his signature on the revised agreement.

A joint press release was issued. The Laurelton papers headlined the "7 cents pay raise" and "the fifth paid holiday" granted "after brief negotiations." In their joint statement the parties said, among other things:

> Only three short meetings, totaling 5½ hours, were required by the representatives to reach an agreement on the new contract. Both union and management point to these brief and amicable negotiations as a symbol of their relationship during the closing year.

The National Labor Relations Board set January 6, 1948, as the day for the election on the union shop. Mr. Mitchell wrote on December 18: "There does not seem to be much doubt about the outcome. The union has circularized forms authorizing an irrevocable assignment of wages for union dues for the year 1948. Only some three or four are yet to be heard from to make the entire workforce unanimous."

Under date of December 18, President Kennedy again wrote to Mitchell, commenting upon the progress in relationships. His letter to Mitchell follows:

> As the year draws to a close, I wish to commend and congratulate you on the splendid progress that this company has made within your area of responsibility.
>
> I suppose that the signing of a satisfactory agreement with our union after only 5½ hours of negotiation is the most spectacular feature of the year's accomplishments. But I prefer to look beyond this to the job which had to be done day in and day out, week in and week out, through this entire past year, to solve our problems with our union on the spot, and at the time they occurred. This seems to me to have been the real cause behind the effect—which was a short, satisfactory negotiation.
>
> I don't suppose that chronic conflict between the personnel man and the works manager is a great deal newer than the Industrial Revolution. Therefore, it is especially pleasing that you and Jim [James Hurst, plant manager] have gotten along so well in finding solutions for our problems. The cost figures bear witness to the fact that, in addition to each of you doing your own job, Jim has done a good Industrial Relations job and you have done a sound Production Job.
>
> May I wish you and Mrs. Mitchell and your family a very happy Christmas.

On January 6, 1948, as scheduled, the regional director for the NLRB held the "consent election" on the union shop at the cafeteria of the Laurelton plant. The official "Tally of Ballots" recorded the following results: Over 92% of the eligible voters in the bargaining unit cast ballots on the "proposition" (union shop). Over 95% of those voting cast their ballots "for" the union shop. Under the requirements of the Taft-Hartley Act, accordingly, the regional director certified that, "A majority of the eligible voters have cast valid votes for the proposition."

The day after the election, the local union officers sent the following letter to Mr. Mitchell:

Dear Mr. Mitchell:

Kindly accept our sincere thanks for the wonderful cooperation extended to our Organization by your Associates and yourself in the recent election conducted by the National Labor Relations Board.

Personally, we feel the result of the election was, in reality, a vote of confidence for both the Company and our Union. As we embark on a New Year, we do so with the feeling of trust and confidence, with the full knowledge that Management and Labor shall enjoy a harmonious relationship unexcelled anywhere in the United States.

On behalf of the entire membership and myself, please accept our best wishes for your continued success.

Respectfully yours,
Frank Schultz,
President

A week later, the officers of Local 8 invited Mr. Mitchell to give a course in labor relations for the union's officials and shop stewards.

DISCUSSION QUESTIONS

1. Evaluate Mitchell's opening of this session—and Wagner's response to it.

2. Evaluate the resolution of the differences regarding "seasonal employees."

3. Would you endorse Mitchell's statement of the company's policy on wage bargaining? Interpret his probable reasons for making the concession on the beef boners.

4. How would you characterize the post-negotiation activities?

5. Review the impact of the Taft-Hartley Act in this negotiation and what followed and preceded it from the viewpoint of (a) specific adjustments, and (b) underlying relationships.

6. Discuss President Kennedy's letter to Mitchell, giving your evaluation particularly of the interrelations he suggests between (a) successful negotiation and continuing relationships, and (b) the plant manager and the manager of industrial relations.

7. If Mr. Mitchell asked your advice on his reply to the union's request regarding a training course, detail the pros and cons you would urge for his consideration.

8. Review critically the strategy and tactics over the two-year period.

PILGRIM OIL COMPANY (A)

NEGOTIATING THE SHUTDOWN OF A REFINERY

I

At the Crown Point refinery of the Pilgrim Oil Company the operating, laboratory, and chemical workers are represented by the Oil Workers International Union. The agreement is automatically renewed from year to year unless either party, within 60 days of any expiration date, gives written notice of desire to change it. The negotiations recorded in this case were initiated by the union, which presented 47 demands for contract changes embodying revisions in practically every article of the agreement. Charles Raymond, manager of labor relations, came from New York headquarters to lead the management negotiating committee; he participated throughout the proceedings until the strike went into effect. He then returned when negotiations were resumed to end the strike.

Behind the parties were over 14 years of relationships—as each side reminded the other during their sessions. But these reminders also brought recurrent references to stormy episodes, disputes, strikes, or other "tough" negotiations. Some local union officials and management executives had participated almost from the start. Perhaps the most continuous service in such bargaining roles had been held by Michael C. Flynn for management, and Joseph C. Arnold for the union. Woody Davis and Burton Chadwick on the union side also had relatively long terms of service. Most of the stressful episodes had occurred during the administration not of the present general manager, Mr. George Metcalf, but of his predecessor. Flynn had then been assistant to Andrew Holden, the former manager, who had been retired during the war years.

On January 20, as the proceedings opened, the union negotiators asked to discuss first one of their demands that they announced was "basic"—that their negotiators be paid by the company for time lost from work through these proceedings. They argued that other companies in the area paid for negotiating time and that the costs had been exceedingly heavy for the local union; yet democratic procedure as well as joint interest demanded rank-and-file employees on the negotiating committee. They also emphasized that the company paid for negotiating time in another branch plant (Dobie), where an independent union represented the employees. This preliminary argument occupied hours of the opening session and was reintroduced time and again throughout the proceedings.

Preliminary exploration of the union's remaining 46 demands then followed: revisions of the no-strike clause that would bind the union only on matters referable to the grievance procedures up to and including arbitration; rate adjustments in some 69 individual jobs in the operating departments and a like number in the crafts, exclusive of the laboratory, which was covered by a separate negotiating subcommittee; joint discussion of qualifications for and classification of jobs in new plants; changes in the provision for accrual of seniority on temporary assignments; a union shop and checkoff; revisions in current benefits, including allowance for clothing damaged on the job; severance, sick leave, and other insurance benefits; paid holidays and vacation allowances; increased meal allowances on overtime work; time off with pay for attendance at the funeral of a member of an employee's family; and pay to men serving as jurors or court witnesses. Finally the union asked for the current cost-of-living bonus to be converted into basic wage increases of 18 cents per hour retroactive for the last quarter of the contract year just ending, and for a 25 cents per hour increase for the new contract year. Explanation by the union of the "meaning" of its demands occupied both sessions of January 20, the morning session of January 21, and part of the afternoon session.

II

As this initial stage of negotiations drew to its conclusion, company officials submitted 22 counterproposals. They were focused upon provisions regarding contractual coverage and revision, seniority, no-strike obligation, the grievance machinery, and union security. They sought to remove hourly rated supervisors from the bargaining unit; to establish the affirmative obligation of the union to refrain from work stoppages of any kind; to give management the right to appoint temporary (as well as permanent) supervisors without regard to seniority rules; to make the job the basic unit for seniority purposes instead of the department and the plant; to establish a six months' probationary period for new employees; to deduct unexcused absences from the record of continuous service for seniority purposes; to accord management the right to "try out" the top several men in seniority rank prior to assignment to a higher rated job vacancy; to bar an employee summoned for conference with a superior from calling his union representative if only questions of fact were to be asked; to require union stewards to obtain permission from supervision before leaving the job to transact union business; to make the American Arbitration Association the agency to name arbitrators under the grievance machinery; to eliminate the right of job preference among jobs in the same classification; to eliminate the maintenance of membership clause; and to define "valid union business" entitling an employee to leave of absence. The company's first wage offer postulated a formula arrangement yielding a 12½% cost-of-living bonus effective February 1 to June 1.

After scanning the written draft of these management counterproposals, the union representatives interrupted management's exposition with a protest that none of them really touched on the union's demands and that the company was not presenting its "new demands" within the contractual time limit. The session closed on this argument. The next day, January 22, a group of union members entered as "spectators." The protest against the company's counterproposals was vigorously continued. There were no union spectators at the afternoon session; and management's proposal that the negotiators collate the union's and the company's proposals serially with the articles of the expiring contract was accepted. Discussion of the agreement went forward in this manner on the fourth and fifth days' sessions, January 23 and 24.

On the fifth day, the parties concluded their preliminary explorations of the union's proposals and the company's counterproposals; and a night session was held. Pointing out that wide differences persisted while the contract was due to expire on January 31, the union proposed that the parties meet with the Federal Mediation and Conciliation Service.

III

Beginning with the appearance of the Federal conciliator, John D. Parkman, negotiations continued for 10 days. During this period, the current contract, which had expired on January 31, was extended three times.

The conciliator did his utmost to avert a shutdown. He proposed possible compromises; he tried to "narrow differences." He engaged in separate conferences with each side. He made a point of "checking off" articulately any issue on which "tentative agreement" was reached. He sought, by very specific questions, to crystallize the boundaries of difference and within them carve out an area of agreement.

On the sixteenth negotiating day, it began to appear that a deadlock would be inescapable. The conciliator at this point proposed a somewhat different approach: that one side produce a concession, or a new offer, on one of the differences and then the other side make a concession on another. The conferees proceeded to offer alternative concessions until these offers also ceased. The parties then withdrew for separate conferences.

IV

Upon resumption of joint discussion, a union representative proposed to the management that the 14 to 18 remaining issues be submitted to arbitration. Upon the refusal of the management to accept this proposal, the union representatives called a union meeting on the night of February 12, at which the members voted to strike. Representatives of management waited to be informed of membership action. At 1:22 A.M. on February 13, union officials brought notification of the strike vote to the Crown Point refinery and the meeting proceeded, with the following in attendance:

For the Union

Woody Davis, Local President and Chairman of Negotiating Committee
Joseph C. Arnold, Secretary-Treasurer and full-time local union official
Burton Chadwick ⎫
Robert Marsh   ⎬ Members of the Negotiating Committee
Price E. Bennett ⎪
Albert Hill   ⎭
Elmer Smith, Chairman, Strike Committee
Also, eight members of the strike committee and three regional representatives
    of the union

For the Crown Point Refinery

George Metcalf, General Manager
Michael C. Flynn, Director of Industrial Relations
Edward Peters, Assistant Director of Industrial Relations
Donald W. Turner, Assistant Superintendent
Paul C. Parsons, Production Manager
Adam Jeffreys, Assistant Production Manager
Charles Raymond, Manager of Industrial Relations, and other representatives
    from New York headquarters and the legal staff

Excerpts from the stenographic transcript follow:

Davis (u): Mr. Metcalf, we have come out to plan an orderly shutdown.

Metcalf (m): If you will talk a little louder; the cat cracker [1] makes such a terrible noise.

Davis (u): I say we have come to plan an orderly shutdown with management.

Metcalf (m): Mr. Parsons has the plan we would like to follow.

Parsons (m): Well, we must be careful to hold our steam load, so we plan on shutting the Dubbs units down first. The flashers will be the first ones and then Dubbs 9, followed by the reformers. Shortly thereafter the topping plant will come down, to be followed by the other operations. We plan next on shutting down the cat cracker. The treating department will have to go on as long as the cat cracker is producing, but just as soon as the products stop coming over, the treaters will be shut down. By the third shift the operating people, with the exception of the boilerhouse and treaters, and most of the maintenance personnel can be released. The alkylation plant shutdown will take about 24 hours. We will want some maintenance men to take care of leaks that might develop.

Davis (u): We have asked all the crews to stand by to be used as needed.

Metcalf (m): We appreciate those instructions, and our thought is to use them only as long as needed to get the units in shape for the standby after the shutdown.

Arnold (u): We are vitally interested in that and we don't want any friction.

Parsons (m): We might discuss here whether we keep men on for the full eight-hour shift or release them as they are finished. It is immaterial to us.

Metcalf (m): Using them for part of a shift, we would probably need them for the entire eight hours.

Arnold (u): That's right. You would want to be sure that everything was done.

Davis (u): Are you going to notify the men through the supervisors?

Parsons (m): Oh, yes. All department managers and assistants will be out on the line during the shutdown, instructing the men as to the units which

---

[1] Abbreviated name for catalytic cracker in which crude oil is refined into various products.

come down first and how fast they should bring them down. There shouldn't be any misunderstanding on that.

Davis (u): Is there anything further, Mr. Metcalf?

Parsons (m): I have one question. Is it your feeling that the men will not work more than eight hours if a marginal half hour would be required to complete the job?

Davis (u): Mr. Parsons, I think that that should be governed by the rule of reason. Have you made any plans about continuing construction of the new plant?

Metcalf (m): I naturally would like to see all construction go on because it will create more jobs later on.

Parsons (m): I think the interest of keeping Pilgrim competitive is mutual because it is a unit which your people are going to run.

Arnold (u): Well, of course, when it appeared this afternoon that it might come to this now, we discussed it with the A. F. of L. building trades. They say they have some mechanics they can't make work behind a picket line. However, where no picket line affects them they don't think they will have any trouble with the membership.

Metcalf (m): I gather from that, Joe, that you don't intend to put pickets up at the road that comes in by the baseball diamond?

Arnold (u): No, sir. Of course, that is the present status. The A. F. of L. will work with us on a twenty-four hour basis.

Chadwick (u): You will be shutting the Hollis pipeline down, Mr. Metcalf? [1]

Metcalf (m): The Hollis pipeline will be shut down. But the crude oil lines will continue to operate until we get the tanks filled up.

Arnold (u): There is another question. A lot of the mechanics have tools in here and all they will have to do is approach the gate and get clearance to get those without any difficulty?

Metcalf (m): Oh, yes. They will be permitted to take their personal tools out.

Arnold (u): As we understand it on the shutdown now, it probably will range between thirty to thirty-six hours.

Metcalf (m): Maximum of forty-eight, Joe. It may take a shorter time, but a maximum of forty-eight because of the cat cracker.

Arnold (u): I see. Maximum forty-eight. Will there be a request for any crews after you are totally down?

Metcalf (m): No. It is our idea to set up crews to take care of emergencies that might arise. The biggest emergency that we could anticipate would be a direct hit by lightning on a tank or something like that; and, of course, we will have staff members operate that part of the boilerhouse generator necessary to provide steam and electricity for lighting and for running water pumps to fight fires with.

---

[1] Mr. Chadwick elaborated upon a "misunderstanding" that delayed shutdown of the Hollis pipeline for some days during a strike in 1945.

Arnold (u): We feel that emergency crews would be the answer. However, management has made a different decision. There will not be any difficulty on plant managers, their assistants, and department heads going back and forth. On any others, the membership feels that they will go and come, if they do, through the picket line without the clearance or goodwill of the organization. Now, that instruction was given to the committee when we left and it was unanimous. That was the procedure used in 1937 when we had another dispute. We felt you should know the membership had taken that action. After all, they are your employees.

Metcalf (m): All of you present remember the difficulties that arose in 1945 with the emergency crews that we requested to stay in. With that experience behind us, we thought that we wouldn't attempt that again. It embarrassed you fellows and it embarrassed the men themselves. So we felt we would use our own men during the shutdown. It is difficult for me to understand why your membership would take a sort of discriminating position with respect to the men in those assignments. As I understand it, you are saying that the top staff members could come and go as they pleased. But those in the other staff positions to whom we assigned jobs couldn't come and go with the goodwill of the membership and the pickets. Why take that position?

Arnold (u): Because the management apparently is increasing the number of employees in the plant during shutdowns. There was immense friction and widespread hard feeling during the last shutdown.

Metcalf (m): Of course, we reduced the number considerably by transferring a great many of them in town—precisely because we didn't think it well to have too many people coming and going. We thought we would confine it to those needed for all emergencies. Now, it is difficult for me to understand why a certain number of those individuals can come and go and the other group cannot. They aren't doing operating jobs.

Arnold (u): We understand that. But you have to be a union man, Mr. Metcalf, to understand how they feel. They are out, and they aren't going to have any income. They want the company's property protected. In fact, they will throw down a picket sign to go in to protect any part of the plant at any time. They always have. There was no fracas except unfortunately in 1937 when some of those who stayed in threw beer bottles out at the pickets. We finally got the authorities to stop that. We had to get the authorities to do it, though. And some of the boys haven't forgotten that, unfortunately.

Now there they are on the picket line, losing pay, and they feel you shouldn't have any hesitancy in walking out to a picket and saying, "I need some help." When a man stands on his principles and makes that sacrifice, he can't feel too kindly toward those who are drawing their pay whether they are actually needed or not—especially when he recalls how in the past some of them have made light of the fact that the union members were picketing in all sorts of weather, and having to lose pay as well, in carrying out a strike.

Right now, moreover, the membership feels so strongly on this because they can't understand why the shutdown is necessary at all. There are now very few plants that aren't under a contract with the union. The other plants are negotiating, and many of the things that we are apart on have been in contracts for years in the other companies in the area. When the members took this action, it was reluctantly. It wasn't hasty. It wasn't vindictive. Each fellow feels like he is forced to fight for his working conditions, while someone else is able to go back and forth and have his income continue without any trouble. Naturally, he can't feel happy about that sort of thing.

Metcalf (m): Perhaps he doesn't, but what right has he to interfere with that other fellow coming and going to his job that is still available? I have 767 men here who are in the nonbargaining group. I am going to use 247 for the various assignments. Now, those men aren't in on this strike, and the jobs that we have for them all along and still have for them are available. It seems to me that they have an individual right, too. Now, your members have decided that they have an individual right. They have decided to strike. These other men haven't struck. So I don't feel that your men have any right to interfere.

I don't think either that it would be right for me to have the whole 767 coming and going. We have made other arrangements for the remainder so that we only have those necessary to protect the company's interests. Now, whether you fellows agree with the number that I have chosen or not, the fact still remains that it is my responsibility and I have decided that that is the number we should have. I would be extremely derelict in my duty if I would agree that part of this group would have to be locked in while others would be permitted to come and go. I just can't see it, Joe.

Arnold (u): Well, I am sure you can't because you are manager of the plant. If you worked out there you would understand better. Since we are still on the record, you said "interfere." We don't say "interfere." We said "goodwill."

Metcalf (m): Well, I will retract the "interfere." You did say "goodwill."

Arnold (u): If any of those people belonged to a union, then they wouldn't feel any obligation to remain in except for absolute emergency needs. Unfortunately, they don't belong to a union, so they feel that if the management says they should be here, their only recourse is to be here.

Metcalf (m): Well, what other objections are you going to raise if I take the position that all of them are to come and go freely on the shifts that I assign them on?

Arnold (u): The only position that we can take would be that they are hurting themselves. If the management wanted a stipulated number of people here regularly, or a stand-by arrangement for emergency, and worked that out with us, that would be one thing. But our fellows feel these jobs are theirs just as property belonging to the management. Some of them have over twenty years' service. That is a big investment, and they can't take it lightly.

Metcalf (m): Yes. I don't deny that. I have about thirty-one years, and being management's representative, I think seriously about the general protection and safety of the millions of dollars' worth of equipment that we have. I am not trying to exaggerate what that responsibility is. I have endeavored to be fair. I would like to mention one other problem, the people living in the staff houses. I presume that those people, while they are living in company houses, will have a right to come and go as they please with the goodwill of your people.

Arnold (u): That was understood and, in fact, was approved by motion.

Metcalf (m): Of course, that also includes the children going to and from school.

Arnold (u): Definitely.

Metcalf (m): Now, at the start we will have some clerical help coming and going to take care of the hourly payroll.

Arnold (u): In other words, the pay procedure will continue and be completed, and you will need people for that.

Regardless of the fact that we don't seem to be together on a portion of the planning, there is one thing that is important. Whether it is an individual or a bus going in, if they will just slow down a little bit instead of giving us dust in the teeth when we are carrying the picket signs, it will help. We would just like to know what you are sending in.

Metcalf (m): I will be responsible for the actions of the people on my side and I assure you I have already mentioned to them that I want them to conduct themselves properly. I don't want them to get into any verbal or any type of clashes with the pickets. I don't want them to kick dust up in their faces or be discourteous in any way. And I, of course, expect you fellows to be responsible for the acts of your people.

Arnold (u): We would like to know of any irregularity. We aren't going to tolerate drinking on the picket line. We aren't going to tolerate any improper acts. Just as we call you if there is anything that isn't proper, we would like for you to call us, and Elmer Smith is going to have the worry of the discipline of the pickets. He is the vice president of the Pilgrim group and is chairman of the strike committee.

Metcalf (m): Does that mean if I have any points to take up with your group that I will contact Smith?

Arnold (u): Yes, sir.

Metcalf (m): I intend to be here to handle those things. In my absence, of course, Mr. Parsons will handle them. May I ask at this stage: When do you plan to put up your pickets?

Arnold (u): Sometime between now and morning, probably 6 or 7 o'clock, something like that.

Metcalf (m): You intend to put your pickets up even before we get the refinery shut down entirely?

Arnold (u): It hasn't been definitely decided yet, but it is felt we should have the pickets in position mainly for observation in the shutting down.

Metcalf (m): Also, do you intend to have pickets on other stations besides the one here at the main entrance?

Arnold (u): The main entrance, the rear gate, the dock gate, and the railroad right of way. The membership has given the committee authority, *if* the management is inclined to work it out, to clear construction material that may be coming in the railroad right of way. If not, then we will just be forced to picket.

Metcalf (m): I don't quite follow you there, with respect to the management's inclination.

Arnold (u): Well, if the management orders cars kicked in there without regard to what is in them, it leaves us no alternative but to picket the right of way. We would like to clear, if we can, anything that is not detrimental to our interests.

Metcalf (m): What do you consider detrimental to your interests?

Arnold (u): Well, making it comfortable for some people that will be drawing pay while we aren't, if you know what I mean. If it is construction material, that is another matter. We are being very frank. We are out there on the picket lines. We don't feel we should pass anything to prolong the strike itself and make it comfortable for someone who has been in the plant.

Metcalf (m): Of course, the men I have chosen to guard the plant will be out there night and day, too, Joe, guarding the plant that you have chosen to shut down.

Arnold (u): I know that. Unfortunately, we are having to fight for them, too.

Metcalf (m): You say you have your responsibility to your men. I have my responsibility to my men.

Arnold (u): Surely. We appreciate that.

Metcalf (m): And I intend to fulfill the responsibility to the fullest.

Arnold (u): Right.

Metcalf (m): I am not threatening by making such a statement.

Arnold (u): No, no.

Metcalf (m): It is a plain statement of facts.

Arnold (u): I think you see now what I meant when I said that if we can't reach an understanding on what comes in by rail, then we will just picket.

Metcalf (m): I hope in our disagreements we don't have any trouble as time goes on.

Chadwick (u): On that, what Joe is trying to say, Mr. Metcalf, is this, that he would propose when cars are to be pushed into this refinery, if it is construction material, the union has no disposition other than to clear it.

Metcalf (m): That was the way the situation was in 1945.

Chadwick (u): Yes. But, when it comes to cars with material that would be detrimental to this shutdown, then that would be another matter. If we can work out an understanding, then most of it is going to be cleared. Otherwise our picket line would be established. That is the only trouble that you would be running into. No clashes at all. Just no traffic if we didn't come to an agreement.

Metcalf (m): You will picket on the railroad right of way?

Chadwick (u): Somewhere where the county road crosses it. If we just tell the Brotherhood that there is an invisible picket sign up there, we don't have to carry it.

Arnold (u): Well, I believe that is all we have now, Mr. Metcalf, unless management has something else.

Metcalf (m): Is it your thought that as soon as we leave this meeting you wish for the plant to shut down?

Arnold (u): That was one of the last questions we were going to ask you. We repeat that we see no reason why we can't settle this dispute. We repeat again that if we can't negotiate it out, we think we should arbitrate. But if management feels the same as they did when we were in conference, then it leaves us no alternative but to ask you if you will begin the shutdowns as soon as the committee leaves.

Chadwick (u): You wouldn't even let Mr. Parsons arbitrate it, would you? [Laughter.]

Metcalf (m): I am afraid I wouldn't let myself arbitrate it.

Arnold (u): We hope the company won't attempt to make transfers or dispositions of products after we shut down, because we are going to make all the contacts we can to let it be known we have a dispute here.

Metcalf (m): Did you understand me when I said that the crude oil pipe lines would continue to run crude in here until we filled the space that we have in the storage tanks? The reason for that is very obvious—that you can't stop an oil well quickly.

Arnold (u): Well, what is the estimated amount of time on that?

Metcalf (m): About thirteen days.

Arnold (u): I am afraid we have hit a snag.

Chadwick (u): Who operates those tanks over there?

Metcalf (m): The pipe line.

Chadwick (u): Those are pipe line tanks and pipe line gauges?

Metcalf (m): That is right.

Arnold (u): Well, we hope that you won't do it, Mr. Metcalf. All we can do is request those who are making that transfer not to make it. They may make it anyway, but we hope you won't do it after the forty-eight hour period.

Metcalf (m): I don't see what harm it would do, Joe, to continue to fill up. That crude would merely come into the tanks and rest there until the strike is over. It is not a product.

Arnold (u): I know, Mr. Metcalf, but if you don't put the crude in here, you will have to put it some place; and we hope you won't try to move it in here. It is natural for us to feel that way. It is going to inconvenience you, but we are going to be inconvenienced, too.

Metcalf (m): Well, I am afraid there is nothing else for the pipe line to do but to put the crude in, Joe. I am afraid it comes down to a conservation problem, conservation of crude oil, and I, for one, would be the last one to interfere with that at the moment.

Arnold (u): Well, I don't suppose we can dispose of that one, and the men are getting anxious, Mr. Metcalf. We would rather that we go ahead and start now so that it will be orderly. If we can't agree on that, why, we just can't agree.

Metcalf (m): Would you excuse me just a moment. Mr. Parsons has a point he wants to discuss.

[Messrs. Metcalf, Parsons, and Flynn, and the representatives of management from headquarters and the legal staff left the conference room.]

Metcalf (m): We have just had a discussion with respect to the railroad feature, and we feel that to clear material car by car is going to be quite a problem. For that reason we are willing to take the position that the materials that will come in will be construction materials and if we deviate from that, we would let you know twenty-four hours ahead of time.

Arnold (u): Well, that poses a problem for us, Mr. Metcalf. There could be a reshuffling of those cars, say, without your personal knowledge and it would appear to be bad faith on your part maybe when you were not aware of that situation happening.

Metcalf (m): It doesn't worry me a bit, Joe, because I believe I am going to be aware of most everything that goes on.

Arnold (u): Suppose we have a chance to go into that fully ourselves, say during the day tomorrow.

Metcalf (m): But there will be materials coming and going in the meantime. I mean coming. Materials going, no. There will be no products.

Arnold (u): Surely. We understand that. All right, sir. I believe that is all we have, then.

Metcalf (m): All right. Then we will start up the machinery to immediately start shutting down.

[The conference was adjourned at 2:55 A.M.]

Discussion Questions

1. Outline the plan of shutdown prepared by the management. List the concerns of each side regarding the period of shutdown as indicated in discussions of this plan; what would you name as mutual concerns, and what as concerns particular to each?

2. What would you say is the strategic value of such a plan of shutdown from the viewpoint of (*a*) protection of property; (*b*) effect on negotiations; (*c*) effect on continuing relationships?

3. Outline and evaluate picketing arrangements, again from viewpoint of (*a*) protection of property; (*b*) conduct of strike; (*c*) effect on continuing relationships.

4. Evaluate Mr. Metcalf's handling of this conference from viewpoint of (*a*) immediate emergency of imminent strikes; (*b*) attempt of union to resume negotiations; (*c*) continuing relationships.

5. What insights do you get as to the relationship between company and union prior to this negotiation and strike?

6. What sentiments are expressed in this case—explicit and implicit—as to status, rights, privileges of stockholders, management, supervisors, unions, and employees?

7. What clues do you derive from this case on the strategy and tactics of Company and Union?

PILGRIM OIL COMPANY (B)

NEGOTIATIONS DURING A STRIKE

I. INTRODUCTION

After the strike at the Crown Point Refinery had run 5 days, the parties convened again at the request of the union. Messrs. Metcalf, Flynn, and Butler represented management. Conciliator Parkman also participated. In addition to the union negotiating committee composed of Messrs. Davis, Arnold, Chadwick, Marsh, Bennett, and Hill, and Regional Representatives Kenny and Warren, a considerable number of union members were present as spectators.

Excerpts follow from the stenographic transcript.

II. FROM THE SESSIONS OF FEBRUARY 18

MORNING SESSION

Conciliator: This conference was arranged, as I understand it, by consultation between the company and the union. I am here to give any assistance possible.

Arnold (u): We shouldn't have any trouble in settling the dispute if the difficulty is as voiced by management. A number of responsible staff members have made the statement that it would be no problem at all to settle the dispute if Arnold were out of the way. With that in mind, I am prepared to resign if the management is prepared to grant these issues proposed by the organization. But if management wasn't in good faith, we think it will clear up quite a lot here.

Flynn (m): I don't know to whom Mr. Arnold is referring. We have never made a proposal that we were agreeable to the union demands on the basis of Arnold's resignation. We reached the end of our negotiations because the remaining items were of a nature that we weren't in position to grant. I am afraid that would have to be our position whether Arnold stayed or left the organization.

Arnold (u): Well, that is unfortunate, Mr. Flynn, because we definitely know the persons who made the statements. We had hoped that management meant it because we would like to settle this dispute.

Since there is quite a bit of discussion among the supervisory group—and we are pretty well posted—we will make another proposal: We believe that we can settle this dispute if the management committee is prepared to let Mr. Ellis (New York headquarters) and Mr. Metcalf take the lead.

Flynn (m): As I said, it is not a question of personalities, on our side. I

321

don't know whether it is from your side. Mr. Ellis and Mr. Metcalf have been in on every decision we have made. Both of them will say they are in agreement with the position we have taken.

Mr. Arnold is referring to statements that are coming to him. I don't mind saying that I have had people tell me: "If Arnold weren't here, it would be easier to reach an agreement." I don't mind saying also that our people in the plant have heard from the outside that if both of us were out, that negotiations would proceed smoothly.

Chadwick (u): Are you making that as a suggestion?

Flynn (m): No. Regardless of personalities, we are talking about a final request from the union that we just aren't in position to grant.

Arnold (u): Management proposed in this negotiation to take out of the contract twenty-two things. Our experience with other companies is that they line up three or four that may be bothersome to them.

Now, another thing, we have arbitrated in this company forty-some cases. The aggregate arbitrations of the six companies we compare with in this area haven't yet reached that number, meaning that they must do a lot of bargaining short of arbitration. Those are relationships of two or three years, while our relationship here has been about fourteen or fifteen years. I wanted to mention that before we went into the actual issues themselves.

Flynn (m): I am glad you did, because I think it does have some significance in connection with our relationship. We did make twenty-two requests for contract changes. Of course, the union made some forty-seven requests. I don't know how you bargain with other people; I don't know whether it is a practice to sign contracts with which everybody seems to be happy, yet on their expiration make demands for wholesale changes. At the end of our negotiations in 1941, we signed a contract that the union committee said was very satisfactory. But we had some forty issues up for negotiation in 1942.

In 1946 we were again presented with some forty contract changes. This year the union started with forty-seven. Now, if that is the way we are to receive requests, I can't see anything but protracted negotiations.

Again, if we are going to arbitrate anybody's grievance on the theory that there is nothing to lose and there is always a chance the average arbitrator will try to find some middle ground, that is something we can't control. When we don't feel that the request is justified, we are going to have to resist it even though it means arbitration.

We have bargaining relationships under some sixty contracts in the United States. And we have more trouble negotiating a contract in Crown Point, more trouble administering a contract, more arbitration cases, than anywhere else in the country. Now, I don't think that policies vary that much from one location to another. It still is the same company, the same top management, the same outfit who ultimately pays the bill on anything we agree on.

Arnold (u): In our local union we have four other contracts. In two of them, most of these issues have been settled for a year or two. In three of them, relationships now, even in two or three years, have developed to the point that grievances are settled by telephone without even being put in writing. With us, too, these are the same people and the same local union with which you say Pilgrim has such trouble.

Davis (u): You say we take up any grievance without any justification and arbitrate it. I would like to point out that we have won our share of the arbitrations; and, if there wasn't any justification, I don't understand how we would have won our share of them.

Flynn (m): By the wording of your own organization's booklet, you are instructed to go through a contract with a fine tooth comb and find language that will apply. So long as that is the attitude, we can reasonably expect grievances to arise and go to arbitration.

Chadwick (u): Did you say that you ran across a book of instruction in our organization wherein people were instructed to go through the contract with a fine tooth comb?

Flynn (m): Yes. It is a booklet put out by your international: *How to Win with the Union.*

Chadwick (u): I am fully acquainted and most of the rest of the people here are acquainted with that booklet. It is a book of instructions on how to proceed with grievances under a contract. It does advise people that, before they make a grievance, they familiarize themselves with the wording of the contract so that they will know whether they have a grievance. There is no book of instructions that does, or was intended to, cause people to make grievances on the technicality of wording which are not founded in principle. I think that probably we will want to read that book into the record before this is over to show exactly what was intended and what it says.

Flynn (m): I don't want to belabor the point. However, it does contain some very unfortunate language that the idea is to win the grievance somehow. However, that is a little bit away from the negotiation of this contract.

Chadwick (u): I don't think it is a side conversation since you made that statement before all this group.

Conciliator: May I ask this question? Some reference was made to forty arbitrations. Was that during the whole period of your relationships? In fourteen or fifteen years?

Arnold (u): Yes.

Davis (u): Well, Mr. Flynn, if we are through discussing that, we would like to start off on these issues.

Flynn (m): Fine.

[Davis thereupon reviewed the fourteen to eighteen—the figure differed according to the manner of grouping related items—issues still remaining in dispute between the parties. His review concluded the morning sessions.]

AFTERNOON SESSION [1]

Chadwick (u): Mr. Flynn, we also wanted to discuss that speech you made to the gallery about this little book that we put out.

---

[1] At the opening of the session, Mr. Davis reported to Mr. Metcalf complaints from union pickets on the excessive speed at which cars had been driving into and out of the plant. Mr. Metcalf replied that he had noticed this and had instructed the company

Flynn (m): You want to do that now or after I complete my answer to Davis' review of area practice on the outstanding issues?

Chadwick (u): Well, we would rather wait until after your answer.

Flynn (m): At the morning session considerable time was spent in discussing area practice. When we consider the competitive industry we have always spoken of the six refineries of the major companies in this area. Five of them have contracts with your union. What I will have to say will be restricted to those companies. They are the big plants and the big companies, so if there is any such thing as a pattern, they would be a representative group.

In the negotiations and in the press, considerable space has been devoted to the fact that Pilgrim is out of line with industry practice. It is difficult for us to understand such a charge. Maybe we haven't done a very good selling job in acquainting our people with what they have received over a long period of time in benefits.

To start off, our savings fund enables a man to invest 10% of his money and double that investment through company contributions plus interest; it enables him to lay up a nest egg that I don't think is touched anywhere in any industry. Our pension plan is one of the few in the oil industry at no cost to employees. Most plans have some contribution from the employee. On vacations, we are the *only* one with two weeks' vacation with pay for one year of service.

Holidays: we have agreed in this negotiation to four paid holidays if an employee is scheduled to work but is not used. Those same holidays are paid at double time if the employee works. Of course, on two additional holidays we pay time and one-half for hours worked. One company has six paid holidays and another has four. But in both of those companies, employees who work receive time and a half instead of double time. Another company pays straight time on three holidays scheduled and double time for hours worked. Still another pays straight time on two holidays scheduled and double time if worked. The remaining company has no paid holidays as such, and pays time and one-half for work done on six holidays.

We have agreed to allow an employee time off with pay in case of death in the immediate family. Among the other five companies only one has such a provision.

We pay time and a half for hours worked on the sixth day worked, double time for hours worked in the seventh day worked. Only one other company has this same provision.

Pilgrim pays time and a half for all hours worked on the first day of a changed schedule, with limited exceptions. Of the five other companies, only one has a similar provision except that their provision does not apply if the schedule change is due to vacation relief.

I think we are the only company in the area that doesn't have some type

---

guards to keep the gates "down," so that cars would have to stop. He urged the union to let him know of any further complaints.

of probationary period for new employees. We had proposed a probationary period; but in an attempt to reach a settlement, we have dropped our request.

Now to get to issues still in dispute: first is the composition of the Workmen's Committee and your request that union officers who aren't Pilgrim employees be permitted to attend regular grievance meetings. All of the contracts of these five companies dealing with your union provide that committeemen be member employees. None of them provides for attendance of nonemployee union officers.

Chadwick (u): Mr. Flynn, we know that no contract has that provision in it. But no other company raises any question if any officer is requested by the committee to attend. Ever since we have had our relationship here, we have had to secure permission each time for each individual officer to attend.

Flynn (m): I think that is correct, Burt.

Chadwick (u): And the only reason that we have asked to include this is that their contracts read the same as yours, but your practice is different.

Flynn (m): You are asking us to contract that right to you and I am saying that I have analyzed the contracts and given you my best information based on that analysis.

Chadwick (u): Would you be willing to state here that you will practice the same thing that they do, if we withdraw our request for writing it into the contract?

Flynn (m): You mean without restriction?

Chadwick (u): Any time the committee requests the presence of officers— as is the practice in other companies.

Flynn (m): I wouldn't be willing.

The next subject is committee pay. Other companies do pay some negotiating pay. However, we go further than any other company in paying for attendance at grievance meetings. We do pay also for time lost the first day of a negotiating meeting called by the company.

On the wage reopening, we feel that at the time of entering into a contract the union should join the company in guaranteeing that those wages remain effective for the period of the agreement. The union, however, has proposed that they could open wages and strike the plants if no agreement was reached. As to area practice, two companies have no wage reopening. Two companies have contracts providing for wage reopening, and one agrees that wages shall be discussed six months after the signing of the agreement.

The next subject is check-off. In two contracts no provision is made for check-off. Two companies have a voluntary revocable check-off. And one has a voluntary, irrevocable check-off.

Next is the subject of arbitration of qualifications for new plants. Of course, you can arbitrate the propriety of classifications. In all the other companies, management determines job qualifications and classifications for new plants, and only in one does the general right of union protest up to and through arbitration set no specific exclusion for this type of controversy.

Next we come to arbitration of rates involving alleged intraplant or interplant inequities. With the exception of one company, no other agreement permits arbitration of such inequities.

Now, as to arbitration on rates based on changes in job content: Two companies have a contract provision which calls for the arbitration of rates resulting from changes of job content. That has been an endless headache to one of these companies and, perhaps people on the other side of the table will agree, to the union as well.

One more general item—the general wage adjustment. We had information that there were wage settlements in effect in three companies: Amtex, Rio, and Alstate. Our final offer before the strike is as good or better than any of these settlements.

That just about covers the matter of area practice. It should be sufficient to point out that there is no such thing as an area practice. No two contracts are identical; each company does the best job of negotiating on specific items. In other words, we have to look at the entire picture when we decide if we can go along with a request to add still another encumbrance in the contract. We are proud that we do for our employees as much or more than most other companies do. We want it to be that way. All of you know a good many of these policies have been extended without any request on the part of the union at all. But we just don't feel that we are under an obligation to meet the best conditions that can be selected here and there from other people's contracts.

I think it is your duty to weigh very carefully what we do for our employees as against what other people do for their employees. I don't believe that you will come up with an answer that we are stingy, that we are trying to chisel on what is commonly done.

Conciliator: Are there any other points of comparison the union would like to explore?

Arnold (u): We would like to make some comments at this time. First, there is only one plant in the area where the bargaining agency was won by the union earlier than at Pilgrim. That is Amtex. Some of the companies being compared have as low as three years of contractual relations. Practically none of the companies like to pioneer on more than one or two things at a time. When you weigh a three-year relationship and its accomplishment against 14 years, it gives you an idea of why some of the other contracts may not have yet been brought up to the standards of others.

[Mr. Arnold thereupon answered at some length Flynn's survey of comparative area conditions. He pointed out the union had withdrawn its requests for liberalized sick-leave benefits and vacations and that liberalized holiday provisions granted during the negotiations were "a little light" in view of "potentialities" in other negotiations under way. With regard to pay for workmen's committees, and qualifications for new plants, he urged that explicit contract provisions did not tell the whole story since customary practice on these matters generally supported the union's position. Finally he insisted that every major company in the area but Pilgrim "had either a voluntary revocable or a voluntary irrevocable check-off."]

Davis (u): Well, Mr. Parkman, if Mr. Flynn doesn't have anything else, may we get our committeemen straightened out on this booklet about handling grievances?

Chadwick (u): What page of this book were you quoting from this morning?

Flynn (m): On page thirty.

Naturally, the steward should always be ready to give a union member the benefit of the doubt on all borderline cases.

The steward's greatest difficulty will come on grievances which do not appear to be covered by the terms of the contract. . . . In such a situation, the steward, or plant committeeman, goes through his contract with a fine-tooth comb to find some provision which will cover this particular situation. . . . In practically all cases where a worker has a legitimate complaint it will be possible to find some clause of the contract which, with a little pulling and hauling, can be made to cover the situation. Lawyers have been able to use a Constitution written over one-hundred fifty years ago to cover the complex issues of modern life. A bright steward should be able to do just about as well with his contract.

Now, I am not purporting to say what is meant by that. I say this: I think it is unfortunate language and unfortunate advice that we feel has been followed in a lot of grievances.

Chadwick (u): To begin with, I am sure that you read what went before that page.

Flynn (m): Yes.

Chadwick (u): But you didn't quote it this morning.

Flynn (m): No. ·

Chadwick (u): But the people who were listening to you this morning may not have read all the things in this book like this:

Don't give your foreman reason to believe that you are trying to bluff him. A reputation for honesty and good judgment is essential to your success in collective bargaining.

Then further,

No grievance should be made an issue between the union and management before complete information concerning the case is available to union negotiators. Too often, good union people have pounded the table, threatened drastic action on a grievance—only to find that their picture of the situation was incomplete or inaccurate. And management has always been quick to swing the axe when the union's neck is stuck out.

[Laughter.]

On page twenty-eight:

If you are not sure you have a full picture of the situation, take things easy until you hear the foreman's side of the case. For instance, one of the men in your department comes to you with the complaint that he has been transferred to a new job and had his rate cut 10 cents per hour. . . .

You may find from the foreman that the man was demoted because there was no work on his old job and that he is being paid the proper rate on his new job. If that is true, then you have no reason to take action. There is no grievance.

Now, we are reading these to show you that the union is advising people not to take up unfounded grievances.

Flynn (m): Keep reading on that page.

Chadwick (u):

It should be remembered, of course, that where there is conflict of testimony—your man saying one thing, the foreman the opposite—the testimony of your man should be accepted as correct. A steward's job is to represent his man, not act as an impartial arbitrator.

All right. Many times we have told you that as long as there is any doubt as to whether the man had a grievance, we were bound to push it until you proved to us that he didn't have, and we will always do that.

Further, on page twenty-nine:

Obviously, when a complaint is not founded on facts, the steward is making a dangerous mistake in trying to make a grievance out of it. By so doing he damages the union's position both with the union membership and plant management. The workers are led to expect results when none could possibly be obtained, and the union's reliability is discredited with management.

As to the practice of pulling and hauling to see if something is or isn't covered, I would guess that might have been written by men who worked with Pilgrim about nine years ago [laughter] when that practice was invented by your top executive in charge of the refinery before Mr. Metcalf came on the job. [Laughter.] You, Mr. Flynn, had to carry it out for him.

We aren't going to deny that we have people every now and then who try to pull and haul. We have a problem trying to correct it. But you have got foremen who react to every grievance as if it is a personal affront to their integrity and good intentions. And they start looking through the contract, combing it with that fine-tooth comb, and pulling it and hauling it, to see if they can't get a hole big enough to get out through. Taken over-all, we feel that this book has instructed stewards in good, sound union practices.

Flynn (m): All I was saying, Burt, was I think some of your boys read page thirty to the exclusion of page twenty-two . . .

Chadwick (u): We just wondered how you pulled it and hauled it to make that charge up. [Laughter.]

Conciliator: Well, gentlemen, I don't know how you desire to proceed here. You got that question, I presume, out of the way. [Laughter.]

Davis (u): Mr. Parkman, we would like a short recess.

[Brief recess.]

Davis (u): Mr. Flynn, we have got a couple of things here we want to throw out on the table for your consideration.

[The union thereupon advanced two compromise proposals on (1) the determination of qualifications for jobs in new plants, and (2) the accrual of seniority on temporary assignments. The union also asked fuller answer on its demands for automatic promotion in the engineering field and the furnishing of tools to machinists and carpenters. The conference was adjourned with the agreement that next morning consideration would be given to the proposals made during the current day's sessions.]

III. FROM THE SESSIONS OF FEBRUARY 19

[When the discussions opened, Mr. Arnold was not in attendance, and no "spectators" were present from the union membership. The union was represented by four local negotiators, participants from the start—Messrs. Davis, Chadwick, Marsh, and Hill—and Regional Representative Martin Kenny.]

Conciliator: Well, in our meeting yesterday the company, I believe, took under advisement three or four proposals or suggestions made by the union.

[Mr. Flynn reported on the company's inquiries into area practice on the four issues raised by the union. On none did area practice support the union's proposals, management concluded, while some of the proposals involved serious operating problems. Management accordingly was not disposed to accept any of these proposals. After this review and the exchanges upon it, the discussion continued as follows:]

Chadwick (u): In this letter which you mailed out to all employees yesterday, you say in the last paragraph:

I want you to know also that we sincerely regret that this strike has taken place. It means hardship to you and your families and a substantial loss to the company. It is my hope that it can be amicably settled and that you can return to your jobs in the not too distant future.

Now, we likewise are desirous of settling this thing. We have come back after it seemed there wasn't much prospect of settling things and have changed our position on a number of issues. The company also has moved mainly on proposals they presented themselves, which were, as we see it, presented for trading purposes mostly—for the purpose of withdrawing them to make their position look better to all interested parties, including the employees. But we are down now to the essential factors; we have fourteen items remaining. The last three meetings have been consumed with the union changing its position to get something started. So far, we haven't seen the management even make the slightest move. So it looks like it is somebody else's move at this time.

Flynn (m): We did propose twenty-two items. The mere fact that six of them have been agreed to is some indication those were not hogwash. As to our right to put in counterproposals for trading purposes, you are no novice at collective bargaining. You have withdrawn a good many of those you put in.

[Mr. Flynn then reviewed the union's demands in terms of those that had been, during the negotiations, withdrawn, settled by agreement, or compromised.]

Flynn (m): Each union proposal on which agreement has been reached constitutes a concession that is very substantial. To be perfectly frank, under less serious circumstances than a threatened shutdown, a good many would probably not have been granted voluntarily.

I will agree that since the strike we have been able to arrive at practically nothing that would bring us closer together. But that is why we went as far as we could before the strike.

Chadwick (u): Well, in your letter and in your statements to the paper, you have gone into great detail to explain the fairness of all your proposals. Now, if you feel that can be backed up, why are you unwilling to submit them as we have requested to a tri-partite panel of three people, one chosen by you, one by us, and one or more by the two so selected?

Flynn (m): Well, Burt, we have said in the letter that we aren't opposed to the principle of arbitration. Once we have entered into an agreement, we are willing to go to arbitration for any disputes arising out of its application or interpretation. But what you are asking now is to allow a third party to tell us, the principals, what the terms and conditions of that bargaining should be. We aren't agreeable to that type of arbitration. The job of the arbitrator is to make his decisions on the contract; otherwise he has no standard by which to be guided except his own ideas.

Chadwick (u): The law gives us the right to bargain collectively with respect to hours of work, rates of pay, and working conditions in that plant. Although we don't own any of Pilgrim's stock, nevertheless, to the extent that the law gives us the right to bargain with respect to working conditions in the plant, we own a part of that house. That is why we think our differences as co-owners become a matter of equity and subject for arbitration.

Flynn (m): This company will never agree voluntarily to substitute arbitration for collective bargaining. You spoke a while ago about sticking some demands in for trading purposes. If the parties know arbitration lies ahead, you come into negotiations with twenty-four times as much as you expect to get from anybody. You simply enlarge your demands and let everything go to arbitration, hoping the arbitrator will "split the difference."

Don't forget that of all the issues that are left only one is our original request; the balance are all union requests. Anything further that you would get out of the arbitration panel would be concessions to you, not to us.

[After further discussion and efforts by the conciliator, it became increasingly clear that neither side was prepared to offer further concessions. The conference thereupon was adjourned at 5:10 P.M. until further notice.]

IV. The Settlement

The strike lasted for 64 days. Negotiations were resumed during the last week at Parkman's initiative, and after he had held exploratory conversations with each side. Raymond, manager of industrial relations from the Corporation headquarters, led the management representatives, and the international president of the union led the union delegation. Neither Mr. Flynn nor Mr. Arnold participated. Conferences were held on April 11, 12, 15, and 16. No stenographic transcript was made of these final meetings. A strike settlement was drawn up on April 16. After the members had ratified this proposed settlement, the "Articles of Agreement" were signed on April 18.

A summary of the major provisions of the settlement follows. The notations in brackets after each provision give the final offer made before the strike.

I. WAGES

1. *General Wage Increase.* A cost of living increase to all employees of 22 cents per hour retroactively effective to January 18, and continuing until December 31 unless wages are reopened by either party after 120 days from the date of the Agreement. Whether or not notice of reopening is given, the parties shall, within the 60-day period prior to December 31, enter into negotiations with respect to the continuation, modification, or elimination of the 22 cent per hour cost of living increase; and should they fail to reach an agreement, the entire agreement is terminated as of 11:59 P.M. on December 31.

[This represented the final company offer just before the strike vote.]

2. *Rate Adjustments.* Sixty-one specified increases in individual classification rates.

[This represented 15 additional increases.]

3. *Reclassifications.* Five reclassifications of operating jobs.

[This represented two additional increases.]

II. NONWAGE ITEMS

1. Departmental seniority gained on semipermanent assignments shall not stand in the way of other employees with three months' operating experience claiming permanent vacancies in the starting job on the basis of plant seniority.

[This represented a compromise.]

2. The provisions concerning new plants shall be revised to provide:
a. Classification shall be discussed with the Workmen's Committee. In the event of disagreement the question of whether the employees are properly classified may be submitted to arbitration.

[In essence this represented the company's position *on job classifications* in new plants, which management was willing to submit to grievance procedure up to and including arbitration "because . . . in new plants they aren't jobs that are in existence at the time of the effective contract."]

b. *Qualifications*—the standard qualifications for jobs in the new plant shall be:
For all jobs—high school education or equivalent.
For operator No. 1—six months' prior experience as operator No. 1 or 12 months' experience as operator No. 2.
For operator No. 2—six months' prior experience as operator No. 2 or 12 months of operating experience in the next lower classification.
For any lower paid job above the starting job—six months' prior operating experience.
If, in the opinion of the management, qualifications greater than those listed above are required, management will notify the Workmen's Committee. If no agreement is reached, the selections will be made in accordance with the management's plan, and the matter may be made the subject of negotiations at *any* time the contract is opened.

[Again, this essentially spelled out the company's position on "standard qualifications." Management did, however, now agree to consult with the union at any time these hiring qualifications would be exceeded for new plants.]

3. A plan will be set up whereby each second class craftsman will be automatically promoted to first class craftsman at the end of four years' service in the craft, provided he has had at least one year's service as a second class craftsman and is capable of performing first class work. There shall be no distinction between the work assignments of first and second class craftsmen, as the latter are in training for promotion.

[This represented an approach toward establishing the union's demand for automatic upgrading of craftsmen and for elimination of the distinction between work assignments.]

4. A provision permitting basic wage rates to be reopened for negotiation at any time after 120 days from the date the new contract is signed. If no agreement is reached within 60 days from the date notice of reopening is given, either party shall have the right to terminate the entire agreement on 48 hours' written notice given within the 10 days following the expiration of the 60 days' negotiation period.

[This modified the company's final prestrike position on contract reopening chiefly by providing that cancellation of the entire agreement on failure to agree upon basic wage rates had to be effected by notice within a stipulated time limit. The obligation not to strike or lockout was also explicitly affirmed, as the company had demanded.]

5. The prior provision concerning payment to Workmen's Committee members for time spent in meetings with management shall remain unchanged; except that payment for time lost shall be made to a complainant and necessary witnesses in attending the regular monthly grievance meeting.

[The union thus failed to obtain its central demand of pay for negotiating time; it received a new grant of such pay for complainants and witnesses losing time via participation in grievance procedures.]

6. The new contract will contain a voluntary, revocable checkoff.

[By their final positions before the strike on this issue, the union had demanded a voluntary irrevocable checkoff; the company had refused any form of checkoff. Two other demands of the union were withdrawn in the final settlement: (a) provision for the arbitration of alleged interplant and intraplant wage rate inequities during the life of the contract, and (b) authorization of a nonemployee union representative to participate in the grievance machinery prior to arbitration.]

III. Other Nonwage Items Agreed upon before the Strike

1. Extension of the period during which a laid-off employee's seniority rights are protected from 120 to 180 days.

2. Revision of the provision concerning subdepartmental seniority to insure that the youngest man in the entire department is the one laid off in the event of

a reduction in force; and to provide for the rehiring of an employee having seniority rights in any subdepartment to fill the first opening in the entire department.

3. Revision of the requirements for posting promotions and vacancies to permit an employee on vacation or leave of absence to bid on openings occurring while he is away.

4. Payment of time and one-half for all hours worked in excess of eight in any 24 hour period.

5. Payment of straight time for four (4) holidays per year if scheduled and not worked and double time if worked; payment of time and one-half for work on two additional holidays.

6. Extension from two to three weeks of the time limit on one step of the grievance procedure.

7. Liberalization of the provision concerning leaves of absence for union business.

8. Provision for more and enlarged union bulletin boards.

9. Revision of the provision concerning complaint letters to provide for the arbitration of the contents of the letter if any disciplinary action is subsequently based thereon.

10. Provision for protecting the normal earnings of an employee subpoenaed to serve as court witness.

11. Increase in the overtime meal allowance from 50 cents to 70 cents per meal.

12. Provision granting compensation for damage suffered to clothing because of work accidents if loss immediately reported to foreman and clothing surrendered.

13. Provision for time off with pay to attend the funeral of a member of an employee's immediate family.

14. Renewal of the maintenance-of-membership clause with new 15-day escape period.

Discussion Questions

1. What, on the basis of this case, would you say about the influence of personality in developing relationships?

2. How would you interpret the union's request for the meeting five days after the strike?

3. Evaluate the discussion by the parties on arbitration of the outstanding differences in the negotiations.

4. Evaluate the discussion on the shop stewards' manual from the viewpoint of (a) a training tool for shop stewards; (b) management's reaction to the manual; (c) Mr. Flynn's objectives—and effectiveness—in introducing it in these sessions; (d) the union's response to Mr. Flynn's criticism.

5. In view of the terms of the strike settlement, what clues would you pursue to get a more complete understanding of the strategy and tactics employed by the parties?

6. In what structure of relationship would you place management-union relationships at the Pilgrim Company? What interrelations do you see in this discussion among negotiations, grievances, and arbitration?

APPALACHIAN CHEMICALS COMPANY [1]

THE LAST NEGOTIATING SESSION ON THE EVE OF STRIKE

I

The two-year contract between the Appalachian Chemicals Company and the General Workers Union, covering two plants in Ashland, Kentucky, and Norton, Virginia, was open for renegotiation in May 1952. Wages had been raised twice, in December 1950, by 6 cents an hour, and in 1951 by 5½%. From May 6 to May 16, the parties negotiated almost daily. As usual, numerous large and costly demands were put forth. Until 1952, however, each negotiation had eventually been consummated by an agreement, not without the occasional intervention of the Federal Mediation and Conciliation Service.

The company was in a profitable but highly competitive market. Like so many companies in the South, it had operated until 1941 on a non-union basis. Having enjoyed satisfactory relations with its employees for some thirty years, it was surprised at the militancy which accompanied the advent of the union.

The list of demands presented by the union covered 23 pages. It included, in addition to a wage increase, some 63 contract changes, such as the application of seniority in promotions, demotions, transfers, and recalls; the freezing of the size of crews and the number of job classifications; the union shop; union representation on safety committees; and the presence of a shop steward when foremen contacted employees for overtime work caused by unexpected absences.

The company submitted 15 contract changes, such as the removal of guards, watchmen, and certain hourly paid supervisors from the bargaining unit; the elimination of pay for time not worked in connection with the division of overtime on the basis of the seniority roster; penalties for absenteeism, especially before and after holidays; time limits on grievance procedure; and changes in the application of seniority.

After 10 days of fruitless discussion, the union asked that negotiations be focussed on "money" items. To management's request for classification of the union's demand for a "substantial wage increase," Mr. Heath, the union's district director, replied, "Thirty cents per hour." Management's negotiators pointed out that that would cost some $3,000,000 per year, and that other proposals on wage supplements and fringe benefits would raise this figure to well over 70 cents per hour, or over $7,000,000 per year—plus the undetermined pension and insurance demands.

---

[1] Names of persons, places, the company, and the union have been disguised.

The union, nevertheless, pressed for an offer on "money" items. On May 16, the company presented the following "package":

1. Remove guards and certain hourly paid supervisors from the bargaining unit, with protection of seniority for the supervisors if they return to unit.

2. Provide better liaison with shop stewards in division of overtime but eliminate payment for time not worked in connection therewith.

3. Require employees to work all scheduled hours from 48 hours before until 48 hours after paid holiday, in order to be eligible for holiday pay.

4. Make absence, without justifiable cause, for more than seven consecutive scheduled workdays a reason for termination of employment.

5. Require arbitration cases to be heard within 60 days, unless arbitrator unable to set hearing within that time.

6. Equalize second- and third-shift differentials for day workers with those applying to shift workers.

7. Provide six months' protection of existing seniority in prior department or job in case of company-required transfers.

8. Provide for continuation of Job Evaluation Program according to existing agreement.

9. Guarantee pay on day of injury for employee injured on job.

10. Increase shift differential from 2 cents to 3 cents on second shift and from 4 cents to 5 cents on third shift.

11. Add one additional paid holiday (bringing total to five).

12. Increase wages 3 cents an hour across the board.

After studying this proposal and discussing it in caucus with the union, Heath asked whether the company would insist on "contract" changes *if* the parties could agree on "money." To avoid any misunderstanding about its position, the company prepared the following reply:

In view of the union's position thus far in the negotiations, we are adhering to the position we took in presenting our package proposal this morning. We look upon collective bargaining as just what the term implies. We feel that bargaining implies give-and-take on both sides. As we understand your question, you are inferring that the company should do all of the giving and that the union should do none. We do not believe this is the proper procedure. Therefore, we feel that monetary issues should not be divorced from contract issues in working toward final settlement of the agreement.

Heath closed his notebook and declared the negotiations "adjourned." The company stated that it was ready to continue at any time, and asked the union when it would like to resume. Heath replied he didn't know whether negotiations would be resumed.

Late in May, meetings were resumed for a week on the initiative of the Federal Mediation and Conciliation Service. Again agreement could not be reached; and, on May 29, the sessions were adjourned subject to recall. During the sessions the company had increased its across-the-board wage offer to 4 cents, or 2.6%, at the union's choice; added a sixth paid holiday with time and a half for five holidays if worked; and increased shift differentials to 4 cents and 6 cents. The money offers, however, were contingent on the union's acceptance of three company proposals: (1) elimination of the guards from the bargaining unit; (2) eligibility for holiday pay to be dependent on working as scheduled in the 48-hour periods preceding and following the holiday; (3) provision for better liaison between foremen and shop stewards in the equal division of overtime, eliminating however any payment for time not worked.

On June 9, a second attempt at mediation produced no significant concessions by either party.

The final session was held on June 18, again at the mediator's request. Excerpts from the record follow:

II

The Final Session: June 18–19
2:45 P.M. to 1:48 A.M.

The meeting was held in Washington, D.C., before Randolph H. Claybourne, Federal Mediation and Conciliation Service commissioner.

Present for the Company

William J. Warren	Director of Industrial Relations
Richard M. Johnston	Assistant Plant Manager ⎤ Ashland Plant, Kentucky
Allan G. Stanton	Personnel Manager ⎦
Robert H. Parker	Personnel Manager, Norton Plant, Virginia

Present for the Union

James L. Francis	International Union President
Joseph L. Perrino	International Union Secretary-Treasurer
Kenneth S. Heath	Area Director, Kentucky
George Roberts	Area Director, Virginia
Roger Madison	President ⎤
Guy Henderson	Vice President ⎥ Ashland Local
Malcolm Burke	Committeeman ⎥
Rusty Clark	Committeeman ⎦
Arthur Billings	President ⎤ Norton Local
Henry Dustin, Sr.	Vice President ⎦

Claybourne: At the conclusion of our last meeting, June 9, I urged every possible consideration for agreement. The union is to be commended for not calling a strike. My talks with both sides separately this morning indicated that both sides have made a very determined effort to see what specific further concessions can be made.

Francis (u): First, let me say that any discussion on the other unresolved issues had to be predicated on the assumption that the company could move on the question of a general wage increase. To discuss the other issues with no such possibility would be a waste of time.

Warren (m): Certainly we didn't understand that our coming down here would lead to any assumption that we were changing our offer on the general increase.

Francis (u): We are perfectly willing to discuss compromises. But, if the company expects us to hand over our swords, they got the wrong people, because a strike vote exists.

Claybourne: Bill, under those conditions, I suggest a caucus, unless there is something you might want to say across the table.

Warren (m): Suppose I put on the table what we indicated to you, Mr. Claybourne, this morning. The company looked over its offer to see where it might be possible to extend a little bit in order to try to reach an agreement.

If it would mean an agreement, we would be willing to eliminate the proposal that time worked on the sixth holiday be straight time and we would allow time and a half like the other five holidays.

On the provision requiring employees to work 48 hours before and after the holiday, the company would be willing to cut that to 24 hours.

On the question of the guards—at the last session, Joe Perrino mentioned that, if the company had any legal remedy on this, it perhaps should go to law rather than to the bargaining table. Naturally, we have been looking into the alternatives. One way would be a petition to the NLRB to remove the guards from the existing bargaining unit. That certainly doesn't seem very attractive to either party. If we agreed to a new contract with guards included in the existing bargaining unit, we would be precluded from taking any legal action during the life of that agreement. So another possibility presents itself: to have some provision in the agreement stating that a dispute exists on this point, and reserving the right to have such a determination through NLRB proceedings. That probably would run into a number of undesirable pitfalls. A third way is to agree that guards are not included in this agreement, which seems to be the best way to do it. It might be possible to have some machinery set up for arbitration of the matter in case a dispute arises.

Francis (u): Your comments, Bill, are all well and good—but the fact remains that the union, frankly, can't discuss a settlement until you tell us whether the door is closed on the wage question. Otherwise we are wasting our time.

Frankly, we don't want to strike. We have been put to a lot of trouble. The other night I drove 400 miles, half of it in a fog, to go up and be sure that we had a vote for a strike at Norton; and we got it. Do you think I like to do that?

Claybourne: I apologize for bringing the parties together without a complete understanding. I would certainly suggest that we go back for further caucus; and I can get a more complete picture from the company perhaps, which I agree I should have done in the first place.

[Recess at 3:20 P.M. Session resumed at 9 P.M.]

Claybourne: We started off today's session with the idea of exploring the possibility of reaching some agreement on this guards and watchmen issue. So perhaps we could resume on that.

Francis (u): We feel that the company has introduced a relatively un-important subject and created a major issue over it. The men don't want to work under a Gestapo. Anything done in regard to the watchmen, except leaving them exactly as they are, is going to result in armed men patrolling the working areas—in effect spying upon the people on the job and, possibly, on the supervisors. The word *guard,* of course, also carries the implication that they are going to be armed. So, if there would be a separation of duties—because fire watching and insurance protection do require moving around through working areas—then, the union could possibly agree that guards doing this kind of work be separated from the union.

According to the figures I got from the committee, there are 20 to 23 at Ashland doing a combined job of guarding and watching. Let those people divide up this dual responsibility. Then, those with the sole responsibility and obligations of guarding could by agreement be eliminated from the union. The same thing holds true of Norton.

Warren (m): Jim, we have no intention of setting up an armed Gestapo, or anything like that. Most of your contracts with other companies that I have seen exclude guards and watchmen. And, as far as I know, you haven't run into any Gestapo.

This proposal to split duties is a little unrealistic. It seems only logical that the men who are making the rounds for fire insurance should also have the authority of enforcing the rules, as provided in Taft-Hartley "For the protection of property and the safety of persons."

Francis (u): I don't know how many you checked. Of course, the 75 or 80 contracts that we have won by elections since 1947 naturally excluded it, because under the T-H procedures they were excluded. It happens that we have around 270 contracts. And, in the ones that we had before 1947, we had the watchmen in.

Madison (u): Another thing, in these companies you are talking about, do they wear the uniforms and gun and so forth?

Warren (m): I don't know.

Madison (u): Why do you want them going through the plant wearing a uniform?

Warren (m): Who said anything about their going through the plant wearing a uniform?

Madison (u): We have been told that's what you are preparing for. Put the cards on the table. We have had no denial from you yet.

Henderson (u): The uniform doesn't make any difference, but if he has a gun—that is enough. They just don't want to say that they can't put the pressure on a watchman if he is in our bargaining unit.

Roberts (u): Bill, is your position as to the guards determined on the basis of the needs of the company, or is it what you read in some other contracts?

Warren (m): The needs of the company. We looked at other contracts to see whether it is something that is being done in other places.

Francis (u): If the needs of the company is a fair basis for a decision, we ought to look for the needs of the people. There hasn't been a hell of a lot of consideration given to them in these discussions we have had here.

The United States Government suddenly recognized that there were needs of people on retirement. Social Security benefits are going to be increased by the government $5 to $6 a month for practically everybody covered on account of the increased cost of living. What consideration has the company given to increasing the pension? Will it be increased automatically by that $5 to $6 a month? Just once I would like to have the company pop up with something that we didn't have to scream and clutch our throats and demand. You know that Social Security is going to be increased $5 or $6 a month?

Warren (m): Yes.

Francis (u): And I presume that, under the provisions of the pension plan, that the people at Appalachian will be getting exactly the same thing in November as they are now. Is that right?

Warren (m): That is what the plan provides.

Perrino (u): Well, it could be changed.

Warren (m): It could be changed by mutual agreement.

Perrino (u): Is the company disposed to make any changes?

Warren (m): Not at this time.

Perrino (u): Would you like to take more contracts and also look at some of the other provisions and be bound by all that is in them?

Warren (m): No. As I said, I was merely checking to see whether you had other contracts which excluded guards and watchmen.

Perrino (u): You mean that 10 contracts prove your point?

Warren (m): I wasn't taking a popularity poll. As I told you, I was merely checking the point to determine whether your union had contracts which excluded guards and watchmen.

Perrino (u): One would presume that these guys who come to these tables know what they are talking about. I was just testing your logic, Bill. Your reasoning is kind of bankrupt, I might say.

Warren (m): An examination of the duties of these men might throw light on our position. Would you like to go into the duties at Ashland, Allan?

Stanton (m): We expect these men to report certain things at the main counter as they make their rounds.

Madison (u): What do you mean, certain things?

Stanton (m): Drunkenness or drinking on the part of either employees or outsiders; theft or attempted theft by employees or outsiders; tanks which might be overflowing, which may or may not be the fault of certain employees, it might be the fault of equipment or it might be the fault of employees; reckless or careless driving of trucks or cars on company property; and equipment running unattended that should be attended by an employee.

Burke (u): What the hell do you have foremen for?

Stanton (m): The foreman may see some of these; maybe he wouldn't.

Billings (u): You are not asking for these guys to be insurance watchmen. You are asking them to be a bunch of damn stooges.

Madison (u): What do you expect to get out of it? Do you expect to have a bunch of people going through the plant with uniforms on, with billies and guns, policing the people? Is that what you want from this thing?

Warren (m): No. We want the present people who qualify as guards to be excluded from the bargaining unit.

Perrino (u): Is there a possibility that some may not "qualify"?

Warren (m): We have told you the ones that we think do.

Perrino (u): We want to know whether or not these 23 people at Ashland are going to have jobs. You may well set up a classification of guards and say "You boys don't qualify." And where do they go from there? So, my question is this: are you prepared to say that all these so-called 23 people are automatically guards and satisfy all of the requisites that you have set up or expect to set up? That is my question. You can answer it yes or no.

Francis (u): Let's put it another way and make it very blunt. You can appreciate that, when these people are out of the unit, you can fire them as you see fit. Right?

Perrino (u): Are you perplexed by the simplicity of these questions? We could get down to the point of drawing pictures for you. Can you answer yes or no?

Warren (m): As a matter of fact the answer is yes.

Francis (u): We knew the answer, of course. Now, to follow that through and make the point we have been pursuing to no avail: is there any guarantee that any of them won't be fired if they are taken out of the unit?

Stanton (m): We have no present intention of firing any of them. Such a rumor has been going around. We have no such intention. I would say this, though, we can't guarantee that we are never going to fire a guard. Just as we would with any employee who failed to carry out his duties, he would not remain in the company's employ.

Perrino (u): There are two questions. One is to carry out duties, which comes in the future. The other one is qualifications right now, so that they might be elevated to the status of guards. Do all of them have the qualifications, so far as you are concerned?

Stanton (m): To the best of my knowledge—

Perrino (u): You are qualifying the answer. Do they, or don't they?

Stanton (m): I don't know point-blank if every individual meets requirements.

Madison (u): The rest of the committee wants to ask the same question of the rest of the company personnel.

Perrino (u): We will give them all a chance to talk. Poor guys, they have been so long here without speaking. I don't know if we are ever going to get Johnston to talk.

Heath (u): He is the man behind the scenes [pointing to Johnston].

Henderson (u): Are you afraid to talk?

Johnston (m): No.

Henderson (u): Why don't you come out and talk once in a while?

Johnston (m): Mr. Warren is doing a damn good job here.

Perrino (u): Mr. Stanton, to go back to you. You indicated that, to the best of your knowledge, these people do qualify? Of course, that is not an absolute answer. There is a possibility that some may not qualify? You are not in a position to insure here that these people will be kept as guards? You can't do that, can you?

Stanton (m): I can tell you what our intent is.

Perrino (u): I am not interested in "intent." I would just like to know what you are going to execute. The possibility is that some of these may be dropped? Is that correct?

Stanton (m): Any individual who failed to carry out his job duties would be subject to dismissal.

Perrino (u): That is not the point. I am speaking about qualification right now.

Stanton (m): Right now, I would say they all qualify.

Perrino (u): You give us this assurance that all of them will be brought up into guards? Is that right?

I have one more question, and then I am through. In case a guard should find himself out of a job, can he avail himself of this transcript to defend himself and win reinstatement and win damages if necessary? You see, they are out of the unit; they are at your mercy. You could fire them. Can this transcript be used for them for a defense? You have been free to make a lot of statements here tonight. Some of them sound lousy. Some of them are pretty good. I want to get some equity for these so-called guards. Do you want to caucus?

Warren (m): No. [Pause.]

Perrino (u): Well, what is the answer? I have waited two minutes. Johnston, will you call the play? These guys are stuck here. What about it, Bill?

Warren (m): I don't think he could use the transcript.

Perrino (u): So he is completely at your mercy, and all these presentations that you make here today are not to be used to safeguard the rights of these individuals? Is that right?

Warren (m): We explained our attitudes and intentions.

Madison (u): Bill, put yourself in our position. You have 30 some men all told you say you are going to take out of the unit, and you put forth no good basic arguments. You have run around fences. You have evaded questions. Yet the company is putting itself in the position that they are willing, in all probability, to face a damn good strike over those men!

Burke (u): Bill, we are going to stay here all night for you to answer that question. I would like to know it, so I can tell the people.

Perrino (u): That is why he is not going to tell you. He is afraid you are going to tell the people.

Madison (u): If he can't answer that question, then the things we are afraid of are sure bound to happen. Everything we say here about the black-jacks and guns and patrolling the plant must be so.

Stanton (m): We have no intention of arming our guards.

Madison (u): How about the uniform?

Stanton (m): We may or may not.

Madison (u): For the tenth time, we want to know what to tell the people are the reasons for taking the guards and the watchmen out of the bargaining unit. Cite some cases where they haven't performed the duties. We have to be able to tell the people something.

Warren (m): We think they have been subject to undue pressures.

Perrino (u): Give one case specifically.

Stanton (m): I will mention one.

Heath (u): Look, if Bill Warren discussed this thing with you guys, and he has enough memory, he ought to be able to repeat some of these things now. They told enough damn lies. Let's prove on the record that they are still lying.

Perrino (u): All right, what are the examples?

Warren (m): I am going to call on the representatives of the plants.

Heath (u): Because you don't know. And, when you say you have discussed it, you are a damn liar. You can take that any way you want to take it, see. If you want to take it with coats off, we will take it with coats off as far as I am concerned; or if you want to select anybody on your side of the table to do it, I will take my coat off.

Roberts (u): I would like to ask a question too, and it concerns Macon [the company's one nonunion plant]. There seems to be one thing that the company does down there. It helps its employees out with company property. In the case of Macon, you regard it as an obligation—all the material that these people take out. Any material they may take out in Ashland or Norton, it seems to me, you might regard as theft.

Warren (m): I certainly know of no such obligation at Macon to supply people with company property.

Burke (u): I know, Bill. I was down there on a campaign, and the people told me there at that time "If we joined the union we wouldn't have these privileges to carry stuff home, to stake tomatoes with and to build summer cottages and things."

You all do it to keep the union out. The company is fighting the union to keep those fellows from joining.

Madison (u): Everybody tells us that, if we agree to let that guard go through the departments patrolling the working area as a police force, you could increase it to the extent that you could just do anything you wanted to—by force.

Stanton (m): We have no such intent.

Madison (u): We might end up with more guards than workers.

Perrino (u): Unless the company agrees to use this record on behalf of these people, guards, who may have a grievance and may want to use this record in order to defend themselves.

Stanton (m): What sort of situation do you have in mind when you make that statement?

Heath (u): Why aren't you guys willing to answer some other damn questions here that are pertinent? That guy Warren is supposed to have discussed these things with you. And, if he can't tell today what he discussed with you guys, then somebody on the company's side is a liar again.

Warren (m): I think we would like a brief recess.

[A recess was taken from 11 P.M. to 12 midnight.]

Warren (m): I think Allan has something he wants to say about the fellows at Ashland.

Stanton (m): I believe it was Joe who asked a specific question about the 23 individuals at Ashland, whether or not they would qualify and be able to carry out the job duties that we indicated they should carry out. There are 2 in that group of 23 who are past retirement age and have indicated their desire to retire. With the exception of those 2, the other 21, we feel, should be able to carry out the duties without any trouble.

Francis (u): Is there anything else?

Warren (m): No.

Francis (u): You had quite a long conference. I thought maybe you could do something.

Warren (m): Jim, we have discussed this guard thing. As we previously stated, we don't feel we can go along with the union's proposal to split up these job duties; and we don't feel that we can change our position that we should somehow have these people who qualify as guards out of the unit or, at least, left in a position to get them out.

It is getting pretty late now, 12 o'clock. I wonder if you would like to recess until tomorrow morning.

Francis (u): The committee feels they have made a hell of a lot of trips in here and spent a lot of time. We are of the opinion it might be well to struggle along a little longer. If you are weary of the watchman subject, we have a couple more we can go into. We don't want to subject you to any suffering, but I've got lots of things I would rather do than be here. I would just as soon sleep, too, Bill. But, you know, it keeps coming back to me that a certain fact apparently does not seem to impress the company. We are talking about the destinies, not only of the 4,000 people we represent, but, counting their wives and children, about 15,000 people. We think that it is a pretty substantial responsibility to endeavor to arrive at an agreement. Of course, I won't insist on it if you don't want to.

Warren (m): It would seem to me that we could do just as well if we got an early start tomorrow morning. If you would prefer to go into some of these matters tonight, we will stick around a little while.

Francis (u): We might give you an opportunity to think some of these matters over a little bit. We would like to know what your position is now on equal division of overtime with the shop steward participating as to who should be called.

Warren (m): Jim, there is no change in our basic position on that. As always, we have been willing to discuss the phraseology of the provisions; but we don't feel that we should continue the practice of paying for men who do not report, and do not work.

Francis (u): You mean as long as that phraseology removes the penalty pay for time not worked when the right man is not called. How long have you been with the company, Bill?

Warren (m): Approximately five and a half years.

Francis (u): Then you wouldn't personally know that prior to our union there was discrimination on the part of the company in the division of overtime, would you?

Warren (m): I have been told there was considerable discussion on that point.

Francis (u): Well, there must have been a problem, or there wouldn't be a provision for it in the contract. Is that not right?

Warren (m): At least in some instances.

Francis (u): Do you think the union can depend on the company now, after seven years of mistakes, to be completely fair in the future and carry out the principle if there is no penalty attached? Can you give us that assurance?

Warren (m): I think so, especially with the provision we have offered to give the shop stewards more participation.

Francis (u): Then, in your opinion, it would be a relatively minor problem if that were done in the future?

Warren (m): As I have said before, we think one of the big problems here is the penalty on the company to pay overtime regardless of whether a man can be reached, or even when a supervisor calls in a man out of turn. We can always make up an overtime opportunity for a man.

Francis (u): The problem is the penalty, not the carrying out of the principles?

Warren (m): Well, the penalty is certainly the cause of a lot of friction and the cause of a lot of grievances which don't seem to have any merit and don't have any real relationship to the equitable division of overtime.

In Ashland, for example, nearly 65% of the grievances involved are under this section. Now, many of those grievances don't have much to do with equitable division of overtime as such. To give a recent example, the union was supporting a claim in a situation where an employee had been off on an unscheduled absence—he had been ill. He notified his foreman that he was ready to come back to work. The foreman put him back on the overtime roster. He was low man on the overtime roster. The union contended, however, that the practice in that department was that that man didn't go back on the overtime roster until he actually was back on the job. But anyway, during the period after he called up and before he reported to work, he was called for overtime; and he was the low man, admittedly. But a grievance was filed by the second lowest employee asking for penalty pay. We don't think that that sort of a grievance has much to do with the equal division of overtime.

Francis (u): But you are confident that, with the cooperation of the shop stewards, the principle will be carried out more completely than in the past? The union thinks so, too, I might add.

Warren (m): As I said before, it was the union's position that things would be bettered by more participation by shop stewards. And the company took the position that the big problem was the penalty. Certainly, our proposal on this is to attempt a reconciliation of the two positions.

Perrino (u): If you say "reconciliation," it should be reconciliation; "compromise" should be compromise; and "in-between points" ought to be in-between points. The way you talk, you give the appearance that you have given us a great big deal, you know; and you have not.

Say, did you indicate that the company paid 2,900 bucks for penalties under this article?

Warren (m): Yes, in the two-year period of the present contract.

Perrino (u): At Ashland?

Warren (m): Ashland.

Perrino (u): How much did you pay in Norton?

Warren (m): Four hundred forty dollars.

Roberts (u): Mr. Warren, have you fellows predetermined that this participation by shop stewards would not work?

Warren (m): We think the big problem is the penalty.

Francis (u): The penalty has been upheld.

Warren (m): As I said when we first discussed this subject, we never felt that the obligation to pay for overtime not worked was in the contract. There is no wording to that effect. The practice grew out of an arbitrator's decision about 1945 on a somewhat related case. We didn't think the decision was right at the time. And the practice that grew out of the decision was certainly not intended. Therefore, we want to make it clear in this contract.

Dustin (u): If the company don't want to pay the penalty, then if the mistake is made, take it out of the superintendent's or assistant superintendent's salary.

Henderson (u): If the foreman misses you once and he comes around and says "I will call you next time," and he misses you that time and then comes around again and says "I will call you next time," and misses you that time, what happens then?

Warren (m): This elimination of the pay doesn't take away the right to file a grievance.

Henderson (u): What the hell good is it going to do you to file a grievance? That is a waste of ink. Apparently, you are building up your ink business at our expense.

Madison (u): What the hell would he put on the grievance if the foreman said he would give it the next time?

Dustin (u): A violation of the grievance.

Henderson (u): Mr. Johnston down at Ashland already stated a man that filed a grievance on Article V, Section 3, had no character. He has also indicated lots of times that Article V, Section 3, was going to be done away with.

Perrino (u): Did you make that statement?

Johnston (m): I don't recall that statement.

Heath (u): You are a liar if you say you didn't.

Stanton (m): I was there and he didn't make the statement.

Heath (u): Then you are a liar, too.

Stanton (m): He said some people had sufficient character that they did not want to accept pay for time not worked. Am I right on that, Dick?

Johnston (m): That is approximately correct.

Perrino (u): Mr. Stanton, do you support Johnston's position?

Stanton (m): I do think it is wrong to accept pay for time not worked.

Burke (u): Do you think the arbitrator did not make a fair and honest decision?

Perrino (u): And anyone that does want pay under the contract has no character?

Stanton (m): I don't say that.

Perrino (u): Then you don't agree fully with Johnston, do you?

Stanton (m): I don't agree with what you attach to what he said.

Perrino (u): I don't attach anything to him. You have finally said to us what he said. Now, do you agree with it?

Stanton (m): Yes. "Some people have sufficient character" not to accept pay for time not worked.

Burke (u): That is to indicate that people that did accept didn't have no character.

Stanton (m): That is not what he said.

Burke (u): That is what he meant. What in hell else could he have in mind?

Johnston (m): Guy, you brought that up on a number of occasions, and I pointed out there was no such reflection.

Burke (u): I got paid on more grievances than anybody else, and I think I have more character than you have—because you come down to take the bread and butter out of the kids' mouths in that home town of ours. Don't say you didn't do it, you and them other two guys right aside of you. Sit up and hold your head up.

Heath (u): Don't let anybody on that side of the table say that what I said that Johnston said is a lie, because I am man enough to come over on that side of the table because I know what Johnston said.

Francis (u): I would just like to make a point here. It doesn't impress you people, I know, but Mr. Norton [company president] told me on the phone, when I spoke to him last week in the hope that his responsibilities would leave him free enough to perhaps discuss with a representative of the union some of the principles involved in this dispute, that you were completely competent, Bill, to handle this thing, you and your assistants.

I don't know whether he, or you, appreciates the bitterness that you are generating by your positions. I don't think you appreciate it. I tried to tell Mr. Norton on the phone. But I think, if he does read the record to the extent that he indicated to me that he does read it, I think he is going to get some inkling; and I think too the committee here represents the thinking of the majority of people that work for Appalachian Chemicals. And the bitterness that you are seeing demonstrated here is going to, in the long run, cost you one hell of a lot more than we are arguing about. And that is a prophecy.

You are clinging to this item just like you are on the guards, and it isn't worth a damn to you. You have no sense of values. You won't make a wage offer of a nickel. The things that we are arguing about here are the things that the company is injecting.

Now, on the watchmen, we are trying to do something, trying to search out some means of doing something. You talk about gate guards. O.K., you have to have guys with pistols, uniforms and brass buttons, and blackjacks, and everything. O.K. Keep them around the gates and fences. But, no, you wouldn't be satisfied with that. You have to have them all around. We are quite sure now that you are going to have guys with pistols on their hips and brass buttons and uniforms strutting around the pulverizers and the mixers and the dryers. You haven't said it, but I think that is what you intend to do.

As to Article V, Section 3, the record indicates that there have been violations. Yet you say there is no need for the law—when the very record accuses you beyond all shadow of doubt. Yet you come here and tell us, "Well, we will cure it."

This company has a tremendous plant. It has paid big dividends. The stockholders are prosperous. Some people never do a lick of work and make a living off of these people. You and I know basically, if it wasn't for the work of these people on our side, that you and the others in management would have to go out and dig ditches too, or you wouldn't get any bread. All we are trying to do is to just get a little square deal, to feed a lot of mouths in their homes, and a little pleasanter conditions in the factories where they are working and then a little bit more self-respect. In return for that, they are making a hell of a nice living for people who aren't producing a darned thing. And yet we have to sit up all night arguing about something. And what do we get?

I wish one thing. I wish the 4,000 people we represent could sit here tonight. Ashland would be shaken so damn bad right now, and Norton too, that the walls of those plants would be rattling.

You are not even being human, when you get right down to it. You are perfectly willing if it is necessary—it is obvious to me right now—for these 4,000 people to hit the bricks. It doesn't mean a damn thing to you if we are out on strike a couple of months and the kids may not get all the milk they need.

Warren (m): Don't you men think that in negotiations some real consideration should be given to the problems of the company, as well as the problems of the union?

Dustin (u): We have given you everything but our shirts.

Burke (u): All I can say is it is going to be rough and we are going to make it rough. We will do it by the law, too. The state police can stand there.

Perrino (u): Well, what do you say, Claybourne? You are the mediator. You got us together. Do you have any ideas? Are you recessing, or adjourning? What do you do?

Warren (m): What is your position on the monetary items?

Perrino (u): I am not talking to you, Bill.

Francis (u): What do you want us to do, go down to 3 cents? You sure as hell haven't made any concessions.

Perrino (u): Ten cents, with a productivity increase. Our demand is 10 cents. You are making money. Stop sitting on it.

Claybourne: I would certainly suggest—

Perrino (u): Don't call us to any more meetings. We have exhausted our funds.

Francis (u): All our money is in the strike fund.

Claybourne: I appreciate your cooperation. The only thing I can suggest at this point, while you are together, is to stay together for another day and meet again tomorrow.

Heath (u): Look, we are so damn close, the company can right now, in two minutes, get an agreement. They think that there is not going to be a strike.

Billings (u): Only two damn articles there keeping us from agreement.

Clark (u): If they want an agreement, they can get one.

Billings (u): We've bargained contracts for seven long years. Those things have been in that contract.

Roberts (u): I have been given another assignment and must be leaving; but, for my own satisfaction, I would like to know the company's position. Are you telling us right now that, unless we agree to what you want with regard to overtime and the guards, there shall be no agreement?

Warren (m): I said we wanted something along the lines of what we were talking about on guards.

Roberts (u): And the boys have offered you something that makes sense.

Warren (m): No.

Heath (u): We said don't take your guards and watchmen and combine them together.

Perrino (u): Claybourne, come on, what are you doing?

Claybourne: Gentlemen, all I can do is suggest that we meet tomorrow. If you feel that the deadlock is complete, that it will serve no purpose, the only other thing I can do is, as I did at the end of the last meeting, to remain in touch with you and if there is any change—

Perrino (u): There must be some flexibility on the part of the company, which I fail to see. Why meet again? For a repetition of this damn crap?

Claybourne: I cannot say, except to continue the discussion if that is possible.

Warren (m): We have been flexible.
Burke (u): It all came from this side again.

[Whereupon at 1:40 A.M. the union representatives left the room and returned at 1:45.]

Francis (u): I've got some news for you. If your position is as it was when we walked out of the room, then, you can consider, for the record, there is no contract between your company and our union. Satisfied? That is what you wanted, isn't it? You are a bunch of dumb bastards, all of you. We didn't want it either, but, goddam you, if we stand on the picket line, I hope, if it is blood that flows, I hope it is yours and not that of a poor innocent working man.

Warren (m): Could you tell us when this picket line goes on?
Francis (u): Sure. We will give you notice and wire your damn machines for you, too.

[He and the union delegates start walking out.]

Warren (m): Jim, one further question.
Johnston (m): Bill, don't go after them.
Warren (m): I was just going to ask if the local would sit down with the plant managers and plan an orderly shutdown.

[Whereupon negotiations were broken off at 1:48 A.M.]
The strike went into effect the next morning.

DISCUSSION QUESTIONS

1. On the basis of the record, evaluate the handling of the negotiations and the strategy and tactics of (*a*) the management representatives, (*b*) the union representatives, and (*c*) the mediator.

2. If you were with the Appalachian management, how would you have handled this negotiation?

THE FIRST ARBITRATION CASE UNDER THE COLLECTIVE
AGREEMENT AT THE FORD MOTOR COMPANY

The United Automobile, Aircraft, and Agricultural Implement Workers of America, CIO, won its first major agreement in 1937, when General Motors signed a contract with the union on February 11. Two months later, on April 6, the Chrysler Corporation began contractual relations through an agreement which was modeled closely on that with General Motors. But it was not until more than four years later, on June 20, 1941, that the last of the "Big Three" in the industry, the Ford Motor Company, signed up with the union.

Together with the steel industry, automobile manufacturing had come to symbolize for organized labor the "toughest" resistance to collective bargaining faced by the unions. Manifestly, Ford, the final "hold-out" to be overcome, presented the United Automobile Workers with their stiffest opposition, and, by the same token, their most dramatic victory.

The stormy progress of unionization in the industry as a whole has written one of the most tumultuous chapters of recent labor history. Although labor unions had sought a foothold almost from the beginning of motor-car manufacture—symbolically the International Union of Carriage and Wagon Workers, AFL, had enrolled the first union members in the infant industry that was to end the "horse and buggy age"—it was not until the depression of the nineteen thirties that organization had made any real headway. Many factors had contributed thus to bar effective entry of the unions—not only the determined open-shop policies of the powerful employing corporations, on the one side, and the weakening jurisdictional conflicts among the AFL organizations, on the other, but also the dynamic growth of the prosperous industry and the high wage policies introduced by Ford that attracted migrants from all over the country to Detroit.

By 1933, however, hard times and mounting complaints among the restive automobile workers gave organization a new spirit. The favoring labor legislation of the period accelerated the developments under way. The years that followed saw the workers moving in and out of many different kinds of unions—company unions, craft organizations, and industrial unions, both affiliated and independent, federal locals, grievance agencies, etc.—all of which competed one with the other to aggravate the instability and complexity of the situation.

The finally dominant organization of today had its origins in 1934 in an amalgamation of AFL federal local unions that was chartered the following year as the United Automobile Workers of America. The CIO also was launched in 1935; and, in July, 1936, the UAW speedily transferred its allegiance to the new federation. From that time on, the union's organizing policies became increasingly aggressive.

Yet the UAW's organizing campaigns did not display the carefully planned strategies and control by top leadership that were characteristic of the steel workers' union. Unlike the leaders of labor in the latter industry, those of the auto workers were young, unseasoned recruits to unionism, themselves employees in the mass-production plants or intellectuals who had been forced into industry from college by the depression. They shared the feelings of their rank and file for rapid, militant, novel strategies that would finally batter down the opposition of their employers to organization. Often, indeed, the rank and file forced the pace, initiating strikes and introducing tactics that perturbed their leaders. The men at headquarters would have preferred the restraints of a centrally planned and controlled campaign rather than local outbursts and uncoordinated disturbances.

Nonetheless, the "quickies," or short, localized stoppages, which the men were utilizing in 1936–1937 soon proved a prostrating form of pressure in the highly mechanized, moving-belt industry, as suspension of one department forced the shutdown of the whole plant, and often also of other plants. Next the workers took over the sit-down strike from its successes in the rubber industry. After several turbulent weeks, which startled the whole country, the union in February, 1937, won recognition from "besieged" General Motors.

Thereupon sit-downs "swept through the auto industry." Employees in one plant after another refused to leave their shops and barricaded themselves behind closed doors. Small auto parts were used as ammunition when attempts were made to dislodge the trespassers. Improvised blackjacks and clubs were also used. Auto seats and upholstery materials were turned into mattresses. In some instances steel doors were welded shut. There was, however, no deliberate sabotage; and since the employers did not attempt violently to eject the sit-downers, not a life was lost in these strikes of early 1937 in Michigan. Despite the workers' claim that their employers' disregard of the National Labor Relations Act justified their recourse to the sit-down, public reaction was highly unfavorable.[1]

Naturally, Ford was not unaffected by these developments; but only after four more years of bitter struggle did the company "surrender." The fight embraced every clash familiar to the no-quarter battle for union recognition—from the struggle over "civil rights" to outbreaks of violence, from discharge of active unionists to informal joint dealings, from government intervention on all levels to court appeals. The personnel manager at that time, Mr. Harry H. Bennett, directed the fight against the union; the Ford Service Department under his supervision contained the company guards and plant protection men, who actually barred union organizers from access to the works. One of the famous clashes of the protracted struggle that became known as the "Battle of the Overpass" occurred in 1937, when these guards fought the union men, headed by Richard Frankensteen, who were attempting to enter Dearborn. Similarly violent encounters continuously erupted between the Service Department and the union. A traffic "ordinance" of Dearborn, which the plant protection men helped enforce, forbade distribution of union litera-

---

[1] On February 27, 1939, the Supreme Court (*NLRB v. Fansteel Metallurgical Corporation*, 306 U.S. 240) definitely outlawed the sit-down.

ture in the vicinity of the Ford plant; the union eventually won a court decision that declared it unconstitutional. The National Labor Relations Board ruled that the company was guilty of unfair labor practices in cases involving its plants in eight cities including Dearborn. The company appealed this ruling to the courts; and, on February 10, 1941, when the United States Supreme Court refused to review the circuit court decision upholding the Board on most of the points of its ruling in the Dearborn case, the lengthy, bitter conflict neared its close.

Yet, even from February to June, 1941, the path to eventual agreement proved to be rough going. Discharge of union committeemen evoked a strike in April at the River Rouge plant, which was ended after ten days by the intervention of the Governor. Among the continuing union demands throughout this struggle was the abolition of the Ford Service Department. On May 21, a representation election at the River Rouge and the Lincoln plants gave the union an overwhelming mandate; less than 4 per cent voted against the UAW.

When the first agreement was signed on June 20, it became evident that, having now accepted the union, Ford would go "all out" to establish good relationships. The agreement covered all Ford plants. It made Ford the first motor-car manufacturer to grant the union shop and the checkoff, or to use the union label. All employees whose discharge had been protested to the NLRB were reinstated. Wages, by the provisions of the agreement, were to be at least as high for each type of work as those paid by the major competitor that was to be named by the union.

The first months of operation under this agreement evoked expressions of disappointment from management, particularly because of the large number of illegal walkouts and the continuing turbulence of shop relations. In the meantime, defense production had been launched by the nation; and soon thereafter the needs of the war engulfed Ford as well as other Detroit manufacturers. The joint agreement was renegotiated and signed on November 4, 1942; subsequent supplements were added on May 10 and June 6, 1943.

The supplementary agreement of May 10, 1943, was titled the "Umpire Agreement." It established the office of permanent arbitrator as the terminal step in the settlement of grievances under the contract; hitherto the appeal board, composed of an "equal number of International Union and company officials," had constituted the final rung in the hierarchy of appeal.

On June 3, 1943, the umpire submitted his decision on the first case that was brought to him under the agreement for settlement. The text of that decision follows:

THE UMPIRE

Ford Motor Co. and UAW–CIO

Discipline of Employees for Assault and Mass Disturbance } Case 1 (600-Acft)

This is the first case submitted to and decided by the Umpire pursuant to the agreement of May 10, 1943, between the Ford Motor Company and the United Automobile Workers of America, CIO. This agreement creates the office of standing Umpire finally to resolve disputes between the parties under their general agreement of November 4, 1942, and defines his jurisdiction and powers.

For taking this great forward step in industrial relations, the company and the union deserve the commendation of all their fellow citizens. By this agreement the parties have undertaken to substitute reason and justice for force in the adjustment of the day to day conflicts that attend large scale production. By this agreement the parties have undertaken to comply with their contractual obligations, as determined by an impartial tribunal, until the obligations are terminated or changed through mutual consent. By it, the parties establish order and the rule of reason as the way of industrial life.

It is a real privilege and a cause for pardonable pride to be given the opportunity to start this institution on its way. I do so, by this decision, with a deep sense of the responsibility that the privilege carries. And I do so with the fervent hope that, though the individuals called upon to serve as Umpire may change, the institution will continue to grow strong and become characteristic of industry in a free America.

But it must be constantly borne in mind that the Umpire's office is only one element in the relations between the parties. It is not the whole business. No Umpire could possibly adjudicate all the labor controversies that arise in so large an enterprise, even if the parties were sufficiently unwise to ask him to do so. Smooth, efficient, continuous operation with justice to those involved can hardly be coerced by any outside institution. That can be achieved only by the determination of the parties themselves: the determination to accept each other wholeheartedly as parties in interest, to be patient in the attempt in good faith to explain, to learn and to understand each other's needs and problems, to be patient in an honest search for mutually satisfactory solutions, and to recognize each other as components in a common enterprise rather than as enemies seeking to destroy. That is the process of collective bargaining in which the Umpire's office can play an important part. It can be called upon finally to resolve those relatively few differences which the parties have honestly been unable to eliminate. But appeal to the Umpire must be preceded by sincere effort at mutual adjustment. Otherwise the institution might bog down; the Umpire would not have the time for the study and thought essential to wise decision; and the parties might find the awards harsher than the mutual adjustments that might have been made.

I

This case involves a series of grievances relating to the discipline of thirteen employees for participating in what might have turned out to be a bloody riot at the Aircraft Building in the Rouge plant. All but one of these employees are union officers or committeemen of one kind or another, known in some other plants as union stewards. The evidence as to the several men is widely conflicting. In order to avoid confusion, the story will be told first as presented by the company and the conflicts in the evidence will be detailed as the case against each of the men is separately considered.

According to the evidence introduced by the company, then, the following is the story:

At approximately 11:15 P.M. on the night of March 3, 1943, Tom Hewitt,[1] Financial Secretary of the Aircraft Building, and a day-shift employee, approached Gate 9-A at the Rouge plant. On duty at the gate to check badges and prevent unauthorized persons from entering were James Derry and Albert Hamilton, members of the company's Plant Protection department. Hewitt started to enter through the aisle reserved for outgoing traffic. Derry and Hamilton shouted to him to enter through the aisle used for incoming traffic. They noted then that

---

[1] All names are fictitious, save those of supervision and the umpire. This case is utilized for classroom discussion with the latter's permission.

Hewitt was intoxicated to such a degree that he could not be admitted to the plant —quite apart from the fact, as they claim, that he did not belong to this shift and did not have his badge on. Derry refused Hewitt admission telling him to go home and come back in the morning. Hewitt then became abusive toward Derry, who continued with his job of checking badges. He said that he was financial secretary of the Union, that he was there to attend a meeting, and that he would call out the 12,000 Aircraft Building employees to beat hell out of Derry. Again Derry urged Hewitt to stop obstructing traffic, to go home and return in the morning. He attempted to continue with his work. Hewitt, according to the company's testimony, continued his abusive language, poked his fingers in Derry's back and chest and finally slapped Derry's face. Thereupon Derry struck Hewitt in the face and felled him to the ground. Hewitt then arose from the ground, grabbed hold of Derry and Hamilton, and demanded that they go with him to the union committee room in the Aircraft Building. An unidentified employee called upon the employees entering the gate not to let Derry get away with what he was doing, to a good union man and to take Derry into the building. Hewitt, it is said, joined in this cry for assistance from the crowd. The crowd responded to the incitation of Hewitt and the unidentified employee and pushed Hamilton and Derry to the building. On the way Derry was subjected to some pushing and tripping, and just inside the building Derry and Hamilton freed their arms and exchanged blows with members of the crowd. Finally Derry and Hamilton were brought to the committee room where, it was said, Derry was mistreated again. He attempted to tell his version of the incident but was howled down by the crowd which was shouting that he be hung, beaten up, and so on.

Some one of the committeemen then put in a call for the plant protection supervisor, Mr. De Baecke, known as Murphy, who arrived with some plant protection men. Some of the committeemen advised him to send the plant protection men away lest the crowd be further incited. De Baecke did send the men away, and suggested that Derry be taken to the plant protection office where the matter could be straightened out quietly. (The committee room is a crib near the center of the building partitioned off solely by wire mesh partitions going only part of the way to the ceiling. The plant protection office is a regularly enclosed room on one side of the building.) In the meantime Derry's superior, Mr. Woods, was also summoned. De Baecke and the crowd escorted Derry to the plant protection office and Woods came in presently. There is some evidence that on the way to the plant protection office Derry was tripped and pushed. In the plant protection office he is said to have been given many blows, one or two of which pushed his head through the glass panel of a door in front of which he was standing. Just after his head crashed through the glass the lights in the room went out; and when they were turned on again, the union claims that two or three plant protection men were seen in the back office pointing their guns at the crowd. The company's contention is that the back office is a gun room where guns are checked in and out; that the plant protection men were delivering or receiving their guns in the routine manner; that the guns were not loaded and were not pointed at the crowd. In any event some of the committeemen demanded that the guns be put away. Woods instructed the men to do so and they obeyed. Thereupon it was suggested that Woods go to the crib and see Hewitt's condition and write out a quit slip for Derry. Woods, Derry and the crowd then proceeded back to the crib where, it is said, Derry was again dealt several blows. After seeing Hewitt's condition Woods did write out a quit slip for Derry in response to the demands of the crowd, and further, in similar response, wrote on it that the plant protection man was wrong. Woods wrote this quit slip after inquiring from the committeemen whether they would give Derry safe conduct if the quit slip was written. The reply was that safe conduct would be assured through the building but that no responsibility could be assumed outside of the building. Derry was then escorted toward an exit. As the committeemen saw a number of plant protection men at the exit toward which they were heading they turned and went to a different door with Derry. They stopped at the door to wait for a car to take Derry away. The crowd began to shove and Derry was pushed out of the door. He broke into a run and a number of people ran after him. Derry fell to the ground, having been tripped as he claims, or having slipped as the union claims. While he was on the ground he was kicked. When he arose and held on to the fence to catch his breath, the crowd formed a semi-circle around him and there were cries for a fight between him and members of the crowd. One of the men, a professional boxer, was particularly called upon to fight Derry and was pushed into the center of the semi-circle. Derry fought him in self-defense and knocked him down. Derry then also threw himself to the ground to avoid further punishment. While he was down he was kicked again and called upon to fight others. By this time the car had arrived and Derry was placed in it and driven away to the hospital. He was treated for lacerations and contusions about the face, neck and hands, a fractured jaw, and torn cartilage of the ribs.

Derry's coat had been left in the crib. When it was finally returned to the plant protection office it was torn and cut up into shreds. It is said that the coat was hung on a conveyor and mutilated as it passed along.

As stated above, the evidence is widely conflicting as to the precise roles played by the individuals involved. But the major outlines of the story are beyond dispute. A crowd of varying size did escort Derry from the gate into the committee room, then to the plant protection office, back to the committee room, and then outside. Hewitt did receive at least one well placed and effective blow. Derry was beaten up pretty severely. The crowd was, at times at least, in a threatening mood. And twenty or more union committeemen, including those here involved, were at least present in the crowd.

II

The disturbance on the night of March 3 was, of course, not planned to accomplish any gain for anybody. It might be regarded as an occasional rowdyism which men display, without cause and without reason. But behind the night's disturbance there is a conditioning factor which should be eliminated. There seems to be an hostility against plant protection men and a feeling that somehow their functions are inimical to the workers. The feeling is based not on the current character of the plant protection department or the current conduct of its employees, but rather on the recollection of real or fancied situations prior to the company's unionization.

It is, of course, difficult to change old attitudes. But this hostility to, or suspicion of, plant protection men ought to be eliminated. Plant protection men are not only necessary in this plant, but they are required by the government. Their number has greatly increased during the war for good reason. Many of them are relatively new employees and new to that department. They are fellow workers of the production employees and their interests are not in conflict with those of the production employees. Throughout the country they are frequently organized into unions and affiliated with the same internationals as unions of production employees. Hostilities engendered before unionization should not be permitted to mar relations after a strong union and a good grievance procedure have been established. It is incumbent upon the union leadership to discourage divisive hostility between these fellow workers. Of course, there may be individual plant protection men of less than lovely characters, just as there may also be such men among the production workers. But that merely emphasizes the vice of indiscriminate general condemnation. It is no more just to smear all plant protection men as "stooges," "gestapo," et cetera, than it is to call union men racketeers. Surely the conduct of the plant protection employees who were on the scene during the disturbance was restrained and decent and worthy of praise. It was the crowd, rather than the plant protection men, that was using un-American, "gestapo" methods.

III

No one can fail to regret the disturbance on the night of March 3. No one can take pride in mob violence, whether premeditated or spontaneous. The union does not condone or justify the incident. Its position rather is that the men disciplined were not guilty as charged or did not deserve as severe penalties as they received. If these men were ordinary workers, this position would have greater merit.

But the disciplined men were committeemen, union leaders in the plant. Their position as such imposes equivalent responsibilities. If they were present in the crowd and did nothing to disperse it and restore calm, orderly procedure, they failed to measure up to their responsibilities.

Derry was escorted into the building, according to Hewitt, in order that the grievance against him might be adjusted. This was not the proper way to adjust grievances in the first place. But if this was the object, the crowd and the committeemen interfered with its attainment. A trial or negotiation under such circumstances is a mockery of reason. A verdict rendered by a jury under similar circumstances would have been treated as a nullity and a denial of due process of law. The Supreme Court has said, through Mr. Justice Holmes in 1923: "In Frank v. Mangum, 239 U.S. 309, 335, it was recognized of course that if in fact a trial is dominated by a mob so that there is an actual interference with the course of justice, there is a departure from due process of law. . . ." Moore v. Dempsey, Vol. 261 U.S. Reports, p. 90.

Twenty or more committeemen were not required to settle this grievance. Their mere presence increased the size of the crowd, gave the affair a false appearance of importance and interfered with the orderly collective bargaining required by the contract. Their presence could be justified only if they were there to help restore order. And it is incredible, indeed, that twenty committeemen would not have been able to restore order if they made a real effort to do so.

IV

Before proceeding to the cases of the individual men, a word should be said about the powers of the Umpire in discipline cases. The Umpire has power, of course, to determine guilt or innocence. That is a question of fact to be determined by appropriate investigation. It is to be hoped that the parties will cooperate in the effort to ascertain truth and neither distort nor withhold evidence. While putting something over on the Umpire may give a party a temporary advantage in the particular case, it will in the long run discredit the institution and work to the disadvantage of both parties by depriving them of the protection of impartial and just adjudication.

The Umpire also has power to modify penalties imposed in discipline cases. This is not an arbitrary power. The Umpire is not expected to substitute his own judgment for that of management. His power is to review the penalty and determine whether it is reasonable under the circumstances. Management has considerable discretion in the imposition of discipline. That discretion has not been transferred to the Umpire. His power is to modify only when the penalty is beyond the zone of reasonableness. Where several penalties are all reasonable, the Umpire cannot alter the one selected by management, even though, were he in management's shoes, he might have selected a different one. The reasonableness of a penalty depends, of course, on all the circumstances of the case: the nature of the offense, the prior record of the employee, prophecy as to his future behavior, effect on discipline and morale in the plant, and so on. In arriving at the awards in this case, I have also taken into account the fact that the disturbance occurred prior to the establishment of the Umpire's office and the hope that with this office in operation, attitudes will change considerably and this kind of interference with collective bargaining will not recur.

V

Fitzgerald and Partuzzi. At the hearing no evidence was introduced of any active participation in the affray by these two men. The company's representative conceded this and acquiesced in a modification of their penalties.

But these men were committeemen. They were present in the crowd and in the plant protection office. They had no business there unless they were aiding in negotiation of the grievance or dispersing the crowd. I am not satisfied that they were doing either of these things. Their presence was not necessary for the negotiation of the grievance; as stated previously, it merely augmented the crowd, created greater excitement, and interfered with collective bargaining. Their duty as leaders, if they happened to be present, was to do all in their power to restore order. Even if they struck no blows and did not actively incite violence, they are subject to discipline for their passive interference with collective bargaining.

The penalties imposed by the company were a two weeks' lay-off for Fitzgerald and one week for Partuzzi. These penalties were not imposed on the ground just stated. Indeed, the company did not undertake to penalize committeemen merely for their presence. The company imposed these penalties on the ground that these men actively participated: that Partuzzi "was loud and threatening in the demands that Derry be injured and was striking at Derry whenever he had a chance" and that Fitzgerald "held on to Derry's arms so that a fellow mobster could better assault Derry," that he was "continually threatening Derry and inciting the mob to further violence."

Not one bit of evidence was presented at the hearing to support these grave charges of active participation. Accordingly, by the standard which the company itself set in fixing the penalties in the first place, the penalties must be modified. In so far as the penalties exceed a three-day lay-off, they are unreasonable and are modified accordingly. The award is that the penalties for each of these men should be fixed at three days lay-off and the men compensated for time lost in excess of three days in accordance with paragraph 29 (10) (f) of the contract.

Baker. The only evidence against this man is this: He stated himself that he said to De Baecke, plant protection foreman, and to Derry, that Derry ought to be hanged for what he did. Mr. Baird, assistant plant protection foreman, also testified that he heard Baker make some such remark, that De Baecke then said to Baker something like "Cut it out, George. What do you want to do, start a riot?" and that Baker then did nothing more. On the other hand, De Baecke testified that he did not see or hear Baker do anything out of the way, that Baker was a fine man, a good committeeman and one of whom the union could well be proud. For the reasons stated in the case of Fitzgerald and Partuzzi, Baker deserves similar discipline. The award is that his penalty be fixed at three days lay-off and that he be compensated for time lost in excess of three days in accordance with paragraph 29 (10) (f) of the contract.

Gruber. The only evidence against Gruber, outside of his presence in the crowd, is that, after the affray, he and Bannon were asked for the return of Derry's coat and it was refused. There is no evidence that Gruber had the coat. On the contrary, the evidence is that the coat was being mutilated by others on a conveyor. On the evidence, Gruber had no connection with it whatever except that he happened to be the committeeman to whom the request was addressed. His penalty must be modified in the same way as that of the three men mentioned. The award is that his penalty be fixed at three days lay-off and that he be compensated for the time lost in excess of that in accordance with paragraph 29 (10) (f) of the contract.

Wells. Both Derry and Hamilton testified that when they were first brought into the committee room, Wells, who was there at the time, tried to shove them back into the hands of the crowd with some such remark as "out of here, you stooges." On the other hand, both Wells and plant protection men testified, and it is undisputed that, subsequently at least, Wells made sincere effort to disperse the crowd. Under the circumstances, his penalty should be fixed at three days and he should be compensated for time lost in excess of three days, in accordance with paragraph 29 (10) (f) of the contract.

Barkovsky. He was not a committeeman. But ample evidence was introduced at the hearing to establish that he mingled with the crowd and incited it with remarks about what he had seen and what ought to be done to Derry. On the evidence the penalty of one week's lay-off for his conduct was reasonable and cannot be disturbed. His grievance must therefore be denied.

Martin, Cherowitz and Laird. These men were each given a month's lay-off. Martin was unquestionably a leading character in the event. He asserts himself that he played a leading role. His testimony is, however, that he was attempting throughout to protect Derry from mob violence and to restore order. His testimony is in conflict with that of many other witnesses and hardly fits the logic of the situation. It would be much more credible if he had left Derry in a room and gone out to the crowd to try to quiet and disperse it. Instead, he was at the head of each procession and apparently loud in condemnation of Derry. There is credible evidence that he struck Derry one or more blows. On the evidence presented at the hearing, it cannot be said that the penalty imposed on him is unreasonable and his grievance must therefore be denied.

There is evidence that Cherowitz jabbed at Derry several times and that he and Laird were among the most vocal in inciting the crowd to action. Granting that the amount of a penalty is largely a matter of judgment, it cannot be said on the evidence introduced at the hearing, that the penalties imposed on these men are beyond the zone of reasonableness. The award as to these men must be, therefore, that their grievances are denied.

Barton, Curley and Sheinfelt. These men were discharged.

Barton is said to have been about the most vocal on that night, jumping like a jack rabbit here and there and doing a lot of shouting. No one accuses him of striking any blows. He is said to have chucked Derry under the chin with his fingers—but in a rather playful fashion and without any force or harm. On the other hand, Derry and Baird testified that Barton sought to prevent further violence to Derry when he was down near the fence at the end of the affray. Barton's conduct, on the evidence, was not sufficiently worse than that of Martin, Cherowitz and Laird, if worse at all, to merit discharge with complete loss of seniority. The award must be, accordingly, that Barton should be reinstated without loss of seniority and without back pay.

Curley entered the affray a little late. Derry testified that, while he was in the committee room, Curley struck him several times. While there is no precise corroboration of this, and Curley denies it, there is considerable evidence that Curley pranced around making gestures typical of preparation for a fight. The testimony is in conflict as to what happened at the fence. All agree that the crowd shouted "let Curley take him!" and that Curley was "pushed" into the semicircle around Derry. This is the testimony of Derry as well as Curley and others. Curley claims that immediately after he was so pushed in the circle, Derry kicked him in the groin and he went down. Derry denies that he kicked Curley and asserts that Curley approached him with fists up, they sparred, Derry landed a few blows, Curley went down, and then Sheinfelt stepped forward with "I'm next." There is no doubt that Curley deserved discipline. He had no business to be with the crowd in the building and surely not out at the fence. And he probably did some sparring at least. But to some extent Curley was himself a victim of the crowd. He is a prize fighter of some repute. He was egged on by the crowd and tempted to succumb to the flattery. Judged by the standard set in the punishment of the other men, however, his penalty was unduly severe. The award must be that Curley should be reinstated without back pay and without loss of seniority.

Sheinfelt, too, was one of the alleged leaders. There is considerable evidence that he struck Derry while in the plant protection office, that he tried to fight with him at the fence and there is some evidence that he kicked Derry. In his case, too, judged by the standard set for the others, the penalty must be modified, and he should be reinstated without back pay and without loss of seniority.

Hewitt. We come finally to the beginning of it all. The evidence as to what happened when Hewitt presented himself at Gate 9-A is sharply conflicting. Hewitt says he was not drunk, though he had just had several bottles of beer. Derry, Hamilton, and a non-Ford employee who happened to be at the spot, say that Hewitt was obviously drunk. Hewitt said that Derry pushed him first, that he pushed Derry back, that Derry then struck the blow which felled him. Derry and Hamilton say that Hewitt kept poking at Derry with his fingers, that he then slapped Derry in the face and then Derry struck the blow which felled him.

Derry's story seems to be more credible and more in accord with the objective facts. In view of the difference in the size and build of the two men, it is very doubtful that Hewitt would have even pushed Derry were not his courage stimulated and his discretion dulled by intoxication. Moreover, Derry did not know Hewitt and Hewitt did not know Derry. No reason suggests itself for the beginning of the trouble other than Hewitt's intoxication.

But it may be unnecessary to find the true facts as to this point. For in any event, Hewitt's conduct was highly improper and unworthy particularly of a union officer. His attempt at the hearing to justify his conduct was equally improper and unworthy. While recognizing that his conduct was not in accord with contract obligations, he explained that he wanted to get Derry into the committee room so that supervision could see his condition and adjudicate his grievance. And, he said, production employees charged with an offense are frequently taken from their work and escorted to the labor relations office for determination of their guilt.

It is a little to Hewitt's credit that, in reply to rather leading questions by the Umpire, he admitted that his conduct was improper. The plant protection man's job is to deny admission to persons not authorized to enter or employees seeking admission while intoxicated. To perform his duty, the plant protection man must rely on his observation and judgment. To seek to overcome his judgment by force or undue annoyance is to interfere with his performance of his recognized and proper duty—an interference which cannot be justified. Ample means are available for the orderly review of the plant protection man's judgment. Hewitt might have, as he himself suggested, walked down a way to another gate at which he was better known. He might have waited a few minutes until the incoming employees had entered and then requested to see the appropriate plant protection man who had power to change Derry's determination. Or Hewitt might have sent word into the committee room, with any one of the incoming employees, and thus secured the aid of a committee man from the inside. Or he might have gone to a telephone and summoned aid from the committee room. Any one of these methods is appropriate—rather than persistence in badgering the plant protection man on duty.

Again, to take the plant protection man from his job and forcefully escort him to the committee room is unwarranted and highly improper. In the first place, the committee room is not the designated place for the adjustment of grievances. In the second place, a nonsupervisory employee does not have authority to order another employee away from his job. And in the third place, the entrance to a war plant should not be left unguarded. That Hewitt wanted supervision to see his condition is no justification whatever. He could have resorted to any of the methods mentioned above. And even if they were not available, the advantage to him would not justify his taking the law into his own hands. The suggestion that the company frequently takes a man from his job to the labor relations office is even less of a justification. To the extent that the company has authority to do this, it is in a completely different position from Hewitt who had no semblance of such authority. And if the company's action in that respect is deemed improper, it surely does not justify similar action by Hewitt. He would be the last person to say that, because employees occasionally engage in an unauthorized stoppage, foremen may also occasionally lock out employees.

But Hewitt's penalty should not be measured solely by the consequences of his conduct. He did not plan or intend the riotous action which followed. The testimony is undisputed that he is a quiet, gentlemanly employee who had not heretofore caused trouble. Taking into account all these circumstances, the fact of Hewitt's intoxication and the conviction that he will not again get into trouble of this kind, but on the contrary will be a worthy employee, the penalty of discharge is unduly harsh. The award must be that Hewitt should be reinstated without back pay and without loss of seniority.

VI

In passing on the discipline of the thirteen men it was really not necessary to pass on the quality of Derry's conduct. And his case is not before the Umpire, except as the union claims that he provoked the disturbance, first by his assault of Hewitt and second by his "surly" and "arrogant" manner in the building when surrounded by the crowd. The union relies on the fact that Derry was given a quit slip on the spot and that the quit slip recited that Derry was in the wrong. No inference may justifiably be drawn from the quit slip given Derry. It was demanded by the crowd and given in an effort to quiet it. As stated above, a determination of guilt made under these circumstances is a travesty on justice and cannot be given effect.

It is probable also that what has been termed "surliness" and "arrogance" on Derry's part was rather fortitude and a determination to show no fear.

But Derry's conduct with respect to Hewitt is, on his own testimony, far from commendable. If Hewitt was as intoxicated as Derry claims, and in view of the men's difference in size and power, Derry could have handled the situation without the powerful blow that felled Hewitt, even if Hewitt did strike first. A sober man, and particularly a plant protection man, should not readily resort to violence in dealing with an intoxicated person. Assuming Hewitt struck first, Derry was in no danger or fear from him. Derry, too, might have avoided the subsequent trouble if, in dealing with Hewitt, he had shown the restraint and good judgment which De Baecke and Woods showed in handling the crowd later. They, and the plant protection men then under their control, are to be commended for their wise conduct which prevented the bloody riot that otherwise might have occurred.

VII

The time lost by virtue of the discipline of the men here involved will not be regarded as absence under the vacation plan since the plan specifically provides that periods of lay-off shall not be so regarded. That, of course, refers to disciplinary lay-off as well as lay-off for lack of work.

Harry Shulman
Umpire

Discussion Questions

1. Evaluate the Umpire's distinction between this near-riot and an "unplanned," occasional rowdyism men display at times "without cause and without reason," indicating your analysis of the "causes" of this grave disturbance.

2. Discuss the sentiments that operated as (*a*) factors in this disturbance, and (*b*) its settlement, through the Umpire's decision.

3. Evaluate the handling of the situation by the responsible individuals during the riot episode.

4. Evaluate the Umpire's handling of this situation.

5. What lessons would you conclude exist in this episode for union and management, in terms of structuring relations before and after the union gains entry into a shop?

FORD MOTOR COMPANY

NEGOTIATING THE FIRST POSTWAR AGREEMENT: COMPANY SECURITY AND WILDCAT STRIKES

I

On January 9, 1946, Henry Ford II, in addressing the Society of Automotive Engineers in Detroit on "The Challenge of Human Engineering," expressed the conviction that "there is no reason why a union contract could not be written and agreed upon with the same efficiency and good temper that marks the negotiation of a commercial contract between two companies."

The company at the time was in process of negotiating its first postwar union contract to cover about 120,000 workers. In the context of the tensions that followed V–J Day, the negotiations naturally attracted a great deal of attention. They began during November, 1945, in an exchange of letters—all of which were made public—between the union and the company that laid the groundwork for the actual bargaining meetings. On November 15, 1945, the company replied to the union's proposed contract amendments and its demand for a 30% increase in wages by presenting a list of 31 specific changes in the contract. They included such proposals as general revision to yield more logical and cohesive arrangement of all contract provisions; more accurate enumeration of categories of employees excluded from contract coverage; prohibitions of union coercion as well as company coercion upon employees; company "security" against work stoppages and for increased worker productivity; more inclusive reservations of management rights; reduction in numbers of union committeemen and payment for the time spent on grievances by the union; initial submission of grievances to foremen; modifications in seniority provisions, and various other proposals.

Excerpts from this communication follow:

We want in this letter to state our general position on the question of wage increases at this time. We also draw your attention to circumstances which threaten company security. These circumstances have led us to Proposal Number 3, "The Company proposes that the Union present a plan to be incorporated in the agreement, which will assure the company security through the exercise of union responsibility, which the union shop and checkoff have not provided; further, that such plan provide effective guarantees against work stoppages and for increased productivity on the part of its members."

The Ford Motor Company is today paying the highest wages in the automotive industry. We will pay higher wages whenever we are sure that we can pay them and still maintain this company as a sound and growing business. We want always to be able to pay the highest wages in the industry.

We do not believe that this is the time to attempt to settle on general wage increases. They would have to be based on guesses of what our volume of production and our costs are going to be, and on guesses as to what earnings—if any—we may be able to make. We feel that a general increase such as you propose would amount to a very heavy mortgage on the future of all of us—the Ford Motor Company and its employees alike.

We are now finishing reconversion and shooting as hard as we can toward maximum production. Every dollar of company profits during the war years is already committed to plant expansion, improvement of working conditions and installation of methods and machines to gear our operations to sharp postwar competition. Today our materials are costing us more than they ever have before. More important, our work productivity per man is at the lowest mark ever.

The wage rates we will be able to pay will, after reconversion is completed and we have reached volume production, depend entirely on these two questions: Whether we are able to keep other costs down while obtaining better productivity from our employees. . . .

The company agreed in 1941 to the union shop and checkoff provisions. Its purpose in so doing was not only to give the union the benefit of membership and financial security, but to eliminate a great deal of friction, dispute and downright industrial strife.

In return, the company was assured by union representatives that it would receive greater security and that disturbances of the type then prevalent in other plants would be avoided. . . .

Our experiences in the last four years have substantially dispelled this hope. The peaceful relations have not materialized. The experiment has been an unhappy one. The record shows, for example, 773 work stoppages since the signing of that contract in 1941.

During this period, the cost to the company of maintaining the checkoff system has been huge. Last year, for example, the company spent $2,814,078.36 in the Dearborn area alone to collect these dues and fees, and to pay more than 1,000 union men in the company's plant who spent all or part of their time handling union business.

From August, 1941, through October, 1945, the company collected for the union in dues, initiation fees and special assessments a total of $7,799,924.65.

Last year the union's income through the checkoff system was $2,050,563.71.

The result has been that the union has had membership and financial security, but the company has had no compensating security. . . .

The company accepts the principle of union membership for its employees and collective bargaining with union representatives. But if we are to reach production efficiency essential to our common objectives, we must insist upon guarantees by the union against work stoppages and losses in productivity.

Our record since 1941 indicates that these guarantees have not in fact been provided by the union shop and checkoff. We therefore propose that you come to our forthcoming negotiations prepared to give us some better plan for giving the company the same degree of security as we have given the union itself.

Because a majority of the company representatives who will attend the negotiation meetings have other pressing duties, the company proposes that the committee representing the company and the union meet on alternate days, beginning Nov. 29.

We suggest that the meetings be held from 1:30 to 5 P.M. the first week, from 9:30 A.M. to 12:30 P.M. the second week, and follow this alternate schedule until negotiations are concluded.

In reply to this letter, Richard T. Leonard, then national director of the Ford Department of the UAW, wrote:

The statement issued to the press today by the company is a union-busting, irresponsible and strife-provoking document.

The company's statement makes it clear that the Ford company has joined the conspiracy of profit-swollen corporations to perpetuate present starvation wages or open the gates to inflation through unjustified price increases. . . .

We had hoped that our differences with the company would be peaceably adjusted during negotiations, but the company, without waiting for negotiations to begin or making any attempt whatever to determine if our problems could be settled by collective bargaining, comes out with a wild and threatening attack upon the union.

This is certainly not bargaining in good faith. The only interpretation we can put on the statement is that the company is anxious to provoke a strike. . . .

The attitude of the company is medieval. It says that it won't discuss paying a living wage but at the same time it expects more effort from the workers. We say that the living wage comes first—as it must—and that we are determined to get it.

Workers enjoying a decent wage will produce everything that is needed. There won't be any production problem. Our production in wartime was no fairy tale, as the fate of the Nazis and Japanese attests.

This is the time for better wages but it is exactly the wrong time to discuss greater production. The company is still engaged in reconversion. Volume is low. It is impossible at this time to compare productivity against a peacetime period of volume production. When production gets into full swing then it will be possible to make an analysis of individual or group productivity. We are satisfied that such an analysis will show that Ford workers are putting in a very fair day's work.

The company recently purged its managerial staff. One of the chief reasons for this purge of top management was to get men into the Ford plants who can organize productive efficiency. That's tantamount to an admission that the company's production problems were the result of managerial inefficiency. . . .

The company says it wants "company security" in exchange for union security. Since the company keeps its financial affairs largely a secret it's hard to tell how much "security" the company has. We do know that the company's assets are now well over a billion dollars, having increased during wartime by more than $300,000,000.

That looks like pretty good security. Contrast it with the shocking lack of security of the Ford workers. . . .

The company claims its security has been injured by work stoppages since 1941. There is a very simple way to avoid work stoppages. That is to stop provoking them. Every work stoppage in Ford plants has been provoked by the unfair practices of management. . . .

We also challenge the statement that there have been 773 stoppages since 1941. That is the grossest kind of exaggeration. The company must have blamed on the union every occasion in which management closed down a department, a section of a department, a plant, or sent a handful of workers home.

In this connection we point out that the company boasted about the prôduction of its workers when Army-Navy "E" awards were made. Maybe it was pixies that did the work.

The company's statement on collection of dues and assessments is distorted and misleading. The UAW–CIO dues are $1 a month and there are very few assessments and they are never more than a dollar.

The company also makes a misleading complaint about the costs of union committeemen engaged in union business. It conveniently forgot that whenever a committeeman is on union business he is also directly engaged in company business. Or would the company say that its labor relations is none of its business?

The company spent far more on "labor relations" prior to the union than it does now. The company spent ten times as much money on several thousand nonproductive employees and servicemen whose only function was to keep out the union by spying, sabotage and brute force.

II

From the outset, the company insisted that an agreement must be reached on the question of company security before wage discussions could begin. Its original plan projected union responsibility, the union to guarantee payment of $5.00 a day for each worker participating in an illegal walkout. On December 10, in reply to this initial suggestion, Leonard declared:

We oppose the company's proposal because we are convinced it wouldn't work. In addition, it would be a device that could be used to break the union. . . .

It simply is not humanly possible to guarantee that there never will be a wildcat strike. Human beings are emotional and complicated—and when there are 80,000 or 90,000 as there are at Rouge—it is just not sensible to assume that things will never get out of hand.

Nor is there any guarantee that members of supervision will not provoke strikes. They have done so in many instances. The company cannot always control all members of supervision.

There are also individuals who do not like either the union or the company. By instigating a wildcat strike they could injure both the union and the company if the proposal went into effect.

There are also irresponsible individuals who act before they think. Whether their grievance is real or fancied is largely irrelevant. Such people are not going to be concerned by the fact that the union might have to pay heavy damages for their action.

There have not been anywhere near 773 unauthorized stoppages [since 1941] and most of those which have happened have been of a minor character. Nevertheless, we say also that there have been too many of them.

We are convinced that the way to reduce such stoppages to the minimum is to penalize the individuals who instigate wildcat strikes. The other side of that penny is to put an end to provocation by management supervisors. . . .

The union negotiators are willing to support a proposal that punishment for instigators of wildcat strikes be swift and sure.

(1) Any employee or employees found guilty of instigating, fomenting or giving leadership to an unauthorized stoppage of work shall be subject to discharge.

(2) Those workers who are charged with participation in (as distinguished from instigating, fomenting or giving leadership to) such unauthorized stoppages and whose guilt has been determined by the umpire shall be subject to penalties, not to exceed the following:

First participation penalty—fine—$3 for each day of the stoppage (or major fraction of any subsequent day).

Second participation penalty—fine—$5 for each day of the stoppage (or major fraction of any subsequent day).

In the event of a financial penalty, the company shall deduct the fine from the earnings of the worker involved. It is agreed that all fines levied under this section shall be donated to the President's Infantile Paralysis Fund.

(3) The Company therefore agrees, for itself, its supervision and representatives:

That they shall not, either by language or conduct, engage in any provocation leading to such an unauthorized strike.

(4) That upon complaint and proof by the union of the violation of any of the terms or the spirit of this agreement, the company shall promptly impose appropriate financial penalties upon those representatives of the company responsible therefor, it being understood that in the event of dissatisfaction by the union with the disposition of such charges the guilt or innocence of the accused and the penalty to be imposed, including the penalty of discharge, shall be determined by the Umpire.

The reply of the company follows:

The plan which you presented is a hopeful step forward in union acceptance of its responsibilities, for which you are certainly to be commended.

We are giving your proposal sincere and careful study, and it will be several days before we can form an intelligent judgment as to its workability.

As you realize, it varies basically from our suggestions. . . . We proposed that the union itself take financial responsibility . . . some insurance that the union itself would exercise control over the conduct of its members—a control which we believe you must have if we are to move forward in the conviction that both the company and the union are going to live up to their agreements. . . .

Instead of this, you now propose that the individual worker be made to take this financial responsibility.

Also there is some doubt as to our legal right to penalize individual workers and this point we must examine with some care.

In the meantime, we are now prepared to start the second phase of our discussions—the proposals . . . for an increase in wages. . . .

Between January, 1941, and July, 1945, we granted wage increases totaling 36.65 per cent (this does not include "increases" in the form of vacation pay and shift premiums). We are today paying on the average wages 7 per cent higher than the average wage of the next highest among our major competitors.

Even though there is no increase in wages, and even though we reach maximum production of motor cars and trucks during the calendar year of 1946 we will, at present OPA prices, and even with an increase of 16 per cent in the present low rate of individual productivity, lose about $27 on every motor car and truck we make—or a total of about $35,000,000.

It is inevitable, therefore, that our discussions on wages must consider our joint ability to increase the productivity of the employees in this company and upon our ability to get into full production. We hope that you will approach this basic problem with us with the same constructive thought which you and your associates gave to the question of unauthorized work stoppages.

III

Ford's first official wage offer was announced on December 18, 1945, in a statement which again restated the company's basic objective "to arrive at workable and equitable solutions to the problem of wages and the problem of company security which involves worker productivity and unauthorized work stoppages." The statement proceeded as follows:

On the other hand, you have repeatedly maintained that these statistics do not answer the pressing and real problem of the employees you represent—the problem of meeting family budgets without the overtime pay taken home during wartime.

Theoretically, we could ask the Government to raise ceiling prices enough to cover a wage increase. We do not think it wise to go that road at this time, because present Government policy is based on the belief that only rigid adherence to OPA ceiling prices can prevent inflation.

That puts the problem squarely up to the Ford Motor Company and its employees. Unless we give up the problem as insoluble, we have no alternative but to take a gamble.

The management of the company has done its best to calculate carefully the risks in such a gamble. It has decided to risk an additional $33,000,000.

Behind this important decision is our belief that we may be able to win these things:

1. The confidence and cooperation of our employees.

2. We can stay in production and keep men employed.

3. In prompt all-out production we can sharpen our production skills and efficiency to meet and beat competition.

4. We may help to break the log-jam of postwar mass production.

5. By bringing the supply of new cars up to demand, we can do our share in halting inflation.

Therefore we propose:

1. That a wage increase of 15 cents per hour be granted, this increase to become effective at the beginning of the calendar month during which total production reaches a volume of 80,000 units, including Fords, Mercurys, Lincolns and trucks.

(This represents a 12.4 per cent increase in our present average wage and approximately 21 per cent more than the present average of our major competitors.)

2. That these new rates remain in effect for two years from the date they become effective.

3. That this proposal be made subject to agreement on the following items involved with the problem of company security:

A. Elimination of unauthorized work stoppages.

B. Management prerogatives.

C. Reduction of the number of union committeemen.

4. That if the OPA should raise price ceilings on our products, such action shall not be made the basis for additional wage proposals by the union.

This wage offer was rejected by the union as "completely unacceptable" and "full of jokes."

At the same time, a new company security plan was also suggested by the company. It provided that instigators of wildcat strikes be subject to summary dismissal, subject to appeal, and that participants be fined $1.50 a day for the first offense and $2.50 for the second one. These amounts were to be deducted from the wages of the offenders and turned over to some organized charity, and the union was to be liable to Ford for equal amounts to be taken from the sums collected by the company under the checkoff system.

Negotiations were recessed until January 7, 1946.

Throughout the negotiations the union had been stressing the benefits that would accrue to the company if Ford would become the first major producer to conclude an agreement. By such pioneering, the union representatives argued, the company would win highly valuable goodwill.

As January drew to a close, rumors of an impending agreement at Chrysler began to spread. Thereupon Leonard hurriedly invited the negotiating committee to meet in "emergency session." The committee on January 26, 1946, announced agreement upon a wage increase, "beating" a similar announcement from Chrysler by a few hours. The Ford negotiations established a wage increase of 18 cents per hour, working out to about 15%; Chrysler granted 18½ cents per hour, or about 16%. At the same time, Reuther announced for the G.M. workers, then in the 67th day of their strike, that they would not settle for less than the 19½ cents an hour recommended by the President's fact-finding board.[1]

---

[1] On May 8, 1946, Leonard, speaking before the Industrial Relations Council of Metropolitan Boston, explained the settlement in part by saying, "We did recognize,

The full contract at Ford was not completed for another month, becoming effective on February 27, 1946, and running to May 30, 1947. Comparison of its terms with those of the agreement it superseded revealed many changes: the revisions tightened the scope and coverage of the central provisions, marked the transition to permanent continuing joint relationships, and spelled out mutual rights and obligations with explicit particularity.

IV

The major innovation of the 1946 agreement was embodied in its Article V, titled "Union Responsibility," which follows:

Article V

Union Responsibility

The Union recognizes that the primary objective of the Company in entering into this Agreement is the promotion of orderly and peaceful relations with its employees and the attaining of efficient and uninterrupted operations in its plants.

It is recognized that this contract is intended to set forth the rights and obligations of the Company to the Union and the employees it represents, and that the grievance procedure set forth herein gives the Union members full and complete redress for any grievance arising from this Agreement.

To protect the Company against violation of this Article, the Union agrees as follows:

Section 1. The Union and its members, individually and collectively, agree that during the term of this Agreement, they will not participate in any strike in respect to any controversy, dispute or grievance.

a. Which may properly be considered under the grievance procedure provided herein and which may be finally determined by the Umpire, whose determination with respect to such matters shall be conclusive and binding on the parties as specifically provided.

b. Which may relate to any matters specifically provided herein as Company responsibility, or committed to the Company's discretion, as to which matters the Company has the express right to determine and decide.

c. Which has as its objective an avoidance of the effects of a decision of the Umpire or of obtaining a change in or addition to this contract or any agreements supplementary thereto so long as this contract remains in force.

Section 2. For the purpose of Section 1, the term "strike" includes a sit-down, stay-in, slow-down, walk-out, curtailment of work, stoppage of work, interference with work, stoppage of any of the Company's operations, or picketing of any of the Company's plants or premises.

Section 3. In the event of any controversies, disputes, or grievances relating to the matters other than those specified in Section 1 hereof, the Union and its members, individually, and collectively, agree that they will not participate in any strike until the specific issues in dispute have been presented in writing by the National

however, that management had a financial problem which was concerning them to a very serious extent. We took that into consideration when we settled for 18 cents. We also took into consideration the differential in the wages paid at Ford and those paid at General Motors and Chrysler. . . . The company's representatives said that the average Ford rate is nine cents above General Motors and seven or eight cents above Chrysler. I do not know if the differential is quite that much, but I am satisfied that it is not less than 5 or 6 cents. That, of course, represents a lot of money when you consider that the company employs well over one hundred thousand people."

Ford Department and negotiations have continued with respect thereto for a period of fifteen (15) working days and until strike action has thereafter been fully authorized as provided in the constitution of the Union, upon the issues as presented to the Company. In no event shall the strike take the form of a sit-down, stay-in, slow-down, or comparable curtailment of work as contrasted with a walk-out.

Section 4. Any strike contrary to and in violation of Sections 1 and 3 above, shall be deemed to be an illegitimate strike for the purpose of this section.

Section 5. In the event of an illegitimate strike:

a. Any employee or employees found guilty of instigating, fomenting, actively supporting or giving leadership to such illegitimate strike shall be subject to discharge. In the event the penalty of discharge is invoked and the affected employee denies his guilt, the Local Union having jurisdiction may conduct an immediate investigation to determine the guilt or innocence of the discharged member. If the Local Union's investigation substantiates the Company's claim, no grievance will be filed in respect to such discharge. In any event an investigation must be conducted prior to a grievance being filed.

If the Local Union's investigation does not substantiate the Company's claim, a grievance will be processed in accordance with the grievance procedure as hereinafter outlined, but only for the purpose of determining the guilt or innocence of the employee. The Umpire shall have no authority to modify such penalty with the sole exception that if he determines the employee not to be guilty of violation of this sub-paragraph, but to be guilty of participation in such illegitimate strike, he may reduce the penalty to that appropriate for such participation.

b. Any employee who participates in an illegitimate strike but who is not guilty of instigating, fomenting, actively supporting, or giving leadership to such strike, shall be subject to the following penalties: First offense—reprimand to two weeks' suspension; second offense—reprimand to discharge.

In the event discipline consists of suspension, Management shall have the sole discretion as to time such penalty shall be applied, but shall be required to give notice of alleged guilt and extent of penalty to the employee and his committeeman within seven (7) days from the date of the alleged offense. . . .

Employees guilty of two or more offenses of participating in an illegitimate strike shall be treated as instigators and the provisions of sub-paragraph (*a*) of this paragraph shall be applicable to them.

Participation in illegitimate strikes occurring prior to the date of this Agreement shall not be counted for the purpose of determining the number of participations under this sub-paragraph.

The Company has agreed to withdraw its demand for financial penalties in cases of illegitimate strikes or work stoppages upon the Union's representations and assurances that it would exert every possible effort and means at its disposal to stop or to reduce to a negligible minimum such illegitimate strikes through its regular Union procedures. However, if the experience between the execution date of this Agreement and May 30, 1947, shows that the Union either cannot or does not so reduce such work stoppages, then at that time the parties may renegotiate this Agreement to include a clause providing for financial penalties.

DISCUSSION QUESTIONS

1. What seems to have been the chief objective of the company and of the union in these negotiations from the viewpoint of (*a*) immediate goals, and (*b*) continuing relationships?

2. Review critically the strategy and tactics pursued by each of the parties in promoting its objectives.

3. Analyze the strategy advanced by each of the parties in the various letters and proposals exchanged between the two.

4. Evaluate Article V—Union Responsibility—written into the 1946 agreement.

5. Do the 1946 negotiations represent any shift in the "structure" being built between the parties from that of 1941?

FORD MOTOR COMPANY

NEGOTIATING THE 1947 AGREEMENT:
WAGES, TAFT-HARTLEY ACT, AND THE ALTERNATIVE VOTE

I

During the early weeks of negotiation of the contract that expired on May 30, 1947, which began May 5 and continued for more than three months, the parties debated the "improvements in the present contract" they respectively desired. On May 27 the union issued a statement blaming the company for the alleged stalemate in the bargaining sessions, and called a secret strike vote. The next day, Ford released the following letter:

When we started our negotiations three weeks ago, our objective was to arrive at a new contract by the time the old one ran out on May 30, 1947. We knew our employees would want to have, as of May 31, the benefit of any wage increase the contract might provide.

This is still our objective, although only two days remain. In order to expedite matters, we wish to make two alternative proposals, either one of which would be acceptable to us.

1. Although we would like to see improvements in the present contract, it has on the whole worked well for both of us. We are prepared to renew this contract immediately for a minimum period of one year, amending it to provide a 15 cents per hour average wage increase to become effective May 31. Three and a half cents of this 15 cents would be used for six holidays with pay, in accordance with the pattern established in the industry,[1] and details of the distribution of the balance of this increase would be worked out between us.

2. We are prepared to agree now that our new contract will become effective on June 15, this contract to consist of the present one amended by any changes we have agreed upon by that time and to run for a minimum period of one year. As part of that contract we are prepared to agree now to a 15 cent per hour average wage increase to become retroactively effective May 31. Three and a half cents of this 15 cents would be used for six holidays with pay, in accordance with the pattern established in the industry, and details of the distribution of the balance of this increase would be worked out between us.

Both proposals assume prompt ratification by your membership so that there will be no delay in passing on benefits.

In accordance with the company's desire to pay the best wages in the industry, the Ford average hourly rate is about seven cents per hour greater than the average hourly rate of its principal competitors. This differential, which will be maintained by the proposed increase, has been recognized officially by your union.

But a wage increase can be considered only against the background of the rest of the contract. Before we can make any reasonable estimate of wages we can afford to pay, we must know the conditions under which we are going to operate to make the money to pay those wages.

We ask you also to keep constantly in mind the fact that Ford Motor Company

---

[1] During April, 1947, General Motors had established the industry pattern in settling its wage revisions with the United Electrical Workers (CIO) on the basis of 11½ cents per hour increase and six paid holidays equivalent to 3½ cents more per hour.

is extremely concerned with the necessity for keeping the prices of its products down. We gave evidence of this concern in January 1947 when we reduced prices.

The increase we are now proposing will add approximately $43,000,000 annually to the company's labor costs. This added cost to the production of cars and trucks at this critical time must somehow be compensated for by high productivity, continued freedom from unauthorized work stoppages[1] and sustained high production if we are to escape the unsound position of simply passing the bill on to our customers.

This is added reason why the nature of the new contract as a whole is extremely important to us and why any wage increase must be considered part of the whole "package."

Simultaneously the company announced that it was raising wages of 20,000 salaried employees by 10%.

II

In rejecting both of these alternative offers, the union negotiators now brought into central focus their demand for a pension plan.

The issues between the company and the union involve more than just a wage increase. Equally important factors are the human needs of the workers involving old age retirement and social security benefits.

When the expiration date of the contract arrived, its term was extended, pending continued negotiations. Reports from the bargaining sessions indicated that the June sessions concentrated upon formulating in basic outline an acceptable pension plan and dovetailing it with the wage and other provisions of the emerging contract. As the negotiations were drawing to a successful conclusion, the Labor-Management Relations Act of 1947—the Taft-Hartley Bill—was enacted into law over President Truman's veto on June 23. Four days later a joint statement made the following report of progress in negotiations:

After eight weeks of intensive bargaining, the Ford Motor Company and the UAW–CIO have reached tentative agreement on a new labor contract that marks an important step forward in providing security for Ford Motor Company employees. Included is the first retirement plan for hourly rate employees in the automotive industy.

The contract provides for a straight 7-cent an hour wage increase. Other financial gains will be in the form of the retirement program which will be put into effect as soon as possible after ratification of the contract by the union and the company.

When finally signed, the contract will run for a minimum of two years. It can be reopened for negotiation only on economic matters, and only once during the two years. The wage agreement will be retroactive to May 31, 1947, the date on which the old contract expired.

With the wage increase, the average hourly pay of Ford employees will be approximately 3 cents an hour more than those of major competitors. An additional 5-cent an hour increase will be given to 10,000 maintenance employees and to coremakers and jobbing molders.

---

[1] In 1946 there were only 27 unauthorized work stoppages throughout the United States at all Ford plants, resulting in the loss of 112,000 man-hours of production. In contrast, about 2,071,000 man-hours of production had been lost for the three-year period 1943–1945 because of some 608 unauthorized stoppages.

The parties projected the retirement plan as a voluntary program which employees would join at their own option. A summary of its major provisions in the formulation of June 27, with the differences on detail between the parties, follows:

Company Contributions. 5% of payroll, equaling on the average $146.60 per man per year, or an annual total of about $17,600,000. An additional $200,000,000 it was estimated would be needed over the first ten years "to get the plan started."

Employee Contributions. 2½% of the first $3,000 in annual earnings, 5% of all earnings above $3,000. It was estimated that the average employee contribution would come to $73.30 per year, totaling annually about $8,800,000, or half of the estimated company contribution.

Benefits to Employees. Pension. 1% of "pay" multiplied by the number of years worked. Retirement would be placed somewhere between the ages of 55 and 65; pensions would be paid only after a minimum number of years of service. Both figures remained still to be negotiated; regarding years of service the union was asking five, the company was stipulating ten.

Full Disability. Employees would be eligible after a minimum of 15 years of service. The amount of benefit and minimum age limit were still to be negotiated.

Death. Entire employee contribution plus interest would be payable to survivor.

Savings. Upon withdrawal from the plan, an employee's entire contribution plus interest would belong to him.

Administration. No final decision had been made. Some form of joint company-union management was projected as probable, while it seemed likely that the plan would be financed by deposits in trust rather than through insurance policies.

III

As the negotiations stretched through July, the union charged the company with receding from its verbal agreement upon details of the pension plan, while the company emphasized the unreasonable demands of the union to "by-pass" the Taft-Hartley Act.

Three provisions of the new law in particular were impinging upon the negotiations. These were:

(1) Sections 102 through 104 providing that no performance of an obligation under a collective bargaining agreement entered into prior to the effective date of the Taft-Hartley Act would be deemed an unfair labor practice, if it had not constituted as such a violation of the Wagner Act, as for instance, the union shop. The effective date was set at "sixty days after the date of the enactment" of the act, or August 22, 1947.

(2) Section 302 regulating the payment and delivery by an employer of "any money or other thing of value to any representative" of his employees. Specifically this section prohibited, among other things, the checkoff of union dues without written assignment from each employee involved.

(3) Section 301 (*a*) and (*b*) permitting damage suits against unions for contract violations, as follows:

(*a*) Suits for violation of contracts between an employer and a labor organization . . . or between any such labor organizations, may be brought in any district court of the United States having jurisdiction of the parties, without respect to the amount in controversy or without regard to the citizenship of the parties.

(*b*) Any labor organization . . . shall be bound by the acts of its agents. Any such labor organization may sue or be sued as an entity. . . . Any money judgment against a labor organization . . . shall be enforceable only against the organization as an entity and against its assets. . . .

As July drew to a close, negotiations had apparently broken down. On July 30 the union negotiating committee informed the company negotiators that the committee was powerless to consider further suggestions for averting a general strike in the Ford plants, scheduled to begin on August 4. The union was asking a contract provision that would exempt it from Section 301, quoted above.

On July 31 Mr. Ford telephoned Philip Murray, requesting a conference. At 5 P.M. as the conference convened in New York, Mr. Ford handed Mr. Murray the following letter:

Dear Mr. Murray:

I am writing you because of the critical situation which faces Ford Motor Company today. We are threatened with a general strike next Monday which we are sure could be avoided by the use of patience and reason.

We believe in collective bargaining. We have, moreover, scrupulously followed the practice of negotiating across the bargaining table. It is our conviction that no good purpose can be served by turning the bargaining table into a public forum.

We find now, however, that we are no longer bargaining with the representatives of our employees. The negotiations have become a marionette show with hands far distant from the bargaining table pulling the strings.

For this reason we feel we have no choice but to bring to your immediate attention a proposal which we have made to the Ford UAW–CIO, and one which the union claims it is powerless to consider.

The union is asking us to include in our new agreement a provision which would in effect nullify certain provisions of the Taft-Hartley law. This we cannot agree to do. We respect and obey the laws of the land and cannot be party to placing unions above the law.

On the other hand, we are aware that irresponsible factions in Ford UAW–CIO could inspire incidents over which the union leadership might have little or no control, and that the union might in consequence suffer financial penalty for an act it could not prevent.

To eliminate this possibility, we have suggested a contract provision which would leave no question as to our good faith under such circumstances.

We have, to be specific, proposed that the company will agree not to institute suit against the union for damages arising out of illegal strikes under the following "good faith" conditions:

1. If the union has not inspired or authorized such an illegal strike, and

2. If the union will agree promptly to denounce publicly such an illegal strike, and

3. If the union and its responsible officers and agents will agree to use prompt and honest effort to prevent or end any such illegal strike, and

4. If the impartial umpire, who, by agreement with the union, decides other points of difference arising out of our contract and who has always had the com-

plete confidence of both the union and the company, can be the final judge as to whether the union has taken these reasonable steps in regard to illegal strikes.

In short, this provision merely asks that the leadership of the union act in good faith and with reasonable diligence to avoid illegal strikes or the threat of such strikes. In turn, we are pledging the good faith of Ford Motor Company not to claim damages, if, in the opinion of the impartial umpire, the union meets these reasonable conditions.

Finally, I would like to point out that the strike which is threatened against this company would not really be a strike against Ford Motor Company at all. It would be a strike against the government and the laws of the land.

In this connection, may we say that we sharply question the wisdom of a strike or a threat to strike under these circumstances. Our customers, our employees, our management—none of whom is at fault—will suddenly suffer loss of cars and trucks, wages, and income, simply because Ford Motor Company has been chosen as the guinea pig in an effort by UAW–CIO to veto those parts of a federal statute which it does not happen to like. In our opinion, it is things like this which cause people to lose confidence in labor leadership, which we will both have cause to regret.

We do not want a strike. We believe our employees do not want a strike. To avert a strike we have made a proposal which we are sure you will find fair and reasonable in every respect. Since Ford UAW–CIO seems powerless to act in this matter, we are calling on you to act.

The top-level conference in New York reached no definite conclusion, and Mr. Ford announced at its close that the company's discussions "with the Ford Union Bargaining Committee" would be resumed "in Detroit, Friday, August 1, at 2:30 P.M." When these discussions resumed, the strike threat still hung over the negotiations. Each side increased its public announcements. The company sought particularly to make clear that allegations ascribing the deadlock to differences over the pension plan were misleading; that the true heart of the controversy centered in the Taft-Hartley Act. Thus under date of August 2, 1947, it released a letter sent to the union:

You have stated publicly that you intend to press for a general strike against the Ford Motor Company. You now give as one of the reasons for this threat the failure to reach immediate agreement on all details of the Ford Employee Retirement Plan, although you know there is little disagreement between us on the general terms of the plan, and despite the fact you have refused to discuss these few differences with us during the past week. . . .

We have no objection to withdrawing our proposal. The financial burdens involved are tremendous. What we do object to is misrepresentation, which we think happened when you called our proposal "inadequate."

Before we could entertain any thought of an Employee Retirement Plan at Ford Motor Company, we had to answer two basic questions. The first was the question of company security. If the company's ability to go on as a profitable, progressive institution would be threatened, it was obvious that such a program could not be considered.

On the other hand, if our employees were not encouraged to their best efforts and top efficiency by fair treatment, good working conditions, good wages, and a reasonable sense of security in their jobs, the ability of the company to succeed in competitive enterprise would also be placed in danger.

The Employee Retirement Plan we proposed meets these requirements. Moreover, to the best of our knowledge it is as progressive a step in the direction of employee security as has been taken by a large mass-production industrial concern.

To state it as simply as possible, the plan is designed to assure our employees a better old age through added comforts and enjoyments, and most of all, a sense of dignity and independence. . . .

The following day, the company took the admittedly unusual step of appealing to the union membership over the heads of their leaders.

To All Members of the Ford UAW–CIO:

You may shortly be required to take part in a general strike against the Ford Motor Company. Your Union representatives have publicly announced that one reason for such a strike would be because they had been unable to reach agreement with us on details of an employee retirement plan.

Ordinarily, the Ford Motor Company conducts its affairs with you through the men you have chosen to represent you. At this time, however, we do not think that your representatives have given you a clear idea either of the proposed employee retirement program or of the attitude of the Ford Motor Company in this matter.

We are proud of this plan. We regard it as a most progressive step in the direction of better employee relationships. Why, of all issues, this progressive proposal should have been chosen as an excuse for calling a general strike is something we cannot understand.

We know such a plan will give our employees additional assurance of security and a sense of dignity and independence in old age. In spite of its great cost to the company, we feel it also answers what must be a basic concern of ours—the question of company security.

Because the plan involves well over 100,000 people with varying years of service, rates of income, and for many other reasons, it is necessarily very complex. However, I want you to know the main points and benefits of the plan. Therefore, I am attaching a copy of a letter sent . . . to your Union representatives on this subject. I am confident that if you study the brief summary of the plan closely, you will agree with us that this is a great step forward in industrial democracy.

Sincerely yours,
HENRY FORD II

As the strike deadline approached, the union negotiators requested that Mr. Ford join the conferees in an effort to reach a settlement. Mr. Ford replied by the following telegram:

With other members of the policy committee, I have been in close touch with negotiations over the week-end. In spite of our very best efforts to conciliate differences with the union, it is now quite clear to us that you propose to strike unless we agree with you to establish for all industry what seems to us a disastrous precedent for scuttling the union responsibility provisions of the Taft-Hartley law.

We have made many proposals to you, all within the spirit of the Taft-Hartley law, but intended to give full protection to responsible union leadership. We offered to pledge the good faith of Ford Motor Company in return only for a pledge of good faith on the part of the union that its leaders will prevent or bring to an end illegal strikes.

It seems to me a mistake to leave the impression that any major difference between us centers in our ability to settle at once on the few remaining details of the proposed employee retirement plan. I must remind you that during the last ten days of negotiation, you have refused even to discuss this retirement plan. And in the eight hours of yesterday's negotiations, only the final 15 minutes were spent in discussion of the plan, and that at our insistence.

Bluntly stated, the strike you seem determined to call will not be an attack on the labor policy of Ford Motor Company but a strike against a law.

We do not want a strike. We are prepared to continue negotiations to prevent one. Under the circumstances, however, I do not think my attendance at this morning's session could add anything helpful.

Tension mounted as the nation watched to see if the negotiators would avert the biggest stoppage of manufacturing workers thus far in 1947. For almost eighteen consecutive hours the negotiators remained in session. Finally in the dawn hours of August 5, union spokesmen emerged to call off the strike. The parties announced the agreement in the following joint statement:

> Ford Motor Company and the UAW–CIO have reached agreement on a contract provision covering the financial responsibility sections of the Taft-Hartley law which have been under discussion in negotiations between the company and the union. The agreement represents a compromise between the final proposal of the union and the final proposal of the company. Strike action was cancelled by the eleventh-hour agreement on this issue. . . . Agreement on the Taft-Hartley issue is of course contingent upon agreement on the whole contract. . . .

IV

In the course of the day the exact wording of Article 5, Section 6, of the contract embodying the provisions regarding union financial liability was made public, as follows:

ARTICLE V—UNION RESPONSIBILITY

Section 6. In consideration of the undertaking by the Union hereinbefore provided to avoid unauthorized strikes and work stoppages, it is agreed that a four-man committee, composed of two chosen by the Company and two by the Union, will be appointed forthwith to work out a solution of the question of the liability, for damages by suit for breach of contract, of the International Union, the Local Unions covered by this contract, and their officers, agents or members. If the committee fails to arrive at a unanimous solution within three (3) months from the date of this Agreement, it will choose a fifth member of the committee (or, if it cannot unanimously agree upon the identity of such fifth member, the Umpire shall serve as such). The committee shall if necessary continue its efforts to arrive at a solution for an additional three months' period and for such further periods of three months (limited as provided below) as the committee by majority vote of all its members may determine. The committee's solution of such question shall be submitted in writing, must be by unanimous consent of all of its members, and thereupon will be conclusive and binding upon the Company and the Union.

Should the committee fail both to arrive at a solution and to extend the period of its deliberations as above provided, the Union may re-open direct negotiations on this question with the Company, which either party may terminate at any time; provided, however, that the total period (hereinafter referred to as the deliberation period) which may be devoted to such question both by deliberation of the committee and by such reopened direct negotiations, shall be limited to one year from the date of this Agreement. There shall be no liability by suit for damages on the part of any such Union, their officers, agents, or members for breach of contract by reason of any strike or work stoppage on the part of the members of any such Union, their officers, agents, or members, which may have occurred during the deliberation period; and the Company shall institute no suit for damages against any such Union or any of their officers, agents, or members in case of such breach of contract alleged to have been committed during the deliberation period.

It is further agreed that in the event suit for damages shall be instituted by the Company in violation of its undertakings in this Section, or for the purpose of invalidating any of the provisions of this Section, the Union reserves the right to terminate this Agreement forthwith.

If at the end of the deliberation period, no solution of such question acceptable to both parties shall have been worked out by the committee or agreed upon by the parties, the Union shall have the right to strike for that reason only, without liability by suit for damages for breach of contract based thereon on the part of any such Union, their officers, agents, or members. The preceding sentence shall not be deemed to limit the right of the Union to strike at the same or any other time on any other issue with respect to which a strike is not prohibited by the other Sections of this Agreement, including the right to strike over a failure to agree upon wages in the event the wage issue is reopened pursuant to the termination provisions of this Agreement.

It is further agreed that in the event of and notwithstanding such strike all the provisions of this Agreement shall remain in full force and effect for the full term of this Agreement.

Mr. Ford issued a statement expressing his gratification:

The agreement to refer to a joint study group the question of the liability of the union for damages by suit for breach of contract seems to us an eminently fair solution to a particularly thorny problem. Any new labor legislation raises problems of human relationships. It has become apparent to us that all of the ramifications of such problems cannot be ironed out immediately around the bargaining table. Under today's settlement opportunity has now been provided for finding, in less hectic surroundings, a solution within the spirit of the Taft-Hartley law, acceptable to both the union and the company.

V

With this hurdle safely passed, the negotiators set their sights on the next deadline: August 21, 1947, so that the union shop could be carried over from the prior contract without a specific vote from 51 per cent of eligible employees, as required by Taft-Hartley. For more than two weeks, conferences were convened and adjourned. New snags appeared to prolong negotiations—for instance, the demand from the company that termination of the paid lunch period of 20 minutes must be part of the contract incorporating the pension plan.

As August 21 came, the negotiators again were meeting in continuous session. With the day ticking to its close, the last compromises were made. Rumor subsequently noised it abroad that the clock had been set back minutes enough to bring the signatures on the dotted lines before midnight. At any rate, the jubilant negotiators announced their new contract under date of August 21, 1947.

VI

The terms of settlement proved complex. No less than seven documents were required to embody a program by which the parties completed a contract, yet left some of its terms open as alternative possibilities to be decided by membership referendum. September 30, 1947, was set as still one more—

and final—deadline; by then the referendum votes would have to be taken and counted to determine—and the company notified—which contract version the union members wished.

Thus on August 21, the parties announced (1) an *Extension Agreement;* (2) a *Settlement Agreement;* (3) *Agreements* to accompany ratification of either of the settlements set forth as alternative proposals in (2); (4) an *Agreement on Union Shop;* (5) an *Agreement on Retirement Plan;* (6) Appendix to (5) setting forth *"Outline of Retirement Plan for Hourly Rate Employees,"* which was to be reduced to writing if the contract embodying such a plan were ratified; and (7) an outline setting forth changes of substance in *Present* [1947] *Master Agreement.*

Agreement 1 provided the mechanism for continuing an effective contract, while the still moot proposals which were set forth by Agreement 2 were submitted to the union members. The two alternative proposals offered the members for vote follow:

PROPOSAL NO. 1

1. Contract provisions as agreed upon including:
    (a) Taft-Hartley Protective Clause.
    (b) Union Shop as agreed upon.
2. Pension Plan as presented.
3. 7 cents per hour general wage increase; 5 cents per hour additional for skilled maintenance and construction employees, jobbing moulders and jobbing coremakers.
4. Paid lunch period eliminated.
5. Termination date, July 15, 1948, for economic matters and Union Shop—balance of contract, July 15, 1949.
6. Taft-Hartley termination one (1) year from date of Agreement (unless under its terms solution is determined sooner).
7. Retroactive date for wage adjustments—May 31, 1947.

PROPOSAL NO. 2

1. Contract provisions as agreed upon including:
    (a) Taft-Hartley Protective Clause.
    (b) Union Shop as agreed upon.
2. Wage Pattern . . . 11½ cent General Wage Increase and 3½ cents for paid holidays. 5 cents additional wage increase for skilled maintenance and construction employees, jobbing moulders and jobbing coremakers.
3. Under this proposal, the Umpire, under the contract, will rule on the company's notification of termination of the paid lunch period.
4. Termination date as above.
5. Retroactive date as above.
6. If either proposal is accepted by September 15, 1947, the Company will agree to the Union Shop provision until July 15, 1948.

Members could also signify their choice of "neither proposal."

Agreements 3 through 6 embodied the varying steps to be taken following ratification of either alternative proposal, the outline of the retirement plan, and the crucial agreement on the union shop clauses of the contract. By the terms covering the union shop, union membership continued a condition of employment until July 15, 1948, if ratification notices for either one of the two contract proposals were received by September 30. Section 4, however, abrogated this part of the contract in any state having a validated prohibition on such a form of union security.

The changes of substance made in the 1946 contract may be classified under three headings: (1) revisions pertaining to normal collective dealings; (2) revisions representing adjustments to the Taft-Hartley law; and (3) a revision withdrawing all portal-to-portal suits.

Three major changes contained adjustments directly related to the Taft-Hartley Act. That dealing with union financial liability has already been cited. The other two stipulated:

Article ii—Union Shop

The parties have heretofore agreed by an agreement dated August 21, 1947, to certain provisions creating a union shop for a period not running beyond July 15, 1948. If and to the extent permitted by law, the provisions of Sections 2, 3 and 4 of such agreement shall be deemed to be a part of this Article of this Agreement as of July 15, 1948, and continued in effect thereafter until the expiration of the remainder of this agreement.

Article iii—Dues and Assessments

Section 1. The Company will deduct from the pay of each employee covered by this Agreement all Union membership dues, provided that at the time of such deduction there is in the possession of the Company a subsisting written assignment, executed by the employee, in the form and according to the terms of the authorization form hereto attached as Appendix D, authorizing such deduction by the Company.

VII

The union immediately launched its program for obtaining ratification of the agreement by its members, including a choice between the two alternative "proposals." For instance, *Ford Facts,* the journal published by Local 600 in Detroit as the "official organ" of the "world's largest local union, reaching 70,000 homes each week," devoted its issue of August 30 almost completely to the new contract. In his front-page "President's Column," Thomas Thompson submitted his report on the negotiations and his recommendation regarding the two proposals. Excerpts follow:

The long, weary weeks of negotiations are over. The National Negotiating Committee fought to the bitter end on each issue. Aside from the length of the negotiations and the several crises, including the threat of strike action precipitated by the provision of the union-busting Taft-Hartley Law which went into effect during the negotiations, the Ford workers made labor history in the battle with the company just ended.

Your committee has reported back to the membership two alternative proposals on the wage increase and pension plan. As President of Local 600 and as Chairman of the National Negotiating Committee, with full knowledge of the entire negotiations, including the technical discussions of the pension plan between the union and company experts, I believe it is my duty to take my position on these alternative proposals.

I have been told that taking a position for or against the pension plan is loaded with political dynamite—that it would be politically expedient to allow the issue to go to the membership without a recommendation from me. That is not the way I see my duty to the membership of Local 600. The issue is too important now and too important to the future welfare and security of our local union membership to permit any pussy-footing on the issue.

As your duly-elected President to whom you have a right to look for advice, guidance, and leadership, I now take my position. I recommend that the membership of Local 600 vote "Yes" for the proposal that contains the Pension Plan (No. 1). The pension plan is within your grasp, despite the fact that many people thought it was a dream.

I cannot say that it is a Utopian plan. I can say, on the advice of the union experts, that it is the best pension plan in heavy American industry today. Despite the fact that it is not all that you, myself, or the other members of the National Negotiating Committee wanted, it is the beginning of old-age security for our workers.

I assure you that when Local 600 leads by adopting this pension plan, the UAW–CIO and the American Labor Movement will follow. Strike your blow for freedom from old-age insecurity by voting YES for the pension plan (Proposal No. 1).

A total of 70,004 union members voted in the ratification referendum; this represented almost two-thirds (65.42%) of the 107,000 Ford production workers whom the union represented. They voted 51,832 for Proposal 2, 16,720 for Proposal 1, and 1,452 against both the proposals. Each of the 43 locals in Ford plants had thus turned down Proposal 1 to register preference for the larger wage increase of Proposal 2; the pension plan was defeated by more than three to one. Mr. Leonard attributed this result to the impact of the high cost of living. Mr. John S. Bugas, before The American Management Association, cited the results on the pension plan as evidence of the fact that "union leaders are definitely out of touch with the thinking and the desires of rank-and-file union members."

On September 30, the UAW–CIO officially notified the Ford Motor Company of its acceptance of Proposal 2. The wage increase it included, retroactive to May 31, according to union officials, would give the production employees on the average about $100 in back pay and bring the average hourly rate in Ford plants to $1.52.

The 1947 contract thereupon went into effect.

DISCUSSION QUESTIONS

1. Divide this negotiation from its opening on May 5 to its conclusion on September 30 into periods to show (a) the changing fulcrum of the bargaining agenda; (b) the major factor or factors causing these changes; and (c) the recourses utilized by the parties to prevent breakdown at the points of tension in each period.

2. Compare the tentative agreement reached by the parties on June 27 with the results of the ratification referendum on September 15; and both in turn with the first offers of the company on May 28. What inferences would you draw on (a) the influence of "wage patterns" in the automobile industry; (b) implications for subsequent bargaining which each side might reasonably draw from these comparisons?

3. Evaluate the strategy and tactics of each of the parties.

FORD MOTOR COMPANY

NEGOTIATING THE 1948 AGREEMENT

I

The 1947 agreement was to remain effective until July 15, 1949, with the proviso that it might be reopened after one year, on 60 days' written notice, for negotiating *economic issues only*.

The year between the effective date of this contract and May 10, 1948, when the union served notice of its desire "to reopen," saw various developments in labor relations at Ford plants. For one thing, the recognition of the Foreman's Association of America, which had begun in 1942, was terminated following a strike lasting 47 days. The strike was not effective, and the men returned to work as individuals after personal letters had been sent to each one by Henry Ford II explaining the company's position regarding unions of supervisors. Management invited their return and their suggestions for future improvements in their jobs. Thereupon a comprehensive program of improving supervisory relationships was launched under the aegis of a special "Management Relations Department."

In various plants, explorations into employee morale were undertaken. A counseling program for supervisors was initiated, and programs for orienting new members as they entered upon Ford jobs were undertaken.

On the union side, Richard Leonard, vice president of the UAW in 1947 and head of the negotiating committee as director of its "National Ford Department," allied himself with the opposition to President Walter P. Reuther and was defeated for re-election. He was replaced by Kenneth Bannon.

II

On May 3, 1948, delegates to the National Ford Council voted unanimously for the following economic demands formally served upon Ford on May 10, 1948.

1. A comprehensive social security–group insurance program, including life, health and accident, hospital, surgical and medical coverage for the worker and his family.

2. A general wage increase of thirty cents per hour.

3. Establishment of a fund adequate to provide equalization of rates by job classifications on a company-wide basis.

4. Revision of present vacation provisions to provide forty hours pay to employees with six months seniority, with graduated increases up to one hundred twenty hours pay for employees with five years seniority; also vacation rights for time spent in the Armed Forces.

5. Provisions for a guaranteed weekly wage of forty hours for any week in which any employee is called to work.

6. Revision of existing contract terms to provide time and one-half for Saturday as such, double time for Sunday as such, and triple time for all holidays worked.

7. Increase in present night shift premiums from five cents to ten per cent.

8. Elimination of merit spreads in all plants of the company.

9. Priorities and 20 per cent discount on all Ford products for all employees covered by the agreement.

10. Employees covered by the agreement to be allowed four hours off with pay on primary and general election days.

11. The establishment of an appropriate retroactive date when the provisions governing economic issues shall become effective.

12. A starting time for the work week.

13. A wage increase, above the general increase asked, for foundry workers, high window cleaners, tool and die workers and employees in the maintenance division.

14. Revision of paid holiday plan.

15. Pension plan—derived from royalty on each unit and service parts produced.

16. Re-establishment of paid lunch period to include all plants.

17. Weekly pay day; subject to the approval of the local involved.

18. Seven day operations. Premium pay for Saturday and Sunday as such. (Working schedules to be mutually agreed upon.)

19. Thirty (30) day reopening clause on economic demands.

Enumeration of . . . the above-listed economic matters is not to be considered as excluding other changes . . . which may be made necessary . . . by reason of matters arising during the course of negotiations.

While this notice is given pursuant to the Labor-Management Relations Act, 1947, the undersigned Union waives none of its rights and hereby expressly reserves all objection to the constitutionality, validity, and applicability of each and all of the provisions of said Act.

It is our understanding that you agree with us as to the desirability of commencing negotiations concerning these matters immediately. Pursuant to this oral understanding, we request that a conference be arranged immediately for this purpose.

When the company replied on May 15, Bugas gave not only management's reasons for rejecting the union's demands but also presented five requests for contract revisions on "economic matters," as follows:

. . . We note . . . that many of the items . . . concern matters on which we are not required to bargain.

This company, which deals with its employees in good faith, cannot help but be disappointed in the attitude displayed by the union in the extremely unrealistic demands served upon it.

In 1941, Ford . . . adopted . . . a policy aimed at giving "union security" to your organization. In 1945, we called on your organization . . . to provide "company security." . . .

In this year's negotiations we propose that top priority be given to the objective of "public security." . . .

. . . the American people are tired of negotiations which seem to have no other aim besides gain for all parties except the consumer. . . . We feel . . . they would . . . welcome . . . a major company and a major union working together constructively in the public interest.

. . . the objective of "public security" is not met in the demands you have sent us, because:

1. Your demands . . . would raise costs and compel us to increase prices on Ford products. . . .

2. Further increases in our costs—hence prices—would reduce markets for our products. . . . Reduced markets mean unemployment. . . .

3. The buying power of workers cannot be increased by jacking up wages. A third round of wage increases would again result in increased prices and decreased buying power for the consumer's dollar.

4. Another round of wage increases will not only be self-defeating; it will cut down now and in the future the real value of Social Security benefits, insurance benefits, savings accounts and savings bonds.

5. Finally, continued rise in wages and prices will bring an end to this period of high employment. This will hurt our employees and every worker in this country.

Our proposals, which we will negotiate on a sincere and good faith basis, are set forth below. They are to the long-term advantage of our employees, the company, and the consuming public.

1. Elimination of the substantial wage differential between Ford . . . and its major competitors.

2. Establishment of Ford wage-rates in all its branch operations throughout the country at community or area wage levels for comparable operations.

3. Establishment of a sound, basic plan for extending the incentive system wherever practicable.

4. Extension and liberalization of present practices relative to operations scheduled to work on Saturdays and/or Sundays.

5. Elimination of payment by the company to union representatives for time spent on union business.

. . . We are willing to start negotiations at a mutually agreeable date in the not too distant future. In line with our expressed desire to conclude negotiations as promptly as possible, it is proposed that the size of the Negotiating Committee be limited to ten persons—five . . . union and five . . . company.

. . . We reserve the right . . . to make . . . additional proposals. . . .

. . . The memorandum also described the offer as "complete . . . throwing away . . . room for horse trading."

Response from the union followed immediately:

The UAW–CIO challenges . . . Ford . . . to make public a complete and accurate financial report to prove, if it can, that a wage increase at this time would require an increase in the prices of Ford products. . . .

Any business institution that has as great an impact on the nation's economy as does . . . Ford . . . has a moral obligation to make public its profit figures. . . .

It ill becomes a corporation that has evaded that kind of responsibility to come forward at this late date with the hypocritical plea that it is concerned about the "public security."

If . . . Ford . . . were really concerned about the public security, it would not have recently and unjustifiably increased the prices of one line of its cars $315 to $420. It certainly can't blame labor cost on that increase because there have been no increases in labor cost.

The Ford workers will be happy even now to withdraw their demands for increases in hourly wage rates . . . if . . . the company will successfully exert its influence on the rest of American industrial management and upon the Congress to effect a substantial roll-back in the cost of living. . . .

The UAW–CIO would welcome a sincere offer from . . . Ford . . . that a "major company and a major union work together constructively in the public interest." . . .

The wage claims of the Ford workers are justifiable from every point of view— from the point of view of equity to the workers, the need of the nation for increased purchasing power in the hands of lower income groups and from the corporation's ability to pay. . . .

Ford's rejection of any wage advance whatever, moreover, buttressed the union's professed suspicion of a "conspiracy," or collusion, among "steel, electrical and other" industrial corporations.

Meanwhile, Chrysler had been on strike since May 12,[1] while negotiations had been going forward at General Motors since March 12. In response to an appeal for financial support of the strikers, Ford Local 600 (Rouge) alone voted $125,000. The Chrysler strike was termed "a fight for a cost of living wage increase not only for themselves but for all organized labor."

III

Formal negotiations opened on June 15. By the end of May, the agreements at General Motors and at Chrysler had been concluded.[2] The negotiations at Ford moved through three general stages: (1) from June 15 to June 21, when the company made its first offer of wage increases; (2) from June 21 to July 12, when Reuther entered the negotiations; and (3) from July 12 to July 22, when settlement was reached.

During the first stage, the company took the position that only "economic matters" could be properly brought before the negotiators; accordingly, various of the union's demands were by this test beyond the scope of current bargaining. The parties also discussed the status of the union shop after July 15, when the requirements of the Taft-Hartley Act set the conditions of its continuation. The company did not regard the question as an issue, since the continuation of the union shop, upon union compliance with the Taft-Hartley Act, had been stipulated by the 1947 agreement. But differences regarding the area of the bargaining unit relevant in the now necessary union shop elections had arisen and were carried to the NLRB. The company urged that each plant be considered a separate bargaining unit, contending that the intent of Taft-Hartley was to give individual workers and local units the fullest opportunity to express their will on accepting or rejecting the union shop principle. The UAW contended, on the other hand, that the company must be held a single bargaining unit in consonance with

---

[1] On February 18, 1948, the UAW notified Chrysler of its desire to reopen their two-year contract dated April 26, 1947, for the purpose of "wage rate negotiations." Formal negotiations opened on February 27, 1948. The union asked a general increase of 30 cents per hour and 23 specific rate improvements. In addition, the union sought adequate social security, group insurance, and pension plans; a guaranteed weekly wage; and increases in vacation payments. Management insisted that the reopening provisions were explicitly restricted to wage-rate increases and that the basic interests of all would best be served by rejecting any wage-rate advances, for they would necessarily exert an inflationary influence. Between March 25 and April 18 the local unions voted to strike if negotiations deadlocked. The union reduced its initial demand for 30 cents to 18½ cents per hour. On April 16 Chrysler offered an increase of 6 cents an hour, which was rejected by the union on April 17 and withdrawn by the company on April 22. Negotiations broke off on May 11 after 33 bargaining sessions and the men struck the next day. On May 25 agreement was reached at General Motors with the "wage formula" settling rate issues. The Chrysler strike ended when the parties announced, on May 28, settlement of their wage issue by a rate increase of 13 cents per hour, which represented the projected application of the GM wage formula to the ensuing two years.

[2] See General Motors Corporation: Negotiating the 1948 Agreement, p. 441.

the development of collective relations. The NLRB upheld the union's position. The union charged that the company's claim had been "based not on fact . . . but on the desire . . . to weaken the whole structure of collective bargaining."

Another sharp controversy arose from the request to hold elections on plant premises. Ford did not give a clear-cut reply; and when on June 16 it asked further delay on the matter until June 19, the union determined to proceed with the election off company property. The elections were completed by July 9, 1948, and the union jubilantly announced the results:

> Here in a nationwide poll—the largest ever conducted outside plant premises— 88,943 workers of all races, creeds and colors and from 25 states in various geographical areas have declared in unmistakable terms that they stand solidly behind their union and will maintain their union shop agreement. . . .
>
> Out of 91,081 workers who voted, 88,943 workers voted to maintain the union shop, the company challenged 924 and 1214 voted against. The union won a 98 per cent majority. Even under the unfair, undemocratic Taft-Hartley provisions which stipulate that votes not cast are votes against the union shop, the Ford workers came through with a ringing 90 per cent majority. . . .

By the time the results of the election were announced, the parties had advanced to the second phase of the discussions. Thus, Bugas submitted to the union's national negotiating committee on June 21 the following memorandum:

> In our talks thus far we seem to be settling down to prolonged discussions that will delay indefinitely a realistic consideration of the important issues.
>
> To avoid this, we should like to get quickly to the main points, and come to an agreement as promptly as possible. . . .
>
> The situation has changed since I wrote you on May 15. . . . Our principal competitors have granted wage increases, and it is no longer possible for us to say as we could before these increases that our average hourly rate is higher, by at least six cents, than theirs.
>
> We therefore propose:
>
> 1. That an increase of 14 cents per hour be added to the straight time earned rate of our employees whose rate is $1.50 per hour or more, and that an increase of 11 cents per hour be added to the straight time earned rate of those employees whose rate is less than $1.50 per hour. This form of increase will erase many of the inequities in our present wage structure of which we are aware and to which you have already called our attention.
>
> 2. That these increases become effective on the day we have reached a signed agreement—whether that day is before, on, or after July 15, 1948, the date on which our present wage agreement expires—provided the agreement is ratified by your membership within three weeks after it is reached. *On this basis, every day we delay in coming to an agreement will mean one dollar lost to each employee.*
>
> 3. That these increases be considered a maximum package; that is, that any other economic adjustments asked by the union and agreed to by the company must be paid for out of this 14-cent and 11-cent offer.
>
> 4. That the new contract be extended to July 15, 1950, except that it may be re-opened with regard to job wage rates once by either party on or after July 15, 1949.
>
> 5. That we agree to extend incentive practices in the company, and that we establish a joint committee to study this matter further.

6. That we revise the overtime and premium pay provisions of our present agreement.

The union publicly rejected the company's proposal as "inadequate to meet the present needs of Ford workers and . . . far short of raising Ford wage standards to those of its competitors." Its counterproposal was presented June 25. Excerpts follow:

We are in hearty agreement that a prompt settlement of issues in our current negotiations is highly desirable. We think not only that a prompt settlement is desirable but also that an interruption in production at Ford's at this time would be unfortunate. . . .
The union believes that an equitable settlement is possible on the basis of economic facts rather than economic power. We do not believe that the Company wants to or would assume the responsibility of forcing its employees to take strike action.
In place of your totally inadequate offer, we propose the following:
1. A fourteen (14¢) cent general wage increase to all workers. . . .
2. A fund equivalent to 5 per cent of payroll for hospitalization, health, and medical care protection for Ford workers and their families. . . .
3. Elimination of differentials in economic standards as between Ford and its competitors. . . . We propose by:
(a) Increasing the afternoon and mid-night shift premiums to five (5%) *percent* and seven and one-half (7½%) *percent* respectively. Ford now pays five (5¢) *cents* per hour for both late shifts. This is two and one-half (2½¢) to six and one-quarter (6¼¢) cents less on the average than was paid by your competitors prior to their most recent wage increase. . . .
(b) Liberalization of vacation payment provisions to provide veterans with credit for time spent in military service and to provide employees with 3 to 5 years seniority with vacation pay equivalent to 60 times their hourly rates. The provision for 3 to 5 years employees has been in effect at General Motors since 1946. . . .
(c) Eliminating so-called "merit spreads." . . .
4. Establishment of an equalization fund to bring wages of tool and die makers and construction maintenance workers into line with prevailing rates . . . and to correct inequities in wage rates existing within and between the company's various plants. . . .
5. Revision of the call-in pay provision to guarantee 8 hours pay for workers permitted to start work on any day. . . .
6. Local negotiation of other economic demands. . . .
7. Agreement to be effective . . . no later than July 15.

By the union's own estimates, its new counterproposal came to a 28-cent "package."

These new proposals dominated the second stage of negotiations from June 21 until Reuther's entrance on July 12. His appearance led to a thorough review. He dilated upon the seven issues that he felt still separated the parties after a month of negotiations. These were as follows: (1) vacation pay, which he summarized as a demand for 40–60–80 hours' vacation for 1–3–5 years' service and for providing allowances for defined breaks in active service; (2) improved vacation rights for veterans; (3) shift premiums; (4) wages; (5) social security; (6) merit spreads; and (7) wage differentials. Reuther elaborated upon similar advances in other companies and urged the company to pioneer without fear of "ideologic windmills." Granting that joint relations were not yet mature, he urged the company to grant the demands for the sake of improving those relations and suggested that the company look forward, not backward.

The company replied by maintaining its willingness to bargain, by restating its offer of the 14-cent and 11-cent wage increases, and by offering "further consideration" of social security if agreement on other differences were to be reached. Such reconsideration, however, could not embrace the principle of a pooled fund, on which the company would have to be adamant. It would not retreat from its position that any insurance program must be on an employer-employee contributory basis.

As the morning session of July 13 drew to a close, Reuther announced he would return when and if the company made a more practical offer. Bannon declared that the negotiating committee desired to report back to the National Ford Council on July 15; he indicated that the committee would unanimously recommend rejection of the company's offers made thus far. The council would then determine what action it deemed expedient. Bugas thereupon specified in detail the company's current proposals as follows: (1) the wage offer of the 14-cent and 11-cent increase was still on the table, an offer that would correct many of the wage inequities about which the union was complaining; (2) continued consideration of social security (to be paid for outside of the wage package) excluding any pool and the principle of joint administration of the fund; (3) company willingness to propose a flat "horizontal" wage increase if the union felt such an offer essential to ultimate settlement; (4) increases of 2 cents and 4 cents on shift premiums; (5) improvements in vacation rights for veterans and regular employees. If these proposals proved an effective basis for agreement, the company would ask in return a 2-year contract reopenable on wages within a year; relief from overtime on overtime; and competitive overtime provisions in steel production.

At a 12-hour session on July 14, some concessions were made by each side. At 8 P.M., the company made its "final offer" in writing, summarized as follows:

1. A wage increase of 13 cents an hour. . . . This increase would again bring the company's average hourly rate above that of major competitors.
2. An improved Group Insurance Plan, to which the company would pay greatly increased amounts as its share.
Benefits to employees include life insurance averaging one year's pay; an additional half-year's pay if death is accidental; benefits ranging from $500 to $2,000 upon dismemberment by accident; substantially higher payments over longer periods for idleness resulting from accident or illness; provision for doctors' fees for home and office visits; and Blue Cross hospital and surgical services.
3. An increase in the afternoon-shift premiums to 7 cents an hour from the present 5-cent rate.
4. An increase in night-shift premiums to 9 cents an hour from the present 5-cent rate.
5. A change in vacation rules to enable reinstated veterans to count their time in uniform as part of their service record. . . .

6. Improved vacation eligibility rules. . . .

7. Provision for a Federal ruling on overtime and premium pay practices in the light of a recent Supreme Court ruling.

8. Extension of the new contract to July 15, 1950, with the provision that it may be reopened with regard to job rates once by either party on or after July 15, 1949.

9. The new contract would become effective July 16, 1948, if accepted by the Union negotiating committee on July 15 and ratified by union membership within three weeks.

The union rejected this offer and proposed (1) establishment of joint committees to study the problem of social security; (2) extension of the company's most recent offer on social security to include the equivalent of Blue Cross hospitalization, the *total cost* of which was *to be paid by the company* "outside of the wage settlement"; (3) a 14-cent wage increase; (4) amended vacation rights; (5) elimination of merit spreads; (6) shift premiums of 5% to 7½%; (7) establishment of a fund to eliminate wage inequities.

When the company declared its own offer of 8 P.M. "final," the negotiations appeared deadlocked. Indeed, the standing strike threat seemed more immediate as the union explained its rejection of the company's latest proposal:

The Ford . . . proposal tonight is unacceptable to the union. . . .

After presenting its proposal to the union, the company broke off negotiations by refusing to consider union counter-proposals. . . .

A continuation of the company's stubborn and unreasonable position means inevitably that it is forcing its employees to strike. . . .

The 13¢ an hour wage offer does not take into account recent and continuing increases in the cost of living since earlier settlements by other major automobile companies; nor does it take into account the competitive advantage enjoyed by . . . Ford . . . because of the lag of two months or more behind its competitors in granting wage increases.

The shortcomings of the company on the social security proposals are: (a) Nearly all the cost is to be borne by the workers themselves. (b) The increased benefits are not in proportion to the cost of living. (c) The plan would be administered entirely by the company. . . . (d) The company refuses to say how much it would pay under the plan as its contribution to the social security program. . . .

The National Ford Council, on July 15, supported the negotiating committee by rejecting unanimously the company's "final" offer of July 14. By July 18, strike votes of Ford union locals were completed when Ford Local 600 by a vote of 3,985 to 81 approved strike action. The international executive board of the UAW–CIO fulfilled the final constitutional requirement for strike action by approving such action on July 19. Immediately, Reuther advised Henry Ford II that strike action had been authorized. In his telegram Reuther added:

Realizing the seriousness of the implications of this action, we are advising the company that the union negotiating committee is prepared to meet with . . . Ford . . . in a further effort to resolve the current dispute, before resorting to strike action.

The company accepted the invitation. On July 20 and 21, the parties took up issue after issue of their respective "final offers" to determine where, if at all, further concessions might be made. The union finally indicated that its bargainers desired that Reuther again enter negotiations.

Reuther joined the negotiators at 7 P.M. on July 21. When they recessed at 11 P.M., 4 hours later, it appeared that the social security demand would be compromised through provision for the establishment of a separate union committee and of a separate company committee, each of which was to study the problem. At 2 A.M. on July 22, when negotiations resumed, the committees addressed themselves to pushing each difference outstanding between them to a compromise agreement. By 10:20 A.M., Bugas felt able to declare apparent agreement on all points but two, the shift premiums and the length of the contract. On these issues he offered the union a choice of the following alternatives: (1) an 18-month contract (with a 12-month reopening option on wages) and 5% to 7½% shift premiums; or (2) a one-year contract with 7-cent and 10-cent shift premiums. After recessing, the union chose the second alternative.

Agreement had been reached after 21 hours of continuous bargaining. In a joint statement, Reuther and Bugas announced the terms of the final settlement as follows:

Thirteen-cent-an-hour wage increase for the 116,000 hourly paid Ford workers in 46 plants in 25 states;

Increase in afternoon shift premium pay to 7 cents from 5 cents;

Increase in midnight shift premium pay to 10 cents from 5 cents;

Agreement to give employes with one year's service 40 hours vacation; those with three years, 60 hours; and those with 5 years and more, 80 hours vacation;

Improved vacation eligibility rules to apply to seniority employes who have been off the active employment rolls for more than one year because of work injury, illness, lay-off or leave of absence;

An improved group insurance plan to which the company would pay increased amounts as its share. In connection with the group insurance program it was agreed that a union advisory committee would be named to discuss over a 10-day period possible changes in benefits under the company plan. The company agreed to consider these proposals provided they were within the cost limits of the plan.

Appointment of a committee to receive and consider suggestions from a union committee relative to administration of the finally approved insurance plan;

Agreement that each party will set up a committee for general study of insurance plans, the company to consider studies presented by the union;

The company agreed to complete a study of its classification structure and, upon completion, to negotiate with the union concerning inequities which may be found to exist;

Liberalization of vacation rules for the benefit of World War II veterans;

Letters are to be exchanged between the company and the union preserving present contract provisions for premium pay, and protecting the company from liability for overtime-on-overtime.

The company and union to negotiate on problems pertaining specifically to tool and die and maintenance and construction workers, and also to seek a new merit increase agreement.

This agreement takes effect July 16, 1948 if ratified by Aug. 16, 1948 and continues in effect for the period of the present contract which expires on July 15, 1949.

During the month that followed, the local unions ratified these terms of agreement; Reuther estimated its "total wage package" of gains as yielding them "an increase of from 16½ to 17¢ per hour." The company's press release offered the following summary:

The agreement between Ford Motor Company and the UAW–CIO concludes acceptance by the union of the final offer of 13 cents made by the company a week ago, plus a few additional fringe adjustments worked out in our negotiating sessions.

DISCUSSION QUESTIONS

1. Discuss the strategy and tactics of (*a*) the company, and (*b*) the union, at the various stages of this negotiation.

2. Viewing the 1948 negotiations as part of a negotiations continuum, what type of relationship structure do you think is being built at Ford?

FORD MOTOR COMPANY

THE 1949 "SPEED-UP" STRIKE

I. Background

On May 6, 1949, the 65,000 members of the Rouge Local 600 "hit the bricks" for the first time since Ford had granted recognition to the union. Contract negotiations, which had been scheduled to open on May 16, were interrupted by the strike. The issue was an explosive one—that of "speed-up."

The question of standards and rates of work had concerned the parties from the very beginning. In 1941, when the first contract was signed, this concern found expression in terms of "a fair day's work for a fair day's pay."

In 1946, when the parties negotiated the first postwar agreement, the company succeeded in having added to the management responsibility section of the contract the following phrase: "the right of the company to establish and determine and to maintain and enforce standards of production is fully recognized." However, the umpire was precluded from hearing cases dealing with standards of production since they were designated as matters of company responsibility. The union also agreed not to participate in any strike over standards of production unless its National Ford Department had approved such action on grounds that health or safety was involved.[1]

Prior to 1946, the company used work standards primarily for costing purposes. These standards were established by a very small staff. In many cases, the pace of production was determined by the nature of the process and the best judgment of the supervisor. As a result, there were instances where identical work assignments were allocated different time allowances.

That year (1946), however, given the mandate "to establish and determine and to maintain and enforce," the company quickly organized itself to realize such an objective. A central industrial engineering department was established and many engineers hired and trained. This new department was put in control of all work standards which previously had been under the direction of the financial department. Working under severe pressure, the new department set standards for all production operations within the space of one year. In an effort to develop guidelines as quickly as possible, many standards were established with little attention to improving methods.

The new standards which were set by time study were used by production supervision in a variety of ways: determination of assembly line speed, measurement of worker performance, and assignment of work. To familiarize supervisory personnel with the many ramifications involved in these standards, an extensive training program was launched.

---

[1] See Exhibit 1.

In 1947, the company took strides in its program of major reorganization which it had entered upon in 1946. Operations were decentralized and responsibility placed on divisions and plant managers. Similarly, with respect to industrial engineering, time study groups were established in all plants. The company then launched an extensive program to improve the methods which had originally been accepted and to revise the work standards accordingly. Simultaneously, continued effort was being directed toward improved and refined techniques for establishing sound work standards.

II. The "Hassle" at the Assembly Line

Thus by 1949, as contract negotiations loomed, the company had been able, through a determined effort at the local plant level, to take most of the "wrinkles" out of the work standards.

One area, however, still remained unresolved—the speed of assembly lines. Management's position on the issue was that it had the right to operate these lines during any portion of a man's working day at a speed faster than the standard rate so long as (1) the average rate of work required during his eight-hour shift was not higher than the standard rate, and (2) health and safety were not endangered. Supervision contended that unforeseeable delays often necessitated running the line at a slightly higher speed so that "lost production" could be made up and required output achieved.

For example: on a particular assembly line the plan might be to complete 400 cars per eight-hour shift. To compensate for delays the line would occasionally be run at a rate of 55 cars per hour. Accordingly at the end of the shift the required output would have been achieved and while during certain periods employees would have worked at speeds faster than the 50-car-per-hour rate, on an over-all shift basis the average rate of work would not have been in excess of the standard.

Such practices, however, aroused the suspicion of workers and local union officials. In November, 1948, for instance, Thompson, president of Local 600, voiced the union's feelings about the matter in the following colorful language:

Drums are beating on the banks of the Rouge. Political drums. "Speed-up," "Speed-up," "Speed-up," they pound out in ever-increasing crescendo. "Mass meeting," "Mass meeting," "Mass meeting," their pip-squeak piccolos pipe. "Strike," "Strike," "Strike," their big bass drums will soon be booming. . . .

For the purpose of the record and so that no one will get any false impressions concerning what I say hereafter, let me state: The Ford Motor Company is making an all-out attempt to speed up production in the Rouge Plant.

. . . This slave-driving piece work system of the auto companies was one of the principal reasons for the almost overnight growth of the UAW–CIO in 1937. . . .

But the Communists, for political purposes, would have you believe that it is something new—and that they and their followers in the Rouge Plant have discovered this new and startling speed-up. . . .

. . . The political opportunists in the plant are engaged in a deliberate attempt to mislead the Ford workers. . . .

There is no royal road to the solution of the speed-up problem. Only hard work by your officers and committeemen in the grievance procedure, right in the plant. If that fails, we can always hit the bricks.

During the early stages of the negotiations in 1949, the parties discussed the assembly line question specifically with respect to the union's allegation that the company had periodically ordered a "speed-up" in the Rouge assembly building "B." But they failed to reach any agreement. On April 16, 1949, Ford Rouge workers by a vote of 2,905 to 92 authorized the local union to take a strike vote; during the next week the Rouge workers approved strike action by the majority of 31,926 to 4,400. Similar action was taken at the Lincoln plant. Both Lincoln and Rouge locals petitioned the International Executive Board for strike authorization. This authorization was required under the UAW constitution and, also, as already indicated, under the terms of the 1946 agreement.[1]

On April 25, Reuther telegraphed Thompson that he had assigned "trouble shooters" to seek an immediate meeting with the company. "If issues are not worked out by the time the union's executive board meets, the board will act on your request for a strike authorization."

On April 28, the UAW Executive Board approved a strike at the Lincoln Plant. Action against the Rouge plant was withheld pending further investigation by a special committee, headed by Mazey, Secretary-Treasurer of the UAW. Reuther addressed the National Ford Council, stressing the fact that the union's strike fund would be greater by mid-July when the 1949 contract expired. He assailed the Communists who, he said, were continuing their disruptive tactics even though numerically they had lost strength. He warned them that the rank and file would rise and throw them out of the union if they did not curb their "divisionist" tactics on the eve of important negotiations.

On April 29, when the investigating committee arrived at Rouge "B" building it was met by committeemen representing this building as well as the offices of the Rouge Local. A dispute arose between the investigation committee and the committeemen as a result of which 22 of the committeemen resigned their posts and walked off the job. A stoppage ensued, idling 1,200 employees, when some of them refused to continue work "without representation." The investigating committee postponed its checkup.

At a meeting the next day, the "B" building membership instructed the committeemen to resume their posts, and to cooperate with the International Union's investigating committee.

On May 2, the investigating committee returned to "B" building and reportedly found the assembly line speed not excessive. The committee then met with company representatives and stated that it was satisfied with the speed of the lines at the time it had observed them and asked that the company agree in writing to maintain the speed at the observed rate.

On the next day the executive board of Rouge Local 600 decided on a

---

[1] See Exhibit 1.

walkout to begin at 10:00 A.M. May 4. In explaining this action, Thompson charged that the company had speeded up its lines on May 3 which so angered the local board that it had decided on peremptory action. Three hours later, Reuther announced official approval of the International Executive Board for a walkout at noon on May 5, the time already approved for Lincoln workers. Reuther then persuaded the Rouge executive board to amend its earlier action and agree to the May 5 deadline.

Reuther also voiced agreement with the Rouge executive board that the "B" building line had been sped up on May 3. He termed it evidence of "double-dealing and bad faith" on the part of management, and said that the International would not "tolerate any kind of speed-up" in any plants under contract with the union, "but until the strike deadline is reached, the union is prepared to exert every effort . . . to reach a settlement through negotiations."

The reaction from the company was immediate. Management had spoken only once before on the "speed-up" issue; now it broke its silence in a telegram on the same day, May 3, sent to Reuther by Bugas:

I have read with astonishment the statement which you have released to the Press.

You have seen fit to accuse the Ford Motor Company of "double dealing," "bad faith," and with a "speed-up in violation of contract," and a refusal to settle the existing controversy on a fair and equitable basis.

I make no accusation of bad faith on your part. But I can only conclude from this intemperate, irresponsible, baseless statement that the Union has for some indiscernible reason determined to call a strike without reference to the facts and without a sincere effort to define the issue and settle it in accordance with the Union's contractual obligations.

The issue is a simple one. The question involved is whether the Company has violated its contractual obligations by taking action which may impair the safety or health of the employees.[1] Although I am confident that we are in the right on this issue, we have repeatedly offered to submit to arbitration under our contract the question of whether our policies and practices are in conformity with our contractual obligations.

. . . These policies and practices do not require any employee to do more than a reasonable day's work in any eight hours. . . .

The Union has persistently refused to bring in an impartial industrial engineer.[2] It appears that the Union is unsure of its position and wishes to preserve this whole matter as a strike issue. . . .[3]

Mr. Thompson's statements in his wire to you, wherein he stated we violated an oral agreement to maintain line speeds at some set rate, and wherein he stated that we speeded up the B Building assembly line today, are pure fabrications and appear to be a prime example of bad faith to drum up a strike atmosphere.

This action on the part of Local 600 came at a time when further efforts to peaceably iron out this matter were scheduled between the parties. The action represents to us a complete lack of coordination between Local 600 and the International UAW, and further epitomizes the absence of an effective sense of responsibility on the part of the Local 600.

A meeting of Company and Union representatives is scheduled Wednesday,

---

[1] See Exhibit 1.
[2] See Exhibit 1.
[3] See Exhibit 1.

May 4, at 2:00 P.M., so we can continue our efforts to settle the matter peaceably. In view of the great importance this matter has assumed it is hoped that you personally will attend.

We wish to do everything within reason to avert a strike.

III. The Strike

During both the afternoon and evening of May 4, negotiations between company and union representatives were held without progress. In a final effort to avert the strike, Mr. Reuther sat in on the morning meeting of May 5. As the session broke up at 12:30 P.M. with no date set for the resumption of talks, the men at Ford and Lincoln had already taken up their places on the picket lines. The strike was on.

On May 6, Henry Ford, 2d, mailed a personal letter to the "Men and Women" of Ford Motor Company, excerpts from which follow:

I want you to know how all of us here feel about this strike.

We don't like it because we don't understand it. We like it even less because we went to great lengths to avoid it. It is the first major strike of hourly employees which has occurred since 1941—the first real break in a record of which all of us have been very proud.

Thousands of men and women are being unjustly penalized by this strike action. You can add to the 62,250 Detroit area employees and their families 43,750 of your fellow-employees in outlying production and assembly plants. You can also add our 7,200 dealers and their 100,000 employees, to say nothing of the thousands upon thousands of men and women in the plants that supply us.

. . . And that does not even take into consideration the most important group of all—our customers, the people who keep these plants going with their orders.

I am most definitely of the opinion that every issue leading up to this strike could have been peacefully resolved by continued negotiation or arbitration, both of which we proposed right up to the moment of the walkout itself. Under the circumstances, we cannot understand why a strike was called, unless it was promoted by some political situation within the union.

There has been a great deal of loose talk about a so-called "speed-up." This is a most unpleasant word which would seem to describe some sort of inhuman treatment of employees. Any time the health and safety of any Ford employee is endangered, we want to know about it—and fix it, immediately.

Moreover, from the point of view of any sane management, "speed-ups" are silly. Efficient work standards mean a smooth and steady production flow which will allow men to turn out their best work without doing them harm of any kind.

I will go even further and say that efficient work standards are the best insurance we have that we can meet competition and thereby assure ourselves of maximum employment at the highest possible wages. . . .

We told your representatives last Thursday when the strike broke off negotiations we are willing to sit down and discuss this matter further. But I want to make it quite clear that this company now and always will hold to its right— fairly and firmly guaranteed under our contract—to establish work standards which will assure efficient operation without impairing in any way the health or safety of our employees.

I am sorry this strike had to happen.

Although negotiations continued with a joint committee representing both Ford and Lincoln workers, reports of "no progress" continued. The company, speaking through Bugas, declined several offers of mediation "prompted either by politics or good intentions."

Both Reuther and the officers of Local 600 answered Mr. Ford in separate letters on May 9. Reuther advanced a three-point proposal: (1) that negotiations be resumed on the morning of May 10; (2) that Henry Ford participate directly in the negotiations; and (3) that, failing resolution of the dispute by May 13, he and Ford debate the issues involved in the dispute at a meeting of all Ford employees in Briggs stadium. Ford immediately telegraphed the company's willingness to resume negotiations at 2 P.M. on May 10, stating that Bugas would be present on behalf of the company. He declined to participate in a public debate.

In their letter, the officers of Local 600 wrote, in part, as follows:

We are writing to you, not only as officers of Local 600, but also as workers with years of service in the River Rouge Plant. In this respect, we believe we voice the sentiments of the many thousands of our fellow workers who are much closer to us, as their chosen leaders, than they are to your supervision and management upon whom you must rely for your information about the operations down on the assembly line of the vast River Rouge Plant.

We are answering your letter mailed to all employees this week, because we believe you are sincere in the convictions expressed therein; and also greatly misinformed as to the true facts in the present controversy. . . .

About two years ago, the Union began to notice a change. No longer did company labor relations men speak with authority. It became necessary to clear everything through channels.

We wonder if this change was brought about by the influx of GM executives into top management positions?

Regardless of the reason, a change took place. The old Ford family of employees concept was replaced by something that smacks of GM, Chrysler and NAM.

We have repeatedly stated that we would not submit this issue to arbitration because there is nothing to arbitrate.

In simple words, the union maintains that the company shall run operations at 100%, *and no faster,* of the production standards established for each job. Your representatives maintain that they will run the jobs at any speed they please.

. . . . .

We emphatically agree with you that this issue could be negotiated between the company and the union. . . .

. . . We will enter into a written agreement . . . provided it embodies *these three points and no others:*

1. Speed of assembly line to remain constant in line with established production standards.

2. Uniform spacing of jobs.

3. Balanced distribution of manpower over entire line so that the individual worker is not required to work in excess of normal work or to make up losses in production resulting from factors over which the worker has no control. . . .

Let's put it in writing so that those hundreds of assistant foremen, foremen, general foremen, assistant-superintendents, superintendents, building and division managers, time-study, labor relations, and all the others who have to do with the management function will know that this is the law of the Ford Plants. . . .

Eight days after the strike began, Cyrus S. Ching, director of the Federal Mediation and Conciliation Service, sent telegrams to the parties, in which he observed that since the stoppage had such a widespread effect upon the delicate balance of the national economy, he would request, unless significant progress were reported within a reasonable time, the parties to meet with representatives of the Service.

Henry Ford replied on May 15:

If you should conclude that the public interest requires your stepping into our negotiations at this time, I want to assure you of all possible assistance.

I should like to suggest, however, that before making your final decision to intervene you weigh carefully other factors in this situation besides the work stoppage itself.

Some of these factors seem to me most definitely to involve the long-range interests of the American people and the balance of our economy.

First, it is basic Ford policy to conduct our relationships with employees on a straightforward, across the table basis. All our efforts are directed towards minimizing the need for government intervention and toward quick and peaceful settlements of arguments within the family.

Second, we anticipated disputes of the technical kind over which this strike has allegedly been called by providing in our contract for appointment of a qualified and impartial expert to arbitrate. The Union has stubbornly refused to use this normal machinery. . . .[1]

Third, this strike thus is both an unnecessary and inexcusable action on the part of UAW–CIO.

Fourth, . . . the thousands of families who are suffering because of this strike are victims of political cross-currents in certain factions within UAW–CIO, and not of irreconcilable Company-Union differences.

Fifth, in our opinion, if the leadership of this unwarranted strike had concentrated as much on reaching a reasonable settlement with us as they have on finding a way of pulling their political hot potatoes out of the fire, this strike would have been ended long since, and perhaps would never have started.

Sixth, the right and responsibility of management to establish reasonable work standards is being challenged so seriously here that we see no course except that of resisting it to the utmost.

Finally, it seems to us that another most significant issue is presented in this strike. It is the question of whether the integrity of contracts mutually agreed to by American labor and management is to be preserved, or whether such a contract and all its careful safeguards of industrial peace can be thrown into the ash can whenever a high political wind blows up in the Union. . . .

Perhaps we could save ourselves the great expense and disruption of continuation of this strike if we were to agree post-haste to any expedient which could save the face of a small group of embarrassed Union leaders. But we feel that in doing so we would be both selfish and short-sighted, and would actually betray for immediate gain the only sound basis for progressive labor-management relations here or anywhere else—that of mutual responsibility under contract.

If you decide under the circumstances to enter our negotiations, I want again to assure you of every possible cooperation.

IV. THE SETTLEMENT

On May 17, the company pointed out that more than 102,000 Ford employees were out of work because of the strike, and yet the dispute was a technical one confined to B building involving directly less than 5,000 men;

---

[1] See Exhibit 1.

accordingly it proposed that the UAW amend its strike authorization to permit all Ford workers to return to their jobs, except those directly involved. Labeling the proposal "fantastic" and "obviously not acceptable," a union spokesman characterized it as "merely a variation of the old employer's trick of divide and rule."

May 19, the day the Conciliation Service intervened, Reuther wrote Bugas suggesting a variety of schedules for meetings between the company and the union, "any of which will permit simultaneous or reasonably continuous negotiations on both the strike and the contract." Reuther concluded, ". . . if the company will not meet on any of the schedules suggested and declines to suggest some alternative arrangement which will accommodate substantially concurrent negotiations on both the strike and the contract, the Union advises that it is unwilling to negotiate on either subject to the exclusion of the other."

Bugas immediately replied:

. . . our full time and effort for weeks has been concentrated on finding means of averting a strike and, once called, of reaching an agreement quickly.

. . . It now appears that you are using the strike to coerce us into yielding to your contention as to the date of commencement of negotiations on the new contract. This is a clear violation, both of our contract and of your duties and our rights under the law.

We do not take the offhand view of the strike which you appear to take. First things come first. . . .

We propose that for the present we both spend full time reaching a settlement of the strike; by following this course we may be able to open our contract negotiations in an atmosphere of peace and not of war.

If you put your ultimatum into effect . . . , you must be held personally accountable for the added distress which will have to be endured by our employees, and the thousands of other people who are being unjustly penalized by the strike.

This met a prompt rejoinder from the union that unfair labor charges would be filed with the NLRB.

The morning of May 23, following negotiations which recessed in deadlock at midnight, Reuther wrote Ford and Bugas as follows:

. . . To remove from the area of dispute the issue which is blocking a settlement of the strike, the union proposes that this question of whether the company has the right under the contract to require an employee to work at a rate of speed in excess of 100% of the established production standards, and to make up production losses resulting from factors over which the employee has no control, shall be submitted to an impartial arbitrator.

Well in advance of the strike . . . we were advised by the umpire that since this dispute involved the application of company policy with respect to production standards, it was of such a nature that in his opinion he doubted that he had jurisdiction or authority to act on the dispute.

. . . The confusion which resulted from the company's use of the terms production standards and work standards has been dispelled in the past several days, since the company has now agreed that work standards and production standards are synonymous.

It is this clarification of the issues and the narrowing of the area in dispute which makes it possible for the union at this time to advance a genuine arbitration proposal that will effectively resolve the real issue in dispute . . . and will permit the parties to resolve the remaining points through direct negotiations. . . .

The company's arbitration proposal would have authorized and permitted the arbitrator to rule on only the technical point of whether the established production standard (100%) was correct, and would not have authorized or permitted the arbitrator to rule on the company's claimed right to work an employee at an "enforced standard" in excess of the established standard of production (100%). . . .

If the Company accepts this proposal to arbitrate this point, the union is prepared to enter immediate negotiations with the company to arrive at a strike settlement agreement. . . .

Beginning on May 24, the parties sought to arrive at a proper statement of the question to be submitted to arbitration. By May 29, a strike settlement agreement was signed under which an arbitrator or an arbitration panel should rule upon the following submission:

> Does the Company under the contract, on the basis of health and safety or otherwise, have the right to require an employee to perform his work assignment on any unit in less time than the Company's time study shows for his assignment, provided the employee is not assigned more than 480 minutes of work as measured by time study in an eight-hour shift?

The "speed-up" strike was over! It had been the longest strike in Ford's history.

V. Arbitration

The arbitration panel included Carl T. Dunn, an engineer named by the company; William Gomberg, management-engineer director of the International Ladies Garment Workers' Union, named by the UAW; and Harry Shulman, umpire under the contract. The panel, the company representative dissenting, issued its award on July 8. Excerpts follow:

> . . . The Union insisted and insists now, that at whatever speed the company chooses to run its lines, each employee should have available for the performance of his assignment per unit of production the time shown by the time study standard. . . . The company has maintained throughout that it may properly allow an actual time per unit reasonably below the time study standard, particularly to overcome recurring minor delays, provided that the total work for the day as measured by standard minutes of work does not exceed 480 standard minutes. . . .
> The truth is that the contract does not expressly spell out either conception . . . the phrases "standards of production" or "work standards" (generally used synonymously) normally mean the quantity of work minutes, per unit of production rather than per any period of actual time. . . . The requirement that the employee meet his standard of production, as actually and necessarily enforced by the company, is not a requirement that he merely finish an eight-hour shift with a given quantity of work. It is rather a requirement that he meet the standard fairly consistently throughout the day from unit to unit. . . .
> In absence of convincing evidence, which is here lacking, that the parties used the phrase "standards of production" in some esoteric way, it should be given its normal meaning as just stated. . . .
> . . . The "right of the company" "to establish and determine and maintain and enforce standards of production" which is "fully recognized" . . . is not a

right to make a final and binding determination. It is not like other "rights" specified in Article IV, as for example, the right to "decide the number and location of plants" or the "products to be manufactured" or the "schedules of production" or the "starting and quitting time." As to these matters, the company may make final determinations which the union must accept for the term of the contract and which may not be made the basis of strike action during that term. Such is not the case with respect to production standards. There the right "to establish and determine and to maintain and enforce" is more in the nature of a right to initiate. . . .

We are required to determine the company's right under the contract. An absolute answer is not possible. . . .

We cannot, therefore, say that the contract prohibits the company in all cases from requiring an employee to perform his work assignment on any unit in less time than that shown by time study. Equally we cannot say that the contract grants the company the right to require an employee, fairly regularly and without countervailing relief, to perform his work assignment per unit in less time than the standard work minutes per unit . . . we believe the conclusion must be as follows:

The company may operate its lines at a speed in excess of the desired production schedule. But at whatever speed the lines are operated, the company must seek to make the individual employee's work assignment as measured by standard work minutes equal to or within the actual production cycle time available to him. That the company has done successfully for most work assignments. For those which cannot be made equal to or within the actual production cycle time, it is not a sufficient answer that the employee is not assigned more than 480 minutes of work as measured by time study in an eight-hour shift. In such cases, appropriate solutions to fit the conditions of the particular jobs must be worked out. . . . The task is not one of achieving unit by unit or minute by minute perfection, but rather one of adopting a proper general plan and practice based upon accepted principles.

The net result of the arbitration decision was that assembly lines could be run in excess of the desired production schedule only by increased manning so that no individual employee would be required to work at a rate faster than standard. In addition certain other guidelines were formulated as a result of the strike settlement and of arbitration decision: (1) each assembly line was to be maintained at a constant speed; (2) during each shift the product mix was to remain unchanged unless appropriate relief measures were taken; and (3) relief men were to be designated in a ratio of at least one to every nineteen employees.

EXHIBIT 1

FORD MOTOR COMPANY

Excerpts from 1946 Contract

V. 1b—"the Union and its members . . . agree that during the term of this agreement they will not participate in any strike . . . which may relate to any matters specifically provided herein as company responsibility or committed to the company's discretion, as to which matters the company has the express right to determine and decide. . . ."

and

IV. 4—"The right of the Company to establish and determine and to maintain and enforce standards of production is fully recognized. . . ."

but

IV. 4—"attempted enforcement by the company of standards of production claimed in writing to the Company by the National Ford Department to impair the health or safety of employees may be, in the discretion of the Union, grounds for waiver [of the no strike pledge in V. 1b]. . . ."

in the case of health or safety

V. 3—"the Union . . . agrees that it will not participate in strike until the specific issues in dispute have been presented in writing by the National Ford Department and negotiations have continued . . . for a period of fifteen (15) working days and until the strike action has . . . been fully authorized. . . ."

however

IV. 4—"during the fifteen (15) working day period . . . the parties (may) agree to retain the services of a mutually acceptable Industrial Engineering Consultant to review the production standard in question and render a decision binding on the parties. . . ."

with respect to arbitration

VII. 18b—"He [umpire] shall have no power to set standards of production. . . ."

DISCUSSION QUESTIONS

1. Analyze the manner in which the company developed standards.

2. Evaluate Reuther's handling of the "speed-up" conflict.

3. Discuss the positions of the company on (*a*) the "speed-up" issue; (*b*) the strike; (*c*) the relation of this walkout to contract negotiations.

4. What impact could the award of the arbitration panel be predicted to have on day-to-day relationships?

FORD MOTOR COMPANY

NEGOTIATING THE 1949 AGREEMENT: WAGES, CONDITIONS, PENSIONS

I

For two years, the company had been planning decentralized operations to provide better management of its various divisions. In February, 1949, Henry Ford II announced formation of the Ford Division as a further step in this plan. In addition, Ford continued to modernize its plant and equipment at the rate of about $100 million a year. The company also launched a management development plan to effectuate a policy that future executives would come from employee ranks. In addition, studies, started three years earlier, had continued in various types of pension, retirement, and insurance programs.

The Executive Board of the UAW, for its part, unanimously adopted January 11 the following demands for 1949: (1) an adequate pension and retirement program; (2) a comprehensive social security program including health, hospitalization, medical, surgical and life insurance provisions; and (3) a wage increase to restore the buying power of wages to the level of June, 1946.

Elaborating on this action, Reuther addressed to all local unions and councils on January 15, 1949, in part:

> . . . Some contracts limit 1949 negotiations to wages. Accordingly, . . . local unions operating under such contracts should request management to open negotiations on pension and social security plans by mutual agreement. If management refuses, a wage demand should be made equivalent to the total cost of a pension plan, a social security plan, plus the cost of living adjustment required to bring wages into line with the buying power of June 1946.
> . . . Slackening of the rise in the cost of living . . . enables us to turn our attention to other urgent matters, . . . pension plans and social security.
> We . . . are no longer willing to tolerate double standards in our industry. . . . Top corporate executives provide generous pensions for themselves while denying them to the workers. . . . We are taking pension and social security plans out of the category of fringe demands and putting them at the top of the agenda. . . .
> To further strengthen the union's financial reserves in support of the implementation of the above demands, the International Executive Board . . . voted to levy an assessment of one dollar per member. . . . Just demands, backed up by the power . . . of the membership and a strong treasury, are a winning combination. . . .

Thomas Thompson, president of "The Rouge," or Ford Local 600, "the world's largest local union," supported this position in *Ford Facts* on January 22: "We in Ford have been fighting for that kind of program for the past three years. At last our efforts have been rewarded. . . . Our program has become the policy of the entire International Union."

The first public translation of these goals into monetary demands came on January 21 when Reuther addressed a four-day educational conference in Milwaukee. A pension of at least $100 a month "in addition to Federal social security which now averages $25 a month" was set as a goal.

A few days later came another proposal from Thompson urging industry-wide bargaining on pension plans. He contended the industry-wide plan would prevent loss of pensions to workers changing jobs, give pension coverage to members in shops now employing few men, and guarantee a financial basis "sufficient to withstand all ordinary business recessions and depressions."

The UAW moved forward in obtaining unified objectives when its International Economic Conference unanimously approved on February 19 the demands recommended by the International Executive Board, and, with only two dissenting votes, the strategy of submitting the demands through normal contract channels with a concentrated drive to break through one important sector at a time and thus establish a pattern. Noting that advocates of the industry-wide approach were making comparisons with coal, Emil Mazey, UAW secretary-treasurer, said, "We can't get along without coal, but we can get along without cars. . . . The best way for us to win our economic demands is to take cognizance of the competitive differences in our industry between Chrysler and Ford and General Motors."

II

First public action on the part of the company in anticipation of negotiations was taken by Bugas on March 2 when he wrote Reuther as follows:

Our negotiations which are to start in May or June may well have a critical effect upon every employee of Ford . . . —and perhaps upon prices and employment throughout the country. In view of the changing situation, we suggested to you several weeks ago that we sit down well in advance and explore informally some of the basic factors that will affect negotiations.

As you know, our negotiations are always a matter of great concern to our employees. We owe it to them to help them understand some of the problems with which we are faced in trying to provide for them the security of stable employment. They should not be misled by loose talk. With this in mind, we are sending to each employee a copy of this letter.

We are now well into an economic period unlike any we have experienced since the war. Food prices and other costs of living are dropping. Workers are being laid off. Most of the post-war consumer demand for things in short supply has been mopped up. Most American producers are no longer in a "sellers market." . . .

Since V–J Day we have effected three large wage increases, totaling 42½¢ an hour, and have incurred substantial additional costs for paid holidays, more liberal vacations, larger shift premiums, and increased insurance benefits.

The cost of living is now declining, and every drop in the cost of living increases *real* wages. . . . There is an increasing tendency for both management and labor to look upon another general wage increase as contrary to the best interests of both.

. . . For a long time, Ford Motor Company has paid a higher average hourly wage than its major competitors. One of these competitors has just reduced its average wage rate by 2¢ an hour.[1] This puts on us an additional handicap in wage costs of about $5,000,000 a year.

Old-age security is a highly desirable goal. But . . . whether financed by a company and its employees directly or indirectly through government [it] must be paid for. It cannot be financed by wishful thinking.

There is no "kitty" from which Ford . . . can draw. . . . Each year since 1945 we have had to spend far more than we have earned for new plants and for modernization of facilities.

Two years ago, after months of negotiations with your union, we agreed upon a liberal pension plan. This was possible only because employees were to forego about 8¢ an hour of a large wage increase to get the plan under way and, in addition, they were to pay a minimum of 2½% of wages in future years as their share of the cost of keeping the plan going.

Your union recommended this plan to our employees; but they voted overwhelmingly to reject it in favor of the wage increase. Is there any reason to believe that our employees now will take the reduction in wages that would be necessary to get such a plan going?

There is only one other way to pay for a pension plan—for our customers to pay for it in higher car prices. But we are convinced that too many of them would not stand for this.

. . . This year—as perhaps never before—it is essential that we go into negotiations with a real understanding of the problems involved.

The first unofficial answer came from Thompson in *Ford Facts,* in part:

John Bugas is merely running interference for . . . Ford . . . in the face of the Union's just demands, the same as he did last year. . . . Speaking in Philadelphia last November 17, 1948, Mr. Henry Ford II said that a fourth round pay raise was "inevitable." I think that Mr. Ford still speaks for the . . . company. . . .

Reuther transmitted the official response to Bugas in a letter dated March 10. He wrote:

Since your letter was used as a press release, it is quite apparent that it was written not in an effort to resolve the problems that confront the Ford workers, but rather as a publicity handout to confuse the real issues in the coming negotiations. Despite the fact that your letter received nation-wide press and radio coverage, we are not releasing our reply to the press or the radio. Our decision is based on a sincere belief that the problems of the Ford workers and their families, will be solved through down-to-earth collective bargaining and not through a publicity contest. No amount of public lamenting, public relations maneuvering or clever playing with words can exempt . . . Ford . . . from its responsibility to provide Ford workers with security against illness and old age.

Your letter is remarkably similar to the letters we have received from you about this time of year, in advance of the 1948, 1947 and 1946 negotiations.

. . . Your letter fails to differentiate between basic causes and effects. Workers are being laid off in America, not because they are being paid too much, but because they are being paid too little, and therefore, lack the purchasing power to buy back the products which their labor has created. . . .

You admit yourself, in your letter, that "old age security is a highly desirable goal." Certainly, high paid executives in the auto industry should know, because they alone have such security. . . . The workers, through their union, are deter-

---

[1] General Motors under the escalator clause of the 1948 agreement.

mined to put an end to these discriminatory, unfair and unreasonable double standards.

You state in your letter, that a social security program, "cannot be financed by wishful thinking." To this we can agree. We are asking that the workers' security program be financed from the same source that is used to finance security for high paid executives.

You complain that . . . Ford . . . has spent more than it has earned since 1945 on capital improvements, . . . that, consequently, "poverty" will be the plea . . . in the 1949 negotiations. . . . Such a plea is unimpressive. Under the free enterprise system, in theory at least, plant expansion is financed by new capital, obtained through investors. . . . Ford . . . on the other hand, stands today as the world's largest family owned industrial empire which was financed almost entirely out of earnings, made possible by the toil and sweat of tens of thousands of Ford workers. . . .

. . . While investing huge sums for plant expansion and improvement, your competitors have been earning greater profits year after year. To assume that . . . Ford . . . was not equally profitable would require us to charge its top executive personnel with gross incompetence. . . .

We are prepared to meet with . . . Ford . . . at your convenience, and it is our hope that the issues in the 1949 negotiations can be resolved through intelligent, constructive, collective bargaining. . . .

Suspicions of collusive action among auto makers were sounded by Thompson on March 12 in *Ford Facts* and he recommended that Local 600 immediately organize all committees essential to strike action.

The actual demands to be served on Ford were formulated by the National Ford Council on April 27–29. Reuther declared, "The negative economic factors which are developing do not in any way detract from the needs out of which our economic demands grew in the first place. . . . Our only answer is to take the offensive." The council elected Gene Prato of Local 600 chairman of the union's 15-man bargaining committee, to be assisted by Kenneth Bannon, director of the National Ford Department, the international officers, and staff members from the union.

On May 2 Bannon served formal notice upon the company:

. . . We propose . . . an adequate pension and retirement program and a comprehensive social security program including health, hospitalization, medical, surgical, disability and life insurance provisions financed by . . . Ford . . . and administered . . . with equal representation from the Union and the Company; . . . a wage increase sufficient to restore the buying power of wages to the level of June 1946; . . . and revised provisions covering paid holidays, vacations and night shift premiums. . . .

We reserve the right to give further notice of additional proposals. . . .

It is our understanding that you agree with us as to the desirability of commencing negotiations concerning these matters immediately. Accordingly, we request that a conference be arranged for this purpose at your earliest possible convenience, but not later than May 16, 1949.

On May 9 a supplementary notice was served upon the company listing additional contractual changes the union was desirous of making, such as: elimination of the prohibition against unionization of executive, supervisory, or work standard employees, and other representatives of management; unlimited right to organize; provision that all work done "for and by" Ford be done by employees covered by the agreement; revision of management's rights clauses in respect to (1) promotion and automatic progression within occupational groups, (2) standards of production, (3) working rules, and (4) overtime; elimination of those contract sections which dealt with union responsibility to prevent strikes and work stoppages.[1] Once again, the union requested that negotiations start "not later than May 16, 1949," the earliest date possible under the contract.

III

Because of the so-called "speed-up" strike which occurred on May 6,[2] negotiations for a new contract did not open until June 2. The company on May 5 had notified the union of its own desire to "modify, amend and supplement" the agreement, and proposed a full reopening of *all* provisions of the agreement in order to (1) examine economic matters "because of their relation to production costs"; (2) define clearly the rights and responsibilities of both the union and the company "in the light of the experiences of the past year"; and (3) present supplementary subject matter for the purpose of bettering the relationship between the union and the company. To expedite negotiations, the company had also proposed (1) to schedule meetings on alternate days, meeting four hours daily, to assure adequate time for preparation and (2) to limit the number of representatives from both sides to six people.

The negotiations moved through four stages: (1) June 2 to June 22, when the parties felt each other out, and the union rejected the company's first major offer on economic proposals; (2) June 23 to July 26, when negotiations moved from economic to noneconomic issues and back again—with little results; (3) July 27 to September 10, when Reuther entered the negotiations and the strike vote loomed important; and (4) September 10 to September 29, when the recommendations of the Steel Industry Board were made public, and settlement was reached.

The first major offer on economic proposals was made on June 18 in the following letter from Bugas to Reuther:

. . . *What agreement can we reach which gives the best promise of providing the largest number of steady jobs to Ford employees?* . . .

Any stabilization pattern must take into account the following considerations:

1. Unemployment is rising. In May there were 3,300,000 unemployed. The way things are going now, this total may reach 5,000,000 this summer—as against 1,900,000 in April, 1949.

2. Industrial production is off 10% from November, 1948.

3. The cost of living has been dropping and further decreases this year appear certain. The drop to date has meant an important increase in the real wages of our employees.

The average rates paid by our major competitor will in all likelihood be reduced.[3] As a result we face the prospect of being at continually greater competitive disadvantage in labor costs—even at our present rates.

---

[1] See Ford Motor Company—Negotiating the First Postwar Agreement, p. 361.
[2] See Ford Motor Company—The 1949 "Speed-Up" Strike, p. 391.
[3] See General Motors Corporation: Negotiating the 1948 Agreement, p. 441.

4. Auto industry economists forecast a market in 1950, 1951, and thereafter of about 4,700,000 cars and trucks annually. This compares with a national market which was running at a rate of about 6,900,000 cars and trucks annually as of June, 1949—a reduction of 32%.

5. So far as the security of our employees is concerned, the important problem is to retain jobs for Ford . . . workers in a narrowing market. Our ability to do that will depend on the price of Ford products. This, in turn, will depend upon Ford costs. Higher labor costs today—in any form—would result in loss of jobs.

6. The recent strike of UAW . . . resulted in a loss of production of 116,587 cars, trucks, and tractors. These are sales lost to competition at a time when the future security of our company and our employees makes it imperative that we better our competitive position. . . .

We will, therefore, reject any change in our contract which would mean higher labor costs—whether in the form of wage increases or pensions and other welfare funds. We must oppose any program which means higher wages but fewer jobs. . . .

This is the stabilization pattern we propose:

1. The union to withdraw all general economic demands for a period of 18 months;

2. The company to maintain present wage rates for a period of 18 months from July 16, 1949;

Provided that on January 15, 1950 and again on July 15, 1950, either party may have the right to reopen the contract for negotiation to adjust the general level of hourly job rates if the latest published B.L.S. index shows a change of four points or more in the interim. . . .

Formal response came in a letter from Reuther to Bugas:

Your proposal is another flight into fantasy. It is the same sort of unsound and unrealistic proposal as those you have previously advanced during negotiations in the past several years.

In 1948 you proposed at the beginning of negotiations that the Ford workers take a wage cut. The result of the negotiations was a 13 cents an hour increase and other economic concessions. Your proposal this year for a wage freeze is no closer to the realities of the situation than was your proposal last year for a wage cut. . . .

The so-called "stabilization pattern" which you propose is a pattern for continued and increasing unemployment. . . .

Your memory should remind you that workers' security and job opportunities did not improve in the early thirties until the government was compelled to take steps to provide the great mass of people with some measure of buying power. . . .

As the parties entered the second stage of negotiations on June 23, the union distributed copies of a 133-page brochure embodying its pension demands. The company rejected these demands because of the uncertain outlook for the general economy and its own competitive disadvantages, particularly with relation to labor costs.

Because of the time-consuming nature of pension discussions, the union pointed out on July 1 that insufficient time remained prior to the expiration of the agreement on July 15. The company concurred, and it was agreed to extend the contract with the understanding that a five-working-day notice would be required for its termination.

The union then presented its second documented brochure, this one supporting its other social security demands. Thereupon the company again set forth, in a letter on July 1 to Reuther, its "stabilization pattern":

We are presenting to the UAW . . . Negotiating Committee again today our proposals for dealing with the major economic issues in our new contract. Since you have not been present at our negotiation sessions, we want to make sure that you are kept fully informed. . . .

1. Our average straight time hourly wage rates are as high or higher than those paid by our major competitors. In 1939 this hourly rate was 90¢. As of April, 1949—only a little more than 10 years later—*this hourly rate stood at $1.66.*

2. To get a true picture of how Ford employees stand today, you must *add about 18½¢ per hour to the current rate of $1.66 for other direct and indirect benefits.*

In 1939, Ford employees had, in addition to wages, other direct and indirect benefits totaling not more than 4¢ an hour. At the present time, Ford employees enjoy such "hidden payroll" benefits of about 18.5¢ an hour.

These benefits are all part of our total labor cost, and include such things as payments for vacations and holidays, social security, unemployment compensation, salaries of Union committeemen, and group insurance.

3. Nor is this all. No overtime or shift premium time payments are included in either the average straight time rate of $1.66 or 18.5¢ an hour for other direct and indirect benefits. We estimate that payments for overtime and shift premiums during the next year will add 7.5¢ hourly to our total labor bill.

We end up, then, with an average true per hour labor cost to the Company of approximately $1.92 at current rates.

4. Since July, 1948, when our present contract was signed, the downward turn in the cost-of-living index has given our employees increased purchasing power of almost 4.5¢ per hour.

This reduction in consumer price levels *has amounted to an automatic 4.5¢ average wage increase for Ford employees* since our last agreement was signed.

5. *Ford employees are already better off, according to any good yardstick, than the vast majority of their fellow employees in other industries.*

The average straight time wage at Ford of $1.66 stands far above the national average hourly earnings of $1.35 for all manufacturing industries.

Bearing these additional factors in mind, we again urge upon you our proposals for settlement of this year's economic issues.

The first is that *the Union withdraw all economic demands for a period of 18 months.*

The second is that *we will agree to maintain our present high wage rates for a period of 18 months.*

Both of these proposals are subject to a general provision that reopenings of the contract on straight hourly wage adjustments will be permitted by either of us if the Bureau of Labor Statistics' so-called "cost-of-living index" moves up or down four points or more.

In a letter to Bugas on July 1, Reuther again rejected as "unsound and unrealistic" the company's position.

At this point, the parties turned to discussion of noneconomic matters, upon the union's proposal to set aside major economic issues in favor of an attempt to arrive at agreement on the other numerous contractual differences.

With little progress being made toward settlement of noneconomic issues, the company on July 18 and 19 elaborated the economic analysis by which it had previously rejected the union's demands by arguments on (1) comparative wages, (2) competitive conditions and (3) uncertainties in the economic outlook. It contended that (1) the ability of unions to raise real wages rested principally upon increases in productivity; (2) the automobile industry was highly competitive and did not engage in monopolistic practices as the union had charged; (3) an analysis of the distribution of national income and of personal savings in 1948 revealed that wage and salary recipients fared well in relation to other economic groups; (4) estimates of consumer expenditure for 1950 indicated a shrinking market for automobiles; (5) lower prices for Ford products were essential to continued sales and job security; (6) the rate of investment, determining as it did the rate at which new job opportunities were created, was dependent to a large extent on the rate of return on invested capital; and (7) lower prices, in contrast to higher wages, offered a better method of economic adjustment since it permitted all sectors of the economy, including fixed-income recipients, to participate in the fruits of increased productivity. On the basis of these criteria, the company contrasted in its presentation the soundness of its own proposed "stabilization pattern" as compared with the union's 1949 economic proposals.

Among the many considerations which the union advanced in support of its position were the following: (1) an 11 cent per hour wage increase was necessary to restore the buying power of wages to the level of June, 1946, when OPA was destroyed; (2) increased wages were necessary to assure adequate purchasing power in the hands of consumers if job security was to be protected; (3) the automobile industry's recent profits reflected more than an adequate ability to pay; (4) a reduction in product prices, with a resulting increase in sales, was economically more feasible than a "self-defeating" limitation on worker income, and hence on consumer purchasing power.

During this second stage of negotiations, the UAW held its Twelfth Constitutional Convention in Milwaukee from July 10 to July 15. Absent were the gusty political tensions that had made prior UAW conventions tumultuous. Reuther and his slate of officers won re-election handily. His own margin over his opponent was 8,021 to 639. The convention's central theme was the drive for pensions and health insurance. The delegates authorized the International Executive Board to levy an emergency strike assessment; they voted down a Reuther-endorsed constitutional change that would have established biennial conventions.

IV

The third stage of negotiations opened on July 27 when Reuther entered the sessions. In the morning he reviewed the union's economic demands and highlighted other points at issue: (1) deletion of union responsibility (management security) clauses; (2) removal of the limitation on the union's right to organize office workers; (3) restriction on the use of outside contractors to perform work formerly done by Ford employees; (4) reduction in the number of committeemen; (5) revision of the grievance and umpire procedure; (6) Rouge area-wide seniority in the skilled trades; (7) elimination of, or reduction in, the 15-day temporary layoff provision; (8) reduction in the probationary period for new employees from 6 months to 30 days; (9) increases in afternoon and night shift differentials; (10) improvement in vacation eligibility rules; and (11) elimination of spread rates for unskilled jobs.

The afternoon meeting was devoted to making arrangements for a state-conducted strike vote. Previously, on July 21, the union had requested the Michigan Labor Mediation Board to conduct such a vote in accordance with the Michigan Labor Mediation Act (Bonine-Tripp Act) which made mandatory, prior to the calling of a strike, a secret ballot among employees of a bargaining unit to determine whether they favored strike action. At the meeting on July 27, the union stated it was unwilling to have the election on company property after Bugas had offered its use for the vote.[1] "We want to cooperate in every way," Bugas had said.

Negotiations were recessed for four days at the request of the company. In a *Ford Rouge News* front-page editorial dated July 29, the company urged every eligible employee to vote on the strike issue:

> . . . the question is not one of voting for or against the Union. Some Union leaders have been telling you that a vote against the strike is a vote to break the Union. That is not so.
> The question is whether you think a long and costly strike in support of the Union's program is better than accepting the Company's proposal for keeping wages and jobs at their present high levels. . . .
> You are already being told that just because you vote for a strike doesn't mean there will be a strike; that the real reason for a strike vote is simply to strengthen union leaders' position at the bargaining table and give them a weapon to force us to yield to their demands.
> But a successful strike vote usually—though not always—results in a strike. And a strike at this time could only result in great hardships for you, for Ford . . . , and for thousands of other people and businesses whose livelihoods depend in one way or another on what we do at Ford. . . .
> It is our sincere conviction that the position we have taken is in the best interests of all employees and the Company as a whole. If we are forced into a strike because of union leaders' insistence on unreasonable demands, we are of the opinion that it will last a long time.
> In our opinion, a vote against a strike is a vote for steady jobs and security over the long pull, while a vote for a strike is a vote for needless hardship.
> But regardless of what decision you make, we urge that you vote in the forthcoming strike election. A secret ballot is not only your right under the law, it is the American way of reaching important decisions.

Reuther termed the editorial a "repetitious statement of the upside-down economics that Ford officials have been advocating throughout our present negotiations," and charged that "the company is trying to threaten its employees with layoffs if they vote to support their union and to back up their just and legitimate demands."

---

[1] Section 9a of the Michigan Labor Mediation Act (Bonine-Tripp Act) requires that the election ". . . shall be held on the premises where those voting are employed unless the Board shall determine that the election cannot be fairly held there. . . ."

On August 1, negotiations were resumed and continued without progress for two days when they were again suspended—this time for a five-day period. During these sessions, Reuther requested the company to furnish cost and profit data.

On August 2, in a letter to the state mediation board, Bugas "emphatically urged" the board to reconsider its decision not to conduct the strike vote on company premises. He emphasized that the union had argued for off company voting to give it a better opportunity to influence voters. Referring to the 1948 union shop vote held among Ford employees, Bugas wrote:

The Board seems to place great stress upon the experience of the NLRB in 1948 in conducting the union shop election off the premises. It is noteworthy, however, that the NLRB was anxious to hold the election in the plant, and chose the other location only when plans to do so fell through for other reasons. Furthermore, results of that election were to be determined by a majority of those eligible to vote, rather than of those voting, so that the Union was under the greatest pressure to see that every eligible voter got to the polls. A similar pressure does not exist in elections under the Bonine-Tripp law.

On August 4 the company telegraphed the mediation board and the Governor again protesting rulings on voting places. The next day, in an effort "to make its position unmistakably clear" prior to the strike vote, the company made a revised stabilization proposal in a letter to Reuther. Excerpts follow:

In an effort to influence the coming strike election under the Bonine-Tripp Act, you and other UAW . . . spokesmen have made a series of calculated misstatements to our employees. . . .

First, that the company is trying to take away employees' seniority rights and holiday pay;

Next, that the company is trying to farm out work now done in our plant here to "scab" shops;

Third, that the company is trying to "break the union," and to eliminate the union shop in Ford plants;

Finally, that the company is trying to reduce wages.

All these charges are absolutely false and you know it. Apparently, however, this knowledge has not kept you from using these arguments to try to influence our employees into voting for a long and needless strike. . . .

To make our position unmistakably clear, we make the following formal proposals:

1. That the noneconomic provisions of our contract remain unchanged in any respect for a period of eighteen (18) months from July 15, 1949, thereby assuring employees of present working conditions without any change whatever;

2. That the economic provisions of our contract—including wage rates and all other economic benefits—remain at their present levels without provision for reopening by either side for a period of twelve (12) months from July 15, 1949.

Your immediate acceptance of these proposals will assure employees continuation of the largest union shop in the automobile industry and of every benefit and right they now enjoy.

An immediate and lengthy response was forthcoming from Reuther. Charging that Bugas' letter was both a "desperate attempt" to confuse employees prior to the strike vote and a challenge to "the honesty and integrity of the union," he wrote in part as follows:

The Union is prepared to prove by quoting the written documents, which you, Mr. Bugas, on behalf of . . . Ford . . . have presented to the Union's negotiating Committee:

1. That the Company did propose basic changes in the seniority provisions which would weaken, if not destroy, full seniority protection of the Ford workers. . . .

2. That the Company did propose to change the contract to make it more difficult for workers to qualify for holiday pay.

3. That in the negotiations you specifically refused to agree to provisions that would protect the Ford workers against the loss of their jobs due to the farming out of work to outside shops.

4. While it is wholly false that we have accused you of proposing a wage cut at the present time, it is true, however, that you proposed a wage cut at the time of negotiations last year, and that in negotiations this year you refused to give us the assurance that your wage proposals would not result in a wage cut.

Your letter significantly does not mention some of the other Company proposals that we did charge the Company with making and which we also can prove with the written documents which you presented to the Union Committee in behalf of the Company. . . .

Since you have charged the Union and its representatives with "calculated misstatements," I am on behalf of the Union challenging you to appear jointly with me to state our respective cases before the Ford employees in the greater Detroit area at a meeting at Briggs Stadium, Sunday, August 7. At that time I shall read to the Ford workers in your presence the written documents which you on behalf of . . . Ford . . . presented to the Union Negotiating Committee and which prove the truth of the Union's position.

There is a reasonable basis for doubt in our minds whether your formal proposal made today through a letter first given to the newspapers and then sent to the Union, is a serious proposal or a last minute maneuver to confuse the issues and to influence the vote in the State-conducted election. . . .

Bugas replied the next day:

. . . Our negotiations thus far have unfortunately been conducted in an atmosphere of emotional outbursts and name-calling by you and other spokesmen for your Union.

I would like to remind you that we have been in constant negotiation since June 2. During that period you personally have been present only at two brief morning sessions. . . . We have, in short, unsuccessfully been asking you to debate at the bargaining table for over two months. . . .

. . . Thus far you have made the air blue with accusations that the company is trying to take away present rights and benefits of our employees, and that we are trying to destroy the Union. We have called this bluff. Our proposal . . . is a firm one.

Finally, we suggest that you spend more time at the bargaining table and less time in propagandizing, name-calling, and efforts to enhance your personal political fortune.

On August 6, the Michigan State Supreme Court denied a motion by the company to block the strike vote on charges that the state Labor Mediation Board had been "unfair" in refusing to conduct the vote on company property and, instead, ordering it held in the immediate vicinity of union offices.

On August 7, the company ran full-page advertisements in Sunday newspapers in the form of a letter from Henry Ford II to the "Men and Women of Ford Motor Company," explaining the company's position on the strike vote. It had already purchased time on four Detroit radio stations for spot announcements urging employees to vote "No." Reuther had responded with a 30-minute radio talk.

The vote was taken August 8–10. By August 13, the results of the vote had been certified as follows: total number of eligible voters = 86,305; total vote = 75,230; for a strike = 65,001; against a strike = 9,549; invalidated and challenged = 680.

Excerpts from union and company comments regarding the results follow:

BUGAS

Results of the vote are not surprising in view of the manner in which it was conducted and especially in view of the statement of the union leadership that a favorable vote does not mean a strike but merely strengthens their position at the bargaining table. . . .

Our position remains unchanged—we desire to reach an agreement which gives the best promise of providing the largest number of steady jobs to Ford employees. . . .

When union leaders call a strike we hope Ford employees realize that it may be a long one.

REUTHER

The union will exhaust every reasonable effort to win justice for the Ford workers through peaceful collective bargaining.

We are determined, however, to obtain justice by the use of the full economic power of our union if the . . . Company continues in its refusal to meet the just demands of the Ford workers and their families.

V

While the strike vote was being taken, negotiations were resumed on August 8. On August 9, the company agreed to reduce the probationary period for new employees in return for some equivalent concession from the union. On August 10, the union, indicating willingness to recognize the company's right to set production standards if adequate safeguards were provided, suggested an exchange of proposals on the matter.

On August 12, further progress was reported in an agreement (1) to revise the umpire procedure by providing for the selection of an additional umpire or umpires as needed, and (2) to add another step in the grievance procedure to cover those matters to be expressly removed from the umpire's jurisdiction, such as disputes on work standards. By August 15, wording was agreed upon regarding the payment of workers on a weekly rather than a biweekly basis.

Commencing on August 16, the pace of negotiations quickened as the parties began to meet daily, without, however, resulting in a proportionally higher rate of agreement. On August 29, therefore, the parties turned their attention to clauses dealing with union recognition and reached essential agreement on this subject except for provisions limiting the union's right to organize excluded personnel. By August 22, it had been agreed that the committeeman structure would, except for a few minor changes, remain unchanged. But complete agreement on this part of the contract was delayed by inability to resolve the question of the number of committeemen. The company did agree, however, to liberalize its vacation eligibility requirements on the understanding that the union would withdraw its proposal to increase vacation benefits.

On August 31, once again the parties began consideration of the economic issues, discussions continuing on the following day without shifts in the position of either party. At this crucial time, Reuther presented a letter stating that unless progress was made a strike deadline would be set. Thus, the third stage of negotiations was coming to an end since the only further agreement to be reached concerned the addition to the contract of a statement relative to the smoking privilege. Discussions of pensions and wage increases revealed both parties remaining firm in the positions they had taken several months before. Because of a 30-day limitation prescribed by law on the validity of the state-conducted strike vote, the strike deadline was extended by the state's acceptance of the existing contract extension agreement as evidence that the strike vote certification should continue valid for so long as the contract extension agreement was in effect.

VI

The fourth and final stage of negotiations commenced on September 10 when the President's fact-finding board for the steel industry made public its recommendations of a maximum 4 cents an hour for employer-paid social insurance, a maximum of 6 cents an hour for employer-paid pensions, and no wage increase. President Truman at the same time requested a postponement of the steel strike deadline from September 14 to September 25.[1]

The session held on September 12 was devoted to a review of each clause of the contract. The impact of the steel board's report became evident, however, when the company requested cancellation of the session scheduled for September 13. On September 14 no progress was made; both parties seemed to be waiting. The break came on September 15 when the company informed Reuther and his associates that it was prepared to discuss a pension plan. During informal discussions over the next few days, the company stated that any money it agreed to spend should be applied to pensions only. The company offered to contribute close to 9 cents an hour for pensions, but stated it would give nothing for social insurance. (The company claimed a deduction of 1¼ cents per hour from the 10-cent steel "package" for contributions it was already making for social insurance.) Employees were to make no contributions. The company conditioned its proposal on the union's withdrawal of all its other economic demands.

On September 19, after a discussion of provisions for funding past service under the company's pension proposal, the union handed company rep-

---

[1] See The Steel Industry: The 1949 Negotiations, p. 466.

resentatives notice of its desire to terminate the contract as of 12:01 A.M., September 29, unless a satisfactory agreement was reached by that time.

The remainder of the 19th and all of the 20th, 21st, 22d, 23d, and 24th was devoted to discussions of noneconomic matters with no discussion of the pension proposal whatever.

On September 25, pensions once again became the focal point of consideration. Reuther indicated that the union would be willing to consider the proposed pension eligibility requirements of 65 years of age, 30 years of service, and automatic retirement at 68. He objected, however, to the company's proposal for funding past service in as short a period as possible under Federal tax laws, inasmuch as the funds needed would be so substantial as to reduce the amount of immediate pension benefits appreciably. The company advanced the argument that unless past service credits were funded, future pension benefits would be uncertain and would depend entirely upon the financial success of the company.

In response to the union's inquiry into the possibility of setting aside 4 cents for a hospitalization program, Bugas stated that the company's offer allowed no room for any upward movement in total costs. The union then urged that the effective date for the pension plan be December 1, 1949, rather than March 1, 1950. After lengthy discussions, agreement was reached on the following points: a qualified bank or trust company was to act as trustee of the pension fund; the right to appoint and contract with the trustee would remain the sole right of the company; no employee would have any vested right under the program except upon actual retirement; and the plan would be subject to the approval of the Commissioner of Internal Revenue. No commitment was made on the company's proposal that benefits from the Ford retirement fund would be reduced when Federal social security benefits were raised. Reuther indicated that the union might accept a two-year contract from date of agreement.

The parties did not meet on September 26 until the evening. At this session discussions were confined to the problems of scheduling reduced work weeks and of temporary layoffs.

The final session began at 2:30 P.M. on September 27 and ended 36 hours later, during which time the parties remained in continuous session. At the opening, Bugas noted the substantial concessions, both in money and in principle, already made by the company. He urged the union to consider with pride the accomplishments they were in a position to announce through acceptance of the company's offer of pensions. He then read the following terms of the "final offer" of the company on the other points at issue: (1) The representation (committeeman) structure to remain as it was except for changes in unit structure. (2) A reasonable restriction to operating extended periods of time at reduced work weeks. (3) Seniority employees to be utilized in maintenance and construction work, but the company to retain its right to contract work. (4) Retention of the right to discipline those participating in wildcat stoppages to be contingent on the umpire's right of review provided the umpire had no power to award back pay except in the case of a finding of innocence. (5) Effective January 1, 1950, an in-hospital medical program with maximum benefits of $280 for 70 days. (6) The union to agree that the prevailing practice for the payment of overtime in integrated steel was to apply to company steel operations. (7) The contract to remain in effect until April 1, 1952, with one reopening by either party on economic matters other than pensions after January 1, 1951.

Bugas again reviewed the pension proposal. He remained firm in his insistence on management's exclusive right to determine how past service credits should be funded. Upon conclusion of his presentation, the parties recessed.

When the bargainers returned, the union sought clarification on several of the company's proposals. The company resisted any additional expenditures. Agreement was reached on most issues except overtime practices in steel operations, temporary layoffs, vacation eligibility requirements,[1] life insurance after retirement, death benefits, and the time period during which the pension agreement would not be subject to renegotiation. Another recess was taken.

Upon returning to negotiations, the parties reached agreement "in principle" on the remaining unresolved issues. The negotiators then divided themselves into subcommittees to develop acceptable contract language regarding the various clauses of their agreement. The settlement was announced at about 2:00 A.M. on September 29, just two hours after the union had telegraphed each of its Ford locals canceling the scheduled strike which was to have been effective at midnight.

VII

Announcement of the settlement and a summary of the major provisions of the pension program and changes in the contract was made immediately. The following statement was issued by Bugas:

Ford Motor Company and UAW–CIO have reached agreement on a new contract to run for two and a half years from October 1, 1949. It will be effective until April 1, 1952, although each party may request one reopening on economic matters only—other than pensions—after January 1, 1951.

The most important feature of the new agreement is a pension plan for all of our hourly rated employees. The plan was worked out by the Company following the report of the President's fact-finding board for the steel industry. In the form now agreed upon, the plan provides for retirement of Ford hourly rated employees at 65 years of age after 30 years of service at $100 monthly, including Social Security benefits. The plan is noncontributory. We estimate that our contribution to the pension fund will be at the rate of 8¾ cents per hour. We regard this agreement as a fresh and significant approach to increasingly better industrial relations in Ford Motor Company plants. Most of all, we believe that it opens the door on a long period of sustained labor peace and productivity.

Full details of the plan still have to be worked out by a Company-Union committee. All major principles, however, have been included in the new agree-

---

[1] The company had withdrawn its proposal of August 22 to liberalize these requirements when it made its final offer matching the steel board's recommendations.

ment, including the following: On retirement at age 65 with 30 years of service an employee will receive $100 a month, including Federal Social Security benefits. Normal retirement will be at age 65, and automatic retirement at age 68 with no increase in benefits after age 65. A "cushioning period" will be provided for employees now approaching 68 or older.

Benefits will be integrated with Social Security benefits. When Federal Social Security benefits are raised, benefits from the Ford retirement fund will be reduced accordingly. Until Social Security benefits are increased, we estimate that our contributions to the fund will be at the rate of 8¾ cents per hour. We are at present contributing about 1¼ cents an hour for social insurance purposes. The pension plan will become effective March 1, 1950 and benefit payments will begin on April 1, 1950.

The pension plan may not be reopened for negotiation until March 1, 1955. At no time prior to that date will either side be required to bargain with respect to the plan and it is agreed that neither party will resort to a strike, lockout or other economic force or threat of force to change or add to the plan.

Employees with 30 years' service may elect early retirement after 60, with reduced benefits, with the consent of the Company. Employees who do not fulfill the service requirements at normal retirement age of 65 will receive proportionately lower benefits. For instance, an employee retiring with 25 years' service at 65 would receive 25/30th of the $100 monthly benefit, including Social Security. Employees may retire for total and permanent disability after 30 years' service at 55 or older with a flat retirement benefit of $50 a month. The benefit would be adjusted for benefits paid under any disability provision which might be added to the Federal Social Security Act.

The Company will retain the sole right to appoint and contract with a qualified bank or trust company as trustee to handle the pension fund, and the period of funding past service will be solely up to the Company.

A Company–Union committee will be established to pass upon qualifications of employees for benefits under the plan. Employees who have left the Company since July 16, 1949 and who would have been eligible had the plan been in effect when they left, will receive retirement payments beginning April 1, 1950.

Past service will be based upon seniority except seniority credited for military service prior to employment by the Company. Future service will be determined on the following basis: one year for each calendar year in which an employee receives pay for 1,800 or more hours; ¾ of a year for 1,300 to 1,799 hours; ½ of a year for 750 to 1,299 hours, and no credit for any year in which an employee works less than 750 hours.

The other major provisions resulting from these negotiations follow:

1. Recognition clauses were developed to define in greater particular those categories of employees excluded from the bargaining unit. The union agreed not to attempt to organize executive or supervisory employees, employees engaged in time study or other industrial engineering activities, employees engaged in industrial relations activities, employees having access to confidential information pertaining to employee and labor relations matters, or "other representatives of management."

2. The union recognized the right of the company to establish and enforce production standards. The union was granted the unrestricted right to process grievances on disputed standards through specialized procedures. Previously the union could challenge standards only on an alleged impairment of the health of safety of employees. The new contract specifically stated that production standards must be set with due consideration for

fatigue and the need for "personal" time. Incorporated also were the provisions of the strike settlement agreement of May 29, 1949, and the rules of manning similar moving assembly lines established by the arbitration award of July 8, 1949. In production standard grievances the union committeemen were given the right to negotiate. A *qualified* union representative could examine all pertinent data and observe and study the jobs. The maximum time provided for reaching an agreement on production standards was 34 days. . . . Failure to reach agreement through the contractually prescribed procedures allowed the union the right to strike. Other issues involving specialized grievance procedures and the right to strike were health and safety, and rates on new jobs.

3. While the company retained the right to prescribe reasonable working rules and regulations, the union gained the right to question their reasonableness through the grievance procedure.

4. The article previously titled "Union Responsibility" was retitled "Strikes, Stoppages and Lockouts." The union reaffirmed its obligation not to permit strikes, stoppages, slowdowns, or any curtailment of work. Power was granted the umpire to review the reasonableness of penalties imposed on employees instigating or participating in unauthorized stoppages, except that he might order back pay only upon a finding of innocence. Previously, the umpire had had no power to modify such penalties, with the sole exception that if he determined an employee not to be guilty of "instigating" or "giving leadership" to an illegitimate strike, he could only reduce the penalty to that appropriate for "participation" in an illegitimate strike.

5. No changes were made in the number of union committeemen or in the provisions for their compensation. Minor changes were effected in the designation of the units such committeemen represented.

6. The major changes in the grievance procedure had as their objective the earlier disposition of grievances. The time allowed for the first step (foreman-committeemen) was reduced, in the Detroit area, from 4 to 3 working days; errors resulting in pay shortage were to be corrected within 5 working days of the filing of a grievance; back-pay awards were to be paid within 30 days; and the umpire was required to rule on a grievance within a specified time from his receipt of the appeal—within 60 days for plants in the lower Michigan area, and within 6 months for all other plants. Should the case load of the umpire become too great he was to notify the parties, and they were to take immediate steps to select one or more persons to act as a temporary umpire under the same procedures and provisions as the permanent umpire.

7. Temporary layoffs (except at times of model changes) during which the company was not required to make seniority adjustments were reduced from 15 to not more than 12 working days, and the company agreed not to use such layoffs in a series to avoid seniority adjustments to meet planned production needs.

8. Scheduling of a continuous period of reduced work weeks was re-

stricted to two weeks for less than an average of 24 hours, to four weeks for less than an average of 32 hours, and to 8 weeks for less than an average of 40 hours—with exceptions negotiable by local agreement.

9. The probationary period of a new employee was reduced from six months to three months. However, an employee had to be on the employment rolls for six months before becoming eligible for holiday pay.

10. Employees laid off by discontinuances of work at one plant were to be given "hiring consideration" at other plants.

11. There was no change in wage rates.

12. Practices prevailing in comparable integrated mills in the steel industry relative to payment of overtime were to be applied to the company's steel operations. For the purpose of determining what those practices were, a joint committee of three union members and three company members was to be established within 30 days. If they were unable to agree by January 1, 1950, all points in dispute were to be referred to the umpire for determination. Any changes in the payment of overtime were to be effective no later than March 1, 1950.

13. Eligibility for vacations was liberalized in that eligibility dated from either June 1 or December 1, depending upon date of hire. Previously employees dated their vacation eligibility only from December 1.

14. The company retained its right to make contracts with outside contractors, but it agreed to inclusion of a clause stating it to be company policy to utilize its own seniority employees in the performance of maintenance and construction work in accordance with its letter to the union of January 20, 1949. In this letter, the company had outlined the policy under which it proposed to continue the use of outside contractors when it felt it was advisable to do so.

15. The company agreed to designate areas in which smoking would be unsafe and not permitted. In undesignated areas smoking would be permitted.

Appraisal of the new agreement was made by the union in a special Ford edition of *The United Automobile Worker* as follows:

The new Ford contract, judged honestly and objectively, represents the most progress that your union has been able to make in any single set of major contract negotiations.

Elsewhere within the union comments were less favorable. Although he urged approval of the new contract, Thompson did so "with full knowledge of the fact that there [was] so much more to be desired." In the October 8 issue of *Ford Facts* he continued as follows:

The new contract when ratified will be effective from October 29, 1949 until April 1, 1952, "except that *economic matters* other than pensions may be opened for negotiations *once* by *each* party before April 1, 1952, but not in any case before January 1, 1951, unless *both* parties agree otherwise." Under the terms of this clause, the contract will be effective for 2½ years or 30 months, reportedly the longest term of any contract in UAW–CIO history. Now from October 29, 1949 to January 1, 1951 . . . is 14 months. So Mr. Bugas got a 14-month wage freeze (where he was only shooting for 12 months last August) *plus* the additional 16-month freeze from January 1, 1951 to April 1, 1952!

Of course, Mr. Bugas might point out that he gave us a new contract, while his proposal of last August was that we continue the old one. But so far as we Rouge workers are concerned, the changes in the new contract, for the most part, merely spell out and grant to Ford workers, nationally, provisions which we at the Rouge had already won in local negotiations and have been enjoying for some time now.

In explaining the contract expiration date of April, 1952, the International union advanced "two basic and fundamental reasons" as follows:

1. Ford, General Motors and Chrysler contracts can now all be lined up so that they will expire within a few weeks of each other, thereby permitting the Union to take maximum advantage of the competitive struggle between the major automotive producers, by playing one corporation against another. . . .

2. Spring is traditionally the period in which automobile producers are stepping up production to take advantage of market conditions. Maximum bargaining power for the Union comes at the time when the manufacturers are stepping up production and introducing new models. Weather conditions in the spring and the summer are such that the workers can better conduct and sustain a strike in support of their demands if necessary.

Open opposition was expressed in a resolution adopted by Chevrolet Local 659 in Flint, Mich., urging Ford workers to reject the proposed contract and declaring that the age limitation, eligibility clauses, and maximum benefits of the pension plan were "wholly inadequate." The local demanded adherence by the International to the original demand for a full 38-cent package as originally adopted by the UAW and endorsed by the annual convention.

Efforts of the International to obtain ratification of the contract were rewarded on October 26 when Rouge workers representing more than one-half of the total of 115,000 Ford workers accepted the agreement by a vote of 32,392 to 7,130. For the 48 Ford locals the total unofficial count was 46,640 to 12,739.

DISCUSSION QUESTIONS

1. Noting that actual negotiations opened on June 2, 1949, indicate the date when you would consider proceedings on the agenda began; and then mark subsequent date of events or actions you would consider significant in this "prelude" to the specific procedure of negotiation. From this chronology, how would you evaluate these events or actions as a part of the "negotiation" procedure at Ford?

2. Analyze the impact of the union as an "institution" upon the negotiations, evaluating particularly intraunion and interunion considerations.

3. Indicate any clues from the case that throw light on the impact of Ford as an "institution" upon this bargaining.

FORD MOTOR COMPANY

NEGOTIATING THE 1955 AGREEMENT

I. BACKGROUND

That the guaranteed annual wage was to be the heart of 1955 negotiations had been made eminently clear by the UAW. This demand was voted "the next major goal of our union" at the 1951 constitutional convention and at the 1953 convention the union's goal was reaffirmed. The first union-wide economic and collective bargaining conference, held in November, 1954, set GAW as the major goal in the forthcoming negotiations, and accordingly endorsed the recommendation to enlarge the strike fund from $8.5 to $25 million by increasing dues $5 a month. In January 1955, the demands outlined by this conference were unanimously adopted by both the GM and the Ford national conferences, for the first time held simultaneously.

The demand for "Guaranteed Employment Plan" included the following:

All workers to be guaranteed a full 40-hour week if working or pay unless notified in advance that they will be laid off for the entire week.

Seniority workers to receive pay for each week of layoff up to 52 weeks, in the ratio of 1 week for each 2 weeks worked. Weeks worked to be credited back to 2 years before the plan.

Unemployment payment to be sufficient to enable workers to maintain the same living standards as when fully employed.

Workers to be available for work and registration with the state employment service, but standards of eligibility to be determined under the plan, not by the state.

Payments by the company to be reduced by the amount of state benefits or other earnings in suitable employment.

The 40-hour week to be financed currently.

The layoff payments to be financed currently up to a certain percentage of each week's payroll.

The plan to be administered by a joint board of administration having equal representation from the union and from management.

Payments beyond the maximum percentage to be paid from a reserve trust fund built up by regular contribution based on the number currently employed and their average wage rates. But no contributions to be made to the fund if the cost of current guarantees has reached the maximum percentage.

The reserve fund to be protected by reinsurance.

A barrage of publicity set forth the union's position. Reuther took every opportunity to predict that the GAW would be won in 1955, by strike if necessary—and without indicating which company should be chosen as a target.

Both Ford and GM kept silence. However, the GM annual report pointed to the existing unemployment compensation system under Social Security, and to the company's own programs for stabilizing employment through timing of model changes at the period of traditionally low demand and through the use of overtime in periods of normally high demand. Ford made a somewhat similar statement in the *Rouge News:*

The only security—the only guarantee—worth anything to Ford employees is that their company will be healthy, competitive and progressive enough to be able to employ them at a high rate of wages and benefits. When any proposed security scheme impairs this healthy condition—no matter how attractive may seem the arguments in its favor—such scheme with dead certainty will impair the real security of the worker.

The union's thinking about the moral, economic, and social considerations underlying the plan was revealed by Reuther's March 1955 "Report to the UAW–CIO Membership."[1]

. . . Again, this year, and to an even greater degree than in 1953, the industry has bunched a disproportionate share of its expected total annual output into the first six months of the year. Again, everything points to mass layoffs and mass hardships in the second half of the year.

. . . . .

Our demand for guaranteed employment is designed to end such corporate irresponsibility and inhumanity.

. . . . .

We in the UAW–CIO have always believed that our demands must not only reflect the legitimate needs and aspirations of our membership but that they must also be morally right, economically sound and socially responsible.

. . . . .

In the last analysis, the only purpose of economic activity is to serve man— to make life better, richer and fuller for people. . . .

. . . . .

From the social and economic standpoints, the demand for guaranteed employment is a demand to minimize unemployment and its effects on community and nation by stabilizing workers' purchasing power and by putting the costs of unemployment on those who are responsible for it and who have the ability, acting individually and collectively, to meet their responsibilities to maintain full employment.

. . . . .

The costs of unemployment are properly chargeable as part of the costs of doing business. Yet management today is largely able to escape them by passing them on to the worker and the community. As a result, many managerial decisions are made which, while profitable to the individual company, are costly to the worker and to the economy as a whole.

. . . . .

Despite our confidence in the plan, and our firm belief that it is one under which our industries could operate without difficulty, we are prepared to give earnest consideration to any other Guaranteed Employment Plan that industry or anyone else has to offer as better or more practical. . . .

. . . . .

---

[1] *The United Automobile Worker,* March, 1955, pp. 3–5.

Other developments had their effect upon the approaching negotiations. The economy had displayed remarkable stability since 1953 with CPI showing a net upward movement of less than one point.   Except for a minor recession in late 1953 and 1954, production generally boomed—resulting in successive increases in total employment.   General Motors announced in 1953 that it anticipated spending $1½ billion over the following two years for new plant and equipment.   In 1954 it raised the figure by another billion.   During these years Ford had completed its program of internal reorganization.   The new engine plant in Cleveland stood out as an outstanding example of automation.

With the advent of the Republican Administration, the political climate became more hospitable to business.   The White House followed a policy of remaining aloof from management-labor disputes.

President Eisenhower repeatedly advocated legislation both to enlarge coverage and to bring state unemployment compensation benefits, which only averaged $25 a week, up to 50% of normal earnings.[1]   Subsequently in August 1954, the earnings base for old age annuity was raised from $3,600 to $4,200 with immediate increases in benefits to a maximum of $108.50 beginning April 1956.

In July 1954 the UAW requested Ford to renegotiate voluntarily its optional pension plan B, so that any future increase in the Social Security benefits would accrue to the retiree.   The company acceded with the result that increases from $5 to $13.50 a month accrued to over 1,100 Ford workers who had already retired.

On the labor side progress toward the long-proposed AFL–CIO merger was made in a no-raiding pact signed in June 1954.   Subsequently terms for a merger were drawn up by the Joint AFL–CIO Unity Committee, subject to the ratification of the AFL and the CIO executive boards and the fall conventions.   Reuther was commonly spoken of as the probable first Vice-president.

Auto production in 1955 consistently passed the 1953 records.   In the race between Ford and GM for consumer preference, GM claimed the leadership for the 19th year; but Ford maintained it was ahead if cars registered by dealers were eliminated.

II. Negotiations

The union opened negotiations with 60-day notices—Ford's was a termination notice for June 1, while GM's was a modification notice for May 29. The union asked for early preliminary conferences to avoid conflict with its constitutional convention opening on March 29.   In these conferences with GM on March 14 and 15 and with Ford on March 16 and 17, the manage-

---

[1] State maximum unemployment benefits ranged from $20 to $35 in amount, with an extra allowance for dependents in some cases.   Maximum duration of payments ranged from 16 to 26½ weeks.

On January 20, 1955, in the *Economic Report of the President,* Eisenhower said, "It is highly desirable that the states change their laws so that the great majority of covered workers will be eligible for payments that at least equal half their regular earnings."

ments heard the union's proposals without giving any intimation of their own reactions. Formal negotiations were scheduled to open with Ford on April 12 and with GM on April 7. It was agreed that there would be no publicity on negotiations without at least 24-hour prior notice to the other party.

Meanwhile, Local 600's *Ford Facts* stated, "It is an open secret that we at Ford have been chosen to go out first, but changing circumstances might possibly lead our top strategists to send GM workers out first instead." Reuther was quoted as saying that he expected to win the GAW without a strike. And at the convention where he was returned to office for his sixth term by an overwhelming majority, he observed that he had heard the rumor that Ford was working out an offer; and he also indicated that for the first time he would take an active part in the complete negotiations.

The union's demands on items other than GAW included an immediate increase of 5.3 cents an hour to bring rates up to the level which would have been attained on the basis of "proper implementation" of the theory behind the 1948 wage formula; improvement factor adjustments "to reflect more adequately actual changes in national productivity"; the transference of the entire cost-of-living allowance to base rates; a recalculation of the cost-of-living escalator table of allowance on the basis of an up-to-date relationship between wages and the index; the future transfer to base rates of any portion of the cost-of-living allowance above a certain unspecified amount; future automatic adjustments in the improvement factor "to protect against inflation"; increases of as much as 30 cents for certain skilled trade classifications; triple time for worked holidays; $25 a month minimum pension for 5 years' service, $2.50 a month for each year of service with a removal of the 30-year ceiling; vested pension rights, a voice in investment of pension funds, and joint administration; company-financed health benefits with joint administration; extension of the bargaining unit to all employees, including office workers; more adequate representation, on a full-time basis, on grievances; no subcontracting of work that could be performed by those covered by the agreement; preferential hiring for workers laid off from other plants of the company and from any plant in the same area under UAW contract; contract duration not to exceed two years if the escalator and improvement factors were included, otherwise one year.

Ford in its demands proposed: to exclude timekeepers and production and quality control employees from the bargaining unit; to substitute part-time representation for full time (2 to 4 hours per day averaged over the week) and to reduce the number to 1 for every 250 employees (Ford's costs in this respect were estimated at $23 per employee per year as compared to GM's $3); to give the company sole discretion on promotion, greater flexibility in assigning overtime and the right to use skilled craftsmen for work incidental to the job to which they were assigned; to authorize the company to use outside contractors without restrictions; and to tighten the grievance procedure, with more effective protection against work stoppages or other interferences with production.

Discussions in April and the greater part of May centered primarily on issues other than GAW. With respect to the latter, Bugas was reported to have said in April that Ford would "never, never" grant the union's demand, to which Reuther rejoined, "Never say 'never,' John." Henry Ford II gave public indication of the company's philosophy in a speech before the American Newspaper Publishers Association on April 28, when he said: "A solid foundation of security . . . [could be put] under every American home and family . . . without piecemeal experimenting with dangerous mechanisms or guinea pig industries, or without creating a special caste of privileged working people whose short-term security is underwritten by the increased insecurity of others—and, in fact, by the long-term insecurity of everybody." [1]

In the meantime, negotiations at GM had been marked by a full-page newspaper advertisement on April 11 which featured the number of new jobs at GM, the all-time high pay, the many benefits gained under five years of labor peace; and ended with an italicized "It's just plain common sense to keep the ball rolling straight through 1955." After the fifth meeting on April 14, Livingston reported "little progress." On April 29, the union gave GM a notice that the contract would terminate on June 7. [2] Livingston commented that "he hoped no one would think the union was being soft on GM because it served a contract modification on GM after Ford."

During the first week of May, the union proposed to both companies that liability under GAW be limited to 8% of current payroll, including contributions of 4% of a base payroll to a reserve fund over a five-year period.

On May 9, the GM and Ford union councils decided to take a strike vote because the companies were "not bargaining." However, in its Management Information Bulletin, Ford said that it had taken no position but was very thoroughly exploring every phase of GAW. It reported that it was also seeking a no-strike pledge and mandatory arbitration of all disputes. On May 24, a vote at GM registered 93.3% in favor of a strike with over two-thirds of each local voting.

On May 26, Ford made an offer which was publicly described by Bugas as "the most challenging and comprehensive" single package in the history of the automotive industry: (1) The opportunity to buy Ford stock combined with the purchase of government bonds. For each $100 put into the plan by an employee, $50 would go into government bonds, and the company would match the other $50 by $100 worth of Ford stock when it became available. (2) Income to be stabilized during layoffs by interest-free loans with repayment to start after recall and at the rate of half of any earnings for work in excess of 32 hours a week. (Loans to be canceled at death or if the worker not recalled within 3 years.) (3) Separation pay to reach as high as $5,980. (4) An annual improvement factor of 2½% to range from 5 cents to 8 cents an hour. (5) Pension after 30 years of service to be increased to $222.80 per month for a married man, including Social Security. (For 40 years' service,

---

[1] *The New York Times,* April 29, 1955.
[2] This is significant, since ordinarily GM's contract would have been expected to have terminated on May 29, 1955, while the Ford agreement was to remain "in full force and effect until June 1, 1955."

$242.80.) (6) Increases in the group insurance program: a new maximum of $6,400 life insurance, plus $3,200 for accidental death or dismemberment; $76.80 weekly accident and sickness benefits; in-hospital medical benefits to include wife and children. (7) The hospitalization-surgical program of other areas to be brought up to the Michigan plan with an effort to arrange for Blue Shield to cover full surgical costs. (8) Vacation for workers of 10 to 15 years' service to be extended to 2½ weeks. (9) The equivalent of a seventh paid holiday to be taken as a half day on Christmas and New Year's Eves. (10) Differential for midnight shift to be increased to 10% except for the steel division. (11) Worked holidays to be paid at triple time except on 7-day operations and in the steel division. (12) Saturday to be at time and a half except on 7-day operations and the steel division. (13) Cost-of-living increases for each .5 instead of .6 in the CPI. (14) Special increases for certain skilled trades. (15) A five-year contract. (16) Finally the company to match any more favorable economic settlement. The management did not put a price tag on its offer, but it was evaluated by *Business Week* as amounting to 37½ cents an hour. Other companies were appalled by its size and not a little disturbed by the inclusion of stock purchase arrangements in a collective bargaining proposal.[1]

As Bugas was reading the offer, he was interrupted halfway through by Reuther; recognizing it as virtually identical with an unpublicized offer made by GM on May 17, he asked, "How the hell do you get a Chevvy on a Ford assembly line?" He very shortly led his team out of the room.

On the 26th a vote of 96.2 in favor of a strike at Ford's was announced by Bannon. That evening the union rejected the company's proposal.

On the 28th, Reuther urged Henry Ford and Ernest R. Breech to attend the next meeting of the Ford Council. Mr. Ford responded:

Your telegram to me was delivered to my office at approximately 1:30 A.M.

I feel that no useful purpose possibly can be served by my appearance—or that of Mr. Breech's—at the meeting of the national UAW–CIO Ford Council today, which you have suggested we attend.

Mr. Breech, Mr. John Bugas . . . and myself—as well as the Ford Motor Company board of directors—are familiar with every phase of the negotiations between the union and the company, as well as with all details of the proposals which the union has made.

We are similarly completely familiar, of course, with the Ford "prosperity partnership package" which has been submitted by us to you at the bargaining table.

I hope that all of your people have taken what you consider to be the necessary time to thoroughly examine the unusual and comprehensive terms of this package.

. . . . .

The union officially sanctioned a strike to start at 12:01 A.M., June 2. Negotiations continued all day Sunday, May 29. The union reduced its demand for layoff benefits from 100% to 80% of straight-time take-home earn-

---

[1] Of all 1955 wage settlements prior to June, 44% had been in the 4-cent to 6-cent range; 10% gave no increase; 61% gave less than 7 cents; and 78% less than 10 cents.

ings for a 40-hour week—its first concession on GAW. The company had already withdrawn the proviso that separation allowance would cancel pension rights. On a union-sponsored local telecast, Reuther urged management to work toward an agreement rather than trying to prove GAW unworkable.

When discussions resumed the next morning, May 30, Reuther suggested that the 140,000 employees be given an opportunity to vote as to whether they preferred GAW or the company plan. The management asked for a recess until the next morning. The union's proposal of a ballot was also incorporated in a letter delivered by hand that same morning to Mr. Ford. It was also released to the press. In addition to suggesting a ballot, the union also indicated that it would accept a modification of its GAW plan that could be financed with the equivalent of the 12 cents per hour that the union said that the company would be paying for its "Partnership in Prosperity Plan."

The company countered with full page advertisements detailing its "Partnership in Prosperity Program" addressed to Ford employees and urging them to read and judge for themselves. The discussions on May 31 were concealed by a news blackout. Reporters noted that the union team twice moved to its caucus room. The first night session ran until 1:30 A.M. Carl Stellato, president of Local 600, called an emergency meeting of the executive board of his local to prepare for possible strike action, held an emergency meeting of union members outside Rouge, and arranged for a meeting of community leaders on the evening of June 1 to hear a discussion of developments in negotiation.

Reuther and Bannon issued a joint statement on June 1, saying that Ford had made a new proposal and that the contract was extended until midnight of Sunday, June 5. The morning papers carried a second letter to Ford employees urging they give the company's proposal a great deal of thought. The official blackout continued as the parties met June 1 to June 3 with frequent caucuses and two night sessions. Rumor had it that the company's new proposal had shifted from the "prosperity partnership package" to a form of supplemental unemployment compensation.

Union officials had no comments on the management's statement that the recent rash of wildcat stoppages around the country had cost the company 25% of its scheduled production in the previous week.

On June 3 the union made a counterproposal. It noted that with the company's shift to a form of supplemental compensation, the parties were in agreement on the principles of supplementation, size of company contribution, and level of the trust fund; however two areas of disagreement remained, level of benefits (the union proposed 80% of take-home pay—the company 60 and 65%) and duration of benefits (the union proposed 52 weeks—the company 26 weeks). The union proposed that the remaining differences be "tabled" until agreement had been reached on the other contract items.

In the event that agreement could not be reached within 30 days of the settlement of other contract issues, the remaining differences would go to arbitration.

Both parties met the press on June 4 after the company had rejected the union's counterproposal. "This latest UAW–CIO proposal," Bugas said, "apparently increases the possibility that Ford Motor Company will be struck sometime after midnight Sunday. This we deeply regret. We are immediately making all necessary plans so that, on our part, if a strike occurs it may be as orderly as possible. . . . We are quite willing to discuss this issue of benefit level and duration across the bargaining table, but it is an important matter of substance and we cannot submit it to arbitration. . . . Now our employees are face to face with a strike, solely because they are fewer in number than the GM employees and to strike them is less costly to the union." He said that Ford stood ready "to continue negotiations as long as necessary to reach settlement without a strike." Reuther commented that Ford had made a "very historic yielding on a basic principle," but added that the "practical effect of the company's proposal was to agree to put up $55 million to finance a guaranteed wage but not agree to spend the money."

Negotiations resumed the next morning, June 5, and continued throughout the night. After nearly 26 hours of continuous negotiation, Reuther stuck his head out and said, "We have an agreement." Then he closed the door. In the corridor pandemonium broke loose. Floodlights went on, flash bulbs were adjusted, some reporters dashed for telephones while their partners waited expectantly for more details.

III. The Settlement

Under the new three-year agreement, a laid-off worker if eligible for state unemployment compensation could receive a total of 65% of his weekly after-tax pay for 4 weeks and subsequently 60% for up to a total of 26 weeks (see Exhibit 1 for more detail on the SUB plan). Other provisions granted: an annual improvement factor of 2½% of base pay with a minimum of 6 cents; an extra wage increase of 8 cents and 18 cents for certain skilled trades, an increase of 10 cents for certain selected classifications; an additional half holiday on Christmas and New Year's Eves; double time plus holiday pay for worked holidays; and 2½ weeks' vacation for those having 10 to 15 years' service. A change was made in the cost of living adjustment factor as established by the 1953 "living document" negotiations. When the cumulative allowance over base reached 6 cents, further increases of 1 cent would be initiated by a .5 increase rather than by the previous .6 increase in the Consumer Price Index. Company-paid pensions were increased from $1.75 to $2.25 a month for each year of service, with the 30-year limitation removed. Disability pensions were increased from $3 to $4.50 for each year of service. Contributory health and insurance benefits were increased and their provisions liberalized.

Management obtained a redefinition of UAW representation rights both in units not under the agreement and in new units; more freedom in offering jobs to workers who exhaust their seniority rights within their own units (a refusal of such offer making a laid-off worker ineligible for supplementary unemployment benefits); and several clauses reducing costs in the steel division.

"Who won?" was the question as the two parties proceeded to the next room for the formal announcement and picture taking. "We both won," Reuther replied. "We are extremely happy to announce that we have arrived at an agreement. . . . Both the Company and the Union have worked very hard and very sincerely at the bargaining table. We believe that this effort we have made together gives lie to the Communists in the world because it proves in a very practical way that free labor and free management can get together, and can find the common denominator for working out their common problems. This is one of the most historic agreements that we have written in the 20 years of our Union. It is the largest economic package that we have ever negotiated. It is in excess of 20 cents an hour. It provides for wage increases from 6 cents an hour to 16 cents and 17 cents an hour. . . . It provides the principle upon which we are going to build the Guaranteed Annual Wage."

Bugas responded, "As perhaps you gentlemen know, we have been for years trying to search out the problem of increased security for our employees, and it was only after a tremendous amount of work and research and internal analysis that we came to a conclusion that one important road to improved security of our employees was this supplemental benefit plan that we proposed. . . ."

"We think it is significant. We think it offers additional security to our employees and particularly in the automotive industry where historically you have layoffs. We thank God they were of rather short duration, but nevertheless they came, and we recognize that in the Ford Motor Company we had some special responsibilities to our employees."

Of more immediate importance was the reaction of GM. Its representatives received from Ford the details of the settlement at 11 P.M. So that it might study the SUB plan, it sought and received, in its 35th bargaining session, extension of the existing agreement until midnight of Sunday, June 12. The settlement, reached at 3:07 A.M., June 13, embraced virtually an identical plan as well as similar increases in other directions—a package which the union estimated at 21 cents. The full union shop also was granted.

The agreement was signed at a public ceremony on June 8. The open door policy contrasted sharply with the blackout that prevailed during most of the negotiations. After appropriate exchanges, Reuther exclaimed, "John, you tell young Henry that we're thinking of tearing down his old house. We'd be glad to give him the painted doors out of the nursery."[1]

IV. AFTERMATH

To what extent would the Ford–UAW SUB plan become a pattern? Negotiations with American Motors Corporation opened the day after GM settled. Reuther had made it clear that while he expected even the smaller firms to supplement UC benefits with a SUB, to guarantee wages, the pattern might be slightly modified. The company was thus able to obtain three im-

---

[1] The old homestead of Edsel Ford where Henry Ford II spent his childhood days, and upon which the union has built its headquarters, Solidarity House.

portant concessions: payments into the SUB fund were deferred for a year; no fund was set up to eliminate wage inequities; and certain increases in company insurance contributions were deferred. In August, Chrysler accepted the Ford pattern.

The Allis-Chalmers contract, reached late in September, was hailed by Reuther as "the new model." New provisions included: 65% of take-home for all 26 weeks; company payment of the entire 65% if state payments ran out; $2 for each dependent up to four; partial credits to be accumulated on a daily basis for less than a full week's work; and pay for short weeks to equal 65% of 40-hour take-home. The union failed in its attempt to remove the requirement of eligibility for state benefits. By the year end, SUB plans were secured in most UAW agreements covering nearly one million members.

Progress on the SUB was shadowed, however, by walkouts of skilled tradesmen at both Ford and GM in protest against the inadequacies of the eight-cent differential which most of them had received under the settlement. Within five months, about 800 had withdrawn from the UAW to join the Pattern Makers League, AFL, or the International Die Sinkers Conference, Indiana. The most serious threat to the UAW in its hold over the 200,000 skilled workers (about 10% of the UAW membership) was the Society of Skilled Trades, formed in Flint by dissident GM employees. Having failed to persuade the executive board to apply to Ford and GM for an immediate 10% wage increase, this group sought and received independent recognition by the NLRB. But it was precluded by the NLRB from obtaining elections for representation rights where the UAW had current agreements. Nevertheless, by the end of the year, the Society claimed membership of 50,000 in Michigan.

The first acceptance of SUB by industries other than autos occurred in shipping. June 17, Atlantic and Gulf Coast shippers yielded the issue in principle. The IUE, whose contract with GM was virtually similar to UAW's, obtained the SUB at Vickers, Inc. At General Electric, however, the union unsuccessfully sought SUB. A new pattern emerged in mid-August in agreements between American Can and Continental Can and the Steelworkers: layoff pay, including state unemployment compensation, would equal 65% of take-home for 52 weeks for employees with 3 years' service with the companies assuming the whole cost if state rulings forbade integration of public and private compensation.

Libby-Owens-Ford and Pittsburgh Plate Glass set another pattern in their contracts with the Glass and Ceramic Workers. In mid-September the parties agreed, in addition to a 14-cent package established in May, to contributions of 5 cents an hour to individual accounts. If an account reached $600, the payment would continue and be credited to the individual's vacation fund. A worker could make withdrawals of $15 to $30 weekly if laid off or ill. There was no tie-in with state unemployment compensation. An employee would be paid his entire balance if he quit, retired, or was permanently discharged. On death it would go to his estate. In September 1956, and again in 1957, the parties would negotiate as to whether an additional five cents would go to individual accounts, be added to base rates, or increase fringe benefits.

A list of supplemental unemployment plans, negotiated during 1955, gathered by BLS, named about 100 companies and 17 unions. About 1,118,000 workers were covered in the automotive, can, glass, textile, sugar, agricultural-implement, appliance, undertaking, shipping, machine-tool, steel, aluminum, and brass-fabricating industries.

The legal machinery also got into action in 1955. The Wage-Hour and Public Contracts Administrator wrote Ford on August 26 in part: "On the advice of the Solicitor of Labor it is my opinion that no part of such contributions need be included in the 'regular rate' or the 'basic rate' of any employee under either of the Acts suggested: Fair Labor Standards Act and the Walsh-Healey Public Contracts Act. . . . The unemployment benefits are, in my opinion, similar to old age retirement, life, accident, or health benefits."

Concerning rulings with respect to the tax consequences of the SUB funds the Assistant Commissioner of Internal Revenue wrote Ford on December 2, 1955, that contributions to the SUB funds would be considered currently deductible company expenses for Federal income tax purposes. In addition, on May 29, 1956, the Commissioner of Internal Revenue ruled that, while SUB payments were not considered wages and hence not eligible for withholding tax procedures, they were considered income and hence declarable for tax purposes by the recipient.

The proviso in the Ford contract that SUB benefits would not reduce or eliminate state unemployment compensation provided an opportunity for opponents of SUB—not only did they carry on propaganda and bring pressure to bear on state officials and legislatures, but also in some states they indicated that as taxpayers they would ask for injunctions if simultaneous state and company benefits were paid.

Ford had adopted the policy that it should take a forthright positive position whenever requested to state its views on supplementation. The company did not, however, undertake a deliberate campaign to "sell" states and the public on SUB plan. As a consequence from June 1955 to November 1956 members of the company's Central Staff made about 75 speeches to management groups, trade associations, university groups and other such public bodies. In addition, they presented a number of formal statements to various states at the request of state legislatures or state study committees.

Action occurred first in Ohio, where on June 14 the Senate killed a bill substantially raising Ohio's unemployment compensation benefits, to which a rider had been attached allowing simultaneous State and company benefits. In November, again, a referendum coupling the two items was lost. Mr. Bugas was quick to point out that the defeat of amendments to Ohio's unemployment law should not be interpreted as a measure of voter reaction to Ford's SUB plan. The referendum measure was initiated prior to the enactment of the Ford Plan and contained many provisions not relevant to SUB.

By May 1956, however, favorable opinions were issued by enough state attorneys general to bring the Ford and GM Plans to fruition. On July 12,

1955, Michigan, where 56% of Ford's employees, 44% of GM's, and over two-thirds of Chrysler's were located, approved simultaneous payment. Massachusetts followed on August 1, Delaware on September 13, New York on October 24, New Jersey on November 10, Pennsylvania on January 26, California on February 10, and Florida on March 2.

Since the opinion of an attorney general might be advisory rather than binding upon state agencies administering the unemployment compensation laws, Ford again sought rulings—this time from the agencies themselves. These followed more slowly.

As the commencement date of June 1, 1956, approached, attention centered on the probable extent of benefit payments. While as of June 1 employment at Ford was down 17,000 from the peak of 140,000, most of the idled employees were not eligible for supplementation. This resulted from a provision in the SUB plan that limited eligibility for payments to employees laid off after May 3. Since automobile production had been slack in the spring of 1955, most of the unemployment was achieved prior to May 3 and to the consternation of the union, few Ford employees were eligible for supplementation in June.

It was not until the August model change-overs that substantial benefits were paid. During this period about 30,000 workers were laid off for an average of 3 weeks. The typical benefits averaged $13. This figure was well under the $25 maximum since in most states, unemployment compensation payments were of such a size that the provision limiting combined benefits of SUB and UC to 65% of take-home pay governed.

The simultaneous payment of SUB and state unemployment compensation was prohibited in only four states: Ohio, Indiana, North Carolina, and Virginia. In these states benefit payments could not be made during the first full year of operation of the plan and would be available only beginning June 1957. Such payments would be based on the so-called "substitute" benefits provisions of the plan.[1]

In negotiating the SUB Plan the parties established a separate machinery for handling SUB grievances including provisions for the establishment of a joint (company-union) Board of Administration, as the level of last resort for SUB grievances. During the period June 1955 to 1956 (the year in which the trust fund was built up prior to the payment of any benefits) the Joint Board spent most of its time establishing the administrative procedures of the plan. As a result of the careful planning which preceded the payment of any benefits, grievances have been resolved in a mutually satisfactory manner. In fact, by November 1956 it had not been necessary to appoint the seventh and impartial member of the Board since all problems that had reached the last stage had been settled by the company and union representatives.

While the experience of the first year under SUB was not sufficiently representative, the company felt that the initial experience was favorable. In November 1956 the fund stood at 32% of maximum and the few problems that had arisen had been quickly settled.

---

[1] See Exhibit 1.

EXHIBIT 1

FORD MOTOR COMPANY—NEGOTIATING THE 1955 AGREEMENT

The Ford Supplemental Unemployment Benefit Plan [1]

The Plan

Ford Motor Company's newly-established Supplemental Unemployment Benefit Plan was conceived by staff executives who have had long experience in the fields of finance, law and industrial relations.

Founded on the twin principles of limited liability and predictable maximum costs, the Plan is compatible with and complementary to the free and competitive economy of the United States.

Purpose of the Plan

The purpose of the Plan is to supplement, by private means, the State Unemployment Compensation payments received by hourly-rated Ford men and women during layoffs. The Company believed that a decision to supplement state benefits would be particularly justified with respect to short-term layoffs, when the employee's opportunity to find other work is relatively limited.

Basically, the Plan is intended to assist eligible employees in weathering layoffs. Benefits paid under the Plan will not be so high, however, as to discourage a worker from seeking other employment, particularly when his layoff is of long duration.

The Company has always paid the full cost of State Unemployment Compensation benefits received by its employees when they are temporarily out of work through no fault of their own. By adding to these benefits, Ford is simply extending and enlarging upon a concept which has long been firmly established in the laws of the 48 states.

Understanding the Plan

A knowledge of the mechanics of the Plan is essential to understanding the principles underlying it and the management philosophy which will govern its operation.

Under the carefully-drawn provisions of the Plan, an eligible employee could receive cash benefits ranging up to a maximum of $25 a week. Eventually, these payments could extend to a maximum of 26 weeks during any one layoff. The number of weeks for which benefits may be paid will depend on the amount of money available in the applicable Trust Fund and the employee's individual status under the Plan.

Eligibility

Employees will become eligible to participate in the Plan only when they have acquired one year of seniority. Benefit payments will be made only when an employee is laid off through no fault of his own, as in the case of a reduction in force, discontinuance of a plant or operation, or because of a temporary suspension or curtailment of work. However, for certain layoffs—such as those caused by labor disputes involving Company employees or property, or by acts of God, enemy action or sabotage—no benefits will be paid.

Special and Regular Benefits

Within the limitation of the $25 maximum, the benefits—when added to State Unemployment Compensation—could give an eligible employee an amount equal

[1] From The Ford Supplemental Unemployment Benefit Plan, Ford Motor Company, Public Relations Department, Dearborn, Mich., June, 1955, pp. 1–14.

to 65% of his weekly after-tax Ford wages for each of the first four weeks of a layoff, after an annual "waiting week." These 65% benefits are called "Special Benefits." There is a maximum of four Special Benefit payments in a calendar year until the applicable Trust Fund is approximately one-half funded, after which the maximum becomes eight per year.

After the Special Benefits are exhausted, the amount of the weekly benefit would be reduced. An eligible laid-off employee would then begin receiving "Regular Benefits" which could last for a maximum of 22 additional weeks. Regular Benefits, when added to State Unemployment Compensation payments, could equal 60% of the worker's weekly after-tax Ford wages.

In determining all benefits, the weekly wage will be computed on straight-time earnings (highest base rate during the last 30 days the employee worked plus cost of living allowance) for a forty-hour week.

It should be emphasized that the Company did not determine the benefit levels it would agree to on the basis of what the available funds would support, but rather on the merits of the levels as such.[1]

Contributions to Trust Funds

Benefit payments will be made only from two Trust Funds established by Ford Motor Company. The General Fund will cover employees engaged in the regular production activities of the Company. The Defense Fund will cover those in defense work.

The establishment of a separate fund for defense work recognizes that the risks of a layoff in connection with such work are inherently different from those involved in the Company's regular commercial operations. Sufficient flexibility is retained by the Company to assure that such segregation need be made only when it is administratively feasible and when a significant number of employees is involved.

Contributions Sole Liability

The Company's contributions to these Funds constitute its sole liability under the Plan. Ford's financial obligation under the Plan is fixed at and limited to the contribution of five cents for each hour for which covered employees receive pay. However, no contributions to a trust fund are to be made when it is fully funded. Contributions based on pay received by defense employees are to be made to the Defense Fund; all others go to the General Fund. These are not contributions in behalf of particular employees, but represent a reasonable and suitable measure of the Company's financial commitment which will vary with the level of its activities.

Maximum Funding

A limitation, called the "Maximum Funding," also has been placed on the total amount of money to be built up in the Funds. Based on current employment levels—140,000 hourly-rated workers—the Maximum Funding of the two Funds was set at $55 million on June 1, 1955. Every month, a new Maximum Funding amount will be computed. It will vary upward or downward in proportion to increases or decreases in the number of hourly-rated employees.

The initial amount of the Maximum Funding was based on the conservative assumption of a $25 average weekly benefit amount, which is the maximum. This conservatism was justified on the basis that the actual average cannot be precisely predicted, and that any deviations in the early stages of the Plan should be in the direction of building up the Fund more rapidly. Beginning in 1958, the Maximum Funding figure will be varied in relation to experience as to the actual amount of the average weekly benefit paid.

Thus, the total sum toward which the Company will make its contributions will be affected (within the over-all cents per hour limit) by the number of people covered by the Plan and the amounts actually paid in benefits.

---

[1] Note: In negotiation, as in planning, decision on levels preceded decision on duration.

Trust Fund Position

Each month a "Trust Fund Position" of the two Funds also will be computed. The Trust Fund Position will show the market value of assets held in a Fund as a percentage of the current Maximum Funding for that Fund.[1]

When the Trust Fund Position of a Fund reaches 100%—that is, when the market value of the Fund's assets equals the established Maximum Funding figure—the Company's contributions to that Fund will cease. Further contributions, at the rate of five cents for each hour worked by hourly employees, will be made only as necessary to bring the Trust Fund Position to 100% or to maintain it at that level. Subject to certain termination provisions, the Company's over-all obligation to make contributions extends for the length of the three-year collective bargaining agreement signed in June 1955 with the UAW–CIO.

To enable the Funds to build up in the initial stages of the Plan, no benefit payments will be made for the first year of operation, or until June 1, 1956.

Credit Unit System

Employees having the required seniority will become eligible to participate in benefits through a system of acquiring "Credit Units" for weeks actually worked. A Credit Unit has no fixed value in terms of either time or money. It is simply a medium for translating employee service into benefit eligibility and duration under the Plan.

From June 1, 1955, through May 31, 1957, employees with less than ten years' seniority will acquire one-quarter (.25) Credit Unit for each week in which they work at least 32 hours. During the same period, employees with ten or more years' seniority will acquire one-half (.5) Credit Unit for each week in which they work at least 32 hours.

Beginning June 1, 1957, all employees will acquire one-half (.5) Credit Unit for each week in which they work at least 32 hours.

Nonworking hours for which an employee is paid—such as vacation time and holidays—will count as working hours for the purpose of acquiring Credit Units.

In the event of layoff, the employee will obtain benefit payments from the Trust Fund in return for Credit Units he has accumulated. The maximum number of Credit Units he can acquire is 26. The number of Credit Units he actually has at the time of layoff will depend, of course, upon his own employment experience prior to layoff, his seniority and the extent to which he may have used previously-accumulated Credit Units to obtain benefits during earlier layoffs.

Benefit Duration Varies

The duration of benefit payments—that is, the number of weekly benefits an employee may receive—depends on the Trust Fund position at the time of layoff and the number of Credit Units the individual employee has acquired through weeks worked.

When the Plan was formulated, it became obvious that fixed amounts of benefits could not be paid for fixed maximum periods without subjecting either the Company or the Trust Funds to unknown liability.

It was determined, then, that this risk could be avoided if either the benefit amount or the benefit duration were variable. The Company found that if benefit duration were variable, rather than the benefit amount, the average employee would not be adversely affected during most layoffs. The course of variable duration was adopted, therefore, and was accomplished by relating the number of Credit Units required for one weekly benefit to the current Trust Fund Position.

When the Trust Fund Position is 85% or more, only one Credit Unit will be required in exchange for one week's benefit. When the Trust Fund Position is at lower levels—as it will be during the early stages of the Plan, and as may happen

---

[1] Note: Assets were to be held in the form of cash or U.S. government securities.

thereafter because of heavy layoff experience—the exchange rate for Credit Units is less favorable. For example, when the Trust Fund Position is between 13% and 21.99%, an employee with less than five years' seniority would have to surrender five Credit Units for one benefit.

High-seniority employees have an advantage over their fellow workers with lower seniority in the exchange of Credit Units for benefits from the Funds. If the Trust Fund Position is between 40% and 48.99%, for instance, a 25-year employee will be able to obtain one benefit for one Credit Unit, while an employee with less than five years' service would need two Credit Units to obtain one benefit.

The rate of exchange for all employees is the same only when the Trust Fund Position is 85% or more. When the Trust Fund Position falls below that level, the rate of exchange becomes increasingly favorable to higher-seniority employees compared with the lower seniority group. This arrangement is a safeguard against the possibility that the Funds might be depleted or exhausted by payments to lower seniority employees during the early stages of a layoff, with little or no benefits left for higher seniority workers who might be laid off later.

The table [below] shows how the number of Credit Units required to receive the weekly supplemental benefit will vary with changes in the Trust Fund Position. It also demonstrates how the interests of long-service employees are protected by a sliding conversion scale which operates in their favor.

If the Trust Fund Position applicable to the week for which such Benefit is paid is:	And if the seniority of the person to whom such Benefit is paid is:					
	1 to 5 Years	5 to 10 Years	10 to 15 Years	15 to 20 Years	20 to 25 Years	25 Years and Over
	The Credit Units canceled for such Benefit shall be:					
85% or over	1.00	1.00	1.00	1.00	1.00	1.00
76–84.99%	1.11	1.00	1.00	1.00	1.00	1.00
67–75.99%	1.25	1.11	1.00	1.00	1.00	1.00
58–66.99%	1.43	1.25	1.11	1.00	1.00	1.00
49–57.99%	1.67	1.43	1.25	1.11	1.00	1.00
40–48.99%	2.00	1.67	1.43	1.25	1.11	1.00
31–39.99%	2.50	2.00	1.67	1.43	1.25	1.11
22–30.99%	3.33	2.50	2.00	1.67	1.43	1.25
13–21.99%	5.00	3.33	2.50	2.00	1.67	1.43
4–12.99%	10.00	5.00	3.33	2.50	2.00	1.67
Under 4%	No Benefit Payable					

Margins of Safety

The concept of the Maximum Funding and Trust Fund Position was adopted primarily to provide a "margin of safety" for the protection of employees—particularly higher seniority employees—in the event of heavy layoffs, whether repeated or prolonged. The adequacy of the Trust Fund cannot be measured simply by calculating the effects a single heavy layoff would have upon it, since it cannot be assumed that additional layoffs would not follow within a relatively short time.

The effect of relating duration of benefits (through the device of varying Credit Unit cancellation rates) to the relative size of the Fund is to preserve comparable "Margins of Safety" and relative equities as among various seniority groups of employees at all levels of the Fund. For example, if the Fund is just below the half-way mark, the Plan in effect is a 13-week plan for the low seniority employee, assuming moderate layoffs, rather than a 26-week plan. The relative chances of such employees to enjoy the full 13 weeks' protection are comparable to their relative chances to enjoy 26 weeks' protection if the Plan is fully funded. The lower the relative size of the Fund, the more protection is weighted in favor of the higher seniority groups.

Thus, the Plan automatically accommodates itself to any reasonable level of contributions which may be agreed upon, as well as to the volume of layoffs actually experienced.

Apply for Benefits Weekly

Specific application for benefits will have to be made by eligible employees each week. Benefits will become payable after one waiting week per year, in accordance with normal State Unemployment Compensation practices.

The cash amount of a weekly benefit will not normally be affected by the Trust Fund Position. However, should the Trust Fund Position fall below 13%, there would be a 20% reduction in all benefits paid, except that such reduction would not bring a benefit below $5 and would not apply to benefits already below $5. Should the Trust Fund Position fall below 4%, no benefits would be paid until the market value of the assets held by the applicable Fund had risen above 4% of the Maximum Funding.

The maximum benefit to be paid under the Plan will be $25. If the employee would be eligible for a benefit of less than $2, no benefit will be paid. The actual amount of the Supplemental Unemployment Benefit an employee receives will depend on the amount of his State Unemployment Compensation payment, his after-tax earnings, and whether he is receiving Special Benefits or Regular Benefits.

Take the case of a Detroit area employee with a wife and one child. Assume this employee currently is earning $100 weekly straight-time pay before taxes and $87.02 after taxes. He would be eligible under the 1955 bill amending the Michigan act for a State Unemployment Compensation benefit of $42 a week. Assuming, for example, no prior layoffs in that calendar year, an eligible employee would receive in the first four weeks of a layoff (subject to the waiting week provisions) an additional $14.56 under the Ford Supplemental Unemployment Benefit Plan, making his total income $56.56 a week or 65% of his take-home pay.

After the first four weeks of such a layoff, he would receive a Regular Benefit of $10.21 a week, bringing his total income to $52.21 or 60% of his take-home pay.

State Payments Vary

Unemployment Compensation benefits vary in the different states. By comparison with the Michigan employee, take the case of a Buffalo, N.Y., Ford employee with a wife and one child. Assume he is earning, like his fellow worker in Detroit, $100 weekly before taxes and $87.02 after taxes. He is eligible under New York laws for Unemployment Compensation of $36 a week. During the first four weeks of such a layoff, after the waiting week, he would receive an additional $20.56 under the Plan, making his total income $56.56 a week.

After the first four weeks of such a layoff, the Buffalo employee would receive a Regular Benefit of $16.21 a week, bringing his total income to $52.21.

Both cases assume the employee has sufficient credits to receive benefits.

In some cases, an employee can work part of a week and still receive benefits. The agreement provides that if an employee is afforded so few hours of work in a week that, even after working them, he still is eligible under his state's laws to receive Unemployment Compensation, then he also may draw benefits from the Fund.

The amount he can receive from the Fund will be the difference between the 65% or 60% maximum, whichever then is applicable to him, and the total of his Unemployment Compensation benefits plus any pay he received from the Company that week for time worked.

Take again the case of a $100-a-week Ford employee in the Detroit area whose usual weekly take-home pay is $87.02 and who would be eligible under the 1955 bill amending the Michigan Act for an Unemployment Compensation benefit of $42 a week.

Under Michigan law, a worker who earns in a week less than half the state benefit to which he is entitled, may draw the full state benefit. Therefore, if the Detroit-area employee worked, say, four hours in one week, he could collect his full $42 state benefit in addition to the $10 (four hours at $2.50 an hour) he received from the Company in wages.

He then could apply to the Fund for a benefit representing the difference between $52 ($42 Unemployment Compensation plus $10 earnings) and $56.56 (65% of his take-home pay of $87.02). The supplemental benefit would be $4.56.

State Integration Essential

Integration with State Unemployment Compensation systems is an essential condition to the effectiveness of the Ford Supplemental Unemployment Benefit Plan. Before the benefit payments can start, rulings must be obtained in states in which the Company has two-thirds of its hourly working force that simultaneous payment of a Plan benefit shall not reduce or eliminate the State Unemployment Compensation benefit for the same week.

If favorable rulings are not obtained by June 1, 1956, commencement of benefit payments will be delayed beyond that date.

Ford has 56% of its hourly-rated employees in Michigan, 11% in Ohio, and substantial employment in Illinois, New York, Missouri, California and New Jersey.

If appropriate rulings are not obtained from the home states of two-thirds of the employees before June 1, 1957, the Plan will be terminated as of that date.

If the Plan terminates prior to June 1, 1958, Company contributions to the Funds will cease and assets left in the Funds will be used for administration expenses and for payments to eligible employees in the form of benefits until the Funds are exhausted. In the meantime, steps will be taken to negotiate with the union on disposition of the five cents an hour which the Company will no longer pay into the Funds. If no agreement on disposition is reached during 60 days of such negotiations, the Company automatically will grant a five-cents-an-hour general wage increase to all hourly employees represented by the UAW–CIO.

Except in a few cases when state benefits run out before Company benefits, a benefit payment under the Plan will be made only upon proof that a state benefit has been paid for the same week, thus simplifying administration and avoiding duplication or review of state determinations as to eligibility and qualification.

The Plan also provides for discontinuance in any state when specified criteria indicate that the state program is doing a substantially equivalent job. Specifically, it provides for discontinuance of the Plan—on or after June 1, 1958—in states where fewer than 25% of employees with sufficient Credit Units for full benefits would be entitled to Special Benefits of $2 or more if they were laid off. Payment of Regular Benefits would also be discontinued in states where fewer than such number of employees would be entitled to Regular Benefits of $2. However, the Plan could become operative again in such states if an annual review showed that the cause for discontinuance no longer existed.

Nonintegrated States

In the event the necessary rulings are obtained in the home states of two-thirds of the Company's employees, but similar rulings are not forthcoming in one or more of the remaining states, a special set of conditions governing payments from the Plan will take effect for the benefit of Ford employees in such nonintegrated states, starting June 1, 1957.

Instead of Regular Benefits or Special Benefits, "Substitute Supplemental Benefits" will become payable to eligible employees in the nonintegrated states. After an eligible employee who has been laid off receives State Unemployment Compensation benefits for two weeks after the waiting week, he may apply for a Substitute Supplemental Benefit under the Plan. To do this, of course, he would be obliged to forego the state benefit in that week.

The Substitute Supplemental Benefit, under these conditions, would be an amount equal to the Regular or Special Supplemental Benefit to which he would have been entitled for that week if supplementation were permitted, multiplied by three. The number of Credit Units to be canceled upon payment of a Substitute Supplemental Benefit for any week will be the number of Credit Units that would have been required to receive a Regular or Special benefit for the week in question, multiplied by three. If he so chooses, the employee may elect to take a benefit of four times his weekly benefit amount every four weeks, instead of the three week rotation.

Establishment of Trusts

Both the General Fund and the Defense Fund will be established with banks or trust companies selected by and under agreements with the Company. The Company's contributions will be made directly to the Funds and will be held by the Trustees in cash or invested in obligations of the United States Government.

Expenses incurred in the administration of the Plan are chargeable against the funds.

Board of Administration

Although the Company retains complete control over the selection of the Trustees for the Funds and the Union will have no voice in the investment of the Company's contributions, a Board of Administration will be formed consisting of three Company members, three Union members and an impartial chairman.

The board by majority vote will render final decisions on appeals made by benefit claimants, authorizing benefit payments where appeals are granted, and will perform certain other duties of an administrative nature. It will not, however, have any power to decide questions which properly should be decided by State Unemployment Compensation agencies, or to review any determination made under State Unemployment Compensation laws. It will not have any separate staff or facilities of its own.

Federal Rulings

The Ford Supplemental Unemployment Benefit Plan will not go in effect until the Company has received favorable rulings recognizing (1) that the Company's contributions are currently deductible expenses for Federal income tax purposes and (2) that such contributions are to be excluded in computations under the Fair Labor Standards Act.[1]

---

[1] Note: Mindful of the union's insistence that the 1950 five-year contract be amended midterm, which Ford was reported to consider as a questionable action, the company gained the union's acceptance of the following paragraphs in the SUB plan, Article XI: [2]

[2] *Agreements between Ford Motor Company and the UAW–CIO,* June 8, 1955, Ford Motor Company, Industrial Relations Staff, 1955, pp. 153 and 156.

"Section 1. Liability

"(a) The provisions of these Articles I through XII constitute the entire Plan. The provisions of Article IV express, and shall be deemed to express, completely each and every obligation of the Company with respect to the financing of the Plan and providing for benefits and payments. . . . . .

"Section 8. Amendment and Termination of the Plan

"(a) So long as the Agreement concerning the Supplemental Unemployment Benefit Plan shall remain in effect, the Plan shall not be amended, modified, suspended, or

Discussion Questions

1. What was the UAW's strategy? How was it implemented?
2. Why did Reuther select Ford to receive the brunt of the GAW demand?
3. What were the prospects for a strike in 1955?
4. Did the UAW win its goal of GAW? What type of security did the union get?
5. Why did Ford insist on having SUB integrated with state UC?
6. Comment on the "revolt" of the skilled trades.
7. Would you support industry-wide bargaining in the automobile industry?

---

terminated, except as may be proper or permissible under the terms of the Plan or such Agreement."

GENERAL MOTORS CORPORATION

NEGOTIATING THE 1948 AGREEMENT: THE NEW WAGE FORMULA

I

On May 29, 1948, GM and the UAW signed their second national agreement of the postwar years, to run for two years, until May 29, 1950. Relationships between the union and the company began on February 11, 1937, when their first agreement gave the union its first real foothold in the industry. It followed upon the introduction of, and the turbulent struggles unloosened by, the sit-down strike. The union was recognized as bargaining agent only for its members among the employees. Not until 1940, after the "Strategy Strike of 1939," and subsequent NLRB elections did the corporation recognize the union as exclusive bargaining agent for all production and maintenance employees in the 49 plants where it had won elections. Company-wide bargaining developed from that point.

Relationships were formal. The company maintained clear-cut disciplines; and even under the pressure and controls of wartime, it sought to bar concessions on work standards or wage increases via loopholes in the wage controls that might distort the job-rate structure. No form of union security had been voluntarily granted; and in the 1946 agreement, the "directed" maintenance of membership provisions written into the prior contract of the war years were explicitly terminated "in consideration of" the company's compromise formula for checkoff of dues.

Just as it signed the first agreement in the industry, it was also first to establish with the union the office of impartial umpire under the 1940 agreement.

Both sides testified to the orderly character of day-to-day relationships—and this in an industry harassed by wildcat stoppages. From the start, the company firmly enforced disciplinary penalties against unauthorized strikers. It has also pressed for strict construction of the agreement in all grievance cases.

II

But if daily contract administration and shop relationships were orderly, the negotiation of contracts generated sharp conflict at GM. The transition from war production was marked by a particularly protracted struggle. The last agreement of the war years became effective April 1945; it was terminated December 1945, during a strike that began in November and lasted until March 1946. The conflict proved very costly to both sides; employees lost homes and savings, the company $2,000,000 per day—$1,000,000 in direct losses and $1,000,000 in potential profits.

The union's wage demands became the pivot of this long and costly struggle. Formulated under the fears of postwar dislocations and unemployment, the union publicized its case as an effort to safeguard existing levels of "take-home" pay and purchasing power, thus averting the feared postwar depression. An increase in wage rates of 30% was therefore necessary to achieve these objectives. If the company, however, could prove inability to pay such an increase without corresponding advances in prices, the union would reduce its wage demand. The union's publicity focused upon this request for a "look at the books"; it emphasized its willingness to maintain a sound wage-price-profit balance; it stressed the related criterion of "ability to pay" as a fair measure of wage increases.

GM rejected "ability to pay" as a valid criterion in wage determination; it affirmed instead the measure of competitive rates; it urged safeguards against inflation in increased production and retention of the longer work week (i.e., 45 hours as versus 40 hours) until the transition to peacetime schedules had been effected; it denied the union's demand for a "look at the books"; it insisted that pricing policies and profits remained its concern as long as the employees received a fair day's wage for a fair day's work; it deplored the union's "publicity and propaganda" campaigns; and, perhaps most important, it held fast on the strike front despite all counterpressures.

When a wage pattern was set in steel, after government intervention, at an 18½-cent-per-hour increase, GM declared a willingness to settle at the same rate. Subsequently a Presidential fact-finding committee recommended 19½ cents per hour for GM. The company rejected this recommendation. The UAW was willing to settle at this figure. But when the UEW [1] accepted 18½ cents, the UAW eventually had to follow suit, after holding out one month longer on the strike front.

III

The agreement signed on March 19 was to run for 2 years, but provision was made in Paragraph 153 for its reopening on wages and other economic issues.

In the spring of 1947, the so-called "Big Three" of the CIO—the United Steelworkers, the UAW, and the United Electrical Workers—had scheduled a meeting in Pittsburgh on April 19 to confer on wage strategy. The UAW was then demanding an increase of 23½ cents per hour from GM. But the very week of the scheduled meeting, GM again settled with the UEW, which accepted its offer of 11½ cents per hour and six paid holidays. This settlement became the "pattern" for 1947.[2] The auto workers signed with GM on April 24, 1947.

The corporation held negotiations strictly to the economic issues of Para-

---

[1] This union was expelled from the CIO in October, 1949, on grounds of Communist party-line leadership.

[2] By company estimate, the six paid holidays added 3½ cents per hour to make the total increase the "equivalent of 15 cents an hour."

graph 153. The supplemental agreement did provide, however, that the demand for a Social-Security and old-age-retirement program "will continue as a subject for discussion and negotiations. . . ." The expiration date of the contract was also changed from March 19 to April 28, 1948. As the 1947 negotiations drew to a close in basic industries, the following situation was projected for 1948: In steel a 2-year contract had been signed to run until April 30, 1949, except that on April 1, 1948, either party might give written notice to the other of a desire to negotiate general wage rate changes. But if no agreement was reached on or before April 30, 1948, the contract continued in effect *unchanged* until its expiration date. A similar contract had been signed in electrical manufacturing. In GM, notice of desire to amend or terminate was receivable on February 27, 60 days before its 1948 expiration date.

IV

The 1948 negotiations at GM manifestly loomed an important chapter in evolving relationships. Since the whole contract was open, it was anticipated that many continuing and still unsettled issues of the prior negotiations would be resubmitted. The rise in consumers' prices kept sharp the edge of the persisting wage questions. The Taft-Hartley Act had become effective; inevitably its provisions would find some reflection in the forthcoming negotiations. At the 1947 convention of the UAW, Reuther's re-election as president by a complete rout of his left-wing opponents and their allies made his leadership undisputed. Finally the continuing discussions of a Social Security and old-age-retirement program authorized in the 1947 supplemental agreement produced sharp controversy.

The union maintained steady pressure on the issues on the price-wage-profit balance and "the problem of inflation." When GM made its financial report for the third quarter of 1947, an attack upon its figures was publicly made by Reuther. The allocation of $17,500,000 for "extraordinary obsolescence" and "additional depreciation" was characterized as an effort "to lower the iron curtain on part" of profits grown too "embarrassingly large," profits the union estimated as actually 22%.

When GM offered on November 21, 1947, its employees a modification of its group insurance plan in effect for over 20 years, the move was denounced as a futile "management maneuver" to evade collective bargaining. The UAW filed a charge of unfair labor practices with the Detroit regional office of the NLRB, accusing GM of "unilateral action," of "coercion against employees," and of "refusing to bargain collectively" on a demand which the UAW had been presenting since 1945. The board complied with a request for an injunction against the company, which was granted by the Federal Court.

Under date of January 13, 1948, Reuther notified both the corporation and the NLRB of the union's intention to petition for union shop elections under the Taft-Hartley Act. For, under the provisions of the new law, Reuther pointed out, the checkoff could not be continued without prior written authorization of the employees covered. An intensive drive was planned to obtain the signatures authorizing elections (30% of eligible employees) in which the union hoped to secure the necessary majorities. Prizes were announced, none of them GM products. The union explained that it "had planned to give GM cars and other products as prizes but had been unable to get cooperation from the corporation." The petitions for union shop elections were subsequently dropped.

Against this long-term background and in this immediate atmosphere, written notice of desire to negotiate was served.

V

Negotiations opened on March 12, 1948. The union presented 132 demands for contract changes; the company presented 11 counterproposals. The large number of changes requested by the union reflected in part the procedures by which negotiating agenda are prepared in the UAW. The union's GM department is divided into nine geographical subcouncils.[1] These subcouncils together with the local unions of GM members are represented in the national GM council, to which the 85 locals each elect two representatives if its membership totals 5,000 or under, and three if its membership exceeds 5,000. These representatives are instructed by their constituencies as to the contract changes they desire. The council incorporates all these demands into the union's proposals. Among the 132 requests thus compiled there were accordingly varying versions of demands for amendments in identical paragraphs of the agreement. These demands were as follows: (1) a 25-cent-an-hour wage increase, of which up to 10 cents an hour could be allocated for establishment of an adequate old-age-retirement plan; (2) five cents an hour for a comprehensive social security–group insurance program, including life, health and accident, hospital, surgical and medical coverage; (3) equalization of rates by job classification on a corporation-wide basis; (4) revision of vacation allowances to provide, among other things, 40 hours' pay to employees with 6 months' seniority, with graduated increases up to 120 hours' pay for employees with 5 or more years' seniority; (5) a guaranteed work week of 40 hours; (6) time and a half for Saturday and double time for Sunday, as such, and triple time for holidays worked; (7) increase in night-shift premiums, elimination of merit spreads, time off for voting on primary and general election days.

Noneconomic demands included the union shop and checkoff and covered such other general subjects as grievance machinery, seniority, production standards, leaves of absence.

---

[1] Each of the nine subcouncils is constituted by the union locals of the region it covers; each local, in turn, is represented by its president, chairman of the shop committee, and one delegate for every 5,000 workers in the plant. Representatives from the nine subcouncils convene in regular quarterly session and in special emergency meetings as need dictates. The staff of the GM Department, as the continuing administrative agency, meets with these councils to discuss the demands made by the subcouncils and decide negotiating strategy and tactics.

The 11 counterproposals presented by the corporation included the following: (1) establishment of committees to study incentive systems; (2) amendment of checkoff provisions to comply with the Taft-Hartley Act; (3) reduction of committeemen in smaller plants; (4) revision of overtime representation; (5) provision for 5-day notification of any changes in committee personnel; (6) abuse of duplicate investigations in smaller plants to be eliminated; (7) modification of the agreement to discourage excessive and unwarranted absenteeism; (8) provision of a procedure whereby temporary rates on new jobs become part of the agreement after a period of time when there is no disagreement; (9) modification of the provisions under which union representatives may leave the plant during working hours; (10) expansion of the apprenticeship training program for skilled journeyman classifications; (11) provisions to correct the situation of unwarranted attacks on management in union publications.

The bargaining committees when the negotiations opened on March 12 were organized as follows: The union committee, headed by the director of the GM department, was made up of 12 representatives, 3 of them from the international union, and the remainder from the 9 subcouncils. The management committee, headed by the director of labor relations, contained about 4 headquarters representatives and 8 divisional ones. The divisional personnel managers were included to parallel the spokesmen from the subcouncils, men on the union side, and also to afford these plant representatives direct participation in negotiating the contract they would administer.

At prior negotiations, notes had been made by a corporation stenographer. The record kept by him was not given to the union. As the 1948 sessions opened, the union introduced a court stenographer to make a verbatim record. The company questioned the wisdom of this move but when the union persisted, management hired its own court stenographer. Thus two transcripts were made.

Varying internal and external events exerted their influences upon the negotiations. In steel and electrical manufacturing, when the wage issue had been reopened in April, the companies had rejected the unions' demands for increases as a way of halting inflation. Negotiations at Chrysler were approaching deadlock. The union had reduced its original demand from 30 cents per hour to 18½ cents; Chrysler had moved from its original rejection of any increase as inflationary to an offer of 6 cents per hour. But countertrends also appeared; a survey indicated that some 1,200 companies had granted third-round wage increases between November 1, 1947, and May 1, 1948.

On the night of April 20, Reuther was shot in his home; he thus was unable to participate directly in the negotiations, which had then not yet reached the wage issue. Shortly thereafter (April 23) when the rejection of wage increases in steel had been announced, the UAW publicized its intention not to permit developments in steel to influence its own wage policy "in the slightest way." It also differentiated between its own situation and that of the

Steelworkers, who "are bound by their two-year contract not to strike [in 1948] over the wage issue."

On April 28, indeed, the UAW filed its 30-day notice of intent to cancel the GM agreement required under its terms. This made May 28 the terminal date for contract extension or strike action in event of deadlock. Strike votes were taken in GM plants. The so-called "Fisher No. 23" plant, a tool-and-die unit manned largely by highly skilled craftsmen, voted "No." So also did the workers at Buick, who were reported as feeling that GM workers had been in the front lines of the wage fight too often.

It looked as if Chrysler workers this time would hold these "front lines"; they struck on May 12.

This was the situation in which GM approached negotiations—consideration of wage increases. The corporation made its offer on Friday, May 21, at the thirty-eighth bargaining session, as follows:

We have had 37 bargaining sessions with your committee in an effort to resolve our differences and agree on a contract that would improve the relations between your union and General Motors. We have frankly presented our point of view and discussed the problems as we see them. We have also listened to your presentation of your demands and the situation as you men who represent labor see the problem from your point of view. You have ably presented labor's case. We have carefully gone over and reviewed all of your presentations and demands.

We realize that time is running out, that you have dates that must be met.

Due to the developments in our country in the last few months it is now clear that this group (you men representing labor on one side and the General Motors management on the other) face some very important decisions not only as they affect the equities of General Motors and the employes you represent, but thru example, the effect of our action on other industries and labor groups, in fact, on the economics of the whole nation. This is true whether the next few days' deliberations result in agreement or disagreement.

All of us have had first-hand experience with strikes and the effect and aftermath of strikes. We know that you men have the power and responsibility to authorize a strike of General Motors employes if you think that this is the right and necessary thing to do. Likewise, you men know, as we know, that big strikes have many of the same aspects as a war. Some day the conflict will be over, and one party or the other may feel that they have won. This is only a relative matter as both the employes and the employer lose. And what is more important, the whole country loses along with them. Strikes create additional shortages and result in more inflation.

During recent months in various bargaining sessions throughout the country either labor's economic demands have been refused, no solution reached, and work is continuing under a more or less temporary basis with labor dissatisfied; or large and important strikes have been authorized and are now going on. It is clear that the men who represent industry are risking much in their efforts to prevent further inflation—in some cases reducing prices and saying "No" to labor on their demands for increased wages. We subscribe to the importance of this point of view. At the same time we realize the very real problems the employes face in the increased cost of living. We also know that the negotiations just starting between the United Mine Workers and the mine owners, if not peacefully concluded during the next six weeks, will affect adversely all industry and the nation. Perhaps this group here has about the last chance to reach a fair and realistic agreement of the right thing to do and prevent another round of disastrous strikes such as occurred in the fall of 1945 and the spring of 1946. Perhaps the easiest thing for us to do would be to say "No" to your economic demands following the position generally taken by many other important employers and hope that with better crops this summer the cost of living would go down, that in the meantime your union and its members would be patient and would not precipitate a disastrous series of strikes. This would be leaving all of the responsibility with you. We believe we should share this responsibility, and after a careful review of the whole situation we have some ideas that we think might be helpful.

The union now and in the past has interpreted the worker's problem as a dual one:

(*a*) The problem of maintaining the purchasing power of an hour of work—in other words, protecting the worker from increases in consumer prices.

(*b*) The problem of assuring the worker that the buying power of his hour of work will increase as the nation's industrial efficiency improves.

The union has indicated that its economic demands were designed to deal with both of these objectives.

The facts, as reviewed, may be interpreted to support the union's contention that G.M. workers have been placed at a disadvantage by the fact that consumer prices have advanced more rapidly than their hourly earnings.

It has been the record of the past that workers share in the nation's gains of productive efficiency. That is how the standard of living of workers has been brought to new and higher levels over the years. . . . What must be questioned and weighed quite carefully in the best interests of all concerned—workers as well as other economic groups—is the approach to a realization of these objectives.

We have given careful consideration to this problem and have reached certain conclusions on how it might be resolved. A broad outline of these conclusions follows:

G.M.'s Suggestions for Resolving the Problem

The war and its aftermath have made our economy extremely sensitive to influences of all types. What we need to work towards now is greater stability as a foundation for future progress. The suggestions we have to offer for a realistic and practical approach to the problem as it affects our employees take into account both the need for stability and the desirability of future progress. Specifically: We propose,

1. *Re-establish the buying power of an hour of work* on a fair basis—in other words, what the worker has lost through increases in consumer prices during and since the war to be made up on a sound basis;

2. *Protect the buying power of an hour of work* against changes in consumer prices, by making cost-of-living adjustments periodically during the life of the contract;

3. *Improve the buying power of an hour of work* so that over a period of years the worker is assured of an improved standard of living;

4. That the relations between management and labor be stabilized over a substantial period of time.

What we propose can only succeed if we can be assured of stable and cooperative relations with our employees. For this reason our *proposals must hinge upon your willingness to enter into an agreement to remain in force for a long-term period.* Assurance of cooperation and stability over this period is essential if our employees are to realize the benefits our proposals represent.

In order to expedite exploration of these ideas as a possible solution of our problems, we suggest that your group approve a much smaller committee to frankly examine into these proposals as well as other matters, with an equivalent small committee representing General Motors, to see if they provide the basis for a fair and honorable settlement. If this suggestion is adopted, the committee representing General Motors will consist of four people.

Starting the next day, May 22, the respective committees were reduced to four on a side and met in continuing sessions, "adjourning only for a minimum of sleep," until the agreement of 1948 was concluded. Settlement came with the UAW in the early hours of May 25 and with the UEW two days later, on May 27.

VI

The settlement embodied a wage formula with four major provisions which (1) sought to close the gap that had developed since 1940 between living costs and wages; (2) established an "escalator" by which wages would be adjusted up or down each quarter at the rate of 1 cent in hourly wage rates for each 1.14 points in the BLS Consumers Price Index; (3) limited downward adjustment to a maximum of 5 cents per hour; no limit was placed on upward adjustments; (4) advanced by 3 cents per hour, per year, to improve employees' standard of living with anticipated advances in productivity.

Application of the formula yielded an initial wage increase of 11 cents per hour, of which 8 cents represented the amount needed to "close the gap" and 3 cents the "improvement factor" for 1948.

Charles E. Wilson stated the company's view on the settlement before the Rochester Chamber of Commerce on June 2, 1948:

Perhaps the most dramatic part of the settlement was the new formula adopted by the parties for determining fair wages for two years, and the current wage increases resulting from this formula. Perhaps what may ultimately be the more important result was the development of a better understanding of the rights and responsibilities of the parties. We are hopeful that this understanding represents real progress. The agreements speak for themselves but it is worth noting that these agreements could only have been reached in an atmosphere of mutual confidence.

I am sure that those of you who are especially interested in union-management problems will find these agreements very *interesting* reading as much *for what they leave out* as for what they contain.

Some of the major issues thus "left out" follow:

(1) No provision for a union shop.

(2) No abrogation, or alteration, of the no-strike provisions was granted to meet the union's desire for protection against the liabilities for breach of contract under the Taft-Hartley Act.

(3) No provisions regarding insurance or pensions were incorporated into the agreement. It was agreed, however, that if the courts ruled such plans subject to collective bargaining, the parties would appoint a joint study committee to prepare a joint recommendation on the subject.

(4) No amendment in the provisions governing production standards.

(5) No change was made in the grievance procedures to meet the union's demand for a comprehensive shop-steward system.

(6) No guaranteed weekly wage or concessions in "fringe benefits."

(7) No change to make seniority alone controlling in transfers and promotions.

(8) The company obtained more flexible provisions to govern the upgrading of journeymen to skilled craft classifications.

(9) No change in the management-rights clause.

VII

Discussion naturally focused upon the wage settlement. Throughout the negotiations both sides had emphasized directly or by their supporting evidence varying criteria which they would accept—*or reject*—as wage determinants: (1) cost of living; (2) standard of living; (3) rate increases or rejections in patternmaking corporations; (4) third-round rate increases; (5) competitors' rates in motor manufacturing; (6) going rates in communities in which GM plants are located; (7) wage increases in industry as a whole; and (8) maintenance of purchasing power.

Throughout negotiations, the union emphasized that the profit record of the corporation was conclusive evidence of its ability to pay wage increases without increasing the prices of its products.

Appraisals of the mutual interests in avoiding a strike, and memories of both tangible and intangible losses incurred in the 1946 strike came up continuously.

After the agreement had been signed, both sides undertook "educational programs." The company convened in Detroit personnel from its various plants and reviewed with them the complete development of the 1948 contract.

The union recommended the settlement not as a completely satisfactory agreement but as a promising beginning as follows:

Substantial as it is, the UAW–CIO regards this victory as essentially a holding operation. . . . Nevertheless, we are recommending its acceptance . . . workers as their contribution to industrial peace, even though it does not represent all they are entitled to and is far short of the contribution which . . . could and should make to a sturdy, healthy and equitable national economy.

In the first place, the base date for measuring wages in terms of buying power is 1940, when an army of eight million unemployed provided striking testimony that wages were far too low to sustain full employment.

In the second place, instead of sharing its dangerously inflated profits beyond a cost-of-living adjustment based on a depressed 1940 wage, General Motors offered an annual increase of 2 per cent or 3 cents an hour as a gesture toward keeping the workers' purchasing power abreast of the increased output resulting from technological advance in the national economy. This figure itself short-changes the principle involved. But it is important that the General Motors Corporation now has conceded the principle that General Motors workers are entitled to a share in the growing output of an expanding economy. . . .

Third, the UAW–CIO accepts the provision for quarterly wage adjustments to correspond with changes in the BLS cost-of-living index only because most of those in control in government and in industry show no signs of acting in the public interest. They are enforcing a system of private planning for private profit at public expense.

Fourth, the assumption that workers can expect no more than to remain on the economic treadmill, inching up 3 cents an hour per year while management and stockholders reap profits proportionately far in excess of that amount is unsound and unwise. This is still the trickle-down theory of prosperity, slightly modified. The modification is extremely important however, because, in making it, General Motors has accepted the principle that prices and profits ARE a concern of labor. This is progress.

The company's attitude to the settlement was well expressed by Mr. Charles E. Wilson:

I realize that the terms of our settlements with the unions have not met with immediate unanimous approval, perhaps in part because they are not completely understood. I am sure that they have not unfairly prejudiced the collective bargaining in other companies and industries, . . .

If the formula as well as the noneconomic provisions are understood, it will be found that perhaps some real progress has been made in establishing principles. . . .

1. What is a sound basis for determining wages?

2. How do workmen get their real wages increased as the years go by so that they reasonably share in the prosperity of America? Can they only accomplish this by strikes and threats of strikes?

3. If we said "No" to the request for wage increases at this time in face of the recognized increase in the cost of living, how could we explain to 275,000 General Motors workers that while we were asking them to accept the lowest standard of living they had had in eight years we were at the same time selling our cars for hundreds of dollars less than they knew the market was willing to pay for them? . . .

I would like to again point out the essentials of this wage formula.

1. It did not establish a national pattern of so many cents per hour. We do not believe in uniform national wage patterns. If through the years such patterns are set by a few of the large corporations and all industry is forced to follow them through powerful union pressure, we will in effect have national bargaining. . . .

2. We adopted the 1940 relation of our average wages per hour and the cost of living as a sound basis from which to project current wages. Such a 1940 relation was used as a base for wage control during the war. . . .

3. We adopted the Consumer Price Index of the Bureau of Labor Statistics as the most reliable and available measure of the changing cost of living.

4. We thought it was reasonable to maintain the purchasing power of an hour's labor during the term of the agreement. Security of earning power is a natural desire of workmen as well as of all other citizens.

5. If wages were permanently tied to the cost of living, then the standard of living of workmen would be frozen. . . . The annual improvement factor of 3 cents an hour (approximately 2%) we thought we could reasonably underwrite for the people employed in our business for the two years of the agreement. Others may agree on a different improvement factor as applying to their business or may not formalize the amount at all. . . .

. . . . .

. . . A study of the past, particularly of periods of full employment . . . would lead such a student of the past to conclude that present high wages were more the result of fundamental inflationary pressures created by the war than of unreasonable pressure of powerful international unions of which the public is so conscious due to the annual strikes and threats of strikes. . . .

VIII

On May 28, 1948, Chrysler settled the strike at its plants by a wage increase of 13 cents per hour; negotiations under the wage reopening clause of the contract (June 15, 1949) had marked time pending the conclusion of negotiations at Ford. Ford negotiations also yielded a similar increase of 13 cents per hour plus "fringes"; the 1949 negotiations established a non-contributory pension and insurance system.[1]

DISCUSSION QUESTIONS

1. What external or general factors do you believe influenced the various positions taken by the company and the union in this case?

2. What internal factors arising out of the General Motors–UAW relationship itself do you consider important in the positions taken by the company and the union?

3. Evaluate the strategy and tactics employed by the company and the union.

4. What "structures of relationships" do you think emerged at General Motors from 1937 to 1948?

5. Evaluate the impact of this wage formula on the economy.

---

[1] See Ford Motor Company: Negotiating the 1949 Agreement, p. 402.

GENERAL MOTORS CORPORATION

NEGOTIATING THE 1950 AGREEMENT: THE FIVE-YEAR CONTRACT AND THE UNION SHOP

I

Included in the 1950 contract negotiations were two years of experience with the 1948 document. The period had registered the lowest record of time lost through work stoppages. The company felt that its employees had grasped the meaning of the improvement factor and the cost-of-living adjustments. Even on the three occasions when cuts had been made in the cost-of-living allowance little resentment was evidenced among the work force. However, the director of the UAW's GM department stated, "While the UAW–CIO recognizes the technical legal right of the corporation to reduce wages . . . we contend that the profit position of General Motors makes such a reduction morally indefensible."

Manifestly the company had prospered. In 1949, its net income was over $656 million, an all-time record for an American corporation, and, as a percentage of sales, 11.5, compared with 6.3 for Chrysler, 5.8 for Studebaker, and less than 4 for both Packard and Hudson. From 1947 through 1949, GM reinvested over $664 million, compared to $448 million in the 14-year period 1933–1946.

Pensions and insurance had become subjects of joint study. This carried out the 1948 contract's provision that, if the courts ruled that pensions and insurance programs were proper subjects for collective bargaining, the parties would set up a joint committee to examine various types of plans.[1] The committee, which was established in October 1949, met in 13 sessions before the formal 1950 contract negotiations started. The corporation gave the union data on the work force—breakdowns on age, length of service, sex, dependency, etc. Activities of the committee were exploratory with both sides learning the technicalities involved. Bargaining was reserved for the negotiating table. As a result of these preliminary sessions, both union and company representatives developed a healthy respect for the complexity of the whole pension-insurance question. Both sides recognized that it would be foolhardy to get into a frozen position before all aspects of the question had been carefully explored.

---

[1] The courts had ruled that pensions and insurance programs were subject to bargaining in the case of *Inland Steel Company v. NLRB*.

II

Before negotiations opened on March 29, 1950, several significant events occurred:

(1) In late 1949, Ford negotiated a contract to run for two and a half years, which granted a noncontributory pension plan for all hourly rated employees. The contract provided for reopening on economic matters other than pensions after January 1, 1951.[1]

On January 25, 1950, the UAW struck Chrysler over the issue of pensions. The efforts of Federal and state mediators to settle the walkout failed. By late March, the dispute area widened to include general contract issues, which proved equally tough to solve. The company wanted safeguards against alleged abuse of the procedures under which grievances were resolved while union stewards and committeemen were on company time and pay. The union wanted a union-shop agreement, changes in the grievance procedure, promotions based on seniority only, and more. Chrysler presented its side of the story in full-page newspaper advertisements. It charged the union was stalling a settlement, implying that this was being done to establish a pattern that would strengthen its position "elsewhere"—meaning at GM.

(2) On March 1, 1950, the NLRB announced that the International Union of Electrical, Radio and Machine Workers, CIO, had swept the "left-wing" United Electrical Workers out of GM by more than 8 to 1. On the same date, James B. Carey, leader of the IUE, publicized an agreement with the UAW which called for joint consultation on contract demands in GM and provided that neither union would sign a new contract without the sanction of the other. The UAW announced that this agreement would strengthen its bargaining position since the UE could no longer "sign contracts behind the backs of the auto workers, cutting the wage scale throughout the company's plants."

(3) Long before the negotiations started the union began to amass evidence to weaken GM's historical opposition to the union shop. In November 1949, the UAW conducted an intensive membership drive among GM workers. In December 1949, the corporation announced its refusal to permit the conduct of union shop elections on company property.[2] In contrast, every NLRB election to determine union representation previously held among any group of GM employees had been held on company property with company consent. Nevertheless, 87% of the eligible employees turned out in February 1950 to vote. Of the valid ballots cast, 89% were for the union shop.

---

[1] See Ford Motor Company—Negotiating the 1949 Agreement.
[2] The Taft-Hartley Act required that before a union could properly bargain for a union shop it had to receive a mandate from a majority of the union members.

III

When therefore the UAW national GM conference announced on March 3, 1950, the union's 1950 demands, high among them was the union shop. The economic demands, totaling 31 cents an hour, included: $125 a month pensions, comprehensive hospital and medical coverage, severance allowances, and wage increases. The union's proposal also called for discontinuing the cost-of-living escalator clause, although it would retain and increase the "annual improvement factor." Among its noneconomic demands were liberalization of the provisions governing transfers and promotions, an improved production standards clause, increased committeeman representation, and a broadening of the jurisdiction of the impartial umpire.

Similarly, the GM personnel staff prepared for negotiations during the entire two years of the 1948 contract. Knowing that friction points in day-to-day operations often get to the bargaining table, GM collected extensive data on them. Comprehensive analyses were made of all matters requiring umpire decision. Equal attention was given to those provisions of the 1948 agreement which were working well. Several months before the March 29 opening, 20,000 members of GM management were canvassed for their review and appraisal of existing contract provisions and for their suggestions as to improvements. The central personnel staff prepared questionnaires on *each* clause of the contract, which, when answered, provided the GM negotiating team with an extensive record of facts—facts which management considered difficult to refute without other, and equally significant, counterfacts.

The company requested the union to submit to it the make-up of its negotiating team for 1950. GM then proceeded to match the union team man for man from each of its geographical regions.

The corporation took two other preliminary steps. A week prior to the opening of negotiations, it arranged a meeting with the union to discuss several problems which, if left unresolved, would "put unfair pressures on both sides." The first problem was the terminal clause of the 1948 agreement. Under that agreement, either party had the right to serve on the other party 60 days' notice of intention to terminate or to modify the agreement. If notice to modify were given, the pressure exerted on the company to reach an agreement within a stipulated period was weak from the union standpoint. On the other hand, if notice to terminate were given, pressure to settle or to strike could become too great for both sides as the 60 days began to run out, even though satisfactory progress was being made in negotiations. Moreover, the company argued that from a realistic standpoint, when a 60-day notice to terminate is given by either side, negotiations could proceed in an orderly fashion for only about 30 days; during the last 30 days the union representatives would have to devote too much time developing pressure in the local unions for the conduct of a successful strike vote and readying things for a strike in the event a settlement was not reached by the expiration date. The corporation pointed out that a union, even if it wanted to extend an agreement, would have to take positive action which might not always be politic.

Both parties recognized the undesirable pressures inherent in this terminal clause. They agreed therefore to what they termed a "floater" clause. It provided that, if a notice to modify the contract were served, negotiations would continue for 30 days and thereafter until agreement was reached. However, after the first 30 days of negotiations, either party could terminate the agreement on a 30-day notice given at any time. This relieved the pressure on the union to serve notice of contract termination at the outset. As a matter of record, the union never did exercise its right to serve the 30-day notice to terminate. Indeed, at its request, the floater clause was made a part of the new five-year agreement.

The second problem which management wanted to clarify before actual negotiations began was the matter of publicity concerning progress of the negotiations. Management pointed out how difficult it had been to "negotiate in the newspapers" and around the bargaining table at the same time. It claimed that, in the past, it had read union demands in the newspapers before they had been served, and that some of its own offers had been turned down in press releases before there had been a chance fully to explore them. As it had done in 1948, GM asked the union what its pleasure was in this regard. An understanding was reached that neither side would make any public statements for at least 30 days or until hope of a peaceful settlement had been exhausted. With such an understanding, it was hoped that no one would get into a frozen public position.

IV

Finally, on March 29, when the union and the management met, each negotiating team was provided with a separate caucus room adjoining opposite ends of the negotiating room. Every effort was made to make all of these locations as comfortable as possible. At the outset, the parties met three or four times each week, beginning at 1 P.M. and continuing to the first good stopping point after 5 P.M. During the initial meetings, a recess was taken in midafternoon, during which coffee was served to prevent people from scattering. In 1950, in contrast to the 1948 practice, the parties agreed to dispense with a stenographic transcript. However, if either party wanted anything reduced to a verbatim record, it would be done and would be available to both sides. The corporation exercised this option during the early meetings when the union submitted its demands. After this any notes kept were informal ones made by the negotiators themselves.

During the first weeks following March 29, the union presented and explained its 70 proposals for revisions. Chief among the union's demands were those which had been formulated by the UAW national GM conference.

As in 1948, management handled each of the union's demands with careful objectivity and respect. It assigned each group of union proposals to a management committee and asked the committee to prepare a written report. GM's reply to the union's demand to amend production standards totaled 36 pages. The reply reviewed the experience in each of the divisions of GM: Cadillac, Buick, Oldsmobile, etc. Where the record showed a considerable number of grievances over production standards, a detailed analysis was given of how they were handled. The reply then presented a systematic analysis of each of the union's proposals regarding production standards and the problems each of these proposals raised.

GM's proposal on grievances was typical of the type of detailed information that the negotiations evoked from both sides. Both union and management frequently referred to past experience, especially to grievances and to umpire decisions to support their respective positions.

The corporation on April 18 made a presentation of its proposals for contract amendments. Included in the presentation was a review of the day-to-day relations between the union and GM, as follows in part:

. . . . .

Over 2,400 General Motors employees serving as union committeemen and alternates have represented employes during working hours in matters concerning hours, wages and conditions of employment covered by the Agreement terms.

. . . 52,146 written grievances were handled by these 2,400 Union committeemen during the 18-month period (May 29, 1948–December 31, 1949). This means that on the average, one employe out of about eight filed a written grievance once a year. Surveys have shown, however, that some employes file many grievances while 90% of the employes never have found occasion to file a formal grievance. The disposition of the grievances at each step of the grievance procedure is a rather dramatic example of its workability.

Out of the 52,146 written grievances:

25,091 or 48.1% were settled at the first step between the employe, the Union committeeman and the foreman.
19,070 or 36.5% were settled at the second step in committee meetings between local Union shop committeemen and Management usually held weekly at each plant.
6,262 or 11.9% were settled at the appeal step of the procedure where higher representatives of Management and the Union participate.
197 or .4 of 1% were settled by the Impartial Umpire selected and paid jointly by the parties.

. . . . .

The above figures do not take into account the large number of employe matters which are handled informally with supervision in the plant without the necessity for a formal complaint.

. . . . .

As a result of negotiations in 1946, the parties agreed to a check-off system for the collection of Union dues in 1946, wherein employes voluntarily authorize Management to deduct Union dues, assessments and initiation fees. Since that time, this system has continued to prove a convenience to employes and to the Union. . . .

. . . . .

It is interesting to note the growth of the Union membership as indicated by the number of General Motors employes who have authorized dues deductions:

No. of
Employes
Paying Dues

June, 1946	132,080 ⎫
June, 1947	164,391 ⎪ 77.5% Increase in
June, 1948	178,191 ⎬ Four Years of
June, 1949	192,793 ⎪ Peaceful Relationship
March, 1950 [1]	223,009 ⎭

The March 1950 figure represents an all-time peace-time high.

. . . . .

In most of the plants there were no work stoppages due to labor disputes in violation of the terms of the Agreement during 1949. Such time as was lost for this reason, if averaged over all of the employes covered by the Agreement, would have amounted to only about 17 minutes per employe for the entire year. This is an outstanding record.

While the over-all record was good, we should not lose sight of the fact that during the term of the Agreement there were 43 stoppages.

This indicates that while the majority of employes and Union leadership have accepted their responsibilities there are still some sections of local union leadership which have not. In this particular, the record in 1949 was not as good as it was in 1948.

. . . . .

The GM–UAW wage formula . . . has operated in such a manner that General Motors employes today enjoy a greater purchasing power for their hour of work than at any time since the employes have been represented by the UAW. . . . We sincerely believe that this formula contributed, in a major degree, to the stable relations during the existing contract term, since it protected employes against increases in the cost-of-living while at the same time increasing the standard of living by the improvement factor increases. . . .

. . . . .

In addition, the formula provided for an improvement factor in 1948 and 1949 which gave recognition to gradual long-term improvement.

. . . The net effect of the formula has been to provide hourly-rate employes with an upward adjustment as follows:

Quarter Beginning	Increase in Base Rates Per Hour (Improvement Factor)	Cost-of-Living Allowance Per Hour	Total Increase Per Hour
June, 1948	6¢	5¢	11¢
September, 1948	6¢	8¢	14¢
December, 1948	6¢	8¢	14¢
March, 1949	6¢	6¢	12¢
June, 1949	9¢ *	5¢	14¢
September, 1949	9¢	5¢	14¢
December, 1949	9¢	5¢	14¢
March, 1950	9¢	3¢	12¢

* Improvement Factor Increase of three-cents (3¢) per hour added June 1, 1949.

[1] As of March, 1950, the union represented about 270,000 hourly-rated employes at GM.

As can be seen from the above during the two years the formula has operated, the weighted average increase enjoyed by employes was 13⅛¢ per hour as contrasted to the pattern in the durable goods industry of 13¢ per hour.

. . . . .

The joint committee established by General Motors and the UAW in November, 1949, served a useful constructive service in its exploration of the intricate provisions of private pensions and insurance plans. The factual information exchanged in the thirteen meetings of the joint committee should reduce the time necessary to discuss these problems in negotiations.

The above digest covers the high points only. It demonstrates conclusively that the Agreement and the administration of the Agreement by the parties has in the main operated satisfactorily.

The changes which we propose in the existing Agreement do not attack or seek to destroy the basic principles and procedures that have been developed by both parties through experience. But, rather, the changes we suggest are intended as refinements of existing terms where experience dictates such changes should be made in the interest of the relations between the parties and in fairness to the employes.[1] [There then followed a presentation of the company's proposal.]

. . . . .

The company's proposals for changes included: reduction of employed committeemen during slack periods, modification of seniority provisions to insure continuous service during short layoffs, elimination of claims for duplicate payment for overtime work, and cessation of "scurrilous" union attacks on GM.

At about the time that the negotiators completed a second review of contract clauses and proposed changes, the strike at Chrysler ended. Chrysler workers ratified a contract on May 6, 1950, which incorporated $100 monthly pensions and hospital and insurance plans in the three-year agreement.

The next day, May 7, the UAW national GM conference authorized the union's committee to serve notice of cancellation of the contract unless substantial progress were made within 10 days. Management reminded the union that progress was being made, faster in fact than in 1948, that pensions and insurance were intricate subjects, and that resolution would not come from either party's taking a fixed or rigid position.

The pace of negotiations quickened. Management asked the union whether it wanted to negotiate a pattern agreement for two or three years with annual reopenings on wages and perhaps other economic considerations, or whether it was interested in making an effort to settle all matters for a much longer period of time. For the ordinary kind of "pattern settlement" the company would be willing to match the economic considerations recently agreed to by some of its competitors; the union could not expect by ordinary collective bargaining to obtain benefits greater than had been obtained up to that time from other important segments of industry. On the other hand, in line with the principles already incorporated in the 1948 agreement, the company would be willing to do its best to work out an agreement entirely different from the 1950 pattern settlements. Such a forward step, how-

---

[1] General Motors Company, *Presentation of General Motors Proposals to Amend GM–UAW National Agreement Dated May 29, 1948.*

ever, depended upon the union's willingness to break with precedent and agree to a five-year nonreopenable contract.

After careful consideration, the union reported that it was willing to consider without prejudice to either party a five-year agreement. With this understanding, the corporation representatives outlined on May 15 the general framework of the company's offers. Finally, on May 23, after 30 hours of continuous bargaining, a settlement was announced at 2:15 P.M. The new contract continued the wage formula pioneered in 1948—the cost-of-living escalator and the annual "improvement factor," the latter increased from 3 to 4 cents an hour. In addition to the industry's established pension scale of $100 per month including Social Security benefits, guaranteed company-paid minima were set in the event that Federal benefits were increased. The medical and hospital insurance programs were broadened. Vacation pay for employees with 15 years' service was increased to 120 hours' pay. An additional increase of 5 cents per man-hour was granted for certain skilled jobs.

Entirely new was a modified union shop. New employees were to join the union within 90 days but could withdraw if they so wished after a year's membership. Employees who were already members were to remain such for the life of the contract. Those employees already on the payroll who preferred to remain nonunion were not required to become members.

The contract was to run for five years—without any reopening—the longest contract ever signed in a mass production industry.

Reuther hailed the settlement as "historic" and as "the greatest step forward in auto-union history." Wilson called it "unprecedented in labor-management relations" and predicted that "it will have a stabilizing influence not only on our business but on the economy of the whole country."

V

The GM settlement quickly made itself felt across the nation. A half million workers in GM, Chrysler, and Ford plants received wage increases within a single two-week period. In the case of GM, the July cost-of-living index was the basis for a 5-cent increase, the largest since the escalator clause was established. On August 25, Chrysler announced a 10-cent increase plus an additional 5 cents to skilled workers, outside of their 3½-month-old contract. On September 4, Ford announced a totally new contract incorporating an 8-cent increase together with an extra 5 cents for skilled workers. Reached after a "60-hour marathon of collective bargaining," Ford was the second major automobile company to agree to a five-year contract. In addition to a cost-of-living increase and an annual 4-cent wage increase the new Ford contract also provided for: 3-week vacations after 15 years' service, enlarged health and hospital contributory programs, and an increase of the maximum allowable pension to $125 monthly including Social Security. The $125 maximum was accordingly quickly met by GM.

In December, Chrysler became the last of the Big Three to accept the

GM formula when it negotiated for the third time in 1950 with the UAW and reached a new five-year contract to replace the one written in May.

DISCUSSION QUESTIONS

1. List the important elements of GM's planning for the 1950 negotiations.

2. What were the important issues in the 1950 negotiations? To union? To management?

3. What were the major power factors in the 1950 negotiations?

4. What made a 5-year contract possible? Why did the union accept such a long contract?

5. Compare pattern setting in 1950 with automotive pattern setting of previous years. What interrelationships, if any, do you see between these negotiations and those in 1946 and 1948?

6. How would you characterize the union-management relations at GM after the 1950 negotiations?

GENERAL MOTORS CORPORATION

NEGOTIATING THE 1953 AMENDMENTS: THE "LIVING DOCUMENT" PHILOSOPHY

Within a month of the signing of the 1950 five-year agreement, the Korean war started. The war with its resultant economic controls precipitated a number of developments that were to have a significant effect on the operation of the cost of living adjustment and the annual improvement clauses.

Wages and prices were frozen January 26, 1951. On March 1, 1951, the date on which a cost of living wage increase would be due in auto plants, the WSB established Regulation 8 authorizing cost of living wage increases providing prices were not thereby increased. Annual improvement increases, however, met more resistance from industry members of the WSB. The 4 cents due GM employees on May 29 was held up until June 6, 1951, when the WSB passed Resolution No. 22 authorizing such increases if they had been incorporated in agreements prior to the freeze date, and provided they would not lead to a price increase.

The cost of living allowance, however, became complicated by changes in the CPI itself. The contract had specified the BLS CPI "in its present form and calculated on the same basis as the Index for April, 1950, unless otherwise agreed upon by the parties." In 1950, the BLS had announced that it was embarking on a complete revision of the CPI to make it more consonant with the changed buying patterns of consumers since the establishment of the base date of the index (1936–1939 = 100). The new "adjusted" index would be based on 1947–1949 as 100, and when issued would supersede the "old" index.

On March 1, 1951, the BLS released the January cost of living figure for the "adjusted" index.[1] This proved to be .1 point lower than the cost of living figure determined on the basis of the "old" index, a difference too small to change the cost of living allowance. The next day the company and the union drew up a memorandum to: continue the use of the old index plus the .8 agreed upon in 1949 as a correction for the rent factor; shift to the new index if the old one were discontinued, insuring that the transition would not alter the cost of living allowance; and allow either party at any time to initiate discussions concerning the adoption of the new index.

Accordingly, when the BLS announced early in 1952 that the "old" index would be discontinued with the December 1952 figure and that the new index would start January 1953, the UAW initiated exploratory discussions concerning transition to the new index. At the same time it intro-

---

[1] See Exhibit 1.

461

duced its "living document" philosophy, in resolutions passed by the union's GM council:

. . . . .

The five-year National Agreement between the General Motors Corporation and the UAW–CIO dated May 29, 1950, must remain a "living document" giving recognition to the changing scene of the American economy. . . .

. . . . .

Since May 29, 1950, the cost of living, spurred by the unanticipated and unforeseeable war in Korea, has risen sharply so that the cost-of-living adjustment has increased from 3 cents to 25 cents per hour, as of July, 1952. . . . The UAW–CIO–General Motors National Agreement was one of the principal guideposts employed by the Wage Stabilization Board in establishing Regulation 8 governing in part the permissible wage increases in American industry. However, cost-of-living adjustments under Regulation 8 could be added to base rates, which was thereafter done in most other heavy goods' industries.

Moreover, on May 29, 1950, the annual improvement factor was computed at a rate of 2½% which equaled 4 cents per hour, based on the then current average wage of General Motors Corporation employees. Current hourly rates have increased 35 cents per hour since May 29, 1950, so that the 2½% improvement factor translates into a sum of 4.9 cents.[1] Mr. C. E. Wilson, president of General Motors, has publicly stated on numerous occasions that the annual improvement factor is economically sound and represents a 2½% yearly increase to permit employees to share in progress resulting from technological improvements.

. . . . .

BE IT RESOLVED THEREFORE:

1. The General Motors Council wholeheartedly supports the following program to be implemented in discussions with representatives of the General Motors Corporation:

(a) The cost of living float should not at any time exceed five cents and any amounts in excess of the five-cent float should be added to base rates.

(b) The 2½% improvement factor should be established at five cents per year for the remainder of the National Agreement's duration.

(c) The pensions payable to retired workers by the General Motors Corporation under the UAW–GM pension plan should be adjusted to restore the same purchasing power which existed on May 29, 1950.

2. This program merely implements the fundamental principles established in the UAW–GM National Agreement dated May 29, 1950, and therefore should be granted by the General Motors Corporation.

. . . . .

Similar actions were quickly taken by the presidents of the UAW Chrysler locals and by the union's national Ford council.

With the lapse of the old CPI, Reuther declared in a press conference that "the cost of living clause is such an integral part of our contracts that failure to reach agreement on a change from the old CPI to the new would mean in effect 'no contract.' " He also pointed to increases allowed in other industries under stabilization policies and which in many instances were incorporated into base rates not subject to reduction.

Livingston, UAW Vice President of the GM department, wrote Anderson, GM Vice President, on October 28, outlining again the union's demands and

---

[1] By the terms of the 1950 contract the annual improvement factor was 4 cents.

seeking an "equitable" transition to the new index. The company replied that it would be unable to give an answer until after a meeting of the GM operating committee, scheduled to meet the second week of February. Soon after, GM as well as representatives of other industries, President George Meany of the AFL, and the railroad unions urged the new Administration in Washington to reconstitute the old index. The UAW opposed this move on the grounds that it would "further complicate collective bargaining problems."

Late in January 1953, the BLS, on orders from President Eisenhower, announced that it would continue the old index through June, but stated that it would be impossible to issue the January figure before April 1 as it would be necessary to collect back prices and to make estimates for prices which could not be collected. Reuther publicly described any January figure to be published "in the guise of the Old Index" as "the result of political manipulation and pressure by the corporation." He argued that "any reconstruction of those prices must be based on faulty memory, irresponsible guesswork, or unreliable estimating procedures."

By the time formal negotiations opened on February 26, 1953, all wage controls and most price controls had been suspended. On the second day of negotiations the January cost of living figure based on the new index was released. It showed a drop of .3 points.[1] The session, however, was recessed upon the union's rejection of the company's offer: (1) incorporation of 14 cents of the current 25-cent cost-of-living allowance into the base rate, and (2) a 5-cent increase to skilled trades effective June 1. Since the parties had not agreed on the method of conversion to the new index, no wage changes were instituted on March 1.

Reuther spread the whole situation before the 14th constitutional convention of the UAW, March 22–27. He pointed out that "the soundness of the union's position, both from the view of economics and morals, has already compelled General Motors to make certain offers in answer to our demands. Those offers, while reflecting acceptance of the principle that long-term collective bargaining contracts must be 'living documents,' do not provide the full equity to which the workers are entitled."

The convention's response was a nearly unanimous vote for a resolution authorizing resumption of negotiations "with full equity of the auto workers as their goal" and advising managements that "in the event negotiations do not bring about a satisfactory adjustment of the equities involved, the international union and all local unions are directed not to negotiate any further contracts for a period in excess of two years."

With the BLS release of the January and February old index figures on April 6, wages were cut 1 cent over the protest of the union. Livingston said that the international executive board would review the whole matter on April 28 and that negotiations with GM would resume in May. The board's decisions were communicated to Anderson by Livingston on May 7. His letter specified the demands of the union: (1) incorporation of 21 cents of

---

[1] See Exhibit 1.

the current 24-cent cost of living allowance into the base rates; (2) increase of the annual improvement factor from 4 cents to 5 cents; (3) increases in pensions to meet the increase in cost of living and the policy of compulsory retirement at age 68; (4) a special increase for skilled trades; (5) development of a schedule of transition to the new index to reflect the intent of the parties in the original escalator and to preserve the ratio on which it was developed.

As the date for resumption of negotiations approached pressures on the union to reach an agreement mounted. The old index had dropped enough so that a 2-cent decrease was anticipated; the new index was expected to show a rise. There was some expectation of higher wages for the Steelworkers in their coming negotiations. Moreover a week before the negotiations were scheduled to resume the workers in the Detroit transmission plant walked out, a rare occurrence in GM plants. The company sent wires to Reuther warning of court action, and the stoppage ended quickly. On Monday, May 18, the UAW released to the press Livingston's May 7 letter to Anderson authorizing walkouts in foundry plants at Alliance, Ohio, and Danville, Illinois, over rate classifications, one of the few issues which could be a basis for strike action under the contract. The plants were key operations in the GM production cycle and could affect manufacturing operations within a week. By the time negotiations resumed workers had returned to all of the plants.

After three days of nearly continuous sessions without publicity on either side, an agreement was signed on May 22. The major changes were: (1) incorporation of 19 cents of the current 24-cent cost of living allowance into the base rates; (2) conversion of the cost of living allowance to the new CPI with (a) different rates of adjustment above and below the current CPI level, (b) provision, as in the 1948 contract, that downward adjustment be limited to 5 cents below the current wage level, (c) selection of December 1952 as the base date for conversion which avoided an impending 2-cent decrease in the allowance; (3) increase of 10 cents an hour for over 150 skilled classifications and an additional 10-cent increase for a half dozen patternmaker and die sinker classifications; (4) increase of the annual improvement factor from 4 cents to 5 cents; (5) pension increase from $1.50 to $1.75 a month for each year of credited service up to 30 years which would yield, with the addition of the current $85 per month maximum primary Social Security benefit, a maximum of $137.50 a month instead of $130, the $1.75 to apply to those already pensioned; (6) pro rata vacation benefits to retiring employees; and (7) extension of Blue Cross and Blue Shield, or equivalent, coverage at the group rates, optional with the retiree.

In a joint press conference, Reuther remarked:

> We in the UAW–CIO are very gratified that we have been able to work out with the General Motors Corporation these amendments to our present contract that were necessary to make it a workable document. We are pleased that the General Motors Corporation has accepted the principle that a collective bargaining agreement must be a living document under which the workers' equity is maintained

in the face of circumstances impossible for the parties to foresee when the contract was originally negotiated.

We believe that our agreement on these contract amendments shows that free labor and free management, exercising their rights and privileges, facing up to their responsibilities and using their common sense, can, in our kind of democracy, work out their problems across the bargaining table.

Harlow H. Curtice, who had succeeded Wilson as president of GM, described the agreement as "a practical solution to problems created by the Korean war with its resulting inflationary impact and the reconstitution of government controls." He noted that the 1950 contract had had a stabilizing influence on labor-management relations and added, "We expect the understanding reached today will contribute even more to stabilizing relations among our employees for the remaining two years of the contract."

Three days later, Ford matched all that GM had granted and granted an additional 10 cents per hour to patternmakers and die sinkers. Furthermore, it remodeled its pension plan and other fringe benefits which in some respects had been below GM and Chrysler benefits. In modifying fringe benefits Ford moved ahead of the GM pattern in certain respects: extension of the medical care plan to retired workers and incorporation of a vacation pay allowance for retiring workers. Chrysler similarly modified its agreement with UAW on May 27. On May 28, GM in supplementay agreements No. 20 and No. 21 completed the cycle for the Big Three by adopting the additional benefits initiated by Ford.

EXHIBIT I

GENERAL MOTORS CORPORATION—NEGOTIATING THE 1953 AMENDMENTS

Consumer Price Index

	Revised Series	Old Series
Dec. 1950	—	178.8
Jan. 1951	181.5	181.6
Dec. 1951	189.1	190.0
Jan. 1952	189.1	190.2
Dec. 1952	190.7	191.0
Jan. 1953	190.4	—
Feb. 1953	189.6	188.6
Mar. 1953	189.9	188.8
April 1953	190.1	188.3

DISCUSSION QUESTIONS

1. What are the implications of the "living document" philosophy?
2. How do you account for management's initial position on "reopening" the contract?
3. What factors influenced the positions of the parties?
4. What did the company achieve in settling the issue as it did?

THE STEEL INDUSTRY

THE 1949 NEGOTIATIONS

History of Relationship and the Pension Issue

Contract negotiations in steel during 1949 brought into sharp focus crucial issues associated with the swift growth of organized labor since the 1930's. What essentially were the implications of national policy with regard to management-union relations evolving since the war? What about the kind of negotiations that was developing between large unions and large corporations? Did deadlocks impose new responsibilities upon government? If so, what were the requirements—and implications—of government intervention? What specifically about the looming demands for successive rounds of wage increases against the background of inflation? What about relevant criteria in determining wages? What about the demands for pensions and insurance? How large a part did union rivalries play in such demanding? What about the trend toward "pattern bargains"—in focal industries and in the economy as a whole? Was "free collective bargaining" possible in these changing industrial relations?

As the largest manufacturing industry in the United States in terms of value added and number of persons employed, the steel industry has always been sensitive to the effect of its collective bargaining agreements on the economy. Traditionally the steel companies and the Steelworkers union have attempted to justify their contract proposals with elaborate arguments. Both sides have hired well-known economists to analyze the situation; and by the use of pamphlets and advertisements, each side has indicated how its demands would benefit the economy.

I. The Background

Formative unions appeared in iron and steel as early as the mid-nineteenth century. The Amalgamated Association of Iron, Steel and Tin Workers was formed in 1876; but sixty years later unionism had little to show in steel save repeated defeats and a sort of fringe representation limited to skilled workers in the smaller mills. The Homestead Strike in 1892 and the steel strikes of 1910 and 1919 stand out as particularly violent episodes in the annals of later history of the country. Trade unionism had been routed and decimated in the defeats they suffered in these strikes.

Yet, when the transition to organized relationships between "Big Steel" and the CIO did come, it was accomplished amicably. The Steel Workers' Organizing Committee had, of course, been active in steel centers since its formation in 1936. Under the direction of Philip Murray, and with resources and other leaders drawn largely from the United Mine Workers, the organizers concentrated first upon "capturing" the leaders of the employee representation plans, "company unions," which appeared in the industry as early as 1904, and had spread widely after 1933. As CIO organizing efforts were under way, Myron C. Taylor, for the United States Steel Corporation, and John L. Lewis, for the CIO, in direct personal discussions during February, 1937, agreed in principle upon underlying terms for recognizing and negotiating with the union. On March 2, 1937, Murray negotiated with Benjamin F. Fairless, president of Carnegie-Illinois, a preliminary contract that embodied these terms by recognizing the SWOC as bargaining agent only for those employees who were its members. The formal contract, incorporating also a 10% wage increase and the 40-hour week, was followed by the other major subsidiaries of U.S. Steel. Within three months, agreements modeled upon the Carnegie-Illinois pattern were signed with some 140 companies.

The so-called "Little Steel" companies followed U.S. Steel's lead in wages and conditions but not in accepting the recognition "formula." Indeed, the "Little Steel" almost re-echoed the bitterness and violence of the earlier strikes against "Big Steel." The strike called by the union in 1937 against Inland, Republic, and Youngstown, into which Bethlehem was drawn, was lost. In 1941, however, the Supreme Court decision in the Heinz case made mandatory the completion of signed contracts with certified unions. That same year the steelworkers won NLRB certification and recognition from Inland, Bethlehem, Republic, Youngstown, and the Great Lakes plant of National Steel. The United Steelworkers of America was formally created in 1942, when it replaced the Steel Workers' Organizing Committee and absorbed the Amalgamated Association of Iron, Steel and Tin Workers. By 1949, virtually all steel companies, except the American Rolling Mill Company and National Steel at Weirton, had contracts with the United Steelworkers of America, CIO. In round figures, the union was signatory to 1,900 agreements with 1,600 companies in steel and related industries, where it had approximately 1,000,000 members.

II. MANAGEMENT-UNION RELATIONS, 1937–1945

Industry-wide recognition carried the parties to the threshold of World War II; the first agreements with the "Little Steel" companies indeed were signed when the country was already an active combatant. Thereupon the developing patterns naturally took on the impress of war influences. From the predominant prewar pattern of recognition as bargaining agent only for its own members, the Steelworkers union, with the progress of the war, not only was recognized as the exclusive representative of production, maintenance, and hourly rated nonconfidential clerical employees but, in addition, was granted, under NWLB directives, maintenance of membership and check-off of union dues and of initiation fees. These provisions were continued in postwar contracts.

In wages and conditions of employment, the tendency had consistently developed to follow a "pattern"—a course which became well grooved during the war under NWLB directives. All steel companies, even those not yet recognizing the union, granted the general hourly increase of 10 cents, effective March 16, 1937. Another hourly increase of 10 cents, embodied in the U.S. Steel contracts effective April 1, 1941, was universally applied. These prewar negotiations also established premium overtime rates and made beginnings in the providing of "fringe benefits," as, for instance, paid vacations.

As wartime wage, price, and production controls were instituted, it was through the "Little Steel formula" that the pattern of wage stabilization was set by NWLB directive for the period 1942 to 1945. Various fringe benefits were also either introduced or liberalized by award, directive, and ruling.

These conditions were all uniformly carried forward or liberalized in postwar negotiations. Perhaps one of the most impressive cooperative accomplishments was embodied in the job classification and rate inequity program ordered in the NWLB directive of November 25, 1944, and completed after the war (1945–1947), under which several thousands of jobs and rates were reduced to 30 classifications, each with its standard hourly rate, while separate classifications were established for maintenance crafts.

III. 1945–1946 Negotiations

It had been evident, even before the fighting ceased in August, 1945, that the steelworkers, as most workers, had become both restive under wartime wage controls and fearful of the impact of reconversion on take-home pay. In October, 1945, accordingly, the union presented, under the reopening clause of the agreement, demands upon U.S. Steel for wage increases of 25 cents an hour, or $2 a day, retroactive to August 18, 1945. The corporation, pointing to government wage and price policies, rejected the demand. Wage controls had been modified so as to permit employers to make wage increases without government approval, provided such increases did not become the basis for increases in prices; otherwise prior approval remained a requirement.

As the steel controversy proceeded, Fairless repeatedly declared that "as far back as two years ago we asked for new and fair ceiling prices, as provided by law." Required price relief in carbon steel sheerly on the basis of past increases in costs was estimated by the corporation at approximately $7 a ton. The union, on the other hand, argued that "five years of war production" had yielded the industry "over two billion dollars in open and concealed profits" to help satisfy the workers' wage demands to meet mounting living costs and maintain purchasing power.

On November 28, 1945, the union took a strike vote. On December 31, President Truman appointed a three-man fact-finding board to inquire into the dispute. The steel board was the fourth of seven fact-finding boards appointed between November 27, 1945, and January 17, 1946.[1] On January 8,

---

[1] They dealt with deadlocks in the petroleum industry, the General Motors Corporation, the Greyhound Bus Lines, steel, the International Harvester Co., and the meatpacking industry.

1946, Fairless was asked "by a responsible officer of the government" if a $4-a-ton price increase would "enable my company to offer a wage increase." Thereupon bargaining conferences were resumed with the union on January 10 and 11. The company there offered first 12½ cents an hour and then 15 cents an hour, its last pre-strike offer, upon an understanding that some price relief over $4 a ton might be granted. When it became known that the fact-finding board in the General Motors dispute had recommended an hourly increase of 19½ cents, Mr. Murray made this figure the union's "final offer." Deadlock ensued.

President Truman then summoned the parties to continue negotiations at the White House on January 12, 16, and 17. These sessions proved futile. With the strike set to begin on Monday, January 21, the President proposed on January 17 settlement at 18½ cents an hour, retroactive to January 1, 1946. The corporation declared its inability to go beyond 15 cents an hour, "the largest single increase in the history of the United States Steel Corporation, or of the American steel industry." The strike began on January 21 and ended on February 15 in basic steel, and some weeks later in various fabricating plants.

Settlement was made on the President's suggested wage increase of 18½ cents an hour coupled with a price increase of $5 a ton. Something over 1,100 companies with which the steelworkers' union then had contracts settled on the same basis as U.S. Steel.

IV. 1947 Negotiations

By the time negotiations opened in 1947, controls over wages and prices had, of course, been ended. Feared unemployment and recession had failed to materialize. The union urged a second-round wage increase on the basis of the rise in the cost of living. Negotiations proceeded without outside intervention or threat of breakdown until, following a pattern set by General Motors and the United Electrical Workers, an agreement was signed by the Steelworkers with U.S. Steel on April 22, 1947, yielding a "package" of approximately 15 cents an hour. Within several months, contracts modeled on this pattern were signed with other steel producers and fabricators.

The contract was to run for two years with a reopening clause that empowered either party in 1948 to "give written notice to the other party of its desire to negotiate a general and uniform change in rates of pay." If no agreement was achieved by April 30, the contract continued in effect; the union had no freedom to strike.

V. 1948 Negotiations

The Steelworkers invoked the reopening clause on March 29, 1948, for purposes of negotiating wage changes. Negotiations began on April 5; but the corporation steadfastly refused, as did other large companies at the time, to concede any increase in wages, urging the necessity to "hold the line" against inflation. At the same time, it indicated its intention to continue to observe wages and prices against the tests of changing conditions.

Though strenuously protesting management's position, the union honored its obligation not to strike. On May 25, however, General Motors granted a wage increase as a result of negotiations with the United Automobile Workers.[1] Negotiations were then resumed between U.S. Steel and the United Steelworkers, resulting in a settlement effective on July 16, 1948, averaging about 13 cents an hour. The rest of the industry followed this pattern.

The 1948 "Supplemental Agreement" also extended the termination date to April 30, 1950, with the right to reopen in 1949, as stipulated in the following provisions:

. . . sixty days prior to July 16, 1949, either party may serve notice on the other of its desire to negotiate:

a. for a general and uniform change in rates of pay and/or
b. for life, accident, health, medical, and hospital insurance benefits.

Within 30 days after the giving of such notice the parties shall meet for the purpose of negotiating such issues. Failing mutual agreement on such issues by July 16, 1949, the parties may thereupon, notwithstanding any of the other provisions of the Agreement, respectively resort to strike or lockout in support of their contentions, and the Agreement shall thereupon be deemed terminated; provided, however, upon settlement of the two issues above named, the Agreement shall be reinstated in all its terms with the addition of such provisions as may be agreed upon with respect to the two above issues, but no others, and such Agreement shall remain in effect until April 30, 1950. Said provision for reinstatement shall survive and be a continuing obligation in the event the Agreement is terminated as above provided.[2]

VI. 1949 NEGOTIATIONS

On May 16, 1949, the union notified the companies under contract of its desire to negotiate for changes in wage rates, as well as for life, accident, health, medical, and hospital insurance benefits. Separate letters transmitted the union's desire to negotiate also on the subject of retirement pensions.

Negotiations with U.S. Steel and with other companies continued from June 15, intermittently, until July 7. The union pressed three demands, wage increases, social insurance, and pensions, without translating them into precise monetary proposals. On management's side, all the companies rejected the proposal for wage increases; several made offers on social insurance; and all maintained that, with the exception of the Inland Steel Company, pensions were not a bargainable issue at all. No progress was made, since neither side receded from these original positions.

Cyrus Ching, director of the Federal Mediation and Conciliation Service, thereupon invited representatives of the union and the major companies to meet with him in Washington. At the meetings on July 11 with the parties

---

[1] See case, General Motors Corporation: Negotiating the 1948 Agreement, p. 441.
[2] Agreement between Carnegie-Illinois Steel Corporation and the United Steelworkers of America, CIO, Production and Maintenance Employees, April 22, 1947, pp. 90–91.

together and with each separately, Ching found no basis for conciliation. A national steel strike loomed on July 15. Accordingly, on July 12, Ching recommended to President Truman that he request postponement of the strike for 75 days while a fact-finding board explored the issues and made recommendations.

A telegram immediately went from the President to the parties requesting continued operations for 60 days under the current agreement and announcing the appointment of a fact-finding board of three public members to report within 45 days from July 16, 1949.

The union accepted on the following day, July 13. The companies, however, raised questions, urging that, if the President intervened at all, he should do so under the Taft-Hartley Act, which authorized boards of inquiry without power to recommend. By July 15, however, U.S. Steel gave its reluctant acquiescence but declared that it would not consider itself bound by board findings or recommendations. Other companies gave a similarly conditional acceptance; still others pointed out that their contracts had different termination dates; several urged their need for special consideration; a few pointed

Issue	Union Demand	U.S. Steel Counterproposal or Position	Board Recommendation
Wage-rate increases....	12.5¢/hour	None	None
Social insurance.......	(Stipulated benefits for death, total or permanent disability, temporary disability arising from sickness or accident off the job, hospital and surgical care), costing 6.27¢/hour per worker on basis of 2,000-hour year and to be paid fully by the company.	(Stipulated benefits for life insurance, term life insurance for retired employees, accident and sickness, hospital and surgical care), costing net 5.32¢/hour of which employee pays half.	(Details to be negotiated.) Allowance for existing plans to make maximum cost 4.0¢/hour to be met by company.
Pensions..............	($125 per month for each worker retiring at 65 or later; $150 for permanent disability after 10 years' service, to be reduced to $125 at age 65), costing per worker 11.23¢/hour	Not bargainable under 1949 reopening clause	(Details to be studied and ready for negotiation by March 1, 1950.) Allowances as above 6.0¢/hour (noncontributory generally)
Total estimated costs..	30.0¢/hour	5.32¢/hour Divided 2.66¢/hr. by Co. 2.66¢/hr. by worker	10.0¢/hour

out that they had no dispute with the union, nor was there any breakdown in negotiations since none had taken place between them.

On July 15, the Board was formally established with Carroll R. Daugherty, chairman, and Samuel I. Rosenman and David L. Cole, members.

Board proceedings began on July 26 and concluded on August 29. The union and 37 companies had appeared before the board, accounting together for some 90% of the nation's total ingot capacity. Granted an extension from August 30 to September 10, the board on that latter date submitted its findings and recommendations.

The Demands, Counterproposals, and Recommendations. Although the parties had exchanged before government intervention statements of position on the three union demands, it was not until the proceedings before the board that they were reduced to exact terms, as shown in the summary on page 471.

VII. The Issue of "Free Collective Bargaining" and "Pattern Bargaining"

President Murray presented to the board his concept of "good faith bargaining":

. . . From the very beginning of the conferences last month [the various steel producing and fabricating companies] . . . have failed and refused to bargain in good faith with the union. . . . The union . . . furnished to the companies a mass of both oral and written evidence supporting its just demands. The companies have made no genuine effort to meet the union's contentions. . . .

At the very outset of the negotiations, the various companies, through their representatives, expressed their prior determination to deny the Union's demands. The final turndown by the companies is only a reiteration of the decision arrived at before the commencement of the negotiations.

This is not collective bargaining. The duty to bargain means good faith bargaining. Good faith means that the companies are obligated to negotiate with an open rather than a closed mind. Yet it must be apparent that in these collective bargaining conferences the companies throughout have had a closed rather than an open mind.

For their part, the companies generally stressed the implications of "pattern bargaining," implemented by the "monopoly power" of industry-wide unions. They called for a return to "free collective bargaining." Enders M. Voorhees, chairman of the finance committee of U.S. Steel, gave the following articulation to these feared trends:

. . . This is not a situation which in its potentialities is restricted to a few companies, or even to a single industry. The far-reaching issues in this case concern everyone in this land. It is no exaggeration to say that the future economic health of the American people hinges upon the proper solution of the issues in this labor dispute. . . .

Is this Board to recommend a fourth round of wage rate and benefit increases in the steel industry, and recommend it for all companies alike whatever their individual situation, at the instance of this spread-eagle labor organization? And will the driving force of this unfortunate example propel it into the many other industries also under the domination of this single labor organization? Will this Board, in peacetime, needlessly establish national bargaining patterns in the broad wage, insurance and pension fields, thereby firmly enthroning that arch-foe of progress—inflexible, union-dominated, industry-wide and nation-wide patterns? Will this Board lend itself to becoming the guileless handmaiden of big unionism in its campaign to annihilate good-faith collective bargaining? And will this Board do all that in the name of the national interest? I hope not.

The case for the smaller companies was given characteristic summary by their counsel, Judge Robert P. Patterson. He urged upon the board not to make recommendations that would "establish a pattern for nationwide collective bargaining." Looking at the concrete example of the 16 smaller companies for which he spoke, he pointed out:

(1) . . . none of the companies is fully integrated . . . (2) none engages in large tonnage production of standard items . . . (3) none has the facilities to manufacture . . . products in which market demands for any particular period are the most active. These companies face a declining market. . . . They are in competition with concerns which are far larger and have lower-cost advantages. . . . Most are operating at only moderate profit or a loss.

Accordingly, a "single recommendation by the board applying for the entire industry would have serious effects upon their future."

In reply, the union charged the companies with responsibility for the development of the pattern bargaining they now were deploring. As distilled by the board, the union's counterargument ran as follows:

The union . . . complained that the companies' own actions had made collective bargaining meaningless in the present controversy. Although the companies protest that so-called industry patterns in labor relations are undesirable, they all adhered to a pattern in their discussions with the union by maintaining almost uniformly that pensions could not be discussed and that there could be no wage-rate increase whatsoever. . . .

The union contended also . . . that the companies, not the union representatives, were the ones who [long have] insisted on waiting until the major contracts were concluded and then applying the principal features to themselves. . . . All wage-rate increases since the war have been in identical cents per hour, and before the advent of the union the same pattern was followed.

With respect to the smaller companies who are now requesting special attention, the union contended that those companies have followed the traditional practice described and that in any event they have shared substantially in the general prosperity of the steel industry.

The board itself concluded that, "irrespective of whose fault it is," an unusual type of bargaining has evolved in the steel industry "which seems to have stifled the process of collective bargaining" in its "original conception . . . on a plant by plant basis. . . . An agreement is first reached by the union with the United States Steel Corporation or with that corporation and a selected few of the other industry leaders, and is then accepted by all other managements." Conditions in the early postwar years, the board declared, had militated against "normal collective bargaining," but it should now "have a better chance to function." There was merit in the complaint of those individual steel companies who pointed out "that they have been deprived of the opportunity of explaining their own predicaments in collective bargaining and having their own special problems considered on their merits, regardless of what may be done by other companies which have different circumstances." The board concluded:

If a different concept of collective bargaining from that heretofore held is needed, then a study leading to a reappraisal and a redefinition of the terms should be made by the appropriate body, which we think is the Congress itself. We should certainly not undertake to do this, but must limit ourselves to the functions as directed by the President.

VIII. The Issue of Government Intervention

The companies saw one result of these unhealthy deviations from "free collective bargaining" in an alarmingly increasing recourse to government intervention. Thus A. B. Homer, president of Bethlehem, explained this concern in his telegram of July 15 to President Truman:

Our reluctance to approve your proposal for a board that would make recommendations as to terms of settlement is based in part upon our past experience with such boards. . . . When a union which has a virtual monopoly in an important industry threatens a nationwide strike in support of its demands, boards of inquiry have uniformly recommended the granting of some of those demands regardless of the economic justification for them. For example, in the fall of 1945 similar boards were appointed to investigate into and make findings on the demands of unions for substantial wage increases and as a result of their "findings" wages were substantially raised—in the case of steel 18½ cents an hour—which led to a protracted and harmful inflationary spiral.

We are alarmed at the pattern that is emerging of national unions making demands each year for increased wages and threatening nationwide strikes if their demands are not granted, the government appointing boards to recommend terms of settlement, and the boards, under threat of the strikes, following a consistent course of making concessions to the Union in each case. In effect that establishes terms of settlement by government decree and is an abandonment of the process of collective bargaining. It is but a short step to a completely government controlled and regimented economy. . . .

Clarence B. Randall, president of Inland, gave so forceful a statement of this issue that it became the focus for the union's reply. Mr. Randall declared:

When the President announced the formation of this board he was in fact announcing an industrial revolution in America. By doing so he has declared himself as favoring a new social order, and one so different from that under which our magnificent production record has been achieved that unless the process is stopped, and stopped at once, there will be no possibility of turning back.

Through this means, whether he knew it or not, he has proclaimed that wages shall be fixed by the government. This step is always the first one taken by those who set out to establish a socialist or corporative state. The fixing of profits comes next, and then when incentive is killed and production falls, the final step of nationalization follows. Europe came close to starvation because of this tragic sequence, and was saved only by the dynamic quality of a free America. Yet here is the same pattern.

Review the sequence of events. Bargaining was undertaken by this union that turned out to be bargaining in name only. Take Inland Steel Company, for example. . . . We were but an insignificant part in the working out of the global strategy by which the establishment of this board was to be forced upon the government. The wage demand which was presented to you gentlemen was never brought to our bargaining table. We hear of it first here. It was pensions the union asked of us. . . .

We made an offer on pensions. We were confident that our employees liked that offer, but the global strategy of the union required that it be rejected and that no single company be permitted to make an agreement. So we find ourselves pleading our cause before strangers, men of standing but men who are strangers to our company and to our employees. . . . Collective bargaining has been destroyed. It has been repealed by the President. And if this union strategy works this time, collective bargaining will never come back. The precedent here attempted, reflecting the similar attempt made in 1946, would commit us to boards and government wage-fixing forever.

And no thoughtful person should be deceived by the naive suggestion that your findings are to be recommendations only. The moment your announcement is made every power of the government will be brought to bear to compel both sides to accept your conclusions. . . .

Mr. Murray speaks with complete authority. His is the single voice for all unions in the steel business. He holds the power to suspend steel production in every steel plant in the country, and suspend it too in plants that use the production of that industry. Through political alliance with the government he possesses the power to induce the President of the United States to take extra-legal action at his request.

. . . I repeat—this is the repeal of collective bargaining—this is government wage-fixing, the inevitable consequence of labor monopoly.

Murray replied with indignation. He declared that "the attack" was "plainly designed to intimidate the board." He denied the charges both of bad faith and of a "political alliance with the White House." He said:

The negotiations failed not because the union didn't want to make an agreement, but rather because the company [Inland], acting in concert with the rest of the industry, was unwilling to offer anything worth while to the union.

He rejected the implication

of a "political alliance" [as] an insult both to the high office and to the person of the President of the United States. . . . My first knowledge of the appointment of this board came in the wire which I received from the President on the same day that similar wires were received by the companies. I did not know the composition of the board until I read of it in the press.

He characterized Randall's reference to the board as "undermining the private enterprise system as sheer and utter nonsense."

The board set forth its findings on this issue as follows:

We think that in many ways fact-finding boards promote and supplement rather than hinder collective bargaining . . .

First, they serve generally to postpone a strike date, and thus they provide a cooling-off period. A "cooling-off period" imposed by injunction has not been found to create the atmosphere for reaching settlement by bargaining; *voluntary* bargaining and *compulsion* are inherently contradictory.

Second, they provide, often for the first time, an opportunity to the parties to hear from each other, in the course of the presentations to the board, a calm, reasoned recital of the merits which are claimed for their respective positions.

Third, for the first time in the process, they provide an opportunity for the public at large to become informed on the issues of the case. Sitting as the eyes and ears of the general public, they are in a position, as impartial observers, to come to informed conclusions on the facts and to make recommendations as to a fair and equitable settlement of the disputes. These recommendations should cover the framework, rather than the details, of a settlement, which should be left to the parties for negotiation. In doing this they advance the collective bargaining process by helping to provide the public with the facts upon which it can base its opinion. . . .

After all voluntary efforts to reach an agreement have failed, including the inability to agree on arbitration, no machinery more effective than fact-finding boards with power to recommend has as yet been suggested.

IX. The Impact of Union Power and Rivalries

The implications of the growing power of unions and the rivalry of union leaders were stressed by steel executives. To quote Voorhees again:

. . . The competitive rivalry between the leaders of nationwide unions in pursuit of an even greater proportion of what there is for all, cannot be forgotten if fairness is to prevail in this case.

Thus the leaders of the United Steelworkers are confronted with a *fait accompli* of the head of the United Mine Workers, who by the exercise of a complete and uncontrolled monopoly power—a concentration of power heretofore unknown in American life—is able to turn on or turn off at will the nation's production of coal, and has succeeded in wringing from the public, in terms of higher coal prices, a series of special benefits and pensions for the members of his union. . . .

I feel certain that the success of the United Mine Workers' leader—and he is merely a symbol of what is happening in other industries—in establishing new labor patterns at the expense of other segments of the public, arouses other union leaders' envy and goads them to seek equal or greater goals. Hence the origin of the pension demand here made upon us. It is a prime instance of the effect of the virus of big unionism. The company, the industry and, therefore too, the public, our employees, our customers, our suppliers and our stockholders are caught, with the government itself in the bitter race for power of giant labor monopolies. . . .

Murray heatedly indicted this charge as "vicious and insulting" not only to himself but "to those who make Mr. Voorhees' steel and to those who mine his coal. . . . What is Mr. Voorhees for and what is he against?" He answered his own question:

He is for munificent pensions for himself and his associates. He is against decent pensions for his employes. He would compel them to retire without pensions. He is for princely wage increases for himself and his fellow executives. . . . By all the rules of reason, if he was entitled to an increase . . . , then the employes of his corporation are entitled at least to some consideration.

X. The Issue on the Scope of the Reopening Clause

From the outset, one of the major differences between the parties lay in whether the issue of pensions was "bargainable" at all in the 1949 negotiations. The companies stood firmly on the contract clause limiting reopening specifically to general wage changes and social insurance benefits. The union justified pension demands (1) on the basis of a liberal interpretation of wages to include various forms of compensation for services rendered, and (2) on the interpretation of NLRB as affirmed by the courts, in the Inland

Steel case, upholding the union's right to bargain on pension plans. The board made the following findings upon this issue:

. . . We have come to the conclusion that so far as the contract itself is concerned, the subject of pensions does not have to be bargained until the termination of the contract in April 1950. . . .

The presence of the definite clause in the reopening provision referring to social insurance, and the absence of any clause referring to pensions is indicative of the intention of the parties in 1948. If, as contended by the union, the phrase "rates of pay" includes pensions, it would, by the same reasoning, also include social insurance. Nevertheless, one was not mentioned and the other was.

The union urges that apart from the provisions of the contract there is a statutory duty on both sides to bargain about pensions. We agree with that contention. . . .

Under the National Labor Relations Act, before the amendments of the Labor-Management Relations Act, 1947 (Taft-Hartley law), management had a continuing duty to bargain with a union on request on any item included in the phrase "rates of pay, wages, hours of employment, or other conditions of employment." This phrase, it is now admittedly the law [under the ruling of the *Inland Steel* case], includes pensions. This duty existed even though there might be in existence a written contract between the parties which specifically covered the item about which the union wished to bargain. . . .

The Labor-Management Relations Act, 1947, changed this rule but only in part. Although section 8 (d) of that act provides for the continuing obligation of both management and labor to bargain, it [excludes from such obligation any "terms and conditions" specifically written into an effective contract]. . . .

The question here is whether the union is asking for a modification of any of the "terms and conditions contained" in the contract, before the time when such terms and conditions can be reopened. There are, of course, many terms and conditions mentioned in these contracts before us. Although all of them could have been reopened for bargaining at any time under the original National Labor Relations Act, under the 1947 amendment none of these expressed terms in the contract can be reopened until April 30, 1950—except that, by actual agreement, one term "rates of pay" may be opened, and another term "social insurance" (not elsewhere expressly contained in the agreement) may also be reopened. As a matter of fact, even if the reopening clause had not mentioned social insurance, it would always have been a matter of statutory bargaining at any time under the statute because it was not mentioned elsewhere in the agreement. For that same reason, the subject of pensions—nowhere mentioned in the agreement—is a matter of bargaining and always was—from the day the contract was first executed in April 1947. . . .

Of course, as under the old law, the obligation to bargain on either side does not mean any obligation to agree.

XI. On the Merits of a Wage Increase

The criteria about which the union's case for a wage increase revolved were broadly three: (1) the steelworkers' right to, and their need for, rate increases; (2) the ability of the industry to pay such increases by the record of profits, prices, productivity, and break-even points; and (3) the beneficial effects of increasing purchasing power upon the national economy.

The industry spokesmen urged, in turn, that (1) the economic conditions of steelworkers showed them well up among the top tenth of American workers in average hourly and weekly earnings, as well as in real income;

(2) ability to *meet* higher labor costs as projected by the union's data on productivity, profits, prices, and break-even points had been overrated; and (3) the wage increase demanded threatened the whole economy with unemployment, inflation, or a dislocating transfer in purchasing power.

The board rejected the union's argument by the following analysis:

. . . There are no mathematical formulae by which to settle the question of whether wage rates or labor costs should be increased at any particular time in a particular industry or particular plant. The steelworkers' present average hourly earnings of about $1.65 compare favorably with all other manufacturing workers. Their average hourly earnings have risen more in cents per hour since 1939 and 1941 than those of manufacturing workers as a whole, and more than those of the durable-goods workers; in very few industries, manufacturing or non-manufacturing, have hourly earnings risen more in cents. . . .

Groups . . . to be compared with the steelworkers are the corporations themselves, the stockholders, and consumers of steel.

This involves the subject of ability to pay increased wage rates as related to profits, dividends, and prices. Taking up the factors to be considered . . . and other relevant considerations, the Board finds:

The union has not . . . succeeded in proving its contention that productivity has risen by 49.5 percent since 1939. . . . Wage rates in a particular industry should not be tied directly to productivity in that industry but rather . . . to the general industrial rise in productivity, and that any excesses of productivity in any one industry over the general average should provide primarily the means of reducing the prices of the products of that industry. . . .

The evidence before us reveals that for our whole national economy output per man-hour increased from 1899 to 1939 at an annual rate of about 2 percent, but that, in the decade which followed, the general rise in productivity was at a lesser rate. Therefore, the steelworkers' rise of 14 percent in real average hourly earnings during this decade is fairly consonant with the apparent rise in labor productivity in the whole economy during the same period and reflects no inequity in that regard.

. . . The union compared the productivity of 1939, a year of low volume, with 1948, a year of practically maximum volume, which is an unsound comparison.

. . . In computing an index of productivity for the steel industry, the union used the assumption that the production mix of the industry after 1945 was substantially the same as during the war years. This assumption is open to very serious question.

. . . Trustworthy productivity studies can be made only if the companies provide full and accurate data upon which such studies can be made. Such data were not offered in evidence.

. . . The companies also made invalid comparisons in their own productivity claims by insisting that an index of money rather than real average hourly earnings was the proper comparison with the productivity index.

. . . There are no inequities of steelworkers at present which require redress through a general wage-rate increase; and the recommendation is that the union withdraw its request for a general wage-rate increase.

. . . However, with increased efficiency and lowered costs resulting from the plant-modernization program, and with no great decrease in the demand for steel, there should be continued and higher profits. If these profits do not result in benefit to the consumer in the form of lower prices, there would be justification for the union to renew its demand for increase of wage rates in order better to participate in the industry's prosperity.

The cost of living has remained stable within the last year; in fact it has slowly declined. The post-war race between rising wage rates and rising costs of living has been called off by the operation of economic forces. Therefore there is no inequity in respect to other income-receiving groups in the general economy.

. . . With respect to . . . the effect of granting the union's demands on the general levels of economic activity in the country as a whole—the Board finds:

. . . there is a probability that a wage-rate increase in steel would be urged as a pattern to be followed in other industries; this in turn might well cause price dislocations, with adverse effects on the general economy and on the steel industry itself. . . .

While there may be conditions in particular industries which require correction through wage rate adjustments, in general it seems desirable at this time to stabilize the level of wage rates. In the steel industry we have not found such conditions or inequities and, for all the reasons stated, do not believe there should be a wage rate adjustment now. General stability is desirable now in order that consumers and dealers may have confidence in the price structure and resume less restricted buying habits.

XII. On the Merits of Insurance and Pension Demands

The positions of the parties upon insurance and pensions were in many ways integrated into the arguments for and against wage increases. The union stressed the need of the steelworkers for such benefits as well as the ability of the industry to provide them. It maintained also that they must be provided by noncontributory systems. The companies on the whole accepted the fundamental desirability of such benefits. They pointed to existing plans, often long established, challenged the union's cost estimates, urged the desirability of employee contributions in the interests of a sound system, and, as already indicated, insisted that, with the single exception of Inland Steel, pensions were not bargainable until the expiration date of the agreements in 1950.

The content of the union's case may be indicated by the following excerpts from Mr. Murray's statement before the board:

Surely, no one questions in this day and time that workers are entitled to a decent standard of living in return for their labor. This must obviously include provision for illness, accident, old age, and death. . . .

By the Social Security Act the Government has made a start, but only a bare start, at providing old age pensions and survivors' insurance. But there can be no serious suggestion that the Social Security Act even begins to make decent provision for old age. The present average benefits for workers currently retiring from the steel industry is about $37 for an individual and less than $41 for a family. . . . The Federal Government makes no provision whatever except in the railroad industry for incomes to persons who are temporarily ill and no provision for any form of medical care to any workers anywhere. . . .

. . . Now . . . the only group life insurance which the industry provides, with few exceptions, is paid for almost entirely by its employees. The industry contributes the administrative cost which is negligible—in the case of U.S. Steel less than ⅙¢ per hour for each employee. Furthermore, under these so-called voluntary plans providing group life insurance, a substantial number of employees do not participate. In the case of U.S. Steel this non-participating group amounts to 20% of all employees.

The Steelworker wants and is entitled to protection and security, paid for by the company . . . without having to exhaust his savings, borrow money or go into debt.

We will no longer tolerate the double standard whereby machines are preferred over men. Every well-operated company sets aside money for depreciation, repair, and replacement of machinery. Only infrequently, however, does it make similar provisions for the care of its employees—human beings. . . .

It is part of the Union's proposals that the cost of pension and social insurance benefits be paid for by the employers. This is just and entirely logical. Any so-called contributory plan disregards the plain fact that the costs of such benefits are a cost of doing business comparable to the cost of maintaining and replacing machinery. Furthermore, a contributory plan would have the effect of cutting the current wages of employees in the industry, which would be just the opposite of what is desirable both from the standpoint of the employees and of the national economy.

The steel companies summarized their counterarguments on insurance as follows:

1. Most steel companies have insurance programs already in effect. Steel companies are willing to discuss insurance programs and to increase their contributions to them.
2. The principle of joint contributions should be accepted, with employer and employee sharing the cost. Joint responsibility preserves the individual's right to spend or save as he sees fit.
3. Union estimates of the cost of benefits demanded are far short of actual cost figures.

The companies' counterarguments on pensions were as follows:

1. The union, by contract in 1948, waived the right to demand bargaining on pensions until 1950. Contract terms now in effect foreclose bargaining on any issues this year except wage rates and "life, accident, health, and medical hospital insurance benefits."
2. Cost of pensions has been underestimated by the union in many companies where, because of age distribution, costs would be substantially higher.
3. The union should agree to joint employee contributions, in accordance with the sound and traditional American principle of self-help.

The board recommended a total package of 10 cents per hour—4 cents toward insurance and 6 cents toward pensions. Excerpts follow:

. . . Social insurance and pensions should be considered a part of normal business costs to take care of temporary and permanent depreciation in the human "machine," in much the same way as provision is made for depreciation and insurance of plant and machinery. . . .

. . . As indicated in the foregoing economic discussion, the net cost of the social insurance and pension plans herein recommended can be absorbed by the companies without unduly narrowing the profit margin of the industry or its ability to hold or even lower its prices.[1]

. . . Although the steel industry has kept pace with other industries in wages and other industrial relations matters, it has lagged behind other leading basic industries in social insurance and pensions.

. . . The fully integrated companies before us now have social insurance and retirement plans for such of their employees as are in their railroad or coal-mining operations, and this further supports the Board's conclusions that the steel workers are now entitled to these types of protection.

---

[1] The board had estimated the net cost of the two programs "based upon the liberal assumption that labor costs average 50 percent of total production costs" as providing "an increase of only 2½ percent of total costs" on annual operations of 2,000 hours per worker.

. . . Social insurance and pension programs with the types of coverage requested by the union in this dispute have become prevalent in American industry and have been inaugurated either by the unilateral action of employers or, to an increasing extent, through collective bargaining.

. . . The concept of providing social insurance and pensions for workers in industry has become an accepted part of modern American thinking. Unless government provides such insurance in adequate amount, industry should step in to fill the gap.

. . . Government (except in four States) has failed to provide social insurance (as defined herein) for industrial workers generally, and has supplied old-age retirement benefits in amounts which are not adequate to provide an American minimum standard of living.

. . . The recent trend in programs resulting from collective bargaining is toward complete financing of the plan by the employer, or toward lowering the employees' cost in existing contributory plans. . . .

It is recommended as fair and equitable under all the circumstances, that a social insurance plan be incorporated into the collective-bargaining agreements of the industry. The details and specific benefits of the plans should be determined through collective bargaining between each company and the union. The plans should be paid for by the employers without contribution by the employees; but should be limited in net cost to a maximum of about $80 per year per employee, or 4 cents per hour, on a basis of a 2,000-hour workyear.

The subject of pensions is not bargainable at this time under the terms of the reopening clause. . . .

However, the subject of pensions is bargainable under the law as interpreted by the National Labor Relations Board as to all the companies. . . .

Such pension plans as are now in effect in the basic steel industry were the result of unilateral action by employers and are generally inadequate. . . .

It is recommended as fair and equitable under all the circumstances that pension plans be established in this industry, with the cost to be borne by the employers without contribution from the employees. . . .

Pensions should be limited in net cost to a maximum of about $120 per employee per year, or 6 cents per hour on a basis of a 2,000-hour workyear. Based on the union's cost estimates, this will provide, when added to average Social Security old-age benefits, about $100 per month on retirement at age 65 of the average employee. . . .

Since the problems involved in a pension program are more complicated than those faced in social insurance programs, and because the costs are greater and the program less susceptible to change from year to year, it is recommended that a joint study in the industry should be made on pensions.

XIII. DEADLOCK FOLLOWING BOARD'S REPORT

The union expressed disappointment over the denial of a wage increase but accepted the findings and demanded that the recommendations become the basis for settlement. The industry crystallized its position by (1) offering 4 cents an hour for social insurance provided employees made an additional contribution; (2) agreeing to a joint study on pensions, to be concluded March 1, 1950, but without any commitment on the 6-cent figure; and (3) opposing noncontributory pensions. On September 14, Fairless stated:

The most important issue raised by the report of the Presidential steel board is whether such a board, possessing no statutory authority, power or responsibility, is to be permitted by public opinion or otherwise to impose upon American industry for all time a non-contributory system of social security, with the entire cost borne by the employer.

Murray characterized this statement as "a flat rejection by the United States Steel Corporation of the recommendations of the steel industry board," which the union in contrast "has accepted . . . as a basis on which to conclude a prompt settlement . . . in recognition of the public interest in this dispute and in the hope of averting a steel strike." Murray continued:

You presume to dictate . . . that any plan of social insurance and pensions shall be bargained upon only on the basis of a contributory program.

You assert that this is a matter of fundamental principle, notwithstanding that you, Mr. Fairless, and other executives in your corporation and in the industry will enjoy substantial pensions upon retirement based upon noncontributory programs created by the industry for the benefit of its executives rather than its workers.

The union and the public will not and do not accept any such unfair dictates on your part.

The union still hopes that a strike in the basic steel industry can be averted. . . . We are ready and willing to resume collective bargaining . . . on the basis of the board's recommendations.

Fairless, in his turn, rejected the union's interpretation of further mutual responsibility, terming it "nothing more than repetition of your dictatorial message that we must accept" the board's recommendations before the union would resume negotiations. He went on:

I told you yesterday and I now confirm that we decline to accept your ultimatum which is both unfair and contrary to the assurance given us in advance by the President of the United States that the recommendations of the board would not be binding upon either party. . . .

Twice before this week, I have notified you, and I again repeat, that we are ready promptly to resume collective bargaining conferences with your union. . . .

The deadline for your threatened strike on Sept. 25, 1949, is less than ten days away. Time is therefore of the essence, and I ask that you now tell us definitely when your union will meet with us in such a resumption of collective bargaining.

I repeat that the responsibility is yours; not ours.

Both Truman and Ching deplored this "debate by telegraph" and the sparring about "the meaning of words." They pressed upon the parties a resumption of actual negotiations. Truman requested another strike postponement from September 25 to October 1, the third postponement since the dispute began. When the parties assented, last-ditch negotiations began on September 23. Federal conciliators participated; and the company modified its stand by agreeing on September 27 to accept the "10-cent package" as the corporation's contribution but stood firm on the principle of employee contributions. The union persisted in demanding acceptance of the board's recommendations as a whole, including the noncontributory basis.

The final deadlock thus emerged. Protesting the union's use of the recommendations of the board as "equivalent to those of a compulsory arbitration tribunal," U.S. Steel announced its refusal "to bow to such an ultimatum." The strike call thereupon became effective; on the eve of the strike, the union declared its freedom to reinstate its original demand for "a 30-cent package," including a 12½-cent hourly wage increase.

XIV. The Strike

Some half million employees of 37 basic steel companies laid down tools on October 1. The strike was peaceful. The plants were closed down in good shape. Maintenance men were provided by the union as needed. Picketing was quiet and orderly, with management supplying coffee frequently to the pickets and, in one large plant, setting up radios over which pickets could listen to the World Series.

Nonetheless, the pinch was gradually tightening on the whole economy, a pinch accentuated by the concurrent coal strike. Steel was distributed on an allocation basis; workers in automobile and other manufacturing plants were furloughed as layoffs spread and accelerated; railroads curtailed train service. As the strike progressed, relief rolls rose as first the unskilled workers and then others had to seek aid. Most investigators pictured the strikers as neither thoroughly conversant with the subtleties of the narrow issue behind their walkout nor emotionally heated by the controversy. But they were generally determined to stand by their union and particularly their president, Philip Murray. During October, Murray made a tour of the steel centers to explain the union's position in the deadlock. Ching and his associates persisted in their mediation efforts, concentrating mainly upon Bethlehem and U.S. Steel.

XV. The Contemporaneous Strike in Coal

On September 16, about one week after the report of the Steel board was made public, benefit payments—pensions, disability allowances, death benefits, aid to widows and orphans, medical care—had been suspended from the United Mine Workers' Welfare and Retirement Fund. Established in 1946, this fund had been financed in 1949 by a royalty of 20 cents on every ton mined. It had been rumored for some weeks that the miners' welfare fund had been operating on a hand-to-mouth basis, with its reserves reduced to $14 million. Desultory negotiations had been going on between Lewis and the operators for revision of the contract that had expired on June 30. Although Lewis had not submitted formal demands, he was thought to be seeking an increase in welfare royalties to 30 cents a ton, higher wages, a shorter work week, and controlled bituminous production on the model of the anthracite plan. Early in July, Lewis had ordered the miners to work on a three-day-week schedule. Western, Appalachian, and Southern operators differed in policy; and on July 1, the Southern sector suspended royalty payments on the ground that the contract had expired. The suspension of benefit payments followed the same week; and on September 19, the miners quit work.

On October 14, Lewis addressed a letter to William Green, suggesting that nine of AFL's large affiliates join the United Mine Workers in raising each $250,000 a week for assistance to the striking steelworkers to sustain them "in the monumental conflict which is now joined . . ." so that their fight could become "the uncompromising fight of all American Labor." Green's reply raised questions he deemed prerequisite to any further action:

Has Mr. Murray requested the amount of financial assistance referred to in your proposal? . . . Is your proposal based upon a request you received from Mr. Murray for financial assistance?

Murray, in turn, suggested that labor generally furnish assistance to both the striking miners and steelworkers.

XVI. THE CIO CONVENTION AND THE LEFT-WING SHOWDOWN

During this same period also, negotiations had been in progress between Ford and the UAW. On September 29, on the eve of the steel strike, these negotiators announced their establishment of noncontributory insurance and retirement benefits with a $100-a-month retirement allowance including Social Security benefits.[1]

The preparatory sessions of the CIO executive board for the Eleventh Annual Convention, scheduled to meet in Cleveland from October 31 to November 5, opened in that city on October 25. The board unanimously pledged itself to raise a multi-million-dollar fund to aid the steel strikers.

A showdown with eleven left-wing unions that had been developing for some time came to a head in the convention. Murray declared in his keynote address that the Communists were excoriating him because the Steelworkers union had accepted the recommendations of the Board. He described how the Communist press as well as the Moscow radio was denouncing him as "a traitor" to the workers. The convention voted to bar from the executive board Communist Party members, fascists, and those pursuing the policies of any totalitarian organization. The United Electrical, Radio & Machine Workers of America, the third largest union in the CIO, was expelled, as was the United Farm Equipment & Metal Workers of America. A new charter was granted to right-wing leaders in the UE; and immediately throughout the centers manufacturing electrical equipment, the battle began for rank-and-file membership. CIO vice presidents who were leaders of the left-wing unions were barred from candidacy for re-election. Three committees of three board members each were established to hold hearings on the remaining nine left-wing unions; and it was clear by the time the convention ended that they, too, faced expulsion.

XVII. THE SETTLEMENT

In the closing days of the convention, rumors spread that a break in the strike was imminent. At convention headquarters, Murray informed the press in the morning of October 31 that he would have an announcement of great importance for them at 4 P.M. While the reporters kept wires open to flash the news to their papers, the scheduled conference was twice post-

---

[1] See case, Ford Motor Company: Negotiating the 1949 Agreement, p. 402.

poned. Shortly before 8 P.M., Joseph M. Larkin, vice president of industrial relations of Bethlehem Steel, and Murray entered the ballroom of the Hotel Statler "arm in arm . . . the faces of both men . . . flushed" to make the announcement that they had just signed an agreement which ended the strike in the Bethlehem plants.

Bethlehem, Larkin explained, had a 26-year-old noncontributory pension plan. This would be continued "with amendments," subject to stockholders' approval, the principal one of which would increase the present minimum $50 pension to $100 a month for employees of 25 or more years of service at age 65 years or over. The established social insurance program in the company had been noncontributory; the new agreement provided, Larkin declared, a "contributory social program" for death, sickness and accident, and hospitalization benefits. Upon concluding his statement, Larkin left the conference.

Murray thereupon entered upon a lengthier discussion. For the first time, he declared, a company other than U.S. Steel has "taken on itself the responsibility of leadership in setting a pattern for the industry." He emphasized that the Bethlehem agreement had been reached by direct negotiations, and hailed the pension plan as "the most outstanding achievement of its kind attained by any union through collective bargaining in this or any other country." The union gained in the insurance plan even though it agreed to accept a contributory system. Bethlehem employees, instead of paying the full premium as hitherto, would now underwrite one-half of a total cost of 5 cents a man-hour for a "vastly expanded" program. The program, it was hoped, would go into effect on January 1, but in any event, not later than next March 1. The plan would remain unaltered for five years; the contract as a whole would be renewed for two years with a reopening clause for wages in 1950.

The log jam was broken. Jones & Laughlin signed next, on November 8, and then Republic Steel and Youngstown Sheet and Tube. When, on November 11, agreement was concluded with U.S. Steel, the steel strike of 1949 was virtually over. With some minor differences to meet particular situations, the settlements followed the "Bethlehem pattern."

DISCUSSION QUESTIONS

1. Evaluate the strategy and tactics of (*a*) the union, and (*b*) the industry.

2. Evaluate the positions of the union and of management on the major issues: (*a*) industry-wide bargaining; (*b*) pattern bargaining; (*c*) government intervention; (*d*) scope of reopening clauses; (*e*) wages; (*f*) social insurance; (*g*) pensions.

3. Interpret the Bethlehem settlement in terms of the past history of the steel industry.

4. What kind of union-management structure was developing in steel? Explain in detail.

THE STEEL INDUSTRY

THE 1952 NEGOTIATIONS

I. BACKGROUND

In the fall of 1950, a rapid increase in the cost of living and the fear of a wage freeze consequent upon Korean hostilities produced a wave of "voluntary" wage increases. Although the wage clause was not reopenable until December 1, 1950, Murray requested early negotiation citing as reasons "the need of our people," the expected manpower shortage, and the need to produce steel at the highest possible level. Meetings with United States Steel Company began on October 16, 1950, and with the other major steel producers at about the same time. As a result of these negotiations, wages were increased as of December 1 an average of 16 cents an hour; southern wage differentials were reduced by 4½ cents to a remaining 10-cent differential; and wages for iron ore miners were increased an average of 21 cents! The contracts ran to midnight, December 31, 1951.

The union's wage policy committee hailed Murray's leadership "under which wages and working conditions of steelworkers have advanced to the point where steelworkers now stand in the forefront of American industrial workers." Inclusive of vacations and overtime, Murray estimated the total hourly wage increase to be over 18 cents, while Fairless estimated it to be 20 cents. Simultaneously, U.S. Steel announced price increases averaging 5½%, or $5.50 a ton.

By January 1951, Charles E. Wilson, Defense Mobilization director, convinced that voluntary controls were too limited to meet rapidly advancing prices and wages, advocated immediate imposition of wage and price controls. On January 25, Eric Johnston, Economic Stabilization director, pursuant to policies laid down by President Truman, delegated appropriate power to two newly created agencies, the Wage Stabilization Board and the Office of Price Stabilization. The WSB consisted of 9 members, 3 each from industry, labor, and the public. However, on March 16, when the WSB issued Regulation 6, the labor members resigned in a body. This regulation allowed wage increases, including fringe benefits, only up to 10% above rates in effect on January 15, 1950. The labor members had asked for 12%. Accordingly, the WSB was reconstituted on April 21, again tripartite but with 18 members, all to be appointed by the President. It was directed to administer wage stabilization in such a way as to promote collective bargaining. In addition, it was given jurisdiction over any dispute that was not resolved and that threatened an interruption of work affecting national defense under either of two circumstances: (1) if the parties jointly agreed to submit such dispute and the board agreed to accept such jurisdiction, or (2) if the President referred the dispute to the board. In the latter case, the board was to investigate and report directly to the President with recommendations. No action was to be taken incompatible with the Taft-Hartley Act, and recommendations were to be binding only if so agreed by the parties when they voluntarily submitted a dispute.

II. THE 1952 NEGOTIATIONS

With the industry operating at 104% capacity, contract negotiations opened on November 27, 1951. The union submitted 22 demands, the chief ones being: a wage increase averaging 18½ cents; elimination of the geographic differential; an increase in shift differentials; time and a half for Saturday and double time for Sunday; 8 paid holidays, with double time if worked; a vacation of 3 weeks after 15 years; improvement in job eligibility and scheduling; a guaranteed annual wage to employees with 3 or more years' service; a full union shop and checkoff; and a number of substantial modifications in provisions governing seniority, local practices, grievance machinery, and pension and social insurance.

The companies submitted counterproposals. Management asked for the right to "establish, change, or terminate jobs, to arrange and rearrange the duties . . . and to assign the work the company requires to be performed." In addition, U.S. Steel proposed that incentive rates be established by management on the basis of a centralized manual of engineering.

Murray declared that the companies' proposals would turn the clock back to the 19th century and called a special meeting of the union's executive board and the wage policy committee on December 17. At this meeting, the union reported that the steel companies had refused to bargain genuinely on the union's demands. Strike action was recommended, unless contracts were negotiated by midnight December 31. A special convention of the Steelworkers was called for January 3.

Beginning December 20, Cyrus Ching, director of the Federal Mediation and Conciliation Service, met with the parties. The meetings were terminated because, according to the union, the companies would not make counterproposals on the union's demands. Industry representatives, for their part, stated that many of the union demands had not yet been fully clarified or explored. However, on the 21st, Fairless made public a statement that the companies would forego a price increase if the union would forego a wage increase. According to the union, this "offer" was not made directly to it.

President Truman, in certifying the dispute to the WSB on December 22, appealed to the union to remain at work pending completion of the hearings and rejected the companies' request for advance assurances on price increases. The union's executive board and the wage policy committee, meeting on December 27, instructed the membership to remain at work under the terms of the contract, pending action by the convention on January 3. The convention voted almost unanimously to defer strike action until 45 days from the day the hearings got under way.

On January 7, company and union representatives met with WSB officials to set up procedures for the formal hearings to open on January 10 before a six-member special panel. The hearings, exhaustive in nature, took over a month to complete. While the panel was preparing its report, the wage policy committee on February 21 adopted a resolution postponing the strike to March 23—and at the same time castigating the "filibustering" of the industry and its "twisted reasoning" with regard to specific union demands and demanding that settlement be retroactive to January 1. On March 13, the panel submitted to the WSB its 66-page report summarizing the proposals with the arguments and counterarguments of both parties with respect to 23 issues.[1]

Although there was nothing to prohibit further direct negotiation, both sides refused to bargain with each other either by themselves or through the board members. Having been informed by defense officials that a steel strike would imperil the defense program, the public members took the initiative. They met separately with employer members and union members, respectively, to see whether in the event of the impossibility of a unanimous recommendation a majority decision could be arrived at. On March 18, the employer members of the board suggested a 13.7-cent package of 9 cents per hour and fringe benefits. It proved too low for union acceptance. The following day, Nathan P. Feinsinger, the board chairman, proposed to the employer members a 17.6-cent package of 12½ cents plus fringe benefits and a one-year contract. It proved too high for industry acceptance. Then he sought out the labor members; and, after separate and joint conferences of the three groups throughout the night and the afternoon of the 20th, Feinsinger presented his recommendation to the full board.

They were approved at once by the public and the labor members. The industry members dissented. The report was submitted to President Truman late in the evening of March 20.[2] The chief recommendations were: An 18 months' agreement to June 30, 1953, providing for an increase in rates of 12½ cents per hour effective as of the expiration of the contract or the appropriate reopening date for the particular company, a further increase of 2½ cents per hour effective six months thereafter, and an additional increase of 2½ cents effective six months after that; reduction of the present 10-cent-per-hour geographical differential to 5 cents; new shift differentials of 6 cents per hour for the 2d shift and 9 cents per hour for the 3d shift; double hourly rates or average hourly earnings for 6 named holidays worked and 8 hours' pay for the same holidays not worked; three weeks' vacation with pay after 15 years; effective January 1, 1953, time and one-quarter for all hours of work on Sundays, as such; joint consideration during the period of the next contract of the union request for guaranteed annual wages with a view to

---

[1] U.S. Wage Stabilization Board, Special Steel Panel Report, *In the Matter of United Steelworkers of America–CIO and Various Steel and Iron Companies, D-18-C*, Washington, March 13, 1952.

[2] U.S. Wage Stabilization Board, *Report and Recommendations of the Wage Stabilization Board in the Matter of United Steelworkers of America–CIO and Various Steel and Iron Ore Companies, Case No. D-18-C*, Washington, March 20, 1952.

reaching mutual understanding by the time of the next negotiation; agreement on penalty compensation for sporadic rescheduling in violation of contractual provisions and for sporadic change in an employee's starting and quitting time; a union shop provision, the exact form and condition thereof to be determined by the parties in their forthcoming negotiations; submission by the companies of adequate and accurate seniority lists; and remission of the incentive pay issue back to the parties for negotiation.

Proposals on the following were withdrawn: technological demotions; reporting allowance; contracting out; local working conditions; management rights; and job structure.

Spokesmen for the industry immediately denounced the recommendation which would cost 29.8 cents an hour, or over $1 billion a year directly, and would require a price increase of $6 a ton directly and another $6 indirectly through anticipated advances in prices for purchased materials and services. The companies declared at the same time that each would negotiate individually with the union. The union's wage policy committee voted to accept the recommendation, to renew negotiations, and to heed the WSB's request to give the companies 96 hours' notice of intention to strike if no agreement were reached by April 4. On March 21, the six largest companies met with the union in New York City. The meeting was fruitless.

Wilson's reaction to the wage package was pronounced. He thought it was too high. After numerous meetings with all key people, he finally resigned on March 30 saying, in part, "I simply do not believe . . . recommendations and the government's [price policy] meet the principles of equity. . . . I cannot accept public responsibility for national stabilization action which I cannot control."

The major companies and the union resumed sessions in New York on April 3. The companies offered a package of 14.4 cents—a 9-cent wage increase retroactive to March 1, plus 5.4 cents for fringe benefits, as in the WSB's recommendations except for Sunday overtime. Wages would be further increased 2½ cents on July 1 and 2½ cents on January 1, 1953. The union shop was not offered. The contract was to terminate April 1, 1953. Murray insisted that the union shop was a *must* and that both sides should, in the national interest, go along with the complete WSB recommendations. That night, the union sent out strike notices. Attempted mediation by Mr. Feinsinger failed on the following day. The union continuing its efforts to reach contracts with the smaller companies signed on April 6 agreements with four companies employing together about 11,000 workers.

Fairless in a statement over the air on April 6 asserted that the stockholders were the only group that had made any financial sacrifice since the beginning of the Korean war. Wages, payments to suppliers, and taxes had all risen sharply, but profits had gone down 15% in 1951 and were still dropping in spite of increased production. He said that seizure of the industry would "gravely impair, and perhaps destroy, the ability of industry to expand steel production. Ultimately such a course must lead inevitably to the nationalization, not only of the steel industry, but of every other

American industry as well." He declared that the companies had demonstrated the sincerity of their efforts to head off a strike by their April 3 offer of a 14.4-cent wage package but that the union had demanded the entire WSB package, which had "shocked the entire nation" because it exceeded any increase the union had ever won even when no wage and price controls were in effect. He likened a union shop requirement to the old "yellow dog" contract and said, "If the day ever comes when a man in order to earn his living must join one particular party or one favored union, then we may as well join forces with Russia." He emphasized that inflation should be checked and concluded, "There is no time for stubborn uncompromising attitudes, when we are still fighting in Korea and the free world needs our strength. So I appeal to every one of you tonight—to Philip Murray, to company workers in the mills and to colleagues in the industry—to help us compromise our differences in the light of reason and with fair consideration for the welfare of all Americans in every walk of life."

Murray replied in a radio address the next evening. Excerpts follow:

.　.　.　.　.

. . . I am fully aware of the serious consequences of any stoppage of steel production. . . .

Yet, on Wednesday, a strike in steel will begin.

Why?

Simply and plainly because steel management wants a strike. They have openly refused to comply with the government's recommendations for a settlement in our dispute. . . . They have sought to use the present crisis as a bludgeon to wreck our stabilization program and to extort inflationary price increases from the government.

.　.　.　.　.

The facts in this dispute are not complex. . . .

.　.　.　.　.

Fact Number One is this: The Union has voluntarily postponed this strike four times since our contracts terminated on January 1. . . .

.　.　.　.　.

Fact Number Two is this: The Wage Stabilization Board studied the facts of our dispute for almost three months before it offered recommendations for settlement. We honestly believe that those recommendations were too low . . . the Wage Board recommended a wage increase smaller than necessary to meet the rise in the cost of living. . . .

.　.　.　.　.

Fact Number Three—the most important fact for you, the general public—is this: The wage increases recommended by the Wage Board, and agreed to by the union, are not inflationary. . . .

.　.　.　.　.

. . . The industry knows—and has admitted—that steelworkers are entitled to a wage increase to catch up with the rise in the cost of living.

.　.　.　.　.

. . . Mr. Fairless glossed over the fact that the United States Steel Corporation, like every other major steel producer, has voluntarily signed scores of union-shop agreements with other unions . . . for example, union-shop contracts on its company-owned railroads and company-owned steamship lines.

. . . . .

The steel industry could absorb the proposed wage increases in steel without raising prices a single solitary penny a ton—and still make a fair and equitable profit return to the stockholders. Why is there a dispute today? Because the steel industry has taken the position that its tremendous profits are untouchable and preordained. . . .

. . . . .

In 1951, the steelworkers received no increase. But in that year Mr. Benjamin Fairless, President of U.S. Steel, received a pay increase of $47,000. He now receives $261,000 a year with which to fight the wolf from the door of his estate.

. . . . .

Last night Mr. Fairless asked me a question over the radio. I have answered it in this speech. Now I would like to ask him a question:

Mr. Fairless, how do you justify the double-standard practices by your company—a standard under which you and your fellow executives take substantial wage increases for yourselves but deny simple cost-of-living wage adjustments for your employees?

. . . . .

On April 8, with a strike looming at midnight, Feinsinger was in repeated contact with representatives of the industry and the union. Stephens and other spokesmen for the companies indicated a readiness to raise their wage offer to an immediate 12½ cents plus 5.4 cents for fringe benefits, but not to include Sunday premium pay or the further increases suggested on April 3 for July and January. At 4 o'clock Stephens talked with Murray. Neither would disclose the conversations, but at the end Murray said, "The strike order stands."

III. The Seizure

On April 8, an hour and a half before the midnight strike deadline, President Truman made a television address in which he announced that in view of the Korean and the defense situation he had decided upon "two actions tonight": (1) "the Secretary of Commerce to take possession of the steel mills, and to keep them operating"; (2) "the acting director of defense mobilization to get the representatives of the steel companies and the steelworkers down here to Washington at the earliest possible date in a renewed effort to get them to settle their dispute." The President blamed the companies for the shutdown.

The Secretary of Commerce, Charles Sawyer, wired the companies that he was taking possession and ordered them to perform their "usual functions and duties." Immediately, Murray called off the strike. Attorneys for the companies filed suit in the U.S. District Court in Washington challenging the legality of seizure.

The next morning, Judge Alexander Holtzoff, of the U.S. District Court in Washington, denied the request for a restraining order, giving as his view, "It is very doubtful, to say the least, whether a Federal Court would have the authority to issue an injunction against the President of the United States."

That night, April 9, Clarence B. Randall, president of Inland Steel Company, pointed out before a nationwide radio television audience that Mr. Truman had ignored the biggest obstacle, the union's insistence on a union shop; that the WSB had operated as a political agency; that Mr. Truman in seizing the industry had discharged a political debt to the CIO; and that Murray had threatened the safety of our men in Korea.

On April 10, John R. Steelman, labor advisor to the President and acting director of mobilization, brought the companies and the union together in Washington for further bargaining. However, meetings collapsed the next day when the wage policy committee passed a resolution warning that a settlement based on WSB recommendations was "overdue" and that the steelworkers' patience was "not inexhaustible." The companies immediately appealed to the U.S. District Court in Washington, with Judge David A. Pine presiding, for an injunction to force the President to release the steel properties and for a ruling on the legality of seizure. On Friday, the 18th, Secretary Sawyer announced for the President that, if no agreement was reached by the 21st or 22d, the government as operator would grant the recommended wage increase. On the 21st, Feinsinger made a fruitless trip to New York in an effort to effect a settlement. On the 23d, the OPS authorized a $3 price increase, and Sawyer announced he was preparing wage and price increases to go into effect probably the following week. The companies stated their objections in full page advertisements and amended their court petition to request an injunction forbidding any change in wages or working conditions.

On April 21, the Senate voted 44 to 31 to bar the use of any current appropriations to enforce seizure. The Senate and the House Banking Committee began re-examination of powers granted the President in the Defense Production Act. Some senators proposed impeachment of the President. The House voted overwhelmingly that its Committee on Education and Labor make a thorough investigation of the WSB's handling of industrial disputes. And the Senate Labor Committee also undertook hearings on the steel dispute.

On the afternoon of April 29, Judge Pine ruled that there was "utter and complete lack of authoritative support" either in the Constitution or in acts of Congress for the government's position; that the damage to the steel companies would be "irreparable"; and that there was no proof that procedures under the Taft-Hartley Act would not be effective if tried or that, if these failed, Congress would neglect to protect the nation.

Within an hour, steelworkers were walking out on orders from Murray. That evening the White House announced that it would seek a stay of Judge Pine's order and then press the case to the Supreme Court.

The next day, after the government pleaded the necessity of seizure "to keep the mills operating" and the companies argued that the union was striking "against Judge Pine's decision," the U.S. Court of Appeals in a 5 to 4 decision gave the government until 4:30 P.M., May 2, to appeal to the

Supreme Court and gave the government control of the mills until the Supreme Court rendered a decision. The following day, May 1, the Court of Appeals refused, 5 to 4, an industry request to attach a wage freeze to its order. The President asked Murray to call off the strike and requested him (Murray) and the presidents of the six largest companies to be at the White House at 10 A.M. on Saturday, May 3. He opened the meeting with the statement that unless an agreement was reached within 48 hours the government was prepared to order changes in the terms and conditions of employment. As for price relief, the industry would receive whatever it was entitled to under the law. He concluded, "I sent for you for action, and, gentlemen, I want it."

Seven hours later, while the corporation presidents and Murray were still negotiating with the assistance of Steelman, the Supreme Court announced that it would review Judge Pine's decision. It set May 12 for arguments and forbade the government to change wage and working conditions pending its decision. Negotiations at the White House continued until midnight and from 10 to 4 on Sunday, when Steelman announced, "There are a number of issues on which the parties are so far apart that no agreement can be reached at this time." Arthur B. Homer, president of Bethlehem Steel, presented the industry's view that the union's insistence on the entire WSB recommendation, knowing that the union shop was a proposal which the industry could not accept, was the equivalent of a refusal to negotiate. According to Murray, the companies merely repeated their inadequate offers of more than three weeks ago and expressly conditioned them upon the government's approval of a price increase. Thus, Murray stated, the companies were on a strike against collective bargaining. Nevertheless the back-to-work order would not be changed since the union "had no intention of calling a strike against the government."

On June 2, the Supreme Court, in a 6 to 3 decision, found that the President did not have the power to seize the industry.[1] The President ordered the steel properties returned to the companies.

IV. The Strike

Thirty-five minutes after the Supreme Court had rendered its decision, Murray issued a cease-work order and simultaneously called on the various steel companies to negotiate toward agreement on the WSB recommendations. The National Production Authority immediately restricted shipments to ensure defense needs and within a week gave top priority in the nonstruck plants to defense orders. Some small steel companies immediately heeded Murray's request to negotiate; and within three days, the back-to-work order was given to 4,500 employees of the Detroit Steel Corporation when it agreed to a contract on WSB terms.

The major steel producers and the union were asked by Steelman to

[1] 72 Sup. Ct. 863.

send three-man teams to the White House to meet with him. Five days of earnest negotiation began on Thursday, June 5. Industry negotiators were Stephens of U.S. Steel, Benjamin Moreell of Jones & Laughlin, and Charles E. White of Republic. On the fourth day, tentative agreement was reportedly reached on many items, and a recess was called until the next afternoon, June 9. Four hours of negotiation on June 9 brought forth what Stephens termed the industry's "final offer." The chief items were:

1. A general increase in wage rates averaging 16 cents an hour.

2. Six paid holidays with double time for holidays worked.

3. Shift differentials increased to 6 cents per hour for 2d shift and 9 cents per hour for 3d shift.

4. Three weeks' vacation after 15 years of service.

5. Southern differential decreased by 5 cents an hour.

6. Union security provisions of present agreements, which provide for freedom of choice of individual employees to join or refrain from joining the union, not to be changed.

This offer was rejected by the union. Stephens attributed the failure to the union's insistence on "compulsory unionism." Murray attributed it to industry's refusals to grant time and a quarter for Sunday work, to provide genuine union security, to join in study of a guaranteed annual wage, and to its insistence on the union's accepting the companies' unilateral views on many noneconomic aspects.

On June 10, President Truman addressed a joint session of Congress and, stressing the urgency of early resumption of steel production, proposed two alternatives: either that Congress direct him immediately to use the injunction provisions in the Taft-Hartley Act or that it enact new legislation authorizing him to seize the mills. He recommended an act under which the company would face the possibility of receiving less than its usual profits and the workers less wages than those to which they felt entitled. Thus production would be assured, but both parties would have incentive to reach agreement through collective bargaining. Several bills were proposed in both houses; and within hours after the President spoke, the Senate approved the Byrd amendment to its current bill extending the Defense Production Act. This "requested" the President to issue an injunction. The House adopted a similar measure. Mr. Truman refused to heed the Congressional request that he seek an injunction and started looking into the Selective Service Act which authorized under certain circumstances seizure of specific plants vital for defense production. It was quite possible, he said, that the steelworkers might ignore a back-to-work order as the miners had in 1950.

On June 18, the House Labor Committee published its report on the WSB. The majority found that the WSB failed in its union shop recommendation to respect national labor policy as expressed in the Taft-Hartley Act and that the regulations of WSB had been highly unstabilizing and inflationary. The minority found that the WSB had, with the exception of the steel case, done a creditable job and that the union shop recommendation did not conflict with Taft-Hartley but represented, at the most, poor judgment.

On June 20, a full page advertisement by the steel companies featured the June 9 offer and charged that the real reason for continuance of the strike was the union's insistence on compulsory unionism. On the same day, representatives of the major producers and the union met again briefly and unsuccessfully in New York. Unauthorized reports indicated that the primary purpose of the meeting was to plan production of "shooting steel." Later, rumors revealed that discussions also centered on an understanding between Bethlehem and the union which had been reached the previous week on wages and the union shop.

The so-called Bethlehem formula was incorporated on June 27 in an interim agreement between the Steelworkers and Pittsburgh Steel, the first break in the industry front. The union security clause featured: (1) maintenance of membership for present members; (2) present nonmembers to join or not as they wished; and (3) new employees to execute request for membership and authorization for checkoff of dues, assessments, and initiation fees—the request to become effective 30 days after employment unless the employee notified the company and the union to the contrary between the 20th and 30th day of employment. Other benefits included: a basic 12½-cent wage increase, retroactive to April 1, and subject to adjustment in accordance with the "Big Steel" pattern when set; 6 paid holidays, with double pay if worked; 6-cent and 9-cent shift differentials; and 3 weeks' vacation after 15 years' service.

On June 30, after four full weeks of the strike had caused innumerable shutdowns and unemployment to hundreds of thousands of workers in industry generally, President Truman signed the amended Defense Production Act only hours before the old one was due to expire. Wage and price controls were extended to April 30, 1953; but the WSB was stripped of its disputes-settlement function, and appointment of all its members was subject to ratification by Congress. Allocation of scarce materials could continue till June 30, 1953. Also included was the Byrd amendment requesting use of the injunction compelling the Steelworkers to call off the strike under the Taft-Hartley provisions.

By July, the union filed formal charges under the Taft-Hartley Act against U.S. Steel, Bethlehem, Jones & Laughlin, Republic, Youngstown, and Inland Steel. It alleged a conspiracy to prevent any one of the six or any other smaller companies from making a separate settlement. The union also formally requested Attorney General James P. McGranery to take antitrust action against the six major companies. President Truman refused to invoke the Taft-Hartley Act against the union because the Steelworkers had postponed the strike already for 99 days and the companies were engaged in "a conspiracy against the public interest."

Negotiations opened again in Pittsburgh on Thursday, July 10, and continued for four consecutive days. Both sides avoided the press. Negotiations seemed to be centered on the union security clause. Three steel executives left the following day (Friday) for Washington to clarify the price situation. On Saturday, Steelman adjusted an earlier offer of $4.50 by allowing an additional price increase of 70 cents per ton. When the Bethlehem representatives met that same evening with the union, it soon became clear that there had not been a common understanding. The union objected strenuously to details regarding permissible withdrawal of application for union membership by new employees and to an escape period at the expiration of the contract. Negotiations broke off Sunday morning. Murray called for a meeting of the wage policy committee on July 21.

The two parties met again briefly on July 20 at Steelman's request, and he remained in telephonic communication with them far into the night. On July 21, with the temperature at 102 degrees, the wage policy committee again rejected the latest industry proposals on the union shop formula relayed by Murray. But for the first time in history industry representatives took up the routine invitation to attend the afternoon meeting to place their case before the delegates. When the startled workers saw Stephens, Moreell, John M. Larkin, vice president of Bethlehem, and John H. Mors, Bethlehem's counsel, walk in, they burst into applause and cheers. A smiling Murray shook hands with each of the quartet as they peeled off their jackets and sat down on the platform. The union president told the committee he was delighted that the company representatives had come to present their side of the prolonged dispute. He assured all four that there would be "no inhibitions and no restrictions" on what they could say and he called upon the unionists to listen to them with "utmost courtesy."

Before Murray introduced Stephens as the first spokesman, he stressed the three points he regarded as major obstacles to ending the strike: (1) refusal of the same type of union shop already granted coal miners, railroad workers, seamen, and others; (2) insistence on contract changes that would give management increased authority over wage rates and work crews; (3) refusal to bring wages in ore mines up to steel mill levels.

Stephens pushed his tie into his shirt and told the committee that he would not say anything that would add to the heat in the sweltering meeting room. He got applause when he said that any comfort Stalin might derive from the shutdown of the steel mills would be lessened by the knowledge that in America free men were still able to argue out their differences face to face and try to bring their views into accord. He read the offer the companies put before union officials the previous day. The union shop for coal miners, he said, had been forced upon the steel companies by an arbitration award on the day the Japanese struck at Pearl Harbor. Other union shop contracts arose from the desire to follow the prevailing practice in the industries in which steel was a minor factor.

Moreell said his experience as wartime chief of the Seabees had convinced him that it was better to rely on volunteers than on people who had to enroll because they were forced to do so. He had so much confidence in the worth and stability of the steelworkers that it "mystified" him to find the union putting so much stress on forcing workers to join, instead of depending on their signing up voluntarily.

Larkin accepted the cheers that greeted his introduction as proof that he had been right in telling Mr. Murray he had won a "hell of a victory" in the last offer. He said both sides had made "many, many concessions" and that only one point—the 15-day escape clause—remained in conflict. He promised that Bethlehem would go into immediate session with the union to clear away any unresolved issues once the basic pact had been initialed. "We've had splendid relations with your union in the past and we're anxious to get back on the track and renew those relations," he concluded, sitting down amid thunderous applause.

After they had heard the company presentations, Murray asked whether they wanted to alter the resolution calling for the full WSB proposals; the delegates shouted back, "No, hell, no."

V. The Settlement

On the morning of July 24, President Truman talked to Fairless and Murray for 10 minutes and told them that they must end the steel tie-up in 24 hours "or else," which was reported to mean that he would force them into arbitration with both sides bound by the decision. The two went into direct negotiation, with Steelman looking in occasionally. At 11:30, Fairless smilingly read a joint statement that they planned to confer with their committees and meet again at 2:30. Then he gave Murray a ride to the CIO office. When they returned they reported that they had spent part of the recess in joint conference. An hour later, they sent for key assistants on both sides. By the time they arrived, the agreement was virtually ready. While this document was being initialed, Steelman put his signature on an order for an increase of $5.20 per ton. At 4:55, the President called reporters to announce that agreement had been reached.

On the same day, Fairless and Murray agreed to an understanding on the ore dispute and planned a joint speaking tour of the steel plants to afford workers and supervisors a better understanding of one another's problems. As an initial step, Murray invited Fairless to address the coming meeting of the wage policy committee called to ratify the terms of settlement. There Fairless was met with initial politeness, but when he concluded his speech all but a few members rose to applaud. By the afternoon of July 26, both steelworkers and iron ore miners were streaming back to work.

The terms of settlement follow:

1. A general increase in wage rates averaging 16 cents an hour.
2. Six paid holidays with double time for holidays worked.
3. Shift differentials increased to 6 cents per hour for 2d shift and 9 cents per hour for 3d shift.
4. Three weeks' vacation after 15 years of service, effective January 1, 1952.
5. Southern differential decreased by 5 cents an hour.
6. New agreements to run to June 30, 1954, reopenable by either party as of

June 30, 1953, on the subject of general adjustment of wage rates only, with the right to strike or lockout after June 30, 1953, upon appropriate notice.

7. Existing union security provisions changed to provide 15-day withdrawal period for all union members at end rather than beginning of contract. Added was the following provision:

Each new employee shall sign and furnish to the company at the time of his employment an application card, in duplicate, for membership in the union, in a form agreed to in writing by the company and the union. A copy of such card shall be furnished to the employee. Such application card shall provide that it shall not become effective until the expiration of 30 days after the date of his employment and that it shall not thereafter become effective if such employee shall mail to the company a written notice of his election not to become a member of the union, which notice shall be postmarked not less than 15 days and not more than 30 days after the date of his employment. The company shall promptly furnish to the union a copy of each such notice received by it. If such application shall become effective at the expiration of such 30 days, one signed copy of it shall be turned over to the union. The union shall be given reasonable opportunity to inspect all such notices which shall be received by the company.

. . . . . .

The strike had lasted 55 days, the longest in steel history.

VI. The End of an Era

In November, while on his way to Los Angeles where the CIO annual convention was to be held, Murray, whose health had not been in the best of condition for some time, died suddenly. Fairless ordered a minute of silence in all the U.S. Steel Company's plants at 11 A.M., Thursday, November 13, the time of the requiem high mass at the funeral. Messrs. Stephens, Moreell, and Larkin were among those attending the services.

Discussion Questions

1. Compare the attitude of the steel industry toward union security with that of GM and Ford. What form of union security was finally agreed upon?

2. Evaluate the role of the Federal government in the negotiations. Which side benefited? What was the over-all effect?

3. Determine the influence of personalities in the course of events. What impact did Philip Murray have on the negotiations?

4. Consider the charges of "collusion" among the steel companies. Comment on the pros and cons of industry-wide bargaining from the steel industry's viewpoint; from the union's viewpoint.

5. What was the over-all strategy of the companies? Of the union? What were the tactics of both parties in relation to the strike?

6. Identify the various negotiations under way in the case and show their interrelationship.

THE STEEL INDUSTRY

THE 1953–1954–1955 NEGOTIATIONS: THE MC DONALD REGIME

I. Murray's Successors

Philip Murray's sudden death on November 9, 1952, left vacant the presidencies in the CIO and its second largest affiliated union, the United Steelworkers of America. Speculation as to the probable successor in the CIO post centered around Allan S. Haywood, age 65, executive vice president of the CIO, and Walter P. Reuther, age 45, president of the United Automobile Workers. David J. McDonald, age 50, secretary-treasurer of the Steelworkers, was named acting president by the union's executive board until the next regular election.

The CIO annual convention, originally scheduled for November 17, was rescheduled for December 1. A bitter intraorganization battle ended in Reuther's election as president by a margin of 10% over Haywood. Reuther's support came primarily from the larger CIO unions, including his own United Automobile Workers, the Amalgamated Clothing Workers, the International Union of Electrical Workers, the National Maritime Union, the United Rubber Workers, and the Textile Workers Union. Haywood, who had been instrumental as director of organization in building up many of the smaller unions, received heavy support from over 100 unaffiliated local industrial unions. He also enjoyed the backing of McDonald of the Steelworkers, Beirne of the Communications Workers, and Quill of the Transport Workers.

In February 1953, McDonald was elected president of the Steelworkers for a four-year term. He had been associated with Murray since 1922, when he became secretary to the then vice president of the United Mine Workers.

II. 1953 Negotiations

The 1952 contracts were reopenable on or before May 1, 1953, "with respect to a general and uniform change in wage rates" only, and with the right to strike or lock out if no agreement was reached by June 30, 1953. The wage policy committee met on April 28, 1953, and formulated its demands for a general wage increase, amount unspecified; and the elimination of all wage differentials. Although the guaranteed annual wage, pensions, and insurance were not open for negotiation, the Steelworkers requested joint studies on these subjects.

Talks started on May 14. In the course of negotiations, U.S. Steel and several other companies agreed to participate in joint studies on pensions and insurance in preparation for 1954 negotiations but rejected a study of the GAW.

Steel operations were at capacity levels. Deliveries were behind schedule on many items, and backlogs of four to six months were reported. While industry leaders had gone on record that no wage increase was justified, *Steel* magazine and *Iron Age* predicted an increase of about 10 cents per hour accompanied by a rise of $4 per ton.

The settlement with U.S. Steel came in a surprise announcement on June 12, almost three weeks before the deadline date. The accord had been reached in a secret 12-hour meeting ending at 12:30 A.M. McDonald was reported as "shuttling" between the conference room in the Carleton House Hotel and the William Penn Hotel across the street where union district directors were assembled. The terms of settlement were a general wage increase of 8½ cents per hour effective June 12, and the elimination of 5 cents differential in the Southern plants and iron ore operations in two steps of 2½ cents on January 1, 1954, and July 1, 1954. Bethlehem, Republic, Jones and Laughlin, and Youngstown Sheet and Tube also agreed the same day to the same terms and other producers followed shortly thereafter.

Steel Labor, the official union monthly publication, spoke of the "highly satisfactory agreement . . . arrived at with a minimum of wrangling and ill feeling which had marked previous contract negotiations. . . ." McDonald said, "I am happy that we were able to resolve our problems over the collective bargaining table. That is the American system and I like the American system." Stephens called the settlement an "honorable compromise" and said McDonald exercised "statesmanlike conduct."

One of the by-products of the 1952 settlement—and the 55-day strike—was an agreement between Murray and Fairless to tour the corporation's plants and thus give both men an opportunity to observe firsthand relationships at the plant level and help bring about a better understanding on the part of local union and plant officials of one another's problems. McDonald indicated his intention of carrying through the agreement, and the tour was inaugurated in November 1953 by a visit to the Lorain, Ohio, works of the National Tube Division.

In a joint press conference held before the Lorain tour, McDonald and Fairless said they intended to talk to works managers, union grievance committeemen, and rank and file workers "primarily about grievances and why these problems are not always resolved before they reach the desks of the corporation chairman and the union president." Within a period of two months, McDonald and Fairless visited plants at Cleveland, Pittsburgh, and Chicago.

III. 1954 Negotiations

Nine months before the contract was to expire, a rather unusual wage policy conference was held in New York. Such meetings were normally held shortly before negotiations for the purposes of formulating the union's demands. This three-day conference was referred to as "Operation Sound-off" and was designed to communicate to leaders the desires of the rank and file for changes in current contracts. McDonald stressed pensions, insurance, and the GAW as the major demands, but intimated that a strike would not be called to force acceptance of the GAW.

The decline by January 1954 in steel operations to 75% of capacity was accompanied by rising unemployment. Thus McDonald estimated that 190,000 steelworkers were idle in the 2,551 organized plants which normally employed 1,163,000, with an additional 256,000 working less than 40 hours per week. First-quarter sales for the 22 largest companies were down by about 16% in 1954 as compared with 1953; profits before taxes had declined by 35%.

It was in this economic atmosphere that the union's executive committee and the wage policy committee met on May 6–7 and adopted a general statement listing basic objectives and four supplementary statements dealing with the subjects of contract improvements. "Before turning to our specific proposals," ran the general statement, "we wish to call attention to a problem of great concern to the union. The serious unemployment situation in the steel industry has raised the question among many of our members of the possible need for a six-hour day with eight hours' pay. It is essential to restore full employment and expanded production of steel in keeping with a growing America and steady improvements in the standard of living."

The specific demands are summarized below:

Contract Improvements. General increase in wages, elimination of all geographical differentials, two additional paid holidays, eight hours' reporting pay instead of four, higher shift premiums, more liberal vacations, full union shop; changes in provisions governing incentives, job classification manual, overtime pay, seniority, contracting-out, local working conditions, severance pay, safety, and health.

Pensions and Insurance. An across-the-board liberalization of pensions and life, sickness-accident, hospitalization, and surgical insurance plans.

Guaranteed Annual Wage. A 52-week supplemental unemployment benefits plan.

In issuing these proposals, McDonald cautioned against interpreting the contract expiration date of June 30 as a strike deadline.

The morning papers of May 19, 1954, carried a photograph of McDonald and Fairless, taken before the first meeting of the negotiating committees. Indeed, it was the first time that the chairman of the board of U.S. Steel had attended the regular negotiating sessions. It was looked upon as an offer to extend the good neighborliness that had been built up between McDonald and Fairless during their joint visits to the steel plants. Fairless, however, did not participate in later meetings; they were headed for the company by Stephens.

The first meeting was attended by over 100 people and lasted about two hours. The union presented its demands and made supporting statements on the various aspects of its proposals. At the conclusion of the morning meeting, the management representatives announced that they would take the afternoon to examine the union's proposals and ask questions the following day. After the second session, talks were postponed for "at least two weeks" in order to give the corporation an opportunity to do some "homework" on the union's proposals. Negotiations with Bethlehem, Jones and Laughlin, Republic, and other large companies were suspended pending further developments in U.S. Steel negotiations.

Negotiations between U.S. Steel and the union resumed early in June. The union expanded further its earlier arguments by stressing that: (1) elimination of overtime had reduced take-home pay; (2) productivity had risen faster than wages; (3) steel companies had "tremendous capacity to absorb wage increases"; and (4) the UAW's gain under the "living document" approach had set a standard.

U.S. Steel replied to the various union arguments: (1) purchasing power arguments were not valid; (2) unemployment was too broad a problem to be controlled by any one company, it being the concern of the government; and (3) some adjustments in pension and insurance benefits were in order.

The union's wage policy committee was called to meet on June 22. That afternoon the committee voted down an offer of about 5 cents per hour, reported to include a minimum pension provision of $130 a month, inclusive of Social Security, for 30 years of service, a contributory insurance program costing 9 cents per hour, and a 2-cent-per-hour wage increase. McDonald was described as "bitter" over what he considered an attempt by some U.S. Steel executives "to push the union into a strike." He excluded Fairless from blame for these tactics. The committee authorized a strike July 1, failing settlement by that date.

This sudden upsurge of militancy came as a surprise to the rank and file, who had been led by earlier reports to believe that a strike was unlikely. In prior years under Murray's leadership, the buildup for possible strike action had started long before negotiations and had been maintained until either a settlement was reached or the mills were shut down. Since his ascendancy to the presidency of the union, McDonald had been soft-pedaling talk of strikes. The reversal to a tougher attitude therefore was discounted by the press, which pointed to the fact that steel companies were not tapering off operations or banking furnaces as they normally would do in preparation for a strike.

After a series of private meetings between McDonald and Stephens, the wage policy committee was again summoned to meet on June 29. There were reports that a new company offer had been whipped into final shape at a meeting attended by Fairless, Clifford F. Hood, president, and other executives of the corporation. The package was estimated at 12 cents per hour by union officials and approximately 10 cents by company representatives.

On June 30, the *New York Times* carried the following headline: "U.S. STEEL SIGNS FOR 9C 'PACKAGE.' Amount Highest for a Major Industry in '54—Other Big Producers Accept Terms." The terms of settlement included: a general increase of 5 cents per hour and improvements in insurance and pensions and expiration of the basic agreement on June 30, 1956, with a reopening provision on wage rates effective May 1, 1955, and a right to strike or lock out if agreement were not reached by July 1, 1955.

By June 30, 1954, the other companies, representing 90% of steel capacity, had signed agreements embodying substantially the same terms. Steel prices were raised $3 to $4 per ton.

IV. 1955 NEGOTIATIONS

By January 1955, weekly production had reached 83.2% capacity—the highest since the week of November 16, 1953. A steel boom of at least five months was forecast and April and May set a new peak in output. By the time negotiations opened, productive facilities were being strained at nearly 97% of capacity. On January 25, U.S. Steel announced a raise in its dividend rate from 75 cents to $1 a share—the first dividend increase in four years—and a 2-for-1 stock split.

Having reached the age of 65, Fairless retired on May 2 as chairman of the board of directors. He was succeeded by Roger M. Blough, vice chairman, chief counsel, and member of the finance committee.

In accord with the reopening clause of the agreement, McDonald notified the companies on April 27 that the union desired to negotiate "with respect to hourly rates of pay to be effective after June 30, 1955."

The demands, formulated by the union's wage policy committee on May 11, consisted of three parts: (1) Where contracts could be opened only on wages, "a substantial wage increase"—justified by the economic needs of the membership, their high productivity, the prosperous state of the industry, and the economic situation of the country—was to be asked for. (2) A guaranteed annual wage was to be negotiated at the earliest date permissible under present contractual provisions. (3) Where contracts were to expire or could be reopened on subjects other than wages, additional items were to be enumerated.

At this same meeting, McDonald outlined a new procedure. All negotiations would be held in Pittsburgh, beginning with U.S. Steel on June 7 and accompanied by concurrent bargaining with the rest of the Big Six. McDonald would serve as chairman and I. W. Abel, secretary-treasurer, as secretary of the joint union negotiating committee.

The companies were reported as approving the union's change in negotiating procedure as a step toward industry-wide bargaining. But the idea of GAW received little encouragement. The day before steel negotiations opened, however, Ford not only had granted supplementary unemployment benefits but also had settled for a package which the UAW publicized as more than 20 cents an hour.

The union presented its demands to U.S. Steel on June 7. McDonald expressed the union's "hope and determination" to reach agreement before the strike deadline. Stephens concurred in the hope and added his "belief" that the agreement reached would be fair to workers, stockholders, and the public.

The union contended that the time had come to stop linking steel prices and wages.   The companies could absorb up to 30 cents an hour without raising prices or cutting too sharply into profit margins; U.S. Steel's first-quarter report for 1955 showed an increase in net profit of 62% over 1954; the company made a profit of 54 cents an hour on each hour of work in the quarter; the labor bill was nearly $3 million smaller in 1955 than in 1954 while 481 thousand more tons of steel were turned out by over 25 thousand fewer workers—so ran the union argument.

The union also proposed a three-year agreement with annual wage re-openings in exchange for a 16-cent wage increase, a contribution of 5 cents toward a GAW fund, and more substantial pension and welfare benefits than provided in the auto agreement.   The company quickly made it clear that it was interested in negotiating only on the single open issue, wages.   McDonald warned that the union was not interested in "nickels and dimes."   Talks recessed on the 9th, as did those with Bethlehem and Republic, which had taken similar positions.   The company was to notify the union when it had completed its study of the union arguments and was prepared to resume negotiations.

Negotiation with U.S. Steel resumed on June 20.   The company main-tained that its profits, far from being too high, were too low to guarantee that facilities would be kept modern and expanded as the need for steel grew. The company had expended $2.5 billion for this purpose in the postwar period.   The rising cost of new plants had made increasing inroads on profits; for example: profits for the 1955 first quarter were only 8.3% as contrasted to 9.5% in 1940 and 12.6% in 1930.   In each of the last 30 years, steel profit rates had been below the average for all manufacturing industries.   The com-pany argued that wage increases had run well ahead of productivity and that the 1955 increase in profit was attributable in large part to more efficient facilities and to the transition to a higher operating rate.

U.S. Steel's offer, made after consultation with the Big Six, was put to McDonald and three top aides at a private conference on the 23d—a hori-zontal increase of 6½ cents an hour, plus an additional ½-cent increase in the spread between classifications, or an increase on the average of 10.3 cents—or 4½%.   This offer, the company argued, was a full cent above the auto increase.   Hood publicly termed the offer "substantial" and expressed the hope that it would lead to prompt agreement.

But McDonald was far from satisfied.   "I am almost ashamed to men-tion the amount the industry is offering," he reported to his committee; "it is an effrontery in this most profitable year in the industry's history.   It is less than half of what General Motors gave.   What are we—second-class citizens?"

McDonald and Stephens met again privately for two hours on the 25th.

The union issued instructions to all local unions to prepare for strike action.   A meeting of the wage policy committee was set for the 27th at 10 A.M.   But that day passed without any new offer other than 10½ cents from Inland, whose Chicago plant was operating at 107% capacity.   This offer was rejected by McDonald as essentially the same as U.S. Steel's, the difference being due to a larger number of job classifications. And he met Inland's invocation of the clause requiring 120 hours' strike notice—unique in steel contracts—by saying, "I believe there is still time to work out an equitable settlement. However, we will cooperate to the fullest in closing the plants."

McDonald also disclosed that the wage policy committee had empowered him to order a strike—against some or all companies—failing an acceptable offer. The acceptability of an offer and extent of shutdown were to be determined by him. He was an "eternal optimist," he said, and the union was not "strike happy."

The morning papers of the 28th carried a large advertisement headlined, "Why Should the Steel Corporations Force a Crisis?" Beneath a large picture of McDonald were his signed arguments: only 2 out of every 5 steelworkers earned $4,200 annually, required for a modest living; profits had increased by 60% and dividends by 33⅓%, but the wage offer was only an increase of 4½%; productivity had increased by 5 million tons in the first quarter. He repeated these arguments over a telecast that night.

During the day, U.S. Steel stood on its proposal, as did the rest of the Big Six. The companies indicated, however, that they were prepared to bring their offer up to 12½ cents (a figure they had privately considered for some time as final) if the union gave some indication it would settle for less than 16 cents. The union countered that it would welcome a proposal to supplement the 10-cent offer with a 5-cent unemployment fund contribution, the benefits to be negotiated later by a joint committee. With the companies' fresh reminder that the contract prohibited pressing for unemployment benefits that year, an impasse was reached. The companies started to bank their furnaces. Hood called the company's offer "fair and equitable" and condemned the union for forcing a wholly unnecessary strike on the nation.

On the next to the last day of the contract, public statements replaced direct negotiations—except for a perfunctory Bethlehem session. McDonald blamed the steel companies and warned that the time was growing short. He issued an angry retort to Hood's charge and challenged him to take a direct hand in negotiation "instead of spending his time going over press releases." He urged the heads of the other big companies to join negotiations. This was ignored by all but two who stated that they had every confidence in their negotiators. Stephens sounded a hopeful note in an afternoon telecast. He said the industry did not want a strike. He praised the progress made in the last two years in developing more cooperative union-industry relations and voiced hope this progress would continue. He said that the "very substantial" pay offer would bring straight-time earnings in steel 10 cents an hour above the new rate in automobiles. He concluded, "I pledge all of my resources to continue bargaining until the deadline has approached, and in the sincere conviction that if we work hard enough and we both give, we'll produce an agreement." McDonald reasserted the union's readiness to bargain and restated his objections to the 10-cent offer.

Secret negotiations were resumed by U.S. Steel on the 30th. Even as the shutdown of furnaces was being completed and workers were being sent home, various rumors circulated as to the progress. The union canceled a network reservation for 5:20 at the last minute and retained a later radio spot. At the dinner recess, McDonald reported that there was "no settlement yet" but that he was optimistic.

When negotiation resumed at 8 P.M., Stephens returned with an offer of 13½ cents. The union made its first counteroffer on wages alone, 18 cents. The gap narrowed as the deadline passed and pickets were posted. After a two-hour break, in which conferences between U.S. Steel and the executives of other companies failed to clear the way for a settlement, negotiation was suspended until 9:30 A.M. When the four men resumed talks, it took only a few minutes for a meeting of the minds. By 11 A.M., July 1, after the shortest strike in steel history, the union's executive board and wage policy committee announced approval of the new agreement.

Terms of the settlement were a basic increase of 11½ cents and an increase of ½ cent between classifications, averaging 15 cents for most companies.

U.S. Steel immediately announced a price increase averaging $7.50 a ton, with the other companies following the price pattern.

Discussion Questions

1. Why, in your opinion, were the settlements achieved without resort to strikes?

2. Comment on the company's strategy in not reopening the 1955 agreement for a discussion of GAW.

THE STEEL INDUSTRY

THE 1956 NEGOTIATIONS

I. BACKGROUND

In March 1956 U.S. Steel called attention in its annual report to the inflationary consequences of (1) union strategy and (2) Federal monetary policies:

. . . What is good for the nation is twice as good for U.S. Steel. What is bad for the nation is twice as bad for U.S. Steel.

. . . . .

Of great importance . . . is . . . a permanent and alarming peacetime trend of cost and price inflation. . . .

. . . . .

Two basic roots of the inflationary tendency are discernible. The first one is the institution of industry-wide labor unions, headed by leaders who, with power to bring about industry-wide strikes, seek always to outdo each other in elevating employment costs in their respective industries.

The other root is the Government's "full employment" policy under which the money supply must be inflated fast enough to accommodate the inflating employment cost. . . .

The abuse of labor monopoly privilege and the monetary policy that transfers to the public in higher prices the penalty of that abuse appear to be the main elements of institutionalized inflation. . . .

. . . . .

David J. McDonald, president of the Steelworkers, was swift to reply in a public statement:

Instead of congratulating the management-labor team . . . , the Corporation took this occasion [in its Annual Report] gratuitously to insult both the Steelworkers Union and our Government as being the "two basic roots" of an inflationary trend.

. . . . .

Only the . . . managers of the . . . Corporation whose horizons are limited by Wall Street, could regard the efforts of steelworkers to obtain better wages, pensions, and security for themselves and their families, to be solely the result of competition between union leaders seeking "always to out-do each other in elevating employment costs in their respective industries." . . .

The gains won by the workers . . . have not caused inflation. The central fact omitted in the Corporation's report is that the cost of these gains has been more than offset by increases in productivity. Last year, for example, the union won a 15¢-an-hour increase, but each worker, on the average, produced so much more steel per hour that the actual wage cost of each ton of steel went down, not up. . . .

Indeed, the Corporation made a neat profit on the wage increase last year. The theoretical "cost" to U.S. Steel of the 1955 wage increase was approximately 30 million dollars—the actual cost was zero, because of the increase in productivity. But the Corporation, immediately following the wage increase, raised steel prices $7.50 per ton. . . .

Making a profit on a wage increase is nothing new for U.S. Steel. . . .

. . . . .

From the statement, one could easily see an effort to tear down the increasingly better labor-management relations so painstakingly built up between U.S. Steel and our Union. We trust this is not the case.

On May 7 at the annual stockholders' meeting, Roger M. Blough, board chairman, announced that U.S. Steel intended to spend at least $2.5 billion during the next five years for expansion and replacement. In elaborating he said, ". . . We are confronted this month with wage demands which, if granted even in part, would—in the absence of compensating price increase seriously reduce our present profit level and compound the financial problems we must face in the future. . . . During the past ten years alone, our plant and equipment costs have more than doubled. . . . Back in 1930 we built an open hearth plant which cost about 10 million dollars. Today it will cost us about 64 million dollars to replace that plant. Through depreciation we have recovered the original 10 million that we spent on this facility. The remaining 54 million, however, will have to come out of our profits . . . our profits after taxes." The "first and most logical" solution would be a revision of the depreciation laws, he stated, and, failing that action, "the only other possible solution" is to increase profit margins. "This," he declared, "can be done in two ways: First by increased efficiency of operations. . . . And the sole remaining method—the last resort—is by raising prices from time to time. . . . In the absence of a more realistic treatment of depreciation, there simply is no other course."

What effect these intimations of a possible price increase had on the activity of the industry was hard to determine. However, steel operations were at capacity during May, with a three-month backlog of orders.

Some of the things that steelworkers themselves were thinking about were voiced at a kick-off session of the wage policy committee in Chicago on March 6 and 7. Called "Operation Sound-off," the meeting was reported to have emphasized four major points: (1) an increase in wages; (2) supplemental unemployment compensation; (3) premium pay for Saturday and Sunday work; and (4) improvements in insurance coverage.

With the announcement of its demands, the Union notified the companies that it desired to terminate the expiring contracts. The companies also informed the union on May 3 that they intended to terminate the agreements on June 30.

The first clue to industry's objectives was given on May 24 by Joseph L. Block, president of Inland Steel, when he urged the negotiation of long-term steel contracts to avoid "the dubious choice of a nationwide strike or a dose of inflation." He added, "It should be possible to negotiate contracts that will be firm for a period of years and still be equitable to both parties. Such an arrangement would add strength and stability to the economy of our country. Other industries have done this. Surely steel can do likewise."

II. The Contract Negotiations

Contract talks opened on May 28 in Pittsburgh—the Steelworkers meeting with U.S. Steel at 10 A.M., with Bethlehem at 2 P.M., with Republic at 4 P.M. and with other major producers the next day.

Immediately after the first meetings, negotiations were suspended until June 7 to allow the companies time to study the union's demands for:

1. A "substantial" wage increase. McDonald said no figures would be set until negotiations reopened.

2. Time and a half for Saturday work and double time for Sunday work. McDonald urged the seriousness of this demand; 1956 "shall be the break through year on the subject of week-end premium pay."

3. A supplementary unemployment benefit plan to provide 52 weeks of partial pay for laid-off workers, similar to that negotiated with the can companies in 1955.

4. The union shop.

5. A vacation of 1 week for 1 year of service, 2 weeks for 2 to 5 years, 3 weeks for 5 to 15 years, and 4 weeks for 15 years.

6. Shift differentials of 5% for the 2d shift and 10% for the 3d shift.

7. Assumption by the industry of the total bill for welfare and insurance benefits.

8. Two additional paid holidays.

9. An expanded sick benefit, life insurance, and welfare program.

During the 10-day interlude, the "Big Three" agreed to bargain jointly with the Steelworkers. Stephens commented that each company would be bargaining for itself, even though all would be in the same room. He added that the companies had agreed to concurrent sessions hoping thus to dispose of the long list of union demands. The parties also agreed to hold the negotiations in New York hoping for fewer pressures on neutral ground.

When negotiations opened on June 6, the following, in addition to Stephens and McDonald, were present: R. Heath Larry, counsel for U.S. Steel; John A. Morse, counsel for Bethlehem; Tom F. Patton, first vice president for Republic; and, for the union, Howard R. Hague, vice president, I. W. Abel, secretary-treasurer, and Arthur J. Goldberg, general counsel.

The parties met for four hours on the 6th and for two hours on the 7th and then adjourned until the following Wednesday, June 13, when the companies said their proposal would be ready. Meanwhile, previous estimates of capacity operations for the last two quarters of 1956 had been revised downward to about 80%, due in part to the slump in the auto industry, which was down 27% compared to 1955. It also became evident that a good deal of the May–June capacity operation had been due to a rush of orders in anticipation of a possible strike.

When the negotiators met again on June 13, the companies proposed a five-year contract with staggered increases in wages and benefits. Excerpts from the presentation follow:

Were the Companies to grant the union's demands in full and make them effective this year for all their employees, their employment costs would immediately be increased by about 25%.

. . . . .

The Companies believe that there should be no increase in employment costs in the steel industry at this time, but adherence to such a position would undoubtedly mean a prolonged strike which would work extreme hardships upon all concerned. . . .

Accordingly, . . . the three companies are making this proposal for new 5-year nonreopenable agreement.

Such a period of labor stability is sorely needed . . . to plan for and carry out the extensive and costly expansion programs. . . .

. . . . .

Effective Date	Improvement
July 1, 1956	Advance all job class 1 employees to job class 2 and combine the two classes. Increase all standard hourly wage rates by 6 cents and increase increments between job classes above job class 2 by .2 cent.
July 1, 1956	Establish Supplemental Unemployment Benefits Plan with company contributions of 5 cents per hour. (On layoff, employees with 3 years' seniority would receive 65% of their after-tax take-home pay for 52 weeks.)
November 1, 1956	Establish improved insurance program.
July 1, 1957	Increase all standard hourly wage rates by 6 cents and increase increments between job classes above job class 2 by .2 cent.
July 1, 1957	Add a seventh paid holiday.
November 1, 1957	Increase pension benefits. (Primarily involved raising monthly factor from $2.25 to $2.50.)
January 1, 1958	Increase all standard hourly wage rates by 6 cents and increase increments between job classes above job class 2 by .2 cent.
July 1, 1958	Increase shift premiums to 7 cents for afternoon shift and 10 cents for night shift.
July 1, 1959	Increase all standard hourly wage rates by 6 cents and increase increments between job classes above job class 2 by .2 cent.
July 1, 1959	Establish new premium for Sunday shifts equal to night shift premium.
July 1, 1959	Grant jury pay.
July 1, 1960	Increase all standard hourly wage rates by 6 cents and increase increments between job classes above job class 2 by .2 cent.
July 1, 1960	Increase shift premiums to 8 cents for afternoon shift and 12 cents for night shift.
July 1, 1960	Apply new night shift premium to Sunday shifts.

. . . . .

The foregoing proposal is made on behalf of the three Companies, respectively, as a package proposal. . . . None of the items of the proposal can be acted upon or be deemed to have been offered separately, as each is related to all other items in the proposal and is an integral part of a single offer made to settle all outstanding issues.

The package was estimated at 65 cents by the companies, at 45 cents by the Steelworkers.

The proposal was not released to the public until June 15. On the same day McDonald announced its rejection by the union, calling it "too little, too late, and too long." The companies sent letters to all employees explaining their offer in detail.

The proposal was rejected unanimously by the wage policy committee because: (1) wage increase of 6 cents in the face of record profits and productivity was "picayune"; (2) Sunday premium of 10 cents an hour was "shockingly inadequate"; (3) SUB proposal would provide "no benefits whatsoever" in Ohio, Indiana, and Virginia, where authorities had ruled against simultaneous public and private payments; (4) the proposal offered no protection of purchasing power; and (5) the offer included no union shop provision.

On June 16 the companies modified their previous proposal to include a cost of living adjustment. The demand for an escalator clause which prompted the companies' concession indicated that the union had altered its previous policy of obtaining adjustments for inflation by wage reopeners.

On Sunday, June 17, the negotiations reached a deadlock. The union announced abandonment of joint talks with the Big Three and called rank and file representatives to New York for direct negotiations with the 12 major companies.

The next day the wage policy committee authorized a strike for midnight, June 30, if no acceptable contract were offered by that time. Goldberg articulated concisely the union's feeling, "We want more Fairlessness and less Boulwarism."

The meetings between the union and the individual companies resulted in identical offers from each company. After four days of separate talks, the union announced it was resuming joint talks with the Big Three. These opened again on June 20, with little progress. As negotiations approached the June 30 deadline, the union placed full-page advertisements in hundreds of newspapers, and McDonald appeared on TV with the charge that the companies were conspiring to force union acceptance of a five-year no-strike contract with an ultimatum to "take-it-or-leave-it." The union pointed to profits for 1955 of over one billion dollars. A 5-cent increase in net wages was called "shameful" when compared to the rise of 11% in productivity which had contributed to the large profits.

The companies replied in advertisements in more than 350 newspapers that their proposals were "as fair to the workers as they could possibly be without being unfair to all other Americans who also have a stake in the outcome of these negotiations." Moreell of Jones & Laughlin appeared on nationwide television on July 28 and explained that the offer embodied much more than a "nickel increase in net pay"; [1] that it was the largest single package in the history of the industry amounting to 17½ cents in the first year with corresponding increases in each of the following four years; and that purchasing power would be protected by provision for cost-of-living increases. "We believe," said he, "that five years of peace in the steel industry—with no strikes to drain away the workers' savings; no strikes to halt the companies' expansion and improvement programs; no strikes to threaten those industries, large and small, which depend on a steady supply of steel; and no strikes to interrupt the orderly march of progress throughout our economy—that this kind of industrial peace would be a boon to all of us and to our nation."

Patton of Republic linked an increase in steel wages with an increase in steel prices. In press conference, he held that a substantial compensating price increase was inevitable.

Secretary of Labor James P. Mitchell declared that the Administration did not contemplate invoking the Taft-Hartley Act; however, the Mediation and Conciliation Service was available if needed.

On June 27, the 12 companies sent two letters to McDonald as follows:

From Letter No. 1

. . . . .

You have recently reasserted the historical policy of your union of "no contract, no work." If a strike is to begin at midnight, June 30, it will be necessary to start curtailing operations not later than 12 o'clock tonight in order to accomplish an orderly shutdown without risk of serious injury to employees and extensive damage to facilities and equipment.

The companies assert again that they desire to do whatever they can in good conscience to avoid a strike. Accordingly, the companies propose that you postpone any strike at this time, that the parties continue to negotiate beyond midnight of June 30 (should agreement not have been reached by that time) and that you agree to give the companies at least 72 hours' prior written notice, after the date of this letter, of any strike beginning at any time after June 30.

If the union shall accede to this proposal which is, the companies believe, in the interests of employees and the country as a whole, the companies in subsequent negotiations will be agreeable to reducing the 5-year term of the proposed agreements to a shorter term running from the date of the execution of the new agreements to October 31, 1960, with, of course, a proportionate reduction of the benefits provided in their 5-year proposals.

In the absence of an agreement by the union not to strike at any time after June 30 without thereafter giving the companies at least 72 hours' prior written notice, the companies will, for the reasons stated above, be forced to start curtailing operations at midnight tonight.

. . . . .

From Letter No. 2

We have received your reply. In it you propose as a condition of an extension of our existing agreements to July 16, 1956, that benefits which may be resolved

---

[1] In arriving at the figure of a nickel increase, McDonald had subtracted from the wage increase the cost to workers of increased contributions for fringe benefits.

in our bargaining and which are applicable shall be retroactive to the June 30 midnight termination date of the present agreements.

The companies, while desirous of continuing the negotiations and postponement of the strike, cannot, nevertheless, accept the retroactivity condition which you attach to your willingness to extend. Continued negotiations should be conducted with equal pressure on both parties, a condition not present when the union is guaranteed by retroactivity that no matter how it may delay agreement it has nothing to lose.

We agree that the present situation most certainly calls for settlement rather than continued procrastination. Today we tried to meet one of your main objections to the companies' proposals by offering to reduce the term by 2/3 of a year. . . .

The companies must disclaim responsibility for failure to reach agreement. The union has blocked settlement, blocked settlement by insistence upon extravagant concessions far beyond fairness and reason.

On June 28, McDonald made an eleventh-hour plea to the companies to bargain in good faith. He proposed that "the top executive officers of each of the companies—as men who had the real power—come down from their ivory tower and meet with the union." The companies replied that "no useful purpose can possibly be served by changing the present negotiating procedures."

As the parties were drifting toward the deadline, the BLS announced that in May 1956 the CPI had taken the biggest one-month spurt in three years, bringing the index even with the all-time peak of 115.4 reached in October 1953.

As negotiations stalemated, Stephens declared that the employer group was "ready and willing" to meet again at any time. McDonald made it clear, however, that the initiative for another conference would have to come from the industry. "It's up to them; they have given us a 'take it or leave it' offer and we have not taken it."

The companies began to bank their furnaces. Negotiations continued in a lifeless manner until 6 P.M., June 30, when efforts to reach agreement were abandoned. On July 1, 650,000 steelworkers went on strike in an orderly shutdown.

At the government's initiation, separate exploratory conferences were held on July 5 by Federal mediators without any significant results.

Before long 100,000 additional employees were idle in industries dependent on steel, mainly coal and railroads. Steel production was down to 13% of capacity. As a result the Commerce Department ordered a freeze in scarce steel to safeguard defense industries. Actually it was difficult to assess the adequacy of steel stocks. In automobiles, where business had been slack, sufficient steel was on hand to complete production runs for 1956 models. On the other hand, construction, which had been booming, faced exhaustion of steel stocks in two weeks. In general, it was felt that a strike in excess of four weeks might seriously slow down the economy.

On July 12 and 13, the parties came together in Pittsburgh for negotiations sponsored by the mediation service. These efforts, the first time since the strike, proved unsuccessful. Similar meetings were held again in Pittsburgh on July 18, 20, and 21 attended by Joseph F. Finnegan, director of the mediation service, who had flown to Pittsburgh directly from the White House after meeting with the President and key members of the Cabinet. In spite of the warning that the President was concerned and would take action within a week if no agreement were forthcoming, the talks produced no results.

On July 22, McDonald sent to the Cabinet, Congressmen, Federal and state officials, and other leaders two studies entitled *Steel and the National Economy 1956* and *Facts on Steel: Profits, Productivity, Prices and Wages 1956*. Originally the union planned to release the studies at a Washington luncheon for 400 key persons. Senator Wayne Morse and economist Robert Nathan were scheduled to speak on the monopoly aspects of the steel industry. At the last minute the luncheon was called off and the studies were released directly to the press. Excerpts from the covering letter follow:

．　．　．　．　．

Our study refutes any alleged relation between wage increases and inflation: "Experience has proved that wage increases have not caused inflation, that wages can be increased without prices being raised, and that rising real wages give us stable prosperity and growth."

Wage increases, says our report, lagged behind price increases in the immediate postwar and Korean inflations and obviously could not have caused inflation. The pattern of inflation is rising prices, rising real profits and lagging real wages. . . .

．　．　．　．　．

The contrast between the pricing policies of the steel industry and of all manufacturing industries as a whole is rather startling. Steel prices have increased proportionately with wage rates since 1947 ignoring rapidly rising productivity in its pricing policies. For all manufacturing, industrial prices increased considerably less than half as much as wage rates from 1947 to 1955.

The steel industry does not follow the principle of higher volume and lower margins. If there is any single industry that has followed inflationary pricing practices, that has shown a disregard for the economic welfare of the country, especially relative to its key role in the economy, that has truly practiced inflation, that has the least right to hide behind the cloak of favoring a sound dollar and to contend that wage increases are inflationary, it is the steel industry.

．　．　．　．　．

Our study emphasizes productivity as the key to the entire question of wages, prices, profits and the health of the over-all economy.

．　．　．　．

For example, productivity in the steel industry currently has been running at a rate 4.7 per cent higher than in 1955. And the rate in 1955 was a phenomenal 11.2 per cent above 1954. In short, steelworkers are producing more and more steel per many years. . . .

．　．　．　．　．

. . . Far from being in dire straits, profit-wise, the steel corporations under examination have been showing a 1956 profit rate of 15.3 per cent higher than last year and—believe it or not—107.4 per cent higher than in 1954! These are profits before taxes, and it should be remembered that wage increases are offset from profits before, not after taxes. As to profits after taxes, you will find that these companies have been reaping—at the 1956 rate—net profits 13.1 per cent higher than in 1955 and 95.6 per cent higher than in 1954.

，　．　．　．　．

The facts in our study likewise contradict the industry's assertions that increased wages and materials cost have necessitated price increases. The industry has increased prices out of all proportion to increased costs. For each $1 increase in labor costs since 1945, exorbitant price increases have yielded $3.19 in additional revenues. The figures on materials costs are equally startling. Materials costs since 1947 have risen about 28 per cent, but steel prices in the same period have risen 78.2 per cent—an excess of price increases over cost increases of nearly 3 to 1.

. . . . . .

The industry's reply follows in part:

Steel's employment costs per hour have risen to a level now triple that of 1940. They have been advancing since 1940 at the rate of 7.6 per cent each year —meaning 7.6 per cent compounded annually.

Total costs in the steel industry, per hour worked, have advanced since 1940 at the rate of 8.2 per cent a year, compounded.

But figures published by the United States Department of Labor show that the prices of steel products during this period have gone up only at a rate of 5.4 per cent per year, compounded.

. . . . .

Since 1949, the average steelworker's hourly wages and benefits—after being adjusted for price changes—show an increase of 43 per cent. National productivity has meanwhile increased less than 22 per cent, according to extension of data reported by the Joint Committee on the Economic Report.

. . . . .

The package proposed by the steel companies in June, 1956, would increase the hourly cost of wages and benefits by about 23 per cent over a five-year period —or an average increase of more than 4 per cent per year. Since this is considerably more than the average annual increase in productivity, it would further improve the steelworker's standard of living in comparison with that of other workers.

The industry's profit rate per dollar of sales was less in 1956 than in 1940. The decline between these two years was from 8.1 per cent to 7.8 per cent in 1955, according to calculations for steel companies by First National City Bank of New York.

This 7.8 per cent in 1955 was, of course, earned on a much larger volume of sales which totaled $14 billion in 1955 against $3½ billion in 1940. Hence 1955 profits looked much larger, in terms of dollars. But billions of dollars of new investment were necessary to produce the higher sales volume.

The investment of these companies in steel plant rose, for instance, from $3.3 to $7.2 billions between 1940 and 1955. Much of this rise took place in the brief 1950–1955 period, when the investment increased by 40 per cent. In 1955, it therefore took 40 per cent more dollars of profit than in 1950 to pay the same return on the increased investment.

Somewhat similarly, millions of dollars of so-called increased profit now have to be used by the steel industry for use in replacing old plant. The depreciation funds that should pay for this rebuilding are now wholly inadequate because of today's inflated costs.

The amount of so-called profit thus used for replacement might be called "phantom" profit because—as a result of the inadequacy of depreciation reserves—what otherwise would be profit available for payment to owners, and available in some measure for expansion, must be applied to the replacement of present facilities.

Since 1946, about 55 per cent of the total profit, after taxes, of the steel companies has been plowed back into the business for expansion and modernization, while 45 per cent of the profit was used for the payment of dividends.[1]

Against this background, the industry spokesmen proposed on July 22 that contract talks be resumed. As a result, committees representing the Big Three and the Steelworkers met in New York on July 24, and reported at the end of the session that progress was being made. According to rumor, the White House had been putting increased pressure on the companies to reopen idle mills through Secretary of Labor Mitchell and Secretary of the Treasury George M. Humphrey. The bargaining committee worked into the late evenings. On July 27, the Steelworkers and the 12 major companies signed a memorandum of agreement.

III. The Settlement

The settlement embodied the following changes to the companies' initial offer. (The items in parentheses indicate the applicable portion of the initial offer.)

1. *Wages.*

(a) Effective July 27, 1956 (July 1, 1956), all rates to be increased 7.5 cents an hour (6 cents) and increments between job class rates increased .3 cent an hour (.2 cent).

(b) Effective July 1, 1957 (July 1, 1957), all rates to be increased by 7 cents an hour (6 cents) and increments between rates to be increased .2 cent an hour (.2 cent).

(c) Effective July 1, 1958 (July 1, 1958), all rates to be increased by 7 cents an hour (6 cents) and increments between rates to be increased .2 cent an hour (.2 cent).

2. *Premium Pay.* Effective September 1, 1956 (July 1, 1959), a premium of 10% for Sundays (10 cents). Effective July 1, 1957, a Sunday premium of 20% and a holiday premium of 10% (not offered). Effective July 1, 1958, a Sunday and holiday premium of 25% (not offered). [The new holiday premium for holidays was to be over and above the previous double time pay for holidays. The union did not win its demand for premium pay for Saturdays.]

3. *SUB.* A supplementary unemployment benefit plan for employees with two years' seniority (three years').[2] Otherwise the SUB proposal as previously outlined was accepted.

4. *Union Shop.* A full union shop (not offered; a modified union shop already existed).

5. *Vacations.* Effective July 1, 1958, 3½ weeks of vacation pay for all employees with 25 or more years of service (not offered; had been 3 weeks).

6. *Shift Pay.* Effective July 1, 1958, shift differentials to be increased

---

[1] For general statistics on the steel industry, see Exhibit 1.

[2] With respect to the states prohibiting simultaneous payment of SUB and unemployment compensation, the parties agreed to meet prior to August 1, 1957, to make alternate arrangements, to provide if possible lump-sum payments prior to, and after, the payment of unemployment compensation.

to 8 cents for the 2d shift and 12 cents for the 3d shift (7 cents and 10 cents on July 1, 1958, and 8 cents and 12 cents on July 1, 1960).

7. *Contract Term.* Three-year contract (first proposal, five years; second, four years and four months).

8. *Job Classification and Incentive System.* Joint committees, to review job classification and incentive system.

9. *Jury Pay.* Effective July 27, 1956 (July 1, 1959).

10. *Cost of Living Adjustment.* This modification (and the only one made during negotiations) in the companies' proposal had been made on June 16.

The settlement provided for the negotiation of individual agreements by 12 leading companies.

The wage policy committee hailed the settlement as the greatest victory achieved by the union in its 20-year history, pointing to the package of 45.6 cents for three years as compared with the company's original offer of 45 cents for five years, to the breakthrough on week-end premium pay, to the 52-week SUB plan, and to the realization of a full union shop. While the union did not succeed in placing all fringe benefits on a noncontributory basis, it did receive a new monthly pension factor of $2.50, an increase of 25 cents over the auto pattern.

The industry spokesman emphasized the guaranteed industrial peace that had been achieved for the three-year contract period:

These contracts, when concluded, should permit the steel companies of America to proceed, without fear of disrupted production, on their announced plans of adding 15 million tons of new capacity in the next three years.

In striving for a long-term contract providing for an orderly increase in basic steel wages, the companies have sought to retard the advancing pace of inflation, insofar as this can be done within the confines of any one industry.

In this, as in many other respects, the new agreements should be a decided improvement over the previous practice of annual negotiations which presented the repeated possibility of strikes and which actually resulted in five industry-wide strikes in the past eleven years.

. . . . .

After the July 27 memorandum of agreement had been achieved, the task remained of translating the terms into individual company settlements. The pace was feverish.

U.S. Steel signed its contract on August 3; Republic Steel and Jones & Laughlin, that same evening; Pittsburgh Steel earlier in the day. A week-end rush was on to sign contracts. The first of the steelworkers returned to work on Monday, August 6. Estimates of the time needed to return to 90% capacity ranged from ten days to three weeks; and to regain 100% an additional one to three weeks.

IV. Prices and Cost of Living

On August 6 U.S. Steel published a new schedule of prices with an average increase of $8.50 per ton; the other companies promptly followed suit. "In determining the new prices," said U.S. Steel, "consideration has been given to

Exhibit i

The 1956 Steel Negotiations

Steel Industry Statistics

General Statistics	1955	1954	1953	1952	1951	1950	1949	1948	1947
Total Revenue (millions of $)	$13,973	$10,593	$13,155	$10,858	$11,844	$9,534	$7,435	$8,119	$6,704
Total Employment Costs (millions of $)	4,683	3,887	4,476	3,788	3,828	3,150	2,600	2,831	2,464
Net Income (millions of $)	1,097	637	734	541	682	766	528	540	411
Capacity (millions of tons)	125	124	117	108	104	99	96	94	91
Per Cent of Capacity (year's production)	93	71	95	86	101	97	81	94	93
Index Comparison BLS Wholesale Price Index— All Commodities 1947–1949 = 100	110.7	110.3	110.1	111.6	114.8	103.1	99.2	104.4	96.4
BLS Wholesale Price Index— Iron and Steel 1947–1949 = 100	140.6	132.9	131.3	124.7	123.2	113.1	106.0	104.3	81.7
Average *Hourly* Earnings	$2.380	$2.200	$2.160	$1.990	$1.890	$1.691	$1.646	$1.580	$1.439
Real *Hourly* Earnings	2.079	1.916	1.888	1.753	1.703	1.645	1.617	1.537	1.507
Wage Rate Increases	$ .152	$ .050	$ .085	$ .160	None	$ .160	None	$ .130	$ .160

Includes adjustment for changes in purchasing power as measured by C.P.I. 1947–1949.
Sources: American Iron and Steel Institute, *Annual Statistical Report*, 1938–1955.
        Bureau of Labor Statistics.

steel making costs, including the initial costs of the new wage agreement. . . . The new prices do not provide a solution to the problem that Steel faces with respect to inadequate depreciation allowances for the replacement of obsolete and outworn facilities, nor do they attempt to provide a solution to many problems attending the expansion program upon which United States Steel is currently engaged."

The return to normal operations proceeded well ahead of schedule reaching 85.5% by August 14, with full capacity expected by the end of August.

The cost of living showed no signs of abatement: May, 115.4; June, 116.2; and July, 117.0.

Discussion Questions

1. Evaluate the arguments relating wage increases and price increases to inflation.

2. Against the background of the three previous negotiations, why did a strike take place this year?

3. What are the strengths and weaknesses of simultaneous bargaining by the "Big Three"? What were McDonald's tactics in this regard?

4. What was unusual about the bargaining proposals and/or the manner in which they were introduced? Compare this aspect of negotiating skill with that in previous years.

General Statistics	1946	1945	1944	1943	1942	1941	1940	1939	1938
Total Revenue (millions of $)	$4,811	$5,920	$6,613	—	—	—	—	—	—
Total Employment Costs (millions of $)	1,983	2,413	2,729	$2,653	$2,176	$1,679	$1,179	$ 970	—
Net Income (millions of $)	264	184	179	200	221	327	281	140	d. 14
Capacity (millions of tons)	91	95	93	90	88	85	81	81	80
Per Cent of Capacity (year's production)	73	84	96	98	97	97	82	65	39
Index Comparison BLS Wholesale Price Index— All Commodities 1947–1949 = 100	78.7	68.8	67.6	67.0	64.2	56.8	51.1	50.1	—
BLS Wholesale Price Index— Iron and Steel 1947–1949 = 100	74.0	66.5	65.1	65.2	65.2	64.6	63.8	64.2	—
Average *Hourly* Earnings	$1.281	$1.179	$1.157	$1.116	$1.018	$ .941	$ .844	$ .838	—
Real *Hourly* Earnings	1.536	1.533	1.539	1.508	1.461	1.496	1.409	1.410	—
Wage Rate Increases	$ .185	None	None	None	$ .055	$ .100	None	None	—

5. How was a settlement achieved? What were the respective power positions of both parties?

6. List the main contract gains of the union. What effect would these have on bargaining in other industries?

7. What effect did the 1956 negotiations have on the structure of relationship between the companies and the unions?

8. Explain the remark, "More Fairlessness and less Boulwarism."

9. Comment on the tactics of the company in achieving a 3-year no-strike contract.

LEVER BROTHERS COMPANY (A)

THE OPENING SESSIONS OF THE 1949 NEGOTIATIONS

I. Introduction

Lever Brothers dealt with the International Chemical Workers' Union, AFL, at four plants located, respectively, at Cambridge, Massachusetts; Edgewater, New Jersey; Baltimore, Maryland; and St. Louis, Missouri; and with the United Gas, Coke, and Chemical Workers of America, CIO, as the representative of its employees at its fifth plant located at Hammond, Indiana.

The company took pride in pointing out that it had paid better wages than did comparable industries and had been a leader in providing liberal employee benefits. In 1949 such benefits included two weeks' vacation with pay and 7¼ paid holidays each year; paid lunch and rest periods; shift premiums of five and ten cents; time and one-half for Saturdays, and double time for Sundays; free group life insurance; a liberal sickness and accident insurance plan; and a company-financed pension plan.

The company's first recognition of a union came in 1934, after a bitter strike, when Lever Brothers signed its first agreement with an AFL federal local at Hammond. The second contract was signed at its Edgewater plant in 1937 when another federal local was recognized. The Baltimore and St. Louis plants, purchased in 1938, had independent unions at that time. The following year, however, employees at the Baltimore plant changed to a federal AFL local, while the union at St. Louis remained independent. The largest and oldest of the plants, that in Cambridge, was the last to become unionized. A group of employees petitioned for recognition in 1939, but failed to win in an NLRB election. Within two months, however, the company granted recognition without another election, and a fourth AFL federal local was formed.

In 1944, the International Chemical Workers' Union was chartered by the AFL; and the next year, the unions at Baltimore, Cambridge, Edgewater, and Hammond became local units of this international union. In the same year, as the result of a case brought before the NLRB by the firemen and oilers at the Cambridge plant, a separate bargaining unit was established there as a local of the International Brotherhood of Firemen and Oilers, AFL.

In 1946, Charles Luckman became president of the company. He made several addresses and wrote articles in which he expressed his views and philosophy concerning management-labor relations. Among other things he declared himself for pensions, insurance provisions, and ultimately guaranteed annual wages. He said:

. . . no one has a right to manage a business unless he believes in labor's rights just as strongly as he does in management's rights.

The first master agreement between the company and the International Chemical Workers, AFL, was negotiated in 1946. The company also inaugurated the policy of having the managers and industrial relations officials from each plant present in these negotiations. The master contract was then supplemented by local agreements covering seniority and working rules negotiated by each plant. To head the management team in negotiating the master contract, the company engaged Austin Fisher, a labor relations consultant. As a result of the 1946 negotiations, a general wage increase of 18%, or 18 cents, whichever was greater, became effective for all hourly employees.

Although the 1946 contract was not to expire until March, 1947, the AFL unions petitioned for a wage reopening, and the contract was reopened in January, 1947, when Mr. Luckman, referring to the rapid rise in living costs, invited union representatives to meet with management for the purpose of discussing upward wage adjustments and other contract revisions. H. A. Bradley, president of the International Chemical Workers, AFL, headed the union team. Discussions resulted in a new contract, signed in March, 1947, which stipulated an increase of 15 cents—10 cents across the board and the equivalent of 5 cents for job evaluation. A job evaluation program had been instigated as a joint union-management activity late in 1946. The increase of 15 cents was put into effect at the plants in Baltimore, Cambridge, and Edgewater, and was immediately extended to St. Louis, where the independent union still had bargaining rights.

No agreement, however, was reached at this time at Hammond. As a result, Hammond employees worked without a contract or a wage increase from March until August, 1947. In the meantime, as the result of an election, the United Gas, Coke, and Chemical Workers of America, CIO, was certified as the new collective bargaining agent at Hammond. The first agreement between the company and this union, negotiated in August, 1947, resulted in a wage increase of 12½ cents, as well as an increase of 15 cents retroactive to March of that year. The 12½-cent increase was then immediately offered by the company in all its other plants, and was accepted by the AFL unions with the stipulation that a company-wide equalization of rate ranges would be effected when the contract expired in March, 1948.

Concurrent master contract negotiations with the AFL and CIO were held for the first time in March, 1948. An average of 17 cents was gained at all plants, consisting of a general increase of 11 cents, plus an additional 6 cents for an equalization program, under which rate ranges for the same jobs were to be made identical at all plants. Because of previous area wage differentials, the equalization program resulted in substantially different average increases at the various plants, as follows: Hammond, 11 cents; Edgewater, 14½ cents; Cambridge, 18 cents; and Baltimore, 23½ cents.

Shortly before the beginning of 1949 contract negotiations in February, the independent union at the St. Louis plant received a charter from the International Chemical Workers, with the result that management and union representatives from all five company plants were present for the first time at the negotiations.

The total number of Lever hourly employees, as of February, 1949, was 3,093, divided as follows: Cambridge, 1,029; Hammond, 916; Baltimore, 650; Edgewater, 353; and St. Louis, 145.

Before the 1949 proceedings began, the Cambridge, Baltimore, and St. Louis plants had almost consummated their local agreements and Edgewater had begun similar discussions—a procedure in contrast to previous years when local contracts had been negotiated after completion of the master contract.

II. AFL: First Session [1]—February 15, 1949

(9:30 A.M.–1:00 P.M.; 2:30–6:00 P.M.)

For the Company

Representing Company Headquarters:

Austin M. Fisher	Labor Relations Consultant
Thomas A. Gonser	Director of Personnel and Public Relations
Gerald F. Gamber	Associate Director of Personnel
Roy V. Shorey	Personnel Manager
William H. Burkhart	Director of Manufacture
W. Wesley Pear	Personnel Research Administrator

Representing Plant Management:

Albert W. Lamprell	Industrial Relations Manager	Baltimore
John S. Boulden	Plant Manager	Baltimore
William G. Brown	Industrial Relations Manager	Cambridge
Gary G. Grant	Plant Manager	Cambridge
George F. Duncan	Industrial Relations Manager	Edgewater
Frank K. Baker	Plant Superintendent	Edgewater
John B. Buckle	Industrial Relations Manager	St. Louis
Maynard B. Bemis	Plant Manager	St. Louis

For the Union [2]

Louis Belkin	Counsel for the International Union
Joseph I. Barrett	Baltimore, President
John A. Martin	Baltimore, Vice President
Joseph T. Healey	Cambridge, Recording Secretary
Joseph A. De Vincentis	Cambridge, Financial Secretary
James Fitzgerald	Edgewater, Negotiating Committeeman, Chairman of AFL Negotiating Committee
Charles Yurco	Edgewater, Negotiating Committeeman
George Reichardt	St. Louis, President
Edmund Marheincke	St. Louis, Financial Secretary

---

[1] All sessions were held at the Copley-Plaza Hotel, Boston, Massachusetts.

[2] In addition to the negotiating committee, each local had from one to four observers sent from their respective plants.

Burkhart (m): Although I have been chairman of the company's committee for several years, I am just a plain soap maker. So I am happy to relinquish my job to Mr. Gamber, our new associate director of personnel, who has had a wealth of experience in industrial relations.

Gamber (m): Thank you, Bill. I think our schedule calls first for exploring proposals and later negotiating on a continuous basis. As usual, Mr. Fisher is acting as company spokesman.

Fisher (m): Thank you, Gerry. Lou [Belkin], as you probably know, we have a well-established procedure of co-chairing the meetings. If any of the labor representatives wish to be heard, they signify that through you. By the same token, the management representatives will look to me for recognition.

Belkin (u): Mr. Fitzgerald, our chairman, will tell you our demands. We are literally tearing the contract apart. A year ago a wonderful understanding existed, but in the past six months a feeling of hostility has arisen. Now, why? I have here a list of complaints—

Fisher (m): Let me interrupt. It seems you are creating a setting to justify the demands you are going to serve upon us. May we have a short recess?

[A brief recess was taken.]

Fisher (m): You were telling us about some things that have gone wrong. We want to know the facts; so we, at our end, can form some sort of judgment. Will you try to be specific?

Belkin (u): When I was in Edgewater one day processing a minor grievance, I discovered some things that are really astounding. Agreements are being made, so-called gentlemen's agreements—outside the contract, and in clear-cut violation of it. A truck dispatcher's job in the warehouse calls for stenciling cases. The rate is $1.69. But when some extra help was needed, a man was moved up from a $1.57 job and the foreman and shop steward made the agreement that he should only get $1.63. I was told that there were other such gentlemen's agreements, but I didn't go into them. I felt the situation was messy enough and I was there to try and get some peace at that plant. But the local plant management took the surprising position that, although some person might do that particular job of stenciling for two or three weeks without interruption, he should not get the rate for that job because the evaluation program assigned other duties besides stenciling to that job rate.

Fisher (m): We will be interested to receive evidence of irregularities from any of you. But, we want to be sure that they are irregularities and not misunderstandings. Had there ever been any consideration given in the evaluation as to what happens when people stencil full time—has that ever been evaluated?

Belkin (u): The answer to your question, Austin, is, apparently, no. As a matter of practice I checked this issue today with locals other than Edgewater, and they tell me the Edgewater situation would have brought the $1.69 rate at other plants. That is, when someone is assigned work of a different classification, paying a higher rate, he gets that rate even though the work involved is only part of that classification. Now, it is this inconsistency that roils me.

Fisher (m): The thing that puzzles me is why wasn't the matter taken right up through the grievance procedure?

Fitzgerald (u): It was taken to the grievance procedure.

Fisher (m): Why didn't you press it through to arbitration?

Fitzgerald (u): We wanted to bring it up here. There's no reason we have got to go to arbitration when other plants claim they would get the full rate.

Fisher (m): What you are doing is turning a negotiating conference into supergrievance machinery.

Belkin (u): I was afraid at that time to carry this grievance to arbitration. It would so upset the plant that I didn't know what the consequences might be.

Fisher (m): Let us carry on with some of the other things.

Belkin (u): Recently we had this shocking situation at St. Louis. A member's home was burned and afterwards all his remaining possessions were stolen. The next day he left for Kansas City to get help from his parents. En route he ran into a very bad sleet storm and realized he would be delayed in getting back to the plant. So he tried to telephone the plant, but the wires were down. He finally returned to work two days later, explained the situation in full, and received a disciplinary letter stating he should have notified the company he was going to be away. George can probably tell you more.

Reichardt (u): First I want to state that my feeling toward our company has always been the best. I am proud to be a member of the organization, and I appreciate the many considerations extended us. For that reason, when this incident occurred I approached the plant manager as to the possibilities of extending some financial assistance to this individual. He didn't believe the company would consider this case because no serious tragedy was involved. He did tell me he would be willing to present the facts to headquarters. We took up a collection. I have a copy of the letter received by this man.

Fisher (m): Please read it to us.

Reichardt (u): It ends up: "Please see that a situation such as this does not occur again, or I will have to assume that you do not appreciate your job and the responsibilities that go with it."

Fisher (m): By whom is that signed?

Reichardt (u): Mr. Seeley, process foreman. It upset me because I feel toward the boys in the plant just as I do my own people, and when they have trouble I have trouble, and for that reason I was really hurt. After a discussion with Seeley, I saw his attitude was just as stated in the letter, and I am sure it didn't reflect the feeling of the company.

Belkin (u): What was this man's attendance record?

Reichardt (u): He had hardly been absent in his six years with the company.

Fisher (m): I'd like to ask Mr. Bemis his version of the situation.

Bemis (m): I gave permission for the collection to be taken because I felt very sorry for this man. I also told George I would contact Cambridge to see if the company would help him out. The next thing I knew the man left without telling anyone. Mr. Seeley, the foreman, thought he had kicked his job in the teeth as well as having a misfortune and felt he should be given a letter. I finally agreed to a mild letter which would just point out to him that he should let somebody know when he left.

We had a bad situation in St. Louis of people failing to report their absence. It has become a normal practice to write them a letter informing them that they should call in before their shift to inform their supervisor they would be absent.

Fisher (m): I might say this—the fact that I, or any of us, do not give you a reaction doesn't mean we haven't one. But I think it is better to confine this meeting to a statement of facts. We feel this is a good opportunity for you fellows to clear the air.

Belkin (u): Before we leave the St. Louis situation, there is considerable resentment in the ranks because foremen are doing work within our jurisdiction as set forth by the agreement, and when they are consulted about it they blow their tops.

Fisher (m): May I suggest a short recess?

[A brief recess was taken.]

Belkin (u): Let us go to Baltimore. There the company requests men to work overtime and pays them only straight time, even though it is lower than their regular rate.

Fisher (m): Let us get the facts.

Boulden (m): There is a difference between assigning a man to a job and offering him overtime work not in his department. If we go around the plant and say, "Here's a job. Do you want it? It pays so much"—then we pay so much. But if we assign a man to a job, we pay him his regular rate or the rate for the job, whichever is higher.

Belkin (u): From the inception of the labor movement we have fought to prevent one employee from undercutting the rate of another. You haven't any right to offer a job at less than their regular rate. If I am wrong on that I want to know it before we enter into our negotiations.

Barrett (u): You customarily offer overtime on a take-it-or-leave-it basis.

Lamprell (m): I think we ought to distinguish between extra work and overtime.

Fisher (m): Under our contract it is an overtime operation if it is in excess of forty hours, or over eight hours in any one day. But what does that have to do with the *rate* of pay? Our contract states on temporary assignments:

The company shall have the option of promoting or assigning an employee from one job to another, but the employee so assigned shall receive his regular payroll-card rate or the prevailing rate of pay for the work performed, whichever is higher, provided that the temporary assignment shall not exceed five working days.

Lamprell (m): But this is extra work. We are not assigning it to him. We merely ask if anyone wants to do this work.

Fisher (m): And when a man agrees to do something you want, you pay him less than when he does it because you order him to do it?

Lamprell (m): We tell him what the rate of the job is.

Barrett (u): So by being cooperative, the employees get kicked in the teeth.

Boulden (m): If it is a job we really need to have done, we assign a man to it and he gets his regular rate or the rate of the job, whichever is greater.

Barrett (u): It wouldn't be necessary to take people from another department to clean up unless they refused to give people in those departments their overtime rate.

Fitzgerald (u): On extra work, Baltimore has its own contract. It seems to be a management contract! If the Baltimore plant has been doing this thing, they have been going against the contract.

Belkin (u): You gentlemen know what you are doing to the International. You put us in a terrible position. They are entitled to the regular rate for the job.

Fisher (m): The question is whether, under the contract, there is any basis for distinction between voluntary acceptance of overtime and assigning a man to overtime work. I see no such basis. It is a question of whether or not the contract is being lived up to.

Belkin (u): There have been so many things that could have gone to arbitration this year that we would have been in a series of arbitrations, one after the other. If that happens, the whole relationship we have been trying to build breaks down, doesn't it?

Fisher (m): You have one of two alternatives when you have a series of complaints, such as we have heard today. Either you follow your contract— protest these things and take them as high as is necessary, even to arbitration—or the local union and plant management have to work out a satisfactory method of coming to a decision. I agree with you that arbitration should be resorted to only when absolutely essential. On the other hand, I do not believe these things should simmer until they reach an explosion point at negotiation time. You've got to either fish or cut bait—and the trouble here is that we haven't done either.

Now, *assuming* that you fellows are 100 per cent right in every grievance you brought to our attention today, why in the name of heaven didn't you get an answer you could sink your teeth into? If you feel you have legitimate cases, they damned well ought to be processed up the grievance procedure. I don't want to be placed in the position of either agreeing or disagreeing with a plant manager about a decision he makes, and I am sure that neither Mr. Gamber nor Mr. Gonser wants to be placed in that position until the matter is properly before his level of management.

Martin (u): At Baltimore, our relations had been very good, but recently things are piling up and we have several more complaints.

Fisher (m): They are going to get every chance to be aired.

Belkin (u): We can't understand what is happening now. The boys will take it as far as the plant manager, and even though they are right, if he says, "No," in the interest of keeping peace, they have been dropping them.

Fisher (m): It is like getting along with your wife. You think when you don't give her that clinching answer in a dispute with her, that everything is fine. Then, one day about two weeks later, after the third scotch and soda, you let her have it.

Fitzgerald (u): We are just about getting our second scotch and soda now.

Burkhart (m): Mr. Belkin, did I understand that these things had just happened at Baltimore recently?

Belkin (u): I heard most of them within the past month.

Fisher (m): Is this overtime procedure new in Baltimore?

Barrett (u): It has been more general this year than in the past, but it has been a subject of complaint for a long, long time.

Fisher (m): Has it ever been presented at any level as a grievance?

Lamprell (m): No. They just came in and chatted with me informally.

Fisher (m) [to Barrett]: Why did you talk to him informally instead of putting through a grievance?

Barrett (u): I thought that that was more or less of a formal complaint.

Fisher (m): Don't you have a written form?

Barrett (u): The only time we make a record is when we meet with the plant manager and when I ask for minutes. But unless I ask for it, it is not done.

Fitzgerald (u): I might add that none of the other locals knew about this until yesterday.

Fisher (m): All right. Lou, would you like to continue?

Belkin (u): In Cambridge a series of things trouble me very, very much. Some of them are outright violations of the Labor Relations Act. For example, the plant manager discusses with salaried employees who are doing maintenance-production work the question of whether or not they should keep their union affiliation. Now, that is an outright violation of the law.

Fisher (m): Let us pin this thing down. Can you give us the specific names and situations?

De Vincentis (u): I would rather not give the names.

Fisher (m): Look, Joe, in fairness to all, when you make such serious charges you have to support them or not make them. I can't entertain any complaints of violation of the law without being in complete possession of the facts.

De Vincentis (u): I am not complaining about a violation of the law.

Fisher (m): Counsel is.

De Vincentis (u): But I am not, so I will make it as I see it. Some people in the engineering development department complained to me last week that the plant manager approached them and said they had no reason for belonging to the union, that he could see no benefit they derived from being a member, that they were only paying dues. Now I don't want anything to happen to those people, because if anything does, there's going to be trouble—

Fisher (m): Don't get excited. Nothing is going to happen here. Gary, would you care to comment on this?

Grant (m): Those two individuals are not members of the bargaining unit, and therefore I felt perfectly free to talk to them. There was some uncertainty in my mind as to whether they wanted to be in the bargaining unit, and I went and asked them if that was their decision.

Fisher (m): Who are these people?

Grant (m): Plympton and Swenson in the mechanical development shop. I had found that their dues were being deducted by the company—

Fisher (m): Had they signed a checkoff?

Grant (m): Yes, and the cards had been passed to the company to deduct their dues. Since we had never agreed to deduct dues for people not in the bargaining unit, I went to these fellows and asked if they intended to be in the bargaining unit. They said "No," but that they gained a certain amount of seniority by belonging to the union. I said they gained nothing by maintaining their membership as far as seniority protection was concerned. One man has no seniority because he never was an hourly worker. The other man does have some back seniority, which is guaranteed him by the contract.

Fisher (m): Would you agree with Joe's account?

Grant (m): I didn't say they had no reason for belonging to the union. I simply pointed out they had less rights under the union contract than they apparently thought they had.

Fisher (m): I think it is important to determine whether these people have been covered by a checkoff and, secondly, if, in raising the question of the propriety of such a practice, we are following the proper procedures.

Belkin (u): Quite obviously you are not.

De Vincentis (u): They were told if they remained members of the bargaining unit, they would lose all the privileges they now have on a salary status.

Fisher (m): Gary?

Grant (m): I made no such statement.

Fisher (m): I think you see the necessity for getting the facts pretty clearly on both sides, and for everybody to express anything he wants to say on this subject.

Belkin (u): Now, we have these people signed up; and when the company interviews them on the question of whether or not they should be members of our unit, the incident itself is a violation of the Labor Relations Act. Furthermore, when the company points out to them the benefits or lack of benefits in becoming a member of a union, that is a second violation of the law.

If we were to say, for the purpose of argument, that under the contract these men are not members of our bargaining unit, the next step would be, of course, for us to file a petition for representation or request recognition.

Fisher (m): Or to agree by consent to an amendment of the bargaining unit. We have adequate recourse through negotiation to settle whether Swenson and Plymptom are to be in or out of the bargaining unit. That is something we can discuss and decide. Their membership in the union, however, has not been, at least in the past, a subject for discussion.

Belkin (u): What troubles me, Austin, is that intentionally or not, you have been undercutting the union. If we represent these people, you ought to discuss the matter of their representation with us, not with them.

Let's go on to something else. Just prior to negotiations, this year and in the past, a plant manager will call in a member of our negotiating committee and suggest to him that he has been over his record, and, frankly, it would be very easy to fire the person involved. The timing is the thing; it comes just before negotiations.

Fisher (m): Will you please be specific?

Belkin (u): I am very reluctant—

Fisher (m): I am very reluctant to entertain it unless you are specific. You are a seasoned lawyer, and you know it is easy to assassinate a character this way. I would like to say that if there is any feeling on the part of people involved in this that anybody in top management has anything but the most objective desire to give them a fair deal, please put it to bed.

Belkin (u): Joe, suppose you tell them what you told me.

De Vincentis (u): I am a bad boy, I guess. Shortly after several meetings on a series of grievances, I happened to be working on the job when I was called and told that the plant manager was looking all over for me. I finally met him, and he gave me a sad tale of woe—that I had such a terrible record I could be fired for it. Then he asked me if it was unfair to bring that up at that time. I told him it was, because at that time we were in the middle of the third step of a real hot grievance. I think it was the wrong time to approach me on my record. I am well aware of my record.

Fisher (m): Gary, would you like to give your version?

Grant (m): We had tried to locate Mr. De Vincentis during working hours in connection with a grievance. We were unable to find him. We put the call bell on him and sent out for his supervisor to come in and check the equipment which was running and which was supposed to have been shut down. As the supervisor came into the plant, he met Joe coming in from the outside, and it was perfectly obvious that he had been absent for some hour and forty minutes. We had been having other disciplinary cases for this kind of thing during the past year or two; and I felt I couldn't ignore the situation. We have pretty conclusive evidence that he hasn't been in the plant on other occasions. Realizing that here was a delicate time to take the normal disciplinary action, I sought counsel from my superiors. It was their suggestion that I point out to Mr. De Vincentis privately that the usual course of disciplinary action in his case would be very embarrassing to the management. I said it was the first time I had to go to the record of any member of the committee, that I was surprised at that record, and that, had he not been a member of the committee, the record probably would have resulted in his separation. I told him I didn't feel it was fair on his part to put the management in that position, and I still feel the same way about it.

Fisher (m): Are there any other facts that ought to be brought into this? Or other similar instances?

Healey (u): It has been common practice, since we started to organize the plant, to try to intimidate members of the negotiating committee.

Fisher (m): Joe, I would like you to be specific because this is the first time I have ever heard a charge like that in all my years here.

Healey (u): I will be specific. During negotiations, before we ever had a master contract, prior to the present plant manager, the supervisors spoke to each committee member to influence him on the action of the union, and their demands. The former plant manager interfered with the union in many ways.

Fisher (m): Who was this man?

Healey (u): Mr. Cove.

Fisher (m): Heavens! Let's take the present day. Mr. Cove is dead, rest his soul. Are there any recent conversations attempting to intimidate members of the negotiating committee? I don't want to go back to Cove or antediluvian stuff any more than you want us to. If not, shall we recess for lunch?

[A luncheon recess was taken.]

Fisher (m): Well, Lou, in connection with items mentioned this morning, we want to know the facts and what you think. We want also to do the right thing. It is not necessary to labor that point after some ten years with the company. We will do the right thing because we have to live with ourselves, and not because we want to please or displease the union or any other group of people. If there have been errors, we will try to correct them. But, just as you are inclined to be indulgent of shortcomings in your organization, you have to permit us the same luxury. No organization is perfect and all individuals will occasionally make mistakes. Our intentions are of the utmost of goodwill. Now let's get back to some of these things that you raised. I'd like to ask Mr. Grant to repeat what he told us during the recess about questioning employees outside the bargaining unit.

Grant (m): A week or so ago in our local contract negotiations the union said they intended to ask for inclusion in the bargaining unit of some salaried employees—paper cutters, stationery clerks, and printers. I called these employees together and asked point blank whether they wanted to be included, and they said "Yes." I told them that was all I needed to know and that I would act accordingly. And so I did. I told the union of our willingness to take those people into the bargaining unit.

Fisher (m): Is that substantially correct as you understand it, Joe?

De Vincentis (u): Yes.

Fisher (m): All right. There seems to be no need to investigate that one any further. I think I can say this. There is no change in company policy, either in its attitude toward your union, or in its attitude toward you as individuals, or in its attitude toward the other employees whom you represent.

De Vincentis (u): If that is true, why did Mr. Grant ask the foremen what demands the union was going to make? Some of them went around the plant asking what demands the union was going to make. That should come up at contract negotiations and not in the plant level between the foremen and—

Fisher (m): I quite agree with you. Let's be realistic, Joe. In past negotiations we felt we had such inadequate information as to what the union proposals were going to be that we were very often forced to a hasty consideration of the things you presented to us. For that reason we asked our plant managers to anticipate in so far as they could the probable nature of your demands.

Now that was not a signal to engage in improper activities. But to the extent that they had information as to current attitudes of the employees, we felt, and still feel, that it is perfectly proper to ask them what they think is going to happen.

Belkin (u): Well, of course, you know it is a dangerous thing to do. If you want that information, the plant manager can always talk it over with the local committee. But when you go into the matter of questioning our members—

Fisher (m): You don't have to say any more because I agree that it is an improper thing for a foreman to question a union member about a plan. Let me quote from the directive Mr. Burkhart wrote to all plant managers prior to the time that we started to have these talks with the foremen.

These discussions with your staff should be on a positive basis. That is, we do not wish to break down our excellent relations with our union, nor to sabotage their contract or program. But our desire is purely a constructive one to improve the union contract from both a management and a union standpoint so it can be administered more successfully for each of the parties involved.

Now, let me explain what went into that. Many of our foremen, we found, were not entirely familiar with our contract, and that was our responsibility. It was something we wished to correct because we felt we could not rely upon them for accurate administration of an agreement which they didn't understand. Just as you solicit from the rank and file of your own membership, so, too, we felt an obligation to solicit the views of our foremen, who are as much a part of our organization as your members are a part of your union. We thought it was intelligent to attempt to secure a greater participation by the foremen in the business of creating policy. Therefore, the foremen were asked for their opinions. In those cases where we disagreed we told them we disagreed and explained why. All we were trying to do was to create a better level of understanding, greater appreciation, and a greater sense of participation.

I understand that when you undertake a change of that sort there is always danger that it is going to be misconstrued. Now, if they have been irresponsible, the company is in some respects at fault for not having brought them into this thing sooner and more in detail. We have told them before and will repeat a dozen times if necessary that we mean this thing to be a constructive move; we don't want to disrupt, but we do want to bring our labor relations up to an adult relationship.

Reichardt (u): While we don't have much trouble, we do have a few foremen that more or less have done this too.

Fisher (m): Conducting things at an honorable and self-respecting level is what we have always striven to do. This is your first major negotiation, Mr. Reichardt, but I think the record will bear out my statement that we have at all times treated you the way we hope to be treated ourselves. If individuals are guilty of unseeming conduct, do us a favor and let us know about it. If we have a similar problem with any of your people, which, frankly, occurs very rarely, we are going to do the same thing for you. And I am sure that we can very quickly straighten out any rudeness or incivility.

Belkin (u): While we are winding this thing up, I might say our people are touchy and fidgety. We are faced with layoffs now in a greater number than we have ever had, and that is bound to make us fidgety. And, secondly, we sort of feel—although you say that isn't so—that there is a change in management policy.

Now, no one of our people here has any personal resentment against any plant manager. Mr. Grant has been criticized, but, frankly, we feel that because he is closer to your main office he is pushed into a position where willy-nilly he has to act a certain way. That is the story to a lesser degree up and down the line. We don't want any reassurance from you, but if it is true we will meet it as best we can.

Fisher (m): You don't have to worry about that, Lou. And I would know whether it was true or not.

Belkin (u): Frankly, Austin, we wonder if you would.

Fisher (m): I would not be here unless the management told me what their policies were. I have over a period of years been personally close to Mr. Luckman and the members of his top management, and I don't know of any changes in policy or attitude.

Burkhart (m): Perhaps my reassurance would help. After all, I do transmit all policy to the plants, and I can assure you that I know nothing about any policy change.

Fisher (m): It might interest you to know that in several other places where I have negotiated contracts and where I enjoy a pleasant relationship with the union and with the company, I have hit just this sort of thing, particularly during the last six or seven months. I don't think it is just a coincidence that at about that time our national economic picture started to change a little, carloadings started to drop off, and unemployment payments started to rise. I wonder whether all of us aren't suffering from a slight state of jitters brought on by a change in the economic picture and by worry about what is happening abroad. Up until the middle of this last year consumption levels for our products and for the products of many other companies were at all-time highs; the backlog of orders was very great; and inventories were inadequate to meet consumer demands. We were all riding

a wave of optimism. Then along about the middle of the year a change occurred, and people began to wonder.

Now, you fellows know you have your worries. Well, company executives
also have theirs. Perhaps when you both start to worry, you get a little tense
toward each other and assume there is a change of attitude when what has
really occurred is that some of the old ghosts came back to haunt us.

I hope if this three or four hours we have put in today accomplishes anything, it may be a recognition on both sides of the table that these intangibles
have a way of clouding the relationship. It might be good for us to sit down
together and take stock of it before we let our nerves get the better of us.

In passing over these grievances, I don't want you to think that they
are forgotten. They are not forgotten. We will consider them and we will
recommend appropriate action in due course. But let us, at least, try to
enter these negotiations with the air clearer than it was.

[Mr. Belkin and Mr. Fitzgerald then went through the entire contract,
paragraph by paragraph, indicating desired changes, deletions, insertions, and
clarifications involving half of all the contract provisions.

Major wage demands were: a 10% general wage increase [minimum rates:
$1.20 per hour for light task common labor, $1.40 for common labor, $1.95
for top-rate craftsmen]; [1] shift premiums of 7 cents and 15 cents [5 cents
and 10 cents]; bonus of $2\frac{1}{2}$, 5, $7\frac{1}{2}$, and 10 cents per hour for each 5, 10,
15, and 20 years of service; reduction of 13 evaluated labor grades to 10,
each with 10-cent differentials [75-cent total differential]; and liberalization
of overtime provisions. Other demands included: 12 paid holidays [$7\frac{1}{4}$];
pay for 3 working [calendar] days immediately following a death in the
family; vacations of 1, 2, 3, 4, 5 weeks after 6 months, 1, 5, 10, 15 years of
service [1, 2, 3 weeks after 1, 3, 10 years]; one additional paid holiday for
each employee for each year of service with the monetary equivalent of any
days not taken to be given as a Christmas bonus; and severance pay of one
week for each year's service regardless of reason for leaving [physically disabled or ineligible for a pension]. Other economic demands included more
liberal company-paid hospitalization and medical insurance, and a contributory pension plan [company-paid] to be expanded by tie-in with length of
service and convertibility of an increased paid-up life insurance policy.

The important noneconomic demands included the following: inclusion
of stationery clerks and printers in the bargaining unit; union shop, irrevocable checkoff, and company collection of all dues and assessments when
permitted by a change in the Taft-Hartley Act; elimination of all provisions
relating to management's rights, no strike and no lockout, and arbitration;
full five-day work weeks; no work to be subcontracted outside of the company; job evaluation to be accelerated by specified time limits; and the
union to be represented equally with management in the administration of
insurance and pension programs.]

---

[1] Provisions of the contract in effect at the time are bracketed.

Fisher (m): I would like to suggest we recess for a bit to give us a chance to discuss these extremely moderate proposals. Perhaps we will come back with some equally moderate proposals.

[Recess.]

Fisher (m): We have given due consideration to your request, which, it may interest you to know, involves 43 changes, 15 eliminations, and 4 new benefits, a total of 62 new items which you have interjected.

We think you are a hundred per cent right. However, before we make that concession formally, there are a few items we want to bring out, and I am going to ask Roy Shorey to explain that phase of it.

Shorey (m): I would like to give this memorandum to the stenographer and let it go in the record as a recitation of the company's proposal.

[Mr. Shorey then reviewed the company's thirteen-point memorandum, which involved three changes in substance and ten changes in language which incorporated, defined, or clarified in the contract existing clauses and practices. Substantive items were: limitation of the bargaining unit to hourly paid employees,[1] extension of the thirty working day probationary period for new employees, and discussion of policy on leaves of absence [u].[2] The language changes provided for: *inclusion* in the contract of further job evaluation procedures [u] and advance notice of expected absence; *definition* of layoffs (as distinct from shutdowns) and of eligibility for holiday payments; *clarification* of reporting time [u], allowance for relief and lunch periods on overtime shifts [u], and of the paragraph establishing subjects for local negotiation [u]; alignment of the beginning and end of the vacation year with the normal work week; removal of the clause outlining the company's action, when an employee's work was below standard, from the disciplinary section to a new section called Workmanship; and removal of two paragraphs, now unnecessary, which had been incorporated the previous year into the formal benefit program.]

Belkin (u): There is a very strange omission here. Do I understand that you are not making any offer on wages?

Fisher (m): No, we are not making any offer on anything except those changes which we desire to initiate at this time. In other words, we were submitting to you our list of contract changes. We have received your list of contract changes. This, then, places us in a bargaining position.

Fitzgerald (u): And this is the company's total?

Fisher (m): No, don't misunderstand this. This is not a counterproposal. These points represent problems we wish to consider. Just as you have not given an indication with respect to our proposals and you are retiring to consider them, so we, too, do not indicate any position on the proposals you made at this time. We merely accept them, try to understand them; then we will retire to deliberate them.

---

[1] This would involve reclassification of some jobs from salaried to hourly rated work at the Cambridge plant.

[2] [u] indicates items also included in the union demands.

Fitzgerald (u): Do you intend to come back here Monday and hand us another proposal, or work on the contract?

Fisher (m): We will go right to work on the contract, I think, although I want to reserve flexibility for the company to do whatever it thinks advisable on Monday, just as you want to reserve flexibility for yourself. May we have a recess?

[Recess.]

[After the recess Mr. Gamber explained that management had taken under advisement the suggestion made that morning about the number of delegates and their expenses and had decided to offer each local two options: (1) the company would pay all expenses of three delegates, or (2) all expenses of two delegates and transportation for two observers. Under either option all such representatives would be reimbursed for any wages lost during the period of negotiations.]

Gamber (m): We are somewhat taken aback by the number of items suggested in the new contract. We would just like to mention that, starting next Monday, we have only two weeks in which to get the new contract in shape for presentation to your membership on Sunday, March 6th, which I take is an advisable thing. We also have another group to meet with, as you fellows well know, so presumably a portion, up to a half of the time, will be spent with another group.

We would like to have you by Monday take another look at the items presented by you toward eliminating—possibly, some items which are going to clutter up negotiations considerably. We would like to sincerely get down to work Monday; but with the number of items we have to discuss and the number of hours allotted, I wonder how we are going to progress. We would like to suggest that your group stay over tomorrow and organize their thinking on specific changes desired.

If you do stay over, we will treat it the same as Monday or today as far as expenses are concerned. It would be well worth the time spent and would save us a lot of time later on.

[A recess was taken at the request of the union.]

Belkin (u): Mr. Chairman, after due deliberation we found considerable merit in Mr. Gamber's suggestions, and we are going to stay.

De Vincentis (u): How is this thing going to work next week?

Belkin (u): It might be a better thing to meet next week without any interruption from Hammond, and then you meet with Hammond the following week.

Fisher (m): We have a problem. If we negotiate with you the first week, the Hammond group feel they have been discriminated against, and if we negotiate with the Hammond group, you feel you have been discriminated against. Under the circumstances, it seems wisest, based on past experience, to keep the negotiation on a parity of speed. And I am sorry that there aren't any more hours in the day, but it is the best we can do.

Belkin (u): If that is the best you can do, there is no more we can say.

Gamber (m): Would it be possible Monday for the union to have something in writing on your proposal as a result of your meeting tomorrow? Might we look forward to that?

Fitzgerald (u): That I can't tell you. But we intend to go over our contract and do the best we can with it.

Fisher (m): I want to reinforce something, Fitz. You have a hell of a lot of proposals, and if it is possible to eliminate some of them, it will accelerate our discussions.

Fitzgerald (u): We realize that.

Fisher (m): We have tried not to create for ourselves too much of a bargaining position and have confined ourselves to a reasonable number of points. Frankly, you made some proposals that I don't think any of you, in your wildest dreams, expect to get. So cut out the clowning and get down to business.

Fitzgerald (u): If the company is sincere in its efforts, it will get good cooperation from the locals.

III. CIO: First Session—February 16, 1949

(10:00 A.M.–11:45 A.M.)

For the Company

Representing Company Headquarters:

Austin M. Fisher	Labor Relations Consultant
Thomas A. Gonser	Director of Personnel and Public Relations
Gerald F. Gamber	Associate Director of Personnel
Roy V. Shorey	Personnel Manager
William H. Burkhart	Director of Manufacture
W. Wesley Pear	Personnel Research Administrator

Representing Plant Management:

William E. Oyler	Plant Manager	Hammond
Robert J. Barr	Industrial Relations Manager	Hammond

For the Union

Paul Stawicki	Organizer, Chemical Workers, CIO
Michael Krapac	President, Local Union
Harry J. DeFrates	Member of Negotiating Committee
Russell Hammond	Member of Negotiating Committee
Albert F. Kukral	Member of Negotiating Committee
Herman M. Loden	Member of Negotiating Committee
Carl G. Rumps	Member of Negotiating Committee
Elmer W. Smith	Member of Negotiating Committee
Walter J. Swentko	Member of Negotiating Committee

Burkhart (m): We welcome you here for negotiations. Since I have been chairman of the management negotiating committee for several years, I am relinquishing my position to Mr. Gamber. Unfortunately, he had to leave town, but at subsequent meetings he will take over. Mr. Fisher will again act as company spokesman.

Fisher (m): We are glad to have you here again and extend to you, Mr. Stawicki, a special word of greeting since you are new. As you know, we are carrying on concurrent negotiations with the AFL. We would like to continue our past practice of alternate meetings so that neither organization gets any edge. We want to deal with both fairly.

If you wish to go off the record, it is your privilege and ours, too, so the record won't block complete, frank disclosure of anything on anybody's mind. Both sides will reserve the right to call for a caucus whenever they see fit. We are prepared to spend whatever time is necessary in exchanging ideas of what should go into a new contract. Since you fellows served notice of your desire to make changes in the contract, may we ask you to tell us what you have in mind?

Stawicki (u): We are prepared to give you a complete proposal.

Fisher (m): As you go along, we will interrupt to ask you questions. But we will not debate today on the merits of any issues. This is a meeting just to state positions.

Krapac (u): All right. We will now distribute copies of the proposed changes.

Fisher (m): Thank you. May I congratulate you all on your workman-like way of presenting it.

[Stawicki then offered the union's contract proposal incorporating the following economic demands:

1. A wage increase of 27 cents per hour.
   [Minimum rates: 1.20 per hour for light task common labor, $1.40 for common labor, $1.95 for top rate craftsman.] [1]
2. Shift premiums of 10 and 15 cents.
   [5 and 10 cents.]
3. Double time for any work done after eight hours in any 24-hour period or on Saturdays.
   [Time and one-half for such work.]
4. Double time, in addition to holiday pay, on any holiday worked.
   [Holiday pay plus time and one-half.]
5. Nine paid holidays plus Presidential election day.
   [Seven paid holidays plus Presidential election day.]
6. Paid vacations of one, two, three, and four weeks after six months, one, eight, and twelve years.
   [One, two, and three weeks after one, three, and ten years.]
7. Vacation compensation based on 2% of annual earnings for each week of allowed vacation.
   [Based on straight time weekly earnings for each week of allowed vacation.]

---

[1] Provisions of the contract in effect at the time are bracketed.

8. Amendment of pay plan for those absent because of sickness to include pay for first week if the absence exceeds a total of two weeks.
   [Full pay for 13 weeks in any 52-week period; an extra week for each year of service over 10 years up to a maximum of 26 weeks; payment for first week only if absence exceeds 30 days.]
9. Eight hours' pay for an employee "called-in" for whom no work is available.
   [Four hours' pay.]
10. Free lunch period after six hours of overtime.
    [Paid lunch period with food sold at cost and cafeterias operated at company expense.]
11. Pay for three working days for absence in event of death in immediate family (including in-law's); pay for one working day in event of death of any other relative.
    [Pay for three working days in event of death in immediate family.]
12. Amendment of pension plan to permit all employees to work until they have completed their 65th birthday.
    [Noncontributory pension with benefits approximately 1% for each year of service based on highest earnings prior to retirement; retirement on anniversary date of hire nearest employee's 65th birthday.]
13. Pay for time lost on jury duty.
    [Current practice, but not specified by contract.]

The union's noneconomic demands were relatively few: (1) incorporation of power house engineers into the bargaining unit; (2) reduction of the probationary period for new employees from 30 working days or three months, whichever was shorter, to 30 calendar days; (3) checkoff by the company of union initiation fees in addition to the monthly dues which were already checked off; and (4) deletion of clauses stipulating the conditions which the union had to perform in the event of an unauthorized stoppage in order to be free of liability.

After Fisher had again congratulated the union on "as nice a job as I have ever seen done," the company requested a recess.

Following the recess, Shorey presented on behalf of the company a written list of proposals which were practically identical to those given the previous day to the AFL group with the addition of a proposal to reword the provisions of one step in the grievance procedure to conform to existing practice. This revision, as well as a similar one relating to job evaluation procedures, had also been included among the union's demands. The company emphasized that its suggestions did not represent substantive changes in the contract, but rather formalization of existing practices. The union agreed to consider the joint productivity plan (originally suggested by the AFL) which was being considered at the other plants. Each party was to consider the proposals of the other before the next meeting.]

IV. CIO: Second Session—February 21

[This session was largely devoted to exploration of CIO's wage demands.]

V. AFL: Second Session—February 21

(2:20 P.M.–5:05 P.M.)

The union committee had held a series of meetings in an attempt to crystallize some of its proposals. Belkin was absent, his place being taken by Bradley, president of the International. Fitzgerald read off the revised list of contract changes desired by the union, the major changes being a vacation schedule of 1, 2, 3 and 4 weeks, respectively, after 6 months, 1, 10, and 20 years' service, and omission of the demand for hourly service bonuses. The management team then caucused, and when negotiations were resumed Fisher asked Fitzgerald to present the union's reasons for its proposals.

Fitzgerald (u): Well, on the money situation—most of the raises gotten the last month or so by our International have been around 10%. On the labor grades, we find a lot of trouble in the 13 grades which could be taken care of in 10 grades with at least 10-cent differentials.

Fisher (m): Well, Fitz, is your only reason for an increase because the Chemical Workers got 10% increases in the last couple of months?

Fitzgerald (u): Not only the Chemical Workers, but those around in different areas.

Fisher (m): Do you think that other companies, either in the chemical industry or in the areas which you represent, are paying wages as high as ours?

Fitzgerald (u): I am not interested in that particular question. If these other places get raises, they come closer to us. I think that was our argument last year, too, and we want to hold our difference.

Fisher (m): What companies are you talking about?

Bradley (u): I don't know that the companies are of any particular value. The important thing is this. Realizing that unquestionably you representatives of the company are going to point out to us that there is a decline in the cost of living, that your product is down in price, and so on, all of which we would have to admit, the fact remains that the dollar is still worth only 58.3¢. And we are very doubtful that the decline in the cost of living is a permanent thing.

De Vincentis (u): In 1947 there was a downward trend in the cost of living, and we felt at that time that it would continue. But, lo and behold, what do we find? Two or three months later, everything starts skyrocketing and we hit the peak long afterwards. The increase we got in March, 1947, had been wiped out by August of '47. On top of that, most of our people through reductions in overtime have actually taken a cut.

Fisher (m): You mean in hours of work?

De Vincentis (u): Not only in hours, but in their hourly rate. People with long service have taken a cut because the Swan Department is closed down, and they have had to go into other departments to lower rated jobs. Cuts were as much as 25¢ an hour less than they have been getting for years.

Fisher (m): Are there any other general arguments you want to advance at this time, Fitz?

Fitzgerald (u): One more thing should come into this. We are producing much more than we ever did before, per man.

Healey (u): That is right. Every plant has gone up over 10% in their production quotas. And, besides, in '47 and '48 Lever Brothers has had the best profits since they came to this country.

Fisher (m): I am glad you know about profits more than I do. Anything else?

Well, let's take an easy one to start with and see if we can agree on the facts.

[Mr. Fisher then introduced a series of charts. The first charts pictured the straight-time rates paid to No. 1 skilled craftsmen by Lever as compared with local area rates. Area rates were defined as the rates averaged for similar jobs paid by the 20 largest companies drawing workers from the area where 80% of the Lever employees lived. These charts showed a uniform Lever rate of $1.95 for No. 1 craftsmen contrasted to area rates for comparable craftsmen as follows: Baltimore, $1.58; Cambridge, $1.58; Edgewater, $1.76; and St. Louis, $1.68. The union members objected that the companies were "an unfair comparison" since they included "the top rates" and there was "no comparison between our industry and those industries."]

Fisher (m): You are interested only in those companies that pay more than Lever. Year after year you criticize the company's statistics, and yet you never bring in anything in their place. Why don't you give us facts instead of general allegations?

Healey (u): If we based our argument on area rates we would bring them in.

Fisher (m): What is your argument if it isn't area rate?

Healey (u): They have no bearing on Lever Brothers.

Fisher (m): One of the things you mentioned was that our No. 1 craftsmen were out of line. I produced these figures to show you that they are not out of line.

Healey (u): We will be polite and listen to the display of figures.

[Mr. Fisher then displayed a chart comparing total hourly increases given since V–J Day as follows:

	Baltimore	Cambridge	Edgewater	St. Louis
Lever.......	71¢	63.5¢	62.5¢	69.5¢
Area........	41¢	37.9¢	40.6¢	42.2¢

The discussion then continued.]

Fitzgerald (u): You gave us a nice raise last year, and I think you got it well back in efficiency and everything else. If you change your tactics this year, I think it is going to boomerang.

Fisher (m): Well, you are entitled to your opinion, Fitz. What we are trying to do is to examine what reasons support your request for an increase. We were talking about No. 1 craftsmen, and then we got into the general picture of what has happened in these areas since V–J Day.

Healey (u): We don't think those things are relevant.

Fisher (m): What do you think is relevant?

Healey (u): Open up the books there; read some of the profits; compare the profits with these companies; then you are talking our language. Compare our work load per man with some of these other industries.

Fisher (m): What are the facts, Joe, since you bring it up? Why don't you tell us the relevant ones?

Fitzgerald (u): I would like to answer your question there, Mr. Fisher. Last year you gave us this same bunch of charts, and we weren't entitled to a raise last year either, according to them, and still we knew we should get one. Everybody, even you, knew we should get something, and we finally *did* get something. We don't agree with those charts anyhow. We don't go for twenty companies. The more you pick, the further down you go. So let's get on to the next question.

[Fisher then presented a series of line charts showing the relative trends of indexes of the average straight-time hourly rates at each of the Lever plants and the cost of living index as reported for each area by the Bureau of Labor Statistics. The base in each instance was January, 1941, and the points of reference were January, 1941, March, 1946, March, 1947, and then quarterly for the year 1948.

For December, 1948, these charts showed:

	Baltimore	Cambridge	Edgewater	St. Louis
Lever Wages Index..........	267.0	199.2	173.3	247.0
Cost of Living Index........	174.0	164.7	169.2	171.1

Fisher pointed out that these charts proved that, in spite of the increased cost of living, the real wages of Lever employees had increased and that the probable continued decline in the cost of living would even further improve their position. Throughout this demonstration the union argued that the charts were deceptive since there were apparent increases for the early period when none had been given and because an unweighted average should not be considered representative.

After a brief recess there was open discussion as to the probable direction of the cost of living index. The afternoon ended on a somewhat philosophical note:]

Bradley (u): The thing that interests me is that, up until the war when the presidential decree froze wages, most employers' arguments against increased wages were based entirely on ability to pay. As soon as the Government froze wages and said, "No matter what happens to profits, you can only have 15% above January 1, 1941," employers immediately did an about-face. They said, in effect, "Sure, we can afford it; we'd just love to pay you more, but the Government won't let us."

Now that restriction is gone and the employers hold now to an area argument. I think the two important factors are the ability or the nonability to pay, and the amount of money a wage earner needs to live. In the soap industry I understand labor is one of the minor costs in production. So if there is an ability to pay and labor is one of the minor costs, then I think that the area proposition should be left out of it entirely.

Fisher (m): I recognize the force of some of your arguments on a generalized basis, Brad, but this company never discussed ability to pay. We take the position that the company is solvent enough to do the right thing and that, therefore, there need be no discussion of whether we are able or unable. The only time it becomes material is when the company raises the question. We don't raise the question. We haven't in the past, and as far as I am concerned, we are not going to do it now.

Bradley (u): Well, the union doesn't believe in area rates. They believe that it should be based entirely on ability to pay.

Fisher (m): You would hardly take the position that because you are able to pay more than twenty cents a pack for cigarettes that you ought to pay forty cents. Now, I recognize a great distinction between a commodity and a man's labor, but wage rates are set by a community of comparisons, in individual communities like Cambridge or Baltimore or Edgewater, or on a nationwide basis. Wage levels in the United States, fortunately, have not been predetermined by the ability or inability of companies to pay. If they couldn't pay a prevailing rate at the time of a labor shortage, they went out of business. And if they could pay it, by and large, they did.

Bradley (u): In the last few years, but not before.

Fisher (m): That may be. That is one of the reasons why we have felt that the advent of trade unionism was a good thing economically for the country, and we are very free to concede the accomplishments of the American labor movement in bringing wage levels up to where they are now. We also recognize that the labor movement is a dynamic thing and is compelled to forge ahead. But we say there are periods in the economy when you have to be satisfied with the gains you have made. You can't expect the business system to continue to throw off the kind of increments that we have been having over the past five or six years. And we see no evidence why we should go ahead any further than we are now ahead.

Bradley (u): I suppose the place to enunciate the ideas in my mind is, perhaps, in an auditorium. I certainly don't expect that this or any other one company is going to change the situation by themselves.

Fisher (m): Well, Brad, every once in a while one of my clients will start pulling his hair out by the roots and say, "God, when is this thing going to stop? When are these guys going to say, 'We've got enough'?" I say to my client the only answer is *they* will stop when *you* don't want another suit of clothes, another automobile, or bigger house. The point of the matter is that people's appetites for the good things in life are always growing, and our economy continues to expand as it rises. I am not against it.

The only problem is how fast can it safely advance without putting us all in a hole. There are many people who believe the advances made in previous years have been a little bit rich in terms of our ability to support them. We have advanced a little bit too fast and are at the moment suffering some of the consequences of having overreached ourselves.

I am not enough of an economist to be able to appraise that, but I think there is some logic behind the argument and I think it is something that you fellows ought to consider.

It is now 5:00 o'clock. Shall we recess until 9:30 tomorrow?

VI. AFL: Third Session—February 22

(9:30 A.M.–1.00 P.M.)

[Gamber opened the meeting by discussing management's intention to send to the plant supervisors daily bulletins "giving them the gist of the day's happenings." Bradley replied that "if they are going to do the bargaining back in the plants," he would "withdraw from the proceedings" and that he was "not going to be involved in any controversies that would come out of that kind of reporting." He added that he could remember "when relations between the employees and the company were extremely bad, and much of that condition was caused by exactly what Mr. Gamber was proposing to do." Management then caucused, and when the session resumed Gamber stated that management would agree not to send these bulletins.]

Fisher (m): Shall we discuss your modified vacation proposal?

Mr. Bradley, we understand your International has recently added considerably to its research division, and we wonder whether you could give us better information than we have concerning the usual vacation benefits in other I.C.W. contracts.

Bradley (u): Well, only the research department would know that.

Fisher (m): Let me give you what we have and let's see the extent that it is accurate. We have, as in the past, examined some 225 contracts currently held by your organization, and we find that the prevailing practice is to grant one week's vacation after one year. In the majority of the contracts, two weeks' vacation does not start until after three or more years of service. The third week's vacation pattern shows that 4 contracts provide it after 14 years, 28 after 15 years, 14 after 20 years, 14 after 25, and that 165 contracts carry no provision for a third week's vacation.

Fitzgerald (u): Mr. Fisher, I would like to explain our proposal of one week's vacation after six months. You give that to your office personnel and you give two weeks to your one-year service office personnel. That is our reason for putting that in there.

Fisher (m): Well, the principle of uniformity just doesn't work in favor of what you want and cease on the things you don't want.

Fitzgerald (u): You can't blame us for trying to get what the office gets.

Fisher (m): Your new proposal of four weeks' vacation after twenty years of service is not related to anything that happens in the office, is it?

Fitzgerald (u): No; we figure a man who works twenty years for the company deserves four weeks' vacation.

Fisher (m): Our position on the vacation situation relates in principle to a good many other fringe issues, or social benefits. By and large, Lever Brothers provides for what we might call social benefits of vacations, holidays, sickness and accident insurance, pensions, and a variety of other provisions which have been negotiated from time to time or which reflect a long-standing company practice before the advent of the union. They all lump up to a very generous deal.

Fitzgerald (u): Agreed.

Fisher (m): In fact, Lever's social-welfare benefits, taken as a whole, are, I think, as generous as any other company in the United States. Now, it is true that you will find some companies with more generous individual provisions. But we don't feel that it is fair to examine these one by one. We think you have got to examine them as a whole. We have figured the cost in cents per hour per employee for each of Lever Brothers' benefits and they come to a total of 41 cents given you over and above your wage rates. We also checked costs with the twenty companies in your local areas. It is significant that the highest figure reported by any company for their benefit program was 34 cents an hour, and the average cost was less than 15 cents an hour.

Now, one of the Cambridge delegates asked for some more information on how Lever Brothers stands with competing companies in our own industry.

We have tried to get a picture of what our competitors are doing throughout the nation, and to compare our own practices with theirs. The first chart, *Chart B,* reflects the basic male labor rate in all plant areas. This is average straight-time rates. You will see our competitors are paying an average of $1.28 against our $1.40 figure.

Chart C shows the weighted average straight-time rates these competing companies pay for common labor. Our competitors in 1949 average $1.426. Lever's average is $1.47. *Chart D* gives the same type thing for the No. 1 craftsman. Competitive companies on an average paid their No. 1 craftsmen $1.855, and Lever paid $1.950.

The next chart shows the average weekly earnings in Lever Brothers' plants, and the bottom line shows the average weekly earnings in the soap industry.

De Vincentis (u): What is that figure for Lever?

Fisher (m): About $78.50, and the figure for the soap industry about $67. With only one exception, since 1941, Lever Brothers has consistently led the soap industry. There was a period there between 1946 and 1947 when the lines crossed, and there was a slight margin of leadership on the part of the soap industry. That, however, was corrected in March of 1947, and since then there has been a clear leadership.

I would like to show you quickly a comparison for the chemical industry throughout the United States.

Fitzgerald (u): May I ask one question? Why do you go from one group to another? Why don't you stick to the soap industry and compare the figures?

Fisher (m): Let me give you a simple illustration. If you wanted to argue with me that Buick was the fastest car on the market, you would talk about Buick and Fords, and Plymouths, and all types of cars. We are trying to show you that Lever's economic picture is favorable by a good many different standards of comparison.

Fitzgerald (u): I am not being bound by these charts at all, because I just don't believe in charts. Every chart we get is different. It doesn't look good to me.

Fisher (m): Okay. Chart 23, as I said, is a comparison of Lever Brothers and the U.S. chemical industry and shows that the Lever employee enjoys about $20.50 weekly over the average hourly employee in the chemical industry. We will leave copies of these charts with you, and also give them to the stenographer so that they can become a part of the record.

Now, gentlemen, we have tried during the course of the last couple of days to indicate to you the broad position the company feels it must take at this time with respect to monetary issues, and our position, in brief, is that we have heard no evidence that would warrant any change either in our social benefits or in our wage structure.

Shall we meet at 2:30 tomorrow to consider the other items in your proposals?

VII. CIO: THIRD SESSION—FEBRUARY 22

(2:30 P.M.–5:00 P.M.)

[The discussion revolved around cost of living and comparative wages in Hammond, as well as ability to pay. Fisher presented charts showing that in Hammond, too, Lever Brothers compared favorably with other companies in all respects. The session then concluded as follows:]

Fisher (m): We think that is the sort of thing that you might very well want to take back to your membership because we know they sometimes can be critical and not know what the story is, and perhaps not give you credit for doing as good a job as you have done. There are very few companies that come anywhere near providing that kind of a picture. I think, gentlemen, that this is pretty conclusive evidence as to the caliber of jobs provided by this company, and I hope very much that you will give it very serious consideration because we feel that our program, taken as a whole, is of such a generous nature that you should not call upon us at this time to make any changes which would involve additional expenditures. We think that the wage structure is high. We think that there is a reversal in the upward cost of living which plagued us all for a great many years, and we don't think this is the time to ask both for expensive wage increases and for expensive supplementary benefits.

Well, that pretty well completes the charted information that we wanted to submit. Mr. Stawicki, would you like to call a recess for a few minutes?

Stawicki (u): Yes.

[A short recess was taken.]

Fisher (m): Proceed, Mr. Stawicki.

Stawicki (u): We would like a little clarification of the discussion just before recess. Are we to take it for granted that all of the monetary issues the union has requested are refused by the company?

Fisher (m): Yes.

Krapac (u): That is the final answer now?

Fisher (m): Yes. We see nothing in the way of evidence produced so far to warrant, in our opinion, any change in the basic wage structure or in the benefit program.

Krapac (u): With that answer, Mr. Fisher, there is no need for us continuing negotiations. We would like to prepare for transportation home.

Fisher (m): All right, gentlemen. I'm sorry you feel that way about it, but if that is what you wish to do, we will be glad to help you out.

DISCUSSION QUESTION

1. Analyze the negotiating strategy and tactics of union and company in each of these sessions.

LEVER BROTHERS COMPANY (B)

THE CLOSING SESSIONS OF THE 1949 NEGOTIATIONS

I. Introduction

Although the CIO union representatives had withdrawn from negotiations, company negotiators continued meeting with the four AFL locals on eight days between February 23 and March 9. When the parties met on February 28, Bradley, having urgent business elsewhere, was not present. The sessions of February 28 and 29 resulted in language clarification of some clauses and some agreements on principle.

Dennis Moduro, Lever consultant on pension problems, and Arch Price, the company's pension director, joined the all-day meeting March 2, and presented a thorough analysis of the company's pension plan and pointed to its superiority over 80 per cent of those studied in a cross section survey of the United States.

Discussions revealed continued disagreement on the scope of arbitration, monetary questions, and management's rights, as follows:

Fisher (m): We regard the arbitration clause and the management's rights clause as indispensable in any contract. This is not news to you.

Now, you want to know our position on monetary issues. A look back in the record shows, gentlemen, that we think our wage structure is high enough. We think that our benefit plans and fringe benefits are liberal enough. We are not prepared to agree to any increase in wages, nor to any change in the benefit plans that will involve the expenditure of money.

Fitzgerald (u): In other words, all holidays, benefits, and wages stay the same, and you want to go ahead with the rest of the contract?

Fisher (m): That's right.

Discussions the next day, March 3, concerning local contracts led to the following remarks:

De Vincentis (u): There are eleven holidays in our state which we observe whether we get paid or not.

Healey (u): March 17 [1] is not one of these observed holidays, but we may observe it. We are having a union meeting March 15, and our 30-day notice is up on March 16. The Cambridge local doesn't intend to extend the contract, so we will be able to give you a definite answer on Monday morning after our union meeting.

Fisher (m): Well, how can you reach certain decisions on your own if you intend to continue to work as a unit with the other locals?

---

[1] March 17, Evacuation Day (in celebration of the evacuation of South Boston by the British on March 17, 1775) and St. Patrick's Day, is observed as a holiday by some sectors of the Boston community.

Fitzgerald (u): What it amounts to, Mr. Fisher, is that they are going to work as a unit with us, but it could happen that they would not work as a unit with us as of March 17. That's about the size of it.

Further agreements in language and in principle concerning noneconomic matters were reached in the meetings of March 3 and March 7.

The 11th session with the AFL groups, held March 8, lasted only 15 minutes. All noneconomic issues had been explored and most of them resolved. Language changes relating union security provisions to anticipated amendment of the Labor-Management Relations Act of 1947 awaited the return of Belkin. The union still demanded elimination of the no-strike clause and management was firm in insisting that the existing provisions on arbitration and all economic benefits be retained.

II. CIO: Fourth Session—March 9

(10:30 A.M.–11:30 A.M.)

[The CIO negotiators returned to Boston at the request of the Conciliation Service and met with management before two commissioners of the Federal Mediation and Conciliation Service, one of whom came from Chicago and the other from Boston. At their request Stawicki reviewed the union's demands and reasons therefor. Fisher then summarized the company's wage levels and range of current practices as the basis for its rejection of the union's demands. The commissioners then asked to meet with the union committee privately, and the meeting was adjourned.]

III. AFL: Twelfth Session—March 9

(2:00 P.M.–7:00 P.M.)

[The two conciliators were present. After Fisher had reviewed the union's demands and the company's current practices, a recess was taken during which the conciliators met first with the union and then with management.]

Conciliator: Mr. Fisher and gentlemen, as we told you, the gentlemen on labor's side feel they have not had an opportunity to fully discuss their thinking on the issues.

Fisher (m) [to the union]: May I tell you that I am sorry if you have gotten the impression we were trying to foreclose you from saying anything. We would welcome any additional light that any of you care to cast on the issues.

Conciliator: Will you two Joe's now get everything off your chest? The field is yours, gentlemen.

Healey (u): Okay, Commissioner. First, I want to state that we are not as good in dialectics as the company, and you will have to bear with us if we try to explain things in our language.

Conciliator: Be yourself.

Healey (u): We are not business agents or paid representatives of the organization. We work in the plant and we are giving the members' point of view. We are with them 100 per cent, as far as Cambridge is concerned anyway.

For the past five years, we have come to an agreement prior to any of the big industries, and the company took advantage of the fact to get publicity. And the fact that big industries or little industries didn't come to a settlement didn't enter into the picture at that time, so there must be something new behind their position now. Up to now, we feel that we were just discussing things, and I will say, too, that the company was throwing their weight around, and it discouraged a lot of these boys from discussing what was in their minds.

The company has made surveys of the area, of the country as a whole, and of the soap industry, and we took them very lightly because they choose the companies they wish to present and leave out the higher paid industries. We do not have outside influences dictate what our wages should be in order for us to sign a contract and make our members work for a whole year, with a big question mark on what is going to happen from now to next March.

We want to come to some settlement now. We have been claiming that for the last six months there's been a change in the attitude of the company towards the employees. The workers don't feel secure. They can read and they listen to the raido. In *Harper's Magazine*, June, 1947, Mr. Luckman wrote:

> . . . and none of these pension and insurance programs is at all expensive. The funds used to defray the cost help pay their own way by going out as insurance company investments, and these investments aid the national economy by creating employment, purchasing power, when they are poured into housing developments and hundreds of other important projects. Don't forget, too, that if an insurance program helps in the slightest to prevent one small strike, it has paid for itself many times over.

And in last month's issue of *The Atlantic Monthly*, February, 1949, in talking about increased production, his words are:

> Increased productivity is the major need of the moment, if we are to maintain our accustomed living standards at home while nourishing reconstruction abroad. To obtain that productivity, the resultant wealth must be equitably divided in three ways—in the form of better wages to the worker, lower prices to the consumer, and increased profits to the company. The success of our intervention on the side of freedom abroad is thus closely linked with social justice at home.

We in Cambridge also feel, more so than the other plants, that the pensions are too small. So one of our demands has been the fact that even though we kick in and pay part of this cost, we are willing to do it.

From the attitude shown within the plant and at the table here, I feel they don't appreciate what we have done. They figure they are in a better position; they are going to start throwing their weight around. They don't appreciate that we kept everybody in line during the war, that we stopped fellows from drinking to excess and abusing the privileges they had.

The company has been expanding, putting money into cosmetics, margarine, and naturally, the membership knows that they are making plenty of money.

We are some of the few union leaders who take the responsibility to discipline our members. We go out on a limb, like we did on job evaluation, and disrupt the wage structure. We are going to engage in a productivity plan although most labor says, "Hands off." We know we are in a competitive industry. We are going to try to get Cambridge into a position where we can hold our own against competitors and against the other Lever plants. We didn't come in with a lot of unfair demands, although unfair demands have been made—I will say that—but it wasn't the Cambridge local that brought them in.

De Vincentis (u): The big thing that bothers us at Cambridge is these fellows on pension. It's all well and good to say, "You're through at 65," but throwing them to the mercy of the dogs is something else again. We are morally obliged to see that they get enough to live comfortably.

Conciliator: Does anyone else wish to express their views?

Fitzgerald (u): That about winds it up, Commissioner.

[The company requested a recess.]

Fisher (m): There are some things that I am going to say that I wish were not necessary for me to say. Much of the union's statement, if you analyze it, wasn't factual at all. It dealt with opinions, points of view, men's emotions. And it is a very hard thing to talk to people's emotions, because you are never quite sure that you are doing the right thing, hard as you may want to try.

I think in this whole situation there are a number of things at stake. And many of them are much bigger than even our company or your union. Personally, I feel that they are at stake because, over a period of eight years, I have had the privilege of working with your unions and with your company. I have found that your union representatives, even when they were angry and sore and mean—and they get that way just the way we get that way, because we are all human—even in their worst moments, they were all men whose word could be trusted.

They have always been honorable. If they have given a commitment, they have stood by it. I have found in most cases they were men who could be reasoned with. And when the heat of any particular controversy has subsided, we were always able to work out an answer which spelled a fair solution for both sides. In other words, we adopted a philosophy of persuasion as the dominant note in the labor relations that we were trying to build. And persuasion has brought you a long, long way.

Ever since I can remember anything about this company, you were ahead of the procession, and you know it. And today you are even further ahead of the procession, and you know it. Now, you've gotten there not because the company was a great big, generous, good-hearted "Joe"; you had something to do with that; because working through persuasion, you were able to make us see that a position which we had taken ought to be modified. And by the same token, when you were off to a bad start, we were able to make you see that you needed to change some of your attitudes. And that was possible because we all dealt as honorable men who had faith in each other. And at no time have we challenged your good faith, and I don't intend to challenge your good faith today. I think that you are sincerely misguided and mistaken, and I am not content to let any further time go by without speaking to you as frankly as I wish you would speak to me.

What are these things that are at stake that are bigger than either of us? Your union and this company have built a reputation which is the object of admiration in the entire labor movement. And it is a funny thing to me that Lever Brothers is so loved by the labor unions, but it is true. We know that you are proud of us, because if you weren't you wouldn't always point to Lever when you are working elsewhere. And you can't kid us, because we know how much you use Lever's as an example of what other companies should do in industry. But a strike would be evidence that our philosophy of persuasion, the philosophy of a generous labor relations policy, couldn't work; and therefore, it might provide some people with some justification for their own small-minded attitudes. A principle is at stake, and you can either give it a kick in the tail or you can grab its elbow at a time when it needs help.

And that leads me to another point. You fellows in every community have a wage structure that you know is good, is fair, is equitable. I sometimes think we have spent too much time with charts, and too much time with statistics, and too much time with proof. What we really ought to tell you is: Where can you do better? Where is there a place you would rather work? And I know, once again, that inside of you, you would say that you would rather work here than any place else. And you can bluff me on the other side of the table, but I don't buy the bluff, because I know what the facts are just as well as you do.

Now, you say to us you have cooperated. That's right, you have. You say to us that you have given us good productivity. That's right, you have. You say to us that you upheld the disciplinary system in the plant, you have corrected the drunks. That's right, you have. But, by God, that's what you ought to do. You're not doing us any favors when you do that; you're doing what you're supposed to do in terms of being mature trade union leaders and men of responsibility. You've got working conditions and a wage structure that entitles us to expect that kind of cooperation from you. If you were in some little sweat shop, and you gave the kind of performance that you have given, that would be a different matter. But you have given us fine performances as great union leaders, and we appreciate it; and we don't attempt to deprecate it. And it has been your performance as trade union leaders, and it has been your responsibility, and it has been your imagination that has enabled us to get where we are. But once again, gentlemen, we have gotten there through persuasion. And the only way we are going to make progress in the future is through persuasion, which brings me up to the other alternative, and that is force.

I think that some of you think the company has to have the blocks put to it before it will give you what you think you ought to get. But I want you to know that it is a mistake, a very serious mistake. To put the matter more bluntly: if we have a strike here, it is going to be a test of strength. It is going to be a test to find out whether or not pressure can compel Lever Brothers Company to give something that persuasion can't. And we tell you that we can't afford to let that principle get established.

I repeat, gentlemen; you have come a long way by way of persuasion. You have still a long way to go before we round out our lives. And we will make that progress together, provided we do it by persuasion, but we will never do it through force. And if, in the process, we sacrifice some of the things we fought pretty hard to build up, then, believe me, we have lost a lot more than any of the issues that are at stake in this negotiation.

Conciliator: We would like to caucus.

Fisher (m): I feel we should keep at this discussion until we make or break on it. There is not any point in caucusing. The time is getting very short. We want to know where we stand.

Conciliator: Well, we would like to caucus.

IV. CIO: Fifth Session—March 10

(10:30 A.M.–1:15 P.M.)

[The conciliators were present. The first part of the session was devoted to further examination of the demands for wage increases and further benefits. Then:]

Fisher (m): Gentlemen, I think we have demonstrated a willingness to examine your arguments and to weigh them. Now, we think the time has come for some fairly plain talk. We have told our AFL unions that we are not prepared to grant any increase, nor to liberalize any of our benefit plans. We face, of course, the fact that our contract expires with you in three days, and I think that we should indicate that we would regret it if you should see fit to exercise a force which you are entitled to exercise under the law. I think, however, that I should tell you what I have already told the AFL group. I am afraid that some members of this committee have a suspicion that the only way to handle the company is to put the clamps on and the company will give in. I want to make a last-minute effort to give those of you who do not share that point of view an opportunity to give additional evidence in support of your own conclusions.

Now, as you gentlemen know, there has been a disagreement within the AFL. There has been a possibility all along that three of our AFL plants might sign up and that one might not. There has been a possibility that you might not sign up, so Hammond and Cambridge might go down together. Those are two of our largest plants. We know what their production is and what the production loss would be if that should happen. If it does, we will take it. I think you should know that if that happens, the company will then be in a position that it cannot possibly afford to yield to pressure, and so we are determined in our own mind that if we are compelled into a struggle, it will be a very long one. I might say that in the event any plants close, there will be no problems regarding pickets because we will not attempt production.

I have made our position clear not in any challenging sense, but simply to be sure you understand it. We feel you fellows have some of the best jobs in the country. We think you know it. We get a kick out of the fact that you try to bluff us, but, gentlemen, we are not bluffed.

We hope that you listen to our evidence. We will judge the results.

Krapac (u): What you have had to say to us was said to the membership. There was no sales talk on a strike vote. We left it up to the membership entirely. We gave an impartial report when the strike vote was taken.

Fisher (m): Mike, I don't doubt that what you say is true. You fellows have always been square with us, and we have tried to be square with you. If we do have a dispute, it is not going to be an outgrowth of any personal animosity. I think, however, that your committee has the responsibility to do something more than give an impartial report. I think it is much better than to make a distorted and biased report, but it is not as good as exerting the privilege of leadership.

Now, your rank and file will always be ready for an increase, but the test of your leadership, now that the going is rougher, is not going to be your impartiality. It is going to be your ability to face facts, and then convince the people by pure persuasion, within your own group, to accept the conclusion you have reached.

Stawicki (u): Well, Mr. Fisher, we feel that the facts we have presented should merit an increase at this time. We just can't convince ourselves that the company is right in the evidence that they have presented to us, because there will be fourth-round increases.

Fisher (m): Paul, let me talk to you personally since you and I are both professionals. We analyzed 61 contracts that your organization holds to determine the average increase you have been able to negotiate with companies since V–J Day. It has been 40.8 cents. Now, they range from 11 companies, where you have negotiated less than 30 cents an hour, all the way to one company where you got 56½ cents. Lever has granted you 58.1 cents in increases since V–J Day. When you tell me that you are establishing fourth rounds in other companies, I tell you you ought to go ahead and establish fifth, sixth, and seventh rounds. You ought to do it in a hell of a hurry, because you won't catch up with what we have done in the first three. The Lever contract ought to be a Bible for every organizer right in your own union. I think you ought to recommend to your own committee that they accept this thing.

Stawicki (u): If your wholesale price goes up, your retail is bound to go up also.

Fisher (m): Now, if you fellows are worried that you might get caught for a whole year, and this cost of living situation might misbehave, let's talk about it, but let's not get it confused with your desire for a general increase. If you want future protection against a sudden rise in the cost of living, then say so, and we'll listen.

Stawicki (u): I would like to request an adjournment.

[At about 7:30 P.M., the union's request that negotiations be adjourned until March 15 was granted by the company. Both parties agreed to maintain the status quo in the Hammond plant as negotiations continued.]

V. AFL: Thirteenth Session—March 10

(3:30 P.M.–4:00 P.M.)

Conciliator: We have been with the boys for quite some time, and they have also had conferences of their own. They have asked you to come in because they have a few things they wish to say, which I am sure you will be pleased to reply to.

Fitzgerald (u): Yes, we'd like to revise our contract demands.

[All previous demands of the union were withdrawn. The following proposals were submitted in their place: (1) a five per cent wage increase; (2) a hospitalization and sickness benefit program paid for by the company; (3) an additional two and three-quarter paid holidays; and (4) "continued discussion" on the pension plan.]

Fisher (m): All right. Let's see if I understand this, gentlemen, in summary. All of the agreement appears to be in shape, except for a current demand for a 5% wage increase and 10 holidays?

Fitzgerald (u): Yes.

Fisher (m): Hospital and medical plan?

Fitzgerald (u): Right.

Fisher (m): And further discussion on the pension plan? Is that correct?

Fitzgerald (u): That's right.

Fisher (m): Gentlemen, is this your final offer to us?

Fitzgerald (u): No.

Fisher (m): Okay. We'll take a recess.

[At approximately 6:00 P.M., the company sent a written message to the union via the conciliators. Essentially it made four points: (1) the union's counterproposal was unacceptable; (2) the company had stated its final position in regard to economic demands explicitly in negotiations; (3) the management would be glad to work out a formula to provide for a reopening of wage discussions at an appropriate time if the union feared a rise in the price level between March, 1949, and March, 1950; and (4) the company would meet again only when the union was willing to accept the company's final proposal. When the conciliators informed the AFL negotiators at about 8:00 P.M. that the CIO had recessed its negotiations until March 15, the AFL obtained a similar postponement.]

VI. CIO: Sixth Session—March 15

(10:30 A.M.–12:30 P.M.)

[After expressing the union's willingness to settle its differences with the company, Mr. Stawicki explained that the union was amending its original demands by withdrawing the following:

1. Double time for work in excess of eight hours within any twenty-four hour period, and double time, in addition to regular pay, for hours worked on Saturdays, Sundays, and holidays.

2. Revision in the vacation plan granting one week's vacation for six months, two weeks for one year, three weeks for eight years, and four weeks for twelve years.

3. Eight hours' call-in pay.

4. One day's pay for absence to attend the funeral of a relative.

5. Pay for time lost on jury duty.

6. A wage increase of 27 cents an hour, in place of which was submitted a request for a 12-cent increase.

Mr. Stawicki concluded with the following statement: "We have heard rumors that there's something in the company's mind over and above what they have explained to us during these negotiations, and we would like the company to really lay the cards on the table. If there's something in your mind, we wish you would lay it on the table and let us know exactly what it is." After a discussion "off the record," Mr. Fisher requested a management caucus, and the meeting was adjourned subject to recall at a later time.]

VII. AFL: Fourteenth Session—March 15

(4:30 P.M.–2:30 A.M., March 16)

[Mr. Belkin re-entered the negotiations.]

Belkin (u): While we can't tell you what our position is at the moment, we want you to know that we are forming a position. Now, the boys from Cambridge, particularly, are not sure what position our local group should take, and therefore they ask at this time that they be permitted to meet with certain members of management whom they wish to name at this time for a brief meeting. Is that right?

Healey (u): That's right. I suggest we go off the record.

[A recess was taken until 9:30 P.M.]

Belkin (u): We have been meeting, and we are unanimous in our opinion that the proposal we are going to make to you is fair. We don't think it will cost the company much. It will help improve relations, and it is not one of the things we have been guilty of before, of asking for the moon and then seeing whether we can dicker with you. We are not dickering with you now. We have reduced our demands, our proposals—they aren't really demands because they aren't going to be made in that sense—to a real minimum, something we feel you will be pleased to hear.

Fitzgerald (u): We have gone a long way, and we hope the company will give this good consideration. We propose a wage reopening clause in six months, with a ten-day contract termination; hospital and medical service paid by the company; nine holidays; and a pension with a $50 minimum.

Belkin (u): We believe that the policy of Lever Brothers has been that, if their situation permits, they will, of their own volition, improve the lot of the people who work for them. We know that in the past, even though you had no contractual obligation to do so, when the company had additional money, you called us in. We feel that in six months from now we would like to talk to you about the economic picture, and we feel sure you would like to talk to us.

Fisher (m): I think I understand your position. I might say without caucusing that, on a reopening formula, I am somewhat sympathetic. But that is the point at which our thinking stops. In other words, I don't think that we are prepared to reopen the contract and go through these extended negotiations six months from now. On these other things, I am pessimistic, Lou. However, I do want to take a caucus and discuss this with my group.

[A caucus was taken from 9:55 P.M. until 10:45 P.M.]

Fisher (m): I would like to comment briefly on your four items. We would be prepared to have a contract for a year, or we would be prepared to have a cost-of-living reopening along some sort of formula that we could decide. With respect to item No. 2, hospital and medical insurance, we do not feel that we are in any position to add to the expenses that have already been incurred. With respect to the nine holidays, I should like to suggest that we convert Presidential election day, which was observed last year, into an eighth holiday for the future, and that we have an understanding that election day will then become one of our holidays so that we don't continually get into the situation every four years. In other words, we are prepared to agree to eight paid holidays. Now, with respect to the problem of pensions, I would like to make this statement of policy, and let it rest there. If the union cares to bring to the company's attention any case of bona fide hardship by any long-service employee at any time, we will give that problem our most serious and sincere consideration. I think we are very close to an understanding here, and I hope very much that it will be possible to consummate it.

Belkin (u): Well, I think we had better call a caucus.

[A caucus was taken from 11:15 P.M. to 12:15 A.M. The union returned and stated its position as follows: (1) a contract for one year with no wage reopening; (2) withdrawal of all pension proposals, but continuation of discussions during the contract year; (3) reduction of the hospitalization and sickness benefit proposal to include hospitalization only; and (4) retention of its proposal for nine paid holidays. The management asked for a caucus and returned at 2:20 A.M.]

Fisher (m): Gentlemen, I think that you will be pleased to learn that we are unanimously of the opinion that your last proposition is a fair one.

Belkin (u): We are very much pleased that we have come to this kind of a conclusion, and hope this year we will continue the very, very satisfactory relationship that has existed in the past. I want to express my own appreciation to each of these men who represented our people. It seems to me that too often their efforts are not fully recognized by their members. I also want to thank you, Austin, and the company for the sincere method in which you have dealt with us. We really appreciate it.

Fisher (m): Thank you, Lou. I am sure you know that we hold all of you in the highest personal esteem. I should also like to pay the very highest tribute to all of the men on the management side. They have worked hard and participated to an extent which should make the effectuation of our contract and the living under it a mutual experience which can only augur good things for our relations between Lever Brothers and the American Federation of Labor.

VIII. CIO: SEVENTH SESSION—MARCH 16

(11:00 A.M.–12:50 A.M., March 17)

Conciliator: The last session the union gave the company a new proposition. The company has not yet answered it.

Fisher (m): I think, as you know, the answer is "No." We will not grant any kind of a wage increase. We might say that we have been worked on by the Conciliation Commissioners to give some encouragement to a four-point idea. The first was a contract for a year on existing wages; the second, company-borne hospitalization, Blue Cross; third, nine holidays; and fourth, joint analysis of pension problems during the forthcoming year. We think that these points have a certain merit. We also indicated that to the Federation, and we believe that is the solution to our problems with them.

Stawicki (u): Are you certain that is the solution?

Fisher (m): Quite certain. I want to reiterate: we are not going to agree to any kind of a wage increase.

Krapac (u): There is no reopening clause in the contract.

Fisher (m): We are not going to stand on that position. The company would be willing to reopen.

Stawicki (u): I would like to call a short recess.

[A recess was taken from 11:10 A.M. to 12:20 P.M.]

Stawicki (u): Well, we feel we couldn't sell your offer to our people, so we would like an extension of the contract until July 15, and if we can't get it settled by then, we will be allowed to use our economic strength at that time.

Fisher (m): We would like to caucus.

[A recess was taken from 12:45 P.M. to 1:55 P.M.]

Fisher (m): We have faced always the problem of dealing with two groups, both of whom have certain rights, and with a management problem, to preserve our sanity, of adopting a uniform point of view. I told you earlier that the formula suggested had met with approval of the AFL locals and our management. If any doubt resides in your mind, I have just spoken with Mr. Bradley and he too had confirmed the settlement. We have entertained your proposal, gentlemen, and we do not find it acceptable. We have indicated our final position to you, and we will not deviate from it.

Stawicki (u): I don't see why the company should object to the proposal that we have made. All that we are interested in is protecting the future.

Fisher (m): The basis for a reopening was for the contract to remain as is. Our contract has not remained as is because, due to representations made by you and your associates, we were induced to make concessions on fringe benefits.

Krapac (u): As far as we knew, the fringe issues were settled between the AFL and the company. We were left on sort of a limb, you might say.

Fisher (m): Let me tell you why. Until two days ago, you were still at 27 cents. A day ago you were at 12 cents, notwithstanding the fact that we had told you repeatedly that there was not going to be any wage increase. When you first got a turndown you just walked out.

Krapac (u): Sure, got turned down by *you*.

Fisher (m): That's right. AFL got the same treatment, but they stuck around and talked, and we got a lot of problems straightened out.

Krapac (u): What did you talk about?

Fisher (m): We talked about other aspects of the agreement.

Krapac (u): We didn't have anything. There was nothing else but monetary issues.

Fisher (m): I am not trying to tell you how to run your bargaining. What I am trying to tell you is that the discussions were impeded by what we felt was a precipitous move on your part.

Stawicki (u): I think your attitude is unfair.

Fisher (m): You are entitled to characterize my attitude in any way you like. But I will not agree that if there is a fourth round we will have a wage discussion for reasons that I made abundantly clear to you sometime ago; namely, that the increases this company has given since V–J Day are so far in excess of other companies that whether they give a fourth-round increase or not doesn't make any difference. What you want is a broad reopening power?

Stawicki (u): All that we want is a fair reopening clause.

Fisher (m): Would you answer my question? Is that what you are asking for?

Stawicki (u): Yes. That is what we are asking.

Fisher (m): I have indicated at no time that I would be interested in an unconditional reopening. I have indicated we would be interested, in return for a signature on the contract as is, in a reopening in six months based on cost of living.

Krapac (u): The union has never indicated they would accept fringe issues for a year's contract.

Fisher (m): I think that is correct, but it is as far as we are prepared to go.

Stawicki (u): Do you think that if we did finally agree to something along those lines, that we would reopen that contract if there wasn't justification for it?

Fisher (m): I don't know what you would do, because everybody has a different view of what constitutes justification. We felt that somehow our concessions would be something you could take to your membership. One of the things, the holidays, is an answer to a specific request you made. The other locals in the AFL had hospitalization, which was bothering them.

Krapac (u): They also had holidays. And you gave them both their requests.

Fisher (m): It is not a question of giving both requests to one group and none to the other. It is a question of making intelligent social progress for this company.

Krapac (u): It seems the company's thought is only to satisfy the AFL group, because you didn't consider our request whatsoever. Both of those requests are definitely AFL requests.

Fisher (m): As far as your wage requests are concerned, and as far as their wage requests are concerned, the answer is identical. We will not agree to a wage increase. We are dealing with two unions, and the only way in which we can find any peace of mind is to say that we'll listen to both and we'll consider your needs. Neither one is going to be completely satisfied because we can't give everything to one and nothing to the other. If you gentlemen want to reconsider our offer, we will be very glad to have you do it.

Stawicki (u): I would like to call a recess.

[A recess was taken from 2:20 P.M. until 12:15 A.M.]

Fisher (m): I understand from the Conciliators that you would like to report back the proposals to the rank and file.

Stawicki (u): We feel we should let them decide what they want to do.

Fisher (m): Would you consider an extension of the present agreement until a fixed date?

Stawicki (u): We will give you the understanding that everything will remain in status quo.

Fisher (m): This business of status quo is all right during negotiations when we are in constant touch with each other, but it is not quite satisfactory when we are going back to our respective places. Let's have an extension of the present agreement until Monday a week. Let's excute a new agreement for a period of one year containing the terms we have talked about, subject to ratification by the rank and file. Then if the new agreement is ratified, it will supersede the interim agreement. If not, then there is no agreement between us. [The union agreed.]

IX. CIO: Eighth Session—March 17

(10:30 A.M.–6:00 P.M.)

[The parties spent the entire day in resolving noneconomic issues and problems of contract language. Economic issues were not discussed.]

X. CIO: Ninth Session—March 18

(10:30 a.m.–1:15 p.m.)

[The parties concluded their discussions of the noneconomic issues. The session ended as follows:]

Fisher (m): I would like to have you believe that what I am going to say to you is said with great feeling of personal friendship for many of you with whom I have worked in the past, as well as men I have learned to know a little bit this year for the first time. Generally, the arguments that work best in these situations are those which appeal to the selfish interest of the people who are affected; and I would like to tell you why I think in your own interest you ought to recommend this contract to your rank and file.

The chances of a strike in Hammond are rather good because Hammond has always been a money plant. The boys there have always been fellows with an eye for a buck. This is probably the first time that the company has told them they will have to stand still. And they are not going to like it. So I think it is fairly clear that unless you go out and do a selling job, the chances of their taking adverse action are rather good.

We are interested in seeing you recommend this because we feel that a strike will ultimately fail. Unions that have lost a strike have a habit of replacing officers, and it is very likely that you will send back a new negotiating committee next year. We have a selfish interest, and that means we would have to start in with this whole thing all over again. Say what you will, a negotiating conference is an education for everybody who attends it. We learn more about you and you learn more about us. The greatest understanding is possible between people who have met often and frequently.

Now you may ask why I think that a strike would fail. Let me give you several reasons. First of all, you are not going to get teamster cooperation. If you don't get teamster cooperation, the company remains unharmed. Your only other hope is the railway clerks who are independent and hard to get to because in every center where they operate they act in a different way.

My next point deals with the money question. Whatever money your local has been able to accumulate will dissipate very rapidly. In addition, your own International is a relatively new and young organization and, therefore, has not had the advantages that many of the older unions have had in accumulating large sums of money. Therefore, the amount of help they can put at your disposal is limited.

There is another consideration, and that is the extent to which a community will sympathize. If you have a good, hot, emotional issue around which your strike can be built, you can always get plenty of sympathy. But here, the people whom you are going to ask to sympathize with you—at least 80% of them—are making less than you are. They have jobs they would be very glad to swap with you. Those are very practical reasons why I think you ought to calculate the probable outcome of this thing.

Now then, let us assume, however, you decide to strike. What does it cost a man to strike for five weeks? Well, you all know your own personal arithmetic. Take a guy with a $1.57 an hour rate. If he goes on strike it costs him $315. Take the fellow with a $1.69 rate; it costs him $338. Take a fellow with a $1.82 rate; it costs him $364. And you have got to make that up sometime. If he loses the strike, and he doesn't get any kind of an increase, he never makes it up. He is out of pocket. If he wins, and if he gets some kind of an increase—which is impossible in this situation, but you may not face that fact—if he gets a nickel-an-hour settlement, how long before he is even? If he gets a nickel-an-hour settlement, the $1.57 fellow on a five-week strike requires 37 months to come out even—even with a nickel increase. If he gets a 10-cent-an-hour increase, the $1.57 fellow after a five-week strike takes 18 months to make it up. So how in the name of God can you figure there is any arithmetic there, even if you win?

I have told you these things because we like you and respect you as human beings, and because we feel that you would be making a horrible mistake. I think Paul has got a stake in this thing too, personally. He is a young labor leader. He is just coming to the fore. It is not going to do him any good to have a failure here.

I hope very, very sincerely that this thing will work out all right. If it doesn't, we will play fair with you. I think you all know that. We are not dirty fighters. But if you do strike, we will fight back. I have enjoyed meeting with you. I hope next time we meet, it is going to be under happy and productive auspices.

Krapac (u): Thank you, Austin. I would like to say for the record that if a strike develops we will assure the company of a decent shutdown. There will be no harm done to the company property whatsoever.

Fisher (m): Thanks, Mike.

Gamber (m): I would like to say that I have enjoyed having this opportunity to know you a little better, and I hope in the year to come that in working together we can know you still better.

Stawicki (u): I want to say a few words. We have had some fine negotiations. Even though we have had disagreements, I am almost certain that the relationship will continue for the future.

[The AFL unions ratified the master contract and the local agreements Sunday, March 20. A week later the Hammond CIO refused to ratify its contract, but authorized its committee to continue negotiations. Mr. Fisher and the management committee met in Chicago with the CIO group on March 28–29 without making further concessions. The contract was ratified by Hammond on April 3.]

DISCUSSION QUESTIONS

1. Evaluate critically Mr. Healey's statement of union position in the AFL session of March 9. What are the principal factors upon which he based his argument?

2. Analyze the response to Mr. Healey made by Mr. Fisher in this ses-

sion. How does it compare in its nature with statements made by Mr. Fisher in prior sessions? How would you explain Mr. Fisher's opposition to a caucus at the conclusion of this session?

3. Analyze management's discussions regarding the possibility of a strike in its sessions with the CIO on March 10 and March 18. How did management handle the same problem with the AFL? Do you consider management's approach appropriate in each instance? Why or why not?

4. Analyze critically the bargaining strategies and tactics of the AFL, the CIO, and the company at each session, beginning with the thirteenth AFL session held on March 10. What problems did each of the various parties face as the negotiations progressed?

THE FANCO OIL COMPANY

NEGOTIATIONS WITH AN INDEPENDENT UNION

INTRODUCTION

The Fanco Oil Company, a refining and marketing subsidiary of Superior Oil Company, operated its own fleet. Superior's employees, including Fanco's, were represented by independent unions. Thus, the Fanco Boatmen's Union had been certified in May, 1946, by the NLRB to represent the personnel on the company's vessels.

The contract was to expire on August 31, 1951. In May, William Hayes, the union president, approached D. H. Somers, assistant manager of the New York–New England branch, with a new schedule for manning tugboats, calling for 7 days on and 7 days off boats. The schedule then in use conformed to the usual New York harbor practice of 10 days on and 5 days off. The working day of 12 hours began at 6 A.M. Some tugs operated only in the harbor, some went as far as Boston; a few had single crews, but most had double crews. Crews changed every 5 days at 6 A.M., usually in New York. Frequently, however, weather or other conditions delayed the change of crews. At other times, a particular job would require an early change of crews. For all extra days spent aboard, the men received "penalty pay" of time and a half.

Conditions on the New York waterfront were turbulent. The members of the International Longshoremen's Association, then affiliated with the AFL, were seething in revolt in protest against a 10% increase recently negotiated by their leaders—so much so that they finally went out on a wildcat strike in October. The CIO maritime unions virtually had closed the harbor for 11 days in June, 1950, in the process of obtaining a reduction of hours and a 6.4% increase in pay.

THE FIRST SESSION, AUGUST 3

9:30 A.M. TO 3:30 P.M.

All meetings were held in the New York office of the Fanco Company.

Present for the Company

R. W. Downs	New York–New England Branch Manager
D. H. Somers	Assistant Branch Manager
H. R. Fawcett	Port Engineer

Present for the Union

William Hayes	Chairman and President	⎫
Ned Black	Vice Chairman	⎬ Deckhands
Joe Zandoff	Secretary-Treasurer	⎭
Frank Trimble	Stewards' Delegate	
George MacIntosh	Licensed Engineers' Delegate	
Hans Altmeyer	Unlicensed Deckhands' Delegate	
John Riley	Licensed Deckhands' Delegate	

Somers (m): The primary business of the company is to produce and sell petroleum products. Transportation is purely incidental and will be carried on only if we can operate on a competitive basis and enjoy a certain amount of protection. We feel that you should know this policy, and it should be considered in all negotiations. The union has proposed that the men work 7 days on and 7 days off. Capt. Downs has the facts and figures in connection with that proposal.

Downs (m): The 7 and 7 proposition with *monthly* wages the same is not competitive; it puts the hourly rate up $33\frac{1}{3}\%$. We are willing to go along with a 7 and 7 plan but with the same *hourly* rate as now.

Hayes (u): If that is all you have to say, gentlemen, we can adjourn right now.

Downs (m): You mean, if you cannot get 7 and 7 with the same monthly pay, you are not interested in discussing it? We will consider the 7 and 7 deal keeping the hourly rate the same and keeping 3 deckhands on the boat.

Hayes (u): Wages at the present monthly rate is just a living wage for a 42-hour week, which is the monthly average on 7 and 7. We want time off and a living wage.

Downs (m): We thought you people wanted mostly the time off and were not interested in the money.

Delegates (u): Oh, no!

Hayes (u): The outside increase in cost of our plan is 9.25%, but the savings in "penalties" and transportation expenses more than cover any extra expenses. We thought, since the over-all cost of operating the boats shows very little increase in our 7 and 7 plan, that the company would not care about the hourly rates.

Somers (m): We cannot initiate any method which will result in a wage increase per man in excess of what is paid in competition. That is company policy. However, as we have already indicated, we are willing to negotiate around 7 and 7. Do you want to discuss it?

Hayes (u): I don't see where there is any wage raise in the system we set up on the 7 and 7.

Downs (m): There is an hourly rate increase of $33\frac{1}{3}\%$ which may be partially counterbalanced by giving up other items. Our competitors do not have these things to give up; and it would cause confusion and disruption to them and to some of the people from whom we charter boats.

The 7 and 7 is a very radical idea; and I want to point out again that marine transportation is not our main business. We are not the leaders.

Hayes (u): Who are supposed to be the leaders?

Downs (m): In New York harbor, the 600 boats under ILA contracts would naturally be the leaders.

Hayes (u): I don't see why a company of this size should follow the ILA, a union which is full of corruption. Why can't we be the leaders and set a precedent here?

Zandoff (u): This company has been a pioneer in the oil business—why not in transportation?

Hayes (u): It has always been my idea that this company wanted its own union so as not to have labor trouble. When you have your own union, certain things are over and above other unions. When other unions have a strike, they get a raise. Maybe not as large as what they ask for, but they get a raise. If we were to work on the same basis as they, we'd strike when they do; we'd tie your boats up. If you went down to the docks and asked the ILA men if they are satisfied with that 10% raise the union got them, you'd find they aren't. We should be ahead of other unions. Right now, we are behind.

Downs (m): If you add up company benefits, you are way ahead.[1]

Hayes (u): We are interested in our monthly wage and working hours. Benefits are the company's business. They were there when we were hired.

Somers (m): True, but benefits mean nothing? Take some of these people who have been sick and getting paid for over a year. Doesn't that make a job better?

Hayes (u): It still has nothing to do with working conditions or money.

Somers (m): As Capt. Downs has pointed out, we are willing to recognize that you want 7 and 7. It will require more personnel, which will cost us more money to man our equipment. In spite of that, we are still willing to give you a 7 and 7 deal and still have you get vacation, unless you are willing to give that up?

Delegates (u): No, sir.

Somers (m): We are increasing our costs, we are taking on more men, and we would like to have the boats manned with a lesser number of deckhands. We would like to carry 3 instead of 4 and eliminate petty penalties and see some cooperation between the 2 crews in arranging time off. Is there anything fairer than that?

Riley (u): Let's talk about a deckhand's pay—the lowest paid man.

Downs (m): All right. His present base monthly pay is $333. It would come to $249.84 under the 7 and 7, keeping the hourly rate the same, to which you would then add $17.97 a month for Sundays, $13.47 for holidays

---

[1] The company had very liberal benefit plans: pay while sick or when disabled by accident on or off the job or when permanently or totally disabled; hospital and medical insurance at low cost; a savings plan to which the company contributed up to 10% of pay to match the employee's savings; contributory annuities in increased amounts for employees receiving less than $3,000 per year; and low cost group life insurance.

on an average month, and he would be paid $18.75 at home for subsistence, making a total of $300.03. On 10 and 5, which he is working now, he gets a base of $333 and, if you add his Sundays, subsistence, and holidays, you get $383.19. On 7 and 7, keeping the hourly rate the same, he would lose $83.16 a month as compared with the present 10 and 5.[1]

Black (u): Too much to give up.

Downs (m): Even on your own proposal, you lose $50.

Black (u): All our men expect us to give up is just what we state.

Hayes (u): The over-all increase to you of our plan would be only 9.25%, including the extra men you would have to hire.

Somers (m): We are not negotiating on the basis of cost. We have to operate on a competitive basis; and as soon as you increase hourly rates, you are not competitive.

Black (u): The only way the company can remain competitive is on their over-all operating cost. You can't just talk about the hourly rate of pay.

Somers (m): That's not correct. Cost involves the initial cost of your equipment, overhead, and other operating expenses, which include many other items outside of the wages.

Black (u): This year ILA was supposed to come up for a 25% increase, and 50 cents an hour extra for staying on the boat on off hours. They got only 10%. Go to any dock in New York and ask the different men. They voted against it. Don't compare yourselves to the ILA.

Somers (m): The ILA represents a major portion of the transportation personnel in this area.

Let me ask you another question. Your proposal of 7 and 7 cannot be accepted by us, for reasons which we think we have fully explained. And you men have reasons why you do not want our 7 and 7 counterproposal. How about working on a 10 and 5 day basis with a 5-day, 40-hour week with a corresponding reduction in your base? If you work Saturdays and Sundays, you would be paid on premium basis for those days.

Hayes (u): We planned this 7 and 7 with the idea of its being beneficial now and in the future for the company and to the men. Most unions make demands at certain high levels, and then go down half or less. I didn't draw this up that way. You work your boats 24 hours a day and the men stay on the boats. There is no quibble about that. If we cannot talk about this setup, adjourn the meeting.

Downs (m): We have considered your 7 and 7 proposition very seriously. We feel that we cannot accept it; and we are offering you another deal incorporating the 7 and 7 as far as the day's work is concerned and giving you holiday and Sunday pay, which doesn't come too far from the money you lose under your plan. I think that may be moderated a little and it should not be thrown out of the meeting entirely.

Would any change in our 7 and 7 plan be acceptable to you? At present

---

[1] See Exhibit 1.

there is nothing about Saturday. If Saturday overtime were added, it would add $18 to a deckhand's pay per month.

Hayes (u): You don't seem to realize that on top of this reduction you still want only 3 deckhands.

Somers (m): That is not saving us anything. We increase the total number of personnel in our tugboat fleet, just to cover 7 and 7.

Altemeyer (u): How would you work them [the 3 deckhands]?

Somers (m): One on watch, one off watch, and one on call.

Hayes (u): We have come to the conclusion unanimously that under the proposal we set before you there is no increase in our base monthly wage. Using the deckhand's $1.39 [1] hourly rate gives $252.98 for 182 hours. Then 26 weeks on boat at 16 hours a week overtime for 12 hours Sunday and 4 hours Saturday shows 416 for the year, which divided by 12 comes to 36 premium hours per month. Then we have 4.5 average holiday hours per month. That totals $334.43 for a deckhand.[2] The present base wage is $333. It comes to about the same figure. We see no problem. So, if we cannot come to an agreement on that, I think we have nothing more to negotiate.

Somers (m): You are not giving any recognition at all to the hourly rate of pay. Is that correct?

Hayes (u): We are rejecting any plan below our present monthly base wage.

Downs (m): The deckhand would get $334, or 33⅓% increase over present hourly rate.

Hayes (u): We will not take a reduction in monthly wage.

Somers (m): No other system of manning is of interest?

Hayes (u): That's right.

MacIntosh (u): Any plan that can be worked up—Saturdays, Sundays, or holidays—that would bring up pay to what Mr. Hayes has on his sheet would possibly be accepted.

Somers (m): I suggest we take a recess and meet again at 2 o'clock.

. . . . .

Downs (m): This morning we told the union of our opposition to their proposal of the 7 and 7 deal keeping the monthly wage the same. We then offered a counterproposal of 7 and 7 but keeping the hourly rates the same, which the union, as I understand it, did not wish to discuss. Is there anything you wish to discuss?

Hayes (u): All we wish to discuss is our original proposal. The rest is up to you.

Somers (m): We offered you a 40-hour week before.

Hayes (u): That was a horrible offering. You have no real competition. No other boats in the harbor do the work the Fanco tugs do. You would

---

[1] The actual rate was currently $1.369.
[2] See Exhibit 1.

rather have your own tugs do the work. You eventually will do all your own work with your own tugs.

Fawcett (m): If we don't come to some agreement, we may see the outside boats come in.

Hayes (u): I worked before, and a lot of other people did too. If the company wishes to sell the boats, that is their business but we still maintain that the net over-all cost to operate boats on the 7 and 7 setup will not cost you more than it does now on the over-all total.

Downs (m): It would cause trouble with our competitors. We are the followers, not the leaders.

Hayes (u): You don't follow any of the other industries; for instance, in chemical research.

Black (u): Take a ride around and see the people you are following, Capt. Downs. There isn't anything in the harbor worth following.

Downs (m): Moran's new diesel electrics look pretty nice.

Black (u): They are in the minority. Fanco boats are a credit to the company.

Riley (u): It would pay the company to run our boats up and down the harbor as an advertisement.

Downs (m): In appearance our boats have it all over the others.

Riley (u): Your Tug No. 10 can do just as good as a Moran tug. [Nobody disagrees.]

MacIntosh (u): Superior Oil is very choosey about hiring a responsible man, and I believe they should pay for it. You can leave money around on the boats and nobody will touch it.[1]

Hayes (u): The character of our men is above the other outfits. Ninety-five percent are family men from good homes.

Downs (m): I agree with you, Bill, on that point.

Trimble (u): Can you people decide what you can and cannot give us?

Downs (m): We can't give away the company.

MacIntosh (u): If there is any other way, considering Saturdays, Sundays, and holidays, to bring up wages to what Bill has here, we might be interested.

Hayes (u): If other outfits have a strike and get a raise, we also get more money. Meanwhile your boats move. You remain competitive, but we get dirty looks from the ILA men.

Riley (u): Capt. Bradley[2] has his own gang. Go to a meeting and find out. You try to open your mouth and they will take you outside.

Black (u): You are letting men like that set a precedent for you? A bunch of racketeers setting the wage scale.

Hayes (u): The morale of our men on the boats is very bad. More than 50% of the men are not paying dues, and I have instructed the delegates not

---

[1] Pilfering has been a crucial problem in New York harbor.
[2] President of the United Marine Division of the ILA, which bargained for tugboat crews, and later president of the ILA after it was expelled from the AFL.

to collect from them. We are not getting anywhere, so I think we may as well adjourn and let matters take their own course.

Downs (m): You don't want to discuss the situation further?

Hayes (u): I don't think it is necessary.

Downs (m): What about a future meeting?

Hayes (u): I don't know if there is any necessity for a future meeting.

Downs (m): We don't want to see it drop this way.

Hayes (u): If you want to work on anything with respect to 7 and 7 and let us know at a future date, we will be glad to come up.

Somers (m): Maybe an adjournment would give everybody an opportunity to give this whole subject a little more thought.

MacIntosh (u): No sense for further meetings, if we can't agree now on 7 and 7.

Downs (m): Eighteen dollars for Saturday, $18 for Sunday, and $13 for holidays brings a deckhand up to $318.[1]

Black (u): That's "if" money: *If* I work, I get 4 hours' overtime. *If* I don't work Sunday, I don't get this overtime.

Downs (m): If we add $25 monthly income to each man, you would be interested?

Black (u): It makes a lot of difference.

Downs (m): That would make it $343.

Black (u): We don't want $343—we want $334.

Hayes (u): I think we should adjourn this meeting.

Somers (m): Since the union is requesting an adjournment, perhaps that would be the best thing to do. As to a subsequent meeting, we will await word from you.

[Meeting adjourned at 3:30 P.M.]

THE SECOND SESSION, AUGUST 20

10:10 A.M. TO 2:10 P.M.

The same negotiators were present for management with the exception of Mr. Downs. B. Lettieri, an oiler, representing unlicensed engineers, was added to the union team.

Mr. Somers expressed surprise that management had to take the initiative in calling the meeting. He reiterated the company's position. Hayes indicated that the union position was also unchanged.

After lunch, Somers restated the company's "best 7 and 7 offer" in detail: maintaining the same hourly rate, giving a monthly base pay of $249.84; 4 hours' premium pay on Saturday, $17.97; 4 hours' premium pay on Sunday $17.97; time and a half for holidays for men on the boats and straight time for those scheduled off, averaging $13.47; a total of $299.25 a month for the

---

[1] See Exhibit 1.

deckhand.[1]   But, if the men would continue on straight 10 and 5, the company would make a concession.   It would, in addition to the current premium pay for 4 hours on Sunday, be willing to grant 4 hours' premium pay on Saturday.

The union made a "last offer": a two-year contract on 7 and 7 with elimination of "penalty pay" if the company would come up to their $334 demand. Somers rejected this offer as still out of line with company policy and insisted that the union was obligated to present the new 10 and 5 concession to its members.   Hayes agreed, though he contended that it would be useless to do so.

THE THIRD SESSION, AUGUST 28

10:14 A.M. TO 2:20 P.M.

At management's suggestion, Hayes took the chair and reported that the membership had agreed unanimously to stick with the union's original proposal.   The union offered a two-year contract.   Somers replied, "It would not be in the interest of the company or the men because with things moving so fast in the world today too many things can happen to wages and working conditions."

Somers (m): In accordance with the requirements of the Taft-Hartley Act, we are going to notify the Federal Mediation and Conciliation Service of our stalemate and our apparent inability to arrive at a workable agreement. If they do not choose to come in now, it is our intention upon the termination of this contract to *request* mediation.   We are merely advising the union of what steps we intend to take.   By the same token, any time the union wants to call a meeting for any discussion, we are willing to listen.   Mr. Chairman, unless someone else here present has something to say, you might have someone call for an adjournment.

Hayes (u): Just a moment.   I would like to make a request for a meeting of the full membership in the very near future.

Somers (m): Any time you, as president of the union, want to call a meeting of the members, all you have to do is let the company know.   We will notify the crews; and, as a matter of fact, we will bring back every tugboat scheduled out of town.   How much time will you need?

.   .   .   .   .

The union meeting was set for 8 P.M. to 12 P.M., August 30.   Hayes agreed to report the following day the membership's decision "whether negotiations shall or shall not continue, therefore leaving the road open for whatever steps must be taken."   The company volunteered to notify by telephone or telegram all men scheduled off.

---

[1] See Exhibit 1.

[R. M. Harris, Fanco New York Port Captain, joined Fawcett and Somers on the management team.]

Hayes (u): The union held a meeting of its membership on Thursday, August 30, at 8 P.M. The membership was given a choice of one of three alternatives: 10 and 5, as offered by the company, with the inducement of 4 hours' premium pay for Saturdays; 7 and 7, as offered by the company; or the original demands with appropriate action.

The grand count for 10 and 5 was 5 votes. A total of 75 votes was cast for 7 and 7 on the possible best deal; and 32 votes were for pressing our original demands and taking whatever steps were deemed necessary to gain that end. The membership felt also that, due to the fact the company has not met our demands, some of the things we were willing to give up before, we are not willing to agree to now.

So now all we have to do is start working on our agreement.

Somers (m): Our feeling is that the union has made a decision not in their best interest. However, that is the union's business. I would like to go on record as saying that the company agreed to consider 7 and 7 keeping the hourly the same, granting 4 hours' premium pay for Saturdays and Sundays when worked, and premium holiday pay when worked. There are, however, a great many other conditions which have to be considered. We expect that there will be no penalty pay for late or early relief, or for any other purposes. We also expect that the so-called "gimmies," which were instituted or forced upon the company by the union, will be eliminated. Some of these gimmies are as follows: 1. Extra pay for cleaning tubes by firemen. That work is considered normal for firemen. 2. Subsistence pay while on time off. Food is furnished by the company to the personnel when on its vessels. [Several union men interrupted at this point.] We would prefer you fellows make what notes you see fit; and, when any given individual is finished, those notes can be brought up. If we have no interruptions, we will be able to keep a more accurate record of the discussions. 3. Additional compensation to a deckhand called out while not on watch to assist in the hauling of hawsers. 4. While tugboats are laid up for repair in the shipyards, no compensation for board or lodging. The majority usually go home every night. Any man compelled to stay aboard will have a suitable place to sleep. 5. Engine room bilge maintenance. Routine maintenance should not require any extra compensation. 6. Requests to lay over in the shipyards to obtain suitable rest before being assigned to any given job. This privilege has been abused. We are willing to grant lay over, after repairs have been completed, for a period not to exceed 6 hours or one watch. 7. A qualified cook to be aboard while a vessel is in the shipyard. Because of sickness or some other reason, a qualified cook might not be always available. 8. Time off on a working day to renew a license. The renewal of a man's license is his own obligation.

9. Physical examination. This should be taken when a man is on time off.

Now, if we can get together and agree on the elimination of these miserable "gimmies," penalty pay charges, I think we can work out a suitable contract.

Hayes (u): You want working conditions to go back fifty years! First of all, $18.75 grub money was indicated as part of the contract and agreed upon in the minutes as part of the 7 and 7 plan the company offered. We negotiated with you in good faith. Now you want to eliminate grub money.

Somers (m): We have not specifically agreed on anything. Everything up to this point has been merely discussion.

Hayes (u): You have not discussed or bargained in good faith. I took what you offered us back to the membership, and they voted on it. Do you expect me to go back to the men and retract these offers?

Trimble (u): According to the minutes of the first meeting, Capt. Downs agreed on $18.75 as "home" pay for subsistence. Doesn't his statement mean anything?

Somers (m): When the union made the initial proposal of 7 and 7, the company was advised that all the penalty payments could be eliminated and all of the so-called gimmies. What did you have in mind?

Hayes (u): We were willing to give you something, but you have taken everything we offered and not returned anything. Included in the 7 and 7 which we brought back to the membership was the $18.75 for grub money. You made that offer; now you retract it. I have only one thing to say: I think we have reached a stalemate again.

Harris (m): Suppose we set the $18.75 to one side and go on?

Hayes (u): That has got to be settled. Do you admit, Mr. Somers, that that figure was drawn up by management?

Somers (m): It was considered. We were not making definite statements; we were merely discussing the whole problem.

Hayes (u): What can we take back to our membership then?

Somers (m): First, let's work out a new contract before you consider taking anything back for their ratification or rejection. You are making an issue of one specific item that we don't see eye to eye on at this moment. Instead of holding up the meeting, why not consider the others?

Hayes (u): You offered us the $18.75.

Harris (m): You told the men at the last meeting when the vote was taken that you had been offered $18.75 for grub money on time off?

Hayes (u): Yes, but according to what is happening now, that meeting was a farce.

Harris (m): No, it was not. But, as I understand it, those figures were merely being considered with the hopes that this contract could be worked out. Now why not go on to the other items and come back to grub money later rather than delay our meeting?

Hayes (u): I refuse. If we can't believe management, why bother having meetings?

Harris (m): I would like to recess for five minutes.

Hayes (u): Just a moment. I want to read this to you from page 5 of the minutes of the first meeting.

. . . It would come to $249.84 under the 7 and 7, keeping the hourly the same, to which you would then add $17.97 a month for Sundays, $13.47 for holidays on an average month, and he would be paid $18.75 at home for subsistence, making a total of $300.03.

Harris (m): Up to this point, your organization has agreed to that?

Hayes (u): Yes. That was presented to the membership as it was presented to us by the company.

Harris (m): I asked for a recess of five minutes, but I will change it. Let's reconvene after lunch at 1:30.

The Fourth Session, after the Luncheon Recess

1:30 P.M. TO 4:10 P.M.

Hayes (u): Our proposal was drawn up on a give-and-take basis. We would give up so-called penalty pay if management would bring our pay to what base pay is now. Management has not done that, so we certainly cannot consider giving up things from our side.

Somers (m): Mr. Chairman, before I answer your most recent statement, I would like to point out that, in all negotiations between two parties for the purpose of arriving at a contract, it is possible to come to certain agreements with respect to specific items in that contract. All those agreements can be voided by either party as a result of the disagreement of either party with respect to subsequent topics of discussion. Therefore, in order to finalize this deal of 7 and 7, we have to consider all the other clauses within the contract which has just expired. In the meantime we will employ our personnel on the basis of the old contract.

Hayes (u): As long as the negotiations are still in progress, the contract remains valid.

Somers (m): The union and the company are in no great disagreement.

Hayes (u): We tossed proposals back and forth and finally came to a point where we felt that the proposal you made was adequate. We accepted the proposal, and now it seems to be changed.

Somers (m): You're correct, Mr. Chairman. All these things do have to be talked over, back and forth. It is unfortunate, in my opinion, that you took as final some of Capt. Downs' statements with respect to possible take-home pay for grub money. We will now agree to that in principle. How about some of these other things?

MacIntosh (u): Why should we discuss giving up gimmies! Let's discuss other parts of the contract.

Hayes (u): Well, let's start with "hauling of hawsers." You only have two men on watch at any time. One is always sleeping. When you pull hawsers you need three men. So it would be the man who has already put in 12 hours on watch who must come out.

Somers (m): O.K., we will pay compensation for the third man who is required to be called on deck from his time below for hawser work, based on the information you have given me. We will cooperate to that extent.

Hayes (u): "Compensation for board and lodging while in shipyard"?

Harris (m): A fellow who lives on Staten Island will not receive compensation for board and lodging. Myself included. If my home is where my job is, I can't claim lodging for that night.

Hayes (u): If a man is required to go to a hotel and if he does go to a hotel and takes lodging, he should be paid for it.

Somers (m): I will agree to that. He will need to show his receipt.

Hayes (u): Now, "layover in shipyard after repairs for suitable rest." You can't sleep when they are making repairs, and then you have to come up when the other watch comes off.

Harris (m): We want to give the men who have been on watch 6 hours' sleep.

Hayes (u): If you are supposed to be sleeping from 12 to 6 and they are working and you don't sleep, you still have to go on watch at 6 o'clock. The best sleep you could get would be 3 hours if they split the watch.

Somers (m): We will cooperate on that one. We will give a boat 12 hours from the time repairs are completed.

Hayes (u): Now, we come to "qualified cook." What was this about not putting in a qualified cook?

Somers (m): It didn't seem to me that anything as small as that should appear in the contract. It has always been our practice to have a qualified cook on every boat. However, at times when we have had an excessive number of men on claims, we have taken a steward from the boat in the yard; and, under these circumstances, we assumed that possibly the deckhand would throw enough grub together to keep the men happy, until we had time to get a qualified cook.

Hayes (u): I don't think the men would like that. You wouldn't want me to cook for you.

Somers (m): I don't know how good you are. Aren't we giving too much weight to a situation that might not arise?

Hayes (u): We come to: "Time off to renew licenses." They didn't have time to do it on 10 and 5.

Riley (u): As far as license renewal is concerned, the office should notify the man. The men do not realize it and let their licenses lapse.

Harris (m): That's a personal matter. I see no reason why we should be involved at all.

Hayes (u): "Men to take physical examinations on time off."

Black (u): Why should a man go for a physical examination on his time off? If the company wants him to take a physical, they should give him the time to go.

Somers (m): We feel that, with so much free time on 7 and 7, you would have time to go for an examination.

Hayes (u): However, physical examinations should be done on company time.

Somers (m): I will agree, since it is our requirement.

Hayes (u): "Blowing of tubes and bilge work." Bilge work especially is very disagreeable. He is entitled to overtime.

Fawcett (m): I think men who blow tubes by hand should be reimbursed for it. The ones with mechanical soot blowers should not be reimbursed.

Lettieri (u): You mean it takes less time with mechanical blowers?

Fawcett (m): Yes, it takes less time.

Lettieri (u): Shouldn't they be compensated for that less time?

Hayes (u): How much time is spent on blowing tubes?

Fawcett (m): Four hours' premium pay a week.

Harris (m): Would it be fair to split it in half, and treat all men alike?

Hayes (u): I would like to hear Benny's opinion. He is a fireman.

Lettieri (u): If it will help the 7 and 7 setup, I will agree.

Harris (m): Can't we agree on that? No matter what we agree on, some of us are going to be dissatisfied.

MacIntosh (u): Get together, and we lose, lose, and lose!

Somers (m): It would seem to me, in all fairness to union personnel and to the company, that we should give 4 hours' premium pay to men who do not have mechanical soot blowers and 2 hours to those who do.

Hayes (u): There is no reason to change working conditions for firemen in blowing and bilge work. For that small amount of money it should be left in the contract for the men, because it is disagreeable work. Will management concede 4 hours on all boats for blowing tubes?

Somers (m): Harry, how long have boats been fitted out with mechanical blowers?

Fawcett (m): One to two years.

Somers (m): That's a technological improvement that has been made in an effort to lighten the job of firemen. In view of that expense by the company, I believe consideration should be given to 4 hours to men with hand blowers and 2 hours for mechanical.

Black (u): I thought the big idea of installing automatic tube blowers was to cut down on time.

MacIntosh (u): It does save time in tying a boat up.

Somers (m): How often is it necessary to blow tubes?

Fawcett (m): Battleships, once a week; and other boats, 3 and 4 times.

MacIntosh (u): He only paints bilges once a year but cleans them twice a year. While he is doing that, one man has to run back and forth and do two jobs at the same time. That keeps him pretty well occupied. It's a dirty, filthy job on top of that.

Fawcett (m): A man has only gotten bilge money when he actually went into the bilge.

Somers (m): We will let bilge money stand as it is.

Hayes (u): I don't think there is much more we have to discuss right now.

Did you say, Mr. Somers, you could start on a tentative agreement that we could work on?

Somers (m): Yes. But one of the things we haven't discussed was the actual figures for the compensation each man is going to get. Assuming that we came to a final agreement with respect to 7 and 7, the following basic monthly wage scale would be in effect.

[He read the complete list of basic pay for each category, including the amounts for various lengths of service in that category, and pointed out that the hourly rates were unchanged with two exceptions: (1) The steward had been raised 6.4% to compensate for the premium pay the others received for worked Saturdays. (2) Starting pay for firemen and deckhands would be $250.02 on the basis of rounding $1.369 to $1.37 per hour. These increases and the Saturday overtime would have to be authorized by the Wage Stabilization Board.]

MacIntosh (u): If the ILA got a raise, you would match it?

Somers (m): When our wage scale is below competition, our door is always open to discuss it.

[Meeting adjourned to reconvene at 9:30 A.M. next morning.[1]]

EXHIBIT 1

THE FANCO OIL COMPANY NEGOTIATIONS

Alternative Pay Schedules—Deckhand

	Present Pay on 10 and 5 at $1.369	Proposals on 7 and 7			
		Union's Demand at $1.39	Downs' First Statement at $1.369	Downs' Second Statement at $1.369	Somers' "Best Offer" at $1.369
Monthly Base Pay	$333.00	$252.98	$249.84	$249.84	$249.84
4 Premium Hours Sunday	17.97	—	17.97	17.97	17.97
Subsistence at Home	18.75	—	18.75	18.75	—
Holidays	13.47		13.47	13.47	13.47
12 Premium Hours Sunday	—	81.45	—	—	—
4 Premium Hours Saturday	—		—	17.97	17.97
Total	$383.19	$334.43	$300.03	$318.00	$299.25

[1] In four additional sessions the parties reduced to writing the agreements reached to this point without further substantial changes.

FARADAY STEEL COMPANY

THE "LOCAL PRACTICE OR CUSTOM" CLAUSE IN THE AGREEMENT

I. BACKGROUND

During the negotiations of their 1947 Agreement, the United States Steel Corporation and the United Steelworkers of America, CIO, added a new section to their contract, entitled "Local Working Conditions." Incorporated into "Section 2—Scope of the Agreement," it stipulated as follows:

· · · · ·

B. *Local Working Conditions*

The term "local working conditions" as used herein means specific practices or customs which reflect detailed application of the subject matter within the scope of wages, hours of work, or other conditions of employment and includes local agreements, written or oral, on such matters. It is recognized that it is impracticable to set forth in this Agreement all of these working conditions, which are of a local nature only, or to state specifically in this Agreement which of these matters should be changed or eliminated. The following provisions provide general principles and procedures which explain the status of these matters and furnish necessary guideposts for the parties hereto and the Board.

1. It is recognized that an employee does not have the right to have a local working condition established, in any given situation or plant where such condition has not existed, during the term of this Agreement or to have an existing local working condition changed or eliminated, except to the extent necessary to require the application of a specific provision of this Agreement.

2. In no case shall local working conditions be effective to deprive any employee of rights under this Agreement. Should any employee believe that a local working condition is depriving him of the benefits of this Agreement, he shall have recourse to the grievance procedure and arbitration, if necessary, to require that the local working condition be changed or eliminated to provide the benefits established by this Agreement.

3. Should there be any local working conditions in effect which provide benefits that are in excess of or in addition to the benefits established by this Agreement, they shall remain in effect for the term of this Agreement, except as they are changed or eliminated by mutual agreement or in accordance with Paragraph 4 below.

4. The Company shall have the right to change or eliminate any local working condition if, as the result of action taken by Management under Section 3—Management, the basis for the existence of the local working condition is changed or eliminated, thereby making it unnecessary to continue such local working condition; provided, however, that when such a change or elimination is made by the Company any affected employee shall have recourse to the grievance procedure and arbitration, if necessary, to have the Company justify its action.

5. No local working condition shall hereafter be established or agreed to which changes or modifies any of the provisions of this Agreement. In the event such a local working condition is established or agreed to, it shall not be enforceable to the extent that it is inconsistent with or goes beyond the provisions of this

Agreement, except as it is approved by an International Officer of the Union and the Industrial Relations Executive of the Company.

Most of the major steel companies followed with slight modification the pattern set by "Big Steel." One exception was Faraday Steel Company. Its local working conditions clause read as follows:

ARTICLE II—APPLICATION OF THIS AGREEMENT

Section 3. If the Management at any Plant or Works shall change or eliminate any local practice or custom now in effect at said Plant or Works and not covered by this Agreement, an Employee affected by such change may file a grievance with respect thereto and such grievance shall be handled in accordance with the procedure set forth in Article XI hereof for the adjustment of grievances, including the procedure for arbitration set forth in Section 2 of that Article. In the disposition of the grievance the burden shall be on the Management to justify its action. If there shall be any local agreement in writing between the Company and the Union now in effect at any Plant or Works with respect to one or more local working conditions there not covered by this Agreement, such local agreement shall not be changed except by agreement between the Company and the Union, unless such local agreement shall deprive Employees at such Plant or Works of benefits provided by this Agreement or unless as a result of action taken by the Management in accordance with the provisions of Article XIII [1] of this Agreement the basis for the existence of the local working conditions covered by such local agreement shall be changed or eliminated.

After 1947 disputes invoking these "local practices" clauses occurred frequently in all steel companies. Managements were fearful that these clauses were being used by unions to justify grievances that could not be supported by other contractual clauses. The intent of managements in agreeing to the "local clause" had been to assure employees that any local special privilege or condition, even if it did not prevail generally in the company, would be continued. As "customary practice" grievances mounted, considerable discussion was evoked in determining (1) when any given work procedure constituted a local custom or condition within the meanings of the provisions formulated in 1947; (2) the validity of particular managerial actions which the union protested as a "change in" or "elimination of" local practice prohibited by the contract; and (3) the rights and duties of the parties in such situations.

These issues were illustrated by several grievances arising at the Faraday Steel Company.

II. A DISPUTE OVER SPELLING ASSIGNMENTS

The first important case arose in 1948, when the crane operators in the rail mill of the Decatur plant submitted the following grievance:

We, the cranemen who charge rails into the control cooling boxes, request Management to place a speller [2] on each turn when putting hot steel and rails into

---

[1] This clause dealt with management functions.

[2] A speller is an employee assigned as a relief to positions on which the regular assignees need recuperative periods of liberty or assistance on the job because of inherent work conditions of heavy load, heat, radiance, intensity of application, and so forth.

the CC boxes. We request that the speller start when all spellers in the Mill start during the summer months. Also, this speller is to remain on the crane until relieved by the oncoming shift. The request for a speller is necessary due to the extreme heat during the summers. There has been a speller on the job in the past years, but was removed by Management without just cause.

In Step 1 of the grievance procedure, the foreman denied that management had ever regularly assigned a spell crane operator. In Step 2, the superintendent detailed three reasons for denying "the request": (1) The implication that a mill-wide custom regarding summer spell time had been abrogated represented a misunderstanding or error, for no such practice had ever existed. (2) A regular spelling assignment was unnecessary because "normal delays give the crane operator sufficient spell time." (3) "The directing and scheduling of the working forces is the exclusive function of Management," by the contractual definitions of "Article XIII—Management Functions."

The grievance reached arbitration at which time the parties made the following arguments:

The Union's Case. (1) Work at the cooling boxes, in itself a "hot job," is inevitably made more difficult by the heat or humidity often encountered from June through September. By its very assignment of spellers to these crane operators from time to time for summer relief, management itself has recognized the existence of an intrinsic job need, essential to the health, productivity, comfort, and even safety of the operators.

(2) Until the summer of 1948, the men were reasonably satisfied with the discretionary assignment of spellers by their foremen. This relative satisfaction may be witnessed by the fact that no prior grievance to this one has ever been submitted or processed. Men and supervision "got along" and settled these things together.

(3) But about mid-June, 1947, the operators noticed "a tightening up" on these spelling assignments. Even on turns when many tons of rails had to be handled at the cooling boxes, and the heat and humidity were intense, the men's plea for a speller "as usual" was shrugged off.

(4) "Dissatisfaction" mounted and "bickering" in the mill increased as cranemen requested, and foremen refused, spellers "however needed." The men grew convinced that orders had "come down from above to tighten up." The "higher-ups" expected that "postwar demand would be slackening and so everything was to be tightened up." To end such suspicions and bickering, the union was therefore now asking regular assignment of spellers from June through September on this job. So focal a health matter should not be left entirely to supervisory discretion.

(5) The men hoped the arbitrator would visit the cooling boxes at the rail mill "to see for himself" how hot a job theirs is and what a turn must be like for them when summer heat is added to these inherent work conditions.

(6) The union felt no need to stress how widespread and deep-rooted a customary work practice spelling constituted in steel production. For proper spelling involved more than the mere scheduling of operations and work forces within the meaning of Article XIII, defining management's exclusive func-

tions. It concerned the health and safety of the men under the inherently onerous conditions of steel production.

The Company's Case. (1) Although management had explored this grievance with the union through all the stages of the grievance procedures, it wished to enter a challenge to its admissibility for arbitration. By management's interpretation of rights and responsibilities under the agreement, such a grievance was barred for consideration by the umpire.

(2) The cranemen based their request upon the belief that a speller had been regularly assigned to them during the summer months "in the past years, but was removed by Management without just cause." That they had been mistaken about this, and their foreman correct, had been confirmed: the established practice was to assign a speller to cranemen during the summer at the discretion of the foreman. What the aggrieved were requesting, therefore, was not restoration of a once established practice of spelling but transformation of a continuing practice. Discretionary "spelling"—discretionary as to turns and conditions—continues in the rail mill as a part of the functions of the foreman. By requesting mandatory scheduling of a spellman on every turn from June 1 through September 30, the union was also attempting to alter a managerial decision and policy on the direction of the working forces.

(3) The Agreement stipulated the following:

Article XIII—Management Functions

The management of the Plants and Works and *the direction of the working forces* and the operations at the Plants and Works, *including* the hiring, promoting and retiring of Employees, the suspending, discharging or otherwise disciplining of Employees, the laying off and calling to work of Employees in connection with any reduction or increase in the working forces, *the scheduling of work* and the control and regulation of the use of all equipment and other property of the Company, *are the exclusive functions of the Management; provided, however, that in the exercise of such functions the Management shall observe the provisions of this Agreement and shall not discriminate against any Employee or applicant for employment because of his membership in or lawful activity on behalf of the Union.* [Italics indicate clauses on which management predicated its position in this dispute.]

Since the union has not charged management with (*a*) contravening any specific, concrete provisions of the Agreement or (*b*) discrimination, its protest regarding summer spelling constituted a contractually inadmissible invasion of management's exclusive functions to "schedule the work." The dispute by that token lies beyond arbitral jurisdiction.

(4) In raising immediately such a procedural challenge, management is asking the umpire to consider first "certain general principles which apply to cases of this nature," rather than the specific content of this grievance itself. For we see here a growing category of cases which, in management's view, are all adding up to a threatening total trend, precisely because each case in itself does "not appear to ask for very much and does not seem to have far-reaching or dangerous consequences. . . ." But they are cumulating into a disturbing trend. For this trend, at which management now seeks to strike, began in

1943—typically through a "little grievance" that asked reversal of a managerial decision taken under the exclusive rights affirmed in the management clause—now Article XIII—carried forward unchanged from agreement to agreement. The umpire in this early case ruled that, only when the union established the protested managerial decision as so "arbitrary and capricious" or so "unjust and unreasonable" as to impose undue hardship upon the employees concerned, could the underlying grievance become admissible for arbitration.

(5) The apparent "toughness" of these standards for valid union challenge to managerial decisions blurred for a time the fact that this ruling actually set up subjective tests for the managerial decisions themselves. At any rate, management before long found itself on the defensive. Instead of enjoying securely recognized rights in the management clause subject to rigorously defined and limited conditions, the company had to prove in case after case that a challenged decision was *not* arbitrary or capricious, unreasonable, or unfair enough to entail hardship upon the employees. For its part the union could argue by a sort of "scatter-shot" technique, injecting into its evidence at arbitration hearings all manner of allegations in the effort to convince the arbitrator, who is necessarily removed from intimate knowledge of mill conditions and the dynamic problems of daily mill operations, that the "little thing" the complainants were asking justified reversal of a managerial decision. As arbitrators admitted such cases to their jurisdiction, grievances of the type tended to "snowball" until demands for new "comforts" in work conditions, added spellmen, readjustments of work loads, and so forth, cumulated alarmingly throughout the plant and works.

(6) It was to meet this situation that management proposed, in the negotiation of the 1947 Agreement, a revision in Section 2 of Article XI to further define the nature of the grievances that can be appealed to arbitration. The Agreement now adds to the established procedural requirements the added condition that only if a grievance, not satisfactorily settled by the prior joint procedures, "shall involve the meaning and application of the provisions of this Agreement" may it be appealed to an impartial umpire. These new limiting words were purposive. They aimed directly at blocking grievances "which are not based upon any of the substantive provisions of the Agreement"; they underscored the fact "that only substantive rights and substantive obligations can be enforced in an arbitration procedure. . . ."

Section 2. The foregoing procedure, if followed in good faith by both parties, should be adequate to reach a fair and expeditious settlement of any grievance arising at any Plant or Works of the Company. In the event, however, that the procedure hereinbefore in Section 1 of this Article set forth shall have been followed in respect of any grievance and such grievance shall not thereby have been satisfactorily settled *and if such grievance shall involve the meaning and application of the provisions of this Agreement,* it may be appealed, within 20 days after the date of the meeting at which discussion of such grievance under Step No. 4 shall have been completed, or within 10 days after a draft of the minutes of such meeting shall first have been received by a representative of the Union, whichever of those periods shall last expire, to an impartial umpire to be appointed by mutual agreement.

(7) Management's position here can perhaps be further clarified for the umpire by comparing the changes in the now effective provisions regarding "Adjustment of Grievances" in Article XI with the corresponding language in the predecessor contract. The opening paragraph of Section 1, with its definitions of grievances, as well as its subsequent paragraphs detailing the procedures of *joint* adjustment through Step 4 of adjudication are carried forward unchanged. Let the arbitrator note that *two* kinds of differences are defined as submissible grievances by the following identical language in both Agreements:

ARTICLE XI—ADJUSTMENT OF GRIEVANCES

Section 1. Should any differences arise between the Company and the Union as to the meaning and application of the provisions of this Agreement *or as to any question relating to the wages, hours of work and other conditions of employment of any Employee,* there shall not be any suspension of work on account of such differences, but an earnest effort shall be made to settle them promptly and in accordance with the provisions of this Agreement in the manner hereinafter set forth.   [Author's italics.]

(8) Through the four "steps" of joint adjustment, then, management agreed to consider with the union not only differences concerning interpretation of the Agreement but also *any question* that may arise on the job between employees and the union and the company. The revisions introduced in 1947 concern when and if appeal to arbitration may be taken.

(9) With the new language, management was seeking deliberately to differentiate the legislative from the judicial processes in collective relations. Negotiation offers one focal instrument for achieving changes in established practices deemed desirable by either party; without question both utilized it validly to effect new "legislation" formulating the rules and regulations of their work together from day to day and from contract term to contract term. But, in so dynamic a relationship as that between company and employees, management also recognizes that it is salutary to bring the "problems and irritations arising from day to day . . . into the open for discussion and, in many cases, for adjustment without reference to the strict language of the Agreement." That is why, in defining differences that may validly present themselves for "adjustment" in Section 1 of Article XI, management agrees to consider *two* categories with the union: not only those concerning interpretation and application of the Agreement but also any question over their employment troubling employees. But this broader consideration of grievances is valid and acceptable only so long as "the parties to the Agreement are in control, and the interpretation and assertion of their respective rights depends upon their voluntary action," that is, through the successive steps of joint discussion in the grievance procedure, which thus also become "legislative in nature." Thereby the parties together in the grievance meeting, as at the negotiation table, can agree to extend their collective rules or to fit some new remedy to some specific daily situation. But arbitration is henceforth estopped from emerging as a continuation of negotiation or "legislative" process. To that end the new language of Section 2 limits arbitral appeal to only one of

the two categories of differences defined in Section 1: only to *interpretation of the contractual rules upon which the parties have already agreed.* Henceforth there can be no judge-made law under the Faraday Agreement.

(10) In conclusion, then, these newly added restrictions, as applied to the protest regarding summer spelling, bar arbitral jurisdiction from consideration. For Article XIII confers no affirmative or positive rights upon the union and denies even right of challenge save on two explicit grounds: violation of some other contractual provision or antiunion discrimination. Since the request for mandatory assignment of a speller during the summer months has not challenged management's decision on the matter on either of these grounds, it must be dismissed for lack of jurisdiction.

Union Response. The union representatives at the hearing replied that this procedural challenge took them completely unawares. Accordingly, they requested a postponement, during which they could prepare their answer. The legal staff at union headquarters was called upon by the local officers at Decatur for assistance. The union's counterarguments upon this procedural bar follow:

(1) The paragraph opening Article XI on the "Adjustment of Grievances" brings under the procedural steps for the settlement of grievances any differences "as to the meaning and application of the provisions of this Agreement or as to any question relating to the wages, hours of work and other conditions of employment of any Employee. . . ." The present grievance centers upon a difference arising from a question relating to a condition of employment of cranemen—summer spelling. It is therefore admissible to arbitration, just as many similar cases involving conditions of employment have been accepted hitherto by umpires for determination on their merits.

(2) The union has relinquished its right to strike "on account of such differences." But the very prohibition of the strike weapon raises questions regarding the company's apparent contention that there exists an area of potential differences on which the union has simultaneously "foreclosed the right to strike . . . and . . . also surrendered resort to the terminal facilities of arbitration."

(3) The company's argument that this case is representative of the tendency to undermine managerial prerogatives echoes a long history. From the first "safety laws" and earliest protests against bargaining on wages and working conditions, management has feared infringements upon its rights. Instead of the initiation of a process "whereby management is piecemeal losing its sovereignty" in such cases, the union sees "a determined drive by management . . . to monopolize the decision-making process in areas covered by the collective bargaining agreement." The union reaffirms its determination "to protest whenever a management practice endangers the health and safety of its employees."

(4) And this grievance does plainly relate "to the safety and health of the employees." It "raises the simple issue of whether the subjective and unsystematic decisions of a foreman as to when and under what circumstances men will be relieved of the health and safety hazards implicit in exposure to high

temperatures is a reasonable effort to provide safe and healthful conditions of work within the meaning of Article XIV of the Agreement." [1]

III. The Protest on Oxygen Lancing

With the looming demands for increased steel production, the management of Faraday introduced many technical improvements. As these changes in equipment, methods, and processes made themselves felt, differences regarding proper adjustments multiplied between company and union. At one time the Decatur plant was faced with 34 protests stemming from such changes; of these, 19 were withdrawn or settled, and the remaining 15 were appealed to arbitration.

In essence the union maintained that the protested changes in operating techniques imposed unreasonable and unfair work loads upon employees. The company, in turn, defended its decisions as proper exercise of management functions under Article XIII.[2]   The union rested its challenges upon one or more of three provisions in the current Agreement: (1) Article II, Section 3, on "customary practice"; [3] (2) Article V, "Establishment of New Wage Rates and Adjustment of Wage Rates," under which upward revisions of rates or job reclassifications were claimed; [4] and (3) Article XIV, "Safety and Health." [5]

One of these cases serves as illustration of the issues raised.

The first, second, and third helpers in the Open Hearth department submitted the following statement of grievance:

> The Union claims that the Company has put an unreasonable and unfair work load on the above-mentioned employees by requiring that they perform the entire process of lancing the Open Hearth heats with oxygen for the reduction of carbon in the bath, and that if this practice is continued the Company must assign an operator permanently, who should have the entire responsibility for all factors connected with this new and highly technical process.

Oxygen lancing, a new technique in open hearth operations, had been introduced not only throughout the company but also throughout the industry for the general purpose of expediting the basic chemical reactions.   At the time of these grievances the process was still in the experimental stage.

The crews at the Open Hearth operated the new equipment as follows:

Basically the lancing machine was a device for pumping oxygen under the surface of the molten steel.   To do this four lengths of pipe were inserted into the open hearth furnace.   As the pipe gradually burned off more pipe was fed into the furnace.   The second and third helpers prepared the lancing equipment for insertion and the first helper actually performed the lancing process.   Supervisors had counseled the first helper to determine the

---

[1] See Appendix for Article XIV of the agreement, "Safety and Health."
[2] See p. 580.
[3] See p. 578.
[4] See Appendix for the relevant wage provisions of the agreement, p. 586.
[5] See Appendix for text of Article XIV, p. 587.

need for cranking more pipe into the furnace by auditory rather than by visual means—when a "gurgle" emanating from the bath announced that the pipe length already inserted had been burned off.

The Union's Case. The union protested that to require the regular furnace crews to assume these new duties raised safety hazards and altered local practice and custom. The local union had conducted a survey of practices pursuant upon the innovation of oxygen lancing in one other plant of the company and in five other companies. In some of the other companies, additions had been made to the furnace crews that paralleled generally their own demand for "the assignment of two additional crew men per turn or the establishment of two new jobs to be occupied each day of three turns by six assignees." In comparable works, "They have an operator to operate this oxygen lance, and a helper. . . . The men are asking for . . . something similar . . . in our plant here. . . . It is almost a revolutionary change; and to be fair to everybody in the open hearth . . . we don't think that we are asking very much at all. . . . " "The contract states in Article II, Section 3, that, if management changes or eliminates any local practice or custom, the burden of proof shall be on the company. We feel in reality that we have conceded a big point by even presenting our case, because we feel that the burden of proof lies here on the management . . . to show why we do not need an extra man." When asked to specify the local custom thus changed or eliminated, the union's spokesman replied, "The local practice has been not taking care of oxygen. It is a negative practice. The new practice has been introduced and eliminates the old practice."

The Company's Case. For its part, management again challenged the admissibility to arbitration of such a demand for added crewmen on three grounds:

(1) There can be no question regarding management's right to experiment with such a new technique as oxygen lancing. Nor does management, for its part, deny the union's right to ask adjustments as and if they seem necessary. But such must meet the requirements of contractual validity. By no stretch of contractual language can this specific demand of new crew assignees be brought within the coverage of the Agreement.

(2) As for the union's challenge under the local practice clause, management can never identify effective crew composition with local custom, changeable only when it meets the burden of proof to support action here. The union is adding everything "not done" in the past—as lancing heats with oxygen—to the things done that become, by the definitions of Article II, Section 3, "local practice or custom now in effect" at the plant. This projects rigidity and strangulation and becomes thereby the *reductio ad absurdum* implicit in the whole argument. Management can never agree that the Agreement safeguards "past" work loads, crew assignments, crew composition, simply because they *have* existed in the past—or have *not* existed in the past. For efficiency and productivity, management's right to make flexible decisions, as defined in Article XIII, must be maintained.

(3) "The direction of the working forces and the operations at the plant," as well as "the scheduling of work," are expressly enumerated in the management clause, Article XIII, as types of functions that remain exclusively managerial so long as their exercise does not breach any contractual provisions. Crew assignments have always been recognized as a function of management. If the union claims this particular furnace crew needs two additional regular members to meet new hazards imposed by oxygen lancing, it must prove the actual existence of such hazards by the definitions mutually formulated in Article XIV on Health and Safety.[1] The company possesses a top safety record in the industry, of which it is proud; it would not subject its men to avoidable risks. Nor would management deprecate the dangerous potentialities of oxygen as utilized under the typical furnace heat conditions of open hearth operations. "If you blow oxygen out in the open air it won't catch fire at all, but always in the open hearth we have a lot of respect for oxygen." But the use of oxygen is not new; the aggrieved employees themselves have been using it for more than a decade, for instance, to burn out tap holes. And precautions, as the men concede, have been taken which management deems, and the safety record establishes, adequate to the current level of development in the new process of oxygen lancing. The crews, working as teams, and assisted by a pipe fitter, now spend some 37 minutes in $9\frac{1}{2}$ hours at the oxygen lance. But only a minority of heats still are thus lanced; analysis made of the past year's operations show that 1,205, or 19.2%, of the total of 6,273 heats produced were lanced. The process, in a word, is still new, developmental; two large problems still demand solution before wider use of the process is likely: the high cost of oxygen and the excessive roof damage. Certainly, when and if the time comes that all the heats, or far more than the present scanty one in five, are lanced, the union may wish to ask reconsideration of this demand. But that is an "anticipatory and not a [present] issue."

APPENDIX

ARTICLE V—ESTABLISHMENT OF NEW WAGE RATES AND ADJUSTMENT OF WAGE RATES

Section 1. The parties hereto recognize that it may become necessary or desirable from time to time at one or more of the Plants or Works that the Management classify new jobs or reclassify existing jobs or adjust then existing incentive wage rates because of (a) the creation of new positions, (b) changes in equipment, (c) changes in manufacturing processes or in methods or standards of manufacture or production, (d) the development of new manufacturing processes or methods, or (e) mechanical improvements made by the Company in the interest of improved methods or products. An existing job shall not be reclassified, however, unless such changes or events shall alter the requirements of such job as to training, skill, responsibility, effort and surroundings to the extent of a whole numerical classification of 1.0 or more.

Section 2. Whenever after April 28, 1947, any of the changes or other events specified in Section 1 of this Article shall occur and for that reason the Manage-

---

[1] See Appendix, p. 587.

ment at any Plant or Works shall deem it necessary or desirable to classify a new job or to reclassify a then existing job at such Plant or Works, such job shall be classified or reclassified, as the case may be, and the new classification shall be put into effect, in accordance with the procedure set forth in this Section 2 [detailed steps outlined].

. . . . .

Section 4. Whenever after the date of this Agreement any of the changes or other events specified in Section 1 of this Article shall occur and for that reason the Management at any Plant or Works shall deem it necessary or desirable to adjust an existing incentive wage rate for any job at such Plant or Works and thereby to establish a new incentive wage rate therefor, such new incentive wage rate shall be established in accordance with the procedure set forth in this Section 4. [Procedure is then outlined.]

. . . . .

(*c*) The Union may, at any time within 30 days after the effective date of such new incentive wage rate, or, if such rate shall have been made effective for an experimental or trial period as hereinbefore in paragraph (*b*) of this Section provided, at any time within 30 days after the expiration of such period, initiate a grievance regarding such new incentive wage rate, in which event such grievance shall be handled in accordance with the procedure set forth in Article XI hereof for the adjustment of grievances, including the procedure for arbitration set forth in Section 2 of that Article. . . .

ARTICLE XIV—SAFETY AND HEALTH

The Company will continue to make every reasonable effort to provide safe and healthful conditions of work for Employees at the Plants and Works and to provide Employees with any necessary protective equipment in accordance with the practices prevailing at the respective Plants and Works at the date of this Agreement. . . .

The Union will cooperate with the Company in encouraging Employees to observe the safety regulations which shall be prescribed by the Company and to work in a safe manner. . . .

If any Employee shall believe that there exists an unsafe condition, changed from the normal hazards inherent in the operation, so that the employee is in danger of injury, he shall notify his foreman of such danger and of the facts relating thereto. Thereafter, unless there shall be a dispute as to the existence of such unsafe condition, he shall have the right, subject to reasonable steps for protecting other Employees and the equipment from injury, to be relieved from duty on the job in respect of which he has complained and to return to such job when such unsafe condition shall be remedied. The Management may in its discretion assign such Employee to other available work at the Plant or Works. If the existence of such alleged unsafe condition shall be disputed, the Chairman of the Grievance Committee of the Union at the Plant or Works and the Management's Representative or his designee shall immediately investigate such alleged unsafe condition and determine whether it exists. If they shall not agree and if the Chairman of the Grievance Committee is of the opinion that such alleged unsafe condition exists, the Employee shall have the right to present a grievance in writing to the Management's Representative or his designee and thereafter to be relieved from duty on the job as stated above. Such grievance shall be presented without delay directly to an impartial umpire under the provisions of Section 2 of Article XI of this Agreement, who shall determine whether such Employee was justified in leaving the job because of the existence of such an unsafe condition.

ARTICLE XVII—PROHIBITION OF STRIKES AND LOCKOUTS

During the term of this Agreement neither the Union nor any Employee shall (*a*) engage in or in any way encourage or sanction any strike or other action which shall interrupt or interfere with work or production at any of the Plants or Works or (*b*) prevent or attempt to prevent the access of Employees to any of the Plants or Works. During the term of this Agreement the Company shall not engage in any lockout of Employees at any of the Plants or Works. The Company may suspend and later discharge, in accordance with the provisions of Article XII of this Agreement, any Employee who shall violate any provision of this Section. Prior to discharging any such Employee for any such violation, the Company shall furnish the name, check number and address of such Employee to the Director of the District of the Union in which the Plant or Works is located.

INTERNATIONAL MACHINE COMPANY

A COMPLAINT AGAINST A FOREMAN: ADMISSIBILITY TO ARBITRATION

A demand by the union that a foreman be removed was appealed to arbitration. Excerpts from the hearing follow:

Present for the Company	*Present for the Union*
Francis Pennell, Company Counsel	Fred Restuccia, District Director
Richard Hunter, Assistant Counsel	William French, Staff Representative
Ford Tyler, Production Manager	James Cabot, Chairman, Grievance
Orrin Gilbert, Assistant Production	Committee
Manager	Michael Bruckner, Department Steward, and President of Local Union

Pennell (m): I wish to submit a photostatic copy of Grievance No. 623–1885 and excerpts from the minutes of the step 4 meeting.

Employee's Statement of Grievance: *I am filing grievance against the activities of my foreman, Mr. Sinclair, which are in direct violation of the agreement. Mr. Sinclair has repeatedly accused union members of being Nazis, Communists, and Bolsheviks. He persists in inflammatory remarks with the obvious intent of causing feeling against workers of foreign parentage. He tries to stir up race feeling among the men. He has accused the union men of causing the death of his son (who died in battle). Management should prevent its representative from making remarks of this nature. Otherwise, I can only feel that this foreman is acting with the approval of his supervision, who then must accept liability.*

Excerpts from Minutes of Step 4 Meeting: *In this grievance, Michael Bruckner, a machinist, as well as shop steward, and local union president, presented a complaint against the activities of his foreman, Mr. Sinclair, on the basis that those activities violate the agreement.*

The union contended that this grievance is proper because the company should know what is going on in the department; that the company should have equal disciplinary treatment for members of the supervisory forces and for employees; that the only ways the union has of calling such conditions to the attention of the company is to file a grievance or to shut down the department; and that it had selected the orderly way. The union further contended that the employees do not like to work under the conditions existent; that this incident was not the first radical accusation against Bruckner and the union by Sinclair; that Sinclair charged Bruckner and others with being Communists and un-American, and repeated those charges in front of witnesses in February of 1944; that the union filed charges against him at that time; that after that grievance was filed, Mr. Sinclair retracted the statements; that at the same time he refused to bargain with Bruckner and was told by his superintendent that he must bargain with proper union representatives; that since then Sinclair had called Bruckner a Communist and every other name; that he again refused to bargain with Bruckner; that Sinclair should not be permitted to continue his attacks against Bruckner based on the fact that he does not like the union; that Bruckner does like the union and believes in it and in its attempts to keep down labor trouble and to promote harmony; that as a union official he has always worked toward that end; and that on August 7, when Sinclair engaged in a tirade against him, all Bruckner did was to ask Sinclair if anyone had told the employees how to mark certain cards; that Sinclair has made derogatory statements about President Roosevelt which Bruckner believes amount to treason in time of war; that Sinclair did not "blow up" on August 7 because of announcement of the death of his son on that day as alleged, for his son died in April; that Sinclair has been in the department for many years and has continually been "cracking the whip"; that because of Sinclair's actions, Bruckner has been kept busy trying to prevent the men from striking but that if management does not take some positive action against Sinclair, he cannot be responsible for what happens; that the action taken by the management in assigning the assistant foreman to handle grievances is not satisfactory because the assistant foreman is a second-shift man and further because, by removing the responsibility from Sinclair, he got what he wanted, and in the opinion of the union, he should have been disciplined instead; that Sinclair should be made to deal courteously with the union; that the assistant foreman has not been given sufficient authority to act and must report back to Sinclair before making a decision; and that present arrangements are not satisfactory because the union does not consider Sinclair a fit supervisor. The union contended that Sinclair has stated that he hates Bruckner; that in Bruckner's opinion, Sinclair is crazy; that since August 7, Sinclair has repeated a statement formerly made that there is not a real mechanic working in the department; and that what the union is requesting is that Sinclair be fired, as any employee would be under comparable conditions. The union stated that if the company will not agree, it will appeal the grievance to arbitration to see if it cannot force the company to fire Sinclair.

The company stated that this grievance is a complaint about certain statements made by a supervisor; that it is always willing to listen to any employee complaints; that this grievance is not a proper request; it is a function of management to select and discipline supervisors. The company stated that the terms of the agreement are being followed and that it is interested in harmonious cooperation, and that management will continue to watch conditions referred to in this grievance toward promoting harmonious relations. The company stated that it does not condone such alleged statements attributed to Sinclair.

Pennell (m): That concludes the minutes. We have a fundamental objection to the consideration of this grievance. We believe this grievance may not be considered and arbitrated under the agreement. It is not admissible.

French (u): Mr. Umpire, under the agreement, management has the right to discipline employees. But nothing in the agreement gives the foremen the right to use abusive language in the name of discipline. Management has penalized employees for abusive language and has even discharged them. We ask the same consideration. We ask why the company has different rules for supervisors and employees. Management admits that the foreman is not fit to talk to employees or to discuss grievances, since it has substituted another foreman to handle grievances. We feel that Sinclair is not fit to be part of supervision.

Arbitrator: It is a close case, and I shall weigh the issue of admissibility before making any decision on the merits of this case. But we may as well proceed and hear the grievance on its merits unless the company wants to argue further the issue of admissibility.

Hunter (m): Well, you are putting the company in a difficult position that way. While it is not set forth in the grievance form, it is, I presume, the intent of the grievance to ask the company to remove a foreman. Is that correct?

French (u): Management feels that Sinclair is not capable of talking to people when they have grievances, yet he continues to direct them, and causes grievances to arise.

Hunter (m): If we arbitrate the grievance on merit, while its admissibility is under advisement, we are forced to present in an arbitration hearing under the contract testimony on whether or not the company should discharge a foreman, which has nothing to do with the relationship between the company and the union under that contract.

Arbitrator: Another suggestion than discharge may be made.

Hunter (m): My point is that the selection of management personnel is management's business and is outside the scope of arbitration. I don't think the company should be placed in the position, while admissibility is under consideration by the umpire, of having to make a presentation on the merits of whether a foreman should be discharged or some other action taken with respect to what the company's relationship with its own foremen should be.

Restuccia (u): We are placed in a peculiar position by the attitude of the company. We have numerous cases where our members have been discharged for remarks made to a foreman, which were not as objectionable as those made by this foreman.

Such remarks were made to several men, and in particular to the president of a local union, who is also a grievance committeeman. When this union officer is trying to process grievances—we want to know just what our position is going to be. Where are we going? Leave it to the good-will of management? We'll talk to Sinclair, says management, and he won't do it again. But he does it time after time.

And management has had time to remedy the condition. This grievance was filed August 26, 1944, a year and four months ago. It is still unremedied. This provocation still exists. What will happen if Sinclair indulges in one of his regular bouts of name-calling to a man who turns around and smacks him down? Will the employee be fired? I can tell you in advance that such an employee will be taken out of the plant by the police. Yet Sinclair has the right to call the employees anything he wishes. For a year and three months nothing has been done except to assign the assistant foreman to handle grievances.

Arbitrator: I am limited by your joint agreement, Mr. Restuccia. Even if I listen to this case, I am uncertain as to what course of action I may take. I am perfectly willing to listen to it, however, and let matters come out in the open.

Restuccia (u): Well, we certainly would like to have your opinion, so we know what we are going to do from here on. We feel you have the right to hear this grievance under the agreement. If you find that you don't have the right, we would just like to know, so we will know what course we must pursue from here on.

Arbitrator: An arbitrator is not always in the position to evaluate the admissibility of a case at the moment of presentation. He has to think it over. This case has gone through a number of steps. A certain kind of atmosphere has created a certain situation in the shop; and I am inclined to feel that it would be well for me to hear the grievance and leave it for more mature consideration to decide what course of action, if any, is available.

Hunter (m): We realize that there is merit to that suggestion of hearing everything that comes up. Yet there has to be a line somewhere. We had one case in another plant where the union requested a wage decrease for a foreman based upon an alleged inequity. Now, foremen's compensation is something in which the union has no legitimate interest and the umpire so held. The company can't discuss everything that the union brings into the grievance procedure.

Arbitrator: Grievance procedure itself is involved in this case. You have a foreman who is in a very important position, processing grievances.

Hunter (m): But this particular foreman has been removed from that position.

French (u): He is still directing the working force.

Pennell (m): Mr. Umpire, look at Article II. There it is stated that

it is the purpose of the parties to set forth the basic agreement between them in respect of rates of pay, hours of work, and other conditions of employment of the employees.

The term "employee" is defined in Article I:

"Employee" means an employee of the company who is included in a bargaining unit.

It further states,

The unit shall include all production and maintenance employees, except all executives, office and salaried employees, foremen, assistant foremen, timekeepers, watchmen and guards.

You will note that foremen and supervisors are expressly excluded.

Restuccia (u): Mr. Umpire, the term "employees" as used in this agreement gives those employees the right to file grievances. Aggrieved about what? What else but their pay, their hours of work, their seniority, their working conditions? If their complaints about Foreman Sinclair do not come under working conditions, I don't know what would. When men are being called names and insulted every minute of the day—haven't they a grievance against a supervisor and the conditions of work he creates?

If foremen violate seniority, or any other provisions of the agreement, no one denies the right of the employee to file a grievance. Yet Sinclair violates the spirit of the agreement by his relations with union men and union officers. We are filing a grievance against his continuous daily actions.

Arbitrator: Yes, but you are dealing here with intangibles.

Restuccia (u): Wouldn't you say that if an employee is being cussed and abused, he is being asked to tolerate one of the worst kind of working conditions?

Pennell (m): The position the company is taking is that the union is here trying to affect the status of a supervisory employee, and the agreement does not permit such action.

Restuccia (u): The union intends to protect its members from intolerable conditions. There is no comparison between this case and the case Mr. Hunter cited a while ago. We realize that a foreman's salary is outside our jurisdiction, but the welfare of our members is within our jurisdiction. When our members are discriminated against, insulted, provoked, taunted for their beliefs and their origins, working under intolerable conditions—well, just what should we do?

Pennell (m): What is the difference between the union asking us to change a foreman's wage rate and asking us to fire a foreman?

Restuccia (u): A lot. Wages are his personal problem, and concern only his relationship to management. We are asking you to get rid of Sinclair because, as foreman, he is abusing our members. We are not interested in his status as foreman except as it concerns the welfare of our members.

Arbitrator [to company representatives]: Well, I will say this: if you want me to take under consideration the admissibility of this grievance before we hear its merits, I will do so. If you want to press that point, I will yield to you. The company and the union will submit a memorandum to me on admissibility.

French (u): Won't we have a chance to bring out the facts of the case?

Arbitrator: I have to decide first whether I can hear this case.

French (u): There is nothing under the contract to keep you from hearing it.

Arbitrator: I think that, in this case, the company has a right to ask me to make a decision first on admissibility.

French (u): This was not the only grievance filed against this man. Another grievance was filed in February and again in August of 1944.

Restuccia (u): Let's submit our statement on its admissibility under the agreement.

Pennell (m): Before we close, I offer as a company exhibit an arbitration award by Dean Young B. Smith, arbitrator, in a proceeding between Wright Aeronautical Corporation and United Automobile Workers of America, Local No. 669, CIO. The date of that award ruling the grievance inadmissible to arbitration is December 17, 1943, and it deals with the very issue before us in this case.[1]

---

[1] In the Wright case, the company denied the truth of all the charges brought against the foreman by the union.

Arbitrator: Do you want to offer that now or with your memorandum?

Pennell (m): We'll offer it now.

DISCUSSION QUESTIONS

1. How would you summarize the concrete issue here challenged as inadmissible for arbitration?

2. Analyze critically the respective positions of management and union.

3. What decision would you render if you were the arbitrator?

GARDNER BOARD AND CARTON COMPANY

THE DEVELOPMENT OF A NEW STRATEGY IN LABOR RELATIONS

I. INTRODUCTION

The management of the Gardner Board and Carton Company has been giving close attention to modifications in policy toward labor relations in recent years, and particularly since World War II. In reviewing the negotiations of the 1954 contract, management felt that its new approach was paying off.

The company manufactures paperboard and fabricates multicolored printed cartons for food, soap, cigarettes, and various other products. It operates three plants, two in Middletown, Ohio, where the general office is located, and one about 30 miles away, in Lockland, Ohio, a northern suburb of Cincinnati. It consists of two divisions, the Middletown division and the Lockland division, each with facilities for manufacturing paperboard and fabricated paper cartons. Its employees number slightly over 2,000, evenly divided between the two cities.

The company takes its name from the Gardner family, the members of which have maintained close control over all phases of the business since its inception in 1900. The family has been known for its interest in the welfare of the employees. It established, for instance, a dispensary at Middletown in 1918 and group insurance in 1920. In general, the company pays higher than prevailing rates in other plants and maintains stable work even in slack times. Its concern, moreover, has not been limited to its own employees. In both communities the company sponsors a boy scout troop, a junior achievement program, a local radio program and a college scholarship fund.

While the Middletown division has been a part of the Gardner operations since 1900, the Lockland division was acquired in 1932—when the Gardner and Richardson companies merged. In 1946, the Gardners bought out the Richardson interests and thereby gained complete control of the enlarged operations.

In spite of common leadership, however, the Middletown and Lockland divisions differ because of the nature of the communities in which they are located. In Middletown, population 50,000, Gardner with 1,000 employees is the second largest employer; the largest is Armco Steel Co., with 5,000 employees. In Lockland, on the other hand, a part of greater Cincinnati, where companies like Procter & Gamble and General Electric are located, Gardner with 1,000 employees is not a dominant factor. Furthermore, the industries of Lockland have been organized by international unions, but those of Middletown only by local unions. Indeed, Armco Steel Co. is one of the two major steel companies not yet organized by the United Steel-workers.

The history of the two divisions also reveals important differences. In Middletown the employees and company jointly established in 1914 the Mutual Benefit Association—converted in the early 1940's into an independent union, the Independent Paper Workers of Middletown, which by 1954 embraced about 85% of the production and maintenance employees. The only attempt to organize Middletown by an affiliated union failed when in 1948 the Independent Paper Workers defeated the United Paperworkers of America, CIO, by a very narrow margin.

In Lockland, on the other hand, the passage of the Wagner Act was followed by a militant organizing campaign, culminating in 1944 in an NLRB election as a result of which the United Paperworkers of America, CIO, was certified as bargaining agent for paperboard, power house, and maintenance workers. Another NLRB election in October 1946 enlarged the scope of the same union to include carton operations. The United Paperworkers was then certified as bargaining agent for all production and maintenance employees. Union membership grew and by 1954 embraced 95% of the working force.

II. THE LOCKLAND STRIKE

The negotiations of the first contract at Lockland opened in November 1946 with wages and union security the main issues. The union asked for 15 cents; the company offered 6 cents. The company justified its position by the fact that 6 cents was the maximum within the pattern established by automobiles and steel. The union demanded a union shop. The company proposed termination of maintenance of membership, since it was established under the influence of the War Labor Board, but "it was no longer company policy to impose such restrictions on its employees as a condition of right to work."

Little progress was made between November 1946 and January 1947. The union modified its demands to 10 cents and continuance of maintenance of membership, but the company remained firm with its proposals of 6 cents and an "open shop." In January 1947, the union called upon the Federal Mediation and Conciliation Service to intervene. Four sessions were held with a member of the Service during January. The offer of an irrevocable checkoff in place of maintenance of membership was rejected by the union; union's offer to arbitrate the issues was rejected by management.

Concurrent negotiations with the Middletown division resulted during January in a contract embodying a 6-cent wage increase. In general, the company had always maintained a policy of providing the same benefits, paying the same wage scales and making identical offers to both unions.

Since the contract was due to expire, the parties agreed to extend it to April 1. Negotiations continued, but the final meeting of March 31 arrived, with the parties no closer to agreement. As the session broke up, the union's regional director asked, "Where does responsibility for a work stoppage lie?"—

a query sharpened the next day by a walkout which rapidly developed into a full-scale strike. On April 18, the union asked the Federal conciliator to intervene once more. Only one session was held; the strike was to last two months.

On April 30, the company announced an additional increase of 6 cents in both divisions and stated that the first increase had represented a cost of living adjustment, while the second was in conformity with the automobile and steel wage patterns.

After this announcement, the union ran a number of full-page advertisements in the local paper attacking the company. Simultaneously, a "Back to Work Movement" ran full-page advertisements attacking the union. The company wrote a letter to each employee explaining that the real issue of the strike was not wages, as the union had claimed, but the union shop. An offer by the union to leave the issues to a group of local clergymen for decision was turned down.

On June 3, with the strike two months old, a group of 275 employees secured an injunction against mass picketing, limiting them to 10 at any one time, and to the sidewalk across the street from the main gate. The strike quickly ended.

With the resumption of operations, the "Back to Work Movement" converted itself into an independent union in opposition to the United Paperworkers, CIO. The company recognized neither union from June 1947 until July 1948. The United Paperworkers, CIO, filed a charge of unfair labor practices with the NLRB. When the company agreed to sign a six-month contract with the United Paperworkers, the complaint was dismissed in July 1948. The contract provided for an open shop and a representation election by the NLRB at the end of six months.

In January 1949 the membership voted 2 to 1 in favor of the United Paperworkers. Two important contract changes were made during 1949. The company conceded a modified union shop [1] on the understanding that it would never accept a full union shop, and the union agreed to a contributory pension plan.

III. The 1950 Negotiations

The 1948 and 1949 negotiations at Lockland had been carried on by the vice president in charge of operations and the regional director for the union. Negotiations were resumed in July 1950 resulting in the first of a series of two-year contracts. The contract yielded each employee a percentage wage increase ranging from 2 to 7 cents per hour.

Due to the rising cost of living, management again opened the contract for wage talks in October 1950.[2] The company offered an increase of 4%;

---

[1] A modified union shop had been made more acceptable to the company by the provision of the Taft-Hartley law that allowed only two ways by which loss of "good standing" in the union could result in discharge: refusal to become a member of the union at the end of the probationary period, and failure to pay union dues or initiation fees.

[2] The contract provided for voluntary wage re-opening.

the union asked for a flat increase of 10 cents. After some bargaining, the parties compromised on a combination of a flat increase of 3 cents and a cost of living adjustment of 4% for a total wage package of 7 to 9 cents.

Shortly thereafter, the chairman of the 1947 strike became president of the Lockland union. He had campaigned on the issue of a flat as against a percentage increase, making his appeal to the lower paid wage earners who had received in July only 2 cents as compared to 7 cents by higher paid employees.

Shortly afterwards, management changed its strategy. First, it developed its proposals systematically. Economic offers were based on: (1) competitors' rates; (2) industry pattern which was set by industry-wide bargaining on the West Coast, applied in the east by Container Corporation, and by Gair Co.; and (3) area practices. Noneconomic proposals were developed from recommendations of line and staff management.

Secondly, the whole system of communications was revised. The industrial relations department held pre-bargaining and post-bargaining meetings with all levels of line management. These meetings provided a means of interpreting the company's bargaining positions to supervisors and foremen. They also gave supervision an opportunity to register employee reaction to these positions. In addition, the company transmitted a bulletin to all members of management after each session with the union, as well as "fact sheets" as deemed wise from time to time, to help foremen explain the company's proposals to employees. Finally, the company sent letters to the homes of employees throughout the year, including the quarterly business and the annual safety reports. Indeed, letters were frequently sent to employees' homes during negotiations, usually the same evening following the bargaining session, with interpretive comments by company officials.

The new approach is seen in the 1952 negotiations, particularly at Lockland.

IV. 1952 Negotiations

Negotiations were started in July, and completed at Middletown on August 4, and at Lockland on August 5.

On July 11, Colin Gardner III, Vice President in Charge of Operations, sent the following letter to all hourly paid employees at Lockland: [1]

> On July 31, the labor contract between the Company and the CIO Paperworkers will expire. The Union notified us on May 24 that they wanted to end the present agreement and negotiate a new contract.
> The first meeting to discuss the new contract will be held on Wednesday, July 16. After that, there will be other meetings for the same purpose.
> I know you will be interested in these meetings. As they go along, we will try to keep you informed in two ways of the progress being made.
> 1. Some of our management people will attend the meetings. They will tell your foreman about them. And your foreman will pass his information on to you.
> 2. During the negotiations, I will write you and let you know what's happening.

---

[1] Colin Gardner signed all the other letters shown in this case.

That way you and your families will know from time-to-time what progress is being made.

I am sure, too, that the Union will make every effort to keep you informed. That is good. The more facts you have about the bargaining, the more able you will be to help the negotiators on both sides work out the terms and conditions of the new contract.

I am hopeful we can negotiate a new contract before July 31. But it is a short time. Ordinarily, contract negotiators begin their meetings 30 to 60 days before the old contract expires. The Company preferred to begin the discussions during the week of June 16, and we suggested this to the Union. That would have allowed at least 40 days to complete a new contract. However, the Union has said that they do not believe it should take more than two weeks to negotiate a new contract. I can assure you the Company will do everything reasonable to reach a contract agreement with the Union before July 31.

Since we signed our contract two years ago, Gardner people have received wage increases averaging about 24 cents per hour, including job evaluation. And in only one grievance during that time has the Union felt the Company's decision should be reviewed by an arbitrator. In that case the Company's decision was upheld.

. . . . .

The major proposals and the final settlement are shown in the following chart:

Issue	Company's Proposal	Union's Proposal	Final Agreement
Union Security	Status quo—modified union shop	Union shop	Status quo—modified union shop
Wages	Provisions for change based on C.P.I. Cost of living	Cost of living	Cost of living
Shift Differentials	7¢ for 2d 15¢ for 3d	10¢ for 2d 20¢ for 3d	7¢ for 2d 15¢ for 3d
Promotion	Security and Ability	Seniority	Security and Ability
Saturday and Sunday premium pay	Status quo—pay premium if Sat. and Sun. represent working more than 40 hrs. in any workweek	Time and a half for Saturday and double time for Sunday, as such	Status quo
Job Classification	Merit provision	No merit	Compromise
Arbitration of job reclassification	Status quo—no arbitration of job reclassification	Arbitration of job reclassification	Status quo

The bargaining sessions were held at a local hotel in Lockland. In attendance for the company: Vice President in Charge of Operations, Vice President in Charge of Labor Relations and Public Relations, Director of Public Relations; and for the union: the local bargaining committee, two international representatives, and the regional director. In all, seven sessions were held between July 16 and 29.

When the first session opened on July 16, the union wished to present its proposals first. To this the management replied, ". . . [the company desires] to present its proposals first so the union could have something to compare their [union's] proposals against. The company determines the right thing in its offer . . . it doesn't hold anything back." The company proceeded to present its complete offer.

The company remained firm on its proposals throughout. It did withdraw, however, a proposal for incorporation of rotating shifts at Lockland when the foremen reported to the management committee that it was untenable because of strong opposition by senior employees. The union, on the other hand, frequently shifted or changed its position.

The following excerpt from the management bulletin of July 22 illustrates company tactics.

To all Lockland Management People:

At the contract negotiations meeting yesterday, two major subjects were discussed. These were promotions and the job evaluation program.

At the beginning of the meeting the Company gave the Union a letter outlining new language to be used in the seniority clause. This letter has been distributed to all management people. The letter also explained that the Company believed that ability to advance should be a consideration for promotion if it was to manage successfully. Clauses from numerous UPA–CIO contracts were cited in the letter to show that the Company's proposal to make ability to advance a consideration for promotion was a common practice in our industry.

After this letter was read and discussed by the two parties at the bargaining table, a recess was called. Immediately after the recess the Union representatives told the Company that they would accept the Company proposal and recommend to the membership that ability to advance be a consideration for promotion.

At the session of July 29, management rejected a union request for a 15-day extension to present the unsettled issue to employees, on the ground that the company had made its final offer and little could be gained by additional discussion. That same evening, the following letter went to homes:

We had another meeting with the Union Bargaining Committee today. But we were not able to reach agreement with them on a new contract.

The same issues are still in dispute. As I told you in my last letter, the Company feels its position on these subjects is fair and reasonable. And, in addition, the employee benefits proposed by the company are very liberal.

We understand a Union membership meeting has been scheduled for this week to vote on whether or not to accept the contract proposed by the Company. This will be a very important vote—for you and the Company.

Naturally, we hope employees will vote to accept our proposals. They include many new and improved benefits for Gardner people. The wage increases, improved insurance plan at less cost to employees, the more liberal vacation plan and shift differentials are all a part of this contract proposal. These are things which the Union agrees Gardner people want.

The Union disagrees with us on these things:

1. They want a full Union Shop. That would mean that a few long service employees who do not belong would have to join the Union to keep their jobs. We don't believe that is right.

2. The Union doesn't want the Company to pay extra money (in accordance with a merit plan) to our outstanding highly skilled people.

3. The Union wants the right to arbitrate how many people should work on a job and whether we can set up a new job or discontinue an old one. These things depend in part on the needs and desires of our customers. They are also affected by the price our customers are willing to pay for our products. If the Company cannot have control of these things, we would be seriously handicapped in operating our business successfully. We have the right to make these decisions under our present contract. The Union does not claim we have abused it. So we see no reason for changing our contract on this subject.

4. They want some other economic benefits for a small number of people. . . .

The people who attend the Union meeting will decide whether or not we sign a new contract within the next few days. As you know, our present contract expires on July 31. Without a contract the stable and favorable working conditions which we have been enjoying can more easily be interrupted. However, the Company has told the Union that it will do its best to maintain the present wage rates and working conditions during the short period when a contract will not be in force.

I am sure you know how important this Union meeting will be. I want to urge you to attend the meeting, give your opinions and vote for whatever you believe is fair. We hope, of course, that most Gardner people will vote to accept the Company's contract proposal and continue to enjoy steady work, high wages, and good working conditions.

We hope you will think these problems over very seriously. If there is anything you do not understand about the Company's position, please ask your foreman. I know he will be glad to talk to you about it.

On August 5, the membership voted—against the recommendations of the union committee—to accept the company's proposal and sign a 28-month contract.

V. The 1954 Negotiations

With contract negotiations not scheduled to begin until late in 1954, management proposed to the union in June that the incentive system be eliminated. Again the Middletown union quickly accepted the proposal, and new rates went into effect on July 5; but at Lockland, settlement was not reached until August 26, new rates going into effect August 30. Negotiations at Lockland may be followed from company communications.

July 14, 1954

As you know, we met today with your union bargaining committee. We talked over the company's proposal for putting in a new and higher hourly base rate system to replace our present incentive plans. It was a good meeting. Members of the union committee had studied our proposal very carefully. We talked at some length about many of the details.

. . . . .

Unfortunately no change in a pay system ever pleases everyone. But our proposal offers these advantages:

More than half of you will receive wage increases.

You will continue to earn more than people on the same jobs in other companies in our industry with very few exceptions.

You will be paid more fairly in comparison with each other than under any other system we have ever had.

Your foreman has individual job comparisons of rates Gardner will pay under its proposal and the rates paid by some of our major competitors. He will be glad to discuss them with you and show you how we stand.

. . . . .

July 16, 1954

We had another meeting today with the union bargaining committee. The results of the meeting were disappointing. We have no reason to believe any progress was made in reaching an agreement on the company's proposal for a new wage plan.

. . . . .

We do not know where our proposal stands now. Today was our third meeting with the union. So far they have not told us how they feel about our complete proposal. And they did not ask for another meeting.

I am sure the members of the union bargaining committee and your union steward would like to know how you feel about our proposal.

If there are any new developments, we will let you know.

July 27, 1954

A notice was posted on the union bulletin boards today. It says the union bargaining committee is going to talk with us about "improving" our proposal to get rid of our bonus plans.

Naturally, we were disappointed to see this notice. We hoped the union would accept our proposal. Or if they did not do that, we thought they might ask you to vote on it secretly, just as you do in the election of union officers. As it was, we understand that less than 200 people took part in a standing vote. There are about 850 people in the bargaining unit at Lockland.

We made our proposal to the union on June 16. It is a fair way to solve a problem which has been bothering all of us for a long time. And it is a complete and a very liberal solution to a difficult problem.

More important, *we did not hold anything back when we made our proposal.* We don't bargain that way. We believe the union and our employees are entitled to know from the start what our full proposal is on any matter. And that is what we did in this case. We have told all of you what our full proposal is.

I know that a good many of you who did not go to the union meetings have opinions about our proposal. Perhaps you could talk to your union steward and bargaining committeemen about having a full employee vote on our proposal.

If you have any questions about this matter, I know you will find your foreman and superintendent able to answer them for you.

August 26, 1954

A notice posted by your union announces that the company's proposal to get rid of our bonus plans has been accepted by a majority vote of union members.

Naturally, we are pleased about this development. As you know, we sincerely believe that the new base wage system is better for both employees and the company.

We are ready to put the new rates in effect on Monday, August 30, if an agreement can be signed with the union early next week. "Transition pay" checks can be mailed within two weeks after the new rates take effect.

. . . . .

Negotiations for a new contract opened in October. The company's strategy was similar to that used in 1952. Negotiations with the Middletown union were completed on October 29. Again, Lockland proved more difficult.

The personnel in attendance were the same as in 1952 with one exception, the addition of the union's international president. Prior to the first meeting, the company and the union exchanged proposals, and the union distributed its proposals to all employees in a letter. Initial positions and the final settlement are shown in the chart on page 603.

Issue	Company's Proposal	Union's Proposal	Final Agreement
Union Security	Status quo (modified union shop)	Union shop	Status quo (modified union shop)
Wages	5 cents	10 cents	5 cents
Holidays	Status quo (6)	7 days	Status quo (6)
Pension	Noncontributory	No proposal	Noncontributory
Probationary period	Status quo (70 days)	30 days	Status quo (70 days)
Contract Duration	2 years	1 year	2 years

As heretofore, management kept supervisors and employees informed as to the progress of negotiations.

The negotiations opened on October 15 with the company stating, "The facts will substantiate our proposal as a fair and liberal one." When the international president asked for a moratorium on company and union pronouncements, the company answered that "there was no need for a propaganda war but the company might need to write letters to counteract rumors or defend its position."

The company did not recede from its position except for certain changes in the manner of vesting pensions and some union concessions in what the union called nonissue areas.

On October 26, the company sent the following letter to the homes of Lockland employees.

As you know, we are now holding contract negotiation meetings with the bargaining committee from your union.

I thought you'd like to know about the more important proposals the company has made and the reasons we made them.

We drew up our proposals after several months of study. We compared our wage rates and benefits with companies we compete with and which have signed new contracts this year. And we also looked over our benefit plans to see how they needed to be changed.

The proposals we've made to the union are based on this study as well as on four basic ideas I mentioned to you in my last letter. These four ideas are:

1. What Gardner people need and want.
2. Giving Gardner people and the company the best value for money used to pay wages and benefits.
3. Distributing the proposals to benefit many Gardner people.
4. The effect of the proposals on our ability to compete successfully for the amount of business we need to produce full paychecks for Gardner people.

We think proposals based on such ideas are sound and fair. And such proposals can help both you and the company. A company that is soundly financed and soundly managed, offers steady jobs. Gardner always has been able to do this as well as pay wages well above the average for our industry. We want to continue to do this.

In response to the letter, the union handed out a complete report on its version of bargaining progress. Within two days the company had re-submitted to the employees the union's letter with the penciled comments as follows:

REPORT OF THE BARGAINING COMMITTEE
To The Members of Local 1009, UPA–CIO
Lockland, Ohio, November 2, 1954

The union got our proposals in writing on Oct. 15. The same proposals were sent to employees on Oct. 26.

A Union bargaining Committee ordinarily reports to its members at meetings where it can have the benefit of the members' opinions and advice. Due to the fact the Gardner Company has addressed a letter to our members on October 26, your Committee feels an explanation is in order.

The Company's letter was in the mail on the very day your Committee was meeting with the Company. The Union Committee had nothing to report as negotiations were neither concluded nor deadlocked. Your Committee had not indicated either acceptance or rejection of the Company's proposals. The fact is the Company has not, even now, answered on some of the Union proposals

We were doing this at the meeting on Oct. 27. We plan to continue answering their proposals at our next meeting. We haven't told employees anything not told union Committee first.

This implies that only the union should know or be allowed to find out what employees need and want. The important thing is that the needs are known and met, regardless of whether the union or the company is the source.

Now let's look at the Company's letter.

Two of their "basic ideas";

(1) What Gardner people need and want"
(3) Distributing the proposals to benefit many Gardner people",

are what you elected your Committee to tell the Company, For the Company to assume it knows the answers before discussions are completed might well be considered a reflection on the Committee and the members who elected them

We spent 6 months developing our proposals. And we have facts to support them. But we are still open-minded on new facts or good reasons for changing our position.

We can't agree that letters can't be fair. We believe ours. We know they are fair, that's why letters are not complete, that's why we give management people additional details to pass on to employees.

Your Committee wishes to report on progress to date on the Union's proposals. A report by mail cannot be either complete or fair because of limited space but the Company has chosen the method and must suffer its limitations.

First, let us say the Union has asked for nothing, (except in total amount,) that has not already been granted by major competitors of Gardner.

This is an important exception. The total cost of money items is the most important consideration.

UNION PROPOSALS

1. Union Shop -- The Company objects "in principle". They choose to ignore the more basic principle of democracy on which America is founded and the fact their principle competitors have agreed to this provision. The overwhelming majority of employees voted for the Union Shop in a free and democratic election. Over 90% of eligible employees are now members.

Is it "democracy" for the company to force employees to join the union?

2. 10¢ General Wage Increase -- The Company offer, 5¢. The Gardner straight time average rate is now $1.70 per hour. The average for the paper industry is $1.78 in September 1954 and was $1.85 in Pulp, Paper and Paperboard Mills in July 1954 according to the Bureau of Labor Statistics, U.S. Department of Labor.

The non-Gardner figures quoted include overtime, shift differential, vacation & holiday pay. The Gardner figure does not. This is obviously an unfair comparison. Comparable figures for Gardner are about 20¢ higher.

* * * * *

Discussions incomplete on distribution of overtime, contract clarification and other matters

We are not bargaining by mail. We do think Gardner people have a right to know things about the bargaining that affect them.

The Union's report is not complete and cannot be under the circumstances, neither is the Company's. The Union does not approve of reporting by mail and does not appreciate the (Company's efforts to bargain by mail) with the members when these members elected a Committee to represent them.

The implication is the Union Committee does not report the facts to the members.

The Union Committee also does not appreciate the Company's invitation to the members to get their reports on progress of negotiations from the foremen. We understood the (foremen's presence) to be to avoid future errors and for a better understanding of the agreement. If they are to use this information to discuss the merits of the proposals during negotiations then the Union is playing against loaded dice and will have to consider ways to balance the situation.

Our letter of Oct. 9 to all Gardner people (including employee members of the union Committee) said our foremen were going to attend meetings & would tell employees about them.

Your Committee is endeavoring to secure the best possible agreement as instructed by the members. We are aware no agreement can be reached including all of the Union's demands. (We are just as certain no agreement satisfactory to the members can be reached covering only those points mentioned in the Company's letter of October 26th.)

Does this mean the union has closed its mind to an agreement based on our proposals?

Your Union Committee has been negotiating in good faith in a reasonable and responsible manner. (The Union Committee is not responsible for the present delay in negotiations.) When negotiations resume, as they will shortly, your Committee feels it is entitled to the confidence of the members and the respect of the management as demonstrated by deeds not by words alone.

Regional Director Schwenker called on Oct. 28 and asked to postpone the meetings until Nov. 8.

Fraternally submitted,

THE BARGAINING COMMITTEE

Local 1009, UPA–CIO

At the seventh and final session the international president made an attack on the management for lack of flexibility. The company responded by stating that "from experience it knew the desires and the needs of employees, having more access to this information than the union when making these determinations. If the company had offered 2 cents when it could have afforded 5 cents, it would have been dishonest." On November 10 the following letter was sent:

Contract negotiation talks have ended. The union bargaining committee has said it will take the results to the union membership next Tuesday for voting.

We hope you will vote for the new two-year contract. We think it is an excellent one and that it'll make Gardner an even better place to work.

And we hope you'll vote for it because you too think it's a good contract.

I've written you before that we think the improvements in it are fair and liberal. I'd like to list them again and tell you briefly their advantages.

. . . . .

People who attend the union meetings next Tuesday will decide if this new and improved contract is to be signed for the next two years. I'm sure you know how important these meetings will be. I hope you will attend them, give your opinions and vote for the new contract.

On November 17, the membership approved the company's proposals.

INTERNATIONAL HARVESTER COMPANY

THE 1955 NEGOTIATIONS AND STRIKE

I. Introduction

In 1955, following a strike which lasted four weeks, International Harvester [1] and the UAW signed a three-year contract. The negotiation and strike reflected critical factors resulting from both the turbulent relations with the communist-dominated Farm Equipment Workers Union (FE) and the rivalry and conflict in the transition from the FE to the UAW. These two unions dominated the labor history of International Harvester. At its height the FE was the stronger, representing 30,000 to 40,000 workers in 12 plants, chiefly those producing farm implements and tractors. After the FE's expulsion from the CIO in 1949 as communist-dominated, and subsequent merger with the similarly ousted UE, the UAW which had represented workers in automotive operations emerged as the principal union. By June 1955, all former FE locals had voted to join the UAW, giving it 40,000 members [2] out of a total employment of 75,000. The UAW also had organized office workers at eight International Harvester factories. In addition to the UAW, the company bargained with 24 other international unions.

II. Relations with the FE Union

International Harvester was one of the first major companies to introduce a company union in the form of an Industrial Representation Plan established in 1919. It consisted of a Works Council at each plant composed of representatives elected by the employees. These councils met regularly with management to discuss problems of mutual concern.

During the late 1920's the Works Councils experienced difficulty in achieving satisfactory settlements of grievances. Realizing their weakness, the Councils decided to organize secretly a union called the ABC union. During 1934–1936, this union in turn affiliated itself with the Steelworkers Organizing Committee and detailed an outsider, Joseph Weber, reputed to be a communist trained in Moscow, to conduct a membership drive.

Its legal status challenged under the Wagner Act, the Industrial Representation Plan was disbanded in April 1937. Shortly thereafter the ABC union requested recognition as the bargaining agent. The company refused. However, the membership drive continued to make progress and the SWOC had enough support by April 1938 to win a contract. SWOC then established a task force in July 1938 to organize other companies. At the same

---

[1] See Exhibit 1 for operating statistics, p. 621.
[2] See Exhibit 2, p. 622.

time it changed its name to the Farm Equipment Workers Organizing Committee (FEWOC), and Grant Oakes and Gerald Fielde, alleged communists, were elected to the top offices. Thus was completed the transfer of leadership from Works Councils to ABC union to the communist-dominated FEWOC.

By January 1941, the FEWOC had evolved into the FE and fully affiliated itself with the CIO. In that very month, it called a strike against International Harvester, demanding the elimination of all piecework incentives. The strike was to last two months, and was characterized by the House Un-American Activities Committee as follows:

> For weeks the International Harvester plant at Chicago was tied up by the Farm Equipment Organizing Committee under the leadership of Grant Oakes whose communist record included prominent activity in the American Peace Mobilization.
> Oakes and his associates incited the strike in order to cripple the National Defense program which was in keeping with the policies of the APM and the Communist Party during that period.[1]

A settlement came only after intervention of the National Defense Mediation Board had resulted in a directive order granting maintenance of membership.

After Hitler attacked Russia, the FE, in common with other communist-dominated unions, reversed its strategy and denounced stoppages as antiwar and pro-Axis. Nevertheless, relations continued tense.

During the course of the war, FE extended its sway to five other company plants in addition to the McCormick and Tractor Works increasing its membership to 30,000. After the war the FE gained jurisdiction of the employees at the New Louisville plant.

Relations became turbulent again after the war. Because of wildcats and slowdowns,[2] 22 million man-hours were lost during the seven years from October 1944 to October 1951. In the year 1947, management openly charged the union with opposing improved methods and inspiring reduced effort. The union in turn denounced the company and its management in demagogic propaganda. Other factors exacerbated the already hostile relationships—particularly the bitter rivalry between the UAW and the FE, and the fact that negotiations with Harvester, the largest producer, were viewed as pattern setting, both by other unions at Harvester and also by FE locals in other companies.

In 1946, failure to negotiate a new contract led to a two-month strike, during which a settlement was reached only after recommendations were submitted by a fact-finding board appointed by the Secretary of Labor. The union demanded changes in many matters under which it had "chafed" during the war: grievance procedure, rate structure, job classifications, time studies, piece rates, seniority, and union security. It also demanded elimination of so-called "female" rates, the correction of inequities between day and

---

[1] *Investigation of Un-American Propaganda Activities in the U.S.*, Report of the Special Commission on Un-American Activities, House of Representatives, 78th Cong., 2d Sess., H.R. 1311.

[2] See Exhibit 3, p. 623.

pieceworkers, the achievement of uniformity and simplicity in what it termed Harvester's "complicated" rate structure, and the negotiation of contracts on a "chain-wide" (a master contract agreement) basis.

The settlement provided for an 18-cent wage increase and other economic gains and also called for a number of important modifications, such as the "smallest appropriate number" of labor grades and occupational classifications; existing occupational and job descriptions not to be changed without union consent; and further negotiations on interplant rate uniformity. Revisions in piece rates were to be justified by specific changes in materials and methods and only "normal" operating conditions were to be studied in establishing new rates. The union, in turn, agreed to exhaust the grievance procedure for grievances arising out of rate revisions before striking.[1] New employees were to enjoy departmental seniority the first year, and thereafter plant-wide seniority was to govern layoff, rehiring, transfers and promotions.

This 1946 contract was the first company-wide agreement. Long a goal of FE it was made a *de facto* reality by the intervention of the government. Although negotiated centrally, the contract was signed at each plant by local company and union officials.

In early 1947, negotiations over intraplant and interplant rates resulted in a reduction both in the number of grades and also in differentials between Chicago and other plants. These negotiations were accompanied by a 40-day strike at the Louisville plant, and by illegal stoppages instigated elsewhere according to management to support the Louisville strike. The union regarded the Louisville plant as "the company's first effort to flee high Northern rates."

The 1947 contract negotiation resulted in a wage increase of 11½ cents, certain improvements in fringe benefits, reduction in the number of grievance steps, fewer job classifications, and provision for a permanent arbitrator. The request for the union shop was turned down, as were demands for health insurance, pensions and GAW. The FE boasted that, despite the enactment of Taft-Hartley, it had negotiated modifications in the no-strike clauses so that it did not have to get wildcat strikers back to work. In contrast, the UAW had agreed to such an obligation.

In 1948, while the union was content to leave the contract relatively unchanged, management pressed for extensive revisions involving classifications, grievance procedure, arbitration, piece-rate administration, discipline, and union security. Following a two-day walkout, the company settled for a wage increase of 11 cents and no contract changes.

In 1949, the company rejected demands for company-financed, jointly administered pensions and group insurance plans. Few changes were made in the contract.

The same year the FE was expelled, as already indicated, from the CIO

---

[1] By terms of the 1946 contract the arbitrator could not rule on revision of piece rates and consequently the subject was a strikable issue.

along with 11 other unions for communist domination, and soon after joined forces with the similarly expelled UE.

In June 1950, after a two-week strike, the FE–UE signed a two-year contract, embodying a 10-cent wage increase package calling for a contributory health and welfare benefit plan (unilaterally established in 1946) and a noncontributory pension system.[1]

The year 1952 witnessed a "showdown" between FE–UE and International Harvester. In June the union entered negotiation with 122 demands, including a guaranteed annual wage, a 15-cent horizontal wage increase, a one-year contract, elimination of the no-strike clause, arbitration at request of the union, and a union shop. The company offered a four-cent-an-hour annual improvement increase and fringe benefits. Both sides rejected each other's demands.

At the expiration of an extension of the contract for 50 days, the union struck. The men were out for 87 days. The company and union waged extensive publicity campaigns. The latter charged "a speed-up and a drastic pay cut"; the former, irresponsibility as evidenced by the large number of wildcat strikes as well as the "excesses" of the union's demands. Management also announced a policy of keeping its plants open. For the first few weeks only a few returned to work. Soon foremen began to visit homes in a company-sponsored back-to-work movement. By the last week of the strike 8,000 of 18,000 employees involved had returned. One man was killed and 20 employees discharged for disturbances on the picket line.

The contract finally signed embodied the terms originally proposed by management: an increase of seven cents (four as improvement factor and three for increase in cost of living), a liberalized vacation program, a uniform day and piecework wage classification, new "earning objectives" on piecework jobs, payment of stewards only for time spent in grievance meetings with management, a reduction in the grievance steps from four to two, and some concessions on union security; however, two escape clauses permitted resignations from the union and the revocation of checkoff authorization.

The FE's defeat was due not only to the back-to-work movement, but also to the fact that the wage increase had been put into effect for those who had returned to work. FE also found itself weakened by decertification petitions in two plants, possible UAW raids, and hearings in Chicago by the House Un-American Activities Committee. In addition the election of a Republican administration was not without its effect. Indeed, the union leadership explained its acceptance of the company's terms: "management encouraged by the national election results and the return-to-work of some, was prepared to go the limit against our union."

In speculating on the cause of the strike, the company thought the FE had been anxious to gain a settlement above the UAW pattern, as an or-

---

[1] As will be seen later in the case, the company and UAW signed in 1950 a five-year contract patterned after the GM agreement.

ganizational wedge in plants represented by the UAW. It was also rumored that the strike was conducted against the wishes of top UE leadership. Indeed, the defeat was followed by the removal of Grant Oakes and Gerald Fielde from office. Moreover, by the end of the strike, FE membership had dropped to about 50% of its previous level. In fact, FE never regained its original strength.

The new 1952 contract marked a significant turning point. Discipline was tightened and wildcat strikes dropped from about 100 to 8 per year! As time passed, UAW attracted more and more members to its ranks. Starting in June 1954, it initiated proceedings to have the NLRB certify it as bargaining agent for the FE locals. The move was successful. By the spring of 1955 the transformation was complete—all former FE locals had voted to affiliate with the UAW.

III. RELATIONS WITH THE UAW

During the late 30's, the UAW was active in organizing Harvester's automotive operations and by 1941 had obtained contracts at Fort Wayne, Springfield (Ohio), and Indianapolis.

In contrast to those with FE, relations with UAW during and immediately after the war were relatively peaceful. While negotiations with the UAW were held concurrently with those of FE, with generally the same results, they differed in the relative absence of tension and stoppages.

After the war, when the company embarked on a large expansion program in various parts of the country, UAW successfully organized the newly acquired plants with the single exception of Louisville. Thus by 1948, the two unions approached parity in membership: FE—26,000, and UAW—24,000.

The first major strike by UAW occurred in 1950, following the pattern-making settlement at GM, calling for a five-year contract, a modified union shop, annual improvement factor and a cost of living escalator. Early in the negotiations it became apparent that management would not agree to the pattern, nor the union to a contract of five years. The strike lasted 11 weeks and was terminated only after the parties reversed their respective positions and agreed to the automotive pattern and a five-year contract. In granting a modified union shop, the company receded from its previous firm policy.[1]

While the 1950 contract was the first to be negotiated centrally with the UAW, the union spokesmen consisted of four regional directors who consequently found it difficult to agree on a uniform contract. As a result, a number of issues were negotiated locally, such as wage structure, union representation, and seniority.

---

[1] The modified union shop clause which was modeled after the GM contract required all new employees to join the union after 90 days. However, such employees could exercise the right of "escape" after one year. The exercise of this right was limited to a period of 10 days.

These negotiations produced substantial agreement on a place for uniform daywork classifications, but failed when it came to piecework. The piecework books were consequently referred back to local negotiation.

During 1953, UAW criticized Harvester for stalling on the settlement of grievances, most of which involved the setting of piece rates and production standards, and for failing to conform to national wage and pension patterns. The last point was a reference to the company's rejection of the UAW's "living document" concepts. In a letter to employees, president John L. McCaffrey, announcing a wage cut of two cents in line with the decline in the cost of living index, said:

We disagree with the theory that a contract is subject to change whenever one of the parties wants further concessions. Such a document is not a contract—it is a temporary memorandum. The only known reason for having a contract is to settle the issues for a specified period of time.

We also disagree violently with the idea of so-called "patterns" as applying to every aspect of union relations. The pattern idea is an attempt to make everyone wear the same pair of shoes whether or not they fit his feet. We don't believe that just because some large company in another—and much more profitable—industry agrees to something, we are obligated to agree to it also.[1]

In January 1954, with the help of David Cole,[2] permanent arbitrator, the company and UAW were able to agree on a central organization for the union, an arrangement long sought by management to deal with a few union officers on major policy matters rather than with a number of regional directors. The Harvester Department (UAW), as it was called, consisted of Vice President Leonard Woodcock, a staff man for arbitration, and four regional directors, with Woodcock in charge.

In June 1954, the UAW supplanted for the first time a former FE local when the NLRB certified the change at the East Moline Works. Similar victories followed in early 1955 at Farmall, Richmond, Tractor, West, Pullman, McCormick, Rock Falls, Canton and Louisville (see Exhibit 2 for more detail). The procedure was approximately the same at each plant; one day the local FE officials would resign, to be installed or elected the next day as UAW leaders. The shift, moreover, was not limited to the local level; some FE international representatives received corresponding positions in the UAW.

Thus by May 1955, with the approach of negotiations, the UAW claimed 40,000 members, roughly 95% of all production and maintenance workers.

IV. BACKGROUND FOR 1955 NEGOTIATIONS

Prior to the commencement of 1955 negotiations both auto and steel had signed new contracts. Ford "broke the ice" on Supplemental Unemployment Benefits (SUB) with an economic package of about 20 cents, a pat-

---

[1] *The New York Times,* May 23, 1953.

[2] Cole had been selected permanent arbitrator in early 1953. Previously he had been Director of the Federal Mediation and Conciliation Service.

tern soon followed with minor modifications by the other auto companies. In steel, with contracts reopenable only on wages, a settlement of 15 to 16 cents resulted.

President McCaffrey had made the following report in April for the quarter ending January 31, 1955: "Our business in the first quarter of the 1955 fiscal year presented the encouraging picture of an increase in sales accompanied by a sizable gain in estimated net income." This performance was particularly significant in view of sizable sales fluctuations after the war.

Negotiations with FE had been usually accompanied by a strike; the important negotiation with UAW in 1950 had resulted in an 11-week strike. On the other hand, recent years had witnessed a substantial reduction in wildcats, due in large measure to a firm policy, inaugurated in 1952, of disciplining participants in all unauthorized stoppages.

In preparation for the 1955 negotiations management reviewed the history of various contract clauses certain to be issues:

ARTICLE 12, WAGE PROVISIONS

Job Classification. Most plants had too many job classifications, and often similar jobs in various plants were classified differently—a situation found difficult to correct over the years. Management had taken the initiative in 1950 and obtained union agreement for uniform job descriptions, classifications and slotting within labor grades for all daywork jobs.

With respect to piecework the following clause had been written in 1950: "During the negotiations preceding the signing of this contract, both the company and the union gave consideration to the need for replacing the present piecework wage payment system, with a new wage payment system. The difficulties of negotiating such a new wage payment system while the works were not in operation were insurmountable, and both the company and the union, therefore, have expressed a desire to continue negotiations after the signing of this contract for the sole purpose of agreeing upon the terms and conditions of a new wage payment system. . . ."

In UAW plants, however, no progress had been made during the life of the 1950 contract towards streamlining the piece rate job classifications. In the old FE locals the wage payment system had been revised in 1952 during FE negotiations. As a result when the FE locals subsequently transferred to the UAW, they took their uniform piecework and daywork systems with them.

Prior to the commencement of negotiations in 1955 management and UAW agreed to hold exploratory meetings on the entire subject of job classification. The chief distortions were (1) the piecework classification system in UAW plants, and (2) discrepancies produced when FE locals were taken over by UAW.

Classification of Individuals. The Wage and Salary Department at each plant conducted an audit of the classification of individuals in 1951. Labor shortages and rapid promotions had produced many errors. The resultant reclassification of individuals produced many grievances.

Piece Rates. During the war and postwar period the incentive system had gotten "loose." In fact as the last war vehicle was moving down the assembly line in one of the plants, the men attached a sign with the phrase "end of the gravy train." Standards had gotten out of hand primarily from creeping changes.

The first major effort to tighten up the standards was undertaken in 1949 at one of the UAW plants. Most of the jobs were restudied at a production changeover and new standards established. Average piecework earnings dropped from $2.47 to $2.10 per hour.

These new standards came as a result of giving new numbers to parts in model changeovers. The so-called "new parts" concept permitted a restudy of all operations involved in new models. The establishment of a standards department in 1951 in each plant resulted in an increase of time study personnel. Previously standards work had been part of wage and salary administration. With the new department came substantial improvements in techniques and administration.

In the old FE plants, the company had been able in 1952 to secure acceptance of contract language allowing changes in the piecework rates for any changes in specifications, materials, methods, tools or equipment. This liberal clause enabled the company to tighten many of the piece rates and to synchronize the incentive structure with the contractual wage schedule.

The effort to tighten standards met with resistance on the part of the unions and workers—an attitude that produced many grievances.

ARTICLE 6, GRIEVANCES

The multiplicity of grievances was aggravated by the fact that the company had terminated the service of two umpires, and it was not until January 1953 that an umpire had been found who gained an increasing degree of "permanency." Again, management's refusal to reopen the five-year UAW contract in 1953 under the "living document" concept provoked resentment which manifested itself in grievances. By early 1955 it was estimated that nearly 12,000 grievances were awaiting arbitration, 10,000 UAW and 2,000 FE. To rectify the situation, labor relations counsellors were made available from whom foremen were urged to seek help in settling grievances.

In addition, management and union held conferences in early 1955 to establish guidelines that would facilitate the orderly disposition of unresolved grievances. One such agreement was the elimination of the "new parts" concept, and substitution of an arrangement utilizing times for comparable operations on other jobs wherever possible.

Certain decisions of the permanent arbitration provided a basis for disposing of many grievances arising from misclassification of individuals. The net result was that reclassification could be effected without change of duties only if the company could show that it had not acquiesced to the faulty classification or that it was an "evident" misclassification. The arbitrator also upheld the right to establish new job classifications but not by a "carve out," that is, establishing a new job previously part of another job when no change in the "principal function" had taken place.

The 1950 contract had provided that overtime would be equalized over a six-month period by means of allocations at week ends and holidays. In practice this had been difficult to administer. Consequently the company and union agreed instead to assign overtime at week ends and holidays to men at the bottom of the hours' overtime list.

Management and union met regularly during the early months of 1955 in an effort to establish guidelines for grievance settlement. Prior to the establishment of the Harvester Department (UAW) in 1954, with a vice president in charge, it had been difficult to arrive at any company-wide agreements with the UAW. The presence of International representatives who could speak for all UAW locals greatly facilitated the progress made during the spring of 1955.

The Manager of Labor Relations and the Assistant Director of the Harvester Department (UAW) held explanatory meetings with plant managers and shop committees, who were then able to make final settlements on formula jointly developed. Thousands of the accumulated grievances were thus settled. It was estimated that by the time negotiations began, the grievance backlog had been reduced to around 2,000.

V. 1955 NEGOTIATIONS

Towards the end of April, the parties agreed to extend the contract from June 30 until August 23. At the same time the UAW announced some of its forthcoming proposals: (1) modernization of the escalator system; (2) incorporation of past improvement factors in base rates; and (3) incorporation of a retroactive increase in pension benefits. Woodcock added, "We hope International Harvester is sincere in its statement that the company would like to reach an agreement without a strike. But the price of peace is progress for International Harvester workers, including the progress that was denied them over the past three and four years."[1]

Noneconomic Bargaining. Discussions opened on June 30 in Chicago. All sessions were held in a training department building called the "school house." Present for the company was a team of 20 including: the vice president for manufacturing, the vice president for industrial relations, the manager of labor relations who served as chairman of the negotiating committee, and various other staff and divisional personnel. Present for the union was a team that varied in size from 30 to 50 men. On this team were the following: Leonard Woodcock, various international union officers, regional directors, and local union officials.

---

[1] *Ammunition,* May, 1955.

In addition, separate committees were each established to negotiate a contract for office workers and a uniform daywork job classification plan for production, maintenance and office workers.

When negotiations opened on June 30, it was agreed to discuss each article in the order in which it appeared in the contract, except that all economic provisions were to be held in abeyance pending agreement on the other articles. Initially neither side made a complete proposal, but presented its desires on the particular article under discussion.

The progress of negotiations is summarized herewith on a weekly basis with only major issues covered.[1]

Week of July 10. (1) *The union security* article was set aside. (2) *Grievance procedure:* management proposed eliminating the second step between the grievance committeemen and the division superintendent; the new procedure to be: (a) between the employee, steward, and foreman; (b) between management committee and union committee, and (c) arbitration as a last recourse. The company claimed that committeemen were spending too much time on grievance matters with too little results. The company had already obtained acceptance of the 2-step grievance procedure from the FE in 1952 negotiations. The union took the proposal under study.

Week of July 17. (1) *Grievance procedure:* the union advised that the proposal for a 2-step grievance procedure was unacceptable and requested the article be set aside; (2) *arbitration:* the union submitted two demands, (a) a one-year option either to strike or to appeal a grievance to arbitration, and (b) that a specified time limit to schedule arbitration be eliminated. The company replied that the union should not have a right to strike over all grievances and the appeal period should be shorter than one year.

The company further stated that it desired institution of a procedure whereby all grievances be sent, before appeal to arbitration, to the Harvester Department (UAW) for screening and placing on an "unscheduled docket" for appeal to arbitration, and that a period of 90 days be allowed for this screening as against the previous 30 days; and that hearings (except for discipline and other designated cases) be scheduled from the unscheduled docket in such order as the parties agreed. In effect, the Harvester Department (UAW) would determine which grievances to appeal to arbitration with a firm commitment as to the order of such hearings.

The parties agreed to have joint committees negotiate classification descriptions for salaried and piecework jobs. The daywork classification committees previously established had been meeting and making some progress.

Week of July 24. (1) *Arbitration:* the union indicated agreement on the main issues; (2) Article 12, *Wage Payment:* this "knotty" issue was temporarily set aside; and (3) *seniority:* in response to the union's request for local negotiations on seniority, the management stated that it desired to

---

[1] During the negotiations the company sent bulletins to management and letters to all employees. The chronology is based on these communications.

standardize the article to omit needless controversies and excessive costs in "job movements." It proposed a new arrangement based on seniority job groupings—these groupings to be be identified by local negotiations, to be established by department or groups of departments for all employees in labor grade five and above. In addition, two general groupings, one for piecework and another for daywork, would be established in grades one through four. As support for its position, management pointed to its experience prior to 1952, when in applying seniority as interpreted by the UAW, an average of 10 to 12 moves and two to three weeks' time had been needed before a worker finally left the plant.[1] The union requested a written proposal on the matter.

Week of July 31. (1) *Arbitration:* the union stated that complete agreement on the arbitration article was "primarily a case of semantics," and it requested an opportunity to prepare a revision; and (2) the union requested that meetings be held daily instead of two or three times a week to facilitate agreement on all noneconomic matters by August 15, when it would be prepared to receive the company's "full economic" offer.

Week of August 7. (1) *Vacations:* when the union demanded a cessation of the practice of plant shutdown during the summer period, the company replied that if uniform plant shutdown were not accepted the vacations would have to be scheduled throughout the year; (2) *duration of the agreement:* this article was set aside pending completion of the economic issues; (3) *arbitration:* the union was not ready with its revised proposal and requested an extension; and (4) *union security:* it was agreed to discuss this article as part of the economic proposals.

Economic Bargaining. On August 15, management submitted its economic proposal: (1) a 10-cent an hour increase composed of (*a*) annual improvement factor of 2½% or 6 cents and (*b*) a 4-cent cost of living with an additional 18 cents for certain skilled trades; (2) SUB: 65% for 4 weeks, 60% for 22 weeks (Ford Plan); (3) vacations: workers with 10–15 years' service, 2½ weeks instead of 2 weeks; (4) a seventh paid holiday; (5) a full union shop (employees not members would be required to join in 90 days); (6) increased pension benefits; and (7) increased health-welfare benefits. After receiving these proposals, the union requested adjournment until the next day. On August 16, the union responded to three of the proposals: SUB, pensions, and health-welfare, with a four-hour detailed analysis and counter-proposals presented by staff specialists from Detroit headquarters. The company requested time for analysis and comparison with other contracts.

In reply to a request that local plant meetings be resumed to discuss old unresolved grievances, management pointed out that all of these grievances had been reviewed several times by local people, and that the company had no intention of compromising on any grievances stemming from old contracts with FE locals.

---

[1] In negotiating the local seniority agreements, the UAW had usually been able to obtain plant-wide "bumping."

Week of August 21. Management made a full review of its position on SUB, pensions, and health-welfare. Substantial agreement was reached on all three proposals.

With the approach of the deadline, the duration of disability payments remained the only unresolved *economic* issue. Management had proposed that increased benefits be paid over a period of 26 weeks; the union, over a period of 52 weeks. Most of the other issues had been resolved by concessions of the company; for example: agreement that SUB could commence either if states, in which two-thirds of the employees worked, approved simultaneous payment of SUB and unemployment compensation or if the GM and Ford plants commenced operation; extension of the SUB to salaried employees; application of health-welfare benefits to retired workers, and a retroactive increase in pension payments.

While not an economic issue one other matter with SUB implications was still in dispute: reduced work week. During slack periods, it had been the custom to lay off workers rather than shift them to a reduced work week. During the negotiations the company proposed a clause for reduced operations of 32 hours during short periods of four weeks. The union saw in the proposal a possibility for the company to avoid SUB payments by reducing the work sheet.

After its presentation on the economic issues, the company presented a complete review of its position on unresolved noneconomic issues:

Article 6, Grievances. The company demanded a two-step grievance procedure with appeal to arbitration 120 days from the date of the new contract and rejected the request that grievances under former FE contracts be kept "alive" under the new contract.

Article 7, Arbitration. The company accepted the union's proposal for future consultation on matters of contract interpretation.

Article 12, Wage Payment. This complicated article was slowly being "hammered out."

Article 15, Vacations. The company proposed employees take their vacations after March 1; the union proposed April 1.

Article 16, Seniority. Management had attempted in every way to negotiate this article both centrally and locally. It stood ready to continue discussion locally and asked for realistic bargaining to reach local seniority agreements which would eliminate costly and unnecessary job movement.

Article 26, Duration of Contract. The company accepted the union's proposal that the master agreement and all other issues under negotiation expire August 1, 1958.

VI. The Strike

The deadline was August 22. During the last session which ran until 2 A.M. August 23, management and union reviewed the major issues blocking agreement: *grievance procedure,* the union had not accepted a 2-step procedure; and *Article 12, Wage Payment Provision,* the parties were seeking to iron out agreement on job classifications and piece rates. Actually no important issues stood in the way of settlement. The economic offer had been virtually accepted and the full union shop had been granted.

Neither side requested an additional extension and on August 23, 40,000 UAW employees went out on strike, affecting 18 plants in six states. However, the shutdown came as no surprise; indeed, in nine plants workers had "jumped the gun" and stopped work on August 19.

During the strike, negotiations continued on a daily basis, with the chief subject *Article 12, Wage Payment Provision*. The union's demands were (1) greater limitation on the right to correct piecework rates which resulted from "creeping changes," and inflated piecework rates on assembly groups; (2) more control of reclassification; and (3) elimination of delays in setting rates for piecework jobs.

Actually the parties were in basic agreement on the *Wage Payment Provision* article. The difficulty was one of language rather than issues. The issue of piece rates and "creeping changes" had been settled earlier in the year when management gave up its "new parts" concept, and the parties had agreed to a working document of practice and policy. The solution of the reclassification problem had been facilitated by various arbitration rulings; and the demand for minimum delay in setting piecework rates had been met when the company agreed that the rate would be retroactive to the date the job started rather than to the date of the time study. Thus, the parties were in agreement on the principles of wage payment, but a good deal of time was required to translate the understandings into contractual language.

Week of August 28. (1) Negotiations continued on the *Wage Payment Provision*. In an attempt to identify the main problems it was decided to divide into four smaller committees. (2) The piecework job classification committee came to an end. The committee had agreed on about 95% of the job descriptions, but the union balked when the company made a proposal for slotting the descriptions in grades which would have raised 40%, lowered 18% and left 32% unchanged. Interestingly, most of the scheduled reductions were in automotive plants; the UAW plants had never, it should be recalled, received uniform piecework classifications as compared to the old FE plants. (3) The daywork committee also came to an end when the union members refused to discuss slotting daywork jobs. One of the locals, where, by the terms of the company's proposal, a number of stock-handlers were scheduled to be dropped in classification, succeeded in halting further discussions.

Week of September 3. No meetings were held until Wednesday, September 7, when the union offered the company a package proposal for settlement of the strike: (1) a three-step grievance procedure; (2) settlement at each plant of all old grievances, including those under the old FE–UE contracts; and (3) minor changes in the SUB, pension and health-welfare plans. On September 8 after the company had rejected the union's "package proposal," Woodcock proposed that the permanent arbitrator be asked to join the negotiations as mediator. The company agreed.

The last phase of negotiations was influenced by developments in the farm equipment industry in August and September. Caterpillar was the first company to accept the principle of SUB in a contract signed on August 1. Ford, of course, had already accepted the principle with its pattern-making contract in early June, but it did not sign with its farm equipment division until September 5. John Deere signed a new contract on August 8. The most significant contract was the one signed by Allis-Chalmers on September 3. Like the other farm equipment contracts it, too, was signed after a short strike, and it had the following similar provisions: 2½% or 6 cents productivity increase, 10 cents across-the-board increase, seventh paid holiday, triple pay for worked holidays, and a full union shop. However, Allis-Chalmers granted additional SUB features: (1) benefit payments at 65% of take-home pay for the entire 26 weeks rather than the reduction to 60% after 4 weeks; and (2) lump sum payments to workers not eligible for state supplementation. Indeed, Woodcock called the plan "the best we have ever negotiated."

Mediation. Cole, the permanent arbitrator, entered the negotiations on Saturday morning, September 10. Following a brief meeting with each side, he called a joint meeting. After identifying the portions of the contract that had been agreed upon, he called upon the union to outline the issues in dispute. Thereupon Leonard Woodcock indicated about 30 points of disagreement, noting that the large number of issues presented was in sharp contrast to the number mentioned by the papers and subsequently listed by the company in an employee letter.

After Woodcock criticized management for giving the impression that disputed issues were few in number, Cole suggested some "ground rules" regarding future communications: the responsibility for making all public statements about negotiations to be delegated to him. The union accepted, but the company rejected the proposal on the grounds that since the union had on occasion made incomplete, distorted, and inflammatory reports, the company must retain the responsibility for reporting the status of negotiations.

A second proposal to reduce the size of the negotiating teams, about 20 members for the company and 40 for the union, was accepted by management but rejected by the union.

On Saturday evening, Sunday and Monday, Cole held separate meetings with small groups of company and union officials. Throughout the week, separate meetings also were held over seniority supplements, between plant representatives and local union officials.

VII. Settlement

Settlement was finally reached on Friday, September 16, after a 28-hour session, embodying: a wage increase of 11 cents, 3 weeks' vacation after 10 years, disability payments for 52 weeks, with all other economic issues as settled prior to the strike, a full union shop, seniority provisions to be determined by local negotiations, a two-step grievance machinery with review of grievances and determination of an unscheduled docket for arbitration by this Harvester Department (UAW), and a three year contract. The company did not gain the right to schedule reduced work weeks.

The Wage Payment Provision as finally hammered out covered 64 pages of the contract which altogether ran to 286 pages. With respect to three key areas the provision stated:

Reclassification of Individuals. "An employee will not be reclassified under this contract unless his duties are changed during the term of this contract, in which event the employee following such change in duties will be subject to reclassification under the principles of the arbitration awards on classification under the prior contract."

Uniform Job Classifications. "During negotiations the company and the union attempted to reach agreement of uniform daywork and piecework classifications, job descriptions and labor grades for such classifications. It is the continuing desire of both the company and the union that a full agreement be reached on this subject."

Piece Rates. The contract elaborated the previous agreement on the use of comparable standards. The main provisions were: (1) "a piecework price shall remain in effect unless the operation is changed for any reason, such as redesign, change in method, layout or changed time value for the elements"; (2) in establishing new or revised standards, comparable standards already in effect will be used where possible; but (3) standards in dispute will not be eligible for comparison purposes; and (4) standards set on the basis of comparable standards would have all "creeping changes" incorporated.

VIII. Aftermath

After the strike management and union reached several agreements which reduced considerably the number of unresolved grievances. One such agreement invoked a moratorium on arbitration until March 1, 1956—while not automatically disposing of grievances, it gave the Harvester Department (UAW) sufficient time to screen the backlog. As a result the union returned almost 2,000 grievances for settlement at the plant level. When it submitted its first list of "unscheduled" grievances for the arbitration docket, only seven of the 78 grievances listed were old grievances.[1] Most of the old grievances which at one time had numbered about 12,000 had been either resolved by joint agreement or withdrawn as a result of the union screening process.

The new two-step grievance procedure also seemed to be having its effect in reducing the pile-up. Whereas previously a typical local would push 100 grievances per week through arbitration, by the summer of 1956, the corresponding figure was around six or seven. Lower management and union leaders were resolving problems at the first step.

After the signing of the 1955 contract, top management and top union

---

[1] During negotiations the union had pressed for resolution of all prior contract grievances. The new contract provided that if old (including FE) grievances were identified within 120 days, they would be eligible for arbitration.

officials met regularly, resulting in a number of supplementary agreements to clarify, supplement, and interpret provisions in the contract.

As management reviewed the developments leading up to and following the strike, it felt that its relationship with the UAW had improved considerably.

EXHIBIT 1

INTERNATIONAL HARVESTER COMPANY

Operating Statistics

	International Harvester		Industry Sales	
	Sales (1947–1949 = 100)	Net Income (Sales %)	Farm Equipment (1947–1949 = 100)	Motor Trucks & Buses (1947–1949 = 100)
1941	42	8.4	—	—
1942	42	7.3	—	—
1943	53	5.6	22	87
1944	74	4.0	38	102
1945	72	3.9	43	71
1946	56	4.6	52	62
1947	89	6.5	81	104
1948	109	5.9	106	113
1949	105	6.7	105	83
1950	109	7.1	102	102
1951	148	4.9	114	139
1952	139	4.6	103	139
1953	145	4.1	96	123
1954	115	3.7	79	100
1955	135	4.8	90	—

Source: *Standard & Poor's; Moody's.*

1955 Sales Breakdown by Product
(In millions)

Motor truck	$	455
Farm tractors and implements		386
Industrial power		148
Defense		64
Other		113
Total	$1,	166

Source: Annual Report.

Exhibit 2

INTERNATIONAL HARVESTER COMPANY

Status of Plants as of 1950

Note: Unless otherwise indicated representation is for production and maintenance workers.

I. *Organized by FE*

McCormick Works,* Chicago (farm equipment)—shifted to UAW, May 22, 1955.
McCormick Twine, Chicago (binder twine)—shifted to UAW, May 22, 1955.
Tractor Works, Chicago (small tractors)—shifted to UAW, May 22, 1955.
West Pullman Works, Chicago (collateral equipment for farm implements)—shifted to UAW, May 22, 1955.
East Moline, Illinois (combines and corn pickers)—shifted to UAW, June 18, 1954.
Farmall, Rock Island, Illinois (medium-sized tractors)—shifted to UAW, February 11, 1955.
Canton,† Illinois (plows)—shifted to UAW, May 22, 1955.
Rock Falls, Illinois (springs)—shifted to UAW, May 22, 1955.
Richmond, Indiana (cream separators, etc.)—shifted to UAW, March 4, 1955.
Louisville,‡§ Kentucky (small-sized farm tractor)—shifted to UAW, May 22, 1955.

II. *Organized by UAW*

Fort Wayne, Indiana (motor truck).
Indianapolis, Indiana (engines for large and small trucks).
Springfield, Ohio (small motor trucks).
Melrose Park,§ Illinois (diesel motors).
Evansville,§ Indiana (refrigeration).
Memphis,§ Tennessee (southern farm tools).
Emeryville,§ California (trucks).
Stockton,§ California (special West Coast farm equipment).

* At McCormick UAW had organized the tool room and machine repair workers.
† At Canton in 1951 the UAW organized the tool room and machine repair workers.
‡ At Louisville UAW had organized the foundry workers.
§ Plants acquired by International Harvester after the war.

Exhibit 3

INTERNATIONAL HARVESTER COMPANY

Work Stoppage Record (Both Legal and Illegal)

Year Ending October 31	Total Man-Hours Lost (million)	Work Stoppages (number)		% of Total Man-Hours Lost *		Notes
1945	.5	UAW	20	UAW	N.A.	
		FE	130	FE	55	
1946	14.0	UAW	16		1	
		FE	97		97	FE strike
1947	1.4	UAW	15		23	
		FE	155		57	
1948	3.8	UAW	25		51	UAW strike
		FE	172		48	FE strike
1949	1.2	UAW	23		5	
		FE	172		78	
1950	14.3	UAW	32		67	UAW 11-wk. strike
		FE	177		25	
1951	1.2	UAW	40		79	
		FE	118		10	
1952	11.0	UAW	11		22	
		FE	6		73	FE strike
1953	.1	UAW	11		22	
		FE	6		73	
1954	.004	UAW	4		N.A.	
		FE	2		N.A.	

* For any one year the percentages do not total to 100 due to work stoppages by unions other than UAW and FE.

PART IV. CONFLICT AND COOPERATION: PROBLEMS OF ADAPTATION OVER TIME

BARTOLO BROTHERS (A)

HOSTILITIES IN THE CUTTING ROOM

I. INTRODUCTION

Bartolo Brothers, Inc., a manufacturer of men's clothing, dealt for its employees with the Amalgamated Clothing Workers of America. The firm had a reputation for exceptional workmanship. The cutting room, the focus of this case, was organized into working teams of three men each: a "layer," a "marker," and a "cutter."

The layer unrolled the cloth delivered from the sponging room and stretched it flat on a long table, measuring off enough to make one garment according to the specifications on the ticket. A second length was laid on top of the first; a third, on the second; and so on, until enough had been piled up to make all suits of a given size and pattern. The "lay" so produced might contain as many as 40 thicknesses of cloth. It was held in position by iron weights. This operation required relatively little skill and was usually performed by beginners.

The marker next fitted on top of the lay the cardboard patterns for the different pieces of cloth to be cut, such as sleeves, back, side of pants. This required considerable skill, as the prime aim was, of course, to waste as little cloth as possible. Each size, moreover, required a different arrangement of patterns. When he had finally arranged his patterns, he outlined them with tailor's chalk. The marker was considered the most skilled operator of the team.

The cutter, next into the production process, operated an electric machine to cut out the patterns thus marked. This operation obviously required great accuracy, as a single mistake might result in serious loss of material and time.

During the spring of 1939 when a sports model with pinched back became popular, a rate of 84 cents as against 66 cents for ordinary models was established. In the spring of 1940, however, when "plaids" gained popularity, management and union set a uniform rate of 77 cents for all models. Shortly afterwards, the cutters complained that their earnings at the new 77-cent rate were inadequate. Plaid fabrics required two cuts: first, a "rough" cut; and then, a second one to match the stripes. At first it was agreed to allocate the extra or "second" cuts to the markers, paying them an hourly rate based on their "usual" earnings. When this also proved unsatisfactory, the workers' persisting demand for a change in the whole rate schedule was brought to arbitration.

II. The First Arbitration

Excerpts from the stenographic transcript of the hearing before the impartial chairman, T. S. Colton, April 18, 1940, follow:

Present for the Management	*Present for the Union*
Leo Bartolo, President	Frank Santo, Regional Director
Angelo Bartolo, Treasurer	John Pacetti, Business Agent
Arthur Schwartz, Foreman of the	Aaron Kastanian, Marker
Cutting Room	Vito Albani, Marker
Also Present	Don Piano, Marker
Minzio Bonanno, formerly Foreman	Guido Battista, Cutter
of the Cutting Room	Joseph Adelian, Cutter
Rose Bestor, Payroll Clerk and Sec-	Edward Dekran, Cutter
retary to Leo Bartolo	Four Employees from the Pressing
	Department

The hearing was held at the company's office in Hamilton.

Santo (u) [smiling genially]: Now, boys, this always is a better way of handling a situation than walking out or striking and throwing bricks around. Mr. Colton, do you want to have these men begin?

Arbitrator: How long have you had collective bargaining with this firm?

Santo (u): About five years, but we have had a written agreement for only a year or so.

Arbitrator: Mr. Bauer [1] phoned me that there was a situation here which he wanted me to arbitrate, but he really didn't tell me much about it. [To Leo Bartolo.] I wonder if you would be good enough to give me a little background.

Leo Bartolo (m) [speaking very seriously]: For some time we had a lot of trouble with this organization. [He pauses.] When I say some time, I mean about 3 or 4 years. This shop is about 12 years old. For the past 5 years a group of gangsters from the cutters have been causing us a lot of trouble.

Santo (u): Why do you use such language?

Leo Bartolo (m) [decisively]: I want to express myself the way I like. You know what I mean.

Arbitrator: Of course, Mr. Bartolo does not mean gangster in the sense of an Al Capone gang.

Leo Bartolo (m): Of course not. There were times when we could not agree on a wage rate even after the union came in and tried to adjust it. These fellows would not budge. About 3 years ago, they went out on strike for no reason at all. We told them that we would be glad to go to an arbitrator and get the facts settled. It costs us money to stop working. When they struck, they caused another shop here in Hamilton to go out on strike for nothing. Pacetti and Santo tried to patch things up for us.

---

[1] Manager of the regional joint board of the Amalgamated Clothing Workers.

Finally, things got so bad that we became disgusted. It seemed strange for us to consider quitting the business, but we decided last May that we would do just that. We were determined to close down and move out of town. We aren't rich and we couldn't stand it any longer the way things had been going. Mr. Santo came up and after a lot of discussion we finally agreed to sign a contract.

It looked as if things were going to be rosy then; and they were—while they went along to the satisfaction of the cutters and markers. As in everything in life, they have their leaders. [Pause.] I accuse those two men of causing all the trouble. [Pointing.] That man, Aaron [Kastanian], is the leader and the other, Vito [Albani], is his right-hand man. The rest follow along. We have no trouble with most of our employees.

Last July we signed this contract. Lately, because of the conditions in the industry, we decided that the best thing to do was to put the markers on a time basis. The contract states that we have to pay $1.25 an hour to markers or cutters when they are on time work, or, rather, their average earnings which were about that. But when we put some of them on time work, they said that they would like it if the whole cutting floor was put on time. We said that this could not be done because only one group of them was affected by the changes in style. That required the matching of collars in plaid cloth. This talk went on and on; it lasted about a week. We thought that we could convince them to continue, but they didn't like it. We had only one course before us, and that was to arbitrate. During the period when all this happened, production had suddenly fallen down, and we felt that this was caused by some sort of sabotage, some interference with the work by these fellows. We didn't want to harm them financially when we made the change; it simply seemed the best thing all around to do. But they wouldn't cooperate with us in any way.

One day these gentlemen absented themselves voluntarily from the shop. There is always work for the cutters, even though the shop isn't very busy as a whole. It makes no difference in the cutting whether there are 100 lays or 2,000 lays to cut. They have to work the same. They don't suffer as much as the other workers do when the business is a little slack. But this day they didn't report. Mr. Pacetti was good enough to call us and tell us that the workers were in his office. We were very angry. They only work 7 hours a day, and we want to get what we can done in that short time. We had been falling behind right along because of the lack of production. We asked the men to work overtime when they came back. They did, and the following day they walked out again. We were so disgusted and exhausted from dealing with them that we didn't know what to do. We decided that they just don't want to work. [With considerable excitement.] They'll never be cooperative, and I demand that these two men [pointing to Aaron Kastanian and Vito Albani] be fired for their unruliness.

Arbitrator: Is that one of your demands?

Leo Bartolo (m): Absolutely.

Santo (u) [after a pause]: There is something else here that is causing the trouble. I have 12 tickets here. [To Leo Bartolo.] You ought to explain for your side why you are against the week-work proposition; why they want a certain amount and you don't want to give it to them. Then about plaids . . .

Arbitrator: May I interrupt? What are these 12 tickets you have?

Angelo Bartolo (m) [speaking rapidly]: They are specifications for the cutting. [Condescendingly.] We have teams of three in our cutting department. One lays, one marks, and one cuts. Most of them know only the one job they do. They are not very skilled mechanics. We started to study it through with them. Finally, we saw that not one cutter was able to take care of these plaids properly. What they did with the plaids was terrible. It was more of—what shall I say?—a mess than anything else. We couldn't do anything with them except use them for seconds.

Arbitrator: Is it your contention that the work was spoiled and therefore you didn't pay them?

Angelo Bartolo (m): Not for that reason. We had had a lot of trouble. I said that we would fix a price that would be the same and would last and not make a new price every day. We were paying them 66 cents and I went up to 77 cents; that is a raise of 11 cents. What other concern would do this? The markers were also raised so that there would be no argument. We didn't have to pay them that. There's nothing in the agreement to say that we should. There was a loss of time and they didn't deliver me a perfect garment, and that's why we wouldn't pay them.

In order to eliminate discussions, when the plaids came in I took these three markers, the most intelligent of the group, and put them on week-work, so that we would not have to argue about prices any more. Since then the production has dropped way down.

Leo Bartolo (m) [very emphatically]: You see, we signed this contract in order to eliminate disputes and discussions; but what good has it done?

Santo (u): The agreement says that there should be no change in the prices during the middle of the season. But at the beginning of each season either you or the men can ask for a change.

Leo Bartolo (m): What we had in mind was that when the contract was signed, if there was any difference in the work, it could be put through without measuring it within a sixteenth of an inch. That's why we signed the contract. We were paying the markers 66 cents, and by signing the contract we increased it so that matters would be simplified. During the last 6 months, they have averaged $1.26 per hour.

Arbitrator: Mr. Bartolo, I don't get your point about the falling off of production since you put them on the hourly rate. Why has there been this falling off, if there is no reduction in the volume of work?

Angelo Bartolo (m) [rising and speaking rapidly]: The markers force us to put them back on piecework. [With disgust.] They not only want to ruin us, but all the cutters too, because they won't mark. We want them to act like gentlemen. If they have a complaint, all right. But will they wait for Mr. Pacetti to come and straighten it out? No. They pile up mistakes.

I don't know whether it is intentional or unintentional, but they have made more mistakes in the last 3 weeks than in all the time they have been here.

Leo Bartolo (m): A week ago the foreman himself came to me and asked me to put them back on piecework.

Schwartz (m) [rising slowly to speak]: I suggested that to avoid arguments.

Santo (u): What's the matter with piecework?

Leo Bartolo (m): They don't really want to go on piecework. They don't know what they really want. The $1.25 rate was reached on the basis of working in an emergency.

Santo (u): In connection with this question of 77 cents as against 66 cents, remember that the agreement was based on all models, sport and plain. In the question of the plaids and matching the collars, their earnings were affected, and they lost a lot of money because they were losing time.

Albani (u): It took twice as much time to work on the plaids because we have to match the lines on collars and backs.

Santo (u): How much did you make last week?

Albani (u): About $28, and I usually make from $55 to $58.

Kastanian (u) [he spoke slowly with the air of a teacher explaining something]: We had two models, the sport and the plain. The price for the sport was 84 cents and the price for the plain was 66 cents. We also had a lot of extra things which were almost like sport models. We told the firm that we ought to be paid a price between the sport and the plain. All that season we had discussions. We took a licking. We couldn't get together on the rate. Finally, we decided on 77 cents.

Arbitrator: How about the time you went out on strike—to which Mr. Bartolo referred?

Kastanian (u): You want to know about that? Well, in 1937, the general office in New York asked all the manufacturers to raise the wages 12%. On June 15 of that year we were to get our raise. The firm said that the cutters didn't deserve a raise. We weren't going to get it. At the time we weren't working and we had negotiations with the firm through our business agent. Meantime the season was over. There were a few weeks of discussion. We finally got together and received an 8% raise. Then we went back to work.

Four weeks ago, we went to Santo's office about the plaids. We were there from 12:30 to 1:30. We were only a half-hour late in coming back and we planned to work overtime and make it up. When we got back they told us "to get the hell out."

A week ago, Mr. Pacetti didn't come around in the morning, so we went to see Mr. Santo in his office. We were an hour late that day. When we came in, Mr. Bartolo told us to go away. We put on our coats and told our representatives from the union that we had been thrown out. Mr. Pacetti asked them when we should be allowed to come back, and they said not at all. We were out three days.

Arbitrator: I understand that according to the agreement, you are not to go to the union office during working hours.

Schwartz (m): I told them that they couldn't stay out without permission.

Albani (u) [to Schwartz]: I gave you the reason why we were out, didn't I? Could I say a few words please? [He rose.] Two weeks ago we went to see Mr. Santo. We intended to make up the time, but they sent us away. [Walking forward angrily.] But I want to get back to the first point that Mr. Bartolo made. He calls us gangsters.

Arbitrator: He didn't mean that.

Albani (u) [raising his voice]: Am I gangster if I fight for my rights? Am I a gangster if I want extra money when I do extra work?

Santo (u): We know that you're not a gangster.

Albani (u): I have a wife and a child to support. Last week I wasn't paid because I made a mistake.

Arbitrator: Was it the mistake on plaids?

Albani (u): No, on gabardines. Not so long ago our foreman made a mistake on pants. My cutter caught it. If he hadn't caught it, I would have been blamed for the mistake because my signature was on it. My signature was on these gabardines, too, but I didn't do it.

Arbitrator: How does that happen?

Albani (u): We were discharged and were out for 3 days and someone else marked my cloth. I'd like you to see this mistake. [The suit was brought in with the ticket describing the work to be done. Another marker, Don Piano, said that it was his signature and not Albani's. Angelo Bartolo said that it was marked with a ticket that says size 42 but that it was really a 39.]

Piano (u) [who claimed that the mistake was on his cloth]: After my signature was on it someone else may have marked it.

Albani (u): Yesterday my foreman marked the sizes for me. There was no size on a couple of pieces. Should there be anything wrong, I would be to blame.

Angelo Bartolo (m) [showing disgust]: None of these fellows knows what's going on.

Arbitrator: We seem to be getting more and more involved.

Battista (u): Could I explain something to you, Mr. Colton? We cutters haven't been working much and we wanted to do a few singles.[1] While we were loafing they gave the singles to the layers. I loaf three-quarters of a day and they give my work to the layers. We couldn't see Mr. Pacetti until the next Monday so we went to see Frank Santo. When we came back we wanted to make the time up, but we were thrown out.

Schwartz (m) [after several unsuccessful efforts to cut in]: The suits

---

[1] One of the cutting tables was devoted entirely to "singles," the term used to designate custom jobs and special orders for a very few suits. Minzio Bonanno operated this table with his son, Bonanno performing all three operations of the usual team—laying, marking, and cutting—while teaching his son, who assisted him. It was customary to afford layers occasional opportunities to make "singles" as a method of training in marking and cutting.

that this man refers to as singles are custom-made suits and not the regular jobs.

Battista (u): In the first place, I disagree with you; and besides you were just being spiteful when you gave those jobs to the layers. This is a spiteful place.

Leo Bartolo (m) [speaking very rapidly]: These men all learned the trade from me. I taught them all they know about it. [Pointing to Piano.] This man knew nothing when he came here. [Pointing to Albani.] He couldn't hold a piece of chalk when I took him in. Aaron [Kastanian] was the only man who knew a little something when I hired him.

Albani (u) [interrupting]: I beg your pardon. I worked in three places before coming here.

Arbitrator: Please talk one at a time.

Battista (u): We don't begrudge the layers' learning how to cut. It's only when we don't have any work, we don't want them to take it away from us.

Angelo Bartolo (m): He's right that he hasn't any work, but ask him why. [He stood up and pointed dramatically at Battista.]

Leo Bartolo (m): Let me say that the reason why we have had to separate the cutting department was because these gentlemen refused to cut singles and specials. Isn't that right, Bonanno?

Bonanno (u): Well, yes, somewhat.

Leo Bartolo (m): We were forced to establish a department for specials. [To Albani, and speaking very slowly.] You know in your heart that it is the cutters that do the really hard work. The markers have a leisurely job. Even if they did have extra work from the plaids, they have plenty of time to do it in and still not lose any money. We even told them that we would reimburse them for any financial loss they had. [There were signs of resentment at these remarks and Santo cut in.]

Santo (u): Just let me say a few words. We didn't have any agreement until a year ago. Before I entered the picture about 5½ years ago, we used to have a strike here every 3 weeks, even though they didn't belong to the union. The cutters were the most peaceful group then, though. Well, I did a lot of missionary work among the men and we have achieved certain things in the last 3 years. There was a general increase in wages of 12% in the industry. We settled it here for 8%. I was after the firm to sign this agreement for a long time. I must say to their honor that they never refused, but we just never got together. Pacetti told me about a lot of trouble with the cutters lately, but I thought it best not to pay too much attention to them. Finally, in June, 1939, they asked to have this question of the cutters arbitrated. I came here and said that they were entitled to an increase. Also, there was the question of the markers. They finally arrived at the uniform rate of 77 cents, and we signed an agreement. The understanding was that all the models were to be the same price.

At that time, the question of matching the plaids was never made an issue. It was always a question of models. The hourly rate arrived at was based on the average earnings as shown in the company books.

Behind all the complaints made here today are troubles someone must have started. We don't excuse our members if they do wrong, but they are entitled to fight for their rights, and you can't call them gangsters for that. Everyone wants to make a profit at what they are doing and we don't blame them. But the only profit they can make is at their work.

The agreement says, Section 9:

This agreement provides for an orderly adjustment of differences and there is no provocation for direct action. Strikes, stoppages, and lockouts are therefore prohibited during the life of this agreement. If, however, a stoppage shall occur, the union shall immediately order the people to return to work and in the event of any or all of them failing to do so immediately, they shall by such action, and of their own free will, have given up their jobs without recourse.

No one can break this agreement. If they stop, we tell them to go back. They come to the office and it may take hours to convince them to go back, or I may not be there when they arrive, and all that takes time. If we cannot convince them, then we take it to arbitration. If they do not abide by the decision, they lose their jobs. But when they do come back late, after being to my office, or come back the next day, there should be no grievances and no discharges. If they did lose an hour, you [to Bartolo brothers] should have told them in a nice way to work overtime and make it up. But why did you stop all of the men? If two did wrong, there is no reason to stop them all from working.

There is a human element to consider here. I think the lack of tact used here has antagonized these fellows. He [pointing to Albani] is fundamentally a good kid, but you haven't handled him right. This mistake [indicating the suit on the table] is bad; but is it just a human mistake, or is it done in spite? If it is just human, you just have to try to see that it isn't done again. If not, well, the union doesn't stand for sabotage. But let's pin the responsibility down to the person who is to blame, and not blame them all for it.

Schwartz (m) [getting up and speaking with formality]: I would suggest that if you could agree to put a man on to do plaids, singles, and specials, and put them back on piecework, it would work out all right.

Santo (u): We can't have a solution that is based on victory for either side. That only leads to bitterness. They feel that since they can average $1.60 an hour on piecework, why should they go on week-work at $1.25 an hour. If you could arrange to have a person do the extra work, that would solve the problem. [Leo Bartolo started to interrupt, but Santo continued to speak.] If you insist on week-work, they have certain rights to demand certain hourly rates. If there is harmony here, they will produce more. [Several other individuals now began to argue out loud; Santo turned to Leo Bartolo and continued speaking.] You yourself have said that.

Arbitrator [after bringing the hearing to order]: I can see we have not only to solve this immediate dispute but to create a very different spirit here.

After all, it's you here in the firm—management and workers—who have to live together.

Leo Bartolo (m): I have no solution, but I do want to say this. I don't want to treat this meeting as if it were a courtroom. This is no litigation such as you have in a court. I treat it from the moral side. Mr. Santo made a wonderful speech, but that technical way isn't the way I look at it. This affair has been going on for a long time. That is why we signed a contract. Take the question of plaids, for instance. The contract doesn't specifically say plaids, but that is in the spirit of the agreement. A year and a half ago, when there was trouble, we had a peaceful discussion and wages were increased just to smooth things over. Now, that $1.60 an hour, once averaged on piece rates, should be completely disregarded. This is money they found. It was as if I went down the street and found a pocketbook.

Arbitrator: Some of them say that they came down to 77 cents. They don't describe the 77-cent rate as an increase.

Albani (u): I was getting 98 cents.

Leo Bartolo (m): We didn't consider the plaids at that time. They should never have made $1.60 an hour. We have to teach them all they do. We are paying them while they go to school. If one of them is out we have sometimes to spend hundreds of dollars and import a man from New York. We have no fullfledged cutters. We have only helpers. We invest money while they learn. A dollar twenty-five is a very high price. The other 400 workers in the factory don't make this. Besides these cutters work about 46 or 48 weeks a year, which no other workers in the shop enjoy.

Santo (u): How much do the pressers make?

Angelo Bartolo (m): They make about $45 a week, but they only have a few weeks' work. There is plenty of work for the cutters and markers, but two weeks in a row they defied us and stayed out.

Santo (u): How about the suggestion of putting on a man for extras and specials?

Leo Bartolo (m): If I'm waiting for plaids, I can't wait until that particular unit can do it. All of them have to do it or I can't deliver my work. I want my cutting department to be capable of the work that they have to do.

Santo (u): How much do you think they ought to be paid by the hour?

Leo Bartolo (m): I can't say anything; the contract says $1.25. I'd like to pay $1.

Albani (u): A dollar twenty-five is the rate only for regulars. When you have patch pockets, that means extra work. You have to combine the pieces and there is recutting.

Santo (u): Does that rate give you about $45 weekly?

Albani (u): I can average $58 to $60 a week on piecework.

Santo (u): If you were put on week-work, what do you think you ought to get?

Albani (u): Fifty-five dollars a week.

Arbitrator: How much is that an hour?

Santo (u): About $1.50.

Angelo Bartolo (m): The only way of pleasing them is to give them some more money. That's always what they want.

Leo Bartolo (m): To talk of an increase is out of the question.

Albani (u): You didn't give me an increase. I gave you money. I was making 98 cents and I came down to 77 cents.

[Several people talked at the same time here, and the arbitrator was again forced to call the hearing to order.]

Arbitrator: Again I am going to remind you that you all have to live together here. You can't get on with all this bitterness. I want you to help yourselves.

Leo Bartolo (m): We would like to do this, but we've always failed. [To Schwartz, the foreman.] How long have you been with me? [Turned to the arbitrator without waiting for an answer.] He has been a foreman for a year and a half. There is nothing he can do with them and nothing I can do. I give up. [He threw up his hands.]

Battista (u): What happened to the last foreman? We got along all right with him. Everything was peaceful then.

Leo Bartolo (m): You ought to be ashamed to bring that up at all. That foreman was a fellow that I'm ashamed I ever hired. [To Battista.] And you liked him. [Disgusted, he walked to the other side of the room.]

Arbitrator: Why *did* you hire him?

Leo Bartolo (m): I thought I could do something with him—teach him something. [A little sarcastically.] I had to teach all the rest of them.

Schwartz (m): He said that when the other foreman was here they had peace! Why, the whole bin was full of ends of cloth that were wasted.

Battista (u) [to Schwartz]: The firm lost more money since you have been here than in all the time the other foreman was here, my good man.

Albani (u) [to Schwartz, angrily]: What about the mistake you made on the pants last week? Didn't you make a mistake?

Schwartz (m): Yes.

Albani (u): Do they know about that? No.

Arbitrator: This place needs more order and discipline. That's no way to talk to the management and the foreman. [To Santo.] They are insolent.

Santo (u) [smiling]: We look as if we were going to tear each other apart, but we don't mean anything by it. [He laughed.]

Arbitrator: Well, it is they and not we who have to work together.

Santo (u): I have done everything I could. You'll have to arrive at a decision that will help the situation.

Arbitrator: Even when I make a decision that doesn't really settle anything finally. The decision has to be carried out here in the factory. [To Bartolo.] You have a good reputation in the market. But you need goodwill to work together here.

Santo (u) [to the workers]: When this case is disposed of, we'll have to establish strict discipline. If we expect the firm to respect our rights, we have to respect them. [To Leo Bartolo.] The cutters want to be put on week-work as well as the markers, because when the markers have extra work to do, the cutters don't get enough to keep them busy.

Angelo Bartolo (m): We are willing to put all the necessary markers on to supply the cutters. We want to settle this, and we have already lost so many hours in discussion! We put them on week-work without hurting them financially. We don't want to take money from them. If the markers can't keep the cutters busy, we'll supply extra markers.

Leo Bartolo (m): I am willing to do anything that you decide, Mr. Colton, but these two men [pointing to Kastanian and Albani] must be fired. If this were done, we could overload our cutters with work by putting two other markers in their place. They should go out for the benefit of 400 of us. [Angelo Bartolo repeated the demand. Leo Bartolo continued, speaking slowly.] If the decision is against us, then I would ask the privilege of having those two men out for three weeks; I would pay their wages. I'll put markers in their places and they will have more work than they can do, and all of them will make more money. We would like to demonstrate that this can be done.

Kastanian (u) [speaking slowly and bitterly]: It looks as though when you get what you want from someone, the man is good; when you don't, he is bad. [To Angelo Bartolo.] You told me that I was a good marker once. Now it works the other way. Just because I want to take care of myself, I'm no good. Why is that? [To Leo Bartolo.] You're just like a racketeer.

Leo Bartolo (m) [to Kastanian]: It's 3 years since I wanted you to get out.

Dekran (u) [after asking permission to speak]: Mr. Colton, I just want to say this: If these two men are fired, the rest of us seven won't want to work here.

Arbitrator: That's not fair. You're trying to influence me.

Santo (u) [to Dekran]: You're just a jackass, but you insist on talking.

Arbitrator: You are trying to influence my decision. I don't expect threats from either side. Don't you see that you're trying to influence me and tell me that if the decision is against these two men, you'll walk out? That's not fair.

Dekran (u): I'm sorry I said it.

Arbitrator: That's all right, then. I'll have to think things over before making my decision. Meanwhile, I hope that a more amicable spirit may develop here.

III. Arbitrator's Memorandum of an Interview with the Manager of the Union's Joint Board

I expressed my surprise to Bauer over what I found at Bartolo's. I told him that his statement of the case had prepared me only for a routine dispute over wages. Instead I had been plunged into a highly surcharged atmosphere of tense hostility. The hearing lasted for about 4 hours, and practically every minute of it reflected a turbulent emotional situation in the plant. I asked him how he accounted for it. Here is the gist of his answer:

Perhaps I should have warned you, but I did think we might be able to go along on the issue of wages for the cutters—or whatever the issue might be as the disputes come up—while we try to straighten out the deeper troubles there. It is true that there is bad feeling between the management and the workers; I need hardly admit that to you now.

Perhaps we did too good a job in organizing those fellows at Bartolo's. We had had difficulty for years in getting them interested in joining the union. Bartolo Brothers opposed our efforts very strenuously and did everything possible to nullify our organizing campaigns. We even suspect them of having resorted to espionage. Obviously, too, when they established their plant in Hamilton, instead of Capitol City, they were trying to get away from union jurisdiction and union influence. Therefore, prior to signing the agreement, in order to organize those workers we did everything possible to stir up bitterness toward Bartolo Brothers. We succeeded and got them all in the humor, so that the company had no alternative but to sign an agreement.

But it has been difficult since signing the agreement to get the men to quiet down. There has been a carry-over from the organizing campaigns. Of course, you know that is nothing unusual in tough fights like this one had to be. You take such a long hard struggle, you take the company finally forced to give in, and the men are always going to strut about and feel their oats for awhile. It's at that point usually that the union has to step in, establish discipline, and show their new members the difference between the fight they've been through and day-to-day collective relationships.

Well, we've had a problem there because we've been facing the job of training a new local leadership, too, at the same time. As you know, our union is interested in cooperating with management so that a plant can run efficiently. We would like to do that at Bartolo Brothers also, but I must admit we have not succeeded thus far in getting the men into the frame of mind necessary for cooperation. I should tell you, too, that we have had some difficulty with the men themselves over a period of years. Even after we got them higher wages and better working conditions, they were reluctant to pay union dues. From time to time we have questioned their loyalty to the union. We have not always been sure whether some of them have been with us or with the management.

DISCUSSION QUESTIONS

1. How would you define the issue brought to arbitration by the parties in this proceeding?

2. Describe the technical problems of rate setting presented by the dispute. What factors, by the testimony of the parties, enter into the whole problem of rate setting in the cutting room?

3. What indices do the speakers give of deeper disturbances in the cutting room?

4. What clues can you mobilize from this part of the record toward explaining the sources of the hostilities in the cutting room?

5. How would you evaluate the men whom you would designate as leaders on (a) the management side, and (b) the union side, by the behavior at this proceeding?

6. Does the arbitrator obtain any clues regarding possible bench cliques in the cutting room? If so, which of these people would you plan to "follow up" in tracing such an influence?

7. If you were arbitrator, what possible decisions would you weigh for disposing of this case before you?

BARTOLO BROTHERS (B)

"THE SEVEN"

The arbitrator assigned two field workers to interview management, employees, and union representatives.

Interviewing, begun thus after the hearing in mid-April, 1940, continued through the summer of that year. When a second wage dispute arose in the cutting room in July, its issues were assimilated into the "leads" by which the workers and management were approached by the field workers. But by that time they had also established relations of confidence and friendliness.

Their interviews, excerpted below, ran until July 9. While these were progressing, and the arbitrator had not yet rendered his decision in the first case, Aaron Kastanian was discharged by the management. The arbitrator ordered his reinstatement, pending settlement of the case, the conditions of which, he pointed out, could not be altered during arbitration.

I. From an Interview with Leo Bartolo in His Office

Bartolo: I'm glad you came down for I want you to see what this situation really is. It is a terrible situation and our whole business is at stake. [He paused somewhat dramatically.] I will tell you this seriously. We have decided to close our business unless you can do something for us.

We built up this business ourselves, and I believe this—we are good employers. [He paused, then with great emphasis.] We are too good. Ask the priest, ask the storekeepers what the Bartolos have done for Hamilton. Ask the mothers of these girls who work here. This trouble comes from only a few men. We are in their hands. Everyone knows they have us where they want us.

Let me tell you this. The only power the employer has is to discharge a man. Now where is it? Do you remember that boy [Dekran] who spoke up in the meeting and said, "All seven of us will go"? [With great emphasis.] It would be a pleasure to me if they would all seven go. I have not asked for that; I have only asked for two to go. If we cannot discharge these two men, we are *through.*

Interviewer: Who is the seventh? There were only six from the cutting room at the hearing, weren't there?

Bartolo: That's right. But Johnny Salvatore is in with them.

Interviewer: Is the whole shop unionized?

Bartolo: Yes, except for the office force. The rest are all against these men in the cutting room. They are against them; but do they dare say anything at the union meeting? No! These men are like racketeers, like fellows who hold you up with a gun.

Interviewer: Have you talked with the union representatives since the meeting?

Bartolo: Let me tell you this. Santo knows nothing about the details of this business. He is never here. Pacetti, he is all right, but he hasn't got the punch, if you know what I mean. And let me tell you this, too. The laws of this country will have to be changed. We cannot go on this way. We're about through.

Interviewer [after commenting that the rapid growth of Bartolo Brothers despite all these difficulties was very interesting]: How did you start in the business?

Bartolo: I have had a very full career. When I was first a designer in New York, I worked day and night. Just before the war [*i.e.,* World War I] we had a merchant tailor establishment on Fifth Avenue, Angelo and I. We catered to rich people and used to charge $150 for a single suit. When the war came, I could obtain no imported material; I could not have made a suit for $200. I got out of the business and went to Philadelphia as a foreman.

Interviewer: Were you a designer there?

Bartolo [with emphasis]: I have been a designer everywhere. I opened my own shop in Stowbridge in 1927.

Interviewer: I understand that you had stoppages while you were in Stowbridge, and were able to hang on for only a year.

Bartolo: I never knew who was going to hit me first. We lost everything there. The trouble with a union is that we cannot break a contract, but they can. Of course, they can always say that they don't really break it. They can say to the men, "You were wrong. You must go back." But it is always at our expense.

Interviewer: How did the union get in here the first time? How did they get to all your people?

Bartolo: A great many of these people are related. If they get eight or ten families, they have them all.

Interviewer: I believe you said you got rid of the [regional] connection and tied up with New York.

Bartolo: That's right. I saw Mr. Hillman about that and Marconi too. They promised that we need have nothing to do with the regional office. But what did that promise mean? Nothing! My cutters went to this fellow McCarthy [in the regional office] and received advice from him. I believe that they still go there. There is no other way to explain the way they're acting, and I have no doubt [with considerable excitement] that someone in this place is receiving money to make trouble.

II. From an Interview with Arthur Schwartz, Foreman of the Cutting Room

Interviewer [after preliminary exchange]: Schwartz is not an Italian or Armenian name like most of them here, is it?

Schwartz: No. I am German. I am the only "white man" around here, as they say. I know they have no use for me; but listen [slapping his knee], that don't bother me at all. I never saw such a bunch as they have around here. I never saw such lack of intelligence. They don't know right from wrong. I never saw such disrespect and such disregard for everything. They are all members of the Amalgamated Clothing Workers, and all they think of is "the Amalgamated will fix it up for us."

Interviewer: Have you always had trouble with them?

Schwartz: When I started I tried to put them on my side and show them my way of working. I thought I could win them over by fairness, but their aim is to destroy me as a foreman. The Bartolos are looking for unity, but these seven men are against the company. Johnny [Salvatore] is not so bad; he is being led on. That man Aaron [Kastanian] is terrible. They were going to fire him for calling me a rat. Often I have overlooked things they have done. Those markers are working on time now, and you would expect a fair day's work. Once I spoke to Aaron for sitting around and told him I would have to report him. "Go ahead," he says to me. "Go ahead," he says, just like that.

Interviewer: How long has this trouble been going on?

Schwartz: I came here a little more than a year ago. About that time the company was going to move from Hamilton, on account of these men. Mr. Bartolo even had sent away some of the machinery to Parkville. But Santo came in—he's quite a fellow, you know—and fixed things up.

Interviewer: Were you in the clothing business before you came here?

Schwartz: I was a tailor at one time and then I had a good job in an insurance company. But I was sick for a couple of years and had to quit. Then I came here. The Bartolos have always treated me nice. In fact, they have treated everybody nice.

III. FROM AN INTERVIEW WITH AARON KASTANIAN

Interviewer [after exchanging a few remarks about the hearing]: How long have you worked here?

Kastanian [smiling and speaking very quietly]: I've worked here ten years. I used to work with the Belmont Company at Capitol City and came here when Leo started in. I taught Leo a lot about this business. When I first came here, he told me I could stay right along. I had asked him because I wanted to move my wife and mother to Hamilton.

Interviewer: How long has the trouble been going on?

Kastanian: Everything went smoothly for 7 years, and Leo and I used to get on fine. When he was in trouble he asked me what to do. Then when the wage cuts came in the depression—first 20%, then 10%—I took them with the others. I didn't say anything and that was all right.

Interviewer: Then this dispute goes back 3 years?

Kastanian: Yes, that's right. You see he's always trying to get something for nothing. It's always a dispute about rates. Now 2 months ago they brought in those plaids; and, as they are much more work, we expected to get more pay for them. We spoke to Pacetti about it and he said, "That's all right. The boss will fix that." We say to him, "We know him better than you. He always wants more work for the same money." We figure out he pays us one-third less than Belmont in Capitol City for the same work.

Interviewer: There's been some trouble with the foremen too, hasn't there? How long has that been going on?

Kastanian [as if he were trying to explain something which puzzled him]: All these years he never had a foreman. When he wanted something done he would ask me, and after we broke up he ran the floor himself. Then he tried his brother-in-law, but that didn't work at all.

Interviewer: There was another foreman who was on the job before Mr. Schwartz, wasn't there?

Kastanian: Yes. He was a good foreman. He was not a stool pigeon for the boss. He was—you know what I mean—a good diplomat. Then Leo took him out. I don't know why.

Interviewer: Did Schwartz come from another place?

Kastanian: Schwartz was a marker here; and when Leo put him in, he called me personally and said, "We will try him. If he is no good, we will put him back on the bench." Now this man, Schwartz, is a dictator.

IV. From an Interview with Guido Battista and Joseph Adalian

Interviewer: I wonder if you could tell me anything about this situation.

Battista [smiling]: Things went all right until he [Leo Bartolo] began to call us names. Just because he is the boss, he can't call me names.

Interviewer: I suppose this was in 1937.

Battista: That is right. It was when the Amalgamated got us the general raise of 8%.

Interviewer: Is Pacetti running all your union business now? I notice he didn't say anything at the hearing.

Battista: He is business agent, but Santo is there too. Everyone talked at once at the hearing, and they confused Mr. Colton. That hearing was bad; there was a lot of feelings and you got mixed up. [He smiled and shrugged his shoulders.] We should have made our points one by one. Here's a letter I want to show you. [At this point Joseph Adalian came in and sat down on the table.]

Adalian: You see, I have no work now; I am "loafing," as they say. Do you mind if I stay here? There is nothing to do down on the floor.

Interviewer: Of course not. [To Guido.] You were going to show me a letter.

Battista: We got this letter from Mr. Colton, but we couldn't understand this. [He read.] "There will of course always be honest differences between various groups." What does that mean?

Interviewer [after reading the letter]: I think he means that different groups will always have differences of opinion that are partly justified.

Adalian: Is that what he means? We couldn't figure it out.

Interviewer: Did you write to Mr. Colton?

Battista: Yes, we wrote him a letter. We wanted him to know what we were asking for.

Adalian: You know, the four points about which we've all been telling you.

Interviewer: We might as well straighten out these four points. It is easy to get this sort of thing mixed up when you come in from the outside. As I remember it the first one was this: the cutters want a limit on the height of the lay.

Adalian: That's right. They want to protect their weekly earnings.

Interviewer: The second point you want is all week-work or all piece-work for cutters and markers.

Battista: Just now the markers are on week-work. That happened when the plaids came in. You see the plaids had to be cut twice and marked twice to match the stripe. The markers do the extra cut now, but that means they take more time and there is less work for us. Also, the second cut is harder to do.

Interviewer: The third point had something to do with the new worker who came up from New York?

Battista: We don't want an extra cutter here when we haven't enough work for ourselves. If there was work for him we would not mind, but we have a right to have work.

Interviewer: What was the fourth point?

Battista: There should be no cutting given to anyone except us four cutters unless we are busy.

Adalian [interrupting]: That point is very important.

Battista: One day the foreman said, "There is no work for you," but he had just given some cutting to a boy who knows nothing at all.

Interviewer: I think these four points are clear enough.

Battista: Another thing—we want to be paid for the time we lost when we were out from Wednesday through Friday. That is 16 hours.

Adalian: Well, I will have to stop loafing now. [Went out.]

Interviewer [to Battista]: You have been around here a long time, haven't you?

Battista: Seven years.

Interviewer: Are you married?

Battista [smiling broadly]: Yes, I have a boy of 3. Joe Adalian, he has three children.

Interviewer: How long have you been married?

Battista: Only 4 years. Ever since I have been married, there has always been some trouble with the boss. I never come home and feel peaceful.

V. FROM AN INTERVIEW WITH VITO ALBANI

Albani: Everything was harmonious until 3 years ago. It was then that he started to call us gangsters. Now when that business about the plaids came up, he didn't have a leg to stand on. Angelo Bartolo said to Leo,

"What's the use of arbitrating that? You know it's more work." Pacetti heard him say that. Of course, I can't blame the foreman or Bonanno for being on the boss' side; they are obligated. But this foreman they have now, he don't know much. I can teach him plenty. He is no foreman, [with emphasis] not to me. I used to go into Capitol City to get advice from the union people there. One day he come up to my house and said, "Don't have anything to do with those Capitol City people; they will ruin you," he says. Right in front of my wife, he says that. Look, here, we are the only people keeping up the spirit of the union here, and without the union his place would be a sweatshop. Leo'd like to get cutters to work for $20 a week. Last year he approached a kid of 19 or 20 and wanted to make him a cutter at that price. What do you think of that, a cutter making $20 a week!

Interviewer: How much are you fellows making now?

Albani: The markers are on week-work now and make $45 for a full week's work. Week-work is all right if it don't affect your pay, but I could make $55 now. You see he has been experimenting on my time. When the plaids came up, he experimented to see how much time it took. I only made $28 that week, though I told Pacetti I had $15 more coming to me. Pacetti fixed it up with Bartolo to give us all a loan of $15. Then the day we were all fired he took the $15 out of our pay.

Interviewer: What happened when you were discharged?

Albani: We went to Santo's office at lunch time to see about a complaint. He wasn't there but Pacetti says, "Santo will take care of you fellows." When we came back he [Leo Bartolo] did not give us a chance to take off our coats. He just pushed us out.

Interviewer: What was the dispute about?

Albani: A layer was given some of the cutters' work. It should be understood that a layer's job is a layer's job. [He paused.]

Interviewer: A foreman's job must be pretty difficult around here just now.

Albani: They might have had a good foreman. Now Bonanno was our advisor before he became foreman. After he was a foreman, he became a blank. You know there is such a thing as not favoring either side; but if there is anyone who is not good, it is this present foreman. He has no right to talk the way he does. I don't blame him for taking the firm's side, but he plays favorites. He is favoring one of the layers now. You know, in this shop there is a stool pigeon wherever you turn. He [Leo Bartolo] has got his relatives everywhere, and to him we are just racketeers.

VI. From an Interview with Edward Dekran and John Salvatore

Dekran: I've been here 4 years. When we fellows first came in we didn't know much. Aaron [Kastanian] was promised that as the shop grew he would grow too. We always did favors for him [Leo Bartolo], but now we are disgusted. He always claims sabotage and tries to set the others against us. Whenever there's any holdup in the factory he tells them, "Go home. The cutters aren't working. There's nothing for you."

Interviewer: Tell me some more about Aaron. What was he promised?

Dekran: Aaron taught Leo all he knows about cutting, and he sometimes worked as low as $25 a week to help out. Of course, most of us learned our jobs here. I want to tell you another thing. He wants to make a rate difference between markers and cutters just to make us enemies.

Interviewer: The rate setup is pretty complicated for an outsider to understand. I should think your union representative, Pacetti, could take care of that.

Dekran: It's complicated and I don't think Pacetti even understands it. He was never a cutter. You see, we realize that we have a very shrewd man against us; and we have all we can do to fight for our rights.

Interviewer: Are you married? As I remember it, all the other fellows in your crowd are.

Dekran: No, but that doesn't mean I have no one to support. We used to have money when my father ran a store, but he lost it all. My brother and sister have jobs on and off, but most of the time what I earn here is our only support.

Interviewer: How does the union handle things in this shop?

Dekran: The union came in a few years ago. At first the people didn't want it because they thought it meant trouble; then I suppose the Bartolos decided that they needed the label and let the union in. Most of the workers are not really behind it the way we are. We are the only real union people in this shop.

Interviewer: Most of them are women, aren't they?

Dekran: Yes, and a lot of them are against us because they believe what he [Leo Bartolo] tells them. Whenever there is any trouble he just says, "Oh, the cutters are at it again." A lot of them are related, so they are pretty dependent upon this shop; and he can scare them by threatening to move. He tells them we're bandits, but it stands to reason that we didn't become bandits overnight after being good boys for so long.

Salvatore [coming into room]: You don't mind if I join you?

Interviewer: Not at all. Sit down. You're a cutter, aren't you?

Salvatore: Yes, for the last three seasons. I began as a trimmer. Now I have specials and the odds and ends. I don't work with a team, you know.

Interviewer: You've been here quite a while?

Salvatore: 10 years.

Interviewer: How did you fellows manage to get along with the boss in the beginning?

Salvatore: We were all learners or teacher's pets. Aaron was a teacher's pet in those days. We weren't sticking together then. He [Leo Bartolo] don't like the idea of our sticking together. Sometimes he tells me not to bother with those other fellows. Do you know that Leo Bartolo even went to see my mother once and told her how bad I was? She believed him and bawled me out.

Dekran: Every season he scares them by telling them he'll have to move the shop, but the firm makes plenty of money. [With disgust.] They go up and we go down; that's the way it is.

Salvatore [as they left]: You might talk with some of the pressers. They are men; the women will just give his story.

VII. From an Interview with Don Piano, Guido Battista, and Joseph Adalian

Piano: You've heard most of this from the others, but I want just to tell you why this foreman has it in for us. About a year ago, on May 1—that's a union holiday, you know—he and three or four others worked all day. I was on the executive committee and we fined them all $10. Ever since then he claimed he would get even. Now we just have to carry out his dictates.

Battista: Why, you can't do anything with that fellow. He has introduced rules we've never heard of on the floor. He told me once he could fire me if I whistled. Another time he told me, "Better stay away from those other fellows in the union."

Interviewer: I'm a little puzzled about just how the union works in this shop.

Adalian and Piano [together, with considerable emphasis]: So are we.

Interviewer: I would like to talk to Pacetti.

Battista: You know we really don't want Pacetti here.

VIII. A Second Conversation with Aaron Kastanian in the Cutting Room

Kastanian: I see you talk to people who have nothing to do with this case. Why do you do that?

Interviewer: We wanted to get all the information we could.

Kastanian: That fellow you talked to in the sponging room [a "sponger" named Mario Colombo], I think he double-crossed me the other day.

Interviewer [showing surprise]: Is that so? He told me he got along well with the cutters as far as work is concerned; but he feels he hasn't made many friends yet since he moved to Hamilton from New York.

Kastanian: Well, that's good. Of course, we never have anything to do with those fellows. That cutter, Dennis, who came up from New York when we were out, is a friend of Colombo's. I think Colombo told Leo about Dennis. We never have spoken a word to Dennis since he came. But I still don't think you have to see those fellows; they have nothing to do with our case.

IX. From a Second Interview with Joseph Adalian and Vito Albani

Adalian: It's lucky you came out. Do you know what they've done? They've fired Aaron [Kastanian].

Interviewer: That complicates things. What was wrong?

Adalian: Vito [Albani] can tell you better than I can.

Albani [with considerable excitement]: Why, he wasn't doing anything. They just fired him. All he did was to go upstairs to the men's room. You see what kind of a place this is? They say he was loafing. Around here they always think you are loafing.

X. From a Second Interview with Arthur Schwartz, Foreman

Schwartz: I kept warning these fellows, but it didn't do any good. The other day Don [Piano] and Guido [Battista] came in late. I told them they couldn't do that sort of thing, but they don't appreciate anything. Now Aaron [Kastanian] spends a lot of time talking. Whenever he gets a chance he goes over to someone else's bench and starts to talk. Vito always stays at his bench. He may not got anything done, but at least he always stays there.

I couldn't go on this way any longer. I never saw such insolence. Of course, I don't mind what they say about me; and I don't hold it against them personally. I just treat those fellows like tables or chairs, and I don't mean to be unfair to them for what they say about me.

Interviewer: What had Aaron been doing when you fired him?

Schwartz: He left his bench several times that day, and I warned him that he would have to stick to his work. Finally, he went up to the men's room and stayed there about 10 minutes. I know he went up there just to show me my warnings didn't mean anything to him. When he came down, I fired him. Even then he wouldn't go, and I had to send for Mr. Bartolo. [Pause.] By the way, are you from the state?

Interviewer: No; the arbitrator's office under the agreement here is part of the joint machinery.

Schwartz: The reason I asked was that my youngest daughter was fired the other day. She goes to high school and has a job in a store on Friday and Saturday. Some money was missing from the cash register, and they couldn't find out who took it, so they fired the whole bunch, 15 of them. That is very unfair and it leaves a stigma on her.

Interviewer: If they fired the whole group there is no reason to suppose the blame would fall on her.

Schwartz [worriedly]: She will have to get a job when she finishes school, and she will be asked what she has done. It won't be nice for her to say she was fired.

Interviewer: How many children have you?

Schwartz: I have three daughters and two sons and two grandchildren. I live for my grandchildren; they are the only thing that makes me feel young. [He paused.] But I don't know what will happen to them when I am gone. She never should have married him and we warned her, but it didn't do any good.

Interviewer: You're speaking of your daughter? Whom did she marry?

Schwartz: She married a fellow who had a job on a tanker. He only earns $55 a month and is away most of the time, too. [With great decisiveness.] He's no good and never will be any good. Now they are going to have another child. [Pointing to the cutting room.] He's one of them, too.

Interviewer: I don't quite understand.

Schwartz: He's an Italian. He thinks he knows it all. Then I have another girl who is a nurse in a hospital. She wants to do the same thing, too. She wants to marry a fellow who is an orderly in a hospital. He earns $12 a week and his keep. My daughter gets $55 a month on her job. [He paused and then continued somewhat wearily.] I don't know how long I'll last. I don't even know if I'll stay here. Their object is to lick me. Bonanno was foreman for awhile; and they licked him.

XI. From a Second Interview with Leo Bartolo

Bartolo: Mr. Schwartz, the foreman, came to me and said, "Mr. Bartolo, I can't stand this any longer. I'll have to fire this man." I told him, "Why do you come to me? If he is fired, he is fired." Of course, the fellow wouldn't go. If I had been a worker I would have gone under those circumstances. He came to me and told me his case. I said, "If I support you, I let down my foreman. You can go."

Interviewer: Tell me a little more about Aaron.

Bartolo: For 3 years everything was all right. Then he lost, in some way, the use of his mind. He made terrible mistakes. I had him examined by a doctor and sent to a sanitarium for 6 months or perhaps a year.

Interviewer: You mean he had a breakdown?

Bartolo: Yes, that's it. At that time he spoiled a whole lay.

Interviewer: And before that, your relations with him were good?

Bartolo: The best. When he went to the sanitarium, we paid out money for him because we were sorry. [He paused.] Now let me tell you something more. About a year ago at a meeting one of my pressers got up and said he had been offered $20,000 to close this shop.

Interviewer: Who do you think would want to pay $20,000 to close your shop?

Bartolo [shrugging his shoulders]: A competitor, perhaps. I can't prove it, but I believe it's an unseen hand in this affair.

Interviewer: How did you happen to select Mr. Schwartz as foreman?

Bartolo: In my opinion he is a good foreman. For a while my brother-in-law had the job, but they made a fuss and I took him out. Now they want to get rid of Schwartz. When he came to me about Aaron, I said, "Why do you come to me? If he's out he's out. You either run the cutting room or you don't," I said. I want to say this, if one of these men is fired we will all learn something. Either the shop will be first class or we will learn something more is wrong. I believe it is essential that these men should learn that it's possible that someone can lose his job.

On May 9, 1940, the arbitrator rendered his decision regarding the dispute submitted to him on April 18. Excerpts follow:

The difficulties centered in the cutting department, and were concerned particularly with issues of discipline, quantity and quality of output, and wage rates. Subsequent to the hearing, two associates of the arbitrator made several visits to Hamilton where they interviewed representatives of both sides.

While the investigation was under way, Aaron Kastanian was discharged by the management for alleged insubordination. Upon being notified of this by Messrs. Santo and Pacetti, the arbitrator instructed Messrs. Bartolo to reinstate Aaron Kastanian immediately. Obviously the *status quo* must be maintained during a judicial proceeding such as this arbitration.

The decision of the arbitrator is as follows:

(1) The arbitrator confirms the instructions given verbally to Messrs. Bartolo that Aaron Kastanian be reinstated.

(2) The request of the management that Aaron Kastanian and Vito Albani be dismissed is not granted. The arbitrator was impressed, however, with the evidence of insubordination in the cutting department of the plant. It is quite clear that a deplorable lack of discipline does exist. Such a lack of discipline militates against the welfare of the workers as well as against management. This condition should not continue. Therefore, while the arbitrator is ordering the retention of Aaron Kastanian and Vito Albani on their jobs, this is done *provisionally* only. In other words, these two gentlemen are on probation. The management has the right to reopen this case at any time, and if evidence will be presented pointing to continuing lack of discipline or insubordination the arbitrator will have no other recourse but to order the discharge of the guilty persons.

(3) The arbitrator is granting an increase of $2 a week to the markers. Their rate henceforth will thus be $47 a week as against the $45 a week until now prevailing under the hourly rate of $1.25 established by the agreement of June 29, 1939. While this rate of $47 is now established on a weekly basis, the arbitrator expects the maintenance of standards of production in reasonable ratio to what they were when piecework prevailed.

(4) The wage rates of the other workers in the cutting departments are to remain as they are under the agreement of June 29, 1939.

(5) The arbitrator earnestly hopes and expects that more amicable relationships will be developed between the cutters and the management. The Amalgamated Clothing Workers of America has a proud record both for obtaining good working conditions for its members and also for helping manufacturers to carry on their business successfully. This involves cooperation and discipline. It does not mean that differences will not arise from time to time. But orderly adjustment of such differences is an essential part of collective relations, and in recognition of that principle the Amalgamated pioneered in establishing machinery for impartial arbitration. This machinery should be utilized to settle those differences which the union and the management by joint effort have been unable to compose.

As the interviews progressed, reactions to the decision naturally found their way into the statements of interviewees. The judgment of the business agent upon the feeling of the cutters, and relations in general just after the decision, may summarize conditions through the remainder of that spring.

XII. FROM AN INTERVIEW WITH JOHN PACETTI, BUSINESS AGENT

Interviewer: How did they like the decision out in Hamilton?
Pacetti: They thought it was a lousy decision.

Interviewer: It is an interesting situation out there. The business grew up from nothing at all, didn't it?

Pacetti: When those fellows started they were getting $25 and $30 a week and were quite satisfied. That was a lot more than anyone got in the textile mills; and it was a better place to work, too. In those days they were proud to work there, but of course they were all learners then. Now they are getting $45 and they aren't satisfied. [He paused.] The business used to mean a lot to those people. Once when the Bartolos were out of money, some of them came around and showed him their bank books. Then they offered to loan him whatever he needed.

Interviewer: How much did they borrow?

Pacetti: I don't know exactly the total. The Bartolos let it get around that they would have to close, and the workers came around voluntarily and offered to back them up.

Interviewer: He paid them back, didn't he?

Pacetti: Oh, yes. Do you know that there are very few of those people who don't have at least $2,000 saved up? They are very thrifty, and however little they earn they always put away something.

Discussion Questions

1. List "The Seven" as members of a clique in the cutting room, indicating which of the men seems to be the leader, or leaders, and your first judgment upon the places of the others in the group.

2. Trace the motivations behind the hostilities of "The Seven" suggested in these first interviews.

3. Indicate the relationship of "The Seven" to the union, to top management and supervision, and to other workers in the shop.

4. Analyze the history of the company as a factor in present relationships.

5. Evaluate Arthur Schwartz as a foreman in the cutting room.

6. What clues can you note thus far as to the influence of ethnic factors in the cutting room?

7. Discuss the discharge of Aaron Kastanian, in terms of how and why it seemed to have been made when it was, and the policy of top management in confirming it and of the arbitrator in revoking it.

8. Compare the statement of their grievance given by the cutters in these interviews with that at the arbitration hearing. What clue would you find in this behavior?

9. What reasoning do you think lay behind the decision which the arbitrator rendered in the first case presented to him? Do you agree or disagree, and why?

BARTOLO BROTHERS (C)

ANOTHER DISPUTE IN THE CUTTING ROOM

Mr. Pacetti was replaced as business agent for Bartolo Brothers by Vincent Donati. As the spring season's production was drawing toward its close, another dispute in the cutting room was submitted to the arbitrator. Excerpts from the stenographic transcript of the hearing held on July 9, 1940, follow:

Present for the Management	*Present for the Union*
Leo Bartolo, President	Vincent Donati, Business Agent
	Joseph Adalian, Cutter
	Guido Battista, Cutter
	John Salvatore, Cutter
	Edward Dekran, Cutter

Arbitrator: Well, gentlemen, what is the story today?

Donati (u): Since last time, when you arbitrated a case for the cutters and markers, extra work has been given to the cutters for which they have not been paid. It has to do with matching stripes. This requires extra time. In 1939 an agreement was made on prices between the union and the firm, but there were no specifications as to fabrics that required extra work. Let me explain a little more carefully why they have more work to do. After the cutters get the work from the markers, they cut along the first marks. Then to match the collars and the backs, they have to do them individually. They have to be cut over again, one at a time. They make $4 or $5 a week less than last year. This kind of work has been done by the markers ever since they went on week-work. Now it has been given again to the cutters.

Arbitrator: Let's hear Mr. Bartolo's story now.

Bartolo (m): There is a lay, say 35 high. First the cutters cut according to the chalk marks of the markers. That is a rough cut. Then the marker re-marks it and the cutters cut it correctly.

Arbitrator [to Mr. Bartolo]: Have you any data on the payroll to show how earnings are affected?

Bartolo (m): Yes, we have all the material you want, but don't stop on that. [He paused.] I have been bewildered as to how to handle this situation. There is a decided conspiracy among the workers against the management, which I want to emphasize. I really wanted to come here with the purpose of bringing this up. We have quite a few workers who do their work quietly and in peace, and they have been approached by the older ones and threatened in different ways.

Donati (u) [interrupting]: I don't see what that has to do with this case. This word "conspiracy" implies a lot of things but has nothing to do with this case.

Bartolo (m): I may be all wrong, but I want the investigation to go deeper. They have been threatening these fellows by telling them that either they will go along with them, or they will be in trouble. Let your investigator come to us and find out what has been told to them by those that are trying to compel them to belong to their gang. My employees are only trying to earn a living. Why should they be disturbed by these fellows? I want it to be investigated. I may be all wrong, but I want to know. [He paused.] From the time that we put the markers on a week basis, we ran into complications. We signed a contract simply to avoid all of this confusion and disagreement. You [to the arbitrator] have brought them somewhat into line by telling them that they were to give the concern a full day's work. Two weeks ago I told Donati what was going on. He spoke to them and for the past 2 weeks the markers have given me a full day's work. When the markers were not doing a day's work, the cutters didn't have anything to do and I had to send them home. The reason the cutters are not earning what they should is because the markers are loafing on the job. Naturally when they don't mark enough cloth, the cutters don't have enough to cut. Since the cutters are on piecework, they earn less than they would if the markers got out their production.

Arbitrator: You say that you have been getting good production from the markers for the last 2 weeks.

Bartolo (m): No, not good production, but they have done a pretty good day's work.

Arbitrator: Have you a record of the markers' earnings?

[Mr. Bartolo submitted some payroll data.]

Battista (u): There is one thing I'd like to clear up. [To Mr. Bartolo.] Awhile ago you spoke about some threat to some of the workers. What did you mean by that?

Donati (u): Mr. Bartolo has heard that the older cutters and markers have approached others in the shop and told them that either they follow them or else they will suffer for it.

Arbitrator: My investigator will look into that.

Donati (u): The boys have no right to gang up or conspire against the firm. If the firm goes out of business, the boys will lose their jobs.

Battista (u): It's the first I ever heard of it. I never heard of anyone being threatened.

Arbitrator: How often does your local union meet?

Donati (u): They used to meet every month. Lately they haven't been meeting very often, and we want to return to the old system of meeting regularly.

Arbitrator: I think that is a good idea. That would be a good chance for the boys to talk over their grievances. You know the union is what you fellows make it.

Donati (u): I have told them there is a responsibility that they have to the union and that the union means them, not me.

Arbitrator: I'd like to observe earnings for a couple of weeks before making a decision. Since the markers have been doing better during the past 2 weeks, I'd like to see how things go for the next 2 weeks. I'll take their hourly earnings, not their weekly earnings. In other words, I have to pursue further Mr. Bartolo's contention that the markers were not turning out production, and when their production and work improved the cutters' earnings increased. I want to see what their earnings are, say, for the next 2 weeks.

Donati (u): All right, boys, you have nothing to lose. It will show more exactly what you are losing.

I am striving very hard to see that both parties will get together. Both sides have had a chip on their shoulders and have been sarcastic. I want to see peace prevail. I tell the boys and Mr. Bartolo that they all have to try to overlook things. Too much complaining leads to divorces, and we don't want any divorces.

Bartolo (m): I had a solution to this whole thing—that was to get rid of two men. But instead they were given a raise.

Battista (u) [in a disgusted tone]: Is it always going to be like this?

Bartolo (m): As I said before, you, Guido, would give me a good day's work; but I'm afraid of the influence on you from the others.

Arbitrator: Let's see what happens in the next 2 weeks with those boys' earnings. I think you fellows will have to admit that there is something wrong with the spirit of things in the shop.

Donati (u): He means that you boys have to be cooperative and give an honest day's work.

Bartolo (m): They think more of how to present a case now than how to cut more intelligently. We've all had to become lawyers.

Arbitrator: You once had a good relationship with these people. Something happened. Now there's suspicion on both sides and a conflict between the workers and the management. If we could put a finger on what is wrong, you [Mr. Bartolo] would show a profit and they would be happy.

Bartolo (m): I had the cure which would benefit all the 500 or 600 workers, but no one thought it was a good idea. I don't usually want men to lose their jobs. Don Piano is going away and I feel bad about it. I spent hours and weeks with that boy teaching him his business and now he is going away.

Excerpts from the arbitrator's decision follow:

This case relates to the question of compensation for four machine cutters. The latter contend that they are entitled to an increase because of an additional operation necessitated by matching stripes, in the nature of a double cutting—that is, once in the rough and then more precisely to the marking.

The management contends that the lower earnings of the cutters this year are due to the fact that the markers who prepare the cloth for the cutters are not turning out the volume they can and should. The markers have for some time evinced a hostile spirit toward the management; and since they are now on week-work, they are not turning out as much work as last year when they were on piece-work.

It is true that the cutters are earning less per hour during the 1940 season than the 1939 season. It is difficult to ascertain, however, exactly how much of the decreased earnings is due to the process of double cutting, and how much to the fact that the markers are holding back and are not preparing sufficient volume of work.

A comparison of the earnings of the markers indicates that if computed on a piecework basis, they also are earning less during the 1940 season than the 1939 season. There is thus reason to believe that the markers are in part responsible for the reduction in the earnings of the cutters. This is a deplorable situation; and since the men all belong to the same union, and the union has an agreement with the management, the arbitrator recommends that the union look into the situation and take such measures as may be necessary to the end that the markers turn out a satisfactory volume of production. On the other hand, it is obvious that the double cutting process is also in part responsible for the reduction in earnings.

The decision of the arbitrator is therefore as follows: that in those cases in which double cutting is necessary, the cutters be given 5 cents additional per lay, in other words, 82 cents instead of 77 cents. This rate is retroactive to the time of the hearing on July 9, 1940.

DISCUSSION QUESTIONS

1. Discuss the problem presented in this arbitration from the viewpoint of rate setting in the cutting room.

2. What further insights does the proceeding furnish regarding the influence of underlying relationships in the cutting room upon the behavior of and the explicit differences between the parties?

3. Note on a chart, listing "The Seven," which is now to be carried forward from episode to episode to indicate the changes in the clique's internal organization and shop status, the "position" of its members (a) at the outset of the first arbitration; (b) after the decision upon that dispute; (c) by the events indicated in this second rate dispute.

4. Discuss the problem of internal union administration presented by the difficulties in the cutting room. Evaluate the adjustments which the union thus far has been making.

5. Discuss the arbitrator's decision in this case, again in terms of its underlying reasoning and objectives.

BARTOLO BROTHERS (D)

THE "ANTI-SEVEN"

The interviews held subsequent to July 9 naturally carried forward the basic shop situation in terms of the developments indicated at this second hearing, as well as what had gone before. They also reflected the reactions to a change in cutting-room organization effected when management moved one of the cutting teams, together with Foreman Arthur Schwartz, to the nearby shop of an associated company. Shortly thereafter, Minzio Bonanno took over the foremanship in the old cutting room. Excerpts from these interviews, conducted from July 10 until the third hearing convened on September 23, 1940, follow:

I. FROM AN INTERVIEW WITH LEO BARTOLO

Interviewer [after a preliminary exchange of comments on the hearing which had taken place the previous week]: Did you say that Don Piano left you?

Bartolo: He left me and I don't know why. I wish you would find out. Personally I think it is just as if you had asked me to work with you and then I found that I can't stay on unless I do something crooked.

Interviewer: How are you getting on with the others?

Bartolo: You see what they are. Aaron [Kastanian] reads things and thinks he understands them. If he read them upside down, he would understand them just as well. Vito [Albani] knows nothing of what really goes on in the world. Don [Piano] was, I think, a nice boy. He is the kind of boy who is cooperative by instinct. That fellow, Guido Battista, is an honest boy. But he is stubborn; he will see something his way and fight for it whatever you say to him. As for Ed Dekran, you can't tell when he is going to blow up.

Interviewer: I was told Mr. Donati is here today.

Bartolo: I think he is still here. Of course, these fellows think they have to do something or they will lose their jobs. That's why they got rid of Pacetti. He didn't get them enough. Donati was here before that and they finally got rid of him, but now he's back again.

Interviewer: Was Donati here then when your shop was unionized?

Bartolo: I brought the union in myself. Santo was here then, organizing the textile mills, and Hamilton was "on fire." He told me that the times were against me and asked me if I wanted to be known as a "scab" shop. So we decided they had better come in. But let me tell you that the union has no part in this dispute; it has no control over those seven.

II. From an Interview with Vincent Donati

Donati: There is something wrong out here, but I can't find out just what it is. I haven't time to give this situation much attention. Tonight I have to be in Millfield; tomorrow I am in Elliot. Every day this week is full. I wish you could find out just what the situation is. I want to straighten it out. Now there is another thing I want to call to your attention. You know Edward Dekran. His marker—Don Piano—has left. The new marker [Paul Bestor] is slow, and Ed hasn't enough work. That isn't anyone's fault, but he should be given some work to make up for it.

Interviewer: Do you know why Don left?

Donati: He said he was nervous, and when a new job came up he was glad to take it. I told the markers a few weeks ago that the boss was watching them and they would have to keep their production up. Don said he was under a strain and felt badly. The foreman antagonizes all these fellows. I heard him say to one of the boys, "What the hell are you doing?" All the boy had done was to look at somebody's ticket. He jumps on them for every little thing. [Pause.] I hope you can find out something more about what is going on here. All these disputes are exhausting.

III. From an Interview with the Markers and Cutters, Aaron Kastanian, Vito Albani, Guido Battista, Edward Dekran, John Salvatore, and Don Piano

[This conversation took place in the Napoli Restaurant owned by the Piano family. Although everyone except Salvatore contributed to the conversation, most of it was carried by Kastanian and Albani. When Kastanian spoke, the others were always silent. Occasionally, there were two conversations going on at the same time. Albani had originally been asked to come over and talk, and he arranged to bring the others along. Joseph Adalian lived a considerable distance from Hamilton and so did not stay for this evening interview. Albani started off by discussing the foreman.]

Albani: You see, about 1½ years ago, Arthur Schwartz was just one of us. Then one day he worked while all of us were out. It was a union holiday, and he was fined for doing it by the executive board. Ever since then, he's been out to get revenge; and awhile ago, before Don left, he told Don that he was on the spot and had better look out. Of course, we are trying to put him on the spot now, too; and whatever we do, he tells Leo Bartolo.

Kastanian: What I don't understand is why we need to answer all these questions. What has it got to do with our case now?

Albani: That's just what I was saying a few minutes ago. If we were talking about the weather, why bring up the European situation? We had this arbitration to settle rates, and the result was that Aaron and I were put on probation. I'd like to know what crime we were guilty of to be put on probation.

Interviewer: You can see that I can't discuss the merits of that decision.

Kastanian: The decision is over. I want to know why you should ask us to tell you more. What good will it do us?

Albani: He explained that to me. He wants to find out more about the history of it and all that.

Kastanian [speaking very slowly]: If you want to understand labor relations, it is necessary to read books about it. You should read Mr. Hillman's book and a book about the National Labor Relations Board. What they're doing in this shop is against the board's rulings. They want to prevent us from being active members of the union and they have put a lot of stooges into the shop. He has three spies here: the foreman, Bonanno, and that boy Pete.[1] We can ask the Labor Relations Board that they be discharged.

Albani [interrupting]: You know, when we ask that boy, Pete, to do something, he says, "No, I won't do it," in an arrogant voice. He should do what we say. We markers used to be responsible for a machine cutter and a layer. In those days it wasn't—"Do this." They used to say, "We think this should be done." There was never an argument. We used to bowl together and go to the beach together in those days.

Interviewer: When did things begin to go wrong?

Kastanian: It began in 1937 when everyone in all the shops was supposed to get a 12% increase. But the Bartolos thought we were all overpaid and didn't want to give us anything.

Battista: Leo owes a lot of his success to us. [With some excitement.] He says we learned everything from him, but he learned plenty from us. Aaron taught him a lot.

Dekran: About two years after he started, we all loaned him money. He came to us and said, "If you hadn't cooperated, the rest of the shop wouldn't have cooperated." He said, "When conditions are better, you fellows will get a raise without asking for it." But look at where we are now.

Piano: It's the expansion that's going to their heads.

Kastanian: I don't know of any man who has gone up so fast.

Interviewer [to Aaron]: You had a lot of experience in the clothing business before you worked for Leo, hadn't you?

Kastanian: I worked seven years for the Belmont Company in Capitol City. Leo was designer there. Angelo worked there, too.

Interviewer: How did Leo get started on his own?

Kastanian: In 1927 Leo went over to Stowbridge and started a shop. Then there was a strike in Stowbridge and Leo moved out here.

Interviewer: Did you move out here with him when he first started?

Kastanian: I went back and forth from Capitol City. Then finally he says to me, "Why don't you move to Hamilton?" But then I thought, "Why should I move and then get fired?" So I spoke to him about it. He told me, "As long as this business grows, you grow with it." Until 1937 every-

---

[1] Peter Paloti; he will be met in subsequent interviews and hearings.

thing went smoothly; but right after the general raise he said to me, "Now you are a free man. You are no longer obligated to stay here."

Albani: He tried to set us against each other. One day he got hold of me and said, "Look, Vito, if Aaron wants to leave what do we care?" He's tried to set the girls against us, too.

Kastanian: Most of the women give Leo a lot of credit for giving them a little something to do.

Battista: They don't get much, but what little they get helps.

Albani: You see, I won't take the kind of thing that goes on here. The other day the foreman raised his voice to me and I raised mine back so everyone would hear. I said, "That's dictatorship, and I won't take dictatorship around here."

Kastanian: This spring, his brother-in-law, Bonanno, used to get hold of Don and tell him that all us fellows were on the spot and the only solution was to come down on rates.

Albani: You see, he's got stooges all through this shop. Pete and Tom were just hired to be stooges.

IV. From an Interview with Paul Bestor

Interviewer: You began here as layer for Vito Albani, didn't you? How did they get along without a foreman for so long?

Bestor: Leo Bartolo used to be his own foreman. I think Aaron thought he'd be made foreman when the business grew.

Interviewer: Is Arthur Schwartz pretty good?

Bestor: Arthur is good. I've got to give him credit for that. A good many times I've seen him cut down the amount of cloth required for a size. [Pause.] Now let me tell you a little more about what happened to me here. When I came in, all those boys gave me the cold shoulder. For awhile I didn't know why, and then I found out. You see my wife, Rose, had worked with Mr. Bartolo a long time and they thought anything they said would be repeated to him. I finally had it out with Vito and he told me what the matter was. I said, "If you feel that way, just don't say anything." After that, we worked a couple of seasons and I gained their confidence. Of course, I didn't care to hear about their complaints, but we went on picnics together and had a wonderful time for awhile.

Interviewer: How long did that go on?

Bestor: Until just before the arbitration this spring. The layers had always been allowed to cut singles when they were ahead of the marker. That's the way a layer could learn something about cutting and it gave them a chance to earn a little extra money. The cutters finally put up a howl and said that was a cutter's job. I told Ed Dekran that I thought it was all right and asked if I could see Leo about it. He told me to go ahead; he said the small lays wouldn't come in much more anyway. But they did keep coming in and things got worse instead of better. Finally I spoke to Leo and told him all about it. "Look here," he said, "you can cut singles"; so I went on, but the cutters didn't like it.

One afternoon I came in and some of the fellows including the cutters weren't there. I asked Pacetti about it and he told me they were out but that it was O.K. to go ahead with my work. Two days later they came back and I said "hello," but no one spoke to me. When Dennis, the marker from New York, left a few weeks ago, they put me in his place. You know I think he left because none of those fellows in the cutting room would talk to him. The fellows weren't talking to me either; but they used to call me names in such a way that I could overhear them. Finally they said they were angry because I worked when they were out. I told them I had permission from Pacetti. Then they felt a little low because they didn't know that, and they wanted everything to be forgotten. I'm doing Don Piano's work since he left.

Interviewer: You went from layer to marker in one jump. That job must keep your hands full.

Bestor: I'm a little slow now, of course.

Interviewer: Do all the new men begin as layers?

Bestor: That's how they begin to learn.

Interviewer: That boy, Pete Paloti, is a new layer; who is showing him how to do things?

Bestor: He asked me several times how to do things. I used to tell him to ask Vito [Albani]. He is Vito's layer. He said he didn't play around with those fellows.

Interviewer: I don't think he knows many people around here.

Bestor: I didn't even know he lived in Hamilton until a little while ago. You see, I don't see much of fellows in the shop.

V. From an Interview with Tom De Vivio, Layer

[The conversation took place at one end of Tom's table on the cutting floor.]

De Vivio: Of course, I just came on this job recently; but I can tell you that these fellows are hard to work with. They don't give you much help and they make you do things which are wrong. I worked at Vito's table at first and learned a good many tricks of the trade.

Interviewer: What are the tricks of the trade?

De Vivio: Oh, little things that they want you to do. A marker has his own ways of doing things; and he wants you to do them that way, too. For example, if there is a small piece to be marked separately because the cloth is too short, they will slip it into the lay and cut the whole thing together.

Interviewer: How can you cut the whole thing together if one piece is too short?

De Vivio: They can divide it up and put in one part here and one there, so that a single marking will do for almost all of it.

Interviewer: That looks like a pretty efficient scheme.

De Vivio: It's O.K., but they are getting paid for two markings and they should go to the boss and tell him what they are doing. Let me explain another place where the layer can get into trouble. The lay sometimes shrinks a bit after the cloth is down, and I've been caught three times for not having it long enough. If the lay is short, the marker will have a tough time; he may have to work on it all morning to make it fit. So they keep telling me to leave a half-inch. I'd rather talk to the boss anyway. I know what kind of a man he is.

Interviewer: Mario Salvati is a fairly new layer; does he manage to get along all right?

De Vivio: He has the same trouble. You know those fellows expect you to do everything their way. When Mario first came here, he was almost convinced they were the bosses. Sometimes they would wait for him and me down the street and call us names. Mario and I are the same type and don't like trouble; but the other day I said to them, "Go ahead and get fresh if you like; we have plenty of friends in the club now."

Interviewer: What club is that?

De Vivio: The Iroquois Club. Quite a few from the shop belong to it. Tony Feranti, a presser, and Peter Lombardo, foreman in the trimming department, are members and five from the shop downstairs.

Interviewer: How about the union? Do many people go to the union meetings?

De Vivio: The union is a farce around here. I went to a meeting awhile ago and there were only 12 people there—all from the cutting room. The people around here don't care about the union; most of them just wanted to work and mind their own business. Then the big shots came along and the place was unionized.

Interviewer: I had the impression that the management wanted the union to come in.

De Vivio: I suppose it's an advantage for a clothing factory to have a union. All these little stores figure they are sure of good workmanship if they find the union label. But these fellows in the cutting room don't tell the union members about their affairs. They just sort of use the union; they act as if they *are* the union. The rest of the shop don't pay much attention to it unless they think they are going to lose half a cent; then they all turn out. You know the Bartolos have done a lot for these people but some of them don't appreciate it.

Interviewer: You don't work at Vito's [Albani] table any more, do you?

De Vivio: I was moved to Don Piano's table. He's different; that's why I wanted to work with him.

Interviewer: I wonder why Don left.

De Vivio: I think he knew what was right, but didn't want to go against his friends. At one time he was to be a foreman, but he wasn't made for that job.

Interviewer: Who is your marker now?

De Vivio: Paul Bestor. He took Don's place. When he came, he was in the same position. He had to do everything their way. But he wouldn't take any back talk.

Interviewer: Mr. Schwartz must have quite a job on his hands as foreman.

De Vivio: Arthur tells them where they get off. It takes guts for that job. It takes a man who knows right from wrong.

VI. FROM A SECOND INTERVIEW WITH TOM DE VIVIO

De Vivio [who brought up the subject of Aaron voluntarily]: You know Aaron [Kastanian], don't you? What a guy! He takes singing lessons at $5 an hour. Isn't that ridiculous! They sure must have made him think he was good. Of course, all his friends tell him he's good; and he likes that. He's a fellow who wants to appear superior because he's physically weak. He sang at the union meeting the other night.

Interviewer: He must be pretty good if they asked him to sing at the meeting.

De Vivio: They didn't ask him! He just got up and requested it. Then there was some talk going on for awhile and he was sore and wouldn't start. Then someone shouted, "Go ahead, what are you waiting for? Don't you think we can hear you?" Say, did he turn white!

Interviewer: You were pretty young when you went to work here, weren't you?

De Vivio: I was only 16. They thought I had been put in as a stooge.

Interviewer: What did they want you to do?

De Vivio: They wanted me to walk out when they did and keep my eyes closed. If you do anything in favor of the boss in that place, they avoid you.

Interviewer: What kind of things did you have to do in favor of the boss?

De Vivio: Well, for instance, a couple of seasons ago a bunch of work came in and they couldn't rush it fast enough. The boss asked us to work Saturday morning and some of us did. Well, what didn't they do but call us scabs and everything. What they want is to control the room.

Interviewer: Did you ever consult Pacetti?

De Vivio: Sure, but he said it was O.K. He never had any fault to find with me. He said to me once, "What can you do with those guys? They're a pack of tigers." There was a time when you couldn't say a word in this place; they were supreme.

Interviewer: When was this?

De Vivio: About two seasons ago.

Interviewer: Has that changed any?

De Vivio: Since the arbitration, yes.

Interviewer: You think the arbitration decision had some effect on them?

De Vivio: Well, it should have. We all were watching for it. I myself was ready to quit this place a little while ago.

Interviewer: Why?

De Vivio: There was no harmony here. Just quarrels and fights. The only way to have any peace was to do just what they told you. Take Pete [Paloti]; he caught Vito trying to chisel and called the foreman. Say, I saw Don [Piano] yesterday. Is he happy!

Interviewer: Why do you think he left?

De Vivio: He knew he was doing wrong. He saw it was the only way out.

Interviewer: Did he tell you that?

De Vivio: Sure. He called those fellows a bunch of bums.

Interviewer: Don seemed like a nice fellow.

De Vivio: He was. Leo himself knew that. He wasn't the type who wanted to report chiseling. So the only thing he could do was to get out.

Interviewer: How's Pete Paloti getting on now?

De Vivio: He's getting along all right. He's going to join the Iroquois Club. He comes down there every night, you know.

Interviewer: I thought you said there were only a few fellows from the shop in that club.

De Vivio: We were all in the club before we started working here. We're all fellows who live around that region, and have for quite a long time. [Pause.] I've gotten awfully disgusted with this place here, and it's the same downstairs with the pressers. There are a few big shots there and if the boss happens to be in a hurry and a fellow wants to help him, they make life miserable for him. A lot of times Vito has told me, "Give it one or two extra [inches]." He used to do it because he wanted to, and I did it because I didn't know what it was all about. There was one time when the cutters spoiled a whole lay because it was marked the wrong size. Instead of reporting it, they cut it into small pieces. Sometimes, like then, the foreman is out of the room. Of course, they could use some of that cloth on extra pants. But most of it was just wasted.

You see, what they're trying to do is to get everyone under their thumb so the boss won't hear about their mistakes. Of course, it puts a fellow in a pretty mean place to report other people's mistakes. Once I was told that if I kept quiet, I would be made a cutter. They said the union would see to it, and they could handle the union any time.

Interviewer: You thought they could arrange to have a man promoted?

De Vivio: I figured they were the leaders. That's the impression they gave me, but after this season I saw that the boss could put anyone in. When Paul Bestor was made a marker, that showed me.

VII. From an Interview with Peter Paloti

[This conversation took place on a Friday afternoon in the cutting room. The whole shop had been let out on account of the August heat, and the room was almost empty.]

Interviewer: Tell me how you came in as a layer.

Paloti: That was only about three months ago. This is a miserable place to work. They have nagged me and made my life miserable for me. Everything they tell me is wrong. My marker will tell me to leave an inch and a half; I do it and get bawled out for it. They say I'm hired as a stool pigeon for the boss, but I don't want to do that. All I want is to do my own work and not be on either side. But "You've got to be for us," that's what they say. Vito told me, "You can't play both sides. You can only play one deck of cards." I started to say how I got hired. Leo [Bartolo] hired me, you see; but I don't want Vito to know it.

Interviewer: How could he help knowing it?

Paloti: Well, I told him I approached the boss to get a job.

Interviewer: How did you really get it?

Paloti: We met at Bonanno's house—Minzio's his brother-in-law, you know. You see, the girl I've been going around with is a cousin of Bonanno. I was at dinner at Bonanno's place when I met Leo, and that's the reason they got the idea I was a stool pigeon. Vito told me, "Get smart and be a stool pigeon, and tell us what the boss says." But I didn't see where I'd get that way, so one day I said to Ed Dekran, "Does it pay to play politics with the boys? Where do you get by doing that?" Ed's not satisfied now and is all ready to turn to the other side. When I first came in he said, "Don't talk to Paul Bestor." But look where Paul has gotten. Some of those fellows have been here four years, and Paul has come up from a layer to a marker.

Interviewer: Who takes charge of a new layer?

Paloti: Paul helped me out a lot and Arthur Schwartz, too, but that's more than these fellows do. What makes me nervous is the way Vito tells me, "Allow an inch." "Take your time." But a marker should set the patterns in the least possible cloth. You can ruin the boss right here in the cutting room by wasting cloth. I'm not going to let those fellows put it all over me. Mario Salvati opposed them when he first came in. Tom De Vivio came to me and said: "Play your cards right with the boss and you'll get along all right here."

Interviewer: Tell me about how long you three layers have been here.

Paloti: Tom has been here about two years. Mario Salvati has been around about a year and a half. I've only been here three months.

Interviewer: Did you start as a layer?

Paloti: I was in the trimming department first. Then I came here as layer. Paul Bestor was telling me how. Not a soul was speaking to Paul then, and I overheard Aaron say, "That guy has been hired as a stool pigeon."

Do you remember Mario Colombo? He's a sponger. He used to go to lunch with me. Mario's daughter and his son would eat there too in the sponging room. Vito and the others told me not to talk to Mario. I wanted to play in with the boys at that time. One day I did speak to him and he said, "What! No one around now, so you're not afraid!" Why shouldn't I speak to him? Why shouldn't I speak to anyone I like?

VIII. From an Interview with Vito Albani

[The interviewer had just arrived on the cutting floor, and Albani inter-rupted his work to talk for a few minutes.]

Interviewer: I didn't see you Friday afternoon.

Albani: I'm sorry I missed you, but it was so hot they let the whole shop out. We all went swimming.

Interviewer: All the cutters and markers?

Albani: And the layers too—everyone. We get along all right with them outside the shop, you know. It's only when a fellow goes against you that you can't put up with him. The girls over there went too; it's the first time the girls have come with us.

Interviewer: Pete [Paloti] was here on Friday. He must have been the only one who didn't go with you.

Albani: He's a fellow I don't want to see anyway, either outside the shop or inside.

Interviewer: Joe [Adalian] told me as I came in that they had moved Paul Bestor and the rest of his table over to the other cutting room. Arthur Schwartz is over there, too. I wonder why they did that? Is it a permanent arrangement?

Albani: I tell you, they're going to make it tough for us guys. He's go-ing to have us working one day a week pretty soon, if he can.

IX. From an Interview with Aaron Kastanian, Taking Place by Appointment at His Home

[He lived on the second floor of a double house outside of Hamilton. He explained that he preferred a location not too close to other people so he would not disturb them when he was singing. He showed the interviewer some of his music, including the scores of "Carmen" and a number of Italian operas which seemed to please him particularly. He said he had always enjoyed singing, but had taken lessons only in the last three years, and pre-vious to that time was not able to read music. His small daughter, aged about 12, took piano lessons, but he himself did not play any instrument. He planned to give his second daughter musical training, too.]

Interviewer: Tell me a little more about this fellow Scarlati, who had something to do with organizing Bartolo Brothers for the first time.

Kastanian: Scarlati and Vito Albani used to work together. Scarlati was the man who brought the union into this shop.

Interviewer: How do you go about that kind of a job?

Kastanian: They do it in this way: First, they approach the most im-portant of the cutters, markers, and pressers. They have secret meetings and then call a strike. Then the union sends out a man to address a meeting and organize them.

Interviewer: It was the regional office of the Amalgamated, wasn't it, which helped to organize Bartolo Brothers?

Kastanian: There are a number of shops [in this region] and all these shops send representatives to a meeting every week where they discuss their problems. Every Thursday, Scarlati and a couple of other fellows, Mancini and Donshian—Donshian is an Armenian like us—used to go to the meeting. Leo hated that because he used to think that in those discussions his competitors would get information.

Interviewer: Did that scheme work pretty well?

Kastanian: It used to work pretty well, but later on a lot of politics came in. Leo managed to set the pressers against the cutters and the cutters against the markers, so that everyone was against everyone else.

Interviewer: How could he do that?

Kastanian: By bringing in stool pigeons who are really spies and could now be punished under the law. But we have never gone as far as to ask for that. [Pause.] The union here does not work as it should. Every other shop has a shop chairman, a man who acts like an inside business agent.

Interviewer: Do the layers usually act with you union men?

Kastanian: Well, they did before. In 1937, when the general raise came, Leo didn't want to raise the pressers and cutters. We told him, "This doesn't cost you anything; it simply goes on the price of the suit. Every firm is willing to do that, if all the others do it too." That was the time that New York sent up all their best men to organize the textile industry. We stayed out six weeks until it was settled; and when we came back, Leo said, "I don't want John, I don't want Eddie." They were two of our layers then. We phoned Marconi and insisted that they stay. Finally, he promised that they should stay, and we believed him. Leo didn't like it and later in the fall, after we had all been out between seasons, he said he had no more work for Eddie and John. In the meantime, he hired Mario Salvati, a kid from the shipping room, and that boy Tom De Vivio. The trouble was that Pacetti didn't back us up. Pacetti wasn't really with us.

Interviewer: Tell us a little bit about how you got on in the old days before there was any foreman.

Kastanian: Leo used to tell us, "You are as good as a foreman." He trusted us, and we used to work hard to save cloth for him. Very often we'd waste an hour of our own time to save him some cloth. Well, I suppose this new man wanted to make a position for himself, and Leo put him in.

[At this point, Mrs. Kastanian came in and explained some of her own difficulties. She worked in the shop downstairs, and one of her grievances (settled) had concerned the amount of her weekly earnings as compared with some of the girls who were relatively new. The interviewer was asked to supper after that, but refused.]

X. Outline of a Later Conversation with Aaron Kastanian

One day the interviewer spent some time chatting in a casual manner with Aaron Kastanian on the cutting floor and picked up the following information:

He was born in Armenia, and his father was a butcher and grocer. Before the war (*i.e.*, World War I), two older brothers and a sister had come to this country. He was the youngest of the family. During the war, when he was only 10, his father was "massacred" by the Turks; he was executed by a cannon shot, according to Aaron's story. Shortly afterwards, he and his mother and sister made a journey to Aleppo along with many other Armenians, most of whom died on the way. In Aleppo he worked as a servant in a mess hall for German soldiers. He did not like the Germans. Later on, when the British occupied Aleppo, he worked for British soldiers. He liked the English and said they amused themselves and were gay during their spare time, unlike the Germans, who were always fooling with mechanical contrivances. At the end of the war he and his mother came to this country. She had always lived with him. He said his father was a wise and moderate man who never encouraged them to rebel against the Turks.

Aaron continued from here to discuss his personal interests. He said that he always preferred to discuss "serious" topics when he was out with his friends. If he were free to do what he liked, he would choose to be an opera singer. He was interested in love affairs and liked to give people advice on this sort of thing. His first infatuation occurred when he was 16, but this was merely "puppy love" and his mother put a stop to it. Later he fell in love with an American-born Armenian girl, who was very beautiful, very much sought after, but "spoiled." Her mother expected her to have all the luxuries of a Hollywood actress, and, of course, he was unable to provide them. He "suffered terribly" from this incident.

When asked what serious topics he liked to discuss, he mentioned "nature" and "fate." These words seemed to refer to peculiarities of people, and to what happened to them. He was interested in people's personal problems and always read Elsie Robinson's column in the papers. People were worried about many things, such as their business and their wives, he explained, and it was important for them to get rid of fear. He thought many difficulties which people experienced were due to fear. He thought that Christian Science had "the right idea" about this sort of thing, although he himself didn't go to the Christian Science Church. He pointed out that "many great men" had been troubled by fear, but had overcome it. From the topic of personal problems and fear, the conversation shifted to women; and he expressed the opinion that the man should be the master in his house and that women preferred a dominating man.

Discussion Questions

1. On your chart listing "The Seven," indicate the further changes in the clique's position in the cutting room revealed by these interviews.

2. What methods have "The Seven" utilized in their efforts to establish a controlling influence in the cutting room?

3. Trace from these interviews the "defense" clique forming in the cutting room to resist the pressures of "The Seven." List their names and trace the methods of defensive action and counterattack they are developing, as well as the sources of support upon which they seem to place reliance. Contrast those sources of support with those claimed by "The Seven."

4. What further insights do these interviews furnish into the personality traits and shop behavior of Aaron Kastanian?

5. Evaluate the problems of the union field representative as suggested by the interviews and performance of Pacetti and his successor, Donati.

6. List the changes that management has made thus far in the organization of the cutting room, and give your evaluation of their probable objectives.

7. What further insights into ethnic and community factors as influences upon shop relationships are furnished in these interviews?

BARTOLO BROTHERS (E)

THE DISCHARGE OF JOHNNY SALVATORE

As the summer drew to a close, a third dispute was submitted to Mr. Colton. Excerpts from the hearing, held on September 23, 1940, follow:

Present for the Management   *Present for the Union*
Minzio Bonanno, Foreman in the   Vincent Donati, Business Agent
    Cutting Room   John Salvatore, Cutter
Peter Paloti, Layer

Arbitrator: Well, gentlemen, what is this about today?

Donati (u): Last Friday while I was in New York at our union headquarters, Johnny Salvatore was looking all over for me. I came back and saw him, and he told me he was afraid that he had lost his job.

The last decision you gave made the firm feel that they had the right to get quality in the cutting department. So in the matter of matching stripes, they decided to put one person on the job of cutting striped material. Under the old system in matching stripes, when you cut a whole lay through, the cutting was rough, and it had to be cut again. This new way you cut each one right the first time. Mr. Bonanno asked Johnny to do it and told him he could think it over. Mr. Bonanno has recently been made foreman again since Mr. Schwartz was moved to the other shop.

Bonanno (m): I didn't just tell him to think it over. I asked Johnny to do this job for a few hours a day on week-work, and he refused. So I said, "Well, think it over." He said no, that he wouldn't get enough pay on week-work. I said, "You start on it and if you aren't satisfied, you can take it up with the business agent when he comes. Just do the work." I coaxed him two or three times during the day. Then I asked Joe [Adalian] to try to convince Johnny to do the work and not to leave. But he wouldn't do it that day. So I told Johnny to think it over and let me know in the morning. In the morning, Johnny said no again. He had decided that he didn't want to do it. So I said that that was the only work I had for him.

Donati (u): This is Johnny's first time in trouble, Mr. Colton. He is considered a "good boy." Inasmuch as Johnny was wrong—I admit it—I feel that the punishment he has had (he has been out of work for a week) is enough. I have already instructed them that no one else can do this and if they do, I won't take up the case. I admit that he was wrong in not doing the work, but I don't believe in "capital" punishment.

Arbitrator: Johnny, what is your story? Why did you refuse to do the work?

Salvatore (u): I didn't see any future in it. I was a marker, cutter, and layer.

Arbitrator: Did you do singles and specials?

Salvatore (u): I did specials and regulars too. I didn't see any future in doing this work. I like to mark and cut, and if I did this, all my time would be taken up with matching stripes.

Donati (u): Isn't it also a question of earnings?

Salvatore (u): Yes, I would earn more marking and cutting.

Bonanno (m): I would like to ask Johnny a few questions. But first I want to tell you how these seven cutters always make trouble. That is why I brought this man [indicating Peter] with me. He is a learner in the cutting department. He is new and works slowly and holds them up. Sometimes they have been after him not to work too fast. But most of the time they swear at him for not working fast enough. Because he is slow, I kept him overtime, and they objected. They do everything to aggravate the firm. So they call this boy names. One time, a girl made a mistake in the width of the cloth, and to straighten out the lays I took some of their pieces and gave it to Pete because he could cut it at the same time that he was cutting his. They called him a robber and accused him of taking their money away from them. Johnny isn't a man on his own hook. He is one of those seven —there are just five now in my cutting room since Don left, and Ed was moved—and he is highly influenced by the others. He does what they tell him, and he is suffering for it. If he is going to tell me that he won't do some work, I cannot run my floor. Two months ago, he wasn't making half as much as he is now. Isn't that right, Johnny?

Salvatore (u): I guess that's about right.

Bonanno (m): I gave him the chance to make more money by being a cutter. I taught him. Still he quits. I cannot run a floor if they refuse to work. We must have discipline.

Salvatore (u): I thought I was doing right; and, as for being influenced, no one influenced me.

Arbitrator [to Johnny]: Is it your understanding that you can refuse the foreman when he asks you to do something? Do you think the union gives you that right?

Salvatore (u): I thought I was doing right. He wanted to change my job and I was satisfied where I was.

Bonanno (m): Who gave you that job? I didn't give you any signature on it when you began cutting and marking. If I gave you a chance, if I teach you how to do the work, if I waste my time and the boss' cloth, and then I ask you to do me a favor and you turn me down, is that right?

Arbitrator: What makes you think you had the right to refuse?

Salvatore (u): All the time they put me on odds and ends. I was sick of it. I thought I should stay where I was.

Donati (u): I don't think he had the right to refuse. I say that he was wrong to refuse and that Mr. Bonanno is right. But this is "capital" punishment. It is too much for a small thing.

Arbitrator: Is it really a small thing?

Donati (u): He never did it before. He has been a good boy.

Bonanno (m): He walked out with them, when they walked out on their jobs. He always acts with them.

Arbitrator: There is no question that Mr. Bonanno was acting in good faith. [To Johnny.] Do you see that you didn't do right?

Salvatore (u): I thought I was doing right.

Donati (u): What do you think now? [Salvatore did not answer.]

Arbitrator: I am not sure that I can order you reinstated. I can try to persuade the firm to take you back on the grounds that it is your first actual insubordination. But if I do this, I want you to realize the seriousness of what you did. If you have a complaint, then you can come to the union and finally to me. That is the machinery which the union has established. But you have no right to walk out on a job. [To Donati.] Somehow, I can't get the fellows in Bartolo Brothers to understand that. They act as if there were no contract. Every time they think of something they don't like, they take the law in their own hands.

Bonanno (m): Now there is something brewing in the shop. I meant to take it up with Donati before, but I forgot to do it. I had more peace before I was foreman. Those five sit there and waste time. They talk to this one and to that one, tell jokes and stories. Now I don't want them to break their necks, but I want them to work. They sit and chew the rag all day long. When Angelo or Leo comes around they work quietly. But when they aren't around Aaron and Vito talk all the time. As soon as they see the boss, they stop. It's just like I'm nobody there. If Johnny comes back, I'll give up my job. I'll go back on the bench. I have to show discipline.

Arbitrator: How long has he been out of work?

Donati (u): One week.

Arbitrator: That's some punishment for him. I don't want to make a decision that you must take him back.

Bonanno (m): I have nothing against him personally. I have always tried to help him.

Arbitrator: Why not give him another chance?

Bonanno (m): Maybe a little later. Not now.

Arbitrator [to Johnny]: How can you come to the arbitrator and say that you have the right to refuse to do work, and say no when you are asked to do a certain job? It ruins the morale of the whole shop. Mr. Bonanno has to be respected. He represents the firm. You will never get anywhere if there is always bad blood.

Donati (u): The misdeed that Johnny has done was paid for by losing a week's work.

Bonanno (m): Personally I think he paid too much. But for the discipline of the shop, I can't take him back. This is a clean-cut case. I couldn't face the firm if I took him back. Later on, maybe I'll be able to do it. The season is almost over. Next season I'll take him back. I like him personally; he is a good boy. But I must establish prestige on the floor. He wanted to play the hero's part. Now take Vito, he is shrewd. He does things, but you can never pin anything on him. I know these boys; I've worked with them for ten years. Johnny is an innocent boy. He has been misled.

Arbitrator: Why don't you bring charges against those who are responsible? Aaron and Vito are on probation.

Bonanno (m): I know it, but I can't prove anything against them. Aaron is way behind in his production. Vito is much less so. They said they would cooperate. For one day they did, and then the next day it was the same as before. It is nothing you can prove. I can't take photographs. I can't ask Johnny to be a witness against his friends. In fact, Johnny's refusal to work is the first definite thing I could pin on any of that gang. I don't want the impossible. This man Pete works overtime sometimes. They give him hell. Johnny is the victim of all this. I know that; still, if he comes back, I'll tell the boss to get someone else to be foreman. I have to have some satisfaction. There must be discipline.

Donati (u): That has to be the keynote. There must be discipline. This fellow [indicating Bonanno] knows all about unions. [Laughed.] He's a revolutionary.

Bonanno (m): I've been everything. I was a syndicalist; I was a socialist; now I don't know what I am.

Arbitrator: Were you a member of the IWW?

Bonanno (m): No. I was a follower of Emma Goldman ever since I was a kid. I went to Coaltown to picket, and I was in jail for three months. That was the first raw deal I ever got. I was walking along minding my own business and a cop came and beat me up. So I went to jail overnight; and when I went to court, I wanted to have the cop arrested. When I told this to the judge, he gave me ninety days.

Arbitrator [to Peter]: Have you ever done any work like this before?

Paloti (m): This is my first job in the clothing racket.

Donati (u): This is an industry; it isn't any racket.

Paloti (m): All right, industry. It's just a word. I was always good to the other fellows. But I didn't want them to call me names. I was just learning and I don't work very fast, so I came in early and worked overtime sometimes just to help them out. If I didn't get the work ready for them, they wouldn't have anything to do. But they still called me names. I got sore. I asked them why they called me those names and they said because I came in early and worked late. If I lay more, the more they have to mark and cut. I told them I was doing it for them.

Donati (u): No boss can compel you to go into work early.

Bonanno (m): I don't compel him; I just ask him to work overtime sometimes so that we can get the work out. This is only until he learns the work and can work faster.

Paloti (m): I can't help it if I'm not fast; I just wasn't born that way. [To Donati.] If you and I are on one team and I don't produce enough work to keep the rest of the team busy, then I'm no good to the team.

Bonanno (m): This boy is trying to learn a trade. He takes more cloth than is necessary, and it takes him more time. He won't take orders from Aaron and Vito, so they call him names.

Donati (u): When these things come up, I should know about it. If you have a complaint, Pete, you should tell me about it. They have no right to abuse you. This is a good industry and an honorable one. You have the same rights that they have.

Paloti (m): What right have they to tell me what to do?

Donati (u): They have no right to tell you anything. That's what the union is for. You should tell me about anything that isn't right.

Bonanno (m) [to Pete]: He's right. You should tell him of any complaints you have.

Arbitrator [to Donati]: You will have to explain to them just what the union stands for and what it can do for them—what their rights and privileges are as members of the union.

Donati (u): I tried to do that, and they began to mock the union.

Bonanno (m): I think that, between us, Mr. Donati and I can straighten out this problem of Pete's.

Paloti (m): What I'm interested in is my living. I didn't know that I should tell Mr. Donati if anything was wrong. No one told me 'til now. Now I know and I have some support; I have them to protect me. [To Donati.] I didn't know what to do.

Donati (u): I spent three days last week in Hamilton, and what did I accomplish? [To the arbitrator.] You told me to have a meeting of the men. I called one and they were forced to come, by our saying that they would be fined if they didn't. Eight hundred came. They leave and say "Why should we pay dues of 25 cents?" Now this boy [indicating Pete] is wasting his money. It's the use you make of the union that makes it important to you.

Bonanno (m): The boys treated him like a dog.

Donati (u): Then he should come to me and complain.

Arbitrator: I think you have quite a problem in educating the workers. They have to learn what are their rights and what are the management's rights. Johnny thought he had a right to quit.

Bonanno (m): Johnny made one statement in confidence that I don't know if he wants me to repeat here. If not, just let him say that he didn't say it. I'm willing; I won't mind because I'll understand why he denies it. He said, "I have the support of the boys." I feel that you are right, Johnny. It's someone else in back of you that isn't doing right.

Salvatore (u): I did make that statement, but I didn't mean what you say. I meant that the union is in back of me.

Arbitrator: Well, gentlemen, I think that is all we can do today. I'll have to try to get the firm to take you back, Johnny, but I don't know if they will.

Both the union and the management desired a formal decision on this case. Despite his reluctance to render one, the arbitrator accordingly did submit a written decision on the discharge of John Salvatore. Excerpts follow:

In order to improve the quality of the cutting of striped cloth, the management decided to cut single pieces of cloth instead of having it cut in piles as hitherto had been the custom. . . . The management further decided to assign the job of cutting single pieces to John Salvatore. Mr. Bonanno, the foreman in the cutting department, instructed Salvatore on September 12 to do this work. Salvatore refused. When he continued to refuse, after several hours had elapsed, the management discharged him.

The union admits that Salvatore should not have refused to do the work, but should instead, if he had any question as to earnings or any other result, have waited to submit his grievance to Mr. Donati, the union representative. Nevertheless, Mr. Donati pleaded that Salvatore be reinstated because this was his first offense; he had always been a quiet member of the group in the cutting department; to remove him from the job permanently was tantamount to "capital punishment."

The decision of the arbitrator is as follows:

While he realizes the serious implications for Salvatore in not being able to return to employment, he must nevertheless sustain the management in its right to discharge employees for refusing instructions of the foreman. The agreement between the union and the management provides for orderly adjustment of any dispute which may arise. Every workman has the right to invoke this agreement if he feels in any way aggrieved. To permit employees to refuse to carry out instructions of the management would mean the destruction, not only of the efficiency and discipline of the shop, but also of the agreement . . . and the machinery provided under it for arbitration.

The arbitrator cannot therefore see his way clear to order the reinstatement of Salvatore. He hopes, however, that the management will be willing to give Salvatore another chance. He has undoubtedly already learned a lesson from this experience. Such reinstatement, however, must be entirely voluntary on the part of the management. The management as well as the workers have rights under the agreement, and the arbitrator must see to it that the rights of both parties are maintained.

DISCUSSION QUESTIONS

1. Define the precipitating event leading to the discharge of Johnny Salvatore in terms of shop administration.

2. What, in essence, was the case (a) management urged in support of the discharge and (b) the union urged for its mitigation? Evaluate their respective positions.

3. Analyze Salvatore's behavior in the shop situation, stating your hypothesis as to the various motivations that seem to explain it.

4. Evaluate the administrative problems presented to the union by the testimony of Peter Paloti as a member of the "defense" clique, Johnny Salvatore as one of "The Seven," and Foreman Bonanno as a representative of management.

5. Given the arbitrator's emphasis on the gravity of Salvatore's shop offense, how would you explain his reluctance to render a formal decision? Evaluate the decision which he did finally make.

6. On the "clique chart," indicate the further changes made in the make-up of "The Seven" in this case.

BARTOLO BROTHERS (F)

THE FURTHER DISCIPLINE OF AARON KASTANIAN

During the opening weeks of the next year, a dispute submitted for arbitration involved Aaron Kastanian. Excerpts from the decision upon it, dated January 22, 1941, follow:

This dispute arose when a size 40 front was used on a size 38 coat and a size 38 front on a size 40 coat. The mistake was discovered only after a shipment of 82 suits had been made to the customer. The customer returned all of the 82 suits. An examination disclosed that 28 suits in this lot had either size 38 fronts on size 40 suits or size 40 fronts on size 38 suits.

Mr. Aaron Kastanian was the marker on these 82 suits. He claimed that to the best of his recollection he wrote the proper sizes with chalk, and attached pink tickets setting forth these sizes; that generally when Mr. Schwartz, the foreman, did not find a pink ticket on a lay, as he examined the work, he would himself pin a pink ticket on it, and copy the size of the lay on the ticket from the chalk marks made by the marker.

The foreman has no recollection of this particular order, but it is a fact that sometimes he would attach a pink ticket on a lay when it was missing and write the size on it from the chalked information left by the marker. In this instance it would have been necessary for the foreman to have pinned a pink ticket on two lays, marking the ticket on the size 38 lay as size 40 and the ticket on the size 40 lay as size 38.

The question before me, then, concerns the responsibility for this mistake. The company claims serious losses: (1) the cost of altering 28 suits, amounting to $51.76; (2) a resale loss of $3.00 per suit for 82 suits, making a total loss of $297.76; and (3) a probable loss of future business from this customer.

It is agreed that Mr. Kastanian did mark these suits; that it was his duty to mark these suits with their proper sizes and pin on each lay a ticket with the size marked on it; that all subsequent workers in all other sections would depend upon the sizes indicated by Mr. Kastanian as the correct sizes.

I find, therefore, that Mr. Kastanian is responsible for this mistake. I cannot, however, agree that he should be held liable for all the damages claimed by the employer on these 82 suits. Only 28 suits were marked incorrectly. The cost for remedying this mistake was $51.76. I hereby assess against Mr. Kastanian liability for the damage to the 28 suits in the amount of $51.76.

DISCUSSION QUESTIONS

1. Again give your hypothesis as to the reasoning and objectives of the arbitrator in his decision on this shop episode, and give your own critical judgment upon it.

2. On your "clique chart," indicate the change, if any, that this decision makes in the group organization of "The Seven."

BARTOLO BROTHERS (G)

THE NATIONAL STABILIZATION PROGRAM

I

By January, 1941, the stabilization program which the union had been evolving for some years reached the Bartolo shop. The program, in preparation since 1933, was directed in 1939 toward eliminating wage cutting as a form of competition. Garments manufactured were to be divided according to quality and quantity of workmanship into six grades. The operations on each garment were listed, specifications set, and a standard labor cost fixed for each.

At Bartolo's, although the quality of garment produced ranked as Grade 4, its price range and out-of-town location were made controlling to bring its rating down to Grade 3. To the consternation of management, the national union's "enforcement officers," after thorough study and discussion, deemed labor costs per suit 17½% below standard. The demand that they be raised accordingly was submitted to arbitration.

Both sides made this arbitration proceeding a hearing of highly formal importance. Mr. Leo Bartolo, although attending both of its sessions (January 25 and February 8, 1941), was represented by counsel who pressed every possible point to delay application of the program to the Hamilton shop. The union was represented by the national director of its stabilization department and the director of its research department, as well as its usual regional director and local business agent. A large delegation of rank-and-file workers also attended, representing the processes particularly involved—pressing, cutting, and sewing. Among the representatives of the cutting rooms were Aaron Kastanian and Guido Battista.

But through the formalities of the hearing, flares of feeling would occasionally obtrude themselves. Mr. Bartolo, for instance, again aroused resentment by dilating upon his special costs for training labor at Hamilton and his competitive disadvantages against Capitol City. The workers in turn angered him by comparing their earnings with those of comparable craftsmen at the Belmont Company. Ultimately, however, the company's case concentrated upon its financial inability to meet these new "standard" costs; a 17½% increase in wages would, they claimed, force them out of business. But as documents and arguments seeking to prove this financial stringency were presented by company counsel, the attitude of the rank-and-file workers became openly derisive. The following testimony then ensued (Mr. Bartolo's lawyer was Mr. Herbert Kauffman; he, and the presser, Ricardo Scarlati, the marker, Aaron Kastanian, Regional Director Frank Santo, and the arbitrator speak in this excerpt):

Kauffman (m) [interrupting his analysis of an accountant's audit of the company's books]: The union is at liberty to examine our books and see for themselves that there have been no unusual withdrawals and charges, in spite of the fact that the people working there may think that there is a lot of money being made. These gentlemen [indicating Scarlati and Kastanian] seem to be smirking as I read these figures.

Arbitrator: The workers have adequate representation through their union. You have made it clear that the firm is willing to submit its figures to the union experts.

Scarlati (u): I don't know how a firm loses money and expands every year.

Kastanian (u): What we think doesn't make any difference. We are here like a shadow. Our officers are handling this case. But I just want to say one thing. Some of us started with Leo Bartolo when he began the business about 12 years ago. We know what we have seen. We saw them start with about 20 workers in a little shop, and we see them today. I don't know any firm that grew so fast. We can remember when some of us in the cutting room loaned the Bartolos money to keep them going when they struck a hard place. Once the Bartolos felt like one of us; we worked together and were friends outside the shop too. But now—well we think they've grown pretty big. After all, it's funny to hear we are not familiar with things at Bartolo's; we've seen everything happening since the start.

Santo (u): It's a pretty funny thing when a man says he's sick and still gets fat. The workers only know that the firm is expanding. If that is so, how is it that the owners aren't earning much money?

Kauffman (m): The fact that the firm is expanding may be why it is now losing money. They may be making such a low profit on each suit that they have to try to sell a great many suits. They may have to be able to produce a lot to keep their best customers.

Arbitrator [to Kauffman]: Don't be so sensitive about the way the men may look when you make certain statements. They have union representatives to present their case. Your figures are now on the record; and unless they can convincingly challenge them, it will be up to them to explain the situation to the men. The men have a stake in keeping the firm solvent; they want to hold their jobs. On the other hand, the firm wants to pay wages as good as those in comparable shops.

Kauffman (m): It's not that I'm sensitive, but I think the men are important.

Arbitrator: Certainly the men are important, and previous disputes have led me repeatedly to warn all parties of the dangers in the continued hostilities that sour the spirit at Bartolo's. The union has explicitly recognized its responsibility to work for improved shop relations; the men have been warned that they must maintain discipline and production; the firm has accepted decisions that went counter to its desires in these matters in a willingness to see if we cannot all achieve real improvement in the relationships at Bartolo's. I summarize all this as a reminder to all concerned and a recognition of your objective, Mr. Kauffman. The question on which we are focusing today is, of course, related to this basic problem of the spirit behind relationships at Bartolo's. For a national program of standardization must be translated into terms of the local jobs, earnings, and profit sheets.

The arbitrator decided that the company's proved financial condition precluded—for the safety of the workers' jobs as well as of the business—an award of more than 5% increase in wages for 1941. This aggregate increase was then allocated by joint negotiations to the rates paid for specific operations as listed in the union's price guides and production specifications for the Bartolo shop.

II

One year later, in January, 1942, the union again approached Mr. Bartolo, with the demand that, in accordance with the stabilization program, he grant a further wage increase and thus move closer to the standard levels for his grade of output. Again negotiations failed to achieve settlement.
Excerpts follow from the arbitration proceedings:

Present for the Management	*Present for the Union*
Leo Bartolo, President	Frank Santo, Regional Director
	Vincent Donati, Business Agent
	Norman Jacobs, Director ACWA Stabilization Department
	A delegation of 14 Shop Employee Representatives

Jacobs (u): In the arbitration proceedings of January 25, 1941, the union requested that the total labor cost of Bartolo Brothers for a suit be advanced 17½ per cent to bring it in conformity with the standards prevailing under the union stabilization program for out-of-town manufacturers. The arbitrator, moved by what he considered the then delicate financial condition of the firm, decided that only a 5% increase could be granted at that time. The union reconciled itself to awaiting an opportune moment to press for the balance of the adjustment. Bartolo Brothers, along with all other clothing manufacturers, has just gone through a year of unprecedented prosperity. The outlook continues favorable.

Due, no doubt, to opportunities for full-time employment at higher wages elsewhere and the whip of mounting living costs, the workers at Bartolo Brothers have been particularly insistent of late that the union secure the delayed increases. The firm has yielded to these demands to the extent of making a small number of minor upward changes, just as all other clothing manufacturers have had to do in the past seven months. But a comparison [on page 677] of Bartolo Brothers' costs in coats, pants, and vests with the standard costs in Grade 3 work indicates that there is still a wide disparity.

However, there are certain savings to which Bartolo Brothers may be entitled on their coats because they do not utilize operations up to the full

	Standard Costs	Bartolo Brothers	Deficiency
Sackcoats.......	$2.9250	$2.6618	$.2632
Pants..........	.6600	.6314	.0286
Vests..........	.5700	.5312	.0388
Total........	$4.1550	$3.8244	$.3306

specifications for Grade 3. These savings would amount to a credit of about 6.52 cents, and would reduce the deficiency in the above table to 26.54 cents, or an indicated increase of 6.94%.

Arbitrator: What actual increase are you asking for?

Jacobs (u): 26½ cents. We are not stating we want a general percentage increase.

Santo (u): Mr. Colton, the sum total of what Mr. Jacobs has said is, I believe, that for the whole garment—coat, pants, and vest—Bartolo pays something like 26½ cents less. Now we want that 26½ cents to be distributed among the lower paid workers.

Several factors contribute to justify an increase in wages. The cost of living at Hamilton is going up every day in the things that these people buy. Second, the textile workers that live next door to the Bartolo workers have received an increase in wages of 31% in the last 18 months. Some six or seven years ago, wages in Bartolo's were very good in comparison with those paid in the Armstrong Company or some of the other mills. Today that favorable differential has been upset. Finally, within our general case for an increase, some sections contain specific complaints, arising especially out of changes made in operations. Mr. Bartolo has put in an efficiency expert in the last week or two; the firm now demands much better work than they used to. Accordingly, there is the additional complaint that the existing wage rates are out of line with the quality of work demanded.

Our relationship with Mr. Bartolo has always been most pleasant. There had been early troubles, but that is not unusual. One thing we have succeeded in. There has not been a single stoppage of work or cessation of production in the past year. In this shop we have had uninterrupted production and a spirit of cooperation. It may not show on the books as part of the assets. But at the end of the year, it is there nevertheless.

Arbitrator: Well, now, how about the cutting room?

Santo (u): Oh, things are all right there too, now.

Arbitrator: How about Vito Albani and Aaron Kastanian?

Santo (u): Vito Albani left Bartolo's last spring for a job in Capitol City. Poor Aaron Kastanian committed suicide—he hung himself—in August, I think it was. [Interpolating.] I know what you refer to, but with your help as arbitrator, and with the changes in personnel that have taken place, the air has been cleared.

I know Mr. Bartolo will agree with me when I say our relationships are now cordial and cooperative. We want to keep up this good feeling. Discipline has been established. Production has been uninterrupted, and whatever disputes there were have been adjusted in an intelligent and amicable manner.

To continue such relationships, we must now show these people that peaceful means, constructive, intelligent relationships, bring as good results, if not better, than destructive relationships.

Within these past four months, Mr. Bartolo has made several adjustments and we already have agreed that he should get credit for increases already granted.

[Mr. Donati thereupon listed and explained the increases granted to workers on 10 operations; the readjustments of rates ranged from fractions of one cent to one cent per unit of production. They totaled 4 cents out of the 26½ cents the union was asking.]

Arbitrator: Let us now hear Mr. Bartolo on the general question of the increase.

Bartolo (m): I should like to say first of all that each time we are brought here we are made to appear the skunks of the industry, and that is a bad mark which I don't like for a minute. A list is submitted to our people here, and they seem to see that everyone else pays better. Well, you know how statistics are compiled. If we compiled statistics, I could put myself at the top and have a long stream of manufacturers who don't measure up to what I pay.

Now the increase amounts to something like 26 cents. Four cents has already been given. So that we are quarreling over something like 20 cents or 22 cents. First, I want to say this: the management is very concerned about wages. We would like to be in the top ranks. It is one of our ambitions, but we have been absolutely unable to do so; and we have time and again invited the union and also this office to go through and examine just what our conditions are.

We have been working as efficiently as we know how; but my accountant gave me these figures.[1] These are for the union. This is the gross business— $1,700,000.00—for the year 1941, and the net profits have been $20,000.00. Now we have no chair warmers in the place, or people who don't work. Everybody is a worker. Donati knows.

Donati (u): That is true.

---

[1] The figures were:

Net sales	$1,732,986.16
Less discounts and allowances	98,684.98
Net income from sales	$1,634,301.18
Less cost of goods sold	1,485,650.14
Gross profit on sales	$ 148,651.04
Less expenses and taxes	128,336.65
Net profit to surplus	$ 20,314.39

Bartolo (m): We try to manage as well as we know how. All our interests are involved over there. This is our account; it can be checked by the union. Therefore, if, in my estimation, there are some operations which are underpaid, I am willing to hear about them right here and now. We have separate rates for 129 operations and injustices can arise. But when it comes to a general increase, I think that would be very doubtful. When you see conditions like ours, even after a prosperous year, can you tell us how are we going to get along with higher costs?

Santo (u): All right. Suppose then we take up the special operations first. Let's start out with the armhole finishers and take them in rotation.

[The remainder of the hearing was devoted to the testimony presented by the 14 shop employees in attendance. They submitted individual grievances concerning wage rates. The union representatives and Mr. Bartolo participated in questioning these witnesses and discussing each particular grievance. A number of adjustments Mr. Bartolo accepted immediately. The others were submitted, with the major demand for a general increase of roundly 7% within the stabilization program, to the arbitrator for decision. Expressions of goodwill by the workers toward the management were frequent.]

Some days after this hearing, Mr. Colton called into his office Messrs. Bartolo, Santo, and Donati. He informed them that he had decided, in deference to the financial conditions of the company, to award an increase of only 5%, but that he wanted them to make the distribution so that inequities mentioned in the hearing would be properly adjusted. This the parties did, and the results were embodied in a formal decision.

DISCUSSION QUESTIONS

1. Evaluate the principles underlying the "stabilization program" from the viewpoint of (*a*) economic theory; (*b*) the interests of the industry as a whole; (*c*) the interests of the community; (*d*) the problems of management at the Bartolo company; and (*e*) the Bartolo company workers.

2. Evaluate critically the arbitrator's decisions in the stabilization cases.

3. Note the wage criteria urged respectively by the parties. What weights would you accord to these varying criteria?

4. Compare the "spirit" of shop relations manifested in the first stabilization hearing with that in the second.

BARTOLO BROTHERS (H)

THE FINAL BREAKUP OF "THE SEVEN"

One of the field workers who had conducted the interviews of 1940 visited Hamilton to obtain whatever information and insights he could regarding the suicide of Aaron Kastanian and current relationships in the cutting room. Excerpts from these data follow:

Minzio Bonanno: The situation is much better now. A few bad apples will spoil the whole lot. After the arbitrations, they began to feel some responsibility and things improved. You heard that Aaron [Kastanian] committed suicide? He went away for awhile and said he could not work. He was not crazy any more than you or I; he had a nervous breakdown. He had had one before and we sent him away and paid his doctor's bills. This time he was away for several months and said he could not work. The doctor told him to come back and his wife urged him to come back, because it would be better for him. We offered to let him come in and work half a day. He came in and said that he could not do it. He had the ambition to become an opera singer and was very much disappointed. He did not have much of a voice, but he spent a lot of money taking lessons. I don't think his wife liked him to spend that much money.

Vito Albani went away to Capitol City. Eddie Dekran left and got a job at Tarboro. He's in the Air Corps now. Don Piano is still working in town with Mazzola Brothers. Don was a nice boy. Eddie was a nice boy too; he was just misled. You asked about Johnny Salvatore. He got another job after he left here, but he is in the Army now. I told him I would take him back when he came home. Frankly, Aaron was the most intelligent worker of the lot. We have no teams now that do as well as Aaron and Vito did. The men we have now are learners. Joe Adalian and Guido Battista are the only two left from that crowd.

Paul Bestor: Wasn't that a mess we were in a year ago? We are all paid by the hour now, and that would be all right if we earned what we would make on piecework. I am not making what the other markers got after the arbitration, and I would get more if I was paid piece rates. I wanted to do something about it, but could not stick my neck out and be a punk. You can't say anything around here now. I spoke to young Bonanno [son of the foreman] the other day; but he is a relative, so he is in a tough spot. Most of these new men are obligated to the boss in some way. That fellow in the glasses over there is a friend of Leo's [Bartolo]—goes out to his house almost every night. He used to be a shoemaker. The fellow with the green shirt over there is a relative of Angelo's [Bartolo]. The man behind him was brought in from Capitol City.

680

Joseph Adalian: There are a lot of new people around here now. Guido and I are the only old-timers. Did you know that Aaron committed suicide? I do not know why; it was some kind of nervous breakdown, I suppose. We are all on week-work now. It is better that way because they are always making changes. Do you remember the trouble we had about matching stripes? They have girls to do that now. Young Bonanno is marking now. That's all he has ever done. The boss put him in a few years ago and started showing him how to do it.

Peter Paloti: Yes, I have a lot better job than I used to [marking singles]; but I don't get paid enough because I am only supposed to be a learner.

Arthur Schwartz: I am doing a lot of singles now. [Schwartz marked.] I don't know how they happened to get so many; they would not tell me anything if I asked them so I never asked. One thing I do know is that they are not getting the production they did. I don't see how they can get along this way. That fellow Aaron took the hard way out—I suppose you heard about it. He was an erratic fellow—in fact, all that gang were troublemakers. But, God, after all the trouble they had, they went and asked Aaron to stay. They tried to keep him.

My family is fine now [smiling]. Did you ever meet my youngest girl? She is working in the office. They have a fine bunch of girls in this place. It's mighty unusual to find it that way. How do they pick them out? Oh, they are all cousins and mothers and aunts.

Outline of a Conversation with Mrs. Kastanian

Mrs. Kastanian lived in Rome City in a neatly furnished house belonging to her mother, who worked in a nearby factory.

Aaron had committed suicide. It was very hard to bear. Her face and manner appeared to express a perfectly genuine sorrow. The younger girl, aged eight, had found him. It was very disturbing to the child, because she had not been very well. Aaron's picture had been removed from the wall because the child could not stand seeing it there now. He had been extremely fond of his children.

In the spring of 1941, Aaron had felt very bad for some time. In March they went to Morely and took a little apartment, hoping the change would do some good. They left the children in Hamilton with Aaron's mother and came home week ends. It was an expensive arrangement because he was getting only $35 a week down there. The boss said he might get more later on if he fitted into the work. They stayed there about a month, but Aaron did not get any better and they returned to Hamilton. The Bartolos let him come back to work but, she added with emphasis, "the harm had already been done." He had been treated so badly for a long time and "they had always been watching him." When they were starting up, it was Aaron who organized the cutting floor and invented their system for marking cloth economically. He used to come in Saturday and Sunday for nothing, and plan things out. After they got what they wanted out of him, they had no more use for him. She thought the Bartolos were scared because he might have left a suicide note blaming it all on them. That was what she had heard. All the boys were very nice to Aaron. There was nothing that Joe Adalian wouldn't do. Some people had said that Aaron was not getting on with the boys, but that wasn't true.

Mrs. Kastanian explained that she was lucky to have this place to come back to. With prices going up she did not know how they would get on. When Aaron was sick, she had spent a lot of money on doctors; but it did not do any good. She finally took him to a doctor who told him there was really nothing wrong with him; and that "just about finished him." He was sure there was something wrong. He used to feel a pain in the back of his neck. She used to put ice bags on it for one-half hour, but he would say that he couldn't feel them. That spring (1941) she offered to go back to work and let him rest up, but he would not agree. [She had left Bartolo Brothers because she was not feeling very well.] She thought that he was convinced he would always be ill and that was why he did away with himself. He had a nervous breakdown once before. He had always been sensitive.

Aaron's mother had lived with him since they came to this country. Mrs. Kastanian seemed to take this arrangement as a matter of course. Aaron had been very much attached to his mother. You wouldn't find "many of them nowadays who will treat their mother like he did." He was crazy about the little girls too. There was a piano, and the interviewer remarked that Aaron was interested in music. Mrs. Kastanian said he used to sing and could play a little, but she did not show any interest in following up this topic.

DISCUSSION QUESTIONS

1. On your "clique chart" note the changes in the composition of "The Seven" as indicated by these interviews after the stabilization hearings.

2. What seems to be the attitude of (a) the remaining representatives of "The Seven"; (b) the spokesmen who were members of "The Anti-Seven"; (c) cutting-room supervision, present and past (i.e., Bonanno and Schwartz), toward the shop situation?

3. Evaluate the handling of Kastanian, in terms of his whole problem, by the union and by the management.

BARTOLO BROTHERS (I)

THE WAR AND AFTER

Bartolo Brothers, as other clothing manufacturers, adapted its production to fit the nation's needs during the war. The company made military uniforms. Many of the men on its work force left the shop for military service.

After the war, the union negotiated with the men's clothing manufacturers a revised agreement which established, in the closing weeks of 1945, a general increase of 15 cents an hour, various piece-rate adjustments, a retirement fund to be cumulated by payment of 3% of payroll, and six paid holidays. The Bartolo workers, of course, shared these gains.

From particular departments of the shop, disputes had come before Mr. Colton now and then during this period for arbitral decision. But on the whole, they were relatively few in number.

Early in 1947, visits to the shop were resumed. Excerpts from records of interviews held during February and March of that year follow:

I. From an Interview with Minzio Bonanno, Guido Battista, and Joseph Adalian

Mr. Bonanno took me to the cutting room, and a little later to Mr. Leo Bartolo. The foreman proudly told me about the quality of their suits. Wells-Park Avenue had recently become a customer of the firm. Everything was peaceful now and everybody was working happily together.

I spoke later to the two cutters who alone of the original "Seven" remained in the department, Guido Battista and Joseph Adalian. "Everything is all right now," Battista said. "Ever since we have been put on week-work there has been no more trouble. Before, you see, different things used to come up all the time. There were little changes and the prices had to be adjusted constantly. But now that we are on week-work everything is O.K."

Adalian confirmed Battista's remarks, and then went on. "The boss thinks that everything is all right now because the other fellows have left. One of them passed away, you know, and the others all are working over at Mazzola Brothers now. That just shows you if they were really as bad as the boss said they were, they wouldn't be able to work there as well as they do."

Guido told me that a few years ago he was very tired and nervous and had to take a vacation. He went to California for a few months. The boss had asked him to become a foreman. "I tried it for a while," he said, "but I just couldn't take it. There is too much nervous strain involved. You have to be on the boss' side, and yet you don't want to hurt the other fellows' feelings. It drove me crazy. I just couldn't go on that way. I said to the boss that I didn't want the same thing happening to me as happened to Aaron [Kastanian]. He committed suicide, you know." And Joe added, "Yes, it takes a strong nervous system to be a foreman."

Then they talked about Aaron [Kastanian]. "He knew all about the union and what everybody's rights were and he used to defend our rights. Before it all happened, Aaron and the boss were just like that; in fact they promised him he'd grow with the business," Joe said, putting two fingers together. "But after the boss had learned everything he could from Aaron, he figured he didn't need him any more."

Guido took up the conversation. "When they put us on week-work," he said, "they were afraid that they wouldn't get production. But that is wrong. A fellow doesn't like to loaf. He works steadily. But when you are on piecework you get tense and nervous and everything that comes up gets you excited. For instance, when the markers made a mistake, we didn't have time to bother, we just cut; but now we see a mistake, we fix it up. They are getting their production now and they are getting better quality."

II. From an Interview with Vito Albani

Vito was now working at Mazzola Brothers as a marker. "I'll tell you the truth about that case. You see, when you have plaids, they are more difficult to work on than striped materials and it takes longer. We would ask the boss for more money; but when he refused, we went to arbitration. Well, instead of arbitrating prices, they arbitrated our jobs. That wasn't fair. I got the rawest deal from that arbitration. That's right, I got a rotten deal. You can tell Mr. Colton that I think I got a rotten deal; and if you ask me, I'll never go to arbitration again. They put me on probation. Well, I tried to get a job in Capitol City; and when I got one, I went up to Leo Bartolo and told him, 'I'm through here.' He asked me to stay and said, 'After all I have done for you, you are leaving me now.' But I didn't want to stay there any more. We were getting on edge working there. They were constantly picking on us and finding fault with us."

Vito manifestly was still quite disturbed about "the case." "The Bartolos are the most hated people here in Hamilton," he said. "Ask anyone who has had dealings with them; they will tell you so. Money is their God. Angelo Bartolo is a gentleman; you can reason with him, but not Leo. He is excitable and unfair."

He worked in Capitol City for two years and then, he said, Mr. Mazzola gave him a good proposition and he accepted. He preferred working in Hamilton since he was living there. "Mr. Mazzola also," he said, "is a gentleman. He gets excited often, but five minutes later he forgets it—not like Leo Bartolo."

Then he spoke about Aaron [Kastanian]. "They killed him," he said. "He was the finest fellow you could ever think of, but he had a nervous breakdown. He would come to work at that time and would say, 'I can't mark any more, Vito. I can't even hold the chalk in my hand.' I told him to go home and take it easy, and he did. He saw doctors and psychologists and all that sort of thing. One day his wife went out shopping and he was minding the children. When his wife came back, the daughter said, 'Papa is up there hanging.' He hanged himself by his belt."

III. From an Interview with Don Piano

Don returned from the Navy the previous year; he had been in service 3½ years. He liked his work at Mazzola's very much and said that he was happy and he wouldn't return to Bartolo's for anything. He did not, however, display any of the deep antagonism which Vito Albani felt. Even though he was a foreman, he still kept up his membership in the union. He explained that he tried to be fair with the fellows. "I know how it is," he said, "since I've been working myself, and I haven't had any trouble since I've been here."

IV. From an Interview with Johnny Salvatore

Johnny said that he enjoyed his work at Mazzola's. He had spent five years in the Army and took part in the European campaign. He reminisced about the "fellows" back in Bartolo's, though he did not remember too much about the specific disputes. When he was "suspended," Don Piano offered him a job at Mazzola's and he took it rather than wait around. His wife and mother were still working at Bartolo's.

Discussion Question

1. Evaluate the emotional "intensity" of the reminiscences of the five members of the original "Seven," as clues to their roles in the clique.

BARTOLO BROTHERS (J)

POSTWAR PROBLEMS

On November 10, 1947, arbitration proceedings took place on a wage dispute originating in the cutting room. The hearing was held at the plant of the Bartolo Brothers in Hamilton. The following were in attendance:

For the Company	*For the Union*
Leo Bartolo, President	Vincent Donati, Regional Representative
Raphael Macari, Foreman, Cutting Room	August Hansa, Business Agent

For the Company
Leo Bartolo, President
Raphael Macari, Foreman, Cutting Room

For the Office of the Arbitrator
Mr. T. S. Colton, Arbitrator
John J. Warren, Research Associate

For the Union
Vincent Donati, Regional Representative
August Hansa, Business Agent
Joseph Adalian ⎤
Guido Battista ⎟
Paul Bestor ⎟ Cutters and
Arthur Schwartz ⎟ Markers
Angelo Serati ⎟
Samuel Dessandro ⎦

Excerpts from the proceedings follow:

Hansa (u): We feel that there is a little inequality between the wages of the cutters and markers in Hamilton as compared with Capitol City. We also feel that we should have some sort of a graduated scale. We feel that a cutter in Hamilton is just as good as a cutter in Capitol City. We are after $1.99 an hour which is the rate in Capitol City. The rate here is $1.81.

Donati (u): We realize that in Capitol City when an employer needs a cutter, he has only to call the union office. In Hamilton, if he needs one, he has to teach him. I do believe there should be some sort of differential to allow for that. We ask for your consideration a 14-cent an hour raise, which would make a four cents' difference between Capitol City and Hamilton.

Hansa (u): Another thing. A layer moves on to cutting; and, after he has been on cutting for nine months, consideration should be given him regarding a pay increase. The union asks that consideration be given every six months after the first nine months through some three years till he reaches top rate if he shows capacity.

Arbitrator: Every six months after the first nine, for three years? Have you specific rates in mind?

Hansa (u): Yes, I have. A layer will start at $1.17 an hour and stay there for nine months. He should ultimately reach $1.95 within three years.

Arbitrator: You will negotiate yourselves as to what the specific rates between the minimum and maximum should be?

Hansa (u): I believe that, as long as we can get the bottom and top of the ladder set, we can fill in the rest with management. We should also like to have a man learn laying, marking, and cutting, and be a finished craftsman at the end of three years. What has happened here before is that a man has been learning just cutting, and not learning marking.

Bartolo (m): How can that happen? At the end of three years, a man will have a fullfledged cutter's money. When are you going to teach the man to mark? Take any one of these cutters—say they want to go on marking. Am I to pay them, while they learn to mark, the same wage as a fullfledged cutter?

Hansa (u): If you keep a man on cutting, it will take much less than three years to make a machine cutter out of him. Any man after nine months on a machine will be able to produce as much as a man who has been on it five years. He can learn marking too in three years.

Bartolo (m): I have always fought for a 10% differential to cover teaching the men. They compare rates always to the Capitol City market. But when it comes to comparing performance, well, they ignore that.

Donati (u): I want to say again we recognize there should be some differential between a major clothing market and an out-of-town market. But 10% is too much. As a teacher, he has divided his three operations very well. He takes the layers and trains them from the bottom up. Now if a vacancy is created, it would be much easier for you [to Mr. Bartolo] if your cutters were markers as well as cutters. If a cutter has a love for his job, he watches and notices where the chalk mark is made by the other fellows.

Bartolo (m): I will show you that it costs me 10% of the entire payroll to teach these people.

Arbitrator: Let's hear from the cutters.

Adalian (u): Most of the fellows begin here. When they work here nine or ten months, they have some knowledge about the work. When they work a year or two years more, they have more knowledge about the work. So I think if a fellow works two or three years on one job, he is not a greenhorn. When you give him a chance and promote him, he gives more cooperation than if he has nothing else to look forward to. I have been here ten years. Mr. Bartolo promoted many new faces to marking, and many that I had to teach and show them how to work. Maybe I am too good as a cutter and they don't want to change me!

Arbitrator: Do you get the top rate?

Adalian (u): Yes. Mr. Bartolo created this condition himself. Nobody forced him to sectionize the work. He started beginning with the three-man team, and it has been going on right along. A three-man team is more specialized and can produce faster than a two-man team.

Donati (u): I would make a suggestion. A layer has become a fullfledged cutter. I could not expect a firm then to pay him a topnotch rate for marking, which he doesn't know—the same rate, that is, as for cutting which he does know. But to let him go back to the learner's rate, that would be wrong, too. But we could negotiate that.

Bartolo (m): Take individuals: two machine cutters have been here a long time—Guido and Joe—and we get along quite well. These two boys want to go to marking. They get top rate. Should I give them the same amount of money as markers that they have been earning as cutters, or what rate?

Adalian (u): If Mr. Bartolo said that we should go back to the layer's price, that would be absolutely wrong from my standpoint. I think I know something about marking. The only thing I haven't got is the speed, which is going to take time to acquire—three months or six months. But I think it is an injustice to take a man back to $1.17 from $2 an hour. If Paul marks ten sides a day for you, I think I can do seven sides or six sides.

Bartolo (m): I think you are valuable. I don't want a better cutter than you are. How can I take you away from that machine and give you a piece of chalk?

Arbitrator [to Mr. Adalian]: Would you be willing to take a reduction while learning marking?

Adalian (u): I can't say right now.

Battista (u) [interrupting]: I have worked for a long time here; and I have started as a layer. We started cutting on the machine, and I sort of felt more attached to that than any other job. We feel that Mr. Bartolo is right because if he puts somebody else in our place, it will take him more time and more money. Yet we want to learn marking.

Bestor (u): When I was elevated to marker, I marked and soon turned out the same production as any other table. Yet I wasn't getting top marker's pay. You were benefiting from the extra production you were getting from me—until you felt or agreed that we were doing as much work as everyone else. You said, "Paul, next season I will bring you up to top marker." Within that period of time you were using that 10% to teach somebody else. You weren't losing. When I became a fullfledged marker, I was granted an increase in pay.

Arbitrator: You seem to have a pretty stable group among the cutters. These four men have worked here now for a number of years.

Hansa (u): Eighteen, ten, five, and ten.

Schwartz (u): I have worked in a number of jobs; but as far as a marker is concerned, this is the hardest job I have ever tackled. Just because a man has been a good cutter, it doesn't mean that he can do a good job marking.

Adalian (u): If a man has been given a chance, and if he is intelligent enough, I think there is no job too hard for any person to tackle. How did Paul do it? He went on marking and has been a marker for ten years.

[After further discussion in this vein, the arbitrator brought the hearing to a close as follows:]

Arbitrator: I must say that I am delighted to see the kind of spirit that now prevails here.

Ten days later, the arbitrator handed down his award. Excerpts follow:

Before proceeding to the specific problem submitted to me, I must congratulate both the management and the union on the fine spirit which prevailed at the hearing. It was a great pleasure for me to see reflected so vividly in this proceeding the progress that has been made toward mutual goodwill and understanding in the cutting room.

The issue now before me concerns the compensation for men engaged in the cutting department. Considerable discussion at the hearing centered upon the rates in Hamilton as compared with those in Capitol City. On mature consideration, however, I think everyone will agree that while the differential should not be as great as it is now, it also would be neither sound nor fair not to have some differential. In Capitol City, as in other metropolitan markets, trained cutters are available for any concern which needs them. For a smaller, out-of-town market, like Hamilton, the management has to train its own cutters. The considerable investment absorbed into such training should be given due weight.

My decision, accordingly, is as follows:

(1) The top rate for cutters shall be $1.90 per hour; in other words, there shall be an increase of 8½ cents over the rate of $1.81½ which prevails now. [There followed a list of individuals among the cutters and markers who were to receive this top rate.]

(2) With regard to the issue raised concerning progression rates for the cutters, the following procedure is to be followed:

(a) When it is decided to promote a man from laying to cutting, he is to receive, as a "beginning" hourly rate, the average which he earned for the last four consecutive weeks as a layer.

(b) After six months his performance is to be reviewed jointly by the union and management. If he has shown improvement, he is to be given a reasonable increase commensurate with his improvement.

(c) Thereafter his performance is to be reviewed every six months with the objective of giving him a reasonable increase consistent with his improvement, until he reaches the maximum of $1.90 an hour.

(3) There was considerable discussion over the procedure to be followed when a cutter, who has reached the maximum rate, would like to learn to be also a marker, so that he can become an all-around cutter. It would obviously be unfair to expect him to be compensated at the maximum rate of $1.90 an hour, while learning marking. My decision, therefore, is that in such an event, a rate is to be negotiated between the management and the union to cover what they jointly deem a reasonable length of time for learning the marking process.

DISCUSSION QUESTIONS

1. Contrast this rate dispute with those that open the Bartolo cases from the viewpoint of (a) the union's attitude toward the rate differentials between Capitol City and Hamilton; (b) the attitude of the cutters involved; (c) the attitude of management.

2. In what *structure of relationships* would you say the parties are now? How would you classify their relationships at the opening of the case record? How would you classify them at the time of the second stabilization hearing?

3. To what factors would you ascribe the prime influences in the transformations of relationships?

4. Contrast the relationships among Battista, Adalian, Bestor, and Schwartz indicated in this hearing with those existing before the war.

5. Evaluate the arbitrator's decision from the viewpoint of (a) its settlement of the problem of progression rates and the provision of opportunity for promotion; (b) its use of the improved union-management relationship for meeting the job-rate problem.

BARTOLO BROTHERS (K)

THE VETERANS IN THE CUTTING ROOM

During the closing weeks of the year 1947, Mr. John Warren, research associate of Mr. Colton, visited Hamilton. He interviewed various representatives of management and of the cutters; he was also invited to attend a Christmas party given for members of the shop. Excerpts from his records follow:

I. From an Interview with Leo Bartolo

Bartolo: Good morning, good morning, Mr. Warren. Unfortunately this is a very bad day to see me. Once a year the auditor comes up from New York. But I would like to talk to you sometime.

Interviewer: That is all right, Mr. Bartolo. I understand thoroughly. It is very nice of you to let me talk to anyone in the plant.

Bartolo: That is right, you talk with any of them. My people are all good people at heart. My problem is not with the workers. What we need are foremen. Foremen lack two things. First, they cannot teach. The second thing is, my foremen know nothing of human relations. They don't know how to handle the men. My problem is no different from that of all America. In all business—big and small—America needs skilled craftsmen like me who can teach good quality work, and people from college like you who know how to have people get along.

II. From an Interview with Paul Bestor

Bestor: Hello, Mr. Warren. I saw you in the plant today, and I have been hoping that you would come over to our department. You may not know it, but this is the department where we make our quality suits. Everything we do here is made-to-measure.

You will want to watch me mark this piece of cloth. You see here is the ticket. It gives all of the measurements. Do you want to know what this man looks like? This is great fun because we can tell just what shape the man has from these measurements. It is just as if we were artists and were painting. This man has a pot belly. You see this measurement for his waist. What is more, he is short and has broad shoulders.

[Smiling.] You know, people come in the shop and say what an easy job I have got; and I just give them the chalk and say, "You do it." [Paul laughed.] You have to get all of the pieces out of the cloth given you and to make sure to allow just the right amounts in each section of the suit to conform to the body of the man. We really do a fine job here.

You know, actually, Angelo Bartolo is one of the top five designers in

America. Men like him you can count on your fingers. The Bartolo Brothers have done a great deal for our town. They are good people and they have had a hard time getting to the top but now they are beginning to be recognized as being as good as Hart Schaffner & Marx and Hickey-Freeman. You know we have our clothes at Wells-Park Avenue and MacIlvain's and Fletcher-Kingman's. If you buy something at MacIlvain's and it is not what you think, you can take it back. That is a great store. So you see they would not handle our suits unless they were first-rate. That is why I say the Bartolo Brothers have done much for us. Their house is always open to us.

You know, Mr. Warren, this is the life. If I were going to choose my job all over again, I would choose the same job I have now. Clothes is a good business. It is clean and you get a kick out of seeing what you make. I feel I get to know each person for whom I make a suit because I know exactly what they look like. Someday if I get a break I would like to go into business for myself; and, if I do, I would wish to go into the clothes business or have my own little shop.

III. FROM AN INTERVIEW WITH GUIDO BATTISTA AND JOSEPH ADALIAN

Battista: Have you ever seen anyone cut? There are about 40 layers of cloth here. It is very important that I watch the electric knife very closely, for I cannot make a mistake or I will waste 40 pieces of cloth and cloth is very expensive now.

[Guido stopped talking and raced the electric knife with almost no hesitation around the chalk markings on the top layer of cloth. There were a multiplicity of markings, but Guido skillfully followed the correct ones each time. There was hardly a handful of cloth remaining from the 40 lays when he completed his machine cuttings.]

Battista: As I was saying, the price of cloth is pretty high; but so is the price of everything. You know all we were trying to do in that last arbitration was to get a few more dollars in our pockets. You know any boss just naturally doesn't want to give in when money is concerned. Leo is no different than any other boss. The boys say, "Why is it that Leo argues so over a half cent?" But, when you stop to think that there are so many workers in the plant, then a half cent means a good bit of money, especially when it is 8 hours a day, and then many days in the week, and many weeks in the month, and many months in the year. That half a cent costs Leo a lot of money, and it is just natural that the boss doesn't want to give us more than he has to. I like it here very much because I have been here since 1929. If I didn't like it I wouldn't have stayed here that long. The boss likes me because he knows I give him quality and production. The boys don't lay down; he knows that. We give him a full day's work. I guess I will be here until I have long white whiskers way down to here.

Interviewer: Didn't you at one time go to California, Guido?

Battista: Yes, that was after I was foreman. It made me have a nervous breakdown. I would never be foreman again. I thought about everything and kept it all inside myself, but that is no good. You have to look out for yourself. Aaron [Kastanian] kept everything inside himself too. I told the boss I couldn't take it any longer; and he told me to take a vacation, to go away for as long as I wanted, and that I could come back any time, for there was always a job for me here. I like this place and the town—it is where I went to school and it is where my kids are going to school.

Interviewer: How many do you have in your family, Guido?

Battista: I have two boys. They are both in school now and they are doing rather well. You know, it is quite a responsibility now to have a family with living costs what they are.

Interviewer: Would you be a foreman again, now that the foreman has more help?

Battista: No, never again, and I wouldn't want to be shop steward either. What do you get out of it except a headache? All you do is argue with the boss for the men, and then try to tell the men about it, and you have to argue with them. No, I am a quiet man. I like to live in peace. No one wants to be shop steward. In fact, we cutters do not have one. Nobody wants the job.

Interviewer: Everything seems to be working out fairly well without one?

Battista: We don't have any problems here. Oh, there is an occasional one like the arbitration. We always thought there was too much difference between the rates of Capitol City and the rates in our town and we thought that about 5% was enough difference. Of course, we know that Leo has to get young fellows in, and we have to train them. It is not like that in Capitol City where you can get an experienced man. Well, Mr. Colton agreed with us—and he gave us 8½ cents more and we are pretty well satisfied.

Adalian: Did you notice our Christmas tree, Mr. Warren? It really makes the shop look a lot nicer and gives you the Christmas spirit. We each gave 50 cents to buy the tree and the ornaments, and the girls have been decorating it during their lunch hour. Last year we had one and we only paid 25 cents but prices are going up. The girls are kind of pretty too, aren't they?

Interviewer: They certainly are.

Adalian: Why don't you come down to my table with me, Mr. Warren? I will tell you something about the Armenians. You know if you listen to any Armenian you will get a story of the world. We have lost faith in the Christian world. You know, if you read the Bible, that we were the first Christian nation; and during the first World War England told us "You go along with us and you will be right." Then, after the war was over, the Christian world said, "Armenians, you can now be Mohammedans." The Turks came in and massacred most of my people. The few that were left were sent into exile. They only gave our family 24 hours to get out of the country. They told us we could sell our property, but who would buy knowing that we had to leave within a day? My father just shut the door and locked it and then walked away from everything he had lived his life for. Every place we went, it was a bayonet point.

Finally my father, who was a very smart man, said to us, "We can no longer live like this. We must go some place else in the world and start over." I was only 10 years old and all of us owe our lives to our father. He was a professional man—a very good dentist—and he was sending my cousin through medical school in America. Finally he wrote him and said, "Things are going very badly with us. I do not think that we can afford to send you to school any longer. In fact, any moment we may have to run to another city; and I think probably we'll have to come to you, so maybe you had better get a job."

Well, we all came to America, and we got jobs in all the different factories; but we never permitted our father to take a job in a factory. We said to him, "No, you have worked long enough. It is now time for you to take a rest," and we all went to work.

We Armenians are scattered over the world. Is it any wonder we have lost faith with the world? When I say "lost faith," I do not mean that we no longer believe in God; but we have no nation we can call our own. Of course, some of our people went into Russia and we now have the Armenian Soviet Republic. I guess the Russians treat us all right. They don't bother our church or our people, I believe. That is the story of the Armenian people no matter which one tells it to you.

Discussion Questions

1. Contrast Leo Bartolo's distillation of his personnel problems at this time with his appraisal of them at the opening of the Bartolo cases.

2. Contrast the attitudes similarly expressed now—and then—by Bestor, Battista, and Adalian from the viewpoints of (*a*) their craft workmanship; (*b*) the reputation of the company; (*c*) their relationships with management; (*d*) their satisfactions in their job and aspirations for supervisory or union promotion. To what factors—economic, social, interpersonal—would you look for explanation of these changes in attitudes?

BARTOLO BROTHERS (L)

THE CHRISTMAS PARTY

The Christmas party was held December 23, 1947, in the Society of Sicily Hall. Inside it was bright, warm, and clean. At the head of the stairs was Minzio Bonanno. He was "all dressed up" and was exceptionally friendly, smiling and laughing all the time. With him was Raphael Macari, foreman of the cutting room and brother-in-law of Leo Bartolo. Both men were greeting all comers, shaking hands, pointing out the check room at the left, telling the men there was a bar downstairs, indicating seats at the tables in the hall for some, and locating friends for others.

The hall itself was completely filled with tables, which were already prepared with an *antipasto* at each place. The head table, set for about 10 people, was placed across the width of the room in front of the platform near the door. On the platform were the two men who were hired to provide the music with their phonograph, records, and amplifiers. Down the length of the hall were four long tables each set for about 75 people. When Adalian, Battista, and Warren arrived there were only about 30 people in the room. The women were in animated groups of six or eight in different sections of the room. Tables were filling slowly, each group taking their places as they pleased.

Bonanno: Good to see you; good to see you. We will assign you a table if you wish.

Battista: No, Bonanno. We are going to sit over in the far corner where it won't be messy and where people won't be climbing over us. We want a neat place.

Bonanno: Fine, fine. Anything you wish. Go wherever you want. It's all yours. The bar is open downstairs. Some of the men are down there.

[The group proceeded to the farthest corner and sat in the end chairs.]

Adalian: You see, I told you. There are the demitasse cups. [Joe held it up. A woman from across the room called: "Ah ha! Demitasse—this is the Ritz!" Guido then explained each of the items included on the plate of *antipasto*. Two men from the cutting room joined the group but left saying they would soon return so to save them "seats with the gang."]

Adalian: There's Arthur. Oh, Mr. Schwartz, here we are, over here in the corner.

Battista: Well, I see you're all set, Arthur.

Schwartz: Yes, yes. But what are we doing stuck over here in the corner? We ought to be over at one of the better tables.

Adalian: It doesn't look as if many are going to come—there are hardly any men here.

Schwartz [to Warren]: He doesn't know this town. Why, if it's free everyone will come. Where are you from?

Warren: I live in Capitol City now, but my home is in Indiana.

Schwartz: That's where I belong—in Capitol City. I lived there for over 20 years. I've no business being in this town, but I'm 72 years old; it's too late to change another time. What nationality is that name of yours?

Warren: My parents were born here. It's just American, I guess. Originally it was an English name.

Schwartz: That's what I thought. It didn't sound German. I don't know whether you know it or not, but I'm German. I see you pronounce my name right, but they call me everything here. I try to explain to them how you sound the "w" in my name, but what they come out with is just terrible, simply terrible. I tell them and tell them, but that kind never seem to learn.

[Just then Antonio, the shop chairman for the pressers, came over to greet Mr. Schwartz.]

Antonio: Good evening, Mr. Schwartz. How are you this evening? [Antonio showed deference and respect to Mr. Schwartz, but did not pay particular attention to any other individual cutter or marker.]

Schwartz: I'm all right. You're all dressed up.

Antonio: We work in Bartolo's, you know. [Everyone laughed.]

Schwartz: So you're English. How did that fellow who came down here last month ever know my name?

Warren: You mean Mr. Colton, the arbitrator? Of course, he remembers you.

Schwartz: Well, it certainly surprised me. He must meet so many people, and it must have been at least five years since he saw me. I would like to learn how to remember names that way. I was foreman at the time of the first case here. I could have murdered every one of that gang in testimony if I had wanted to, but I didn't want to. Well, one of these guys jumped up and said unless the arbitrator put this one guy back to work, they would all go out. You know what that was? It was perjury, nothing but perjury! But this fellow, the arbitrator, he didn't do anything about that—not a thing. He just let it go past. But in any other court they would all have been thrown out of the courtroom. They were trying to intimidate the court. He shouldn't have let them get away with that.

Warren: You say you could have murdered them? I don't quite understand what you mean.

Schwartz: They were a bad lot. I had plenty on them if I'd wanted to use it.

I still don't see how Mr. Colton knew my name. And he asked me about my family too. I have three grown daughters and two sons; the younger is a senior at Yale. He works hard and is a fine student. He is studying engineering. College does wonders for people, especially girls. My youngest girl got married a little over a year ago, and you should have seen how nice her college friends looked. All my children went to college. We have nice looking girls here too. There are nice girls working at Bartolo's.

They are pretty and see how they are all dressed tonight. Most of them were worried all day they wouldn't have time to get fixed up for tonight. See that one with the long gloves. And almost all of them have what they call the "new look." Yes, these are nice girls too.

About this time other men from the cutting room joined the group. Several of them were accompanied by their wives, who also worked at Bartolo's. The wives were introduced to all. As groups from the cutting room arrived, Guido would call out to them to come "join the gang." They sat elsewhere. Actually, there was no room left in the corner where the cutters and markers were seated.

Battista: Why are Rose and Rita and Celia sitting down there? They should come up and sit with us. Call to them, Joe, and see if you can make them hear.

Adalian: But there's no room here. This is a helluva place to sit. We should have had a whole table on the other side.

Schwartz: Here we are sitting in the corner. This is dumb. We should be up at the head table.

By 7:30 a huge crowd filled the hall and dinner was under way. Bonanno and Macari were seated at the head table. The other places at the head table were taken by other workers—mostly women—but no one of particularly important position in the shop. Everyone was calling out to everyone else as friends sighted friends. The girls would wave and throw kisses to the boys in their department. Battista and Adalian were always saying, "There are some of *our* girls." Calling back and forth, accompanied by much gesturing and sign making, continued throughout the entire dinner.

At this point there was considerable competition for the right to tell Warren the story of a queen of Sicily who had many lovers. As the story was told, everyone would add a little by interrupting, or, at least, agree by nodding his head and saying, "Yes, yes," over and over again. Only Mr. Schwartz did not seem to appreciate the story. Two men came up and wanted to know what kind of manners Guido had—they wanted to be introduced to Mr. Warren. When Mr. Warren introduced himself, they both said, "Oh, we know you. Rumors get around fast here." After the dinner had started, another cutter, Cristo Allegro, a brother-in-law of the Bartolos, came in. He insisted on sitting with the other cutters and markers. There were two empty places immediately adjacent at the next table; but he wouldn't sit there, nor would the other markers and cutters allow him to sit anywhere except with them. Everyone moved his plate, and Allegro crowded in.

Allegro: Arthur, how is the food?

Schwartz: You remember what I told you this afternoon about the wall of China, don't you? They were feeding the Chinese workers Italian spaghetti, and they were dropping off like flies from malnutrition; then they gave them German sauerkraut, and the wall went up.

Battista: Say, Arthur, you sure ate all that Italian cheese.

Schwartz: Yes, it was real good. You know it comes from Northern Italy —they slip it into Italy from Switzerland, and Switzerland imports it from Germany. My parents came from Hanover. That's closer to Northern Italy than Sicily; and you all come from Sicily, except Joe.

[The waiter approached the table with bottles of wine, imported from Italy.]

Allegro: Arthur, you must try this—it's straight from the Rhineland.

Schwartz: I don't like wine; it makes me sick. We are beer drinkers. Give me some wine in this cup, and I'll see how bad it is.

At that moment four of the men from the cutting room jumped up and, standing erect, gave the Nazi salute, yelling "Heil Arthur Schwartz. Heil Arthur Schwartz." Schwartz was both embarrassed and pleased. When the waiter approached with a huge bowl of real Italian-style macaroni, everyone at the table yelled, "Here comes the sauerkraut"; and they insisted that the waiter give it to Schwartz to serve. Schwartz served Warren's plate, then piled the macaroni on his own. Each time that he pretended he was going to serve Battista, and Battista held out his plate, Schwartz would serve someone else. He gave everyone after himself very small portions, and as they yelled about the size of the serving he would chuckle. Cristo served the peas and salad. Schwartz said, "Give me a couple of peas, Cristo." Cristo served him four peas and, when Schwartz objected, Cristo replied, "You only asked for a couple, and I gave you twice that many."

About midway in the dinner, a man entered the hall; and, as he was seen, a great wave of shouts and yells mounted over the hall. Battista said it was Leo Bartolo's father-in-law, whom everyone liked very much. "He comes around the plant from time to time," Battista said. Neither Angelo nor Leo Bartolo had come. In fact, they had not come by the time the cutters left, shortly after 10:00 P.M.

When a broiled half chicken was served, and the men began to enjoy eating it, Schwartz said, "This is a mess. Don't you serve any potatoes or gravy with this? This chicken isn't cooked right. Who ever heard of broiling a chicken?"

The waiter was then passing out a second can of beer to each guest.

Adalian: We will each take two cans a piece at this end of the table.

Waiter: Well, look who's talking; and I suppose this group is something extra.

Adalian: Of course it is; we are the cutting room.

Battista: There are not 10 people in this whole room who are here more years than we are. We taught these other people what to do.

Schwartz: Don't be so dumb. Anyone knows that not everyone can be a marker or a cutter. Of course, we are a special group. We'll take two beers each.

Adalian: Those pressers are noisy. The whole place is noisy. Why can't they settle down?

The girls began singing Christmas songs. The men started to keep time by ringing the side of their glasses with their silverware. The people at each table would lean far to the left, pushing everyone in that direction; they would then lean far to the right. The swaying motion to and fro was accompanied by loud shouting and laughter. Beer cans were stacked row on row in the form of a huge pyramid in the middle of the tables, and then several of the men would throw beer cans at the stack, knocking it all down with a crash.

Schwartz: This is all a mess. Say, you said you were English, and we can't understand these Italians. Let's sing *Tommy Atkins* together.

Warren: I'm sorry, Mr. Schwartz, but I don't think I know that one.

Schwartz: But you said you were English. You don't know *Tommy Atkins?* My, my! I can't understand that. Are you sure you're English? Well, we'll sing one I know you know. You've heard the Michigan College song, haven't you? [Schwartz began to sing, "I wish I were again in Michigan"—he finished the song by himself.] Do you like this kind of food? I don't. You know why I eat? Well, once I went to a wake in South Boston with some other men. One of the fellows at the house where the wake was held offered us a drink, insisted on it. No one wants a drink at a wake; but one fellow said—he was a fellow who wouldn't ever buy a drink—"Let's take it, boys. We don't want to insult him by not accepting what's offered us." Well, that's what I'm doing tonight. I try to eat something of everything tonight so I won't insult them. I don't understand them, but I want to get along with them.

Warren: Everyone has been most cordial to me.

Schwartz: Oh, they all get acquainted quickly in their ignorance. But I don't like their familiarity.

Battista: Did you see that? Pete introduced me to his wife, Rose, and imagine—I knew her when she first came to Bartolo's before he ever met her. That's the trouble. Everyone here is married to someone who works at Bartolo's. You'd be surprised how many husbands got wives in the shop and vice versa. I wonder when Leo is coming. He should be here by now.

Adalian: He will probably come after supper is over.

Minzio Bonanno stood up to speak while the ice cream was being served. No one could hear him, but he got a terrific ovation after speaking only two or three sentences, waving, and sitting down. One of the workers led the group in singing two Italian songs in Italian. Guido Battista excused himself from the table and made his rounds throughout the hall, stopping wherever girls from the cutting room were congregated. At each place he stopped, the girls screamed and laughed and pulled at his hair, as he dared them to come out to the plant the next day with some mistletoe. In a short time, Joseph Adalian started to make the same rounds, stopping to see the girls from the cutting room. Again he kidded them, and there was a considerable amount of horseplay. Finally Arthur Schwartz excused himself from the table saying, "I'll have to go over and see the girls. I see that Guido and Joe have already been over there. We have good girls in our rooms, and I will have to tell them how nice they all are and how fine they look." As Mr. Schwartz approached each group, the girls would stand and shake hands, but he would lay his hands on their shoulders, telling them to be seated, speak to them of their beautiful new dresses, ask them each if they were having a nice time, and inquire how they could ever have eaten that food that had been served them, and then pass on. The girls showed a considerable amount of respect to Mr. Schwartz. There was no horseplay.   .

Soon the dance floor was crowded. Some of the dances were polkas and waltzes; others were jitterbug. Everyone was dancing his own way, disregarding the music. Battista and Adalian asked Warren to dance with "our girls" from the cutting room. After asking one such girl, each girl that was asked would suggest, while dancing, "Why don't you dance with Grace, next? She is from the cutting room, and she likes to dance." Once when Warren sat down to rest, two girls came over to ask if he would dance with them— Battista had dared them to come. Bonanno made the rounds passing out cigars and cigarettes, and loved his job doing it. Macari was always "putting on a show" on the dance floor, making everyone laugh. Beer and wine were served—quantity unlimited.

Celia, a stripe matcher, typified what most of the girls said about the party: "Isn't this fun? I hope they have this every year. We have been looking forward to it. It is much nicer than ever before. You know it is a real privilege to work at Bartolo's. It is very hard to get in unless you know someone already on the inside. My sister works there—that's how I got in. And I'm glad because we have lots of fun. The only thing about the party is that Leo Bartolo didn't come."

Warren: Maybe he thought you'd have a better time this way.
Celia: Oh, no. He is great fun in himself.

En Route to Capitol City on Train after Party

Warren: What are Don and Vito doing now?
Adalian: Oh, they work at Mazzola Brothers. They have been getting along fine. A few weeks ago they saw me standing on the corner and waved; said they were going to Capitol City for a good time; wanted me to go with them. I told them I had to get home to my family. Don did have some trouble a little while ago. He is a foreman, and someone hadn't told him something a foreman should know. Anyway, he got into an argument with this worker, and both Don and the worker quit. Well, they patched it up and they are both working.
Warren: What was it all about?
Adalian: I don't know much more about it. Anyway the fact that they are getting along over there proves Leo was wrong. He shouldn't have called them gangsters. Aaron's widow works. His two daughters are still in school. The older one is very fine on the piano. Aaron would have liked that.

DISCUSSION QUESTIONS

1. List the actions and sentiments expressed at the party that justify its description as a ceremonial symbolic of the transition from conflict to co-operative relationships at Bartolo's.

2. Contrast the impact of the ethnic factor as expressed at this party by the sentiments of Arthur Schwartz and the Italian and the Armenian workers of the cutting room with the influence of this factor as expressed in the earlier structure of relationships.

3. How would you characterize the "cutting-room spirit" evidenced at the party with that of the initial stages in evolving relationships? State the behavior at the Christmas party, verbal and nonverbal, on which you base your judgment.

4. Compare Arthur Schwartz's reminiscences of "The Seven" at the party with those of Joseph Adalian after it as clues to their respective involvements in the original hostilities and their shop roles, as well as the personality traits which they bring to shop relations.

5. How would you evaluate the place of the impartial chairman in this whole developing relationship?

ALPHABETICAL LIST OF CASES